The Presidency of
ULYSSES S.
GRANT

The Presidency of
ULYSSES S.
GRANT

Charles W. Calhoun

UNIVERSITY PRESS OF KANSAS

Published by the University Press of Kansas (Lawrence, Kansas 66045), which
was organized by the Kansas Board of Regents and is operated and funded by
Emporia State University, Fort Hays State University, Kansas State University,
Pittsburg State University, the University of Kansas, and Wichita State University

Library of Congress Cataloging-in-Publication Data

Names: Calhoun, Charles W. (Charles William), 1948– author.
Title: The presidency of Ulysses S. Grant / Charles W. Calhoun.
Description: Lawrence, Kansas : University Press of Kansas, 2017.
Series: American presidency series | Includes bibliographical references and index.
Identifiers: LCCN 2017026679
ISBN 9780700624843 (hardback) | ISBN 9780700624850 (ebook)
ISBN 9780700635122 (paperback)
Subjects: LCSH: United States—Politics and government—1869–1877. | Grant, Ulysses S.
(Ulysses Simpson), 1822–1885. | Presidents—United States—Biography | BISAC:
HISTORY / United States / 19th Century. | BIOGRAPHY & AUTOBIOGRAPHY /
Presidents & Heads of State. | POLITICAL SCIENCE / Government / Executive Branch.
Classification: LCC E671 .C25 2017 | DDC 973.8/2092 [B]—dc23 LC record available at
https://lccn.loc.gov/2017026679.

British Library Cataloguing-in-Publication Data is available.

Printed in the United States of America

The paper used in this publication is acid free and meets the minimum
requirements of the American National Standard for Permanence of
Paper for Printed Library Materials Z39.48-1992.

For Bonnie

CONTENTS

CONTENTS

FOREWORD

The aim of the American Presidency Series is to present historians and the general reading public with interesting, scholarly assessments of the various presidential administrations. These interpretive surveys are intended to cover the broad ground among biographies, specialized monographs, and journalistic accounts. As such, each is a comprehensive work that draws upon original sources and pertinent secondary literature yet leaves room for the author's own analysis and interpretation.

Volumes in the series present the data essential to understanding the administration under consideration. Particularly, each book treats the then-current problems facing the United States and its people and how the president and his associates felt about, thought about, and worked to cope with these problems. Attention is given to how the office developed and operated during the president's tenure. Equally important is consideration of the vital relationships among the president, his staff, the executive officers, Congress, foreign representatives, the judiciary, state officials, the public, political parties, the press, and influential private citizens. The series is also concerned with how this unique American institution—the presidency—was viewed by the presidents, and with what results.

All this is set, insofar as possible, in the context not only of contemporary politics but also of economics, international relations, law, morals, public administration, religion, and thought. Such a broad approach is necessary to understanding, for a presidential administration is more than the elected and appointed officers composing it, since its work so often reflects the major problems, anxieties, and glories of the nation. In short, the authors in this series strive to recount and evaluate the record of each administration and to identify its distinctiveness and relationships to the past, its own time, and the future.

The General Editors

PREFACE

When Fred Woodward of the University Press of Kansas invited me to write this book, I accepted the honor with pleasure. But I also knew that the task that lay ahead was daunting. No scholarly work focusing on Grant's presidency had appeared since the 1930s. Biographies tended to dwell on the war years and gave short shrift to his administration, even though Grant spent twice as much time in the White House as he did fighting in the Union army. As president, he confronted momentous issues, and his administration was steeped in controversy. Yet most biographers drawn to examine his military career seemed relatively uninterested or unversed in the deeply consequential questions that marked his two presidential terms. Those issues of politics and governance have stood at the center of my scholarly concern for more than forty years.

My aim in this book, therefore, was to try to "get it right" in treating the important questions of the Grant era. To do that, I realized that I would need to go beyond secondary works and resort primarily to a close examination of original sources. That has taken time—and space. Assembling the story often required a treatment of some controversial issues or events in considerable detail in order to dispel myth and misinterpretation. It also underscored that a "presidency" is created not only by the president but also by myriad other actors—antagonists as well as allies—and in the chapters that follow, others occasionally take the foreground. In many ways, rethinking Grant's presidency reveals his administration as almost sui generis, for perhaps no other president found his time in office so embattled. I have not engaged in rehabilitation so much as clarification and correction, recognizing that Grant deserves to be regarded as a better president than his reputation suggests, but also acknowledging that he sometimes fell short of his aims. The image of the presidency of Ulysses S. Grant occupies an important place in our political culture. My aim has been to revisit his administration to arrive at an account more serviceable to our usable past.

In preparing this book I incurred a staggering list of debts. For the numerous individuals and institutions that aided me, mention here is compensation wholly inadequate. Historians' principal coadjutors are librarians and archivists. Of the many who helped me, none exceeded the professionalism or dedication of Jeff Flannery and the superb staff in the Manuscript Reading Room of the Library of Congress. Others who went far beyond the call of duty in meeting my requests include Ryan Semmes of the Ulysses S. Grant Presidential Library, Sarina Rodrigues and Erin Mullen of the Special Collections and Archives Department of the University of Rhode Island Library, Irene Axelrod of the Peabody-Essex Museum, Elerina Aldamar of the Oregon Historical Society, and Claude Zachary of the Special Collections Department of the University of Southern California Library. William Gee and Rebecca Harrison of the Interlibrary Loan Office of East Carolina University's Joyner Library provided me with unfailing assistance.

I am also grateful for the courteous and efficient service provided by librarians and archivists at the National Archives; Prints and Photographs Division of the Library of Congress; Senate Historical Office; New Hampshire Historical Society; Massachusetts Historical Society; Concord, Massachusetts, Public Library; Yale University Library; Princeton University Library; Columbia University Library; New York Public Library; New-York Historical Society; University of Virginia Library; Western Reserve Historical Society; Ohio Historical Society; Cincinnati Historical Society; Rutherford B. Hayes Presidential Library; Oberlin College Library; Indiana State Library; Indiana Historical Society; Newberry Library; Illinois State Historical Society; Chicago Museum; Wisconsin Historical Society; and University of Louisville Law School Library.

A portion of the material presented here grew out of research conducted while I held a fellowship from the National Endowment for the Humanities. I also thank John F. Marszalek and the Ulysses S. Grant

Scholars Research Program for helping to fund my research in the Grant Presidential Library. At East Carolina University I received research assistance from the College of Arts and Sciences, the Faculty Senate, and the Department of History's Brewster Fund. I am grateful to ECU chancellor Steve Ballard for his encouragement and support and for his understanding of the importance of political history. Over the course of my academic career, I have had the good fortune to receive good wishes and material aid from several department chairs, including Preston Hubbard, Roger Biles, Michael Palmer, and Gerald Prokopowicz. I am grateful to the latter two for assisting with this project. I also appreciate the support of my History Department colleagues at ECU, especially Anthony J. Papalas, a scholar of ancient Greece who offered valuable perspectives on Grant and his presidency.

In conversation, through correspondence, and in other ways I profited from the insights of Michael Les Benedict, Roger Bridges, Robert Goldman, Lewis L. Gould, Michael Holt, Ari Hoogenboom, John Marszalek, Michael Perman, Frank Scaturro, Brooks Simpson, Mark Summers, and Frank J. Williams. Informal conversations with Ulysses Grant Dietz, Julia Grant Castleton, Frances Elizabeth Griffiths, John Grant Griffiths, and Claire Ruestow Telecki helped me understand the personality of their distinguished ancestor. A specialist in internal medicine, Mark Cervi, M.D., assisted me in framing ways of thinking about Grant and alcohol. I owe a great debt to the late R. Hal Williams, a model scholar and teacher who introduced me to the delights of primary research in Gilded Age politics in a seminar at Yale nearly fifty years ago. I also appreciate the work of Larisa Martin and the production staff of the University Press of Kansas. I am grateful to all these individuals, but I alone bear responsibility for what I have written.

While conducting research for this book I traveled to libraries around the country. I am deeply grateful to friends who opened their homes to me after long days of combing the archives: Connie Shulz in Washington, John and Barbara Van Scoyoc in Boston, Janet and Charlie McClure in Connecticut, Bob Barrows and Leigh Darbee in Indianapolis, and Jon and Susan Art in Chicago.

Once again, I owe my greatest debt to my family. My sisters Judy Blakely and Mary Howard always sustain me with their interest and good wishes. My daughter Liz, a talented scholar in her own right, gave a close reading to the diary of the dyspeptic Benjamin Moran at the Library of Congress. The debt I owe to my dear wife Bonnie defies calculation.

Ulysses S. Grant. (Library of Congress)

INTRODUCTION:

WAR IN PEACE

In American history Ulysses S. Grant's presidency stands as an enigma. After the death of Abraham Lincoln, the victorious and magnanimous Union general stood first among the nation's heroes. He was a shoo-in at the next presidential election, won a smashing reelection to a second term, and garnered substantial support for a return to office for yet another term. And yet, the Grant presidency witnessed extraordinary controversy. In some quarters the eighteenth president was reviled rather than revered. Through most of the time after he left the White House, his administration bore a reputation for spectacular failure. A century later, historian C. Vann Woodward dismissed Grant's two terms as "America's sorriest Administration" and "the lowest ebb" in presidential history. Only in the last few decades have historians and others begun to challenge that view. By the early twenty-first century, some had pushed the pendulum so far that Sean Wilentz hailed Grant "as one of the great presidents of his era, and possibly one of the greatest in all American history."[1]

Historians can never achieve a perfect congruence between their rendering of the past and the "actuality" of what has gone before, but in few cases has their task seemed more challenging than in limning the Grant presidency. Indeed, one may speak of two Grant presidencies. One was the flow of history in real time between 1869 and 1877: the unfolding of events great and small, the policies conceived, the battles joined, the triumphs won, the compromises effected, the defeats endured. The other is the image of the presidency of Ulysses S. Grant that has existed in the nation's collective memory—the place his administration occupies in our understanding of the evolution of the presidency and in our conception of the office. For nearly a hundred years Grant seemed to stand for everything a chief executive should not be, and rankings of the presidents consistently placed him near the bottom. Eventually, new interpretations came to challenge hoary stereotypes, and rarely has a president undergone so stark a change in portraiture. Yet despite the acknowledged significance of Grant's administration— whether for good or ill—the last book-length scholarly treatment that focused on it appeared in the 1930s. A thorough reexamination is long past due. As a political historian, I have approached Grant's presidency not as an incongruous or inconsequential sequel to his military career but instead as the polestar of American public life during a crucial decade in the nation's political development. In the 1870s friend and foe alike recognized Ulysses S. Grant as the dominant figure astride the political landscape.

When Grant became president in 1869, a host of problems confronted the nation, from turmoil in the South to disturbance in the national finances, trouble on the western frontier, and perils in the country's foreign relations. The new chief executive brought to his responsibilities a number of assets, not unmixed with deficiencies. As a commanding general, Grant had won wide recognition for his extraordinary prowess. Although it took time to adapt his skills to fight new kinds of battles, his fundamental traits did not abandon him when he entered the White House. Grant underwent no lobotomy between Appomattox and Inauguration Day. From the beginning, however, antagonists refused to concede his abilities or, in some cases, even his good intentions.

Among Grant's assets was the administrative experience he had gained in the Mexican War and as a commander with ever widening responsibilities during the Civil War. He had learned how to run a large organization, how to assess the totality and the details of a situation, how to delegate tasks and manipulate subordinates to achieve his ends. Yet, even though his service as general of the army in Washington for four years after Appomattox had entangled him in politics, Grant still had much to learn about civilian issues and the workings of the political system. As something of an outsider, he enjoyed a degree of political independence; in 1868 his party had needed him more than he had needed the party. Hence, he momentarily harbored a sense that he could manage his office with little regard for partisan imperatives. He soon learned, however, that to achieve his goals, a president must also be a party leader.

In the military, Grant had exhibited a dogged determination in pursuing his objectives—a drive to push matters to a successful conclusion without being deflected. His presidency posed similar instances when favored projects or policies evoked his fierce tenacity. But in politics, he discovered, what friends might hail as steadfastness, enemies would denounce as obstinacy.

During the war, Grant had justly earned a reputation as a good judge of men. He appreciated their strengths and could detect their weaknesses. In assessing his performance in the White House, however, Grant's critics convinced themselves that he showed little of this kind of discernment. In part, the divergence flowed from the differences between the profession of arms, in which Grant was a natural, and the profession of politics, in which he was a neophyte. In the army, he had developed a sense of what to look for in his subordinates; his shift to politics required new criteria by which to weigh men's attributes. No one, certainly not Grant, would claim that he chose wisely in all his appointments. His cabinet was a mixed lot, and in its deliberations he reserved for himself the power to decide. To assist in administration, he assembled an efficient White House staff. Eventually, as he gained his footing as the head of his party, he looked to state and congressional leaders of the Republican Party to serve as his field lieutenants in the political warfare he waged. He frequently met with members of Congress and, working with strong party leaders, forged strategic alliances that were often cemented by the application of patronage. In the endless strife that marked his administration, the Roscoe Conklings and Oliver Mortons became the new Shermans and Sheridans.

Similarly, as he had in the army, Grant exhibited a deep sense of personal loyalty in forging his new political relationships. A highly sensitive person, he appreciated the fidelity of proven friends and stood by those who stood by him. This mutual sense of loyalty could inure to the benefit of the administration and the country, as in the case of Secretary of State Hamilton Fish, a valued public servant whom the president repeatedly persuaded to remain in government service. But Grant was also loath to dismiss an officer under fire, and he sometimes remained loyal to individuals beyond the time when, by unworthy acts, they had

3

betrayed his loyalty. This tendency to be too trusting sometimes laid him open to charges of countenancing corruption, the most enduring criticism of his administration.

If Grant's war record revealed him as a natural leader of men, he was not a natural politician. The converse of his steadfastness with friends was a wariness with people he knew less well. He could be cordial but was never a glad-hander or a showboat. During the war, he had despised self-puffery by his fellow generals and thought he should let his deeds speak for themselves. But in politics one's deeds inevitably invite attack, and Grant had a thin skin. Political reputation arises from a compound of action and image. But image is open to manipulation, and controversy places a premium on the art of self-advertisement. In confronting the unexpected barrage of criticism against him, Grant's taciturnity did not serve him well. He sometimes proved less than effective in "controlling the narrative," as politicians and pundits of a later era would put it.

For Grant, public speaking was out. He dreaded it and thought Andrew Johnson had demeaned the presidency by his crude rants. Yet, as his memoirs attest, Grant was a powerful writer. He composed forceful messages to Congress, and on occasion, especially when discussing Reconstruction, his messages showed eloquence. He sometimes gave interviews to reporters, and the administration used press leaks to float its ideas and intentions. But as effective as Grant could be when using this kind of communication, he rarely converted opponents or drowned them out. Had he more effectively vindicated his administration's actions, he might have diminished his detractors' impact, both in his time and in historical retrospect. Moreover, after eight years of enduring what he saw as malicious criticism from unscrupulous opponents, when actual turpitude surfaced toward the end of his term, Grant had grown so defensive that he clung with undue tenacity to some associates who no longer deserved his trust. Standing by such men seemed only to confirm what his enemies had alleged all along. One of the unintended lessons of Grant's presidency was that a chief executive should choose his aides wisely and keep them at arm's length. History demonstrates how well that lesson has been heeded by his successors.

The portrayal of Grant as a presidential failure originated in the intense and unrelenting criticism leveled by his contemporary political foes. It reverberated in subsequent historical treatments that made his administration's record seem less than the sum of its parts. Many enemies demonized Grant because he had bested them, and they were determined to see him fail. Some members of the northeastern elite found little to their taste in this mere military man and specimen of "western mediocrity." Democrats in Congress employed the legislature's investigative function to discredit the administration in any way they could. Partisan journalists acknowledged few restraints in their attempts to blacken Grant and his policies. Even within his own party, many Republicans who had failed to receive patronage or other recognition embraced "reform" and became uncompromising critics. Grant's antagonists found him guilty of all manner of vices: an abiding laziness as well as an overbearing Caesarism; ineptitude as well as cunning; vulgarity, brutality, dishonesty, stupidity, avarice, and a hunger for power without the talent to wield it for the public good. Their bitterness drove them to strictures that far exceeded Grant's supposed offenses. Attacking his character as well as his capacity, the president's adversaries managed to put his flaws ahead of his virtues in the minds of many of his contemporaries. Grant had stout defenders and remained widely popular among his fellow citizens, but in retrospective accounts of his presidency, historians and others paid much more attention to the relentless execration by his enemies.

Hence, for decades, most historical writing on Grant's presidency magnified its blemishes and slighted its achievements. Summarizing opinion seventy years after Grant left office, Richard Hofstadter asserted, "Grant's administrations are notorious for their corruption" and otherwise "not much need be said."[2] William McFeely portrayed Grant as "an ordinary American man" who "did not rise above limited talents or inspire others to do so in ways that make his administration a credit to American politics."[3] But the twentieth-century civil rights movement spurred a reconsideration of the Grant presidency, especially its efforts to uphold Reconstruction. Grant won new esteem as a champion of African Americans' rights, and as Brooks Simpson noted, "We see him as on the right side of history."[4] In a brief but thoughtful biography, Josiah Bunting asserted that "the Grant presidency, so far from being one of the nation's worst, may yet be seen as among its best."[5] Still, one must question whether this notion has entered the popular consciousness. A 2015 book reprised the charge that "his administration wallowed in Gilded Age corruption and set an appalling example for the country."[6]

Thus, a central theme running through the pages that follow is that of Grant as an embattled president operating under severe fire from the beginning of his administration to its end. As a newcomer to politics, he did not feel shackled by custom. But many of those who raised allegations of corruption against his administration really aimed to discredit his methods of governing. They attacked him because they did not agree with the innovations he brought to the conduct of his office. Although Grant harbored no express intent to "modernize" the presidency, he instituted new methods that tended in that direction and augured greater presidential activism. Those changes rankled traditional politicians. Long before the major scandals surfaced, Charles Sumner railed against what he called "Grantism," which he equated with "personal government and presidential pretensions."[7]

Grant's critics recoiled against several elements of his leadership style. Early on, many bridled at the independence he exhibited in making executive appointments. In addition, they disliked the expanded staff he installed at the White House to help manage his increasingly complex job. Critics carped about his absences from Washington. Relying on the railroad and telegraph to stay in touch, Grant traveled extensively, embracing a new mobility that presaged the modern notion that the office of the president is wherever the president happens to be. Most important, he played an active role as a legislative president. Although Grant often described himself as merely an executive, he took a keen interest in congressional deliberations and worked closely with allies on Capitol Hill. Tacitly acknowledging his effectiveness, his opponents decried his intervention as executive "dictation." All these innovations represented important contributions in the evolution of the presidency, but in the fog of censure generated by Grant's enemies, historians and others largely overlooked their significance.

A second major theme focuses on the substantive accomplishments of Grant's two terms, despite the incessant conflict. He pursued important initiatives on a variety of fronts. In some cases he posted significant achievements; in others the outcomes fell short of his goals. He obtained substantial legislation to protect African Americans' rights in the South. When he tried to enforce these new laws, however, Democrats and even some of his fellow Republicans denounced his efforts as despotic "militarism." This reflected their own inherent racism and political cupidity more than any genuine fear for the safety of the Republic. But their opposition played into the hands of the South's white supremacists, who eventually prevailed. As president, Grant implemented economic policies that righted the government's financial ship after the storms of civil war. He emphasized fiscal restraint and monetary stability in an era of turmoil and rapid change. Still, the persistence of depression after the Panic of 1873 illustrated the limits of conservative orthodoxy. Grant was the first president to institute civil service reform, but his balanced program fell victim to wrangling between implacable reformers and entrenched spoilsmen. Exhibiting genuine sympathy for Native Americans, he pushed for their more humane treatment, although in the end, his peace policy did not fully eliminate war. Grant's biggest defeat came early when he failed to convince the Senate of the strategic and humanitarian importance of annexing Santo Domingo. The bitter fight over that issue poisoned relations between the president and his opponents and colored impressions of the administration ever after. Indeed, in the perception of many at the time and later, that struggle eclipsed Grant's greatest accomplishment in foreign affairs: the settlement of the *Alabama* claims and the securing of peace with Great Britain through arbitration.

Taken together, Grant's eight years produced a record of considerable energy and success, tempered at times by frustration and blighted expectation. Through it all, he remained popular, winning reelection by a wide margin and coming within a hairsbreadth of being nominated for a third term in 1880. Although he achieved much, his power to reach his goals was limited by the political context in which he operated. A good president can become a great one if he can break restraints and transcend a context that works against him. Ulysses S. Grant could sometimes, but not always, do that.

PROLOGUE:
A TROUBLED NATION

When Americans went to the polls in 1868 to elect a president, their nation exhibited a paradoxical mix of promise and peril. The Civil War had preserved the Union, freed the enslaved people, and opened the way for accelerated development in a land of untold potential. With the acquisition of Alaska, the United States had become the third largest nation on earth. The country abounded in minerals and other natural resources as well as broad, fertile lands that had long made it an agricultural behemoth. Despite the backwardness of the South, Americans were among the best educated people in the world. They applied their inventiveness to innovation, which rapidly transformed the way the nation did business and the way its people lived. In 1868 a reunited America stood poised at the threshold of economic preeminence in the world.

And yet the electoral battle that year took place in a deeply troubled nation. Although the Civil War had ended three years earlier, the country still faced numerous problems spawned by the conflict. The American two-party system, however, had demonstrated remarkable resilience. The first postwar presidential election witnessed a fierce contest between Republicans and Democrats over how best to cure the nation's lingering ills and how best to guide the onrush of economic and social change.

At the top of the agenda stood the South, where political reconstruction remained far from complete. For three years President Andrew Johnson had fought a titanic battle with Congress over the reintegration of the former Confederate states into the Union and the incorporation of former slaves into free society. Soon after succeeding to the presidency, Johnson had initiated a program for the speedy "restoration" of the rebellious states, fostering the creation of new governments that lodged authority in the hands of white southerners and relegated African Americans to second-class status. The Republican Congress countered with the Civil Rights Act of 1866, passed over Johnson's veto, conferring citizenship on the former slaves and guaranteeing them "equal benefit of all laws and proceedings for the security of person and property."[1] The Republicans next embodied the act's essential elements in a new amendment to the Constitution—the fourteenth. By the end of 1866, the differences between congressional Republicans and the president had grown irreconcilable, and the failure of Johnson's "restoration" seemed obvious after riots in the South claimed scores of freed persons' lives.

In early 1867 Congress enacted the first in a series of Reconstruction Acts that required southern states to write new constitutions to establish new governments and institute black suffrage. Republicans also passed the Tenure of Office Act, which stipulated that federal officeholders whose appointment by the president required Senate confirmation could not be removed without Senate approval. Johnson nonetheless suspended Secretary of War Edwin Stanton and replaced him with the head of the army, General Ulysses S. Grant. When the Senate reinstated Stanton, a defiant Johnson attempted a second removal, spurring Republicans in the House of Representatives to impeach the president. In May 1868 he escaped Senate conviction by a single vote. Thus, as the election year got under way, turmoil racked the defeated South, and the government in Washington careened toward dysfunction.

Another vexatious legacy of the sectional conflict stemmed from the metamorphosis in the nation's financial structure. To pay for the Union military effort, Congress had instituted substantial levies on domestic goods and services, an income tax, and large increases in tariff duties on imports. With the return of peace, Americans and their leaders agreed that taxation could be reduced, but many interests had grown comfortable with tariff duties that shielded them from overseas competition, and they hoped to preserve as much of the protective system as possible. The postwar decades witnessed intense debates over how to refashion the tax system in ways that generated sufficient revenue while balancing the interests of American producers and American consumers.

To meet wartime needs, the government had also borrowed heavily. At war's end, the national debt had grown to an unprecedented size, well in excess of $2 billion. This obligation comprised a bewildering array of bonds and other instruments with varied interest rates and repayment schedules. Restructuring this debt remained a major objective in the postwar years. To supplement taxation and borrowing, Congress had enacted the Legal Tender Act in 1862, authorizing the issuance of non-interest-bearing government notes (greenbacks), which had no backing in specie (gold or silver) but putatively possessed the quality of legal tender for all public and private debts. Congress also empowered newly created national banks to issue bank notes secured by holdings of United States bonds. What to do about these new kinds of currency became a central element of the so-called money question after the war.

The shadow of the Civil War also hung over the country's foreign relations, especially with Great Britain. Many northerners interpreted Queen Victoria's proclamation of neutrality early in the conflict as an act hostile to the Union cause. More troubling was the British government's seeming acquiescence when the Confederates purchased ships built in Britain and armed elsewhere. The United States protested, but the British failed to halt the practice before the *Alabama* and other commerce-raiding vessels slipped beyond British jurisdiction to launch careers that were immensely destructive to the American merchant fleet. In the war's aftermath, American ship owners and merchants demanded that the government force Britain to pay restitution. In 1868 the controversy over the *Alabama* claims still festered and threatened long-term relations between the United States and Great Britain.

Besides these war-spawned problems, peace and security remained elusive on the western frontier, where deep animosity still plagued relations between Indians and whites. In addition, the burgeoning federal bureaucracy had outgrown the spoils system as a means for recruiting personnel, and a battle to improve it pitted reformers who wanted no half measures against regular politicians who wanted no measures at all.

On top of all these problems bedeviling the nation, Grant entered the White House at an extraordinary moment in the history of the presidency. The American political system itself suffered profound disarray. The institutional struggle between Congress and Johnson had poisoned relations between the two branches. When Grant became president, many in Congress still hoped to secure the permanent subordination of the executive. Part of his implicit mandate, therefore, was to work to correct the imbalance and put the system back on track.

Moreover, many Americans felt a deep anxiety over the integrity of their government and the nation's political system. As a staple of partisan conflict, allegations of corruption dated back to the early days of the Republic, although citizens' sensitivity to such charges rose and fell over time. During the war, when a vastly expanded public service saw an unprecedented volume of public money flow through the hands of numerous individuals—and stick to the fingers of some—the suspicion of rampant malfeasance reached new heights. It persisted into the postwar years and was confirmed by some noisome outcroppings of thievery, such as the notorious Tweed Ring in New York. At the national level, many jaundiced observers believed the worst, convinced that all sorts of "rings" held the government in their grip.

Depending on the context, "corruption" could refer to any of a multitude of sins. In one sense, it meant the abuse of office—theft, embezzlement, fraud, or other forms of malfeasance—for personal pecuniary gain. But some people applied the term more loosely to criticize excessive government expenditures for purposes of dubious public value. In their minds, spending beyond the barest minimum amounted to extravagance, and extravagance equated with corruption. Although the beneficiaries of such licit "corruption" were legally less peccant than perpetrators of outright malfeasance, critics considered the cost to the public just as egregious. Unfortunately, the fevered cry of "Jobbery!" greeted many proposals for legitimate expenditures, and such imputations discouraged worthwhile programs and nourished distrust of government in general. Finally, "corruption" might refer to making appointments to the public service for partisan advantage—the victors' distribution of patronage to sustain a "machine." The spoils system had persisted for decades, but the great explosion of offices during and after the war called into question time-honored partisan methods of choosing civil servants.

In all these senses—malfeasance, jobbery, spoils—"corruption" represented an offense against republican ideals. In 1868 both political parties promised to clean out the Augean stables. To accomplish this and all the other Herculean tasks the country faced, Republicans believed they offered the ideal leader in Ulysses S. Grant. As one party leader wrote, "The loyal people of the country looked to Grant with an almost superstitious hope. They were prepared to expect almost any miracle from the great genius who had subdued the rebellion."[2]

1
★ ★ ★ ★ ★

POLITICAL APPRENTICESHIP

In 1868 the Republican Party conferred its presidential nomination on General Ulysses S. Grant, by far the most popular man in America. The convention's choice was long expected and unanimous. It nonetheless represented a remarkable turn of events for a man who, seven years earlier, had languished in obscurity before securing a place in the Union army. Indeed, but for the war, Grant in all likelihood would have never entered politics and no doubt would have remained unknown to history.

Grant was born in southern Ohio, the son of a garrulous tanner and farmer, Jesse Root Grant, whose drive to escape poverty won him success in the leather-goods business and enough political capital with his neighbors to become mayor of the town of Georgetown. Little is known of Grant's mother, Hannah Simpson Grant, except that she was as taciturn as her husband was loquacious. Ulysses took after his mother. As a boy, he showed a remarkable talent for training and managing horses. In 1839, more or less at his father's insistence, he set off for West Point. Four years later he graduated twenty-first in a class of thirty-nine and entered the infantry. In these years Grant did not share his father's enthusiasm for politics, though he generally imbibed Jesse's Whig views and agreed with his opposition to the expansion of slavery.[1]

Ironically, in the first serious endeavor of his military career, Grant found himself fighting in a war launched to acquire territory for the spread of slavery. In 1846 the James K. Polk administration picked a

Julia Dent Grant. (Library of Congress)

fight with Mexico, ostensibly over a border dispute but with the ulterior purpose of annexing a sizable chunk of the southern neighbor's land. Grant considered the resulting conflict "one of the most unjust wars ever waged by a stronger against a weaker nation," and he later confessed his regret that, as a "youngster," he "had not moral courage enough to resign" his army commission. But a sense of duty trumped his misgivings, and he served ably. As a quartermaster, he quickly learned the indispensability of well-managed supply, and on the occasions when he saw combat, he impressed his superiors by his bravery, his tactical insight, his judgment of men, and his bulldog determination. His efforts earned him promotion to brevet captain. After the war ended in 1848, he married his West Point roommate's sister, Julia Dent.[2]

Despite his successes in the Mexican-American War, Grant retained his position in the army primarily as a means to support his family. Like other officers in peacetime, he moved from one post to another, sometimes with Julia at his side. During the war, some acquaintances whispered that he had shown a weakness for drink, but his performance then (and later) seemed to belie the notion that he suffered a physical addiction to alcohol. More likely, his metabolism and relatively slight frame were such that a small quantity of alcohol had a greater effect on him than on his bibulous brother officers. Still, in the perfervid moralistic atmosphere of Victorian America, Grant apparently acknowledged a need for personal reform. While he was stationed at Sackets Harbor, New York, in 1851, the twenty-nine-year-old officer took the pledge and joined a local unit of the Sons of Temperance.

In 1852 Grant took up duties on the West Coast, too distant and isolated for Julia to accompany him. At Fort Vancouver in the Oregon territory, he leased and operated a small farm to supplement his salary, but spring floods ruined almost all his crops. Other business schemes also came to naught. The dismay Grant suffered over these reverses was compounded by recurrent ill health and a longing for his family, which now included two sons. The degree to which he turned to alcohol to assuage his distress in this period remains a matter of historical dispute, although his behavior did not prevent his promotion to full captain. The advance in rank proved to be a mixed blessing, however. It required him to relocate in early 1854 to Fort Humboldt, a remote post in northern California, where he suffered contemptuous treatment from the imperious post commander, Robert C. Buchanan, whose ill will toward Grant dated back several years. Buchanan and others later asserted that the commander had threatened a court-martial against the captain because of his drinking, but contemporary records do not substantiate the allegation. Nonetheless, by the end of the spring, Grant had had his fill of army life, and he resigned his commission.[3]

After leaving the army, Grant returned to the Dent family's homestead near St. Louis, Missouri. He took up farming and supplemented the meager return by cutting firewood on his land and selling it in the city. As did many other struggling farmers, he saw his difficulties worsen when a financial panic ruptured the nation's economy in 1857. The next year persistent attacks of "fever and ague" convinced him that he was unsuited to the physical demands of farm labor. He joined one of Julia's cousins in a real estate and collection agency in St. Louis, but the business barely sufficed to support one family, let alone two. Next Grant sought to parlay his West Point training in engineering into an appointment as county engineer in St. Louis, but a political decision by the five-member county court went against him. With his prospects dwindling, the thirty-eight-year-old Grant accepted a position as a clerk in his father's leather-goods store in Galena, Illinois, in May 1860.[4]

The same month that Grant and his family resettled in Galena, 165 miles away in Chicago, delegates at the Republican National Convention nominated Abraham Lincoln for president. Like many Americans, Grant had found the political upheaval of the 1850s deeply disturbing. He later described himself as "a Whig by education and a great admirer of Mr. [Henry] Clay," but by the time he left the army and was ready to exercise the franchise as a civilian, the Whig Party had fatally split over the slavery question. Like other Americans who were fearful of a sectionally divided politics, Grant briefly (for one week) toyed with the Know-Nothings, but he bridled at their nativist agenda. In 1856 he voted for Democrat James Buchanan for president, "not because he was my first choice" but to defeat Republican John C. Frémont, whom Grant had known in the army and held in low esteem. Grant later recalled his apprehension that the election of Frémont, whose party opposed the expansion of slavery, would lead to southern secession and war. But Grant had no love for the institution of slavery, and the only enslaved person he ever owned, acquired from his father-in-law, he quickly manumitted. This was an extraordinary act, given that he might have sold the thirty-five-year-old man for as much as $1,000, which would have gone far to shore up his finances. Still, Grant did not embrace abolitionist agitation, which he believed would drive a defiant South to desperate acts. "I could not endure the thought of the Union separating," he later recalled.[5]

Events during the Buchanan administration deepened Grant's sense of foreboding. In 1860 he watched the election campaign intently but with ambivalence, and he did not mind that his recent move to Illinois left him ineligible to vote. For the presidency, he leaned toward Democrat Stephen A. Douglas, largely because he again feared that a Republican victory would spark disunion. Yet he also helped members of a local Republican "Wide-Awake" club develop their marching skills. Lincoln won the election in November, and the subsequent secession of several southern states confirmed Grant's worst fears. Six weeks after the new president's inauguration, Confederates fired on Fort Sumter in Charleston harbor, igniting the war that Grant had long dreaded.[6]

When Lincoln called for 75,000 troops to suppress the insurrection, Grant's dread gave way to a fervent conviction that every "true patriot" should "be for maintaining the integrity of the glorious old *Stars & Stripes*, the Constitution and the Union." Yet, just a week after Sumter fell, he clearly saw that the fight would be about more than that. He wrote to his pro-slavery father-in-law:

> In all this I can but see the doom of Slavery. The North do not want, nor will they want, to interfere with the institution. But they will refuse for all time to give it protection unless the South shall return soon to their allegiance, and then too this disturbance will give such an impetus to the production of their staple, cotton, in other parts of the world that they can never recover the controll [*sic*] of the market again for that comodity [*sic*]. This will reduce the value of negroes so much that they will never be worth fighting over again.

Grant also foresaw what the coming fight could mean for him. Called on to preside at a pro-Union rally and recruitment meeting in Galena after Lincoln's call for troops, Grant recalled, "I never went into our leather store after that meeting." After years of drifting, he was about to become a man of destiny.[7]

Grant's initial contribution to the fight focused on the recruitment of troops, but he expected that he too would reenter the army soon. He wrote to the War Department in Washington tendering his services, but his letter sparked no interest and got mislaid without a response. He did, however, catch the attention of state leaders, and with a push from Congressman Elihu B. Washburne, the governor appointed Grant in mid-June to be colonel of what became the 21st Illinois Volunteer Regiment. Less than two months later, the shortage of experienced soldiers helped Washburne secure Grant's promotion to brigadier general.[8]

Grant's meteoric career during the Civil War is a well-known chapter in American history. In an early operation in Missouri, the newly minted colonel nervously led his regiment against an encampment of Confederates, and though his pounding heart rose toward his throat, he "kept right on," only to discover that the rebels had fled. It dawned on him that his Confederate counterpart "had been as much afraid of me as I had been of him." He never forgot that lesson and never again "experienced trepidation upon confronting an enemy, though I always felt more or less anxiety."[9]

Despite occasional setbacks, over the next three years Grant achieved success after success and saw a steady rise in his responsibilities and reputation. Key victories in the fall of 1863 confirmed his indispensability as well as his preeminence in public esteem. Congress revived the rank of lieutenant general, previously held only by George Washington, and Lincoln promptly conferred that title on Grant and put him at the head of all the Union armies. Moreover, as the war progressed, Grant fully embraced the end of slavery as integral to the Union cause. Conceding that he had been no abolitionist before the war and "not even what could be called anti slavery," he had concluded "that the North & South could never live at peace with each other except as one nation, and that without slavery. As anxious as I am to see peace reestablished I would not therefore be willing to see any settlemen[t] until this question is forever settled." When he became general in chief, he decided to forgo moving to Washington; instead, in the spring of 1864 he established his command post in the field in Virginia, where subduing the forces of Robert E. Lee became the key to bringing the war to a close. It took another year of hard fighting to achieve that end at Appomattox Court House in April 1865.[10]

Like successful generals in the past, Grant found that many of his fellow citizens believed he could easily transfer his prowess in battle to the political arena, that the qualities underlying his successful leadership of the nation's military arm somehow fitted him to lead the nation itself. Even before the close of the war, in the run-up to the election of 1864, some War Democrats—members of the party who supported the war but not the Republican administration—saw Grant as the ideal candidate to run against Lincoln. But the general demurred. "Nothing likely to happen," he wrote, "would pain me so much as to see my name used in connection with a political office." As he told a former Illinois congressman, being president "is the last thing in the world I desire." He wished only to do his part to whip the rebellion and then hang on to the highest position in the army he could attain. "I have always thought the most slavish life any man could lead was that of a politician."[11]

But become a politician he did. As historian Brooks Simpson has shown, Grant's political education began long before the war was over. Success in military life required skills in managing subordinates and propitiating superiors that partook largely of the political, and Grant had grown increasingly adept at these skills. But on another level, Grant recognized that the fight to preserve the Union and, eventually, to end slavery represented a political struggle. He knew that how he conducted operations would not merely affect the military situation in front of him but also reverberate through the larger political culture. Although he harbored a genuine disdain for partisan politics and politicians as a class, his actions drew him inexorably into the political vortex. As a campaign biography written by two men who had observed Grant in the field put it, his achievements in uniform had "required something in addition to mere soldierly qualities"; they demanded "the talents of a statesman not less than those of a warrior." At the close of the war, Grant had achieved his overt military objective, but as leaders struggled to define federal policy in the war's aftermath, his position at the head of the army put him near the center of a political fight of unprecedented intensity and enormous consequence. His popularity as the victor of Appomattox made him a likely candidate to become the next president, and the fight between President Andrew Johnson and Congress marked the course of events that turned that imagined prospect into the reality of Grant's nomination by the Republican Party.[12]

As the war ended, Grant established his headquarters as general in chief in Washington. Initially he naïvely hoped for a speedy sectional reconciliation and leaned toward policies to hasten that end. He endorsed pardons for Confederate officers and argued against putting Lee on trial. He favored protecting the life and liberty of former slaves but otherwise showed little solicitude for their well-being, giving only tepid support to the Freedmen's Bureau and opposing, as did most national leaders, black suffrage. He posed no opposition when President Johnson set his "restoration" policies in motion in mid-1865, but he considered Johnson's efforts temporary and thought that devising policy regarding the South and the former slaves ultimately rested with Congress, which would reconvene in December. While supervising demobilization, the general recommended the retention of an army of 80,000 men, in view of "the possibility of future local disturbances arising from ill feeling left by the war or the unsettled questions between the white and black races at the South." In August he set off on a triumphal tour through the North and West, which, despite his silence on political questions, enhanced his presidential prospects.[13]

When Grant returned to Washington in October, he found a president eager to win the popular general's imprimatur for his lenient

Reconstruction program. Johnson had received reports of defiance by white southerners, and to counter those reports, he sent the general in chief to examine conditions in the region. Grant's journey was more of a goodwill tour than a true fact-finding mission, for it amounted to little more than conversations with leading citizens in a handful of cities in three states. The general discovered that white leaders who were eager to hold on to power under Johnson's program acted on their best behavior during his visit, so "as to secure admittence [sic] back [into the Union] and to please the general Government." Upon his return, Grant told the president and the cabinet that he considered southerners "more loyal and better-disposed than he expected to find them." This was music to the ears of Johnson and other conservatives such as Secretary of the Navy Gideon Welles, who welcomed Grant's views as "sensible, patriotic, and wise." Massachusetts senator Charles Sumner, leader of the Radical Republicans, vehemently disagreed, telling Welles that "a majority of Congress was determined to overturn the President's policy."[14]

As a battle over Reconstruction loomed, Grant found himself squarely in the middle. At Welles's suggestion, he prepared a written report of his trip, but when he put his thoughts on paper, he was less sanguine about the South than he had been in his oral account. In a brief statement that exhibited more nuance than his contemporaries and many subsequent readers appreciated, the general drew a distinction between the aspirations of white leaders in the South and a lingering resentment among the general population. "The leading men" and the "thinking men of the South" seemed ready to "accept the present situation of affairs in good faith." But after four years of war, during which time force had been the only law, people were reluctant "to yield that ready obedience to civil authority the American people have generally been in the habit of yielding." Hence, government troops must remain in the South until "civil authority is fully established." Grant warned, "It cannot be expected that the opinions held by men at the South for years can be changed in a day, and therefore the freedmen require for a few years not only the laws to protect them, but the fostering care of those who will give them good counsel and in whom they rely." Still, Grant thought whites wanted "to do what they think is required by the Government," and "if such a course was pointed out they would pursue it in good faith." This last observation was striking, for Johnson thought he had already laid out such a course. Grant seemed to be suggesting that Johnson's plan did not suffice, and he looked to "those entrusted with the law-making power" to complete Reconstruction.[15]

Publicly, at least, Johnson ignored the subtleties of Grant's report. In a message to Congress he embraced the general's observations about the views of the "thinking men" of the South while ignoring his warning of persistent ill will in the region. Eight states had already reorganized their governments. Occasional disorder had occurred, but Johnson characterized these events as local, infrequent, and diminishing. The president's Radical critics ignored the balanced assessment in Grant's report as much as Johnson had, and they lumped his message and the general's report together. Charles Sumner blasted Johnson (and, by implication, Grant) for "whitewashing" the situation.[16]

As prospects for cooperation between Congress and the president faded in the winter and spring of 1866, Grant's doubts about a speedy resolution of southern troubles intensified. His actions as general in chief began to foreshadow his defense of blacks' rights as president. Perhaps stung by Sumner's allegation of whitewashing, he ordered commanders in several southern states to report on lawlessness in their districts following the rebel surrender. Their responses painted a grim picture of violence, including forty-four murders, which, according to Grant, necessitated the retention of troops. By mid-January 1866, Carl Schurz observed that the general was "openly express[ing] his regrets" about his earlier report. In response to the discriminatory Black Codes passed by Johnson's state governments, Grant ordered commanders to protect from prosecution any "colored persons" who were "charged with offenses for which white persons are not prosecuted or punished in the same manner and degree." Grant's order echoed provisions in pending congressional legislation to extend the life of the Freedmen's Bureau and to grant citizenship and civil (but not political) rights to former slaves. Johnson's veto of these measures and their passage over his objections foreclosed any hope of cooperation between the two branches. To encircle the guarantees of the Civil Rights Act with even greater protection, Congress embodied them in a new constitutional amendment, the fourteenth, which required no presidential approval before going to the states for ratification.[17]

While these legislative struggles unfolded in Washington, the South witnessed an upsurge of racial violence, including a deadly riot in Memphis in May that cost more than forty lives. Grant decried this "massacre" as "a scene of murder, arson, rape & rob[b]ery in which the victims were all helpless and unresisting negroes[,] stamping lasting disgrace upon the civil authorities that permitted them." In the face of this lawlessness, Grant instituted military arrest and confinement of alleged perpetrators of crime "until such time as a proper judicial tribunal may be ready and willing to try them." Johnson and his attorney general quickly moved to restrict the applicability of Grant's order.[18]

By mid-1866, congressional Republicans and the president stood irretrievably at odds. Although Johnson grudgingly appointed Grant to the newly created position of general of the army, the exasperated president concluded that the time had come to go over his congressional enemies' heads and appeal directly to the people. In the midterm election campaign of 1866, he mounted a three-week trip through the North and took a reluctant Grant with him. The president's anti-Radical stump speeches sometimes degenerated into shouting matches with hecklers, while Grant stayed in the background as much as possible. Secretary Welles alleged that Grant got drunk on one occasion, but newspapers and Johnson himself reported that the general had been ill. Grant told Julia the president's speeches were "a National disgrace." Although he conceded that he still owed Johnson respect as the country's president, a deep personal contempt for the man now joined his skepticism about the administration's policies. Johnson concluded that the general was "looking to the Presidency," while Grant thought that "few people who were loyal to the Government during the rebellion seem to have any influence with" the president. For Johnson, the trip was a disaster. The voters elected a veto-proof Republican majority to both houses of Congress.[19]

After the election, Grant urged Johnson to change his course, but his advice "elicited nothing satisfactory." Indeed, the president was defiant in his annual message in December 1866, demanding that Congress seat members elected from the South. Less than two weeks earlier, Grant had asserted that it would be "necessary to keep a Military force in all the lately rebellious states to insure the execution of law, and to protect life and property against the acts of those who, as yet, will acknowledge no law but force." But despite recurring violence, Johnson claimed that "peace, order, tranquility, and civil authority" existed throughout the region. White southerners took heart from the president's obduracy. Ten of the eleven former Confederate states defiantly rejected the Fourteenth Amendment, finally pushing exasperated moderate Republicans to take radical measures.[20]

In the winter of 1867, while senators and representatives considered new legislation, Grant let his views be known. He argued that a continued military presence would "give security or comparative security to all classes of citizens without regard to race, color or political opinions . . .

until society was capable of protecting itself." He sent Secretary of War Edwin Stanton a detailed report on "outrages committed in Southern States" over the previous year. In the cabinet, Welles charged that Grant was "strongly but unmistakably prejudiced" by the Radicals and had devised his report as "a justification for legislative usurpation." Though not in fact a captive of the Radicals, Grant was coming around to the view that black suffrage in the South was inevitable. In late February he told an interviewer that the work of Reconstruction was "not all done," that southerners had erred in rejecting the Fourteenth Amendment, and that "now . . . they will have to take the Amendment, and manhood suffrage besides. Congress will insist upon this."[21]

As the Thirty-Ninth Congress drew to a close in early March 1867, it passed legislation largely in accord with Grant's views. The Reconstruction Act divided the former Confederate states (except Tennessee, which had ratified the Fourteenth Amendment) into five military districts. Each would be commanded by an army general empowered to suppress insurrection and violence, protect the rights of all persons, and organize military commissions to try offenders. The law made black male suffrage a condition for a state's readmission to the Union. Johnson attempted but failed to block this bill with what Grant privately described as "one of the most ridiculous Veto messages that ever emanated from any President." Nevertheless, Grant insisted that the president, not the general of the army, should select the military district commanders, although the general could reasonably expect to influence those assignments. Congress accepted Grant's view but took other steps to curtail the president's ability to thwart its aims. It required that all orders relating to military operations from the president or the secretary of war be issued "through the General of the Army," and it stipulated that the general could not be removed without Senate approval. The Civil Tenure of Office Act stated that civilian officials whose appointment required Senate confirmation could not be removed without Senate approval of a successor. This law afforded protection to Secretary Stanton, Grant's immediate superior and the only remaining cabinet member with strong ties to congressional Republicans.[22]

Taken together, these measures greatly enhanced Grant's influence over Reconstruction, largely at the expense of the president. Congress's turn to the military reflected Grant's understanding that no realistic alternative existed. Johnson had tried to divorce the federal government from Reconstruction as much as possible and leave it to the states. Congress and Grant recognized that Johnson's approach had failed, and they concluded that the military was the only national institution capable of effecting a true reordering in the South. In the end, Grant refused to accept the notion that "the nation has not now the power, after a victory, to demand security for the future."[23]

As the fight between Johnson and Congress came to a head, the military men closest to Grant became alarmed by his increasingly overt political role. In October 1866, after Grant had repulsed an effort by Johnson to ship him off on a diplomatic mission to Mexico, the general's chief of staff, John A. Rawlins, had called on Secretary of the Interior Orville Browning to assure the administration that Grant harbored no political ambitions. Rawlins, who had worked intimately with Grant since the beginning of the war, told Browning that Grant was "not a politician or statesman—he knows how to do nothing but fight—would fail in other positions." But even though the general was "not a man of ability outside of the profession of arms," many Republicans wanted him to run for president, and according to Rawlins, they were "making some impression upon him." Certainly by the time Congress was framing and passing the Reconstruction Act and other measures, the general was "getting more & more radical," observed another staff member. When the Congress elected in 1866 convened in early March 1867 and hastened to pass supplementary Reconstruction legislation, Grant again consulted with the Republicans, prompting one of his closest aides, Orville E. Babcock, to fear that "the Genl will go into politics too much. . . . I think he makes a mistake to go to the M.C.s [members of Congress] and say anything for it identifies him as opposed to the President, and will result in trouble." Grant felt otherwise, telling one congressman, "whilst there is an antagonism between the executive and legislative branches of the Government, I feel the same obligation to stand at my post that I did whilst there were rebel armies in the field to contend with."[24]

Yet Grant still did not openly break with the president at that time. His immediate task was to advise Johnson on which generals should serve as commanders of the military districts in the South. He ordered Babcock and another aide, Horace Porter, to prepare a list of recommendations—a remarkable demonstration of how he drew on his staff to perform even the most sensitive tasks, a practice he would sometimes follow as president. After working out the details with his aides, Grant met with Johnson to discuss the roster of five commanders. The point of greatest contention was Grant's suggestion of General Philip Sheridan to head the district comprising Louisiana and Texas. Johnson considered Sheridan too prone to side with Radicals in the South and would have preferred William Sherman, but Sherman wanted no part of any quasi-political assignment. Johnson finally signed off on Grant's recommendations, but he never became reconciled to Sheridan.[25]

Noting "a decided hostility to the whole Congressional plan of reconstruction, at the 'White House,'" Grant tried to strike a balance between the district commanders' zealous implementation of the law and the administration's efforts to restrict their operations, especially through the narrow interpretations offered by Attorney General Henry Stanbery. Grant counseled Sheridan, "As district commander I would not be controlled by" Stanbery's views "further than I might be convinced by the argument." Publicly, of course, he could say nothing that directly challenged the president. But in late June a political surrogate of sorts stepped forward in the person of Grant's chief of staff, John A. Rawlins.[26]

Rawlins, a lawyer who had first met Grant in Galena, had served on the general's staff since the summer of 1861. During the war the two men had grown extraordinarily close. A fanatical temperance advocate, Rawlins came to regard himself as the indispensable guardian of his chief's behavior, and his occasional violent blowups against Grant about drinking, including threats to resign, probably did more to damage the general's reputation than any drinking he may have done. Still, Grant placed enormous confidence in Rawlins, and many saw him as the general's alter ego. When Rawlins delivered an address to his (and Grant's) townsmen in Galena on June 21, 1867, many in the audience and around the country believed he was speaking for the general. Indeed, Grant had examined and approved the speech in advance. Thus, despite Rawlins's earlier assurances to Browning that Grant had no political ambitions, the chief of staff now appeared to be the herald of such ambitions.[27]

In his speech Rawlins presented a lawyer-like account of the evolution of Reconstruction policy that clearly upheld the Republican point of view. He defended the Fourteenth Amendment, which was still awaiting ratification, and he endorsed black suffrage not just for the southern states but for the whole country. Once "admitted to all sources of intelligence," the "African" would "rise rapidly in the scale of knowledge and the cloud of ignorance that envelopes him will as rapidly pass away." Rawlins portrayed the Reconstruction Acts as necessary to fulfill the constitutional requirement that the federal government guarantee a republican form of government to the states. He declared that with the settlement of the southern question, years of war and subsequent strife would give way to a "wise and economical administration of public affairs," which, coupled with "the energies of this mighty people," would enable the country to resume its career of greatness. "And if our experiment of manhood suffrage to all, without distinction of race, proves the success we believe it will, we may hope to see our republican principles engrafted upon all the other governments of the world."[28]

The *Cleveland Daily Herald* hailed Rawlins's speech as "emphatically, the platform of the country, and . . . unquestionably, the platform of General Grant." In Washington, however, fellow staff members were less thrilled. "Rawlins's speech has unfortunately been taken up here by the people as a political bid on the part of General Grant," wrote Horace Porter, another close aide. "We are all exceedingly sorry the thing occurred, as it was totally uncalled for." Nor did the speech please Johnson and his allies. A few days later, Welles concluded that even though Grant did not have "much political intelligence or principle, he had party cunning and would strive to be a candidate but not strictly a party candidate."[29]

Congress reconvened in July primarily to devise ways to negate Stanbery's opinions circumscribing the power of the military district commanders. Over Johnson's veto, the Republicans passed a law stipulating that any remnants of the governments established under Johnson's plan were "not legal" and "subject in all respects to the military commanders." In addition, Congress endowed Grant and the district commanders with full authority to remove any civilian official in the southern states, and it further declared that no district commander or election registration official could be bound "by any opinion of any civil officer of the United States," that is, the attorney general.[30]

During the brief session, the House Judiciary Committee took preliminary steps toward a possible impeachment of the president for his resistance to the congressional program. Republican committee members were eager to clarify Grant's attitude toward Johnson's restoration project launched in mid-1865. The general testified that he had been anxious to see civil governments established in the formerly seceded states, but regarding Johnson's program he said, "I was satisfied that every body looked on it as simply temporary until Congress met." He denied he had given Johnson any specific advice about the character of the civil governments the president was erecting. Grant's testimony allayed the anxieties of some congressional Republicans who had questioned whether he sided with them or with Johnson. In the words of the Republican national chairman, "At this moment he stands firm and unshaken in the face of the President and rebeldom. . . . There was at one period a few carping men who doubted General Grant's position, but . . . [h]e seems intuitively to understand the true objects and purposes of those who have been loyal to the country, and he is with them at all times and under all circumstances."[31]

After Congress adjourned, Johnson decided to take bold action. In early August he told Grant that he intended to remove Stanton as secretary of war and asked if the general would accept the position. Grant had little love for the imperious secretary, but he regarded Stanton as a crucial ally in defending Congress's Reconstruction measures. Noting that the Senate was out of session, he insisted that Congress had intended the Tenure of Office Act "specially to protect the Sec. of War" from "Executive removal" without Senate approval. "The meaning of the law may be explained away by an astute lawyer," Grant chided the president, "but common sense, and the mass of loyal people, will give to it the effect intended by its framers." Johnson then decided to *suspend* Stanton, which the law did allow, and he asked Grant to take the position ad interim. Grant agreed as a matter of obeying the commander in chief's orders, but he reminded the president that they held opposite views regarding the Fourteenth Amendment and the Reconstruction Acts.[32*]

Some Radicals feared that Grant's acceptance of the War Department post signified a new accord with the administration. They need not have worried. His new colleagues gave him a cold reception. Browning thought "his crude opinions upon all subjects, and especially upon legal questions," bespoke "a rather ridiculous arrogance."[33] Ten days after he took office, Grant and Welles had an extended political conversation occasioned by Johnson's intention to remove Sheridan as commander in New Orleans. Grant endorsed Sheridan's actions as consistent with congressional legislation, and he went on to defend the constitutionality of the Reconstruction Acts. "The President," he argued, "must like any other citizen submit and obey Congress until the Supreme Court set the law aside." Welles raised constitutional objections, but Grant declined to parse the Constitution and insisted, "The will of the people is the law in this country, and the representatives of the people ma[k]e the laws." He rejected Welles's argument that the former Confederate states were now equal to the other states and should run their own affairs. Believing that such a position smacked too much of "the old State-Rights Doctrine," Grant espoused the Radical position that the seceded states had reverted to the condition of territories. "It was for Congress to say who should vote, and who should not vote in the seceding States as well as in a Territory, and to direct when and how these States should again be admitted." Grant, the military man untrained in the law and inexperienced in politics, held his own. Nonetheless, Welles dismissed his new colleague as "a political ignoramus. General Grant has become severely afflicted with the Presidential disease, and it warps his judgment, which is not very intelligent or enlightened at best. . . . Obviously he has been tampered with, and flattered by the Radicals, who are using him and his name for their selfish and partisan purposes."[34]

When Johnson gave a direct order for the change of commanders at New Orleans, Grant wrote to defend Sheridan, boldly lecturing the president: "It is unmistakably the expressed wish of the Country, that Gen. Sheridan should not be removed from his present Command. This is a republic where the will of the people is the law of the land. I beg that their voice may be heard." An angry Johnson replied that Sheridan's rule in New Orleans had "been one of absolute tyranny." "I am not aware," he added archly, "that the question has ever been submitted to the people themselves for determination." Responding to Grant's lecturing in kind, the president wrote, "This is, indeed, a Republic, based, however, upon a written Constitution. That Constitution is the combined and expressed will of the people." Citing his constitutional duty, Johnson said that removing Sheridan was "absolutely necessary for a faithful execution of the laws."[35]

These letters found their way into the newspapers on August 27, 1867. At cabinet meetings that day and the next, the hostilities continued, heightened by another letter in which Grant declared, "I emphatically decline yiealding [sic] any of the powers given the General of the Army by the laws of Congress." He insisted that only Johnson's stubborn refusal to cooperate had driven the legislature to take extraordinary steps to effect an acceptable Reconstruction. After Johnson labeled this communication "insubordinate in tone," Grant withdrew it.[36]

Johnson and his allies concluded that Grant had initiated his correspondence with the president in large part to shore up his political bona fides with Republicans. Indeed, many Radicals had seen Grant's entry into the cabinet as an implicit endorsement of Johnson's policies, and the general's published letter helped counteract that impression. One newspaper declared that Grant's letter "gives explicit sanction to the idea that he sympathizes with the radical sentiment of the country" and "will materially improve his chances for receiving the Republican presidential nomination."[37]

Yet Grant had hardly won the approval of all Republicans. Massachusetts congressman Benjamin Butler, with whom Grant had tangled during the war, was determined to block his path to the White House. According to Orville Babcock, Butler had the general dogged by detectives, who would "at the proper time prove 'Grant is a drunkard after fast horses[,] women and whores.'" More serious was Charles Sumner, who may have harbored presidential fantasies of his own. Sumner showed scant enthusiasm for nominating a military figure and did not see Grant as having entered the Radical camp. The Massachusetts senator told a newspaper reporter that the general should have refused the War Department office. "Every Presidential order signed by Grant is an encouragement to the old rebel spirit." Ignoring Grant's published letter to Johnson (and Rawlins's June speech), Sumner declared, "We are left in harrowing uncertainty with regard to his opinions. Who can say that, as President, he would give to the freedmen, during the coming years, and through the processes of reconstruction, that kindly and sympathetic support which they need? Can we afford to be in any uncertainty on this point?"[38]

Some Republicans saw a potential president more to their liking in Chief Justice Salmon P. Chase, whose long-frustrated ambition to win that office still gnawed at him. Chase's fervent abolitionism before the war and his support for black suffrage made him a likely vessel for Radical enthusiasm. Yet Chase still had the whiff of the states' rights Democracy about him, dating back to his prewar affiliation with that party. Moreover, his opposition to the Tenure of Office Act, the Command of the Army Act, and military Reconstruction in general hardly squared with the Republican program. Even so, the chief justice had little viable competition for the affection of the Radicals, other than Benjamin F. Wade of Ohio, the president pro tempore of the Senate. Wade possessed impeccable Radical credentials, but his uncouth manner and advanced age (he would turn sixty-eight before the next inauguration) counted against him, and his soft-money notions alienated Republicans who espoused financial orthodoxy.[39]

Moderates predominated within the Republican Party, but they were hard-pressed to offer a candidate from the ranks of civilian politicians. They favored bringing Reconstruction to a speedy close while securing the rights of former slaves, though they stopped short of advocating a nationwide right to vote for blacks. Despite its wide appeal, this position lacked an element of moral urgency to propel any of its adherents forward as viable presidential candidates. Instead, moderates saw victory in 1868 with a presidential candidate whose appeal would transcend intraparty differences over black suffrage and allow the party to sidestep the disruptive money issue. For these purposes, many considered Grant the ideal choice. The general also appealed to conservative Republicans who had no great quarrel with Johnson and favored a presidential campaign that would emphasize the Union military victory and divert attention from the troubles of Reconstruction. As early as July 1867, a gathering in New York calling itself the Union Republican General Committee "nominated" Grant for the presidency.[40]

Observers of all political stripes watched the state and local elections in 1867 for some indication of voters' attitudes toward congressional Reconstruction and the coming presidential election. Democrats castigated Republicans as the party of "the negro," while Grant supporters such as Elihu Washburne "unfurl[ed] the banner" for the general. As the foremost champion of Grant's military career and now a leading advocate for making him president, the Illinois congressman delivered a widely noticed speech laying out Grant's views. Convinced that moderates already tilted toward the general, he framed his remarks primarily to disarm Radical critics such as Sumner. The general "openly and strongly" favored the Thirteenth and Fourteenth Amendments and the Reconstruction Acts, he stated, and had spared no effort to "secure their enforcement in their letter and spirit." By becoming secretary of war, Grant had not allowed "that most important position to be filled by a Copperhead and a Johnson man, who would hinder reconstruction." Moreover, said Washburne, Grant "believes there is no protection or safety to the colored people and the loyal white people in the rebel States *except through impartial suffrage*" and "that consistency as well as impartial justice demand that there should be no discrimination against any class of persons in any of the States." Privately, Washburne expressed the hope that his speech would "satisfy all good Union men in regard to him."[41]

The congressman's wish was largely fulfilled, ironically because the outcome of the 1867 elections proved to be a stunning setback for the Republican Party. In state after state across the North, support for Republicans declined sharply from 1866 levels, even where they managed to win. The falloff in support was large enough in New York and Pennsylvania to result in Republican defeats in those two important swing states. In Ohio the Republican candidate for governor, Rutherford B. Hayes, edged out his Democratic opponent by a margin of just 0.6 percent. The Republicans lost the legislature, thereby killing Benjamin Wade's hope for reelection to the US Senate and whatever chance he might have had for a presidential nomination. Even more alarming for the Radicals, by a margin of more than 38,000, Ohio voters rejected a state constitutional amendment calling for black suffrage. Similar ballot measures were defeated in Minnesota and Kansas. In the South, as expected, the Republicans dominated in elections to call constitutional conventions and to choose delegates, as mandated by Reconstruction legislation, but although these victories were important for moving Reconstruction forward, they offered Republicans small compensation for the losses they suffered in northern states that would play a pivotal role in 1868.[42]

Like many other Republicans, Washburne thought these losses greatly enhanced Grant's prospects for nomination, which he hoped to boost even further by widely distributing his October speech. Grant's aide Babcock, who feared that winning the presidency would be a "great misfortune" to the general, nonetheless conceded that Washburne's address would help offset the loss in Pennsylvania and elsewhere. The outcome of the elections indicated that the party could hope for success only if it assumed a more moderate stance, and for that, Grant was ideally suited. "Our defeat here is owing simply and purely to the question affecting our Sable brother," wrote a Pennsylvania Republican. "Grant is the only man who can save the Republican party next year, and every energy must be bent for that purpose." "Did you ever see anything like the rapidity with which Grant's name is adopted?" Maine congressman James G. Blaine asked Washburne. "The elections have done good. The crop of Presidential candidates were wilted thereby as rapidly as grape vines fall away under the blight of an October frost on the Kennebec."[43]

The men in Johnson's inner circle reveled in the Democratic gains in 1867, but the obvious boost to Grant tempered their gratification. As Welles put it, "the scheming intriguers begin to rally around Grant—speak of him as their candidate for President—not that they want him, but they are fearful he will be taken up by the Democrats."[44]

The notion that Grant would consent to a nomination by the Democrats was preposterous, of course, but would he accept one from the Republicans? He maintained his famous taciturnity, eschewed partisan labels, and at this point apparently had no extensive consultations with Washburne, his key champion. In mid-September Sherman had noted that Grant "writes me in the most unreserved confidence, and never has said a word that looks like wanting the office of President." But Grant knew how deeply Sherman loathed politics, and he may have tailored his comments to comport with his fellow general's contemptuous attitude. After the Republican losses in the October elections, Sherman again wrote that Grant "does not want to be President, told me that fifty millions of dollars would not compensate him therefor." But now Sherman noted Grant's admission "that events might force him [in] spite of inclination . . . to throw himself into a breach." According to Sherman, Grant recognized that circumstances in the South required "some strong power to protect the negroes and union men against legal oppression, or the acts of badly disposed ex-rebels." After the Republican defeats, Grant was not only more willing to be considered; he was also developing a rationale for accepting the nomination out of a sense of duty. In mid-November Horace Porter observed, "Everything is working finely politically. The Gen is the only one spoken of in the East, and he must bow quietly to the will of the people."[45]

Three days later Congress reconvened, and the positioning of Grant for the nomination continued. Impeachment was still on the agenda in the House, where the Judiciary Committee released Grant's July testimony, which drew praise both for defending Robert E. Lee from prosecution and for declaring that he considered Johnson's original restoration program only temporary. Grant's standing up to Johnson was underscored when House Republicans published his August 1 letter to the president, in which he had argued vehemently against the removal of Stanton and Sheridan. Senator Wade told reporters that Grant's letter represented "a sufficient guarantee of his Republicanism." The *New York Times* noted, "Other prominent individuals who have heretofore been non-committal on Grant, now openly favor his nomination by the Republicans."[46]

December witnessed a rush of public meetings calling for Grant's election to the presidency. Cooper Institute in New York hosted a gathering of the city's industrial, commercial, and financial leaders, who saw the election of Grant as essential for ending the political turmoil that threatened the nation's economic stability. The assemblage created a committee to raise funds for his candidacy. In Boston's Faneuil Hall, a similar crowd enthusiastically joined the Grant parade. To Democrats, of course, such meetings showed that moneyed interests saw Grant as a pliant tool. "The rich men of New York," former governor Horatio Seymour asserted, "are looking to the sword for the safety of their fortunes because they see no protection for their fortunes in any other quarter." As for "views of Government and its policy," Seymour insisted, "Grant has none. He is plunged into a sea so deep that he can do nothing but keep a closed mouth."[47]

But in Chicago, the *Tribune*'s publisher Joseph Medill attacked the argument that Grant lacked the experience to be chief executive. In an editorial entitled "Qualifications for the Presidency," the *Tribune* insisted that the duty of a president was "*to execute the laws as he inds them on the statute book.*" A man who has performed "the executive duties of a vast army . . . has certainly an education and an experience in executive duty fully as ripe as any gentleman who has spent his life in committee of the whole, or majestically presided over a court of last resort." Grant possessed the qualities "peculiarly required of a President . . . in a degree not equalled by any other man in public life." In a letter to Washburne, Medill wrote, "I believe I have met the 'want of experience—must have a statesman' objection. We have an 'experienced statesman' now in the Chair who has been everything from a tailor's goose to a traitor."[48]

Amid the swelling Republican chorus for Grant, the most discordant note came from Sumner, who thought Grant was "a good soldier, and nothing more." When House Republicans were preparing to release Grant's correspondence with Johnson, about which the senator had surely been apprised, Sumner complained to a reporter that "no record" existed of Grant's "ever having expressed a political axiom or an idea which could afford the people an insight of his capacity for statesmanship, or of the course he would be likely to pursue if he were elected President." For that reason, Sumner was "opposed to endorsing him as a candidate for the highest office in the gift of the people." "He must say more on our side."[49]

For most Republicans, however, Grant had said enough, and a renewed clash with Johnson in early 1868 sealed their commitment to him. In early January rumors circulated that the Senate Committee on Military Affairs would recommend Stanton's reinstatement. Johnson believed that some time earlier he had received Grant's assurance that in the event the Senate refused to concur in Stanton's suspension, Grant would withdraw from the War Department, "leaving it in the hands of the President as fully as when it was conferred upon him." According to Johnson's secretary, the president also felt that "perhaps it would be well for the Senate to reinstate the Secretary, as he could at once be removed, and in the mean time Genl. Grant be gotten rid of. . . . 'Grant' (the President remarked) 'had served the purpose for which he had been selected, and it was desirable that he should be superseded in the War Office by another.'" On January 10 the Senate committee submitted a resolution of nonconcurrence in Stanton's suspension.[50]

These events pressed Grant to determine his own course. A

rereading of the Tenure of Office Act made it clear to him that should the Senate vote not to accept Stanton's suspension, he, Grant, could be liable for the penalties imposed for violating the act: imprisonment for up to five years and a fine of as much as $10,000. Several months earlier Grant had indicated to Johnson that should the Senate not concur in Stanton's removal, and should Johnson not accept Stanton's reinstatement, Stanton's only recourse to regain office would be the courts. Grant had also told Johnson that if he changed his mind, he would inform the president. His new reading of the act now precipitated just such a change of mind.[51]

On Saturday, January 11, the Senate began debating the committee's resolution, and Grant hastened to the White House to explain his position. He told Johnson that he now realized that the law left him no choice—that upon the Senate's vote of nonconcurrence, his duties as interim secretary of war must cease. But Johnson too had revised his position, abandoning the idea of allowing Stanton back into office to get rid of Grant and then immediately firing Stanton. The president's backers both in and out of the Senate were strongly defending his removal of Stanton, and it was politically untenable for him now to sanction the secretary's return even to face peremptory dismissal. Johnson now insisted to Grant that he had removed Stanton (and appointed Grant) under his constitutional powers as president and not under the terms of any particular law. Hence, the general need not worry about punishment under the Tenure of Office Act. But Grant contended that the law, whether constitutional or not, would be binding on him until overturned by a court. After an hour of repeating their views with no apparent resolution, Johnson said they could talk further later. The president subsequently claimed that the two had agreed to meet on Monday the thirteenth. Johnson also claimed that Grant had promised on Saturday either to relinquish the office so that Johnson could appoint a successor before the Senate vote or to remain in office until the case could be resolved judicially. Grant categorically denied making such a promise on the eleventh and insisted that he had made no specific promise to meet again either on Monday or at "any other definite time." In Grant's mind, he had kept his pledge of the previous fall to inform the president if he came to a new understanding of the situation.[52]

Still, Grant was not averse to helping Johnson (and himself) out of a tight spot. On Sunday, Sherman suggested that Jacob D. Cox, a well-respected moderate Republican about to step down as governor of Ohio, would be an ideal person for Johnson to name to the War Department.

Cox had posted a distinguished record as a general during the war and held views on black suffrage not unlike the president's. Grant encouraged Sherman to push Cox's appointment with Johnson and to convey his own endorsement. Sherman did so Monday morning. His proposal must have made it clear to the president that Grant refused to retain the secretary's office, but Johnson did not warm to the Cox idea, apparently preferring to square off with Grant rather than accept his suggestion for an amicable solution.[53]

On Monday, January 13, the Senate debated the Stanton case until the early evening, when, by a partisan vote of 35 to 6, it resolved not to concur in the secretary's suspension. Official word was immediately sent to Johnson, Grant, and Stanton. Later that evening at a White House reception, the president and the general chatted briefly and cordially, but Johnson did not ask Grant why he had not come earlier to continue their conversation from Saturday, and Grant saw no need to reiterate the position he had taken that day.[54]

The next morning, Tuesday the fourteenth, Grant followed through on his intention as outlined to Johnson on Saturday. He locked the doors to the secretary's office at the War Department, handed the key to the acting adjutant general, and then left for his office at army headquarters. He sent a letter to Johnson informing him that in light of the Senate's vote, under the terms of the Tenure of Office Act, his duties as secretary of war had ceased. With Grant gone, Stanton, who was already present in the War Department building, received the key and took possession of the secretary's office. Grant had had no consultation with Stanton. Indeed, he was angered by what he considered the secretary's precipitate action, which left Grant open to the charge that he had colluded with Stanton to hand over the office and deprive Johnson of the opportunity to make an alternative appointment. Johnson asked the general to attend a cabinet meeting that afternoon.[55]

When the cabinet convened, Johnson delivered a severe tongue-lashing. He accused the general of reneging on a promise to either hold the War Department office until the courts could determine the legality of Stanton's suspension or relinquish the office so that Johnson could appoint a replacement. Grant reminded Johnson that he had informed the president on January 11 that his exposure to penalties under the Tenure of Office Act precluded his adherence to that position. At this, Johnson made the absurd comment that he had told Grant that he, the president, would undergo the penalties, if necessary. Grant cited Cox's appointment as a way out of the crisis, but the president waved that point aside. Johnson further berated Grant for not keeping a promise to renew their conversation on Monday. Grant denied making any such promise, although, in an effort to mollify the agitated Johnson, he noted that a number of things had kept him busy that day. Johnson and his cabinet considered Grant guilty of "duplicity" and thought that, as he rose to leave, he looked downcast at being found out. Instead, he was shocked by what he considered Johnson's blatant lies. Given his lifelong tendency to grow silent when crossed, Grant's quiet departure likely represented an effort to rein in his anger at the abuse he had endured. Afterward, Johnson "laughed at the fact that the Radicals had actually legislated Grant, their favorite for the Presidency, out of the War Dept."[56]

Nor was Johnson finished. Either he or a member of his cabinet fed their version of events to the administration's organ, the *Washington National Intelligencer*. Grant, accompanied by Sherman, immediately confronted Johnson at the White House and asserted that the article contained "serious mistakes." Johnson denied any knowledge of the piece and stuck by his story. Relations between the two men were beyond repair. Over the next few weeks, each stoutly defended his position in an angry exchange of letters that found their way into the press. Johnson accused Grant of insubordination, and Grant charged that Johnson had assailed "my honor as a soldier and integrity as a man" in an attempt to "destroy my character before the country."[57]

If Johnson and his allies thought these letters would blast the general's presidential prospects, their efforts backfired. An Illinois Republican reported to Washburne that "Grant's scorching letters are creating a sensation. Everyone is wonderfully pleased with them." Even Horace Greeley's *New York Tribune*, no champion of Grant, declared that the general had "shown qualities that add to his great fame, and justify the confidence of loyal men."[58]

The fight with Johnson further eroded Grant's reluctance to run for president. In the midst of the crisis, Sherman wrote, "Grant tells me that he will avoid the nomination if he can." But Grant then proceeded to point out the weaknesses of the other potential nominees: Salmon P. Chase lacked popularity, Democrat George Pendleton had opposed the war, Indiana senator Oliver Morton suffered from paralysis and could not stand, and New York senator Edwin Morgan, though "a good man," was not a candidate. "All sorts of names are bandied about," Sherman noted, "but Grant's seems to be the favorite."[59]

The growing inevitability of Grant's nomination drove the die-hard advocates of other candidates, especially Radicals who favored Chase, to desperate efforts to besmirch the general with allegations of drunkenness. In January a Treasury official informed House Speaker Schuyler Colfax about a *"dastardly calumny"* circulating through Washington that Grant had "been seen 'beastly drunk'" on the fifth of that month, a Sunday. A week later, a Grant supporter in the capital reported to Washburne that "the Chase men are industriously circulating the statement that Gen. Grant is frequently *drunk,* that he looks as if he were constantly on a bender, is slovenly in his dress, and is very dissolute in his habits, both as to *women* and . . . *wine!* This statement is the common talk of the city." The story soon went national. The January 5 incident was embellished by a Washington woman who wrote to Theodore Tilton, the Radical pro-Chase editor of the *New York Independent,* that she had seen Grant "very much intoxicated" and leaning on the arm of a companion on F Street that day. Tilton repeated the story in the *Independent,* calling on Grant to take the pledge, while Wendell Phillips urged temperance societies to investigate. But the accusation gained little traction outside the circle of those who were already opposed to Grant. Although some temperance backers, especially in rural regions, expressed concern, the insincerity of the defamatory statements seemed clear to many, and even one of Chase's closest associates noted, "There is nothing in his appearance, most certainly, indicative of a drinking man. I *would* believe the statements against him to be untrue." Most politicians gave the whispering campaign little credence. From New Hampshire, former senator George Fogg assured Washburne, "Grant needs no defense *here.* Nobody believes him a drunkard, and nobody dares *charge* it."[60]

The greatest concern at the moment for Fogg and the New Hampshire Republicans was a hard-fought state election, during which they heartily linked their campaign to Grant's presidential candidacy. In early March the GOP carried New Hampshire with 51.6 percent of the vote. The state's Republicans took pride in their reversal of the party's losses the previous fall. Grant, of course, made no comment, but a few days later, Sherman noted that Grant "thinks that the Democrats ought not to succeed to power, and that he would be willing to stand a sacrifice rather than see that result."[61]

Other spring elections proved less cheering for the Republicans. In Connecticut the party faced a more robust Democratic opposition rooted largely in urban immigrant neighborhoods. The Democrats showed little restraint in appealing to the racism of the state's whites, both immigrant and native. Their candidate for governor won reelection by a slightly increased margin, and although the Republicans increased their majority in the legislature, the Democrats claimed a victory. The Connecticut Republicans had closely identified their campaign with Grant's candidacy, and those who saw the glass half full argued that their loss in the toss-up state would have been far worse with any other man as the putative presidential nominee. But in the more reliably Republican state of Michigan, voters rejected a new constitution that contained a provision for black suffrage. The import of the mixed outcome of the spring contests seemed clear. "The results of all the elections show we cannot moot the suffrage question in the free states," a Pennsylvania Republican wrote to Washburne. "General Grant is a sufficient platform—and he should not be obliged to carry weight."[62]

Meanwhile, affairs had taken a dramatic turn in Washington. Johnson attempted to oust Stanton again with the appointment of Adjutant General Lorenzo Thomas as secretary of war. Stanton did not budge, and the House of Representatives finally took the fateful step of voting to impeach the president—by a strict party vote—on February 24. Johnson's trial commenced in late March and proceeded off and on for more than two months, with Chief Justice Chase presiding. Many Republicans believed that Chase's rulings tilted in the president's favor, and some ascribed his behavior to his hankering after the Democratic Party's presidential nomination. Chase's Republican prospects were now dead, and he had indeed transferred his hope to convincing the Democrats to tap him as a kind of hybrid candidate—opposed to much of Congress's Reconstruction program but in favor of black suffrage—to challenge Grant in the fall.[63]

Impeachment also affected, and was affected by, the fortunes of one aspirant for the second spot on the Republican ticket: Benjamin Wade, who, as president pro tempore of the Senate, would succeed to the presidency upon Johnson's conviction. Wade's hopes for the presidential nomination had withered, and he had lost reelection to the Senate. He now hoped that occupying the White House for even a brief period would enhance his chances of receiving the party's nod for the vice presidency. In light of Grant's reluctance to address issues publicly, Wade had special appeal to Radical Republicans who remained skeptical about the general's views. Yet Wade's position on the extreme left wing of the party in favor of universal black suffrage alienated other Republicans who feared a repeat of the losses of 1867. In addition, hard-money men scorned Wade's unorthodox views on the currency, and low-tariff supporters abhorred his commitment to high protectionism. Moreover, putting Wade in Johnson's place would require the party to switch the thrust of the upcoming campaign from the offensive to the defensive. In the end, the prospect of Wade's ascension to the presidency did not further his candidacy for the vice presidency and undermined the chances of convicting Johnson.[64]

Wade sought to cultivate Grant's goodwill, but the general required little coaxing to favor Johnson's conviction. Personally, Grant thought Johnson deserved removal because he was "an infernal liar," but the general also thought the president's ouster would "give peace and quiet to the country." Steadfastly keeping silent publicly, he discreetly lobbied wavering senators, with mixed success.[65]

But Johnson and his allies were also working on the doubters, promising good behavior if he were acquitted. As an earnest, Johnson submitted to Congress two state constitutions devised under the terms of the Reconstruction Act that would supplant the constitutions implemented under his plan. Most important, he nominated General John M. Schofield to replace Stanton in the War Department. Republicans considered Schofield acceptable, and Johnson's "idea was to relieve some of the Senators of the opposition." To most observers, the last of the eleven impeachment articles, a summary of Johnson's transgressions, seemed most likely to pass in the vote scheduled for May 16. That morning the *New York Times* carried the statement, no doubt unauthorized, that Grant believed "the President ought to be removed, because the Government cannot go on practically or safely in its present demoralized condition." But whatever Grant's hopes, by that time he had concluded that "impeachment is likely to fail." Indeed, the Senate acquitted Johnson on the eleventh article by a vote of 35 to 19, one vote short of conviction. Later votes on other articles showed the same result. Seven Republicans voted with twelve Democrats against conviction.[66]

One of the most outspoken of the seven Republicans, Missouri's John Henderson, insisted that he remained a firm supporter of Grant and that "one of the purposes of impeachment" had been "to destroy the General politically." In fact, however, neither conviction nor acquittal in the impeachment could have derailed the general's candidacy. After a stormy apprenticeship in politics, Ulysses S. Grant was about to assume the mantle of leadership of the Republican Party.[67]

2

★ ★ ★ ★ ★

"LET US HAVE PEACE"

The vote on May 16, 1868, to acquit President Johnson did nothing to dampen Republican enthusiasm for Ulysses Grant when delegates streamed into Chicago for the party's convention four days later. The previous day, a boisterous gathering of veterans had called Grant's election essential to "secure the fruits of our exertions and a restoration of the Union upon a loyal basis." At the convention itself, no formal nominating speech was offered, and Grant won a unanimous nomination amid deafening cheers. The band struck up "The Battle Cry of Freedom," and the delegates joined in the chorus while a curtain dropped bearing a painting of Liberty upholding Grant: "Match him."[1]

For the second spot on the ticket, Republicans aimed to avoid repeating the mistake they had made in selecting Johnson in 1864. When nominating speeches got under way, Carl Schurz of Missouri assured the delegates that "if Ben. Wade is put behind Gen. Grant, there is not a Life Insurance Company in the world, that will not at once want to take a premium on the life of Gen. Grant." With friends like Schurz, Wade needed no enemies. No one had forgotten that enough Republican senators had, in essence, said they preferred Johnson to Wade in order to defeat impeachment. Although Wade led on the first four ballots, House Speaker Schuyler Colfax overtook him on the fifth, and the convention nominated Colfax in a rush. Less outspokenly radical than Wade, "Smiler Schuyler" would help put a moderate stamp on the campaign.[2]

The Republican ticket for 1868. (Library of Congress)

The party's embrace of moderation showed in the platform as well. The convention asserted that the right of black men to vote in the South "was demanded by every consideration of public safety, of gratitude, and of justice, and must be maintained; while the question of suffrage in all the loyal States properly belongs to the people of those States." (Republicans in Congress would repudiate this craven hypocrisy at the next session—after the election—with passage of the Fifteenth Amendment.) Optimistically, the delegates congratulated the country on "the assured success of the reconstruction policy of Congress." The platform endorsed economic orthodoxy by calling for payment of the nation's bonds at full value, refunding of the national debt at lower interest rates, a reduction in taxation, and economy in expenditures. The resolutions committee also called for a "liberal" immigration policy and for the protection of naturalized citizens. From the floor, delegates added resolutions vaguely endorsing the lifting of restrictions on former Confederate leaders when "the spirit of disloyalty" died out and embracing the principles of the Declaration of Independence. The convention condemned Andrew Johnson for "persistently and corruptly resist[ing], by every means in his power, every proper attempt at the reconstruction of the States lately in rebellion."[3]

When news of Grant's nomination reached the War Department,

one of his aides observed "no shade of exultation or agitation on his face, not a flush on his cheek, nor a flash in his eye." Grant did, however, signal his approval of the platform, especially its upholding of the sanctity of the national debt. The next evening he greeted a crowd of 2,000 or 3,000, including many women, gathered at his house: "Being entirely unaccustomed to public speaking, and without the desire to cultivate that power [laughter], it is impossible for me to find appropriate language to thank you for this demonstration. All that I can say is, that to whatever position I may be called by your will, I shall endeavor to discharge its duties with fidelity and honesty of purpose." A week later the convention's notification committee presented the nomination to Grant, stating, "We know that you will not seek to enforce upon the unwilling representatives of the people any policy of your own devising, for you have said that 'the will of the people is the law of the land.'" At this pointed reference to Johnson's behavior, Grant readily promised, "I shall have no policy of my own to interfere against the will of the people."[4]

Grant reiterated this theme in his formal letter of acceptance. He praised the convention for reflecting "the feelings of the great mass of those who sustained the country through its recent trials." He endorsed the platform and asserted that "peace, and universal prosperity—its sequence—with economy of administration, will lighten the burden of taxation, while it constantly reduces the national debt." Beyond this he offered no policy prescriptions, arguing that new issues and changing public attitudes made it "impossible, or at least eminently improper, to lay down a policy to be adhered to, right or wrong, through an administration of four years." Instead, he insisted, "a purely administrative officer should always be left free to execute the will of the people. I have always respected that will, and always shall."[5]

Before Election Day Grant said little else publicly. His brief acceptance letter, followed by a studied silence, served the purpose of Republicans, who believed the campaign should stress his image as the savior of the Union—an apolitical leader above the fray rather than a spokesman for party doctrine. After three years of institutional wrangling in Washington, Grant would be the un-Johnson. He closed his letter with these words: "Let us have peace." This simple yet exquisite plea was open to all kinds of readings: peace between the races, peace between the sections, peace between the parties, peace among Republican factions, peace among the branches of government. The phrase became the hallmark of the campaign, during which Republicans asked Americans to accept the leadership of a victor in war who was strong enough and selfless enough to become a champion of peace. "Your nomination," Senator John Sherman wrote, "was not made by our party but by the People and in obedience to the universal demand that our Candidate should be so independent of party politics as to be a guarantee of Peace and quiet."[6]

Grant cultivated this image of self-sacrifice in his own mind and in the minds of others. He wrote to General Sherman that his position was "one I would not occupy for any mere personal consideration, but, from the nature of the contest since the close of active hostilities, I have been forced into it in spite of myself. I could not back down without, as it seems to me, leaving the contest for power for the next four years between mere trading politicians, the elevation of whom, no matter which party won, would lose to us, largely, the results of the costly war which we have gone through." Grant's aide Adam Badeau later recalled that despite his reluctance to leave his secure army post, the general found solace in casting the move as answering the call of duty. "Indeed he had been told so often that he was indispensable at this crisis that he might be pardoned if he believed it."[7]

At the White House, however, the president and his allies were in no mood to pardon the man they considered a central player in the impeachment intrigue. To Johnson, "Grant represented all the worst principles of the radical party," and his former cabinet colleagues thought they "could not support him without disgracing themselves." Welles called Grant "a man of low instincts" who "is wanting in truthfulness and sincerity, and is grossly, shamefully ignorant of the Constitution and of the structure of the government." Grant's calls for "peace" notwithstanding, he could expect no goodwill from these men who hated him to the core.[8]

Although a host of Democrats angled for their party's nomination, none emerged as the clear front-runner to challenge Grant. After the general's nomination, a gust of speculation wafted the perennial hopes of Salmon Chase, who assured party chairman August Belmont that, in his political views, he had long been a Democrat. The desperate chief justice even stooped to attenuate his commitment to black suffrage, writing to another party leader, "On this question I adhere to my old States rights doctrines." But Chase's protestations made little headway among skeptical Democrats who saw him only as a radical. No one placed his name in nomination, and despite machinations on his behalf to capture a deadlocked convention, he never received more than four votes.[9]

Among the openly avowed candidates, no one showed greater strength than former Ohio congressman George Pendleton, the party's vice presidential nominee in 1864. Pendleton based his campaign on a fervent advocacy of the so-called Ohio Idea, the inflationist precept that the Treasury should pay the principal on a portion of the nation's bonds in greenbacks. His currency notions appealed to distressed farmers in the Midwest but won scant support in the East, where several state party organizations backed favorite-son candidates to await developments at the convention. A few Democrats favored Andrew Johnson, who was eager for vindication. Others backed General Winfield Hancock, who, as military governor in Louisiana, had hewed a line far closer to Johnson's Reconstruction policy than to Congress's.[10]

Hancock enjoyed some popular support, but his candidacy aroused little enthusiasm among those Democrats who aimed to lash the Republicans for employing the military to fix "the iron heel of the conqueror upon the South." In opening the national convention, Belmont stirred the delegates' fury by insisting that the Republicans' nomination of Grant could mean but one thing: *They intend Congressional usurpation of all the branches and functions of the Government, to be enforced by the bayonets of a military despotism!* The Democrats required a two-thirds vote to nominate, and in a convention riven by doctrinal differences and personal, sectional, and factional animosities, that threshold proved elusive. Finally, on the twenty-second ballot, the delegates chose the convention's president, former governor of New York Horatio Seymour, who had earlier refused to be a candidate. As a hard-money supporter, he still hesitated to accept, in part because the Pendleton forces had put a plank in the platform endorsing the Ohio Idea.[11]

But the money question aside, the Democrats embraced Seymour as a perfect exemplar of the party's animus against Reconstruction. He had stood out as a critic of the Lincoln administration, and in 1863 he had addressed murderous anti-draft rioters in New York City as "my friends." He had backed Johnson in his fight with Congress. After the Chicago convention chose Grant, Seymour had declared, "The Republicans, by their nominations and resolutions, are pledged to keep up the negro and military policy," using taxpayers' money "to keep up military despotism, feed idle negroes, break down the Judiciary, shackle the Executive and destroy all constitutional rights." With no apparent sense of irony, he had told a Cooper Institute crowd, "Every man who is not blinded by hate or bigotry looks forward with horror to the condition of the South under negro domination."[12]

For vice president, the Democrats nominated Frank Blair, a former Union general from Missouri who had bitterly rejected Republican Reconstruction policies. As a presidential aspirant himself before the convention, Blair had called for the election of a Democratic president who would "trampl[e] into dust the usurpations of Congress known as the reconstruction acts" and "compel the army to undo its usurpations at the South." Although he failed to win the top spot on the ticket, this attitude suffused the Tammany Hall proceedings, which featured prominent ex-Confederates such as Nathan Bedford Forrest, founder of the Ku Klux Klan. The platform condemned the Reconstruction Acts as "unconstitutional, revolutionary, and void" and called for "the abolition of the Freedmen's Bureau and all political instrumentalities designed to secure negro supremacy." All in all, the Democratic gathering proved a godsend to Republicans, who wished to focus their campaign on allegations of Democratic disloyalty during and after the war.[13]

Beyond issuing his letter of acceptance, Grant played almost no overt role in the general election campaign. In midsummer Sherman and Sheridan joined him for a tour of the West, reaching as far as Denver. Although Grant made no political speeches, he accepted the warm greetings of crowds along the way. In a campaign that exalted the general's military triumphs and stressed Republicans' commitment to the results of the war, Grant's travels with Sherman and Sheridan won press coverage across the nation and spurred his supporters' fervor. By August 7, the candidate was back at home in Galena, where he largely remained for the rest of the campaign. On the few times he did venture out for ostensibly nonpolitical visits to nearby towns, he noticed that "the turn out of people is immense when they hear of my coming." But, he confessed to a friend, "I am not a very good hand at entertaining such crouds [sic]," which he considered a "very good reason why I should want to avoid them."[14]

During his travels, Grant stopped to visit his father in Covington, Kentucky, where he conversed for two hours with David Eckstein, a Jewish Republican from Cincinnati who was concerned about the general's attitude toward Jews. The question dated from late 1862, when Grant had issued an order expelling "Jews, as a class," from the area of his command in Mississippi for violating trade regulations. The ill-advised order reflected his frustrations in trying to control illicit commerce behind the lines, and Lincoln countermanded it as soon as it came to his attention. Both before and after his nomination, Grant's enemies brandished that document as evidence of his prejudice against Jews as a religious group. Leaders of both parties recognized that despite their relatively small numbers, Jews might provide the winning edge in key swing states such as New York and Ohio. Loath to inject himself into the campaign, Grant initially left the task of explaining his order to Washburne and his army aides. But in September he wrote to former Illinois congressman Isaac Morris: "The order was made and sent out without any reflection, and without thinking of the Jews as a sect or race to themselves, but simply as the persons who had successfully . . . violated an order, which violation innured [*sic*] greatly to the help of the rebels. . . . I have no prejudice against sect or race but want each individual to be judged by his own merit. . . . I do not sustain that order." Morris shared Grant's letter with Jewish leaders, and one of them, Adolph Moses, publicly exonerated him: "While it lies in the power of any one to do a wrong act, it requires a higher type of manhood to make a reparation. . . . [T]he best interests of our country are subserved by the election of General Grant."[15]

The "Jew order" controversy did little to shake Grant's confidence, and he saw no need to exercise much personal direction over the national campaign. In late September he wrote to a relative, "I have had the most quiet, pleasant time this summer . . . since the opening of the rebellion in /61. I want to make the most of it not knowing when the same opportunity will present itself again." At Galena, Washburne and Badeau maintained communication with the party leadership in the East. At campaign headquarters in New York, detailed management fell largely to Republican national secretary William E. Chandler of New Hampshire, a political operator with boundless energy and infinite devotion to the party. He worked closely with Thomas L. Tullock, the secretary of the Republican Congressional Campaign Committee, which had headquarters in Washington.[16]

Although Chandler and his staff coordinated the assignment of surrogate speakers around the country, the campaign remained largely decentralized. The national committee mainly gave financial assistance to the various state committees, especially in doubtful states, such as Indiana, or to those where local Republicans had scant resources of their own, such as in the South. Prominent business leaders such as Jay Cooke, A. T. Stewart, and Moses Grinnell participated, both in contributing funds themselves and in soliciting donations from others. Former New York governor Hamilton Fish kicked in $5,000, not entirely for selfless reasons, perhaps, for Grinnell assured him that in case of Grant's victory, Fish would likely have the opportunity to display "*court dress* . . . in some foreign land," that is, win appointment to a diplomatic post.[17]

Chandler got help in fund-raising from Tullock and the congressional campaign committee, which levied "assessments" on the salaries of federal government appointees. This traditional mode of collecting campaign money proved tricky in 1868, for Johnson had replaced many Republican officeholders appointed by Lincoln with Democrats who had scant sympathy for Republican policies and feared the loss of their jobs if Grant should win. Nonetheless, ample numbers of Republicans remained on the federal rolls, and Tullock and Chandler pursued them relentlessly. The national committee sent much of the proceeds to state committees, but Tullock also devoted a substantial sum to producing and distributing a variety of campaign pamphlets targeted at specific groups of voters. By the last month of the campaign, he was mailing from his "busy hive at the Capitol" 100,000 to 150,000 pamphlets per day.[18]

Although the Republicans probably outdid their opponents in raising funds through assessment, the Democrats obtained substantial sums from other sources. Belmont, New York party chairman Samuel Tilden, and farm implement manufacturer Cyrus McCormick each gave $10,000. Other men of means chipped in, and the Democrats amassed a war chest comparable to the Republicans'. One potential source of funds for the Democrats gave the Republicans particular anxiety. The high federal tax on whiskey—$2 per gallon—had given rise to a conspiracy in which distillers bribed internal revenue officials to falsify their production reports so that the producers could evade a portion of the costly levy. Republicans feared that money from this so-called Whiskey Ring would find its way into Democratic coffers. From Indianapolis, the state party chairman warned Chandler, "Unless the whiskey tax is reduced to twenty-five cents on the gallon or even less, it will be almost useless to continue the fight in Indiana." Congress did lower the tax to 50 cents in July, but the new rate would not take effect for two months. Although the ring's impact on the outcome in 1868 is impossible to gauge, it persisted and became the target of a massive investigation by Grant's Treasury Department during his second term.[19]

Raising money was a minor worry for the Democrats compared with the general disarray of their campaign throughout the summer and fall. Each party suffered internal divisions over the currency question and hence de-emphasized it, but that issue proved more problematic for the Democrats, whose hard-money presidential nominee stood diametrically opposed to the platform's endorsement of the inflationist Ohio Idea. Both parties tried to turn voters' attention to Reconstruction, but a number of Democrats complained that the nomination of Seymour and Blair had surrendered the loyalty issue to the Republicans. The delegates had hardly escaped New York's heat when prominent lawyer and Tammany sachem Edwards Pierrepont, who had hoped for a Chase nomination, assured Edwin Stanton that no War Democrat could support the ticket: "I would as soon vote for Davis and Lee. . . . The Spirit of the Rebellion was the life & soul of that convention, controlled it, led it—selected its candidates." Pierrepont made speeches for Grant and gave $20,000 to his campaign. Lobbyist Samuel Ward thought the Republicans had a double "war cry against our candidates . . . First—against Seymour because he was opposed to the last war and Second—against Blair because he is in favor of the next one."[20]

Nonetheless, many other Democrats believed that the key to victory was hammering the Republicans on Reconstruction with blatantly racist appeals. As early as February, Tilden had urged that the "paramount issue" be a demand for the "restoration" of the former Confederate states "with their local government in the hands of the white population" and a *condemnation and reversal of negro supremacy.* Both Seymour and Blair devoted their letters of acceptance exclusively to a searing indictment of congressional Reconstruction, the latter declaring that Republicans had "substituted as electors in place of the men of our own race . . . a host of ignorant negroes, who are supported in idleness with the public money." Georgia's Robert Toombs denounced "absolute negro supremacy" as "the corner stone of the Congressional plan." Many northern Democrats spewed similar venom. New York congressman S. S. Cox told a Brooklyn audience that Reconstruction had "but one purpose—that is, to perpetuate radical power by negro votes." If the election were close, "these black votes will rule. We are then a black republic! It is a terrible peril." Speaking in Omaha, Blair declared that the Reconstruction measures had subjected "all the people of our race in ten of the Southern States" to a "hideous black barbarism." At Indianapolis, he attacked blacks as "addicted to indiscriminate concubinage" and, in politics, "content to be the tools of those who gratify their brutal lusts."[21]

Such vitriol contrasted sharply with Grant's call for sectional and racial peace, and even some Democratic leaders feared it could alienate Republican voters they hoped to attract. Tilden reversed course and called on Democrats to exercise "the greatest moderation, prudence, and forbearance." William Rosecrans, a former Union general whose enmity for Grant dated back to their clashes during the war, tried to enlist Robert E. Lee's help in softening the Democrats' image. He asked the former commander and other southern leaders meeting at White Sulphur Springs if they were "willing to pledge the people of the South to a chivalrous and magnanimous devotion to restoring peace and prosperity to our common country." In his published reply, signed by more than thirty ex-Confederates, Lee assured Rosecrans that white southerners "earnestly desire tranquility and the restoration of the Union." They had shown their willingness to cooperate under Johnson's program, but their efforts had not "been met in a spirit of frankness and cordiality"; what they now desired was "relief from oppressive misrule" resulting from congressional policies. Lee denied that southern whites were "hostile" to blacks, yet he decried "influences exerted to stir up the passions of the negroes." The southern states simply wanted "the right of self-government" but were "opposed to any system of laws which would place the political power of the country in the hands of the negro race."[22]

Republicans dismissed Lee's statement as typical "Southern gammon," offering "specious promises" no more palatable than the truculence of Toombs and company. One journalist said it would make "a first-class campaign document for the Republicans."[23] The GOP countered by soliciting a public endorsement of Grant by John A. Dix, a prominent War Democrat and Union general, whom Lincoln had dispatched to New York after the draft riots in July 1863. Having been appalled by Governor Seymour's efforts against the draft, Dix now declared that his election would be "one of the greatest calamities that could befall the country. . . . I see but one source of safety for the country under existing circumstances, and that is the election of General Grant."[24]

Dix's letter reflected the dominant motif in the Republican campaign: the indispensability of Grant's election to sustain Reconstruction and thus secure what he termed the "results" of the war. "If the Democratic party succeed in the election of a President and Vice-President," James A. Garfield told an Ohio audience, "all we have gained by the war will be lost. . . . But elect General Grant, and four years more will settle all these questions, and secure an honorable peace." Union veterans fell in line. A gathering of more than 20,000 in Philadelphia shook the rafters in response to a one-sentence message from Phil Sheridan: "Say to the Boys in Blue that it is as essential to have a political victory this Fall as it was to have an Appomattox in '65, and that every man who loves his country should vote for Grant." A desperate, if not delusional, Seymour believed that old soldiers would oppose Grant because he had "slaughtered them too ruthlessly." He thought a speech by George McClellan, a popular favorite among veterans, could "wipe out the effect of the soldiers' convention." But neither McClellan nor Winfield Hancock felt inclined to mount an overt effort against the architect of Union victory.[25]

Grant's champions asserted that he possessed great attributes of leadership not only as a military captain but also as a "statesman." Former secretary of war Edwin Stanton declared that while Grant was fighting to preserve the Union, "his capacity and integrity for civil administration were equally manifest." In a popular campaign biography, *New York Sun* editor Charles A. Dana argued that, in the three years after the war, Grant had dealt "constantly with civil matters, of the most rare, complex, and delicate character," wielding "his vast powers rather as a civil magistrate, than as a military commander," doing so with "zeal, urbanity, patience and ability." According to the *Washington National Republican*, "It is his peculiar *forte* to study men and laws—principles, and their application to government. . . . He will be a sound, clear-headed, patriotic statesman."[26]

Democrats sought to counteract such claims with renewed allegations that Grant was a drunkard. The editor of the *Hartford Times* circulated the rumor that "Grant is drinking all the time & drunk a good part of the time." On the stump, Democratic speakers revived the earlier charge that Grant had been seen "staggering drunk on the streets of Washington." Grant, of course, said nothing, but his defenders fought back. Through an intermediary, Admiral David Porter publicly said that, having had "intimate" contact with the general for years both during and after the war, and having *"had every opportunity of learning his habits and knowing his conduct . . . , I have never known him to taste, nor have I ever heard of his touching, intoxicating liquors of any kind, not even wine!"* In a Brooklyn speech, the Reverend Henry Ward Beecher, the nation's premier Protestant divine, cut to the heart of the matter: "I would rather have General Grant drunk than Governor Seymour sober."[27]

As the campaign grew intense, a handful of state and local elections occurred during the weeks leading up to the national balloting. In September Republicans easily prevailed in Vermont and Maine, but both parties fought mightily for the key swing states of Pennsylvania, Ohio, and Indiana, where mid-October elections would serve as barometers for their prospects in November. Indiana in particular witnessed months of hand-to-hand combat. Both parties raised funds for the state and dispatched speakers, including vice presidential nominee Schuyler Colfax, who hailed from South Bend. Two days before the Indiana election, the Republicans' western chairman wrote to Grant, "I have never seen so much excitement nor so much bad blood in any canvass. Not a day passes without somebody being killed. Everybody goes armed."[28]

But the Republicans' work paid off, resulting in victory in Indiana by 0.28 percent of the vote and in Pennsylvania and Ohio by similar margins. "We had a jolly time here the night of the election," Washburne wrote to Chandler. "I have never seen the General looking or feeling better." Despite the narrowness of the victories in the doubtful states, the October wins opened the wallets of government employees who hoped to hang on to their jobs in the putative new administration. "Everybody is for Grant now," wrote an official responsible for hitting up clerks in the Treasury. "The fear is we shall have altogether too many *original* Grant men here on the fourth of next March, for the comfort of outside expectants."[29]

Among Democrats, the October losses triggered a grim foreboding if not outright panic. A proposal sprang up among western Democrats to scrap Seymour and Blair, reconvene the national convention, and nominate a new ticket. Some favored tapping Chase, while others leaned toward Thomas A. Hendricks of Indiana, Hancock, John Q. Adams II of Massachusetts, or even Andrew Johnson, whose heart skipped a beat at the mention of his name. Relishing the Democrats' discomfiture, a bemused Adam Badeau wrote to a friend in New York, "The latest phase of the political campaign is the strangest, and to me the most unexpected imaginable. Gen. Grant, however, said to me, almost a half dozen times, and as far back as August, that if the October elections went for the Republicans, he considered the withdrawal of Seymour & Blair and substitution of other candidates one of the most probable contingencies. Doesn't that look very like political foresight and sagacity, especially in one not trained in political life?" Fearing disaster, Democratic leaders tried to emphasize the party's strong showing in October and dismissed the notion of changing the ticket as "absurd."[30]

Resolved to fight back, Seymour broke with tradition and hit the campaign trail himself. In several speeches he tried to paper over his party's internal differences with regard to the money question and soften Blair's rhetoric while still condemning the Republicans' Reconstruction policies. He drew large crowds, but the trip betrayed an air of desperation. At one stop Seymour conceded that the Republicans were likely to retain control of Congress and observed that a good reason to elect him president was to hold them in check. Johnson, still passionate in his hatred for Grant, urged the candidate to warn the people "against the encroachments of the despotic power now ready to enter the very gates of the citadel of liberty." Nonetheless, after only a week, Gideon Welles concluded that Seymour's speeches were "likely to be unavailing." Grant, meanwhile, stayed put in Galena, in "tip top" shape and determined to avoid any appearance of campaigning.[31]

As a Republican victory seemed increasingly likely, some men who had shown no great solicitude for Grant's candidacy began to rally to his cause, with an eye to their own advancement as much as his. Among them was John Lothrop Motley, a Harvard-educated Boston Brahmin and one of the nation's foremost historians. Motley had served as minister to Austria from 1861 to 1867, when he resigned in a huff after Secretary of State William Seward questioned him about some disparaging remarks he had allegedly made about President Johnson. Some observers saw him as a possible successor to Seward under Grant, an appointment he would relish as vindication. In the first political campaign speech he ever delivered, billed as a "lecture," Motley hailed Grant's military common sense as a species of "genius." "To be a great soldier necessarily implies many of the highest intellectual faculties. No man can be a great soldier without being a thinker." Yet, Motley declared, "Not because he is a great soldier—deep as the debt of gratitude is which the nation owes him—but because during the whole of his career he has manifested those civic virtues which inspire confidence, do we wish him for our chief magistrate." Backhandedly, he added, Grant "seems utterly without ambition, and this is the reason why he is one of the few successful soldiers of history whom it will seem safe for the people to have trusted."[32]

Motley's friend Charles Sumner, a more prominent prospect for secretary of state, had reviewed the historian's speech in advance, but in taking a speaking role himself, Sumner could not quite match his townsman's ardor. Except for a brief comment in September, he had turned aside requests that he campaign for Grant, pleading a problem with his voice. Not until five days before the voting did he step forward to deliver an address in Cambridge on "Issues at the Presidential Election." After presenting a lengthy rebuttal to critics of his own record, Sumner defended the Reconstruction Acts, denounced states' rights, and upheld orthodox financial views. He mentioned Grant only three times in passing and offered nothing about his fitness for the presidency except to say, "if you are in earnest against the rebellion and seek just safeguards for the Republic, then vote for Grant and Colfax." Republicans welcomed the senator's participation, but no one could blame the party's nominee if he found little to be grateful for in Sumner's faint—barely existent—praise.[33]

In his speech Sumner donned his accustomed mantle as the country's preeminent champion of the newly enfranchised former slaves, but other Republicans felt an equal solicitude for the party's special wards. Republican strategists sought ways to acculturate these inexperienced voters participating in their first national election. The national committeeman from Georgia urged national headquarters to produce a pamphlet providing a brief biography of Grant "in a very plain style," as well as a "plain, large print" account of the Democrats' drive for the "defeat of negro suffrage and establishment of a 'white man's government.'" He also called for the creation of a weekly campaign newspaper for African Americans, the hiring of "good speakers, white and colored," and the organizing of barbecues and other entertainments. All this would cost money, but the national committee could allocate only small amounts. One suggestion it did act on was the distribution of tens of thousands of colorful Grant badges designed to appeal to African Americans. The chairman of the Memphis Republican committee thanked Chandler profusely for the 5,000 badges he had given to black voters: "Simple-hearted and imaginative, they regarded those badges with as much veneration and affection as ever Napoleon's veterans did the famous Crosses of the Legion of Honor. . . . Poor, noble-hearted, generous creatures! What grand capacities for good they have exhibited and retained in spite of all the degradation of their race! They have suffered so much in this very campaign for their principles, dimly as in some respects they comprehend them."[34]

Such tokens might exhilarate the freedmen, but they could do nothing to protect them from violent assaults against their right to vote. The campaign in the South witnessed numerous incidents of intimidation. No state escaped unscathed, but the worst outbreaks occurred in Georgia and Louisiana. From the latter state, Republican officials apprised Chandler of a "reign of terror" in which "hundreds of Republicans have been killed. Republican residences, churches, school houses, printing offices are being sacked, flags & fixtures of club rooms destroyed, Registration certificates of Republicans taken by armed bands. Democratic secret organizations, press, & party are in resistance to the laws & advise overthrow of [the] state government." However much the situation may have been exaggerated in this and similar reports, violence was pervasive. State forces proved inadequate to quell the mayhem, and the Johnson administration showed scant inclination to do so. Although the violence sometimes occurred under the auspices of the Ku Klux Klan or similar groups, more often the outbursts were localized and uncoordinated. Yet the attacks' spontaneity testified to the depth of white conservatives' hostility toward blacks, and the outcome showed that blacks' participation in Louisiana and Georgia was markedly lower than in earlier local contests. Because he was a candidate, Grant refrained from intervening as general in chief to stop the outrages. The endemic violence remained a problem that would confront the new administration.[35]

On November 3 Grant walked to his polling station in Galena, where he voted for Washburne for Congress and for other Republicans. He did not cast a ballot for president. In the evening he awaited the returns with a small group of friends at Washburne's house. As the night wore on, Washburne recorded, "The General was very cool yet anxious." Before the balloting, he had handicapped the result in each state, predicting which candidate would win and by what margin. As the news arrived from around the country, the general made "much sport" of his prognostications, appearing, as one reporter noted, "much more pleased at his political sagacity than at his success." If his behavior bespoke a fundamental confidence, it was justified. Grant and the Republicans prevailed.[36]

Yet the result was not a rout. In the Electoral College, Grant posted a comfortable margin over Seymour of 214 to 80. The popular vote showed a much closer division; Grant amassed 3,013,650 votes to Seymour's 2,708,744, or 52.7 percent to 47.3 percent. The preponderance of Grant's electoral votes—157—came from states free of slavery before the Civil War; Seymour carried only three "free" states with 43 electoral votes. In the northern and western states, Grant won 54.7 percent of the popular vote. Of the former Confederate states that cast popular votes in 1868, Grant won Alabama, Arkansas, the two Carolinas, and Tennessee, but the violence in Louisiana and Georgia proved so effective in deterring black voters that Seymour won those states handily. Throughout the old Confederacy, the Democrat garnered 51.5 percent of the votes cast. In the Border States—former slave areas that had not joined the Confederacy—Seymour won 58.7 percent of the total. These results taught Republicans that the political structure they had created with the Reconstruction Acts and the new state governments had failed to provide adequate protection for black suffrage in the former Confederacy.

Moreover, that political structure had entirely neglected the question of suffrage in Border States such as Maryland, Delaware, and Missouri, whose black populations were large enough to affect the outcome in future contests. In addition, although the African American population in the northern states remained small, the potential black vote could swing close states such as Indiana and New York. In the latter state, where property qualifications thwarted black voting, the number of potential African American voters was around 10,000, approximately equal to the margin by which Grant lost the state to Seymour. Republicans won lopsided majorities in both houses of Congress but did not wait to act on suffrage. When the Fortieth Congress returned for its lame-duck session in December, Republicans took up the question of a constitutional amendment to end racial discrimination in voting throughout the nation.[37]

Questions related to section and race had dominated the campaign, and for many observers, Grant's victory signified the final triumph of the cause for which Union men had fought since 1861. A Boston Republican told Washburne that Grant's "success is the one thing needed to secure the results of the war," and *Harper's Weekly* saw his "triumphant election" as the "final interpretation of the war." Businessman and reformer Edward Atkinson assured Secretary of the Treasury Hugh McCulloch that Grant's election "practically settles the southern question." But McCulloch and other men around Andrew Johnson took no solace. "The truth is," wrote Gideon Welles, "Grant is elected by illegal votes and fraudulent and unconstitutional practices. He would not have had a vote south of Washington but for the usurping and inexcusable acts of Congress." As for reuniting the country, Welles thought Grant lacked the "comprehension" to "reconcile these differences, and before his Administration will be half served out, serious calamities are likely to befall the country."[38]

Nonetheless, Grant took justifiable pride in his election and his successful thwarting of the Democrats' "most desperate and unscrupulous effort of their lives" to prevent it. Following "the bitterness and animosity" of the campaign, he wrote to a friend, "I hope now for national quiet and more looking after material interests." The day after the election, the president-elect told a huge crowd of well-wishers in Galena that he could perform his duties as president "if I can have the same support which has been given to me thus far." He added, "The responsibilities of the position I feel, but accept them without fear." Seasoned Grant watchers detected an echo from the general's remarks in March 1864, when President Lincoln had assigned him to command all the Union armies. On that occasion, Grant had ascribed his success to the "noble armies" he led and had told the president, "I feel the full weight of the responsibilities now devolving on me" but promised an "earnest endeavor not to disappoint your expectations." The final year of the war had shown the wisdom of Lincoln's decision. The four years now to come would test whether Grant could transfer his capacity for leadership from the battlefield to the White House and vindicate the American people's decision to entrust him with the highest office in the land.[39]

3

★ ★ ★ ★ ★

GRANT TAKES COMMAND

Two days after the election, President-elect Ulysses S. Grant left the quiet of Galena and headed to Washington. He had four months to choose cabinet advisers, and speculation abounded. Would he gather a "team of rivals," as Abraham Lincoln had done? Would the cabinet be dominated by Radicals, men at the ideological forefront of the Republican Party, or would it be leavened by a moderate contingent representing those who had always viewed Grant as the party's best hope for victory? Would it be political at all, or would it be a more "personal" group of individuals with whom Grant felt comfortable?

Suggestions about the cabinet and other offices grew to a torrent, and Grant worked to educate himself about men and measures. He took several trips, attending dinners and receptions in Boston, New York, Chicago, Philadelphia, and elsewhere. On these trips and at army headquarters he held countless private conversations. As aide Adam Badeau wrote, "He receives all, he is willing to be informed of the various views, and he weighs the opinions advanced. He gives all respect to those especially whose positions in the party which elected him entitle them to be considered." On occasion he journeyed to the Capitol for tête-à-tête sessions with Republican leaders. He listened more than he spoke, and whatever the source of advice, he did not tip his hand. His choices for cabinet seats remained a secret—even to most of the nominees—until after he had taken the oath of office. Although his silence frustrated politicians and the press, most observers hoped that Grant's reputation for tapping able subordinates during the war presaged his selection of an exemplary cast of civilian advisers. As one political reporter put it, "I question whether an incoming President ever before knew as much of the individuals from among whom his Cabinet must be selected as Grant; of their individual antecedents, their clique affiliations, and their respective capabilities."[1]

Among the men mentioned, none drew more attention than Charles Sumner as a prospective secretary of state. Never a shrinking violet, Sumner believed his preeminence in the Republican Party, his broad foreign acquaintance, and his eight years as chairman of the Senate Foreign Relations Committee not only equipped him for but also entitled him to the top cabinet post. Nor did he wait for lightning to strike. In the midst of the impeachment crisis, Sumner had consulted with Senate president pro tempore Benjamin Wade about becoming secretary of state in an abbreviated Wade administration, which would have positioned him to retain the office under Grant. The ploy did not pan out, but Sumner's ambition persisted. The day after the election he wrote to a friend that if a cabinet place "were offered to me . . . my country has a right to determine where I can work best." In the succeeding days he distributed pamphlet copies of his lone campaign speech as evidence of his service to the Grant cause. His good friend Congressman Samuel Hooper noted that if Grant should make Sumner secretary of state, "it would be received as an indication of his policy to look to the republican party for the support of his administration."[2]

Others, however, scoffed at the notion of Sumner as the avatar of Republicanism and considered him singularly ill-suited to become the nation's chief diplomat. *Chicago Tribune* proprietor Joseph Medill reminded Washburne that "Sumner has never been a friend of the General's." With the critical question of the *Alabama* claims still pending, Sumner would be "so intent on peace with England that he would sacrifice all rights, dignity and self respect to maintain it. He would let England p[is]s all over him rather than resent it." James G. Blaine—slated to be Speaker in the new House of Representatives—warned, "Thousands of men in our party would be offended" by Sumner's appointment. "We want a strong healthy *American* feeling in Grant's Cabinet—not braggadocio & bluster but dignity & firmness, & you will not have it if Sumner is put in the State Dept."[3]

Such objections amounted to so much preaching to the choir. Despite their shared commitment to Republican principles, the modest, plainspoken general had little in common with the pretentiously erudite and egotistical Bostonian who insisted on pronouncing the president's name "Grawnt." As one observer put it, "Mr. Sumner was an extremely intolerant man; a species of Sir Anthony Absolute in politics; very easy to get along with if you always humbly agreed with him." In later years Grant recalled that Sumner was "the only man I was ever anything but my real self to; the only man I ever tried to conciliate by artificial means." As he prepared to become president, he saw no need to go so far as to invite the senator into his official household. In early December the president-elect traveled to Boston and gave Sumner no indication that he was under consideration for the State Department post. Sumner began telling friends he did "not wish to leave the Senate."[4]

In his feeling of superiority over Grant, Sumner was not alone. At a dinner in Boston the general met Charles Francis Adams, the son and grandson of presidents, who had recently completed seven years as America's minister to Great Britain and was now on many handicappers' short lists for secretary of state. At the dinner Adams saw "wisdom" in Grant's reserve, but he also thought such reticence was "partly due to a consciousness of inability to converse with any fund of resources to sustain himself." Adams confided to his diary, "My instincts seem to repel me so much from him, that I am relieved to think there is no probability of my being tried by any offer of confidence." Still, Adams believed that "on any principle of public service I ought to be the secretary of state." When rumors persisted that he might be selected, he told himself, "I cannot flinch or shirk danger." But the rumors proved false, and a week before the inauguration, Adams concluded that Grant wanted only "second rate men." Like Sumner, Adams could not muster respect for the mediocre man who had the temerity to forgo his services. At least, he observed, "I have had the . . . good fortune in not being called to the hopeless task of educating him."[5]

Another ambitious Bostonian suggested for the State Department, John Lothrop Motley, tried to ingratiate himself with the president-elect. During Grant's visit, Motley managed to cross paths with him several times. Afterward, he gushed to Badeau that if the general "liked Boston only half as well as Boston was delighted with him . . . we shall all be deeply gratified." Grant did find his visit to New England "very pleasant" but did not warm to the pompous Motley. "He parts his hair in the middle and carries a single eyeglass," Grant told Badeau, in a comment whose "tone, as much as the words, indicated that the historian was too foreign in his ways to please the President-elect." Eventually, cold realism told Motley that he should lower his sights toward becoming minister to Great Britain.[6]

Adams's son Henry, who also entertained hopes of winning a job and suffered rejection, claimed to "pity the man that goes into that Cabinet." "We here look for a reign of western mediocrity," he sneered. But the Boston Olympians were blind to the virtues seen by others in the modest general. After a "most delightful talk," Ohio governor Rutherford B. Hayes marveled at "how completely and wonderfully he remains unspoiled by his elevation." He went on to note that "after he warms up," Grant was "cheerful, chatty, and good-natured, and so sensible, clear-headed, and well-informed." "Western mediocrity" held few terrors for most Americans outside New England.[7]

Washburne's name appeared on most cabinet slates, penciled in as secretary of state or more often as secretary of the treasury. As chairman of the House Appropriations Committee, he was known as the "Watchdog of the Treasury." In a speech two months before the inauguration, he took aim at "speculation, profligacy, extravagance, and corruption" and hailed Grant as "emphatically an honest man and an enlightened statesman, who would faithfully administer the laws without fear, favor, or affection." The speech not only warmed the hearts of those who decried the malfeasance under Johnson but also enhanced Washburne's bona fides as a cabinet prospect. But Washburne suffered from ill health, and some thought he might prefer a less taxing post overseas such as minister to France. Other possible appointees to head the Treasury Department included Massachusetts congressman George Boutwell and special commissioner of the revenue David A. Wells, whose recent report calling for reduced tariff rates pleased people leaning toward freer trade. The *New York Herald* saw "no one better to fill the post" than wealthy New York merchant Alexander T. Stewart. The likelihood that political attention would shift from sectional to financial issues heightened interest in the appointment.[8]

Speculation swirled around the other cabinet slots as well. One seemingly well-grounded rumor had General John M. Schofield, who had replaced Stanton as secretary of war, remaining in office, at least for awhile, and Admiral David Porter becoming secretary of the navy. This notion encountered the objection that military men ought not to be appointed to fill civilian posts. Sumner raised his voice against the idea, and Vermont senator George Edmunds submitted legislation to bar such appointments. Some party leaders thought the Radical element deserved particular recognition, such as the appointment of Benjamin

Wade as postmaster general, but Wade received no seat. Nearly all Republicans agreed that representatives of the large states of New York and Pennsylvania should have cabinet posts, but those states were so riven by infighting among rival factions that Grant struggled to choose persons who would not alienate large segments of the party. Oddly enough, some men in Johnson's cabinet, especially Secretary of the Treasury Hugh McCulloch and Attorney General William Evarts, harbored illusions that Grant might ask them to stay. But there was slim chance that Grant would tap either Evarts, who had been Johnson's counsel during the impeachment, or McCulloch, who had earned Grant's undying hatred for publicly endorsing Johnson's version of their controversy. Whatever the prospects for individual selections, the nation's general expectations were high. One New York party leader told Washburne, "You cannot overstate the anxiety which agitates thoughtful and good men all over this land, respecting General Grant's selections for his Cabinet—not in the ordinary political sense but as the authentic exponents of his civil ability. Men are looking to him for the formation of a new party—not for politics—but for country."[9]

While mulling his cabinet choices, Grant also monitored issues pending before the country. In his annual report as general, he advocated (unsuccessfully) the transfer of the Indian Bureau to the War Department from the Interior Department, where corruption was notorious. He opposed any reduction in the size of the army, not only because of continuing troubles between whites and Indians in the West but also because of threats to peace in the South. In December Grant clarified the military's responsibility to assist in the enforcement of judicial orders issued under the Civil Rights Act of 1866. In January he assured delegates to an African American civil rights meeting in Washington, "I hope sincerely that the colored people of the nation may receive every protection which the laws give them. They shall have my efforts to secure such protection."[10]

Grant also weighed in on a proposed constitutional amendment outlawing racial discrimination in voting. Sumner thought it would be more expeditious to enact equal suffrage by simple statute, but Grant and other Republicans sought to place voting rights beyond the power of courts or legislatures to undo. As one of his confidants reported, "Gen'l Grant's view is that there can be no quiet in the rebellious states without a final settlement of the suffrage right both as to the election of state & national officers—this by amendment to the Constitution—not by bill, as Sumner favors." Sumner absented himself during key roll calls, thereby leaving Grant as a leader on the issue more advanced than the vaunted champion of blacks' rights. A week before he took office, Congress passed the Fifteenth Amendment and sent it to the states for ratification.[11]

Another issue pending in Congress—repeal of the Tenure of Office Act—would help determine whether Grant would be able to clean the Augean stables of the federal bureaucracy. During the campaign, Republicans had condemned pervasive corruption in the Johnson administration. To effect significant reform would require the replacement of officeholders the Republicans held accountable for malfeasance, but as a former congressman warned Washburne, reform was impossible "if Genl Grant must submit to the Senate *his reasons* for making removals and appointments." Many Republicans concluded that a law they had passed to prevent Johnson from firing good men should not keep Grant from firing bad ones. Grant himself told reporters, "Because one horse needs a curb-bit you should not crowd a curb-bit into another horse's mouth." In addition, party leaders hankered after the patronage that repealing the law would unleash—none more so than Massachusetts representative Benjamin Butler. Seeking to bury the hatchet with Grant, Butler sponsored a repeal bill, and in January, before Grant took office, the House voted to wipe the law off the books. But the Senate dragged its feet, many of its members reluctant to relinquish a power they had secured in the Johnson years. Finally, Sumner and other GOP leaders convinced the party caucus to put the question off until the next Congress. "Distrust of Grant is the real explanation of this proceeding," concluded the *New York Herald*. "Sumner has no faith in Grant."[12]

That distrust arose in part as a reaction to Grant's silence regarding his cabinet picks, which kept many a Republican on edge. The flood of advice and queries continued, and on February 13, in response to the congressional committee that officially notified Grant of his election, he explained his reasons for keeping mum:

> There is not a man in the country whom I could invite to my Cabinet who would not immediately after the announcement, be the object of all kinds of adverse criticisms, in the hope to prevent his selection and confirmation, even among my own friends and those of the party which elected me. Many would attempt to change my determination. I have, therefore, concluded not to make known, even to the gentlemen themselves, the names of the Cabinet officers until I send their nominations to the Senate. If I should notify the gentlemen at all

whom I may choose, in advance of their nominations, it would not be more than two or three days previously.

In a few instances, Grant strayed from this rule. He had already offered the Treasury post to Alexander T. Stewart, and a week before the inauguration he informed Philadelphia philanthropist George Stuart that he was under consideration. During the war, Stuart had headed the US Christian Commission, which had provided religious services and material aid to soldiers. But abjuring politics, Stuart declined.[13]

Before approaching Stuart, Grant had had a conversation with Philadelphia journalist and politician Alexander McClure, who had urged the president-elect not to waste a Pennsylvania cabinet slot on someone like Stuart, who was not an active partisan. Instead, McClure encouraged Grant to select a "fair representative of the Republican Party." Grant defended Stuart and, according to one account, pointedly told McClure, "I am not the representative of a political party myself, although a party voted for me." According to another report, when McClure said that Stuart had not been identified with the party organization, Grant replied, "The same objection applies to me. I have never been active in politics, but a party voted for me." This conversation appeared in newspapers around the country and warmed the hearts of many Americans who had been turned off by the nation's rancorous politics. Former New Hampshire congressman Mason Tappan told Washburne that Grant's statement "meets my ideas of republicanism. . . . [I]f he thinks it best to go outside of the more prominent politicians of the country for his help to carry on the Government, the people will say *Amen!*"[14]

Tappan's enthusiasm exemplified the soaring expectations that surrounded Grant's accession to the presidency. As Congressman (later Senator) George Hoar recalled, "The loyal people of the country looked to Grant with an almost superstitious hope. They were prepared to expect almost any miracle from the great genius who had subdued the rebellion." Historian George Bancroft assured the new president, "You have exactly that power which is required for the success of an administration, comprehensiveness of view, joined with sureness of judgment & force of will to direct." A Massachusetts Republican said, "The true friends of the country have in Genl Grant the man for the times." According to *Harper's Weekly*, "The national confidence is unbounded." And on and on. Could any mortal meet such stratospheric expectations?[15]

Certainly the current occupant of the White House harbored no illusions about his successor's genius. To Andrew Johnson, Grant would always be "a liar, guilty of duplicity, false to his duty and his trust." Gideon Welles labored to convince Johnson and his cabinet colleagues to boycott the inauguration "of this ignorant, vulgar man." Grant may have heard of Welles's efforts, for he let it be known that he would not ride to the Capitol with Johnson. The inaugural committee suggested separate carriages, but in the end, Johnson refused to go at all. On the morning of March 4 the retiring president busied himself signing bills, and at noon he and his allies departed the White House. Later that day Welles confided to his diary that Grant had ridden up Capitol Hill followed by "a long procession, mostly of negroes,—at least two thirds, I should judge."[16]

Upon arrival at the Capitol, the president-elect walked to the Senate chamber for the swearing in of Vice President Schuyler Colfax. During that ceremony, according to one observer, Grant exhibited "his imperturbable expression as unchanged as ever. . . . There he sits, quiet, 'calm,' self-possessed, as though he were at his own fireside, instead of being in the presence of the assembled wisdom, wealth, intelligence and power of the country, whose destinies have been confided to him." By the time Grant moved out to the inaugural stand at the Capitol's east front, the rain clouds of the morning had given way to fair skies. He was sworn into office by Chief Justice Chase, who no doubt felt that he should be taking the oath rather than administering it. A reporter described Chase as "very nervous. He fumbled with the paper on which the oath of office was written, and he was far more embarrassed than President Grant." Afterward, the new president delivered his inaugural address in a clear but quiet voice. As he read the half dozen manuscript sheets, "his thumb and forefinger went to his lips" as he turned each page without the "least affectation."[17]

Grant had written the address himself and had kept it secret from all but a few intimate friends.[18] He repeated a line from his postelection speech in Galena: "The responsibilities of the position I feel, but accept them without fear." Now he added, "The office has come to me unsought; I commence its duties untrammeled"—again underscoring his sense that he entered upon his duties unfettered by political obligations. Yet he also used the address to begin repairing the grievous damage inflicted on executive-congressional relations during the past four years. He said he would veto measures he opposed but would enforce all laws on the books whether they met his approval or not—unlike the imperious Johnson, who had striven to subvert legislation such as the Reconstruction Acts. "I shall on all subjects have a policy to recommend, but none to enforce against the will of the people." Citing problems lingering from the rebellion, he urged his countrymen to approach them "calmly, without prejudice, hate, or sectional pride, remembering that the greatest good to the greatest number is the object to be attained." He pledged to enforce all laws to uphold the "security of person, property, and free religious and political opinion in every part of our common country, without regard to local prejudice."

Grant devoted half his speech to financial matters. He gave the obligatory nod to "a faithful collection of the revenue" and "the greatest practicable retrenchment in expenditure," but he also addressed the important financial issues left over from the war. Regarding the more than $2 billion in bonds still outstanding, he declared, "Every dollar of Government indebtedness should be paid in gold, unless otherwise expressly stipulated in the contract." Moreover, making sure that "no repudiator of one farthing of our public debt will be trusted in public place" would enhance the national credit and enable a refinancing of government bonds at lower interest rates. He also called for a return to specie payments "as soon as it can be accomplished without material detriment to the debtor class or to the country at large." Sounding like the general who had disdained councils of war, he added: "How the public debt is to be paid or specie payments resumed is not so important as that a plan should be adopted and acquiesced in. A united determination to do is worth more than divided counsels upon the method of doing." In high-flown language, he cited an untapped natural endowment waiting to lighten the nation's debt burden: "Why, it looks as though Providence had bestowed upon us a strong box in the precious metals locked up in the sterile mountains of the far West, and which we are now forging the key to unlock, to meet the very contingency that is now upon us." It might be necessary for the federal government to assist in creating "the facilities to reach these riches"—that is, provide aid to railroad construction—but such aid should wait until after the resumption of specie payments.

In foreign policy, the new president invoked a Golden Rule for international relations: "I would respect the rights of all nations, demanding equal respect for our own. If others depart from this rule in their dealings with us," he quietly warned, "we may be compelled to follow their precedent." On a long-standing problem closer to home, he declared, "The proper treatment of the original occupants of this land— the Indians—is one deserving of careful study. I will favor any course toward them which tends to their civilization and ultimate citizenship."

Before closing, Grant returned to Reconstruction, urging ratification of the Fifteenth Amendment, which Congress had just passed. "The question of suffrage is one which is likely to agitate the public so long as a portion of the citizens of the nation are excluded from its privileges in any State. It seems to me very desirable that this question should be settled now."[19]

One of the shortest inaugural addresses on record, Grant's speech won general approval. *Harper's Weekly* opined, "It suggests, by its nobility and manliness, the golden words of Washington and Lincoln." According to the *Washington National Republican*, "The president meets the two leading questions now before the nation, that of the public debt finance and impartial suffrage, with a square and unshrinking firmness which is worthy of the highest statesmanship." Even Charles Francis Adams conceded that Grant's address was "a clear, business-like declaration of his views on specific measures," although he was still convinced "there will be no breadth or loftiness of view, no comprehensive policy, nothing above commonplace." Gideon Welles dismissed the address as "a mess of trite, flat, newspaper partyism. . . . Still, it is lauded as a remarkable state paper." And indeed it was. "What is the general prospect?" asked the *New York Herald*. "It is one full of promise, prosperity, progress, development, and power at home and abroad. And so opens the new book of American history."[20]

Up until the moment of his taking the oath of office, Grant had retained his position as general of the army, not only to maintain his salary but also to prevent Johnson from naming his successor. In his first substantive act as president he nominated William T. Sherman to fill the post. On March 5 the president sent the Senate his cabinet nominations. For secretary of state, he chose Washburne. Observers had long predicted a cabinet post for him, despite his rough-hewn western demeanor. (One wag later joked that Washburne had wanted to be named minister to Great Britain, but "his want of knowledge of the English Language was insurmountable.") Most had thought Washburne would get the Treasury Department, but a month earlier Grant had tapped Stewart for that job. Grant believed the New Yorker's business acumen would give him unparalleled insight into economic issues. For secretary of war, Grant asked Schofield to remain in office briefly, primarily to compliment the general for his past service in both war and peace.[21]

The continuing matter of Reconstruction would involve complex legal questions, and Grant chose for attorney general Ebenezer Rockwood Hoar, a well-respected Massachusetts Supreme Court justice who had fought in the ranks of antislavery lawyers. To appeal to the moderate wing of the Republican Party, he nominated for secretary of the interior Jacob D. Cox, a former Union general and governor of Ohio who had won Grant's respect during the war. Cox's reputation for integrity augured reform of the corrupt bureaus in the Interior Department. Desirous of reaching out to the South, Grant named former Maryland congressman and senator John A. J. Creswell as postmaster general. A relatively recent arrival in the political arena, Creswell had championed the antisecession cause in Maryland.[22]

The biggest surprise was Grant's selection for secretary of the navy: Adolph Borie, a wealthy Philadelphia merchant with virtually no political experience. A strong supporter of the Union cause, Borie had contributed liberally from his own pocket to support the troops, a fact that impressed Grant. Borie (like Stewart) had also made a substantial donation to a fund to buy a house for the Union victor, spurring severe criticism when the president gave him a cabinet post. But Borie also drew fire from some Republican leaders as the most blatant example of Grant's apparent refusal to listen to their advice. "Who the mischief is Borie?" Joseph Medill asked Washburne.[23]

Clearly, Grant had assembled no "team of rivals"—men of independent public stature whose own bases of political power could lend support to the administration's standing. To some observers, this was a serious blunder. As one Pennsylvania Republican put it, "I don't believe a personal administration, such as the present Cabinet seems to be, with no wish other than the President's and no counsel or advice or policy of its own, can or ought to be successful." Rumors circulated that Sumner could not "conceal his wrath and indignation" at being "offered nothing" nor "even consulted in regard to the Cabinet." Others, however, applauded. Harvard law professor Emory Washburn wrote to Elihu Washburne, "If he will only go on as he has begun & cut himself loose from a set of party hacks who undertake to run the machine themselves for their own advantage, the country will thank him enough to overshadow all the curses which disappointed politicians may cast at him."[24]

The charge that the cabinet was too "personal" missed the nuanced considerations that informed Grant's selections. In Borie's case, he did not expect the new secretary to stay long or to closely supervise the Navy Department. The president planned to assign real direction to Admiral Porter, but he bowed to the prejudice against making military officers heads of departments and nominated Borie instead. Borie's appointment also made good political sense. For months, adherents of the warring factions of the Pennsylvania Republican Party had pressured Grant to choose this or that man. He conceded that the Republican victory in the state in October had boosted his own campaign, and for this, Pennsylvania deserved recognition, but he understood the pitfalls of tilting one way or another among the factions. Hence he chose Borie, who was not closely identified with any of them. Grant had envisioned the same role for George Stuart, but when Stuart declined, he turned to Borie.[25]

New York, another large state deserving to be rewarded with a cabinet slot, also witnessed intense animosities among leaders such as Horace Greeley, former senator E. D. Morgan, and Reuben Fenton, who had defeated Morgan for reelection. Grant aimed to avoid exacerbating these rivalries, and Stewart's recent entry into politics offered a way out of the factional conundrum. Both Pennsylvania and New York were large swing states where it was imperative to keep the party united, but even the staunchly Republican state of Massachusetts exhibited similar factionalism. Charles Sumner and Charles Francis Adams held each other in contempt, and both of them despised the unpredictable spoilsman Ben Butler. Given this nest of vipers, Rockwood Hoar's wit, sociability, intellect, and literary culture seemed well suited to ward off attacks. In the end, it was not that Grant had failed to listen to the politicians. He had listened. But the advice he heard moved him to frame his cabinet in a way that he hoped would minimize infighting, both within the group and in the party at large. "It contains no Presidential aspirants, and may therefore be regarded as organized for harmony," wrote Rutherford Hayes. "No man being conspicuous, Grant's leadership and rule is beyond question."[26]

Upon receiving Grant's nominations on Friday, March 5, the Senate confirmed them unanimously. Within hours, the president's handiwork began to unravel when the lobby erupted with suggestions that Stewart might be ineligible to serve. The 1789 law establishing the Treasury Department included a provision barring from the office of secretary and other positions any person "carrying on the business of trade or commerce" or engaging in several other types of business, including the "purchase or disposal" of federal or state bonds. The statute had lain unnoticed for years, and the Senate certainly overlooked it in its unanimous vote. Stewart immediately sought advice from Chief Justice Chase, who responded that the only apparent way to avoid the law's stipulations was for Stewart to divest himself of all his holdings. But according to Stewart, it would take five years to extricate himself. Later in the evening he discussed the problem with Grant, who was just as surprised at the turn of events as Stewart. The president promised to ask Congress the next day to modify the law to permit Stewart to serve.[27]

On Saturday, New Hampshire senator James Patterson proposed a bill to repeal the disqualifying portion of the 1789 law. Smelling blood, Sumner objected to its immediate passage and called for referral of the bill to committee, but the Senate had yet to form its new committees. This brief discussion ended inconclusively, and shortly thereafter Grant's message arrived requesting that, in view of Stewart's unanimous confirmation, "he be exempted by joint resolution of the two Houses" from the act's prohibition. John Sherman introduced a repeal bill similar to Patterson's but including a provision barring the treasury secretary from acting "on any matter, claim, or account in which he is personally interested." Sherman sought to address the concern that the treasury secretary had jurisdiction over cases involving the tariff laws, which could affect Stewart's import business. Again, Sumner blocked an immediate decision. A day earlier the House had adjourned for several days, delaying any attempt to introduce a repeal measure in that body.[28]

By these maneuvers, Sumner and others gained time to arouse public opinion against Stewart. Henry Bowen, editor of the *New York Independent*, told the Massachusetts senator that repeal of the statute would be "a monstrous outrage. . . . Can a man be lawyer, judge, and jury all at the same moment in his own case[?]" Stewart's defenders insisted that some previous treasury secretaries had served in technical violation of the law with no detriment to the nation. More important, asserted the *New York Herald*, the law "is manifestly unconstitutional; for it is a prohibition against any American citizen holding office who is at the moment engaged in promoting the prosperity of his country by using his brains, treasure and energies in business pursuits." Some of the secretary's allies argued that it was absurd to assume that Stewart—one of the richest men in America—would manipulate his office to add paltry sums to his immense wealth.[29]

Nonetheless, in an age of heightened sensitivity to allegations of corruption, defenders of the law won the public relations battle. On Monday, March 8, after the Senate Republican caucus took no action on the repeal proposition, Stewart told Grant he could place his assets in a trust. He thus proposed a device that became common among federal appointees in the twentieth century and went even further by offering to donate the proceeds to charity. Grant believed that, under this plan, the secretary would no longer be in violation of the law. The next day, after running the proposal by several congressmen, Grant withdrew his request that Stewart be exempted from the statute. Stewart presented the president with a detailed trust agreement as well as a letter of resignation, should Grant conclude that this was the wiser course. Stewart's magnanimity won praise, but questions remained about whether the trust plan could really circumvent the prohibitions of the law. Stewart might not reap any profits, but his assets would nonetheless be vulnerable to loss, a circumstance that still exposed him to a potential conflict of interest. Grant soon concluded that the politics of the situation had become untenable. Before the end of the day, he accepted Stewart's resignation.[30]

To replace Stewart, Grant turned to George Boutwell. A former governor and congressman from Massachusetts, Boutwell enjoyed an impeccable reputation as a Radical and had served as one of the House managers during the Johnson impeachment. He had earned his financial credentials during the war as the first commissioner of the Internal Revenue Service. Before the inauguration, many had considered him the likeliest choice for secretary of the treasury. In late February Grant had talked with Boutwell about cabinet possibilities. By then, he was committed to appointing Stewart to the Treasury, and he offered Boutwell the Interior Department, which he declined. Boutwell now won easy confirmation as secretary of the treasury.[31]

Although the controversy surrounding Stewart's appointment was ostensibly about his legal ineligibility, other issues were in play. Some observers intimated that the seventy-four-year-old Stewart lacked the vigor to meet the challenges of such a complex job. Others criticized his involvement in raising money to buy General Grant a house in Washington after the war and then raising another fund to buy the house back, at a handsome profit to Grant, in order to present it to Sherman on the day before the inauguration. Moreover, Grant may have overestimated Stewart's acceptability to all the New York factions. Senator Roscoe Conkling, for instance, showed little enthusiasm for the merchant.[32]

Most important, however, Stewart's views on the tariff aroused the ire of the Republican Party's dominant protectionist wing. Stewart supported the low-tariff ideas espoused by special commissioner of the revenue David Wells, but protectionist Republicans considered Wells a traitor and found Stewart no more acceptable. When the New York Free Trade League called a meeting to celebrate Stewart's appointment, protectionists sprang into action. In the words of one reporter, "The discovery of the [1789] law was a Godsend to them, not so much on account of its provisions, but it gave them an ostensible ground for opposition—a rallying point." But the assault shocked midwestern tariff reformers. Horace White of the *Chicago Tribune* pleaded with Washburne, "If anything can be done to keep Mr. Stewart in the Cabinet, it ought to be done." In the end, however, salvaging the nomination proved impossible. Boutwell's appointment pleased his fellow protectionists and left the low-tariff men cold. That the president had appointed two men with radically different views on the tariff suggested that, as New Yorker John Bigelow delicately put it, "Grant has no prejudices upon that subject to conquer."[33]

The Stewart imbroglio tended to confirm the impression that Grant had failed to consult party leaders, obliterating from the public consciousness the nearly nonstop conversations he had held with Republicans since his election. Had he "asked and taken the advice of a few Senators and members who know something about these things," one congressman groused, "he would not have run himself and the party into this awkward predicament." Such second-guessing conveniently overlooked the Senate's unanimous confirmation of Stewart. As the *New York Times* noted, senators who were "satirically alluding to the first day's work of the 'President General' . . . as a 'bungling piece of business'" had forgotten "the proof of their ignorance of the law." Sumner, who had joined in the unanimous vote, sniped a week later, "I hope General Grant will make no more mistakes."[34]

While the Stewart struggle was unfolding, reports filtered through Washington that ill health would soon force Washburne to resign. Washburne had been ailing for weeks, and Grant had long intended to make him minister to France, hoping that a sojourn abroad would restore his health. His original choice for the State Department had been Iowa representative James F. Wilson, who was leaving Congress. Shortly before the inauguration, however, Washburne told Grant that before he left for France he would like to briefly occupy a cabinet position to enhance his standing in the important diplomatic post. He preferred the Treasury Department, but Grant had already recruited Stewart, so they agreed that Washburne would become secretary of state, with the understanding that he would soon step down. Wilson accepted this arrangement only reluctantly, and when Washburne did not resign upon confirmation and even began suggesting appointments in the department, Wilson backed out. Grant next turned to Hamilton Fish, a former governor and senator from New York. Grant had planned to give Fish the plum job of minister to Great Britain, but when Stewart's resignation opened up a cabinet slot for a New Yorker, Grant thought of Fish for the State Department. The sixty-year-old Fish declined at first, but when Grant urged him to accept to "avoid another break," he relented.[35]

Once again, Grant's benign intentions opened him to criticism. Although appointments based on personal motives had a long history in American politics, members of the previous administration affected shock at Washburne's selection. William Seward thought it "extraordinary that Grant should have taken a man so notoriously unfit as Washburne for Secy of State merely to pay him a compliment." Gideon Welles found the appointment "in character," for Grant bestowed offices "on favorites for their personal service and devotion to him, not for qualification of the recipient nor for the public welfare." At least, thought Welles, the patrician Fish offered an improvement over the "coarse, boorish, village demagogue" Washburne.[36]

What Seward and Welles did not realize was that Fish, too, owed his appointment to a personal acquaintance with Grant. Since early 1867, both men had served as trustees of the Peabody Education Fund, which fostered education for both blacks and whites in the South. Grant had formed a deep respect for Fish's intelligence, sound sense, and public-spiritedness, and their encounters at board meetings nourished a warm friendship. In December the president-elect attended the wedding of Fish's daughter in New York, and in early February, on one of his listening trips to New York, he dined at Fish's residence. When Fish initially declined Grant's invitation to join the cabinet, the president assured him, "Should you not like the position you can withdraw after the adjournment of Congress." Fish accepted, became a trusted adviser, stayed for the entirety of Grant's two terms, and earned a reputation as one of ablest secretaries in the nineteenth century.[37]

If Grant's "complimentary" appointment of Washburne raised eyebrows, few saw anything amiss when he did essentially the same thing by keeping Schofield at the War Department for a short time. "I did this to mark my approval of his course in going into Johnson's Cabinet," Grant later said. He soon replaced Schofield with his longtime associate John A. Rawlins, who resigned as army chief of staff in order to accept the position. Afflicted with tuberculosis, Rawlins suffered ill health worse than Washburne's. Grant had contemplated putting him in command of the army in Arizona, where the climate could do his friend good. But Rawlins believed his experience and past service entitled him to head the War Department, and Grant acquiesced. The Senate confirmed Fish, Boutwell, and Rawlins on March 11, one week after the inauguration.[38]

Grant's bruising first week in office took a toll on his political capital. During the period after the election, he had listened to the advice and pleas of numerous Republicans. Contrary to an erroneous impression at the time and in historical retrospect, he had not walled himself off from party leaders. But his persistent refusal to test his thoughts with them had deprived him of their valuable insights regarding potential pitfalls in his cabinet selections. Democrats reveled in his discomfiture, and Gideon Welles exulted that Grant "has been humbled and subdued in a measure by the exposure of his ignorance." Most Republicans, however, strove to put the best face on the situation, portraying the troubles as a reflection of the president's inexperience and naïveté rather than a sign of weakness or incompetence. "This is a strong and safe Cabinet," asserted the *New York Tribune*. Horace White told Washburne, "I have 'got over' my apprehensions concerning the Cabinet imbroglio, sufficiently to think we can now take a fresh start with a good chance of success." The important thing now was that "the Tenure-of-Office law must be repealed, 'if it takes the shirt off our backs.'"[39]

The president agreed. Described as "*intensely* anxious about the Civil Tenure of Office act," he let it be known that he would make no removals or appointments until Congress removed the impediment. As House Speaker James G. Blaine later put it, "Grant was resolved that neither he nor the members of his Cabinet would go through the disagreeable and undignified process of filing reasons for suspending an officer, when in fact no reasons existed aside from obnoxious political opinion." Five days after the inauguration, the House passed a bill to repeal the law by a vote of 138 to 16. The Senate Judiciary Committee rejected outright repeal and offered an amended bill that simply suspended the act until the next session of Congress. Grant would thus be able to replace Johnson administration officeholders with new appointees, presumably recommended by Republican members of Congress, who would then be secure in their positions and safe from further presidential interference. Grant's allies attacked this proposal, which, said Senator Oliver Morton of Indiana, would be "interpreted as putting the President of the United States on trial, on probation."[40]

After days of fruitless debate over repeal versus suspension of the law, the Senate Republican caucus met and called for a substitute bill that would do neither but would eliminate the obnoxious features of the

Tenure of Office Act while preserving the law itself. This proposal would give the president a free hand to choose his cabinet members. It would eliminate the requirement that he inform the Senate of his reasons for removal, requiring him to simply report, not justify, any removals he made during a congressional recess. Once the Judiciary Committee had written the new bill, it submitted the text to Grant, who acquiesced, and the Senate passed it.[41]

The amended bill next went to the House, whose refusal to accept the Senate's changes sent it to a conference committee. When the process threatened to drag on without a resolution, thus leaving the law intact, Grant pressed for a settlement. The Senate bill stipulated that if the Senate failed to approve the suspension of an officer or to confirm a successor, the suspended officer would be "entitled to resume the possession of the office." The bill as it emerged from conference eliminated this language and merely stated that "the President shall nominate another person as soon as practicable." Both houses approved the conference committee's version.[42]

But the drama was not quite over. When Lyman Trumbull reported the conference bill to the Senate, he stated that even with the new language, if the Senate failed to approve a replacement for a suspended officer before the end of a congressional session, "the old officer takes possession of the office. . . . The authority of the President to suspend extends to the end of the session, and no further." On this assurance, the Senate approved the conference report. In the House, however, Ben Butler asserted that in the case of a suspended officer, if the Senate failed to confirm a substitute, "then the place becomes vacant and the officer is removed in that way." Butler's conference committee colleague John A. Bingham added that "no authority, without the consent of the President, can get a suspended officer back into the same office again." On these assurances, the House approved the conference report. As Blaine observed, "It was certainly an extraordinary spectacle, without precedent or parallel, that the report of the conferees should have one meaning assigned to it in the Senate, and a diametrically opposite meaning assigned to it in the House, and that these antagonistic meanings should be made on the same day."[43]

The next day, April 1, Grant and the cabinet discussed the anomalous outcome. The president's initial impulse was to veto the bill, but he then considered signing it and accompanying his approval with a list of objections. Attorney General Hoar said this was the sort of thing Andrew Johnson would have done—the sure kiss of death for Grant.

Arguing that such a message would imply division within the party, Hoar persuaded Grant to hold his objections for his annual message in December. Grant examined a certified copy of the bill to make sure of its wording and decided to regard the House interpretation as correct. He signed the bill on April 5.[44]

Although the outcome of the Tenure of Office Act struggle is sometimes labeled a defeat for Grant, in that the law remained on the books, the changes gave the president virtually everything he wanted. As Blaine noted, "It was freely predicted at the time that so long as the Senate and the President were in political harmony nothing would be heard of the Tenure-of-Office Act." The Republicans retained control of the Senate throughout Grant's two terms, and the prediction came true. As the legislative struggle wound down and it became clear that Grant would make wholesale removals, the behavior of office seekers went from sullen waiting to clamorous beseeching. Office seeking, the president wrote, "is getting to be one of the industries of the age. It gives me no peace."[45]

To manage the patronage and other administrative burdens, Grant resolved to model the organization of the executive office after the staff system he had used in the army. In 1857 Congress had begun paying for a small presidential staff, and since then, presidents had employed private secretaries to assist them, especially with correspondence. Grant went further. He not only increased the number of staff members but, drawing on his wartime experience, also gave them substantive responsibilities. Nominally, his official private secretary was Robert Douglas, son of the late Illinois senator Stephen Douglas, but Grant gave Douglas relatively little to do. To a much greater degree he turned to the men who had served as his military aides. Under an arrangement with Sherman, staff officers who had served under General Grant were now detailed to the White House as President Grant's private secretaries. They kept their army salaries and did not require Senate confirmation. Horace Porter and Orville Babcock, both West Point graduates, handled the burgeoning correspondence and other paperwork, most of which related to patronage. Frederick Dent, Grant's brother-in-law, manned the reception room, an innovation in the executive office. Occupying a separate space outside the president's office, Dent screened all visitors and much of the mail. With the help of two messengers, two doorkeepers, and a clerk, he kept the crowd of office seekers at bay, and no one saw the president or the other secretaries without his permission. From the beginning, Grant relied heavily on this staff, which, as the *Washington*

National Republican observed, relieved him of "a vast amount of useless labor."[46]

Nonetheless, Grant's bureaucratic streamlining sparked complaints almost immediately. Members of Congress and cabinet secretaries claimed that staff aides blocked their access to the president and, by filtering the flow of information to him, exercised undue power over decisions. That these aides were all career military men compounded the suspicion. "God only knows," a Democratic congressman complained, "how this Administration is conducted in its arcana, its secret recesses. It is run by aid[e]-de-camps and military people, who even come to the floor of this House for the purpose of assisting us in our legislation."[47]

Over time, Babcock drew the most criticism. After graduating third in his class at West Point in 1861, he had gone immediately into the war. He joined Grant's staff in 1864, where he remained after the war with the rank of brevet brigadier general. Originally reluctant to see Grant become embroiled in politics, Babcock eventually embraced the inevitable with gusto.[48]

Thirty-three years old at the time of the inauguration and completely devoted to his chief, Babcock emerged as the president's political majordomo, if not his jackal. He injected himself into patronage matters, dug up dirt on the administration's critics, and fed political matter to friendly newspapers. "It is time," he told a friend, "that we have some discipline in the Republican Party." He often performed delicate special assignments for the president. According to one fawning press account, "He is in fact the executive officer of the President, and it is through his hands that nearly all the business of the Government passes." But Babcock's intervention, especially with regard to appointments, greatly irritated the cabinet. Fish conceded that Babcock "has brains & very many excellent & gentlemanly qualities but is spoiled by his position & a want of delicacy & consideration for the official responsibilities & proper authority (official) of civilians. He runs the 'Military' a little too hard." In 1875 a Treasury Department official alleged that the war and navy secretaries "are completely under Babcock's thumb." This was an exaggeration, but it nonetheless reflected the impression of Babcock's arrogance and pervasive power. There was nothing inherently wrong and much that was right with Grant's staff system. It enhanced the efficiency of his office and broadened the range of issues the president could deal with effectively. Yet the presumptuous—some would say insolent—Babcock proved inapt for Grant's administrative reform. Moreover, many saw Babcock as a man of questionable personal honesty, or at least one with dubious notions of conflict of interest. Critics viewed him as a Svengali leading the president onto unrighteous paths. Grant paid little heed to the criticisms, however, and his aide remained at his side for seven years. His loyalty to Babcock and other less-than-worthy assistants handed his enemies a weapon and disappointed many of his supporters.[49]

Babcock's longevity contrasted sharply with the rapid turnover in the cabinet. During Grant's eight years in office, two dozen men occupied the seven posts, several of them for less than two years. Five served as attorney general, and four each headed the War Department, the Treasury Department, and the post office. In 1876 an Ohio Republican quipped, "The cabinet of Genl Grant seems to be a kind of genteel lunch, where gentlemen stop for refreshments for awhile, & if they stay too long are told to 'move on' by the police, so everybody can have a chance. In the Atty Genl's office I believe they keep an *Artist* all the time, as an occupant scarcely stays there long enough to be painted."[50]

In the beginning, as is true of all new administrations, Grant and his advisers were feeling their way, and they had scant experience to draw upon. In the group that remained after the initial shuffling, only one of them had ever sat at the cabinet table before—Grant himself, who had been interim secretary of war. Only three members had occupied positions in the civilian federal government, two only in the legislative branch. Fish, Boutwell, and Cox had served brief terms as state governors. Moreover, Johnson's embittered secretaries did not personally hand off their departments to their successors, who were forced to rely on subordinates to acquaint them with modes of operation and pending business.[51]

In establishing a routine, Grant and the cabinet adopted some traditional patterns, such as holding regular meetings on Tuesdays and Fridays. During times when business was intense, especially when Congress was in session, these discussions could be lengthy, complicated, and occasionally contentious; in slack periods, the meetings were less focused and sometimes almost breezy. Hamilton Fish kept a diary, which became the most complete source of information about how the cabinet operated, although the fastidious Fish sometimes betrayed a sense of punctilio that contrasted with Grant's more relaxed approach.[52]

At a typical meeting, Fish observed, the president and each of the secretaries would raise questions for discussion. Grant would solicit their views and "then reach his own conclusion, and direct the course to be pursued which he thought best." "He was never arrogant," wrote

Attorney General Edwards Pierrepont; "he was considerate of others; but I don't think the opinions of others, when he had made up his own mind, influenced his action at all." On occasion, a trying circumstance might move the president to a rhetorical outburst to let off steam. At one point during a discussion of American fishing rights in waters off Canada, Grant exclaimed that he wished "Congress would declare war with Gt. Britain, when we would take Canada, & wipe out her commerce as she has done ours, & then we would start fair." When Fish and Boutwell shook their heads, he cooled down but added, "I am tired of all this arrogance, & assumption of Gt. Britain." Sometimes an outlandish statement betrayed the president's wry humor. In May 1873, when Union veterans complained that their southern counterparts planned to decorate Confederate graves at Arlington Cemetery on Decoration Day, Grant said that he was "disposed to order the marines there with ball cartridges." The secretary of war played along and said, "The Grand Army of the Republic could take care of the matter."[53]

In general, Grant enjoyed amicable relations with his advisers, but not all the secretaries adapted equally well to his leadership style as he worked to make his own will the basis for a unified outlook in the cabinet. In private settings with close acquaintances, Grant could be delightful company, but in more formal situations, he was less comfortable with verbal give-and-take. Occasionally when someone disagreed with him, he would clam up, sometimes in anger. Interior Secretary Jacob Cox thought Grant lacked "the faculty of drawing out the opinions of others, and of presenting matters for consideration and discussion." As a result, Cox believed, the cabinet secretaries remained disunited and compartmentalized. What Grant ought to do was lead the cabinet as a whole in developing "a common policy on which the Administration should be a unit & not drift into a bureaucracy in which each Department minds *only* its own business."[54]

Yet, when the president and Cox found themselves engaged in a serious policy dispute that led to the secretary's resignation, Cox sang a different tune. Now he complained that the president was acting like an "absolute ruler over the judgments and decisions of his Secretaries," treating them as if they were "subordinate in the sense of his division or corps commanders in the field; his only *advisers* being his military family of *aides*." Grant recalled after leaving the White House, "I never allowed the Cabinet to interfere when my mind was made up." That attitude was abhorrent to men like Cox, who apparently failed to realize that, as the elected head of the administration, the president, not the cabinet secretaries, bore the ultimate responsibility for executive actions and must have the final say. Grant's notions represented an important step in the creation of the modern presidency, but ten years after Grant's death, Cox published an influential article in which he still bridled at his cabinet members' having been "shorn of their power" by "mischievous influences."[55]

Those alleged "mischievous influences" included not only the White House staff but also various members of Congress who Cox and some other cabinet members believed exercised too much sway over the president. Grant formed close associations with several senators and representatives, but he was hardly their captive. Before becoming president, Grant had expressed disdain for "mere trading politicians," but he soon realized that as president he lacked the absolute authority he had wielded as a commanding general and could accomplish little without working with congressional allies. During the period of congressional Reconstruction, General Grant had worked amicably with Republicans to frame legislation. But the tortured Johnson years had left a thick residue of institutional resentment on Capitol Hill. As Fish observed, "The habit of criticism, if not of opposition, became somewhat fixed & could not even on the accession of a friend to the Executive Chair, entirely & at once subside." The Stewart impasse and the fight over the Tenure of Office Act taught Grant that he could not simply let his wishes be known and expect Congress to comply. "An Executive must consider Congress," he observed after leaving the White House. "A government machine must run, and an Executive depends on Congress. The members have their rights as well as himself. If he wants to get along with Congress, have the government go smoothly, and secure wholesome legislation he must be in sympathy with Congress."[56]

Among the president's formal methods of cultivating that sympathy, one of the most important was the presentation of annual and special messages to Congress. Grant wrote all his own annual messages, although he drew on departmental reports from the cabinet secretaries and read drafts to them and solicited their suggestions. The president also wrote his own special messages about specific issues or events, although for technical matters or those related to legal or other arcane questions, he often asked the appropriate cabinet member for a draft. In the fall of 1871, as he labored over his third annual report, he joked to a good friend, "I always feel unhappy when the time comes to commence the job of writing a Message, and miserable until it is comple[te]d. I believe I am lazy and dont get credit for it." He was hardly lazy, for

President Grant and his cabinet study bills in the President's Room at the Capitol at the close of the Forty-Fourth Congress. (*Harper's Weekly*, March 24, 1877)

he composed that message, which totaled more than 6,000 words, in just three days. Jocose bellyaching aside, Grant fully realized the importance of these messages, the principal means by which nineteenth-century chief executives outlined their policy objectives. Both houses of Congress examined them at length. Newspapers printed them in full and assessed their every detail. Grant had the gift of strong, direct prose, and his words carried the potential to inspire allies and galvanize opponents.[57]

Grant used other methods to gain support in Congress. In some instances, the administration provided draft legislation to accomplish particular ends. The president regularly applied the personal touch, and hardly a day passed that several senators and representatives did not visit him at the White House. Grant used these encounters not merely to gauge congressional opinion but to shape it. On occasion he would invite the entire membership of a congressional committee to meet with him to discuss a pending measure. Sometimes he made the trip up Capitol Hill to lobby for legislation, often undertaking that pilgrimage in the final hours of the last session of a Congress before it expired on March 3.

In 1875, for instance, in the waning moments of the Forty-Third Congress, a group of senators interrupted a cabinet meeting to report that important financial measures were in trouble. Grant adjourned the cabinet early, corralled the secretary of the treasury, and headed up the Hill. After the legislation went through, one senator noted, "the President saved us again."[58]

Grant understood that, in forging long-term friendships with powerful Republicans in Congress, many saw patronage as the coin of the realm. As he later put it, "In a government where there are senators and members, where senators and members depend upon politics for success, there will be applications for patronage. You cannot call it corruption—it is a condition of our representative form of government." As Fish noted early on, the president intended to "withhold political patronage from those recommended by Senators & others in opposition to the policy or attitude of the Administration." For supporters, the bestowal of patronage could be lavish. Grant even developed a friendship with his old nemesis Ben Butler. The marginally competent political general who had disappointed Grant during the war rarely did so as a civilian political lieutenant. Although the Massachusetts congressman still considered himself smarter than Grant, he respected power and had initiated the rapprochement by pushing for repeal of the Tenure of Office Act. In short order his relationship with the president grew so strong that some observers thought Butler must be blackmailing Grant and threatening to reveal some deep secret. The evidence for that is slim, but it is undeniable that Butler wanted patronage recognition and got it. Butler did not always agree with Grant, especially on monetary issues, but he along with Oliver Morton, Simon Cameron, Zachariah Chandler, Roscoe Conkling, and others formed the core of a loyal administration party on whom the president could generally rely to fight his battles on Capitol Hill. After he left the White House, Grant privately faulted his successor, Hayes, for failing to exercise much "influence" over legislation, largely because of his "Utopian ideas . . . of running a government without a party."[59]

But support for Grant in Congress was hardly universal, and the path to success was rarely smooth. Indeed, he and others in his administration always considered working with Congress a struggle, even with substantial Republican majorities in each house. Part of the difficulty arose from the intense partisanship that marked both the House and the Senate in this era, when the minority Democrats believed their main function was obstruction and attack. As Grant's first Congress assembled in December 1869, New York representative S. S. Cox wrote, "There is only one way for a Dem in opposition,—that is, to *charge the other side*. I charge them with making all the mischief & failing in any remedy. Isn't that *tactics*?" Committee investigations provided the Democrats with a potent weapon against the administration, and after they won control of the House in the election of 1874, they possessed almost unlimited firepower. "We must press the enemy vigorously now," a Maryland Democrat insisted. "The whole country must understand . . . that the chief duty of the next Congress will be *investigation*." Grant took deep offense at these tactics, and shortly before leaving office he complained to the Democratic national chairman, who also served in the House, that that body had "raked up petty accusations" against him with no "evidence of a desire to do him justice."[60]

But it was not only congressional Democrats who were gunning for Grant. Some Republicans, represented most vocally by Charles Sumner, could never bring themselves to regard the unprepossessing president as worthy of their respect. As Sumner's biographer noted, he had "always had a low opinion of soldiers" and felt that "the real victories of the recent war had been won in the Senate chamber." On patronage matters, Sumner exhibited an overweening sense of entitlement. Grant recalled that Sumner was "among the first senators to ask offices for his friends. He expected offices as a right." He succeeded in pestering Grant into giving the prestigious post of minister to Great Britain to John Lothrop Motley, but he was hardly satisfied with that success. One evening he spent two hours at the White House pushing for patronage, and the next day he wrote to a Senate colleague, Henry Anthony of Rhode Island, "I am tired of dancing attendance & arguing these questions. It is very wearisome—very." The obeisant Anthony replied, "I can well understand how insufferably annoying it must be to you with your perfect familiarity with our foreign relations to force your views upon men who ought to seek them and to follow them."[61]

Anthony served up just the sort of deference that Sumner craved but Grant and Fish were increasingly disinclined to supply, especially when policy critiques joined patronage carping in Sumner's catalog of supposed grievances. At bottom, Sumner proved incapable of seeing anyone but himself as the true leader of the Republican Party. In a moment of inadvertent candor after Fish could not meet one of his patronage demands, Sumner wrote to a friend, "I am tired of unsatisfied aspiration & longing." Over time, he sank into self-absorption. Eighteen months into the administration, Fish wrote to another senator

Charles Sumner. (Library of Congress)

that Sumner "nourishes his supposed griefs & seems to take comfort in imagining that every thing that is done without a curtsey to his wishes is a personal offense aimed at him." Solicitor General Benjamin Bristow saw the senator as "a learned fool" who, despite his intellectual attainments, "hasn't an ounce of 'horse-swapping sense.'" "The Pres[iden]t got off a good thing on Sumner yesterday," Bristow wrote to a friend. "A member of Congress was abusing Sumner in the presence of the Pres[iden]t, and among other things said that Sumner didn't believe the Bible. 'Of course he don't,' said the Pres[iden]t, 'for he didn't write it.' This illustrates Sumner's character very fully."[62]

Even before the inauguration, Charles Francis Adams had concluded that Grant "must contend with Sumner, or follow him implicitly." When Grant saw no need to do the latter, Sumner became a bitter enemy, determined to discredit the president and his administration. He engaged in abusive personal attacks that traveled beyond his private correspondence and onto the Senate floor. After one such eruption, another senator wrote to an administration official, "I think I never found a more depraved man—except a professed leader of a gang of counterfeiters whose only binding oath was on his *bowie knife*." An exasperated Fish wrote, "No wild bull ever dashed more violently at a red rag than he does at anything that he thinks the President is interested in." But Sumner insisted, "I utterly deny that I am controlled by personal motives." Rather, he said, "Possibly my own personal experience has enabled me to see the absolute unfitness of Grant in a clearer light than I should otherwise have seen it." Grant later confided to Fish that he did not regard Sumner as "an ordinary falsifyer [*sic*] of the truth because he was so egotistical, so infal[l]ible in his own estimation, that he believed what he said, and would try to force his statements upon the credulity of those who knew better." The clash between these two leaders wrought tragic results. Sumner slid into a crippling obsession, and over time, his assaults sullied Grant's reputation in the eyes of his fellow citizens. Perhaps even more, Sumner abetted the general besmirching of President Grant's standing in history. The record of a presidency is made not only by those who serve in the administration but also by those who engage it, for good or ill. Charles Sumner bears a large responsibility for the dark cloud that hangs over the Grant presidency to this day.[63]

Henry Adams bears a similar responsibility. After serving as his father's secretary during his tenure as minister to Great Britain, the thirty-year-old Adams settled in Washington in the summer of 1868, intending to launch a career in journalism and thereby influence public policy. He

had nursed an ambition to obtain a position in the incoming administration, but by January 1869, with his prospects exhibiting scant vitality,
he decided to make his mark as a reform writer. Adams believed that
American democracy had degenerated since the days of the Founders (including his great-grandfather John Adams). "The whole root of
the evil," he concluded, "is in *political* corruption," by which he meant
devolution from the nation's original republican ideal. He aimed to do
whatever he could to set things right by educating the citizenry, even
at the risk of making himself repellent to those who held power. "I . . .
care very little for the new administration," he confessed. "I want to be
advertised and the easiest way is to do something obnoxious and do it
well." Thus, before Ulysses Grant ever placed his hand on the Bible to
take the oath of office, Henry Adams was primed to vie for attention, if
not influence, as a political scold.[64]

That Adams received no appointment fueled his determination. In
less than two months, he was saying that Grant was "less capable than
Johnson" and that the new administration was "far inferior to the last."
The Grant administration had not had time to do much in the way of
policymaking to merit Adams's censure, but it had had time to neglect
his ambition. "My hopes of the new Administration have all been disappointed," he wrote to an English friend.[65]

Spared the burdens of office, Adams set to work on an article he described as "very bitter and abusive of the Administration." Appearing
in the October 1869 issue of *North American Review*, "Civil Service Reform" took Grant to task for abandoning his supposed original intention
to reject the entrenched system of appointments based on congressional
patronage and the replacement of officeholders on partisan grounds.
Adams conceded that previous presidents had followed these practices,
but Grant's administration had descended "lower than the worst of
its predecessors in the scale of self-degradation." Remarkably, Adams
told Jacob Cox that he "lived in the hope" that Grant would endorse
his ideas in his first annual message to Congress. The president said
nothing about civil service reform and instead condemned the Tenure
of Office Act, which, he said, forced the retention of officials "against the
will of the President."[66]

A week after that message, Adam Badeau took Adams to the White
House, where they found the president enjoying a postprandial chat
with friends. Grant and the First Lady treated Badeau's companion po-
litely, if not warmly. As Adams later confided to his friend Charles Gaskell, he "performed the part of guest, though you can imagine with what

an effort." Julia Grant showed him scant attention, but the young man took revenge, privately mocking her strabismus: "She squints like an isosceles triangle, but is not much more vulgar than some Duchesses." Adams "chattered" away as the evening wore on. Perhaps jokingly, but no less tellingly, he told Gaskell, "I flatter myself it was I who showed them how they ought to behave. One feels such an irresistible desire, as you know, to tell this kind of individual to put themselves at their ease and talk just as though they were at home." Such was the man who craved influence with the successor to two Adamses.[67]

Before leaving Washington to teach history at Harvard College and edit the *North American Review*, Adams fired another blast in "The Session, 1869–1870," published in the July 1870 issue of the *Review*. Again he expressed disappointment at Grant's supposed failure to live up to the nation's hopes. In less than a year, he wrote, "The Administration was marked by no distinctive character. No purpose of peculiar elevation, no broad policy, no commanding dignity indicated the beginning of a new era. The old type of politician was no less powerful than under other presidents."[68]

Administration defenders responded vigorously. In a long article, Wisconsin senator Timothy Howe attacked Adams's assertions as vague, inconsistent, inaccurate, and illogical. The government had acted on a large number of "difficult, anomalous and sharply debated problems," but Adams had offered "a great deal of theory and but few facts; an intolerable quantity of sack and not much bread." Grant read Howe's article "with great gusto." The Adamses, he believed, "do not possess one noble trait of character that I ever heard of, from old John Adams down to the last of all of them, H. B." Two years later the Democrats distributed Adams's article as a campaign document against Grant's reelection.[69]

Grant had suffered some severe criticism during the war, but nothing had prepared him for the attacks he encountered as the nation's political leader. Early cabinet troubles and patronage fights ensured that the administration's honeymoon would be short. Indeed, within a year, Grant found the "assaults made upon him in the press" so wearing that in a burst of fury he told Fish that he was "very seriously . . . contemplating a resignation of his office." During his eight years in office, the Democratic press rarely missed an opportunity to cast the administration and the president in the worst possible light.[70]

But sharp criticism came from some Republican papers as well, in some cases after their editors' ambitions for office had been frustrated.

None outdid *New York Sun* editor Charles A. Dana in showering the administration with undiluted bile. Dana had cowritten a campaign biography of Grant in 1868, but Grant's cabinet selections made him skeptical of the new president's judgment. After Dana failed to be appointed the collector of customs for New York, his skepticism gave way to excoriation. The *Sun* labeled Grant incompetent, accused him of nepotism, and called him a corrupt gift taker; it also bitterly trashed the policies pursued by Hamilton Fish. Grant was convinced that Dana had been paid for these "assaults" on him, and Fish damned the editor as "a Blackguard" whose newspaper was like "a 'house of prostitution' . . . of the lowest & filthiest character." But Assistant Secretary of State J. C. Bancroft Davis expressed the administration's frustrations: "If I begin answering Dana, where am I to stop? He can make up stories faster than I can deny them, and when I stop denying he will say, well! at last here is something he can't deny."[71]

Grant ordered that the government's advertising business be denied to any paper that "personally assault[ed] any member of the Administration." On the positive side, he and other officials planted favorable stories in friendly newspapers. In one case, a congressman observed that an "associated press dispatch was dictated to the agent by Grant himself." Some cabinet members manipulated the press with skill. Fish no doubt envied them, for he often found himself under fire. On more than one occasion Grant leaned on editors to give Fish more favorable coverage. Such ad hoc efforts had limited effectiveness. As Babcock noted, "the President likes the idea of a permanent organization for the press," but no such system emerged. What was needed, Fish thought, was "a reliable sound organ."[72]

The closest the administration came to having such an organ was the *Washington National Republican*, owned and edited by William Murtagh, a sharp businessman with an eye for the main chance. Enjoying government largesse in the form of a seat on the District of Columbia police commission as well as contracts for government printing, Murtagh gave Grant unstinting praise. On the occasion of the president's second inauguration, the *Republican* declared that he was "President of the whole people more than any one of his predecessors since Washington. . . . Once [and] for all, parties and politicians had better understand that he is the master of them all; master because the people are master, and have made him the minister and executor of their will." But to many observers, the very extravagance of the *Republican*'s rhetoric vitiated its influence. The *New York Tribune*'s Whitelaw Reid dismissed the paper as "simply a sewer for the kitchen slops of the White House." Moreover, Murtagh did not treat all members of the administration with the reverence he accorded the president. He particularly criticized Fish, sometimes implying that the secretary was pursuing a foreign policy contrary to the president's wishes. On one occasion Fish complained to Grant, who promised to tell Murtagh to publish nothing about the administration's foreign policy without first securing Fish's approval, but two days later the *Republican* carried yet another editorial censuring the secretary. The lack of coordination compounded Fish's general dismay at the press, which "scatters flippant skimmings; and 'news' whether true or false, makes no difference so long as it [is] sensational, & can sell the paper."[73]

Others shared Fish's frustration. Six months into the first term, Postmaster General John Creswell wrote to a senator, "Never since I have been cognizant of the management of affairs at Washington . . . has the governmental machinery been run so well or so honestly, so smoothly or so economically. And yet we have made comparatively little impression upon the country, simply because we have not reached the popular heart or ear." Two years later, little had changed. "Genl Grant is so good and pure," Creswell confided to his mother, "that all he needs for his perfect vindication is simply that the people shall know him, and his works."[74]

Nonetheless, Grant himself rarely mounted the public rostrum to pursue the vindication Creswell and others thought he deserved. "Speaking before the public," he once confided to a friend, "is a terrible trial for me." In messages to Congress and other written communications, he effectively represented administration policy, and in small private encounters, he could speak with ease and handle issues deftly. In a conversation with John M. Harlan, he impressed the future Supreme Court justice "as an honest, well-meaning man, with more intellect than I ever supposed he had. He has a clear well-balanced mind." An hour's chat made a similar impression on *New York Times* editor John Bigelow: "He spoke at length of all the domestic questions of his administration and very well." But confronting a large audience of listeners, no matter how friendly, was another matter. Once, when asked to say a few words at an army reunion, Grant confessed, "I would like to write all that I think about this, and have you read it, for you know it is not one of my gifts to stand up before you and say what I wish to say. I can take two or three of you in a private room and say all I like to say on an occasion of this sort, but there are others to follow me who are not troubled with my diffidence."[75]

Nor did the oratorical achievements of his two immediate predecessors inspire him to conquer his natural diffidence. No one, certainly not Ulysses Grant, could hope to match the spoken eloquence of Abraham Lincoln. And no one, certainly not Grant, wanted to risk the condemnation that had greeted much of Andrew Johnson's public rhetoric. The *National Republican* interpreted his taciturnity as a virtue: "Grant never 'slops over'" and "does not talk for the sake of hearing his own chatter." Unfortunately, the great "silent man" often left a vacuum that his enemies eagerly and adeptly filled. This need not have happened, for Grant and others sold his speaking abilities short. His inaugural addresses were certainly creditable, if not masterly. One other notable time that he ventured onto the speaker's platform, during the off-year election of 1875, his remarks, according to one party leader, "met with well-nigh universal favor" and helped the Republicans secure a narrow victory in Ohio. But the power of that speech derived in large part from its rarity. If Grant had employed such rhetoric more often to explain his policies and defend his administration, he could have diminished his detractors' impact, both at the time and in historical retrospect. He did not, however, and throughout his presidency he seldom went beyond a few innocuous, sometimes self-deprecating words spoken to crowds gathered to greet him during his travels.[76]

And yet, those travels were not without significance. Grant was the first president to use the railroads to travel extensively around the country, at a time when accidents were frequent and sometimes deadly. Grant considered it important to get out of Washington and mix with citizens. Most of this mixing occurred during ceremonial occasions, but he also found that wherever he went he encountered individuals who wanted to bend his ear, sometimes more than he bargained for. Although he refrained from making political speeches, his trips often had an implicit political purpose. Republicans around the country begged him to visit, and he frequently traveled to states holding elections, where his mere presence gave a boost to the party's nominees.[77]

But politicking was only one reason for Grant's sometimes prolonged absences from Washington. In the days before air-conditioning, the capital city's beastly heat drove Grant and his family to seek the more salubrious climate of the shore at Long Branch, New Jersey, where they typically occupied a spacious cottage for several weeks each summer. He later remarked, "During the months of August and September the White House is one of the most unhealthy places in the world. . . . Scarcely any of the people who stay there during these months but suffer from chills and fever." With the president's blessing, most cabinet members also escaped to their home states or elsewhere, and Congress fled too.[78]

Yet, even though Washington experienced a general exodus during the summer, Grant took severe criticism for his absences. Sumner, who spent his summers in Boston or Europe, sneered at the president's "seaside loiterings." Grant rejected any suggestion that he neglected his duties. His staff accompanied him on his travels and relocated to Long Branch in the summer. He used the telegraph—with a cipher, if necessary—to stay in touch with Fish and other officials, and the nation's intricate railway infrastructure expedited a return to Washington if the need arose. He invited cabinet members and favored congressmen as well as friends and political associates to make extended visits to Long Branch, where leisure activities alternated with discussions of policy and politics. "The theory of government changes with general progress," the president declared in his second inaugural address. "Now that the telegraph is made available for communicating thought, together with rapid transit by steam, all parts of a continent are made contiguous for all purposes of government."[79]

In the last year of his presidency, the Democratic majority in the House of Representatives passed a resolution asking Grant to report any acts or duties he had "performed at a distance from the seat of Government." In an early assertion of executive privilege, Grant adamantly refused to provide the information solicited by this blatantly political request. He enlisted the careful lawyer Fish to draft his response, which stated that the House could ask a president for information for purposes related only to "its powers of legislation or of impeachment." The resolution made no pretense to the former, and Grant implicitly dared the House to attempt the latter. He argued that virtually all his predecessors had "been in the habit" of absenting themselves on occasion and insisted that during his own absences he did not neglect his responsibilities. The "rapidity of travel and of mail communication" and the "almost instantaneous correspondence" of the telegraph gave the president the power "to maintain as constant and almost as quick intercourse with the Departments at Washington as may be maintained while he remains in the capital." Dismissing the House's request as an infringement of his executive function, he asserted that "no Act of Congress can limit, suspend, or confine this constitutional duty." The message hit the bull's-eye. Grant made it clear that the office of the president existed wherever the president happened to be. In doing so, he struck a blow for the independence of the executive as well as for the use of modern technology in conducting the government's business.[80]

In many ways, Ulysses S. Grant was a novice in civilian affairs upon entering the presidency. His lack of experience compounded the difficulty of meeting the challenges he confronted, but it also made him more open to innovation than a seasoned political hand might have been. "Grant will learn, seems willing to learn," Illinois Republican P. N. Reed wrote to Elihu Washburne on the eve of the inauguration, "& when he has learned we shall have the best President the United States ever had." During the war, adaptability had been central to Grant's success; as president, he again proved willing to try new ways of doing things. He assembled an efficient personal staff, recruited able lieutenants in his cabinet, cultivated strategic friendships in Congress, and readily adapted technological developments to extend the reach and mobility of the presidency. But he had little time to ease into the job. Echoes from the inaugural ball had scarcely faded before a host of pressing problems made it clear that his new endeavor would require every skill and all the agility at his disposal. As Reed told Washburne, "Genl Grant has a *harder* task now than he had when he took charge of the Armies of the United States."[81]

4

RECONSTRUCTION:
CONSUMMATION WITHOUT CLOSURE

In 1868 the central policy motivation that led Ulysses S. Grant to leave his comfortable berth at the head of the army and run for president was his determination to preserve "the results of the costly war which we have gone through." For Grant, perpetuating those "results" connoted not simply securing the permanency of Confederate defeat and reunification of the nation. Indeed, secession was dead beyond resuscitation. At stake now was the shape of the newly configured southern society that the death of slavery had wrought. His campaign watchword, "Let us have peace," signified not only the cessation of hostilities between North and South but also the fashioning of a peaceful coexistence between blacks and whites. After four years of fighting between Andrew Johnson and Congress, Grant's accession to office opened the possibility for an essential congruence between "presidential" and "congressional" Reconstruction. For most of the next eight years, the southern question stood at the top of the administration's domestic agenda.[1]

As president, Grant first aimed for the speedy restoration of the southern states as "peaceful and orderly communities" that would "effectually secure the civil and political rights of all persons." This goal was consistent with his role as leader of his party, for he fully embraced the notion that the completion of Reconstruction not only depended on but also would ensure the retention of power by the Republicans. But framing a "southern" policy posed enormous difficulties. For one thing, "the South" was a term of convenience that obscured wide variations among individual states, each with its own history, factions, and demographic makeup. Some southern states had black majority populations, while others, especially the Border States, counted relatively few African Americans. From state to state, the proportion of blacks, carpetbaggers, and scalawags in the Republican coalition varied, but in each state the party risked disruption by factional fights over offices as well as policy. Blacks, shut out of government's beneficence for centuries, sought redress through programs such as state-funded education, while many whites favored either pursuing austerity or, conversely, devoting state resources to economic development. Some states had shown robust two-party competition before the war, and now quondam Whigs saw much to admire in the Republican Party's economic policies, while Democrats clung to minimalist notions of government. On top of the social and political multiformity in the South, at the national level the truce between Republican radicals and moderates that had enabled Grant's nomination proved transitory. Before long, new antagonisms encumbered efforts to frame a coherent southern policy.[2]

Despite these difficulties, however, Congress and the president provided immediate evidence of a new working relationship. Less than two weeks after Grant's inauguration, Congress passed a law to eliminate the word *white* from statutes relating to the District of Columbia so as to ban discrimination in office holding and jury service. Grant did not hesitate to affix his signature. Although the measure had limited scope, as a New England newspaper observed, it provided "an indication of the character of the administration."[3]

In the South, the first order of business was to deal with the three states not yet readmitted to the Union under the congressional program adopted in 1867: Virginia, Mississippi, and Texas. Grant aimed to expedite their return and thereby conclude Reconstruction. In the administration's early weeks, Washington teemed with southerners angling to influence the president and Congress. Grant met with a group from Mississippi, where a year earlier a popular vote had defeated the adoption of a new state constitution that would have guaranteed suffrage and other rights to blacks but also included provisions disfranchising ex-Confederates. Grant and the Mississippians discussed the possibility of holding a new referendum, with separate votes on the main constitution and the disfranchisement sections. As one conservative put it, the president "proposes that the constitution be again submitted to the people so that they may vote upon those parts which are acceptable and against those parts which are objectionable." In early April Grant and a committee of Virginia conservatives discussed a similar separate vote for that state. Convinced that this procedure offered fairness to all interests, the president ordered Attorney General E. Rockwood Hoar to draft a message asking Congress for the authority to set such a vote in the Old Dominion. Although little time remained for action in the current short session, Grant believed the question "concerns so deeply the welfare of the country" that he pushed ahead anyway.[4]

In his brief message, Grant underscored the nation's commitment to "the absolute protection of all its citizens," but he also asserted that when the people of a formerly rebellious state showed their readiness "to enter in good faith upon the accomplishment of this object," it was "desirable that all causes of irritation should be removed." Allowing a separate vote on the disfranchisement clauses of the constitution would do just that. He expressed his "confident hope and belief" that the people of Virginia were "now ready to cooperate with the National Government" and "give to all its people those equal rights under the law which were asserted in the Declaration of Independence." At the end of the message he tacked on a paragraph proposing a similar revote in Mississippi.[5] Congress acted quickly, adding provisions for a separate-vote referendum in Texas as well. Three days after his message, the president's recommendations were law.[6]

Grant's early foray as a legislative leader won praise. Calling his action a welcome departure from "the policy of Andy Johnson," the *New York Herald* declared that Grant's backing of "the restoration of Southern white men's rights while enforcing Southern black men's rights" had "shown political wisdom and conferred a material benefit upon the whole country." Charles Francis Adams welcomed the new cooperation between the branches, as well as Grant's inclination "to accelerate the complete restoration of the Southern States, which is the most essential point of all." Charles Sumner tried unsuccessfully to convince his colleagues to enact additional Reconstruction legislation, but even he expressed the hope "that six months of a vigorous and loyal executive will make affairs in the South wear a different aspect."[7]

In early May 1869 Grant engaged in symbolic reconciliation by accepting a courtesy call from Robert E. Lee, who was in Washington on business connected with railroad construction. The two did not meet in private; John Lothrop Motley, the new minister to England, and two of Lee's friends were present for the conversation, which avoided public issues. At one point, Grant quipped that he and Lee had "had more to do with destroying railroads than building them," but the frosty ex-Confederate ignored this attempt at levity. Although reporters (and later historians) read more significance into this brief conversation than it possessed, the president's meeting with his old rival, even if only for a personal chat, signaled to white southerners that he saw no profit in perpetuating wartime bitterness.[8]

In the ensuing weeks Grant set elections in the three states, where voters would not only decide on the new constitutions but also select men to fill the offices the documents established. Virginia's came first in early July, and as expected, voters approved the constitution and rejected the clauses disfranchising ex-Confederates. But in the balloting for state officers, a coalition of Democrats and dissident conservative Republicans triumphed over the Republicans, winning the governorship as well as a majority in the legislature. Although twenty-nine African Americans won seats in the legislature, conservative whites exulted that Virginia had escaped radical control. The conservative victory disappointed the administration, but in the end, Grant concluded that the government could not reject the outcome of an election conducted in accordance with the policy he and Congress had outlined.[9]

Shortly after the Virginia election, Grant called for elections in Mississippi and Texas on November 30. He chose a date after Election Day elsewhere, hoping to avert any damage that bad news might do to Republican prospects in northern states. In Mississippi, Democrats and conservative Republicans combined in hopes of duplicating the victory in the Old Dominion. To ward off any wariness the president might have felt after the Virginia outcome, the Mississippi fusionists nominated Julia Grant's brother, Lewis Dent, for governor. The ploy failed. Putting personal concerns aside, Grant told Dent that, as a matter of "public duty," he intended to "throw the weight of my influence in favor of the party opposed to you." He explained, "I am . . . thoroughly satisfied in my own mind that the success of the so-called Conservative Republican party in Mississippi would result in the defeat of what I believe to be for the best interest of the State and country."[10]

The president stuck by this position even more tenaciously after a disappointing result in the mid-August election in Tennessee, which had been readmitted to the Union years earlier. There, the conservative Republican governor running for reelection sought to woo Democratic support by permitting the registration of ex-Confederates; he won a smashing victory himself and secured a conservative majority in the legislature. In Texas, Grant originally tried to stay out of the factional disputes among Republicans, but after the conservative victories in Virginia and Tennessee, he tilted toward the regular Republican nominee for governor, Edmund Davis. The administration moved aggressively to replace conservative Republican patronage appointees with Davis followers as a way to bolster his candidacy. The effort paid off; in the November balloting, Davis squeaked by his opponent. In Mississippi, Dent's conservative coalition faltered without Grant's support. A month before the election, the president's secretary Horace Porter confidently wrote, "Brother Dent we think will go under, and be handsomely tomahawked right through the centre of his head." A large turnout of African Americans on Election Day gave Mississippi's Republicans a substantial victory.[11]

The readmission of Virginia, Mississippi, and Texas, plus the seating of their senators and representatives, rested ultimately with Congress, and that question became more complicated because of events in Georgia. In the spring of 1868 an election under a new constitution had resulted in the selection of a Republican governor, Rufus Bullock, but a legislature dominated by conservatives. Several of the conservative legislators were ex-Confederate leaders disqualified from holding office by the Fourteenth Amendment. Moreover, when the legislature convened, it replaced more than two dozen black members with their white electoral opponents. In the fall presidential election, widespread violence against black and white Republicans had resulted in a victory in the state by Democrat Horatio Seymour. Lawless conditions persisted into 1869, and Grant ordered General Alfred Terry, commander of the Department of the South, to investigate. Terry reported that "in many parts of the State there is practically no government. . . . Murders have been, and are, frequent; the abuse in various ways of the blacks is too common to excite notice." He recommended that the federal government "resume military control" while Georgia authorities reorganized the state's government in accordance with the law.[12]

When Congress convened in December 1869, Grant submitted Terry's report and advocated new legislation authorizing the governor of Georgia to convene the legislature as originally elected, which would put the black members back in their seats. He advised an additional stipulation that each member take a test oath (as prescribed in the Reconstruction Acts of 1867) swearing that he either was not disqualified under the Fourteenth Amendment or had been relieved of such exclusion by Congress. Several months earlier Attorney General Hoar had issued an opinion that cast doubt on the applicability of such a test oath, leading one radical member of the Georgia legislature to declare that if Hoar's decision were sustained, "the days of the Republican party in the Rebel States are numbered." Grant now asked for a statutory provision upholding the oath. Two weeks later Congress sent Grant a bill that did all he asked. Further, the measure specifically prohibited the exclusion of any duly elected member on account of race, color, or previous condition of servitude, and it required that the legislature ratify the Fifteenth Amendment in order to gain admission for the state's senators and representatives. Congress also authorized the president to use the military to enforce the act. Georgia reverted to military reconstruction, and a reorganization of the government proceeded under Terry's watchful eye. In July 1870 Congress readmitted the state to representation.[13]

In his 1869 annual message, Grant mentioned the other three states still moving toward readmission. Once they had met all requirements, including ratification of the Fourteenth and Fifteenth Amendments, he said, Congress should accord them readmission "and thus close the work of reconstruction." Yet, in light of events in Georgia and the conservative makeup of Virginia's new government, many Republicans saw a need to impose further requirements on the Old Dominion. On January 26, 1870, Grant approved a new act that readmitted Virginia but required every officeholder to take the test oath; prohibited the state from changing its constitution to deny the franchise to anyone guaranteed the right to vote; barred the state from depriving any citizen of the right to hold office on account of race, color, or previous condition of servitude; and stipulated that the constitution could never be changed to deprive any class of citizens equal "school rights and privileges." Over the next several weeks, Congress passed identical bills for Mississippi and Texas. By mid-1870, every southern state was again eligible for representation in Congress. Thus, after carefully tailoring policies to the individual states, Grant had consummated Reconstruction, at least in the sense of restoring all states to the national legislature.[14]

Meanwhile, Grant also worked for approval of the Fifteenth Amendment. Within his first four months in office, seventeen states had ratified it, but the pace slowed during the second half of 1869, prompting Grant to exert his influence. He pushed the governor of Nebraska to convene a special session of the legislature, citing "the earnest desire I have to see a question of such great national importance brought to an early settlement, in order that it may no longer remain an open issue, and a subject of agitation before the people." In December he reported to Congress on the status of ratification, and after the first of the

The Fifteenth Amendment and its results. (Library of Congress)

year, several more states joined the list. In the end, the question came down to Texas, and Grant pressured authorities there to get a report of ratification to Washington as fast as possible. Once Texas's approval was secure, the question arose as to whether it had legal force prior to the state's readmission, leading the administration to push Congress to complete that process. On March 30, 1870, the House passed a bill readmitting Texas; the president signed it immediately and released a proclamation announcing ratification of the Fifteenth Amendment.[15]

Grant considered the amendment of such "vast importance" that he decided to go beyond the customary proclamation and celebrate its adoption in a special message. He said the amendment overthrew the notion set forth in the *Dred Scott* decision that "black men had no rights which the white man was bound to respect." Its ratification "completes the greatest civil change and constitutes the most important event that has occurred since the nation came into life." He encouraged "the newly enfranchised race" to recognize "the importance of their striving in every honorable manner to make themselves worthy of their new privilege." He entreated whites to "withhold no legal privilege of advancement to the new citizen." In framing his ideas, Grant had solicited the advice of Massachusetts congressman George Hoar, brother of the attorney general and a leading advocate of education for the freed slaves. Adopting Hoar's views and some of his language, the president noted, "The framers of our Constitution firmly believed that a republican government could not endure without intelligence and education generally diffused among the people." He called on Congress "to take all the means within their constitutional powers to promote and encourage popular education throughout the country, and upon the people everywhere to see to it that all who possess and exercise political rights shall have the opportunity to acquire the knowledge which will make their share in the Government a blessing and not a danger."[16]

Announcement of the ratification sparked celebrations throughout the land, none more exuberant than those among the African American citizens of Washington. At an evening serenade at the White House, Grant told the crowd, "There has been no event since the close of the war in which I have felt so deep an interest as that of the ratification of the fifteenth amendment. . . . I have felt the greatest anxiety ever since I have been called to this House to know that that was to be secured. It looked to me as the realization of the Declaration of Independence."[17]

In the weeks leading up to the proclamation, Grant's euphoria led him to consider a simultaneous announcement of a general amnesty and pardon for all men who had participated in the rebellion. Several cabinet secretaries immediately objected to the word *pardon*, but a consensus emerged that amnesty might be offered to all who "by some affirmative act" asked for it and promised to abide by the law. But Grant soon backed away from the idea. He realized that many white southerners had experienced no real change of heart, and after the adoption of the Fifteenth Amendment, they might be even more determined to resist social and political change. When the cabinet returned to the question two weeks after the proclamation, the president said that if the "entire pacification" of the rebel states had been "accomplished & quiet fully restored," he would "have been glad to recommend a general Amnesty." But because reports from several states still showed "lawlessness & opposition to the Government," Grant did "not think it wise to move in the direction of a general Amnesty which would make [Confederate Vice President] 'Aleck Stephens, Jeff. Davis & Robert Lee' & others eligible to seats in the Senate or House." When one cabinet secretary suggested excluding top Confederate officials, Grant said it would simply "invest the persons exempted with the character of martyrdom. . . . [I]t is better to wait." Putting southerners on notice, he told a reporter that "so long as the state of society in those districts is such as to call for military aid to preserve order it would be useless to recommend to Congress the removal of disabilities."[18]

Grant changed his mind about amnesty after receiving "many complaints about outrages in the South and requests for military intervention." Terrorist organizations such as the Ku Klux Klan operated in many parts of the region, and the violence that had marred the elections of 1868 continued through 1869 and into 1870. In March 1870 Grant sent a regiment of federal troops to North Carolina to help the beleaguered governor maintain order, and he later followed up with additional troops and arms. But by then, Republicans had recognized that piecemeal measures would not suffice to meet the widespread threat. Both the Fourteenth and Fifteenth Amendments authorized Congress to pass enforcement legislation, and Congress proceeded to act.[19]

Debate revealed anxiety among Republicans over how far the federal government could go to protect the rights guaranteed by the amendments. Senator Carl Schurz of Missouri saw danger in "undue centralization," but he insisted that the outcome of the war and the amendments had rescued individual rights from the "arbitrary discretion" of the states and "placed them under the shield of national protection." Most Republicans agreed, passing an Enforcement Act in late May 1870. For all elections—local and state as well as national—it enacted criminal sanctions for violating the Fifteenth Amendment's ban against discrimination in voting based on race, color, or previous condition of servitude. It outlawed interference with voting by force, bribery, intimidation, or economic sanctions such as threatening the loss of employment or eviction. The law granted exclusive jurisdiction over its provisions to the federal courts and authorized the president to employ the armed forces to assist in its enforcement. Aiming at groups such as the Klan, the act outlawed conspiracy to deprive any citizen of "any right or privilege" granted by the Constitution or laws of the United States. It mandated that all persons receive the same treatment as "white citizens" in such areas as court proceedings, punishments, taxes, and license fees. This omnibus law also struck at a variety of election abuses committed mainly in northern cities dominated by political machines, usually in the interest of the Democrats. It outlawed fraudulent registration, repeat voting, and voting in the name of another person, "living, dead, or fictitious." Grant signed the bill on May 31, 1870.[20]

The law's provisions regarding election fraud had the endorsement of northern Republicans such as Edwards Pierrepont, the federal district attorney for New York City. Pierrepont told Grant that he had carried New York by 20,000 votes in 1868, but cheating by the Democrats had cost him the state. If Congress would pass "a wise law under the XV amendment," Pierrepont wrote, "the national power [could] be used for national success." Grant agreed and saw the need for legislation that went beyond the Enforcement Act's protection of urban elections. At the time—mid-1870—Boss William Tweed and Tammany Hall dominated New York City's politics, their power resting largely on the fraudulent naturalization of immigrants. Republicans became convinced of the need for new naturalization legislation to break the Democrats' grip on the city and state. New York representative Noah Davis introduced a bill outlawing fraudulent naturalization and the false claim of citizenship, and it assigned jurisdiction over such violations to federal courts. In the Senate, Roscoe Conkling went further, proposing that in congressional elections in cities of 20,000 or more, federal judges be empowered to appoint federal supervisors to observe voter registration, voting at polling places, and the counting of ballots. The supervisors could challenge voters thought to be engaged in fraud and certify the results of congressional elections. Behind the scenes, Grant lent the full weight of his office to this bill and argued that Conkling's amendments would "go far to prevent the fraudulent 'repeating' &c in N.Y." He urged Davis to adopt the amendments and offered him appointment as district attorney in place of Pierrepont, who had resigned. Davis accepted, and the amended bill went forward.[21]

In the Senate, Sumner proposed to strike the word *white* from all naturalization laws to rid the process of any "distinction of race or color." The move sparked an impassioned debate about the complex mix of race, citizenship, and suffrage. Sumner's measure failed, although the final bill did include a provision opening naturalization to persons of African "nativity" or "descent." In the end, the debate over Sumner's amendment diverted attention from the momentous step authorized by the main bill—the injection of federal supervision into congressional elections in big cities in the North. Grant signed it on July 14, 1870.[22]

While the Enforcement Act and the Naturalization Act outlined new federal action, Republicans saw a need to centralize federal legal authority. The office of attorney general had existed since Washington's time but had exercised little control over the government's subordinate legal officials, such as the district attorneys and marshals working in the states. The government's burgeoning legal business wrought by the Civil War and its aftermath spurred efforts to vest greater control in the attorney general and his staff. Passage of the new enforcement legislation heightened this concern, resulting in the passage of an act to establish the Department of Justice, approved by Grant on June 22, 1870. In addition to clarifying the attorney general's authority, the law created the post of solicitor general, who would serve as the government's principal litigator and supervise the work of the department's officials in the field.[23]

The work of reorganization and enforcement fell not to Hoar, who resigned as attorney general in mid-June, but to his successor, Amos T. Akerman. Over the months, Hoar's position in the cabinet had grown increasingly shaky. In the early days of the administration, when Grant turned to Boutwell to head the Treasury Department, Hoar had assured the president that if the presence in the cabinet of two persons from the same state (Massachusetts) caused problems, he would gladly bow out. Grant did come under severe political pressure regarding Hoar, especially from senators and representatives who found the attorney general insufficiently attentive to their patronage requests. But the president held Hoar in high regard, and in December 1869 he saw a way out of the dilemma by naming him to a seat on the Supreme Court. The nomination met strong opposition, however, with southerners claiming that because the circuit associated with the seat was in the South, the appointment should not go to a northerner. Within a few days the Senate tabled the nomination. Both Grant and Hoar dug in their heels, and Grant refused to withdraw Hoar's name; in early February the Senate rejected his nomination. Four months later, when Grant was earnestly seeking senators' approval for his project to annex Santo Domingo, he finally accepted Hoar's offer to resign as attorney general.[24]

Akerman took up his duties in early July. A native of New Hampshire and a graduate of Dartmouth College, he had moved to Georgia in 1842. An unenthusiastic supporter of secession, Akerman had served in the Georgia State Guard during the war, intermittently and without distinction. After the war he supported the Republican Party and campaigned for Grant. The president rewarded him with appointment as US attorney for Georgia, a position he held until assuming the office of attorney general. Akerman became the first former Confederate to serve in the cabinet. To fill the new office of solicitor general, Grant chose Benjamin Bristow, a Kentuckian who had led a Union regiment during the war. Bristow had served as US attorney for Kentucky for four years, amassing an impressive record of successful prosecutions under the Civil Rights Act of 1866.[25]

In appointing Akerman and Bristow, Grant chose men committed to federal legal protection for African Americans in the South. But before the midterm elections of 1870, the officers of the new Justice Department did relatively little to uphold the suffrage rights of the newly enfranchised citizens. Indeed, Bristow did not even take office until mid-October. And Akerman, like many other Republican leaders who remained optimistic about racial harmony, tacitly accepted the notion that the mere existence of the new enforcement legislation would somehow envelop southern black voters with the necessary protection. The administration gave much greater attention to the election in New York, which, being the largest state, Grant regarded as "certainly the most important state to secure a fare [sic] election, in, and to secure to the republican party." Three weeks before the election, Grant ordered Akerman to authorize the US marshal in New York to appoint 5,000 special deputies, and he placed at the marshal's disposal 1,200 regular soldiers and 250 marines. Akerman himself traveled to New York City to organize the operation. Grant's aim, as Fish noted, was that "no person entitled to vote must be prevented & if possible none not entitled be allowed to vote."[26]

In the end, the administration's efforts yielded only modest gains for the Republicans. On the eve of the election, the federal attorney and marshal reached an agreement with city officials about keeping the peace at the polls. On Election Day the city was quiet and saw only a handful of arrests. Republican performance improved over previous elections; support for the Democrats declined somewhat, but not enough to defeat their municipal ticket. Moreover, Republicans charged that Tammany had dispatched many of its repeat voters to rural areas, where they contributed to the victory of the Democratic candidate for governor and the addition of four seats in Congress.[27]

If the administration's robust enforcement program achieved little in New York, benign neglect produced malignant results in the South. Violence and intimidation had a telling impact in several states, especially Georgia, Alabama, and North Carolina. In congressional elections alone, at least fifteen House seats shifted from Republican to Democratic control. Although southern Republicans suffered from infighting and corruption that deterred some voters, the lesson of the 1870 election was clear: without adequate federal action, blacks' right to vote remained in jeopardy, and the Republican Party's prospects in the region were dim. In his annual message a month later, Grant welcomed the readmission of Virginia, Mississippi, and Texas, but he noted that "violence and intimidation" had denied "a free exercise of the elective franchise" to citizens in some states and "the verdict of the people has thereby been reversed." Calling for renewed dedication to secure "a pure, untrammeled ballot," Grant conceded that after nearly two years, this major goal of his domestic program remained far from fulfilled. The Union stood intact again, but the work of Reconstruction was not yet done.[28]

5

★ ★ ★ ★ ★

RECONSTRUCTING THE
NATION'S FINANCES

Besides the southern question, the other major item on the domestic agenda cited by Grant in his inaugural address concerned the disordered state of the nation's finances, another consequence of the war. Preserving the Union had required enormous changes in the government's financial system, including a vast new tax structure, borrowing that saddled the country with a huge debt, the issuance of legal-tender paper money unbacked by gold or silver, and the creation of a system of national banks that issued notes of their own. For years, controversy regarding fiscal and monetary policy had pitted hard-money forces, who generally defended the interests of creditors, against soft-money supporters, who believed that inflation would benefit debtors. The argument created deep rifts between sections of the country, between economic interests among the people, and between two wings in each of the political parties. During the 1868 campaign, Republican leaders embraced economic orthodoxy, especially condemning the Democrats for endorsing George H. Pendleton's Ohio Idea, which proposed that the principal of some government bonds be paid with greenbacks. After the party's November victory, conservative Republicans like James A. Garfield said, "It was solemnly decided by the great majority which elected General Grant that repudiators should be repudiated and that the faith of the nation should be preserved inviolate."[1]

In his inaugural address, Grant came out foursquare for the party's conservative monetary position. "No repudiator of one farthing of our public debt will be trusted in public place," he declared, and "every dollar of Government indebtedness should be paid in gold, unless otherwise expressly stipulated in the contract." Grant also called for specie resumption but added an important condition: "as soon as it can be accomplished without material detriment to the debtor class or to the country at large." The new Congress acted immediately. Two weeks after taking office, Grant approved the Act to Strengthen Public Credit, the first law to receive his signature. The statute called for the payment of all the government's interest-bearing bonds in coin, unless the original bond authorization stated otherwise. In addition, the law pledged that the government would "make provision at the earliest practicable period" for the redemption of greenbacks in coin. The law was more than mere symbolism. Grant and his allies in Congress were determined to undergird faith in the solvency and credit of the government, as well as drive a stake through the heart of the Ohio Idea. As the act itself explicitly stated, its aim was to "remove any doubt as to the purpose of the Government to discharge all just obligations to the public creditors."[2]

In framing the administration's policy, Grant relied heavily on Treasury Secretary George S. Boutwell. The new secretary laid out two central objectives: to reduce the national debt and to move the nation closer toward specie resumption. During the war, the US government had borrowed enormous sums, and in March 1869 the outstanding interest-bearing bonds still totaled more than $2.5 billion. The previous administration had reduced the debt somewhat, but Boutwell aimed to accelerate the effort. The resumption question grew out of the Legal Tender Act of 1862, whereby Congress had tried to make up for the crippling insufficiency of specie to meet wartime needs. The law authorized the Treasury to issue new US notes, a non-interest-bearing currency unbacked by gold or silver that came to be called greenbacks. The notes were legal tender for all debts public and private, except for customs duties and interest on the national debt. They were "payable to bearer, at the Treasury of the United States," but the law set no date or term for their payment. They represented a kind of forced loan; the government obligated citizens to accept greenbacks as currency while making only an implied promise to pay coin for them at some unspecified time. By war's end, $400 million in greenbacks was circulating in the economy.[3]

What to do with this new currency dominated the money question in the years after the war. Some Americans—a minority—believed that the government should leave the greenbacks as they stood, a fiat paper

Secretary of the Treasury George S. Boutwell. (Library of Congress)

currency inconvertible for coin, thus implicitly abandoning a specie standard. The general opinion, however, was that the Treasury should resume specie payments at some point, but how to get there remained a matter of contention. Some insisted that the Treasury should simply plow forward, that "the way to resume is to resume." But at the war's end, the greenbacks remained an inflated currency; on the open market, $100 in gold commanded about $150 in greenbacks. With this difference, known as the premium, if the Treasury were to begin paying gold for greenbacks at face value, its gold stocks would soon be drained away. Others argued that the greenbacks must first be brought up to par with gold in the market in order to permit a safe resumption of specie payments. But how to raise their value was the question. One way was to contract the volume of paper currency by withdrawing and destroying the notes until they reached par. The fewer the greenbacks, the greater their worth. In 1866 Congress authorized contraction, and Johnson's secretary of the treasury Hugh McCulloch began a steady reduction in the number of notes. But after a severe business recession, Congress halted withdrawal in early 1868, leaving the volume of legal tender at $356 million. This abortive contraction policy and its political ramifications formed the backdrop for Grant's proviso in his inaugural address that specie resumption should begin when it could "be accomplished without material detriment to the debtor class or to the country at large."[4]

As a member of Congress, Boutwell had opposed McCulloch's contraction, and soon after taking the Treasury post he launched another approach. He posited that if the greenbacks remained in use, over time the country's expanding economic activity and "the condition of its industries" would enable the nation to "grow up" to resumption without "any special legislation." Rebuilding of the South, the construction of railroads, and growth in other businesses would accelerate the need for paper currency. Of necessity, the public use of greenbacks would increase, and their value relative to gold would naturally rise. In addition, increasing exports would decrease the amount of gold leaving the country to settle international trade accounts. Because "these changes will tend to diminish the difference between paper and coin," the greenbacks would eventually reach par with gold, at which point the Treasury could safely offer specie in exchange.[5]

Although some dismissed Boutwell's growing-up policy as a do-nothing approach, he understood that the nation's economic health was "more or less dependent upon the general policy of the government." Hence, he pursued government action to enhance the overall credit of the United States as a way to bolster faith in greenbacks. He launched an aggressive program to reduce the national debt by redeeming or buying back government bonds, paying for them with greenbacks. Some observers thought Boutwell's purchases violated the spirit of the Public Credit Act, but he paid for the bonds with greenbacks at their face value plus the premium, essentially the equivalent of their value in gold. At the same time, he used Treasury gold to buy greenbacks, which had the effect of raising the greenbacks' value and lowering the price of gold—a necessary step toward reaching par. Thus, Boutwell's policy aimed to reduce the national debt, underscore the government's commitment to meet its obligations, and move the country closer to a safe resumption of specie payments. From Paris, Minister Elihu Washburne thanked the secretary: "Under the direction of the President, you hold the key to the prosperity and honor of the country and the success of the Republican party."[6]

But Grant and Boutwell knew that financial policy would not remain exclusively under their direction. When the Forty-First Congress convened for its first regular session in December 1869, the legislative hopper overflowed with proposals, and Grant used his annual message to underscore the administration's determination to enhance the nation's credit. Central to that effort was the need to fashion a policy to manage the national debt. In his message Grant "heartily concurred" in Boutwell's bond-buying program, which had reduced the debt by some $75 million. But the president also advocated legislation to fund (refinance) the government's bonds. Their current interest rates of 5 or 6 percent were "too high and crippling to the industrial interests of the country," and leaving them in place unredeemed would put a substantial tax burden on citizens. Instead, Grant proposed that Congress authorize the replacement of existing bonds with a new issue that would run for a longer period at an interest rate "not exceeding 4½ percent." In essence, this amounted to paying for the Union war effort over a longer stretch of time. In his annual report accompanying the president's message, Boutwell elaborated on the proposal, suggesting the issuance of $1.2 billion in new bonds at interest of no more than 4½ percent, divided into three classes of $400 million each, to be payable at different periods.[7]

Grant's aim in this funding proposal was not only to undergird the nation's credit but also to ease Americans' tax burden. He strongly favored a general tax revision but asked Congress to postpone action until after the funding scheme took effect, when it would be clearer how much reduction was feasible. In the meantime, he suggested a modification of the income tax, which had been on the books since 1862. Over the years, the tax had undergone several revisions; the latest one in 1867 had set the rate at 5 percent on incomes over $1,000. The annual form filed by taxpayers required them to specify sources of income as well as taxable personal property. The assessment and collection of the tax embodied a degree of official prying into citizens' lives to which nineteenth-century Americans were scarcely accustomed. Although the levy tapped only about 250,000 out of 40 million Americans, it remained controversial. It was set to expire in 1870, and when Grant raised the question of its extension, it drew criticism in the cabinet. But Boutwell defended the income tax and said that its replacement by other taxes that affected more people would be politically unpopular. In his message, Grant called for a three-year extension and a reduction of the tax rate to 3 percent.[8]

On the politically treacherous question of the tariff, Grant trod lightly in his first annual message. He favored a revenue reduction of $60 million to $80 million per year, a portion of which could come from a cut in tariff duties. But he also observed that American manufactures were "increasing with wonderful rapidity under the encouragement which they now receive." He noted that manufacturing had spread to all areas of the nation and provided "employment and support to hundreds of thousands of people. . . . Self-interest, if not self-preservation, therefore dictates caution against disturbing any industrial interest of the country." Grant's gingerly treatment of the issue showed that he recognized its complexity and was aware of the divisions within the Republican Party over protectionism favored in the Northeast versus freer trade favored in the West.[9]

His comments found little favor among the small cohort of low-tariff Republicans who began styling themselves as revenue reformers. More to their liking was the report of the special revenue commissioner, David A. Wells, which charged that current tariff rates were "*excessive and unnecessary, and opposed alike to the highest interests of civilization and humanity, as well as to the proper and healthy growth of all domestic commerce and industry.*" With his post as special commissioner set to expire, Wells had hoped to enter Grant's cabinet as secretary of the treasury, but his low-tariff views made him anathema to Republican protectionists. He became a hero, however, to the revenue reformers, one of whom, *Chicago Tribune* editor Horace White, hailed his 1869 report as "the most important & valuable state paper ever produced in this country on any financial or economical subject." Although White's low-tariff views were genuine, he, like some other critics of the president, harbored a grudge over his lack of patronage influence. "Horace White never suffers a re-sentment to die out," an administration ally from Chicago reported to Washington. "He will never forgive Grant for not making some appoint-ment he asked for." Under White's editorial hand, the *Tribune* followed the path of free trade, gave "bitter, cold-blooded, & vindictive" treat-ment to the president, and "scarcely cover[ed] it with a decent mask."[10]

In this early fight over the tariff, revenue reformers made the reau-thorization of Wells's office, which would require an act of Congress, their rallying point. The commissioner himself took an active part in this movement and also curried favor with low-tariff Democrats. He presided at a strategy session of free-trade luminaries in Henry Adams's Washington apartment, where they discussed organizing support, re-gardless of party affiliation, for a low-tariff candidate to run against Grant in 1872. Wells enjoyed considerable support in Congress, but his allies were not numerous enough to secure the renewal of his post. When he had first undertaken his study, he had favored a protective tariff, and now many Republicans considered his about-face an act of treachery. "The workingmen of this great country are moving together," one New York congressman declared, "and they know their true inter-ests too well to be influenced by either false reports, false statistics, false deductions, or false logic."[11]

According to statute, the treasury secretary had the authority to appoint the special commissioner. The avowedly protectionist and turf-conscious Boutwell considered the post superfluous and, as con-ducted by Wells, pernicious. In early June 1870 Grant informed Wells that he would not recommend a reauthorization of his office. Since Boutwell never would have reappointed the commissioner anyway, some low-tariff backers concluded that it was better "to let the office disappear by default" and make Wells a martyr. "By all means," *New York Evening Post* editor William Cullen Bryant wrote, "General Grant should be admonished, with all plainness, that the country expects bet-ter things of him than to join the confederacy of the mill-owners because Mr. Boutwell has done so."[12]

As such overheated rhetoric made clear, by focusing on Wells's fate, many of the "revenue reformers" outside of Congress failed to recog-nize or chose to overlook the president's tacit support of a careful tar-iff reduction during the months following his annual message. In early May 1870 he even contemplated sending a special message calling for "a decided reduction," but in the end he decided to forgo so public a drive. Eventually, Congress agreed on a compromise implementing a moderate reduction in the tariff, with which Grant fully concurred. The move did not assuage the wrath of the low-tariff men.[13]

Congress tinkered with financial measures until the very end of the session. At 9:00 p.m. on the last day, July 14, 1870, Grant and cabinet members journeyed to the President's Room at the Capitol, where they pored over bills for several hours. The president could take satisfaction in the fact that much of the financial legislation reflected the recommendations of his annual message. The Funding Act called for the issuance of three classes of new bonds: $1 billion at 4 percent interest payable in thirty years, $300 million at 4½ percent payable in fifteen years, and $200 million at 5 percent payable in ten years. Refinancing the debt opened the way for tax reduction. An omnibus reform act reduced the levy on incomes to 2½ percent on earnings over $2,000; after two years it would end altogether. Internal revenue taxes ceased on nearly all domestic items except alcohol and tobacco. The tariff provisions reduced duties on some favorite consumer articles such as coffee, tea, sugar, and spices—imported commodities that generally did not compete with American products. The law also removed all duties on more than a hundred other noncompeting items, many of which manufacturers purchased as raw materials. Some protected items such as steel rails, marble, and nickel received an increase in duties. Estimates placed the aggregate decrease in revenue from all sources at as much as $80 million per year. The *New York Times* hailed the new tax law as "a successful stroke of strategy as well as a wise measure of relief."[14]

Republicans, and Americans in general, saw cuts in government spending as concomitant with a reduction in taxes. In his inaugural address, Grant had called for "the greatest practicable retrenchment in expenditures in every department of the Government." His first annual message did not abandon that notion, but it did imply an emphasis on what was "practicable." The president knew military matters best. The budget for the army, he said, had been "reduced wherever it has been deemed practicable" to a level "as low as it is believed can be relied on." "Looking to our future," he recommended "a liberal, though not extravagant, policy" toward funding for the navy. Public opinion, he declared, gave "an emphatic sanction" to the large outlay for veterans' pensions. As for internal improvements, he would accept "whatever amount Congress may deem proper to appropriate." These comments in favor of adequate spending were unexceptionable, and the parsimonious Elihu

Washburne found them consistent with his own belief in "enforcing a rigid economy."[15]

Hence, Grant was genuinely surprised when, shortly after his message, House Appropriations Committee chairman Henry L. Dawes appeared at the White House to complain about the government's estimates for the coming fiscal year. The Massachusetts representative had just replaced Washburne as head of the committee and was eager to prove himself as resolute a fiscal guardian as his predecessor. Dawes and other committee members had first visited the cabinet secretaries, only to learn that none of them saw any room for further cuts in their departments' funding. Frustrated, Dawes laid the question before the president, who promised that his "influence would be exerted to the utmost to bring down these estimates."[16]

Not long after this interview, however, Dawes took the floor of the House and presented a stinging indictment of the administration for proposing higher estimates than the last ones submitted by Johnson. Despite the administration's "professions of economy," he said, all but one department was asking for increased funding. Dawes made no mention of his conversation with Grant and instead told his colleagues that they could expect "no aid from the other end of the avenue."[17]

Dawes's attack met immediate challenge. Ben Butler asserted that in several instances his colleague's figures were misleading or erroneous. Johnson's estimates had been lower because of lingering surpluses from previous years and also because his department heads had deliberately understated their projections to embarrass the incoming administration. Grant was livid. He had no inkling from his conversation with Dawes "that he intended to make an open attack, but supposed he would consult with the different Cabinet officers on this matter." When a committee of citizens met with the president to discuss improvements for Washington, he denounced the congressman's speech, pointing out its "many inaccuracies." At a cabinet meeting, he said he thought the Democrats should "take him [Dawes] as a candidate" at the next election. Three weeks after Dawes's speech, Grant still fumed, claiming that the congressman had been prying into his private investments. Fish recorded in his diary that because of this episode and other "assaults made upon him in the press," Grant said he was "very seriously . . . contemplating a resignation of his office."[18]

While Dawes basked in the praise of Democrats and conservative Republicans, administration officials fought back. Assistant Secretary of

State J. C. Bancroft Davis told a Massachusetts Republican that Dawes's "erroneous, unreliable, and in some respects absolutely false" speech had "certainly done more than any one thing to sow the seeds of division in the party." "The truth is," Davis asserted, "unless Republican members of Congress can put some confidence in the administration elected by the Republican party, unless they can give up the assaults upon its policy, unless they can believe that it honestly has the good of the country at heart, unless they are willing some times to take counsel from it as well as give counsel to it, unless they can believe that it knows something about the affairs of the country and has sound ideas about the business entrusted to it, it will be impossible to keep the party together or to carry on the government with efficiency."[19]

Davis's point had immediate relevance in state contests in March, when New Hampshire's Republican governor faced a hard fight for reelection. As was usually the case, observers would see the outcome of the state race in part as a referendum on the national administration, and Grant worried about the political impact of the spending controversy. After Dawes accepted an invitation to campaign in New Hampshire, Grant met with him at the White House and enjoined him to set the record straight: "Tell the people of New Hampshire that during my administration there shall be no ascending scale of public expenditures, but wherever and whenever the closest scrutiny shall disclose the possibility of cutting off a dollar, it shall be done." Dawes complied, and in a speech at Nashua he quoted Grant directly. Moreover, at the president's behest, he pointed out that expenditures during Grant's first year in office were $60 million less than during Johnson's last year. Dawes insisted that the president and Congress were united in "an earnest, conscientious effort . . . to see to it that there shall be not a dollar more appropriated for the next year than for this." This message registered. The Republicans won the New Hampshire race with 51 percent of the vote.[20]

Yet the retrenchment dustup bore larger implications. In his defense of the administration, Butler rejected Dawes's philosophical approach to spending as too conservative. "He dislikes to take any step forward," Butler complained. "Recommending an appropriation for these many millions which the necessities of a great nation and a great people require to be expended seems to him a step in advance from which he shrinks." Dawes's fellow conservatives, however, saluted him as a virtual savior of the Republic. They regarded the expenditures he had targeted not simply as excessive but as a species of "corruption" that must be rooted out. He received numerous congratulatory letters studded with terms that equated government spending with moral turpitude: "demoralization," "tide of corruption," "reckless disbursements," "wicked prodigality." Former Pennsylvania congressman Charles Naylor wrote that "reckless selfishness, unprincipled doings, [and] low, debasing sentiments," borne of "a long unchecked possession of absolute power," had smothered the Republican Party "in an atmosphere of moral pestilence." Men like Naylor saw little need for government action or spending to meet the challenges of a changing economy and society.[21]

Grant also embraced economy, but unlike Dawes and his allies, he saw a greater potential for good in government activism. Two months after Dawes's speech, for instance, he sent Congress a message lamenting the diminution of the nation's merchant marine, which had led to a large portion of the nation's commerce being carried on foreign ships. He called on Congress to provide not only "general assistance" to the industry but also "a direct money subsidy" to individual shipping lines. In cabinet discussions he indicated a willingness to spend $5 million annually in government subsidies to mail steamships as a way to "rebuild & restore our Commercial Marine." Although all Americans recognized the problem, the president's recommendation for a remedy fell on deaf ears. Such a program, said the *New York Herald*, "would open the door to innumerable evils . . . and at one blow would overthrow the long established policy of this country." Congress took no action, and pinched notions of fiscal conservatism hampered government activism for years to come. After the enormous spending of the war years, Americans believed that the return of peace demanded a return to the thrifty ways of peacetime, with a minimalist conception of government that inextricably linked honesty to frugality. During the 1870s the House of Representatives, where money bills originated, adopted several rules that set up new roadblocks to the spending of public revenue. Throughout Grant's term, the federal government never ran at a deficit, and appropriations dropped by 25 percent. Nonetheless, that record did little to dispel doubts about Grant's commitment to responsible spending, prompted by Dawes's unwarranted attack during the president's first year in office.[22]

Hard-money conservatives who were prepared to see the worst in Grant's financial policies found another point of criticism in his handling of a series of Supreme Court decisions known as the *Legal Tender Cases*. This episode became one of the most controversial of his presidency. Contemporary critics as well as later historians argued that in reaction to a decision undercutting greenbacks, Grant packed the Court with new justices to gain approval of the suspect paper currency. A closer examination reveals the complexity of the incident and underscores Grant's essential commitment to a stable and dependable currency.

In early February 1870 Boutwell's strategy of growing up to specie payments through the gradual enhancement of greenbacks' value encountered a potentially serious setback. In *Hepburn v. Griswold*, Chief Justice Salmon P. Chase, speaking for a five-to-three majority, ruled unconstitutional the portion of the Legal Tender Act of 1862 that made greenbacks legal tender for debts contracted before the act's passage. Although Chase had supported passage of the law as secretary of the treasury in the Lincoln administration, he now decried the notion that creditors who had made loans before 1862 should be required to take payment in paper instead of the gold they had expected. The chief justice's opinion delighted hard-money proponents.[23]

The Court's decision sparked anxiety that the value of greenbacks would plummet and that gold prices would shoot up, but these fears proved unfounded. The market remained stable, in part because the decision affected relatively few debts, but also because few observers expected the Court's pronouncement to endure. Although it pleased hard-money Democrats and laissez-faire liberals, Republicans responsible for making monetary policy denounced the decision. Senate Finance Committee chairman John Sherman denied the Court's authority to rule on the question. Grant and Boutwell believed the decision would delay rather than hasten a resumption of specie payments. Denying the greenbacks' applicability to a certain class of debts threatened to diminish the notes' desirability, thereby undermining the administration's policy of gradually increasing their value toward par.[24]

Doubts that the *Hepburn* decision would stand arose in part because several cases dealing with the legal-tender clause still remained to be adjudicated. Moreover, the dissenting justices deplored the handling of the case in the Court's private conference. During that discussion, Justice Robert Grier, who for years had suffered physical and mental decline, voted to uphold the constitutionality of the legal-tender clause, leading to a four-to-four split. This result would have sustained the lower court's decision but, importantly, would have set no precedent. In the consideration of a companion case, however, Grier had leaned the other way. When Chase and the justices allied with him, all Democrats, pointed out this apparent inconsistency, the befuddled Grier reluctantly changed his mind on *Hepburn*, leading to the five-to-three outcome. The three dissenting justices, all Republicans, thought that because of this brazen manipulation, the *Hepburn* decision ought to be deprived of any precedential character. And this was all the more reason, they believed, to open the Court to argument on the remaining undecided legal-tender cases. Shortly after the conference on November 27, 1869, Chase and Democratic justice Samuel Nelson urged Grier to submit his resignation. He did so in early December, effective February 1, 1870. That the Court did not announce its final determination in *Hepburn* until February 7, a week after Grier's departure, led some to regard it as a decision by four justices rather than five. This cast further doubt on its status as a precedent.[25]

The vacancy occasioned by Grier's resignation presented Grant with his second opportunity to appoint a new justice. The other opening stemmed from a law passed by Congress in April 1869 that raised the number of justices to nine, effective in December. Not surprisingly, the president confronted an abundance of candidates for the two lifetime positions. In mid-December he nominated Attorney General Rockwood Hoar to the newly created position and Edwin Stanton to replace Grier. Stanton won confirmation instantly, but four days later he died. On Thursday, February 3, the Senate rejected Hoar. This came as no surprise to Grant, who had been canvassing possible replacement nominees for some time. He held up both new nominations until after Hoar's official rejection, and on Monday, February 7, he nominated William Strong of Pennsylvania and Joseph P. Bradley of New Jersey.[26]

Grant sent his nominations to the Senate on the same day that Chase issued his *Hepburn* opinion, leading some to charge that he intended to pack the Court to achieve a reversal. Henry Adams published an article asserting that if the newly constituted Court should issue a ruling reversing the decision, it "would establish beyond dispute a precedent for packing the Court . . . and destroying the independence of the Judiciary as a coordinate branch of the American government." Wisconsin senator Timothy Howe responded that the president had settled on Strong and Bradley before the Court issued its judgment, "and their opinions upon the legal tender question had no more influence upon their selection than had their opinions upon the question of papal infallibility." Hoar later maintained that the nominations had been filled out and signed before the Court's announcement of its decision, and both Grant and Hamilton Fish confirmed Hoar's recollection.[27]

Questions about the precise timing of the nominations notwithstanding, Grant had been considering Bradley and Strong long before February 7. For months, politicians from Bradley's home state of New

Jersey had been pushing him for a federal judgeship, and their efforts accelerated after Grier's resignation.[28] Similarly, the administration had long recognized Strong's professional attainments and the vigorous support for him. He hailed from Pennsylvania, as did Grier, and enjoyed the backing of its Republicans, including Grant's chief ally in the state, Senator Simon Cameron.[29] Nearly seven years later, Grant recalled the buildup to the appointments in a conversation that Fish recorded in his diary:

> Although he required no declaration from Judges Strong and Bradley on the Constitutionality of the Legal Tender Act, he knew Judge Strong had on the bench in Pennsylvania given a decision sustaining its constitutionality and he had reason to believe Judge Bradley's opinion tended in the same direction[;] that at the time he felt it important that the constitutionality of the law should be sustained and, while he would do nothing to exact anything like a pledge or expression of opinion from the parties he might appoint to the bench[,] he had desired that the constitutionality should be sustained by the Supreme Court[;] that he believed such had been the opinion of all his Cabinet at the time.[30]

The cabinet secretary most concerned with the monetary issue, Boutwell, echoed Grant's recollection. "Judge Strong," Boutwell wrote, "as Chief Justice of the Supreme Court of Pennsylvania, had sustained the constitutionality of the Legal Tender Act, and it was understood that Bradley was of the same opinion." To Boutwell, it was perfectly legitimate and logical that the seats on the Court should go to nominees "in harmony with the opinion of the person making the appointment." Boutwell also claimed that Chase had notified him of his opinion two weeks before announcing it. As early as November 20, 1869, nearly three months before Chase's opinion, Grant and Fish had sparred over the constitutionality of the act. During the same conversation, Grant had alluded to filling federal judgeships and said he wanted to appoint persons "whose views on questions growing out of the war, & its incidents, are sound." The greenback question was certainly a major "incident" of the war, and Grant's philosophy regarding appointments obviously would apply most forcefully to members of the Supreme Court. Unlike fastidious legal purists, Grant, the realist general who focused on results, harbored no illusions about the high court's Olympian judicial detachment. He believed the justices' predilections inevitably influenced their approaches to the questions before them. He selected Strong and Bradley accordingly.[31]

Whatever the circumstances of their appointment, with Strong and Bradley secure on the bench, Grant proceeded to undo the damage done by Chase's opinion. Just days after the new justices were confirmed by the Senate, the attorney general appeared before the newly constituted Court to push for adjudication of other pending legal-tender cases. Without naming him, Hoar cited Chase's "differing opinions at differing times of his life" as treasury secretary and as chief justice. Chase tried to stymie the consideration of these new cases, resorting, according to a Republican justice, "to all the stratagems of the lowest political trickery to prevent their being heard." But to no avail. The new justices joined the previous minority to form a new majority, which in May 1871 upheld the Legal Tender Act as it applied to debts incurred both before and after the law's passage. After the new decision, Chase confronted Boutwell: "Why did you consent to the appointment of judges to overrule me?" Boutwell assured the chief justice that "there was no personal feeling on the part of the President." But, he added, the *Hepburn* decision "operated as a limitation of the constitutional powers of Congress," and "its full and final recognition might prove injurious to the country." As Grant had wished, greenbacks were now distinctly sanctioned by the Constitution.[32]

The outcome of the second round of *Legal Tender Cases* capped two years of successful fiscal and monetary management. Working with Boutwell and Congress, Grant had achieved re-funding of the government's bonds at a lower interest rate and a substantial reduction in federal taxation, and he had advocated a balanced approach to spending. He and Boutwell had also championed a gradual enhancement of the value of greenbacks as the surest route to specie resumption. Along the way, however, in the fall of 1869 their carefully calibrated monetary policy came near to destruction at the hands of Wall Street buccaneers.

6

★ ★ ★ ★ ★

BRUSH WITH DISASTER
THE NEW YORK GOLD CORNER
CONSPIRACY

While tax and funding legislation wound its way through Congress and the Supreme Court wrestled with the legal-tender question, Congress spent considerable time in the winter of 1870 investigating an episode from the previous summer that had threatened to upend the Grant administration's monetary policy of "growing up" to specie resumption. This was the so-called New York Gold Corner conspiracy, a nefarious manufactured panic that reached its climax and collapse on Black Friday, September 24, 1869, when Grant and Treasury Secretary George Boutwell moved to shut it down. The financial impact of the episode proved relatively short-lived, but its political impact endured and cast a shadow over Grant's performance as president that persisted long afterward.

This scheme to corner the gold market in the nation's financial capital was the brainchild of the notorious financial speculators Jay Gould and James Fisk Jr. The shrewd and sinuous Gould stood in marked contrast to the volcanic and vulgar Fisk. Yet the two shared a love of making money, an attenuated concept of fair play, and scant regard for the public weal. On the eve of Grant's administration, they were savoring their victory over Cornelius Vanderbilt in a "war" for control of the Erie Railroad. Gould had emerged with his position as president of the Erie relatively secure, but the road's financial condition was less firm. He

Jay Gould. (Library of Congress)

concluded that it could reap large returns from an increased shipment of agricultural products over its routes from western states to the East Coast for export. The key way to increase the export demand, he believed, was to maintain a high premium on gold. Gold priced high in greenbacks would enable foreign customers to obtain a greater quantity of currency to purchase American products, which railroads would

James Fisk Jr. (Library of Congress)

carry eastward.The higher the price of gold, the greater the exports; the more traffic, the higher the Erie's income.[1]

Gould later claimed he "had no idea of cornering" the gold market, but he did admit that with an aggressive program of gold purchasing, "the price of gold would go up while the movement was going on," and "we could make money both ways by buying it then, and selling it on the rise." By bidding up the price, Gould and Fisk stood to turn huge profits when they made gold available to merchants and others who needed it for foreign trade exchanges and customs duties. Whatever the merits of the crop-movement theory, and whether or not they intended an absolute corner of the gold market, Gould and Fisk saw an opportunity for immense gains from a manipulation of the currency.[2]

From the beginning, the two schemers understood that success required a change in Boutwell's policy of selling gold for greenbacks. If they sought to bid up the gold price, gold sold by the Treasury would tend to push it down. Starting in late April 1869, as part of his long-term plan to reduce the premium, Boutwell regularly sold Treasury gold, reaching a total of $15 million within two months. This rapid selling of gold lowered its price, resulted in a severe tightening of the currency market, and ran directly counter to Gould and Fisk's purposes.[3]

Gould, the mastermind of the duo, saw little hope of successful consultation with Boutwell and therefore sought other means to influence the administration's policy. Most notably he cultivated a relationship with Grant's brother-in-law Abel Corbin, who had long been a friend of Julia Grant's family. In 1842 Corbin had accepted the position of clerk of the House Committee on Claims in Washington, where he moonlighted as a lobbyist. He abruptly resigned the clerkship in 1858 when he was accused of accepting payments from manufacturers to influence the passage of tariff legislation in 1857. He avoided criminal prosecution, moved to New York, and became a successful speculator in real estate. In 1865 he sold General Grant a house in Washington, the cost of which was promptly defrayed by a group of wealthy New York businessmen. In March 1869 Corbin attended the inaugural events in Washington, where the sixty-one-year-old widower met the new president's unmarried sister. Two months later, ever watchful for the main chance, Corbin married Jennie Grant, nearly twenty-five years his junior.[4]

The congressional committee investigating the allegations of influence peddling in 1857 concluded that Corbin had had less impact on the legislation than he claimed; indeed, he had "sneer[ed] a little at the blindness and stupidity" of the businessmen who had paid him for his services. The committee's report wryly observed that Corbin's testimony "shows how capitalists may be fleeced by parties who pretend to be able to exert an influence over legislation, of which they are wholly destitute." It is doubtful that this obscure report ever came to Jay Gould's attention before Black Friday a decade later, but if it did, he chose not to see it as a cautionary tale.[5]

When and how Gould and Corbin became allies in the gold scheme is not clear, but both espoused the idea of pushing up the price of gold to promote agricultural exports. They also agreed that an important first step was to secure the appointment of a sympathetic assistant US treasurer at New York, the official responsible for implementing the Treasury Department's monetary policy, including gold sales. According to Corbin's step-son-in-law, who refused to be considered for the job, they believed they "could operate with safety when they were acting on a certainty." Gould and Corbin turned to Daniel Butterfield, an army general who was well connected in the city's business circles and had spearheaded the effort to raise funds to pay for Grant's house in Washington in 1866. Butterfield also enjoyed the support of other New York businessmen, and he received the appointment. Gould later claimed that about a month after Butterfield took office, the new assistant treasurer asked Gould to buy gold for him. Gould said he complied to the tune of $1.5 million, but Butterfield denied ever making the request and explained that a $10,000 check he received from Gould was a loan.[6]

Besides favoring Butterfield's appointment, Gould and Corbin saw the importance of directly lobbying the president. In mid-June 1869 both Gould and Fisk availed themselves of an opportunity to speak with Grant about the administration's financial policy. The occasion was the president's trip to Boston to attend the National Peace Jubilee, commemorating the end of the Civil War. Grant stopped briefly in New York City to drop his family off at Corbin's house, where a group of businessmen waited to escort him to a boat owned by Gould and Fisk. That Grant made this trip to Boston on a privately owned vessel was hardly unusual; with negligible government support for executive travel, railroads and other transportation companies frequently provided free passage to presidents. During the voyage Grant enjoyed an evening supper, followed by conversation with several men, including Gould and Fisk. Corbin was not present, and Gould and Fisk did not speak with Grant alone. As Gould later recalled, the group discussed "the state of the country, the crops, prospects ahead," and the like. "The President was a listener," Gould said; "the other gentlemen were discussing. Some were in favor of Boutwell's selling gold, and some were opposed to it." When someone asked Grant's opinion, he "remarked that he thought there was a certain amount of fictitiousness about the prosperity of the country, and that the bubble might as well be tapped in one way as another." In essence, the comment represented an endorsement of Boutwell's policy, and Gould and Fisk concluded "from that conversation that the President was a contractionist." Gould warned that Boutwell's policy "would produce great distress," spark "strikes among the workmen," cause factories to close, and perhaps "almost lead to civil war." He argued that the government "ought to facilitate an upward movement of gold in the fall" to stimulate agricultural exports and spur the economy. But he made no headway with the president and concluded that the "interview on the way to Boston was a wet blanket." As Fisk recalled, "When we got to Boston, Mr. Gould and myself made up our minds that the prospect did not look promising."[7]

For Grant, the shipboard conversation was an incidental happenstance unrelated to the larger purpose of his trip to Massachusetts. Although the jubilee excursion was nonpolitical, the president lent his prestige to the state's Republicans, including Governor William Claflin, who had chaired Grant's 1868 campaign and was now running for reelection. Grant also visited Boutwell at his home in Groton, where he likely recounted the conversation on the steamer from New York. The president then returned to New York, where he spent a few days relaxing at Corbin's house. He also attended two plays, including one at the Fifth Avenue Theater, partly owned by Fisk.[8]

As it happened, Gould and Fisk had approached Grant at a time when, in part because of the Treasury's monetary operations, money was exceedingly tight and the downward pressure on the gold price was great. Businessmen throughout the country felt the pinch, and Boutwell felt their concerns. Although he "consider[ed] it for the interest of the country that the premium on gold should diminish," he also believed that "for the Treasury to force down the price of gold at any time below what the natural condition of the country would dictate, would be bad policy." Hence, he decided to continue the sales but to scale them back to $2 million per month in July and subsequent months. The president generally relied on Boutwell's judgment regarding this kind of decision. In early August he enthusiastically explained to *New York Times* editor John Bigelow how the secretary's policies had reduced the debt and raised the value of the bonds. The next day Bigelow published an editorial praising "the promising financial results" the administration had achieved.[9]

Grant traveled extensively during the summer of 1869, often combining leisure trips with "nonpolitical" political appearances. (Repair work at the White House made the mansion uninhabitable for several weeks.) He frequently stopped at Corbin's residence when he passed through New York, more to enjoy the company of his favorite sister than to listen to unsolicited advice from the tiresome Corbin. Even so, his brother-in-law continued to push the crop-movement theory, and on a couple of occasions he arranged for Gould to speak with Grant. Although the testimony of both Gould and Corbin regarding these encounters was hazy, Corbin noted that "the President was always hitching a little from him [Gould] whenever he began to go at all into the policy of the government. The President would talk on general principles, but the moment the conversation led to the subject of what the administration would do, he uniformly became very reticent." One such encounter occurred on August 13, but Gould obtained nothing conclusive during this brief conversation. Indeed, his recollection of it was so indistinct that he confused it with another that took place weeks later.[10]

Nor did Fisk get much further when he spoke with Grant on August 19 as the latter was preparing to leave New York for a trip to New England. Fisk laid it on thick, presenting a letter from Gould stating that 300 ships were in the Mediterranean heading for England laden with grain that would undercut American exports. Fisk later testified, "I talked with General Grant on the subject, and endeavored, as far as I could, to convince him that his policy was one that would only bring destruction to us all." He also claimed that Grant told him he would see Boutwell and then get back to Fisk, or all three of them would get together. But according to Grant, he told Fisk it would not be fair to give him any advance information about the government's intentions and that whenever the Treasury Department changed its action or policy, it gave notice in the press to be fair to all. No further meeting with Fisk took place, and Fisk received no assurances of a change in the administration's gold-selling policy from either Grant or Boutwell. Indeed, Fisk later said, "the thing began to look scary to me," and he did not commence buying gold until Gould convinced him to do so several weeks later.[11]

After these fruitless efforts to persuade Grant directly, Gould and Corbin hit upon another tactic. They concluded that even without an actual pledge from the president to withhold Treasury gold, their scheme to push up the price of gold might work if they could convince the public that the administration would not sell. At Gould's request, Corbin wrote an editorial to be planted in the *New York Times*, purporting to convey the administration's intentions. Gould approved the piece and enlisted a friend to pass it along to the *Times* as coming from someone knowledgeable about the administration's aims. Corbin's article rehashed the crop-movement theory, but Caleb Norvell, the paper's astute financial editor, immediately noticed that the article contradicted the administration policy Grant had outlined to Bigelow a few weeks earlier.

Doubting that the piece was authoritative, Norvell altered it to align more closely with the newspaper's position and Grant's earlier statements. He added passages, including one indicating that the administration might insert gold into the market to moderate the price. The last paragraph in Corbin's draft asserted that "a high price for gold, during the next three months, would be productive of great good to exporters of produce. . . . Hence, [the] government will not so act as to lessen the value of this year's abundant crop." Seeing in this passage "a sinister purpose to 'bull' gold," Norvell cut it out entirely. In essence, Norvell left intact those passages indicating that the administration would not take steps to lower the price of gold, but he altered the article to remove the implication that it intended to take steps to push it higher. The *Times* printed the revised piece, "Financial Policy of the Administration," on August 25. It failed to alter administration policy, as Gould and Corbin had hoped. Three days later, Assistant Secretary of the Treasury William A. Richardson informed Butterfield that the purchase of bonds and the sale of gold would continue in September "to the same extent and in the same manner as in August."[12]

According to Norvell's later testimony, Gould fumed that Corbin's article had been "mutilated" and "reversed in its position by some editor." Though foiled again, Gould did not give up. He wrote Boutwell a letter redolent with what a later generation would call "spin." Gould treated the *Times* article as if it had reported that Boutwell *embraced* the crop-movement theory, and he observed how "peculiarly fortunate" the country was "in having a financial head who can take a broad view of the situation." He asserted once again that "only by making gold high and scarce" could American grain compete in European markets. But if Gould hoped for an endorsement or a rejoinder by which he could divine Boutwell's intentions, the secretary resisted the ploy. His brief and "very evasive" reply gave no hint regarding the Treasury's intentions. Boutwell later recalled that the crop-export idea had "never made much impression upon my mind."[13]

When Corbin's article appeared in the *Times*, Boutwell was traveling with Grant through New England. Whether or not they discussed gold sales, nothing in the record suggests that Grant ordered Boutwell to curtail them, for on August 28, three days after the article appeared, Richardson told Butterfield to continue sales in September as in August. But back home in Groton, Boutwell concluded that market conditions were such that larger sales—$4 million to $6 million in gold, and more likely the latter sum—would be necessary in September, a stance directly counter to Gould's purposes. On Thursday, September 1, Bout-well alerted Richardson to be ready to give notice of the sale on Sunday, September 5.[14]

After his brief tour in New England with Boutwell, the president joined his family, including Corbin and Jennie, at the well-known resort in Saratoga, New York. There he ran into A. T. Stewart, with whom he discussed the gold question at length. In contrast with Grant's encounters with Gould and Fisk, Corbin said of the talk with Stewart: it was "the only time I ever heard the President speak unreservedly on the subject." The substance of the conversation went unrecorded, but Stewart's attitude can be inferred from the later congressional testimony of others. He opposed increased gold sales by the Treasury. Stewart considered it inappropriate for the Treasury to engage in operations such as selling gold that would make it a participant in the struggle between two sets of speculators—those who bulled gold and those who were short of gold and gambled on a decline in price. Although the Treasury appointment fiasco had strained Grant's relations with Stewart, the president still had immense respect for the merchant's business acumen.[15]

Shortly after his conversation with Stewart, Grant apparently wrote a letter to Boutwell regarding gold sales. In later hearings, Boutwell failed to produce this letter, but he recollected that it was dated September 2 and he received it on September 4. He said that Grant had "expressed an opinion that it was undesirable to force down the price of gold" because doing so would retard the movement of crops from the West. The letter gave Boutwell the "impression" that the president had "rather a strong opinion" on the subject, but "in the letter he said he had no desire to control my purpose in regard to the management of the Treasury; . . . and he left the matter to my judgment entirely." Since he had become secretary of the treasury, Grant had "never" given him a direct order regarding gold sales. Moreover, Boutwell noted that opposing a move to reduce the price of gold was not the same as favoring an increase, which the conspirators wanted. "I do not think the President, in writing or in any other way, indicated his desire that [the price of] gold should advance. The suggestion was that it should not be forced down during the month of September when the crops were to be moved; that they could not be moved as well upon a falling market as upon a *stationary* one."[16]

Some observers at the time and later saw Grant's purported September 2 letter as evidence that he was somehow in league with or had been duped by the gold conspirators.[17] But in fact, for weeks Gould had failed to gain any traction with Grant. Nor was the crop-movement idea Gould's exclusive creation. Others, including House Banking and Currency Committee chairman James A. Garfield, understood that "an amount of currency amply sufficient for the winter and spring might be wholly insufficient for moving the fall crops." A modern historian has claimed that Gould "laid out a cockamamie theory," but in fact, he simply espoused a commonplace notion that a nation can enhance its exports by devaluing its currency. Indeed, it was precisely the crop theory's plausibility that led Gould to adopt it to mask his ulterior motives in bulling the gold market. As the harvest season drew near, and after Grant had talked the matter over with Stewart, the president apparently sent a suggestion to Boutwell that he avoid taking steps that would force the price of gold down during the period crucial to farmers' success.[18]

As it happened, Grant's September 2 letter occasioned no substantive change in Treasury policy. When Boutwell received the letter on September 4, he wired Richardson in Washington, "Send no order to Butterfield as to sales of gold until you hear from me." This was not an order to stop sales; instead, it referred to Boutwell's September 1 letter to Richardson about the possibility of *increased* sales, an idea that he now put on hold. The sales program for September had already been set in Richardson's order of August 28, and Boutwell did not change that. As Butterfield later testified, he received no directive "other than the regular orders" for the month. Gold sales continued, and by September 17, they had reached a total of $2 million, equal to the total for each of the entire months of July and August. Grant did not halt gold sales in the interest of the conspirators.[19]

Sometime in late August or early September, Gould took steps to bind Corbin more tightly to his project by offering to purchase gold on his behalf so that he could benefit from the anticipated rise in price. Corbin hesitated, but he accepted Gould's gesture as long as the account would be carried in his wife's name. On September 2 Gould gave Corbin a written statement of the purchase of $1.5 million in gold. As with his similar purchase for Butterfield, Gould did not ask Corbin to pay a margin (down payment). The transaction was not quite the "friendly thing" Gould later claimed, however; although Corbin and Butterfield stood to gain if the price of gold rose, they would also bear the cost of any decline. Congressional investigators later zeroed in on Gould's aim: "Was it to interest them in establishing the policy of the country?" they asked. Gould replied, "I supposed that what interest they had would be thrown in that way." "And you considered that an anchor thrown to windward, did you?" Garfield asked. "Yes, sir," Gould responded. After only four days, when the gold price had risen somewhat, Corbin asked Gould to sell "his" gold and pay him the proceeds. Gould gave the insistent Corbin a check for $25,000 but kept his account on the books, trying to keep him on board with the scheme. Corbin's hope for a quick, profitable exit clearly echoed his skinning of tariff interests for his "lobbying" in the 1850s.[20]

Gould could hardly regard Corbin's desire to sell as an expression of confidence that the gold price would rise further, so he once again attempted to work on Grant directly. He appeared at Corbin's house on the evening of September 11, when Grant and his family were visiting.[21] In later testimony, Gould claimed that "the President had changed his views" and that Grant "had said then that he was satisfied the country had a very bountiful harvest; that there was to be a large surplus; that unless we could find a market abroad for that surplus it would put down prices here; and he remarked that the Government would do nothing during the fall months of the year to put down the price of gold or make money tight." But even if Grant said all this, it was not an endorsement of a *rise* in the price of gold. Gould also claimed that Grant told Corbin that Boutwell had given an order to sell gold and Grant had countermanded it, but Corbin vehemently denied Gould's assertion. In his testimony, Gould tried to massage this conversation into a presidential endorsement of his project, but Grant's secretary Horace Porter, who had been present, testified that Corbin had done most of the talking about the crop theory. Grant had said virtually nothing and in fact had been irritated by Gould. In a rare show of displeasure with a servant, Grant had chided the Corbins' doorman "a little peevishly" for being "a little too easy in allowing Mr. Gould to have an interview." Corbin remembered this incident "because it was such an unusual thing for the President to exhibit impatience. He then turned around to his wife, who sat near by, and remarked, half ejaculatory, that Gould was always trying to find something out of him."[22]

The next day Grant dined with A. T. Stewart, who no doubt reiterated his opposition to the government's interfering between speculative rivals in the gold market. Certainly that was the tenor of a letter Grant wrote to Boutwell just before leaving New York for a trip to western Pennsylvania. Grant was enduring another conversation on the subject of gold prices with Corbin when he apparently became so alarmed at his brother-in-law's persistence that he broke off the talk to write a cautionary letter to Boutwell, who would be arriving in New York a few days later. Dated September 12, the day after his annoying conversation with Gould, Grant's letter warned Boutwell that the combat between competing interests was heating up:

> I am satisfied that on your arrival you will be met by the bulls and bears of Wall Street, and probably by merchants too, to induce you to sell gold, or pay the November interest in advance, on the one side, and to hold fast on the other. The fact is, a desperate struggle is now taking place, and each party want the government to help them out. I write this letter to advise you of what I think you may expect, to put you on your guard. I think, from the lights before me, I would move on, without change, until the present struggle is over.

Grant asked Boutwell to let him know "your experience with the factions." Again deferring to the secretary, he closed by stating, "No doubt you will have a better chance to judge than I, for I have avoided general discussion of the subject." Boutwell later testified that he understood Grant's letter to mean that "he would allow the existing order to remain, which was, as I recollect it, to sell a million of gold on alternate weeks" in September, a position directly counter to the conspirators' wishes. Again, Gould had made no headway with the president, who did not order a halt in the sale of gold.[23]

On September 15 Grant arrived for a relaxing family visit at the home of Julia's cousin William Smith in Washington, Pennsylvania. Included in the party were Horace Porter and *New York Herald* reporter DeB. Randolph Keim, who had traveled with Grant extensively during the previous weeks. On September 16 Keim and the president engaged in an extended conversation, which Keim briefly recounted in a letter to his boss, James Gordon Bennett. During this talk, Grant let down his guard enough to mention his recent letter to Boutwell, warning the secretary, as Keim put it, "to beware of Wall Street and to sell no gold except by his (the President's) directions." Grant wanted no publicity that would aid one side or the other in the speculative struggles, and Keim alerted Bennett that "nothing should be said of the letter."[24]

Of course, Keim knew nothing about the behind-the-scenes lobbying over gold prices, but Grant had said enough to make the reporter wonder whether the president suspected some sort of nefarious manipulation by at least some of the contending parties on Wall Street. As Keim wrote to Bennett, "I am trying to unravel the Boutwell intrigue. I alluded to it to the President. I saw it struck him and I am in hopes of getting what he thinks about it, to use indirectly, after he has considered it thoroughly. He insinuated that there might be something in it." A week later, Grant and Boutwell's action to halt the gambling on Wall Street on Black Friday confirmed Keim's inference; he concluded that Grant's September 12 letter to the treasury secretary had been a "piece of strategy on [the] part of [the] President to break the gold ring." Keim's reference to "the Boutwell intrigue" was unclear, but it may have reflected Grant's concern that, while in New York, the hard-money treasury secretary might become captive of the bears who were short of gold and laboring to push the price down. Boutwell's general monetary policy called for a reduction of the gold premium over time to ease the country back to specie payments, and Grant fully agreed with that policy. But the politics of the moment called for placing that strategy on temporary hold. Gubernatorial elections loomed in the key states of Ohio and Pennsylvania, and with a bountiful harvest already tending to undermine agricultural prices, any government action that resulted in a further reduction in farm prices could damage Republican prospects in those states and Grant's political standing as well.[25]

Meanwhile, Gould's September 11 conversation with Grant had left him unconvinced that the president would aid his plan by halting gold sales, and Boutwell's visit to New York did not set his mind at ease. Soon after his arrival on September 15, the secretary dined with Butterfield, who warned him of the impending struggle between "railroad men" who favored higher-priced gold and "innocent" merchants who favored cheap gold. Butterfield urged Boutwell to listen to both before making his judgment. A. T. Stewart also warned the secretary that he would be "besieged" by both factions and advised him "not to interfere on either side." In a meeting with businessmen the next day, Boutwell asked banker George Opdyke his opinion of the crop-movement theory. Opdyke replied that a higher premium on gold "produced by natural causes" would benefit the farmers, but "an attempt to produce that result by combination, or by any other artificial means, was certain to fail in the end, and that the reaction would produce infinitely more mischief than the temporary advantage."[26]

By the time he spoke at a Union League dinner on the evening of September 16, Boutwell had become "satisfied that there were speculative movements in gold, the nature of which I did not learn more than that there appeared to be an opinion that Fisk and Gould were concerned in it." In his speech the secretary declared, "Nothing should be done for the purpose of giving any opportunities of making money out of the Government's operations. That could not always be prevented, but it should never come through the aid or connivance of his department." The next morning the *New York Herald* noted that the Treasury held between $80 million and $90 million in gold, and "Secretary Boutwell will sell gold and buy bonds whenever he thinks it to the interest of the government to do so, without regard to any combinations of the gold gamblers." On September 16 and again on September 17, the subtreasury in New York sold half a million dollars in gold.[27]

Gould was so upset by Boutwell's New York visit that he once again called on Corbin. "I have made an honest effort to maintain the price of gold," the frantic speculator declared. "And now here is Mr. Boutwell, represented by all of his leading friends in the city as being disposed to crush down the market. . . . This report he does not deny, and his silence causes it to be believed by the operators that there is to be a great thrust of gold on the market." Corbin tried to calm him down by assuring him that Grant would override any attempt by Boutwell to sell gold. To substantiate his assertion, Corbin cited Grant's September 12 letter to the secretary, but as Gould later testified, "that did not satisfy me," especially when Corbin admitted he had not read the letter. For his part, Corbin was now worried about maintaining his credibility as a man of influence with the president, his only stock in trade in the enterprise. He agreed to write Grant a letter making their case one more time. Gould got Fisk to supply one of his most trusted agents to hand-deliver Corbin's letter to the president.[28]

Shortly after Corbin wrote to Grant, Gould wrote directly to Boutwell. "My theory," he stated, "is to let gold go to a price that we can export our surplus products. . . . In my judgment, the government cannot afford to sell gold during the next three months, while the crops are being marketed, and if such a policy were announced it would immediately cause a high export of breadstuffs and an active fall trade." Again, Gould's objective was not merely to persuade Boutwell to follow a certain course but also to get an announcement of such a policy that would enable him to bull the market. Boutwell did not reply and did not halt the sale of gold.[29]

With no assurance of help from the administration, Gould feared that the considerable quantity of gold he had bought would fail to appreciate, so he turned to Fisk to help him push the price upward. Fisk had held out scant hope for the success of Gould and Corbin's summer campaign, and now he feared that "if we bought gold up the government would unload their gold onto us." But Gould was intent on enlisting Fisk's aid, and according to Fisk, Gould assured him, "This matter is all fixed up; . . . Corbin has got Grant fixed all right." Fisk also alleged that, according to Corbin, of the gold Gould had bought on Corbin's behalf, $500,000 was earmarked for Julia Grant, and a check for $25,000 had already been sent to her. Corbin denied making such a statement, and Fisk himself admitted that Corbin could present no evidence to substantiate the claim. But rather than these professions of administration support, which neither Gould nor Corbin could substantiate, Fisk was apparently most influenced by Gould's own willingness to plunge into the market: "I did not go into the transaction until I considered that Mr. Gould was undertaking to carry a pretty heavy burden, when I said that of course my entire resources were at his disposal."[30]

About the time Fisk was deciding to join the buying scheme, his agent was making a breakneck trip to deliver Corbin's letter to Grant in Pennsylvania. Called in from a game of croquet, the president stepped aside to read his brother-in-law's letter, which went on for "page after page" on the crop-movement idea. Although no one preserved the document, Corbin later described it as "a strong letter" that "took up all these old theories very much at length," including the assertion that "a change of policy . . . would affect the elections very seriously, and most certainly would affect the prosperity of the country." The letter told Grant nothing new, and he showed little reaction, telling the messenger he had no reply. But when Porter informed him of the manner of the letter's delivery, direct from New York by special messenger, alarm bells went off. This letter, Porter later recalled, "urging a certain policy on the administration, taken in connection with some rumors that had got into the newspapers at that time, as to Mr. Corbin having become a great bull in gold, excited the President's suspicions, and he believed that Mr. Corbin must have a peculiar interest in those speculations; that he was not actuated simply by a desire to see a certain policy carried out for the benefit of the administration."[31]

Indeed, Grant was so disturbed by Corbin's urgent entreaty that he asked Julia to write to his sister and have her tell her husband that if he were engaged in gold speculation to get out immediately. As Julia Grant recalled in her memoirs, she told Jennie that if Corbin did not break off his speculation, "he will be ruined, for come what may, he (your brother) will do his duty to the country and the trusts in his keeping." As Corbin later testified, Mrs. Grant "spoke with such directness and feeling that, while but few words were used, they evidently were upon the assumption that there was something about it so terrible, so disgraceful, that it wonderfully excited my wife, to whom the letter was addressed."[32]

The Corbins received Julia's correspondence on September 22, and Jennie was so distressed that Corbin showed the letter to Gould and told him, "I *must* go out of this matter," and "the matter must now end." Corbin asked Gould to sell the gold he had purchased for him and pay him the $100,000 profit resulting from the moderate rise in price thus far. Gould declined to do so. Corbin was anxious to be able to tell Grant that he was not involved in speculation and wrote a letter to that effect, adding the sentence: "I tell you now, as a man who has studied this matter impartially, that if you give an order to sell gold, you will commit a grave mistake." Corbin included this statement more for Gould's benefit than for Grant's, but as Gould later put it, "I did not bite at it." He understood that Corbin's influence with the president, if it had ever existed, had collapsed. He offered to give Corbin a check for $100,000 "on account" if he would remain in the pool, but Jennie insisted that "Ulysses thinks it wrong, and that it ought to end," and Corbin declined the offer. His refusal "astonished" Gould, and as Corbin recalled, "he looked at me with a look of severe distrust, as if he was afraid of treachery in the camp."[33]

Julia Grant's letter to Jennie Corbin, with its clear indication that Grant would not assist the speculative venture and that Corbin had been bluffing about his influence, forced Gould to change course radically. Realizing that Grant and the Treasury would in all likelihood sell gold to break the attempted corner, he knew it was time to exit the scheme. He proceeded to sell gold quietly at the higher prices, buying "merely enough to make believe that I was a bull." While others around him were plotting to send the gold price even higher, Gould later said, "I had my own views about the market, and had my own fish to fry."[34]

To fry those fish, Gould was willing to cook Fisk's goose. He told Fisk that Corbin "feels troubled and nervous," but otherwise he did not reveal how much Julia Grant's letter had changed the situation. Hence, while Gould surreptitiously sold gold, Fisk continued to buy it and bull the market upward. On the afternoon of Thursday, September 23, he stormed into the New York Gold Room, booming orders to buy. According to an editorial in the *New York Times* the next morning, Fisk and his allies had "talked freely of the warrant which they had from Washington that the Government would not interfere with them. . . . Although this must have been known to be false, there were abundant rumors and suspicions insidiously spread around the Street to create the belief or fear with good men that the Administration would *not* interpose by further sales of Gold from the Treasury." Gould surmised that this "editorial was written for the purpose of being telegraphed to Washington to frighten the officials," and it "led me to believe that the government would sell." When the market opened, Gould said, "I sold all the morning."[35]

At the end of the day on Thursday, gold closed significantly higher at 143⅛, and Boutwell rushed to the White House to consult the president, who had recently returned to Washington. After examining the matter at length, the two men decided that "if gold advanced materially the next day, it would be our duty to sell." The bulling continued on September 24, which came to be known as Black Friday, one of the most tumultuous days in the history of American financial markets. At the opening of the market at 10:00 a.m., gold stood at 150; it continued upward through the morning, reaching 160 before 11:30. Each upward tick spurred clamor in New York and Washington for the Treasury to step in. Shortly after 11:00 Boutwell left the Treasury to consult with Grant next door at the White House. The secretary suggested selling $3 million in gold; Grant proposed $5 million. Boutwell wired Butterfield to sell $4 million. Meanwhile, the bears in the Gold Room had not been supine, having concluded that "a bold proceeding, such as giving them all the gold that they would take, would probably kill the bull." By the time Butterfield released Boutwell's sell order, the bears had broken the bulls' momentum, and a total rout followed the order's publication. The price stood at 160 at 11:59, fell to 140 at 12:07, and tumbled to 133 at 12:32. At 3:00 p.m. gold closed at 133⅛. Even though the government sale was only $4 million, the bulls knew, as Fisk put it, that "the government had eighty or ninety millions right behind it" and "had made up its mind to break up this clique." Grant and Boutwell's order made it clear that they would not brook continued bulling, and the so-called gold corner, which had actually exhibited a palpable shape for less than a week, was beaten.[36]

Fisk and Gould could not resist concluding that Corbin had hoodwinked them. "You damned old scoundrel, do you know what has happened?" Fisk yelled. "If we had not had confidence in you, do you suppose we would have gone on?" Gould recalled telling Corbin that "it looked as though he [Corbin] had been rather assuming on the President; that he had assumed to know what the President would do, and had counted without his host." To assuage the temper of his erstwhile allies, the old influence peddler made one last try, offering to go to Washington to see Grant on Sunday. The three agreed that he would propose that the Treasury withdraw its order to sell gold on Monday and allow the bulls and bears in New York to confer and agree on a price to settle the mélange of sales that had occurred during the panic. Corbin was to appeal to the president on the grounds that such a course would "mend up the matter, bind up the wounds," and "save large losses to all concerned." If Corbin succeeded, he was to telegraph Fisk and Gould immediately so that they could arrange meetings to settle the price.[37]

Once again, Corbin had counted without his host. After an all-night train ride, he went to the White House on Sunday morning and hit a brick wall. He told the president that if Treasury gold sales could be halted until November, "it would be of great benefit both to the bulls and bears in settling up." Grant cut him off: "This matter has been concluded, and I cannot open up nor consider the subject." According to Horace Porter, Corbin pleaded that "a great many people are ruined. The bulls and the bears have both suffered very severely." At this, "the President turned around and said, 'I am not at all sorry to hear it, and I have no sympathy with gold gamblers.'" That same day Boutwell gave additional orders to sell gold twice a week until November 1, a policy that was later extended to the end of the year. Corbin's game was over. He did not telegraph Gould but simply took the train back to New York. As Fisk put it, "It was no use." It was now "each man drag out his own corpse. Get out of it as well as you can."[38]

In the end, Fisk managed to "get out of it" by repudiating his purchase contracts with the help of compliant judges. Gould obtained a series of court injunctions that enabled him to secure a settlement of gold sales from Black Friday at 135, near the price at the close. Although Gould and Fisk suffered tainted reputations, neither man was ruined financially. Others were less fortunate. Many gold brokers and more than a dozen firms on the stock exchange went under. The panic caused tumult in the stock market, with the usual casualties that accompany such disturbances.[39]

Legitimate businessmen generally execrated the attempted corner and consequent panic, but they did not agree about the overall impact. Merchant William Dodge told a congressional investigating committee that "for several weeks, business was almost entirely paralyzed," while banker George Opdyke conceded that the situation was "very injurious" but "failures were not numerous." More important, Opdyke believed, the attempted corner suggested to "the mercantile and financial mind, not only in this country but all over the world, that we here are a set of gamblers, and that it is not safe to enter into any contracts with us, when it is possible for a small combination of speculators to monopolize one branch of our currency, the coin." Many observers thought that nothing short of a return to specie payments could avert future Black Friday–type speculation.[40]

Before Black Friday, the public had known little beyond a general awareness that Gould and Fisk were at the bottom of an attempt to corner gold, but accounts of their machinations soon began to appear in the press. Within a week, Fisk and Corbin were exchanging accusations in newspaper interviews. Neither man was burdened by scruples, but Fisk's bombast clearly overpowered Corbin's sniveling. Fisk claimed the ring had relied on the president's brother-in-law as a go-between with the government, and he insinuated complicity by the president. Grant at first refrained from commenting, but with little more than a week before the elections in Ohio and Pennsylvania, he could not ignore the potential political damage. In an Associated Press interview he said he had "done nothing whatever to influence the money market or to afford any advantages to private parties." He noted that during his stay in New York he had had "many voluntary advisers," but he had repeatedly told them that the administration would do what was best for the public interest. He specifically recalled his August 19 encounter with Fisk, who had asked for some "little intimation" as to what the administration was going to do. "The President replied that the giving of such information would not be fair, and asked Fisk if he did not think so himself. Fisk admitted it would not be fair." Grant also recounted his decision to sell gold on Black Friday. Significantly, he said nothing about Corbin, exculpatory or otherwise. The report of the interview closed by stating: "It may be repeated that the President had informed no one whomsoever of the purposes of the administration on financial subjects, and the same remark is equally true of the Secretary of the Treasury."[41]

Fisk did not let up. He charged that Gould and Corbin had planned the corner and that Corbin had actually married Jennie Grant with that purpose in mind. "The President himself was interested with us in the corner," Fisk told an astonished reporter for the *New York Herald*. "I had several interviews with him on the subject, and finally, with Corbin's influence, everything was arranged and we set to work. . . . Grant got scared, however, when the crisis came, and gave Boutwell instructions to sell." The reporter dismissed these preposterous charges as "vile slanders." On the editorial page, the *Herald* defended Grant's "simple, straightforward honesty" and observed that the "lobby jobber" Corbin and the other conspirators had taken "the wrong tack in gauging him by their own measure." Even the rabidly anti-Grant *New York Sun* conceded that no evidence "incompatible with his innocence" had surfaced.[42]

The administration strove to carry on as usual. At the urgent request of Pennsylvania Republicans, Boutwell traveled to Philadelphia to deliver a key campaign speech that touted the administration's financial policy, especially the effort to reduce and refinance the national debt. On October 12 the Republicans narrowly won gubernatorial elections in Pennsylvania and Ohio, but both states showed a steep decline in the Republicans' margin compared with Grant's victories in 1868. The next day the president issued a more direct denial of complicity in the gold ring. In a published letter to *New York Ledger* editor Robert Bonner, Grant wrote that he had previously "never thought of contradicting statements or insinuations made against me by irresponsible parties," but now "I will say that I had no more to do with the late gold excitement in New-York City than yourself, or any other innocent party, except that I ordered the sale of gold to break the ring engaged, as I thought, in a most disreputable transaction."[43]

Despite the closeness of the elections, some Republican leaders took heart. In France, minister Elihu Washburne thought, "We can hold the country and re-elect Grant" despite "the infamous attempt of the infamous copperhead gold ring in N.Y. to connect the President with their fiasco." "The truth is the Administration is strong," James G. Blaine wrote to Washburne. "The gold excitement in N.Y. looked at one time as if it might prove *nasty*, but the President is unscathed. Old Corbin, however, has his fingers in the trap & I guess Dan Butterfield also."[44]

But still the insinuations came. Gould cast Julia Grant's letter conveying her husband's demand that Corbin cease speculating as evidence of the president's complicity in the ring. Once again, Grant gave an interview denouncing as "untrue" any assertion that he had been influenced by Corbin. He admitted communicating with Corbin a good deal during the summer, but he had never intimated what he "intended to do or what would be the financial policy of the government." On Fisk's attempts to wheedle information out of him, Grant pulled no punches: "I don't know but I should have felt insulted by such a proposal had it come from any other but a person like Fisk. But coming from a man so destitute of moral character I didn't think it worth noticing." In a companion interview, Boutwell dismissed Corbin as "a knave and a fool" used by Fisk and Gould. He conceded that while Grant was at his brother-in-law's house, Corbin may have "drawn him into conversation" about gold sales, and on some occasion Grant "may have dropped a few words unwittingly which were magnified, twisted and made the most of by Corbin to advance his speculative interests." Indeed, Corbin may have gone to Fisk and Gould and "represented to them certain things that the President had said or was about to do, on the strength of the fact that Grant was a guest at Corbin's house." But the idea that Grant "had any knowledge of the combination formed to bull gold" Boutwell called "utterly false." The press also dredged up the congressional report that had condemned Corbin for his tariff influence peddling in 1857. It now seemed clear that Corbin could expect no defense from the White House.[45]

Nor did the administration rally around assistant treasurer Daniel Butterfield, against whom allegations of involvement in the ring began to surface. When Gould released evidence that Butterfield had shown Boutwell's sell order on Black Friday to a Gould agent before informing anyone else, Boutwell suggested that Butterfield resign, and he complied. As Blaine put it, Butterfield's resignation was "a sort of suicide that amounts to confession." He stayed in office long enough for Grant to find a successor, and then he was gone.[46]

When Congress convened in early December, Grant used his annual message to condemn the speculation that had roiled the market two months earlier. Hoping to push discussion of the episode to a higher plane and to draw a policy lesson from it, the president noted that fluctuation in the price of gold in greenbacks not only made "the man of business an involuntary gambler"; it was also "detrimental to the interests of trade." The root of the problem lay in the nation's "irredeemable currency," one of "the evils growing out of the rebellion." Hence, he lectured Congress, "one of the highest duties of Government" was to "secure to the citizen a medium of exchange of fixed, unvarying value. This implies a return to a specie basis, and no substitute for it can be devised."[47]

Democrats pushed hard to extract political benefit from the episode. In the House they called for a special committee to conduct an investigation "and especially to inquire if the President, the Secretary of the Treasury, or any officer of the Government was in any manner interested in causing" the fluctuations in the price of gold in September. The Republican majority removed the specific references to Grant and Boutwell and assigned the task to the Banking and Currency Committee, which, because of the political makeup of the House, was overwhelmingly Republican.[48]

Before taking testimony, committee chairman James Garfield "reconnoiter[ed] the field" in New York and surmised that the inquiry "perhaps will lead us into the parlors of the President. I don't think it will touch him, but it may a member of his family." During hearings in January and February 1870, the committee questioned more than fifty witnesses, focusing on the four principal conspirators—Gould, Fisk, Corbin, and Butterfield—as well as Boutwell. Their testimony exhibited myriad contradictions and outright lies, which defied synthesis into a coherent narrative. The committee's two Democrats (out of ten members) wanted Grant and his wife to testify, but the Republicans overrode that idea. The Democrats also pressed for a summons of Jennie Corbin, but Jacob Cox convinced his friend Garfield, no doubt at Grant's behest, to defer to her precarious health and leave her out of it. At the Democrats' urging, Garfield met with Grant at the White House and offered to show him the testimony touching on him and his family and invited his response. The president thanked the chairman for the committee's courtesy but declined to read the testimony or make any statement.[49]

Garfield and the Republican majority issued a report that laid bare the machinations of Gould and Fisk and condemned Corbin's attempted influence peddling:

> Mr. Corbin, using the opportunities which his family relationship to the President afforded, and under that worst form of hypocrisy which puts on the guise of religion and patriotism, used all his arts to learn something from the private conversations of the President which could be made profitable to him and his co-conspirators. But with this and all the efforts of his associates, the testimony has not elicited a word or an act of the President inconsistent with that patriotism and integrity which befit the Chief Executive of the nation.

The majority report asserted that Grant's cautionary letter to Boutwell on September 12 "exhibits both the wisdom of the President's opinions and the prudence of his conduct in reference to the gold movement." Moreover, Grant's message to Corbin via Julia's letter to Jennie and the order to sell gold on Black Friday, "which laid the strong hand of the government upon the conspirators and broke their power, are the most significant declarations that the President held and treated them as enemies of the credit and business of the country." The Republicans on the committee condemned the assertion that Julia Grant had received $25,000 from the gold speculation as a "groundless and wicked charge" devised by either Corbin or Fisk to divert attention from their own misdeeds. Garfield and his colleagues concluded that "the wicked and cunningly devised attempts of the conspirators to compromise the President of the United States or his family utterly failed." Echoing Grant's call for specie resumption, they also declared that as long as "we have two standards of value recognized by law"—that is, gold and greenbacks—capital would "be used in this reckless gambling which ruins the great majority of those who engage in it, and endangers the business of the whole country."[50]

New York Democrat S. S. Cox, assisted by Kentuckian Thomas Jones, wrote the committee's minority report. Cox's general philosophy as a minority House member was that Democrats should "*charge the other side . . .* with making all the mischief." The gold investigation gave him a golden opportunity to do so. He admitted that the minority "substantially concur[s]" with the majority report, which "faithfully details" the machinations of the chief conspirators. Nonetheless, Cox insinuated, "Unconsciously, or consciously, the President in his letters to Mr. Boutwell worked in unison with the conspirators." Cox erroneously alleged that Grant had had "frequent meetings" with Gould, ignoring that these few encounters had left Gould frustrated and that he had obtained no assurances from the president. Having presumed Grant's complicity, Cox decried the majority's refusal to secure testimony from Grant, Julia Grant, Jennie Corbin, and Julia's brother and presidential secretary Frederick Dent. Because these individuals had failed to appear, Cox claimed that he and Jones were left for "guidance in these matters entirely to the mysterious, unexplained, conflicting, and nebulous testimony which points to, but does not enter, the inviolable chambers of the White House." A few days before the release of the minority report, Cox privately referred to it as "my Report on the Grant family." "I did not at first believe they were in it. I now believe so," he wrote to a New York editor. But, he added, he "could not say it outright." Guilt by innuendo would have to do. Grant was so outraged by the report that several months later at a cabinet meeting he was still denouncing it, "with a good deal of feeling," as an example of the unwarranted "abuse heaped upon public men."[51]

Cox forbore from speculating about what motives might have led the president to assist the conspiracy, leaving unstated the supposition that the Grant family wanted money. In truth, Grant did feel financially pressed during this period, as he did for much of his life. In his mid-September conversation with reporter Randolph Keim in Pennsylvania, Keim asked the president if he had thought about reelection. Never wishing to appear ambitious, Grant responded, "I am exceedingly anxious to retire from public life, for which I have no taste. I wish to retire at the earliest moment." As for reelection, he said, an "extraordinary condition of affairs might bring me to consent to a second term but certainly if my circumstances . . . are satisfactory no other consideration will." Grant's concern about his "circumstances" was genuine. Serving as president cost him more than his $25,000 salary just "to keep up the barest appearance of respectability." He intended to ask Congress for an increase in the president's pay, which would not apply to the present term but would "benefit my successors who should have at least enough to live on." As for retirement, Grant said, "My circumstances are not such now as to permit [it] but I hope they will be before my present four years term is over."[52]

But just one year after his predecessor had been impeached and nearly convicted, would Grant take the huge risk of jeopardizing his presidency as well as his place in history by engaging in a highly dubious and visible scheme such as the gold corner simply to provide himself with a competence for retirement? Certainly the congressional investigating committee adduced scant credible evidence that he had done so. Moreover, Grant had already devised a reasonable financial plan: if the properties he owned in Chicago and St. Louis "increase in value as I anticipate I can retire comfortably for the rest of my life." Of course, if Grant were involved in the gold corner, he would not tell Keim, but the question remains: if he had reason to expect a comfortable retirement, would he take the extraordinary risk of countenancing the scheme in his own interest? The absence of clear, credible evidence of his willing complicity suggests that he did not. Indeed, the conspirators kept going back again and again to try to get him on board—only to be repeatedly refused—until Grant finally got fed up and had Julia write the letter to Jennie Corbin.[53]

Nonetheless, the attempt to corner the gold market left an indelible stain on Grant's presidency. As soon as the chief conspirators began exchanging recriminations in public, newspapers carried references to Grant's attendance at "all these splendid dinners, balls, parties, picnics and steamboat excursions in his honor by New York financiers, gold and stock gamblers." A close reading of the congressional report shows

this to be a gross exaggeration, but testimony regarding the very few actual encounters of this nature that occurred, unsought by Grant, tended
to confirm rather than dispel the impression of intimacy between the
president and the conspirators. Indeed, constructing that impression for
public consumption had been at the heart of the conspirators' strategy.
Fisk's Erie Palace in New York exhibited a large oil painting of Grant,
Gould, and Fisk over the caption, "See the Conquering Heroes Come!"
Such a gimmick was a telling symbol of the conspirators' larger stratagem of exploiting Grant's cachet. By a bizarre alchemy, Fisk's clown-
ishness morphed into a degradation of the president. As one worried
Grant ally observed, "There are thousands who think the administration compromised."[54]

Moreover, these events confirmed the biases of those who were
disposed to see the worst in Grant. Henry Adams exulted that "such
a dramatic scandal was Heaven-sent." He pored over the published
committee testimony to devise a damning article about the episode. In
his autobiography he depicted the gold corner as a "dirty cesspool of
vulgar corruption" and an example of "the incredible and inexplicable lapses of Grant's intelligence." More than two years later, Charles
Sumner delivered a general arraignment of Grant, claiming that he was
"surrounded by rings" and placed his "personal aims and objects . . .
more prominent than the public interest."[55]

The episode damaged Grant's presidency in subtler ways, providing
fodder, for instance, for the Machiavellian purposes of James Harrison
Wilson, who eventually became one of Grant's most insidious detractors. Wilson saw the gold corner commotion as an opportunity to fulfill
his own ambition of obtaining an appointment in the administration. An
1860 graduate of West Point, "Harry" Wilson had served for a time on
General Grant's staff and had formed a deep admiration for John Rawlins. When the secretary of war died on September 6, Wilson conceived
the notion that, despite his youth (he had just turned thirty-two), he
could be Rawlins's successor. While the Black Friday conspirators were
exchanging recriminations in the newspapers, Wilson wrote to Horace
Porter and expressed the opinion that Grant was "as honest a man as
ever lived" and "entirely innocent of complicity with the Gold Ring."
But Wilson had convinced himself that Grant was also "as unsuspicious
as a child, and almost as easily trapped." The "scoundrel" Corbin had
gulled him, but this was "only one of a thousand instances in which
the President has been duped." "Practically," Wilson told Porter, Grant
needed "a mentor as sleepless as fate and as watchful as Cerberus."

Wilson felt confident that as Grant's new guardian, he could "perform the duties that Rawlins did" as "his conscience keeper."[56]

Fearing that his chances for appointment were slim, Wilson then recommended Porter for the vacancy. But he may have concluded that Grant would not want to transfer Porter from his own staff to the War Department, and advocating Porter gave Wilson an opening to defend the appointment of a young man to the post. Porter was Wilson's classmate at West Point and the same age. Wilson wrote to Grant, "The 'politicians' will probably object to his [Porter's] appointment (to an office which they consider as a political perquisite), on the score of *youth*, coupled with the fact that he is a graduate of West Point, but as you have not hitherto regarded these as fatal objection[s] unless coupled with others more worthy of consideration, and as *you will probably have to fight the politicians anyhow*, I hope you will not allow them to exert an undue influence in the choice of your advisers and most trusted subordinates." Such an argument applied to himself as well as to Porter. But Wilson's ploy failed. The job went to neither Porter nor Wilson but to William W. Belknap, a relatively unknown Union general from Iowa whom Porter had been urging on Grant since Rawlins's death. Wilson also endorsed Belknap, although he told Porter that "compared with you he is entirely unfit for the place." Through it all, Wilson betrayed no sense of irony at his own duplicity. Offering to protect the childlike president from exploitation, he tried to capitalize on insinuations against Grant to weasel his way into the administration. Chagrined by his failure, he grew increasingly alienated from Grant. After the president continued to ignore his ambition for other positions, he became one of his bitterest foes. Eventually Wilson rivaled Henry Adams in his determination to besmirch Grant's reputation.[57]

7

★ ★ ★ ★ ★

RECONSTRUCTING AMERICAN FOREIGN POLICY

In his inaugural address Ulysses S. Grant devoted one brief paragraph to foreign affairs. He said nothing about any specific issue but instead spoke in generalities about his commitment to peace and to equitable relations with all nations. With the nation's internal war now four years in the past, he spoke with a quiet yet fervent confidence in the capacity and will of the newly united nation to defend its interests in the world. "I would respect the rights of all nations, demanding equal respect for our own." But, he warned, "If others depart from this rule in their dealings with us, we may be compelled to follow their precedent." The *New York Herald* called the speech "a simple enunciation of our desire for strict justice" and argued that it would "do more to effect a cordial and immediate understanding with foreign Powers than all the Machiavellian statesmanship of the past four years."[1]

The new president's focus on domestic affairs mirrored his constituents' concerns, but it could not mask the potentially dangerous problems the new administration faced in framing its foreign policy. At the head of the list, a host of differences fed mutual suspicion between the United States and Great Britain, the most important being the festering dispute over the *Alabama* claims. A bloody conflict in the colony of Cuba between insurgents and Spanish authorities outraged Americans' moral sense, jeopardized commercial and other economic interests, and challenged the viability of the Monroe Doctrine. The administration could not treat these questions in isolation: an impulse to concede official recognition to the belligerency of the Cuban rebels, for instance, ran directly counter to American accusations against Britain for unneutral acts during the United States' own fight against insurgents during the Civil War. In a larger sense, the country's growing economic might augured a fundamental shift in its geopolitical position and demanded a more forceful, perhaps expansionist posture. Opportunities beckoned for naval stations and commercial outposts, most immediately in the Western Hemisphere. Hardly less than in domestic affairs, Grant's accession to power heralded a reconstruction in the nation's foreign relations.

At the outset, however, Grant's ideas about foreign policy were fairly inchoate. His chief guiding principle was an adherence to the Monroe Doctrine, a position he held in common with most Americans. Toward the end of the war, he had kept careful watch on French emperor Napoleon III's attempt to erect a New World empire in Mexico under Maximilian of Austria. After Appomattox, Grant had even sent troops to western Texas, where, should events require it, they would be on hand to confirm the Monroe Doctrine "as a code of international law, to be observed by all Nations." Maximilian's regime fell without an American invasion, but Grant continued to embrace the doctrine as "a security for our future peace." Not surprisingly, affairs in the Western Hemisphere stood at the center of his administration's concerns.[2]

One of the important lessons Grant had learned from naval operations during the Civil War was that the United States needed to pursue a more active policy to defend its strategic interests in the hemisphere. Of particular concern was the string of islands held by Great Britain in the Caribbean Sea, as well as its outposts in Central America and British Guiana in South America. This circumstance, coupled with Spain's possession of Cuba, made the Caribbean a virtual European lake. Having to pass through these "foreign waters" endangered the US coasting trade and the safety of the nation itself in the event of foreign war. Early in his administration, Grant concluded that an obvious first step in redressing the strategic imbalance in the Caribbean lay in American acquisition of some sort of outpost in the region.[3]

Grant took more interest in foreign affairs than in most other business coming before his administration. In pursuing his goals, he enjoyed the able assistance of Secretary of State Hamilton Fish. The scion of a distinguished New York family, a wealthy lawyer, and originally a Whig, Fish had served a single term each as congressman, governor, and US senator from 1851 to 1857. As a conservative in the 1850s, he

Secretary of State Hamilton Fish. (Library of Congress)

deplored the destruction of the Whig Party, which he saw as a bulwark of national unity. He opposed abolitionist agitation as "senseless" and "useless," and he allied only reluctantly with the nascent Republican Party. As a senator, he opposed the expansionist projects the Democrats pushed southward into the Caribbean. He not only recoiled at the acquisition of new slave territory but also questioned the capacity of the people in those regions to absorb American democratic values. As a member of the Foreign Relations Committee during his last two years in the Senate, he gained valuable experience in monitoring the nation's overseas relations. Reluctant to leave retirement, he initially resisted Grant's invitation to head the State Department. Once in office, however, he showed a patrician sense of duty, a great capacity for sustained labor, and a legalistic approach to diplomatic questions that stood him in good stead when grappling with issues such as the *Alabama* claims. Before the administration was very far advanced, Grant was completely convinced of the wisdom of his selection of Fish.[4]

In these years the State Department staff numbered scarcely more than two dozen. Fish persuaded Grant to appoint his fellow New Yorker, J. C. Bancroft Davis, as assistant secretary of state. With a privileged background, commitment to duty, and intellectual tastes not unlike Fish's, Davis proved an adept and loyal right-hand man. On occasion Fish also enlisted the aid of men outside the department, most notably Caleb Cushing, a renowned international lawyer, former minister to China, and former attorney general. It soon became clear, however, that the administration could expect only trouble from Charles Sumner, whose obsession with asserting control over foreign affairs became a persistent menace during Grant's embattled presidency.[5]

At the outset, Fish recognized the importance of establishing good working relations with the chairman of the Senate Foreign Relations Committee, with whom he had enjoyed a long friendship. Even before he reached Washington to take office, the ever-polite Fish wrote to Sumner that he had "little taste & less fitness" for his new job but that "in yielding, I hoped that I could rely upon your friendship & upon your experience & ability, for your support & aid to supply my manifold deficiencies." The senator responded with requests for State Department patronage. He was disappointed not to be heading the department himself, and according to Charles Francis Adams, "the next worst position for harmony" that Sumner could occupy was as "chief of the Foreign Committee in the Senate." The prediction proved correct. Sumner could never reconcile himself to the president's assumption that the administration could get along without him. Not infrequently over the ensuing years, his actions betrayed a selfishness and recklessness that compounded the difficulties confronting Grant and Fish. From the beginning, the senator was determined to reclaim what he considered his rightful preeminence in the framing of foreign policy.[6]

Sumner soon concluded that the best way to burnish his credentials was to use the dispute with Great Britain over the *Alabama* claims, the most pressing question in the nation's foreign relations. Taking a bold stance could go far to efface the impression that, as James G. Blaine put it, "Sumner is a complete toady to England & everything English." The administration was scarcely ten days old when rumors circulated that Sumner would soon deliver what Adams forecast as a "warlike speech against England." The occasion was Senate consideration of the recent Johnson-Clarendon Convention establishing a procedure for the adjudication of the claims.[7]

The issue dated from the early years of the Civil War, when the Confederacy had sought to augment its minuscule navy by purchasing vessels in England. The southern government commissioned the construction of several ships from British builders, who, to avoid outright violation of Britain's Foreign Enlistment Acts, constructed them without arms. Guns and other armaments were added later at ports outside of British waters. The ships, especially the *Alabama*, *Florida*, and *Shenandoah*, saw duty as raiders against Union commerce, with deadly effect. After months of protest by American minister Charles Francis Adams, the British government finally moved to halt the construction of additional vessels in the spring of 1863, but that did not curtail the success of the ships already released. All told, they destroyed or captured some 250 northern merchant vessels. Not merely those who suffered pecuniary losses but Americans in general held Great Britain largely responsible for the depredations.

For years, however, British recalcitrance had stymied efforts to settle American claims for compensation, until a change in government brought more conciliatory leaders to power. Responsibility for conducting negotiations fell to seventy-two-year-old Reverdy Johnson, whom Andrew Johnson had appointed in the summer of 1868 to replace Adams, and British foreign secretary Lord Clarendon. The Johnson-Clarendon Convention called for the creation of a four-person commission, comprising two members from each nation, that would adjudicate not only the *Alabama* claims but also any other claims raised by the citizens of either country since their last claims convention in 1853. In the event that a majority of the commission could not agree on a particular claim, it would go before an arbitrator chosen by the two nations; if they could not agree on an arbitrator, that individual would be selected by lot. The treaty included no admission of wrongdoing or expression of regret by Great Britain. Indeed, it implied a moral and legal symmetry between British losses from the sinking or capture of British blockade-runners and American losses inflicted by the *Alabama* and its fellow commerce raiders. Johnson's agreeing to the treatment of the *Alabama* claims as merely one kind of claim among many struck most Americans as a craven surrender. Moreover, he gained no friends for his treaty in America by hobnobbing with wealthy and titled Britons and making speeches oozing with honeyed references to Anglo-American kinship.[8]

Signed on January 14, 1869, the Johnson-Clarendon Convention was dead on arrival when it reached the United States. President-elect Grant made no secret of his opposition. He felt a reflexive contempt for just about anything bearing the stamp of the Johnson administration, and he regarded the treaty itself as fatally bad. Within days he suggested to Sumner that the Senate delay consideration of the convention until after the inauguration. Once in office, he pushed for its swift rejection. Rather than a mere question of dollars and cents, he thought the dispute with Britain involved more important considerations of international law and the rights of nations. He urged swift action by the Senate before its special session adjourned in mid-April. Sumner agreed, but he was unwilling to let Grant take the lead on the issue. Recognizing the convention's widespread unpopularity, the senator sought to step out front with a major foreign policy address at the outset of the new administration.[9]

Rising in executive session on April 13, Sumner denounced the pending treaty as "a snare" that failed to settle "the massive grievance under which our country suffered for years." For the next hour he gave no quarter in a sustained attack on the British. He emphasized two central themes: the offenses for which Great Britain was culpable and the just compensation it owed for those offenses. He described the construction and escape of the Confederate vessels and alleged that during their commerce raiding careers, they had received "welcome hospitality and supplies in British ports." But Sumner went further, insisting that Britain's offense had begun with its recognition of Confederate belligerency in a neutrality proclamation issued by the British government in Queen Victoria's name on May 13, 1861. This proclamation, he declared, marked "the first stage in the depredations on our commerce." Sumner brushed aside British arguments that the proclamation merely recognized the state of war acknowledged by President Abraham Lincoln in calling for a blockade of southern ports. England could not have become "an 'arsenal' for the rebels . . . unless the [queen's] proclamation had prepared the way," he insisted. "Had it not been made, no rebel ship could have been built in England."

Sumner proved even more audacious in his calculation of Britain's liability. He estimated individual losses to citizens caused by the destruction of merchant vessels and their cargo at $15 million. But under the rubric of "national losses," Sumner posited two additional categories of Britain's liabilities. First was the financial loss the nation sustained by the reflagging of American merchant vessels in foreign countries and the consequent diminution of the nation's merchant fleet, the rise in insurance rates for American ships and cargo, and the reduction of the country's imports and exports. Sumner invoked the estimate of an unnamed "intelligent statistician" and pegged these losses at the huge sum of $110 million. His assertion of another category, however, was truly breathtaking. The Union government had expended $4 billion in suppressing the rebellion. Because of Britain's pro-Confederate offenses, "the war was doubled in duration," and therefore Britain was "justly responsible for the additional expenditure to which our country was doomed." This added another $2 billion, bringing the aggregate to $2.125 billion. This "colossal sum-total," he concluded, represented the losses to individuals, "the destruction of our commerce, and the prolongation of the war, all of which may be traced directly to England."[10]

To no one's surprise, the Senate rejected the Johnson-Clarendon Convention by a vote of 54 to 1. More important for Sumner's purposes, at least in the short term, his speech yielded precisely the political effect he desired. Michigan senator Zachariah Chandler, who, among others, had suspected Sumner of harboring pro-English feelings, moved that the Senate take the unusual step of lifting the secrecy of its executive session and permitting the publication of Sumner's speech. Sumner lost no time in ordering a large number of copies from the government printer, and he used his franking privilege to distribute them widely. The response was gratifying. Frederick Douglass hailed the speech as "grand and masterly." The *New York Herald*, no friend of Sumner, noted that the settlement of the slavery question had "caused the people to lose sight of him. Now, however, he throws himself to the front" with a "firm and masterly speech" that "showers . . . trenchant blows upon our hereditary rival." Indeed, said the *Herald*, Grant ought to replace Fish with Sumner "to take charge of this great business in the State Department." Sumner returned the favor by granting the *Herald* an interview in which he boasted that his speech had "met with a response from the press and the people almost as unanimous as it had received from the Senate."[11]

But the praise was not universal. Henry Adams was convinced that as soon as "Sumner found that popular feeling ran very strongly against the Treaty, he was inspired by the passion of seizing the direction of our foreign affairs." He was "like a school-boy in vacation," eager to "ride the whirlwind" with a dangerous denunciation of the British. Similarly, Charles Francis Adams thought the senator raised "the scale of our demand of reparation so very high that there is no chance of negotiation left, unless the English have lost all their spirit and character." Such "blundering impracticableness" could "drift us into a war."[12]

The English press condemned Sumner's speech, which, as the Adamses suggested, did nothing to promote a peaceful settlement. The British minister in Washington, Edward Thornton, dismissed Sumner's notion about Britain's liability for the prolongation of the war as an "absurdity" calculated to "excite the passions of his impulsive countrymen" and inflame their "animosity" against England. Yet Thornton did not despair. He had reason to believe that the Grant administration considered "the tone of Mr. Sumner's speech to be somewhat more hostile towards England than is expedient at present." The minister advised his government that the best way "of bringing the people of this country to reasonable ideas" was to "show a firm but courteous and decided resistance" to the senator's "exaggerated pretensions." In London, Lord Clarendon told Reverdy Johnson that Sumner's speech was "insulting" to the English people, who "would not stand" such remarks. Johnson himself publicly leveled "violent abuse" against Sumner for destroying the crowning achievement of his career.[13]

Grant and Fish welcomed the treaty's defeat, but Sumner had so poisoned the atmosphere that fashioning an alternative became highly problematic. Newspapers circulated the story that Grant had dismissed the speech as "good rhetoric" but "bad logic," which dealt a setback to serious negotiations. Fish assured Thornton that the senator "could not be considered as the exponent of the opinions of the people in general or of his colleagues," some of whom had voted against the Johnson-Clarendon Convention on other grounds. The administration concluded that negotiations for a new agreement should be delayed to allow tempers to cool, and when talks did begin again, they should take place in Washington.[14]

On the same day Sumner delivered his speech, the Senate confirmed the nomination of John Lothrop Motley, one of his allies, to be minister to the Court of St. James's. Motley possessed an impetuous temperament, as evidenced by his abrupt resignation as minister to Austria in 1867 following a petty dispute with Secretary of State William Seward. Even one of Sumner's closest associates thought the learned historian Motley had shown no evidence of "practical or diplomatic capacity." Grant and Fish considered him hardly equal to the delicate task of negotiating with the British. Still, Fish could not avoid addressing the claims question in the new minister's initial instructions.[15]

In writing to a friend shortly after Sumner's speech, Fish conceded that the United States had a "national" claim and that Britain's "early recognition of belligerent rights to the Rebels" had been "a grievous wrong." Yet that point contradicted the notion that "our whole history & policy has been one of sympathy with rebellion & revolutionary movements," and "we should not ask indemnification for the practical enforcement or application of our own habitual policy." America's national losses might amount to $1 billion, but "no nation will and can consent to such a verdict. The value can never be paid in money." The United States "may be compensated by a territorial concession," he wrote, thereby acknowledging the demand that Britain turn Canada over to the United States, as favored by some expansionist politicians and a portion of the press. "But," Fish said, "to suggest this to G. Britain is to ensure its refusal. It is difficult therefore to make any counter proposal" to the defeated arbitration convention.[16]

Not surprisingly, Sumner offered his help, suggesting to Fish that Motley prepare a paper detailing his understanding of the claims controversy. Motley presented a "memoir" that exceeded 10,000 words and went beyond even Sumner's speech in its extravagant condemnation of Britain's conduct. Motley denounced the queen's May 1861 proclamation as a "virtual recognition by Great Britain of the independence of the so-called confederacy," after which the existence of the United States government "was virtually denied." The United States suffered a "prodigious accumulation of debt," in large part because of "the protraction of the rebellion through the direct agency of Great Britain in virtually recognizing the Rebellion as a state, in the very first hours of its existence, and by the aid and comfort given to it by British subjects." In Motley's view, the "individual claims, although amounting to several millions," were "far less important than the national injury," but he declined to place a dollar figure on the latter.[17]

Fish considered Motley's memoir unacceptable, calling it "neither sound nor politic;" although he assured the minister that he "would very gladly have availed of your memoir" if his instructions had not already been dispatched. Honeyed words aside, Fish thought the document disqualified Motley to carry on the delicate negotiations with Britain. Anger in both nations had reached such a point that an "intermission of discussion" was required. He frankly told Motley, "The public feeling in this country has been very much excited by Mr. Sumner's very eloquent speech, which at the same time has produced no little irritation in Great Britain. It is better therefore to take [a] breath."[18]

Delay in renewing negotiations with the British would allow time for the possible resolution of another issue complicating the claims question. In October 1868 insurgents in Cuba had launched a revolt against Spanish control of the island. Representatives of the rebels organized juntas based in New York, where they solicited American aid in men and matériel. They played on widespread American sympathy for their struggle to throw off European monarchical chains, and their chief diplomatic aim was to win recognition from the United States government. In pursuing that end, they enjoyed substantial support in Congress and in the press.[19]

The administration approached the question cautiously. A movement toward establishing a constitutional monarchy was under way in Spain, and some members of Grant's cabinet hesitated to jeopardize these seemingly liberalizing efforts by conceding belligerency status to the Cuban insurgency. Fish kept leaders of the junta at arm's length and told the Spanish minister in Washington, Don Mauricio Lopez Roberts, that even though Spain had granted belligerent rights to the Confederacy, the United States would not be "over hasty" in recognizing the Cuban revolutionary government. Yet, President Grant sympathized with the Cubans. On April 6 he told the cabinet that "strict justice w[oul]d justify us in not delaying action" in granting them belligerent status, but he also acknowledged that "early recognition might prejudice our case with Great Britain with respect to our claims." Although the Cubans' staunchest supporter in the cabinet, Secretary of War John A. Rawlins, urged "more speedy action," Grant "decided not to entertain it at present." Four days later the House of Representatives, by a vote of 98 to 25, passed a resolution tendering its "constitutional support" in the event the president recognized the independence and sovereignty of Cuba.

Nonetheless, Grant kept recognition in abeyance, although he sent naval vessels to Cuban waters to report on conditions there and protect American citizens if need be.[20]

Initially, Grant was concerned that granting belligerency status to the Cubans might injure the American case in the *Alabama* dispute. But after Sumner's speech, the president was more concerned that denying the queen's right to recognize the Confederate belligerency would negate America's right to recognize the Cubans. Grant ordered Fish, who was preparing Motley's instructions, not to press the question of England's concession of belligerency to the South. By mid-May, Fish had prepared a draft that stated, "The President wishes it to be understood that he does not complain of the fact of the accordance by Great Britain, or by any other nation, of belligerent rights to the insurgent population during the late rebellion within the U.S. He recognizes the right of every power, when a civil conflict has arisen within another state, & has attained a sufficient complexity, magnitude, & completeness, to define its own relations, & those of its citizens & subjects toward the parties to the conflict." The timing and manner of the queen's proclamation were "important only as they foreshadow subsequent events."[21]

Fish showed his draft to Sumner, who was aghast at this "fatal" provision. If these instructions were allowed to stand, he said, "I will make Motley resign." "Let him," Fish said. "We will find a better man in an hour." After thus suggesting that Motley was at his command, Sumner calmed down and wrote an alternative passage that characterized the queen's proclamation as "hasty & without just foundation" and "the beginning of the unjustifiable conduct of England." Fish rejected this substitute as directly contravening Grant's intent. The next day the senator capitulated. He sent Fish a second draft stating that the American claims were "founded on actual losses suffered by individual citizens or by the nation," a substantial retreat from the position in his April 13 speech. He characterized the queen's belligerency proclamation as "a part of the case only so far as it shows the beginnings of that course of conduct, which resulted so disastrously to the U. States. It is less important in itself than from what followed." This new draft essentially echoed Fish and Grant's attempt to minimize the proclamation as a factor in the American case.[22]

Sumner quickly realized his tactical error, and the next morning wrote to Fish to withdraw his second proposed passage. He could not, he wrote, "be a party to a statement which abandons or enfeebles any of the just grounds of my country." He suggested that Motley be allowed simply "to speak according to his own enlightened discretion," a notion that Fish could not entertain. The senator tried to regain the ground he had lost by sending lawyer Caleb Cushing to the State Department, where he and the secretary worked for several hours on the instructions. After Sumner heard back from Cushing, he claimed in a letter to Motley that Fish's "clause abandoning our position on belligerency is given up." In fact, Fish had done no such thing.[23]

The secretary unequivocally stated the position he had sketched out in his initial draft. "The President," said the final instructions, "recognizes the right of every power, when a civil conflict has arisen within another state, and has attained a sufficient complexity, magnitude, and completeness, to define its own relations and those of its citizens and subjects toward the parties to the conflict." In the present case, the "necessity and the propriety" of Britain's original concession of belligerency were "not admitted" and were "questionable." But, adopting language from Sumner's second proposal that he himself had disavowed as "inadequate," Fish noted that "the President regards that concession as part of the case only so far as it shows the beginning and the animus of that course of conduct which resulted so disastrously to the United States." Fish drew a distinction between Great Britain and other countries that had conceded belligerency status to the Confederates, emphasizing that "it was in England only that the concession was supplemented by acts causing direct damage to the United States." Fish ordered Motley to "place the cause of grievance against Great Britain, not so much upon the issuance of her recognition of the insurgents' state of war, but upon her conduct under, and subsequent to, such recognition."

In another section, Fish noted that Grant approved the Senate's rejection of the Johnson-Clarendon Convention because it failed to remove the "existing grievance." Yet, with a not-so-veiled swipe at Sumner, he added that the "tone of the press and the proclaimed opinions of some public men in each country suggest that the present is not the most hopeful moment to enter upon a renewed discussion." When negotiations did resume, Fish wrote to Motley, the president hoped for some agreement as to the rights and duties of neutrals in time of war. The lack of such a provision had contributed to the defeat of the convention.[24]

If the official instructions to Motley left any doubt as to the United States' position, Fish hastened to offer reassurances to Edward Thornton. Sumner's speech, he told the minister, had included "pretensions [that] were most exaggerated" and could not "be taken as explanatory of the opinions of the U.S. Gov't upon the subject." According to Thornton's report to the Foreign Office, Fish insisted "that the government had their own responsibilities and could not allow themselves to be dictated to by Mr. Sumner or by the Senate upon matters for wh[ich] the former were alone accountable." Moreover, because of "the notorious friendship & identity of views" held by Sumner and Motley, the administration "would hesitate to entrust to the latter so delicate a matter lest he should be controlled by the influence of Mr. Sumner." Meanwhile, Fish tried to mollify the senator, telling him they both had "but one object" and differed "only as to some incidents—they may be of more importance than I suppose, or of less than you think. But [they] can hardly be of sufficient importance to break up an effort at negotiation, or to break down an Administration." Less than three months into his tenure, Fish could scarcely have missed the irony that while he felt he could speak to the British minister with perfect candor, his handling of the mercurial Foreign Relations chairman and the nation's envoy to London taxed his diplomatic skills to the utmost.[25]

Fish also discreetly sought to counteract the unrealistic expectations Sumner's speech had raised among the American people. He sent New York civic leader Samuel Ruggles the purport of his instructions to Motley, especially playing down the belligerency question, and asked him to prepare "some well considered articles in this direction." Similarly, he wrote to reformer and political scientist Francis Lieber that Sumner's "startling presentation of the magnitude of the losses pleased the American pride" but raised the "danger that our people will accept Sumner's standard as that which they ought to demand." He had spoken "only as an individual Senator," but if "pride of passion" should "force the adoption of Mr. Sumner's *standard* upon either the Republican Party or the country, there can be no pacific settlement."[26]

After his fight with Fish, Sumner launched a letter-writing campaign to demonstrate that he had not been marginalized and to reassert his authority in foreign affairs. In a flagrant misrepresentation, he wrote to the Duchess of Argyll that Motley's "instructions were submitted to me & altered by me in order to make an important point clearer"— neglecting to add that he had withdrawn his suggestions. "Of course Mr. Motley agrees with me." When news accounts alleged a difference of opinion between the senator and the administration, Sumner insisted to his friend Henry Longfellow, "The Presdt, the Secy of State, the Minister to England & the Chairman of the Senate Comttee. of Foreign Relations are *all agreed*," and he even informed a prominent member of Parliament that Motley "will tell you to what extent my speech represented the views of all here, from the President down to the doorkeeper." Sumner continued to distribute copies of his address and told Lieber that Motley "accepted it *verbatim* & was willing to meet Lord Clarendon & all English Society on that basis." Or so Sumner wished. As he confessed to a friend, Grant had appointed Motley on Sumner's recommendation, and that "makes me peculiarly responsible for the success of the mission."[27]

The British people anticipated Motley's arrival with some anxiety, fearing that Sumner's speech augured war. Hence, they were pleasantly surprised when, upon his arrival at Liverpool in late May, Motley spoke of Grant's desire to "cultivate faithful, friendly, and equitable relations" and promised his own "strenuous efforts" to nurture "the most thorough and mutual good understanding between the two nations." American newspapers carried reports that, "after contrasting Mr. Sumner's speech in the Senate with Mr. Motley's language," the British press expressed satisfaction that Grant was pursuing "a policy of conciliation and peace." After this evidence that Motley intended to hew to the administration's line, Grant himself told Sumner that Motley was "the best man for England now." Even so, Grant appointed his old army aide Adam Badeau as second secretary at the London legation and asked him to report privately on the minister's performance.[28]

If Grant felt momentary satisfaction with the minister after his welcome in Liverpool, Sumner wrote to Motley and expressed his own dissatisfaction. "A good deal mystified" by Sumner's criticism, Motley replied, "I could not answer their friendly welcome, without saying that the President wished amicable, equitable & honorable relations bet[ween] the two countries. He does certainly & so *do you* & so do I. . . . There is an awful responsibility upon me. I can bring on a war with this country—or at least a decided rupture—in a very few days' notice." The chastened minister assured Sumner that privately he defended the senator's position, having told a British cabinet member that Sumner's "speech, considered as a statement of our case, as a setting forth of the sentiments on the great national wrong which had been sustained, was accepted by a very large portion of the people as a legitimate & not exaggerated expression of grievance."[29]

Both Motley and Sumner knew that what really counted was the minister's presentation of the American position to Clarendon, and here Motley did all that Sumner wished. In their first substantive meeting, he noted the president's recognition of the right of nations to proclaim neutrality in a war between insurgents and a lawful government, but he added gratuitously that "such measures must always be taken with a full view of the grave responsibilities assumed," implying that Great Britain had failed to recognize its responsibilities. He followed Fish's instructions to the extent of alluding to the president's wish that the American case should cite the queen's proclamation "only as showing animus," but then he asserted that the president regarded the procla- mation as "the fountain head of the disasters which had been caused to the American people, both individually and collectively, by the hands of Englishmen." He further alleged that from "Great Britain alone there had come a long series of deeds, injurious to the United States, *as the fruits of the proclamation.*" Clarendon testily replied that he would "al- ways maintain that the English neutrality had been a fair and sincere neutrality on the part of the English government." He cut Motley off from any further discussion.[30]

Motley's exchange with Clarendon appalled legation secretary Benjamin Moran, a career diplomat who had worked at the American legation in London since 1853. Moran, who had taken an almost instant dislike to the snobbish and imperious minister, thought Motley's con- versation with the foreign secretary had "more of Mr. Sumner than of the President in it. He was too warm with Lord Clarendon and made the relations between the two countries more dangerous in appearance than they are. I don't think it expresses the President's intentions."[31]

Fish did not think so either. He complained that Motley had repeated "in almost the identical words, the strong expressions, adjectives, and expletives, the stinging allusions, and the cutting observations which had been submitted in his 'memoir,' and rejected by this Department, and none of which were authorized by his instructions. . . . He was not instructed to threaten Great Britain, or to refer to her responsibilities." In a conversation with Thornton, Fish practically disavowed Motley, not- ing that he had been "a little too emphatic upon certain points, much more so than he need have been. . . . Mr. Motley must begin to learn to keep to his instructions." On the question of the queen's proclamation, Motley had used "phrases exactly similar to those employed by Mr. Sumner," which Fish found "objectionable." The secretary reassured the British minister that nations had a right to judge for themselves when to issue such proclamations, and even if they were considered unfriendly, such declarations "could not be made a ground for claiming pecuniary compensation even if they might be taken in connexion with subsequent acts as showing the animus of these."[32]

Grant thought Motley's insubordination warranted his immediate dismissal. Fish agreed that they should remove the minister from any responsibility for the *Alabama* question, but he persuaded Grant to hold off on firing him. Looking ahead to the time they would need Sumner's approval of an agreement with the British, Fish convinced Grant that it was best not to "stir him up again" by cashiering Motley. Instead, Fish delivered a tempered rebuke to the minister for failing to present the American conception of the belligerency question "in precise conformity" to the president's view. The secretary stroked Motley's ego by acknowledging that his "excess was in the right direction," but he also stressed Grant's determination that when negotiations were resumed, they would "be conducted in the United States."[33]

Sumner, in contrast, was pleased with Motley's performance and asked Fish to send him a copy of the minister's account of the meeting. The secretary reluctantly broke long-standing practice and provided the dispatch, but he enjoined the senator to maintain total secrecy. Sumner promised, "Nobody will know from me any thing about it." Yet on the very same day, Sumner wrote to the Duchess of Argyll, whose husband served in the British cabinet, "Mr. Motley's report on his conference with Ld. C. has been sent to me from Washington. Every thing is excellent except where he alludes to excitement here as an excuse for suspension of negotiations." The next day Sumner informed Fish that he had returned the dispatch to the State Department, "nobody having seen it or knowing anything about it." The "excitement," of course, had arisen largely because of Sumner's April speech, but he wrote to the secretary that he remained convinced that "I did not go too far in the statement of our grievance."[34]

In London, Motley blanched at Fish's admonition, which, according to Moran, "reduces him to a cipher." Moran confided to his diary, "Mr. Motley says he knows he overstated the case in his first official interview with Ld. Clarendon, and exceeded the letter of his instructions. But he defended himself to me for doing so." The minister immediately set about composing a reply to Fish. With the assistance of George Bemis, an American lawyer in whom Sumner had great confidence, the minister produced what Moran described as "an imprudent composition" that "takes ground in direct opposition to the views of the President." Motley argued that he thought the British proclamation of belligerency had stimulated privateering, in violation of the 1856 Declaration of Paris. "I did not, therefore, suppose myself to be transcending the lucidly and carefully-drawn limitations of the instructions in which you explain the President's views on the subject of belligerency." In Moran's view, Motley's reply to Fish was "labored and disingenuous." In his talk with Clarendon, Motley had failed to accurately represent the American position regarding belligerency, "although he knows that this very important point in his instructions was put there by Gen'l Grant himself."[35]

As if Motley's impertinent self-defense were not enough to irritate Fish, two weeks later Motley informed the secretary that in his report he had neglected to inform Fish that he had submitted his summary of the conversation to Clarendon for his approval before sending it to Washington. Although showing such a summary to an interlocutor to ensure accuracy was accepted diplomatic practice, Motley erred in not telling Fish he had done so in this case. Grant again wanted to fire Motley, but Fish thought it best to leave him in place temporarily to continue work on naturalization and consular agreements. Fish ordered Motley to explain to Clarendon "that your presentation and treatment of the subject discussed at that interview were, in part, disapproved by me." As Fish later wrote, from that time forward, "Mr. Motley's retention in his position was with the reluctant approval of the President, and with his frequently declared intention to name a successor at no distant day."[36]

While Motley was demonstrating his unfitness for his mission, Fish looked for alternative avenues for renewing discussions with the British. He held several conversations with John Rose, the Canadian minister of finance, who was in Washington to push for commercial reciprocity. Rose would be leaving for England shortly, where he had close connections with the government. Fish seized the opportunity to set forth his notion of the parameters of a possible agreement, which, he said, must be "something much beyond Mr. Reverdy Johnson's treaty." He projected a settlement that included "some kind expressions of regret" by England, "a competent indemnity," and "some agreement as to the laws of neutrality for the future, between the two nations, so framed that we may assume a recognition of our views as to the past, without their positively admitting any wrong on their part." Rose carried Fish's views to England, and the secretary soon heard that they had been "well received." Although the talks produced no immediate result, the two men had planted the seeds for the Treaty of Washington of 1871.[37]

While Fish dealt with the refractory Motley, he still had to contend with Sumner. Throughout the summer, the senator badgered Fish for "a vigorous presentment" to the British, noting ominously that "something of this nature must be done before the meeting of Congress, or there would be dissatisfaction." Fish decided to call Sumner on the question and invited him to prepare such a declaration, but the senator claimed he was too busy; "besides," he added, "I had made my statement."[38]

Deep down, Fish believed that the "two English-speaking—progressive, liberal—governments of the world should not, must not, be divided." But he found himself engaged in a delicate balancing act, wishing to offend neither the British, with whom he hoped to secure an agreement, nor Sumner, the acknowledged foreign policy leader of the Senate, whose approval he would need for any deal. In September Fish decided to send Motley a dispatch laying out the American grievance in strong language, with the dual purpose of demonstrating American earnestness to the British and staving off fractious criticism when Congress convened in December. He enlisted Caleb Cushing's help, but he did not inform Sumner about the preparation or the existence of the dispatch until weeks after he had sent it.[39]

Completed amid the turmoil of the gold panic, the dispatch was the culmination of several weeks of work. In general, the September 25 note conveyed an assessment of America's grievance in considerably stronger language than Fish had employed in his original instructions to Motley. Yet most of the tough new verbiage referred to the British government's negligence in allowing the construction and release of the "Alabama, at least," as "gross and inexcusable and such as indisputably to devolve on that government full responsibility for all the depredations committed." The southern rebellion, Fish contended, "was continued, and obtained its enduring vitality, by means of the resources it drew from Great Britain." On the delicate question of the recognition of belligerency, Fish echoed the assertion of his original instructions. The United States believed Great Britain "had prematurely, as we deemed it, and without adequate reason, awarded the status of belligerency to our insurgents. But this act of itself, and by its inherent nature, was of neutral color, and an act which, howsoever we might condemn it in the particular case, we could not deny to be of the competency of a sovereign State." Still, by "virtue of the proclamation maritime enterprises in the ports of Great Britain, which would otherwise have been piratical, were rendered lawful, and thus Great Britain became, and to the end continued to be, the arsenal, the navy yard, and the treasury of the insurgent confederates." These subsequent overt actions "translated a measure indefinite of itself into one of definite wrong to the United States," thus rendering the proclamation "a virtual act of war." Grant and Fish made no specific demands, forbore estimating what compensation might be due, and left to future discussions the nature of new rules for neutrals that might be added to maritime law.[40]

When Fish's dispatch arrived in London, Moran thought Great

Britain would have to either "acknowledge she was wrong in grant-ing the rebels belligerent rights or fight." But when Motley read the note to Clarendon, the foreign secretary listened "in the most friendly spirit and said that his greatest desire was to preserve the peace," add-ing "emphatically, 'We shall have no war.'" Privately, Clarendon and Prime Minister William Gladstone found the overall tone of Fish's note "malignant" and "offensive," but Gladstone quickly guessed that it was largely "bunkum" designed by Fish for no "other purpose than as a tub to the whale for Motley and Sumner." Indeed, Fish's conciliatory tone in the concluding passages gave Gladstone "a hopeful view of it." Clar-endon wrote privately to Thornton that he looked "upon this dispatch as not being of a strictly official character." In a formal reply conveyed through Thornton in Washington, Clarendon said that he and the gov-ernment "fully agree with Mr. Fish" that the two nations should turn their present disagreement "to good account" by devising new interna-tional laws to avert "similar difficulties hereafter." Clarendon appended an unsigned memorandum that defended the queen's proclamation of neutrality and denied the British government's complicity in the escape of the Confederate cruisers, points he chose not to address in his dis-patch. Fish focused on the foreign minister's official response and as-sured Thornton that he thought its "general tone" was "friendly" and that it required no response.[41]

Thus, Fish's calculated risk paid off. In his September 25 instruc-tions he made a bold assertion of the American position without causing a rupture in relations with the British, and he did so without instituting a fundamental change in administration policy. Indeed, he told Thorn-ton that he did not expect a reply "unless the British Gov. thinks it nec-essary." Moreover, he soon stepped back from the heated rhetoric. As Moran noted, Fish sent instructions to Motley, "telling him in substance to apologise to Ld. Clarendon for his overstatement of our case" during their first interview. Fish told Sumner that "under any other Govern-ment than this, such violation of instructions" as Motley had committed "would not have failed to be followed by the most severe censure, & probably by an immediate recall." Yet the minister remained recalcitrant. Sumner shared with Fish a letter in which Motley admitted that even though "I am expressly instructed to avoid the subject[,] semi-officially I continue to throw out the skirmish line as far as possible—& very likely a good bit out of supporting distance." "Can we," the astounded Fish asked Sumner, "preserve peace if the accredited representative of our Government should endeavor to 'make such a detestable record against

Gr. Britain that it is almost too inflaming for the public mind in both countries to preserve peace[?]'" Within weeks Grant again told Fish that he "would not be sorry" if Motley were to resign.[42]

With the focus of the negotiations shifting to Washington, a principal motive for Fish's September 25 instructions to Motley was to fend off sniping at home. "I wish to retain the control of the question," he confided to Thornton, and "without something of the kind the question would have been discussed violently in Congress." This confirmed Gladstone's inference that the instructions were "meant to shield the Govt., and pay off Motley with moonshine." It worked; Motley complimented Fish and told Sumner that it was "a capital paper . . . & just what was wanted." Similarly, an intent to disarm critics informed Fish's drafting of a passage for the president's annual message in early December. In a sentence Fish lifted substantially from his September 25 note, the message stated that the Johnson-Clarendon Convention had done nothing to satisfy injuries beyond ordinary commercial claims— "injuries resulting to the United States by reason of the course adopted by Great Britain during our late civil war—in the increased rates of insurance; in the diminution of exports and imports, and other obstructions to domestic industry and production; in its effect upon the foreign commerce of the country; in the decrease and transfer to Great Britain of our commercial marine; in the prolongation of the war and the increased cost (both in treasure and in lives) of its suppression." Elsewhere in the message, however, Grant upheld a nation's right to recognize belligerency, and Thornton expressed his satisfaction at the message's "manner & tone." Soon afterward, Sumner secured passage of a request for all correspondence with Britain on the subject since the defeat of the Johnson-Clarendon Convention. This move played right into Fish's hands, giving the administration an opportunity to exhibit the September 25 note publicly. Senators could read the correspondence during the Christmas break, after which Fish hoped they would return "with a determination to leave the settlement of the question entirely in the hands of the Administration." The tactic succeeded. Vice President Schuyler Colfax spoke for many when he thanked Fish for his "masterly & unanswerable" presentation.[43]

While Fish spent much of the fall maneuvering Motley out of the way, he also began serious preliminary discussions with Thornton. In early November the British minister asked the secretary, in light of his September 25 note to Motley, what kind of settlement the United States envisioned. Fish declined to make a specific statement until he could consult Sumner, but when Fish laid the question before the senator and invited him to formulate a "proposition," he refused. Sumner replied that "what the people will require" could "be seen in the probable debates of Congress." This response threatened precisely the sort of interference Fish aimed to forestall, so he decided to move forward on his own.[44]

A week later, Fish sketched out for Thornton his personal notion of a possible accord, largely along the lines of his intimations to Rose that summer. The United States would expect some "kind word with reference to the past," an "agreement settling the laws of Maritime Neutrality," and Britain's payment of a gross sum for the claims or the creation of a commission to arrive at a figure. Thornton said his government would not confess to wrongdoing without submitting the question to arbitration, but Fish noted that many British statesmen had, in effect, already "admitted it." As for additions to international law, the secretary proposed an understanding that a proclamation of neutrality amounted to a recognition of belligerency, a ban on arming a vessel at sea (as had been done with the *Alabama*), a stipulation that the nationality of a ship could "not be changed by sale or on the High Seas," and perhaps a ban on privateering if the British agreed to "the doctrine that private property on the ocean is protected." After this conversation in mid-November, Fish and Thornton returned to the discussion only intermittently over the next several months. In one conversation Fish suggested that a reason for devising rules for neutrals in wartime was that in the event Britain became involved in a European conflict, "it would be impossible to prevent retaliation, & the ocean would swarm with 'Alabamas.'" When Thornton replied that England would then declare war on the United States, Fish rejoined that the minister was thus admitting that the United States had grounds for a declaration of war based on England's behavior in the 1860s.[45]

Grant left the *Alabama* question largely to Fish, but he did on occasion draw a connection between a settlement of the controversy and Britain's abandonment of its control over Canada. For decades, many Americans had embraced the idea that the acquisition of Britain's remaining North American provinces would be a glorious final chapter of the American Revolution. No less a figure than Charles Sumner envisioned a union that "all American hearts" would regard as "the harbinger of infinite good." During a couple of cabinet meetings in November 1869, Grant raised the possibility that a delay in resolving the claims issue might move Great Britain to cede Canada as a way to secure a settlement. But Boutwell cautioned that cession would entail acceptance of the financial liabilities Britain had assumed on Canada's behalf. And Fish noted that the British government would not relinquish the Dominion until the Canadians themselves had agreed "unequivocally," and it certainly would not do so as "a satisfaction for any claim." Grant and the cabinet concluded that it was best not to propose any conditions that might delay the *Alabama* settlement but to demonstrate a willingness to negotiate whenever the British were ready.[46]

Fish saw an opportunity to raise the Canada question in late December. He and Thornton were discussing the problem of the Fenians, a strongly nationalistic Irish group in the United States that saw filibustering raids into Canada as a way to spark Anglo-American conflict and thus hasten Ireland's independence from England. As Fish recorded in his diary, "I suddenly remarked, 'why not withdraw entirely from Canada, & remove the pretext of these Fenian threats, & at the same time we can settle the Alabama claims immediately[?]'" When Thornton replied that the Canadians did not favor British withdrawal, Fish countered that "a very large preponderance of sentiment" endorsed separation. The secretary returned to the point sporadically, arguing in March 1870 that "if Gt Britain would make the Provinces Independent," all "irritating questions—Indians, Fenians, disorderly soldiers, &c"—would be removed. Still Thornton demurred.[47]

The potential for trouble over the Fenians burst forth in late May 1870 when paramilitary groups gathered at points in northern New York and Vermont, threatening to make raids across the border. Grant sent troops to the region and issued a warning proclamation, ordering federal officers to "prevent and defeat" any "unlawful proceedings" and to arrest all persons involved. In short order the US marshal captured thirty tons of arms, which Grant ordered to be deposited at a US arsenal. In addition, the president refused to help the Fenians return to their homes. He told Fish, "The people along the Frontier have been sympathizing with these movements & aiding these People, & if it is annoying to them both, it is well that they 'should sweat a while.'" The next day Fish assured Thornton that the US government would not return the arms to the would-be raiders. Grant and Fish wanted no pretext for the British to draw a parallel between American laxity regarding the Fenians and British culpability for the *Alabama*—an idea that had occurred to Gladstone. A few months later Grant followed up with another stinging proclamation against "evil-disposed persons" contemplating such raids, although he also issued pardons for nine Fenians who had been jailed.[48]

Although the government's quick action squelched the Fenians' designs, an exasperated Grant exclaimed to the cabinet in early June, "If Gt. Britain would evacuate Canada the 'Alabama' claims could be settled instantly." Once again, Fish and others explained that even though Britain might be ready, Canada was not. Fish thought he might ease a settlement of the claims issue by calming British fears about American imperialist designs. He told Thornton the administration favored independence for the provinces, not annexation. But this was a distinction without a difference, Thornton insisted; Canadians assumed that independence would lead to annexation, and this they did not want.[49]

While Anglo-American relations remained tense, the European war that many had feared broke out in mid-July between France and the North German Confederation headed by Prussia. "What a time this would be," Assistant Secretary J. C. Bancroft Davis wrote to Fish, "to strike in London for the independence of Canada, and the settlement of the Alabama claims." But England managed to stay out of the conflict and thus avoided any worries about a "swarm" of *Alabamas*. Because of France's recent abortive attempt to establish an empire in Mexico, most Americans detested Napoleon III and initially tilted toward Prussia. Grant shared these feelings, remembering French loans to the Confederacy and German sympathy for the Union cause. The United States offered its good offices to help secure peace, but military success left the North German government unreceptive. As matters went from bad to worse for France, its minister in Washington pleaded with Fish for the United States to expostulate against North Germany's annexing of French territory. Fish privately expressed his hope to the American minister in Berlin, George Bancroft, that France not be dismembered, but publicly the administration refused to intercede. For Grant, the issue was simple: "France having without provocation entered upon the war, with a scarcely concealed intention to dispossess Prussia of a portion of her Territory, could not complain, & was not entitled to sympathy if the result of the war deprived her of a portion of her own territory."[50]

Officially the administration maintained strict neutrality. The president issued two proclamations enjoining Americans against enlisting in the service of either belligerent or arming any ship to be used by a belligerent and imposing severe restrictions on belligerent warships in American harbors. The administration did not, however, regard the sale of arms to the belligerents by private individuals as a violation of neutrality, as long as such sales were available to both sides. Fish told the French minister in Washington that arms constituted "an important staple of our manufacturers." More bluntly, he wrote to Davis, "Why should the manufacturer or dealer in arms three or four thousand miles off, be expected to shut up shop whenever Lou Nap. & Bill Hohenzollern take off their coats & go to fisticuffs to settle which is the better man, or whether their boundary fence should be this or that side of the goose pond[?]" The United States government itself had sold surplus arms since the close of the Civil War and continued to do so during this period, but Grant forbade the sale of government arms to either belligerent or to anyone suspected of being an agent of either. At one projected auction in October, the Remington Arms Company put in the highest bid for a quantity of War Department weapons, but the government blocked the sale when it discovered that Remington was an agent for France. Two months later, to avoid any unintended transfer to France or Prussia, Grant suspended government arms sales altogether. The issue had the potential to damage the American position in the *Alabama* case, but Fish carefully explained the American policy to Thornton, who accepted the difference between government sales and private sales.[51]

More ominous for achieving an *Alabama* settlement was a resurgence of the so-called fisheries question, which had plagued Anglo-American relations for decades. At issue was Americans' right (or privilege) to catch fish in the waters of Canada. After the Revolution, the British government had barred the newly independent Americans from fishing in the rich Canadian waters. They regained limited access under the Anglo-American Convention of 1818, but New England fishermen still bridled at that treaty's severe restrictions. In 1854 the United States and Britain negotiated the comprehensive Marcy-Elgin Reciprocity Treaty, which secured more generous privileges for American fishermen in Canadian waters, as well as establishing free trade between the two countries in more than twenty-five classes of commodities. In 1866, however, the United States abrogated the 1854 treaty, in part in reaction to Canada's lax policing of its borders during the Civil War and, more important, because Americans perceived that Canadians had reaped far greater profits from the trade reciprocity, outweighing any American gains from broader fishing privileges. As a result of the abrogation, Americans' fishing rights reverted to a much more circumscribed area outlined in the Convention of 1818, and the Canadians instituted license fees and other restrictions against American vessels that hit New England fishing communities particularly hard. At the opening of the fishing season in the summer of 1870, the Canadians intensified their enforcement procedures, angering American fishermen and further aggravating tensions between the United States and Great Britain.[52]

As a way to strike back, the administration contemplated barring the transshipment of goods in bond from one point in Canada to another across American soil. As Davis wrote to Fish, the United States could "give the Canucks trouble in that way if they continue obstreperous." Grant fully endorsed such "retaliatory measures," telling Davis that he was "tired of yielding, and thought that it was about time to do something on our side." Through the fall of 1870, Fish complained to Thornton about "the vexatious conduct of the British & Canadian authorities toward our Fishermen." At one point the minister suggested a revival of reciprocity: trading Americans' fishing rights and navigation in Canadian canals in exchange for the duty-free admission into the United States of such commodities as grains, animals, hides, furs, butter, cheese, ores, and timber. Fish gave Thornton no encouragement, and the cabinet, recognizing that western states would object to increased imports of several of these items, squelched the idea. Thornton also proposed submitting the fisheries question to arbitration, which Fish rejected "very decidedly." Grant concluded that "the question had better be left open for settlement with the Alabama Claims."[53]

Yet the fall of 1870 witnessed little progress on that front. At the outset of the Franco-Prussian War, Britain had rushed to revise its Foreign Enlistment Act, in part to prevent the construction of vessels like the *Alabama* for either side in the new conflict. Fish pointedly told Thornton that this new British legislation represented "a practical admission . . . of their fault in not . . . discharging their international obligations toward us" during the Civil War. But Thornton insisted that Great Britain could never concede liability except as a result of arbitration. Fish in turn argued that rejection of the Johnson-Clarendon Convention amounted to a rejection of arbitration in the *Alabama* case. "Without some other principle or concession," Fish said, "we would stand at a deadlock."[54]

There matters stood until events in Europe again intruded. In November 1870 Russia announced to the other European powers its intention to abrogate the Treaty of 1856, which had banned its ships in a general demilitarization of the Black Sea. The move threatened Turkey, exacerbated the so-called Eastern Question potentially to the point of war, and posed a menace to British interests in the region. An anxious Thornton confided to Fish that it looked as if England might be "drawn into the controversy." In London, officials warned that if England was "on the verge of a Russian war," it was "very important that all cause of difference with the United States should, if possible, be got out of the way." Settling the *Alabama* question was "a matter of national exigency."[55]

After weeks of sparring with Fish, the next time Thornton showed up at the State Department, a new mood prevailed. When the minister reiterated that Britain would be willing to submit the *Alabama* question to arbitration, Fish replied that the United States would consent to refer the issue of the amount of damages to third-party adjudication but not the issue of Britain's liability. Beyond the actual financial loss from the destruction of property, the United States had a national grievance against Britain and "must have some recognition of a wrong *done, some expression of regret, some kind word.*" Noting the recent amendments to Britain's Foreign Enlistment Act, Fish assured Thornton that the British would not suffer "any humiliation" if they were now "to say that under the previous laws by accident or carelessness a wrong had befallen us for which they are ready to make satisfaction." Without specifically mentioning Britain's European complications, Fish further observed that "the precedent of granting compensation in this case would be invaluable for Great Britain in case she should herself be involved in war, and her commerce exposed to depredations of a like nature." Regarding rules governing neutrals, Fish elaborated suggestions he had made a year earlier: the outlawing of privateering, protection of a belligerent's non-contraband goods by a neutral flag, the inviolability of neutral goods on a belligerent ship, the legality of a blockade contingent on its effectiveness, a ban on changing the nationality of an armed vessel at sea, no arming of a vessel on the high seas, and protection of the public mails. Thornton told the Foreign Office that Fish was "much more serious and plain than usual" and suggested that his points "be taken into consideration." Fish had seized upon Great Britain's current vulnerability in Europe to drive home the American case.[56]

Fish kept up the pressure while preparing the foreign policy section of Grant's second annual message in early December 1870. Grant wanted no letup and dismissed as "pure fiction" a rumor that the United States would not press the *Alabama* claims. He noted with regret that Great Britain appeared to be unwilling to admit any negligence or the commission of any act that gave the United States "just cause of complaint." He insisted, "Our firm and unalterable convictions are directly the reverse." The president urged Congress to authorize payment of the private claims by the United States so that the government would have "responsible control of all the demands against Great Britain." He dwelled at length on the fisheries question, alleging that the Canadian government, as a "semi-independent but irresponsible agent," had inflicted "unfriendly and vexatious treatment . . . designed to bear harshly upon the hardy fishermen of the United States." He called on Congress to authorize him to suspend the transportation of goods across US territory to Canada and, "should such an extreme measure become necessary," to bar Canadian vessels from American waters. "The President's quiet way of stating the case, and the course proper to be pursued," observed the *Washington Evening Star*, "will undoubtedly give Great Britain more uneasiness and a greater disposition to settle her little bill than any amount of bluster on our part."[57]

Indeed, the British had already decided to move. In late November John Rose, now serving in London as a principal in the Anglo-American banking firm of Morton, Rose, had sent Fish a letter signaling England's eagerness to reach a settlement. Although he professed to be writing "entirely of my own accord," Rose had conversed with the British government on the issue. His motives ranged beyond civic-mindedness; as a prospective agent for marketing US bonds, his banking house would benefit from the preservation of peace between the United States and Britain. Without revealing his personal interest to British officials, Rose had sought to convince them that the Grant administration was eager for a diplomatic settlement in order to facilitate the sale of new bonds in England in an effort to refinance the national debt. Rose wrote to Fish that he well understood the administration's hope for an equitable settlement and asserted, "*a desire equally strong exists here*." He offered himself as a go-between for "informal & confidential communications." When Fish presented the Canadian's letter to the cabinet, Boutwell noted Rose's attempt to leverage a settlement by linking it to the refunding plan. The president did not leap to accept Rose's offer to intercede, however, believing that negotiations conducted by a new minister in place of Motley might suffice. But Fish convinced him that informal discussions could pave the way for formal talks. To keep the pressure on England, the administration sent Congress draft legislation to carry out Grant's threat to stop the transshipment of Canadian goods and to bar Canadian ships from US ports. Within a week after writing to Fish, Rose received approval for his mission from the British cabinet, and a few weeks later he was on his way to Washington.[58]

Thus, as 1870 drew to a close, the administration faced a brightening prospect that it could at last achieve an acceptable settlement of the vexatious *Alabama* question.

8

REVOLT IN CUBA

As the *Alabama* question evolved during the summer and fall of 1869, the United States' acknowledgment that a nation could determine for itself when to recognize a state of belligerency was intertwined with the administration's effort to define its position regarding the insurrection in Cuba. Grant was "very fixed in his adherence" to the view that a nation had every right to accord such recognition if circumstances warranted. But acknowledging the right of recognition differed from embracing its advisability. In the Cuban case, many Americans favored recognizing the insurgency against Spain not only on humanitarian grounds but also as a way to help terminate a war that damaged American commerce and other economic interests. The rebel Cuban junta based in New York nourished these sympathetic feelings, while Spanish authorities alleged that a lax enforcement of US neutrality laws allowed Americans to provide material aid to the rebels. Grant felt deep sympathy for the Cubans' fight against the anomalous vestige of Spain's faded but arrogant empire. But he also came to see a need to strike a balance between fervent interventionist calls for US recognition of belligerence and a watchful reserve dictated by international law and a prudent calculation of the nation's true interests.[1]

Within the cabinet, Rawlins emerged as the Cuban insurgents' staunchest supporter. Like Grant—and many Americans—the secretary of war saw the Monroe Doctrine as a linchpin of the nation's foreign

Secretary of War John A. Rawlins. (Library of Congress)

policy. He eagerly anticipated the final withdrawal of all European powers from the Americas, which would rid the hemisphere of "the influence and dangers of monarchism."[2] Yet Rawlins apparently had less lofty motives as well. To garner support, the junta freely gave journalists and government officials large quantities of bonds that would gain in value in the event of a Cuban victory. From time to time, Spanish minister Don Mauricio Lopez Roberts showed Fish lists of purported recipients of such bonds, and Rawlins's name appeared next to a figure of $20,000 or $25,000. Fish apparently did not inform the president, but shortly after Rawlins's death in early September 1869, Grant, serving as executor of the estate, learned that the securities were among his papers. He ordered them destroyed. Six years later, however, as the Cuban war continued, Grant discovered that the bonds still lay in the safe Rawlins had used. When he consulted Fish and Secretary of the Navy George Robeson about what to do, Fish revealed that he had seen Rawlins's name on Roberts's list. Robeson suggested that the bonds be sold, but both Fish and Grant squelched that sketchy idea. Instead, the president burned them.[3]

Whatever Rawlins's motives, his voice was potent with Grant and echoed a sentiment widespread in the country. "Let us talk no more of the Monroe Doctrine, of sympathy with any brave people struggling for their independence," declared the *New York Herald*, "if we do not promptly accord to the Cubans belligerent rights." Grant toyed with the idea of issuing a proclamation recognizing the insurgency in precisely the same language Spain had used in according belligerency status to the Confederacy in 1861, and he even floated the idea with Charles Sumner. The senator, no friend of the Cuban junta, advised against it.[4]

The most formidable opponent was Fish, whom the *Herald* labeled "a timid old fogy." Eager to avoid hostilities with Spain or any complication with England, Fish believed that the United States should not "be in haste to prematurely recognize a revolutionary movement until it had manifested the capacity of self sustenance & of some degree of stability." Fish feared that a precipitate recognition would encourage a movement for American annexation of Cuba, which he adamantly opposed. It would be contrary to Americans' interests, he believed, "to undertake the management of a race so different from their own and so unaccustomed to such laws and institutions as those of the U.S." Nor did Fish exhibit any desire to acquire Cuba in the interest of freer trade. In its present state of debt, the United States could not afford to take on the expense of managing the island and at the same time forgo the $32 million per year the government collected in customs duties on Cuban imports, nearly 18 percent of total tariff revenues. The United States, he told Edward Thornton, favored independence for Cuba, not annexation.[5]

In this frame of mind, Fish leaped at what appeared to be an opening for American mediation that could end the conflict and thus relieve the administration of the vexatious recognition problem. Bankrupt and bowed by crushing debt, the Spanish government in Madrid informed American businessman Paul Forbes that Spain would be willing to let Cuba go for an appropriate pecuniary consideration. Grant and Fish welcomed the proposal not as a chance to buy Cuba but instead as an opportunity for the United States to mediate between Spain and the insurgents. The secretary worked out the details of a response grounded on certain conditions: (1) Cuban independence, (2) Cuba's payment to Spain of a sum to cover its loss of revenue and loss of buildings and other public property, (3) the abolition of slavery, and (4) an armistice during the negotiations. Cuba would raise the money for the indemnity by issuing bonds. Fish added that with congressional approval, the United States could guarantee the bonds, using Cuba's customs revenues as security. Sumner thought the mediation plan would allow the United States "to keep on good terms with Spain" and also "do more for Cuba & at less cost than by any system of filibusterism or unjustifiable concession [of belligerency], with the hazard of war & infinite expense." Hopeful for a speedy resolution, Grant gave Fish the go-ahead. Before putting the proposal to the Spanish, Fish sounded out the leaders of the Cuban junta, who responded enthusiastically.[6]

Although Fish spoke frequently with Roberts, the Spanish minister, he thought it best to present the offer in Madrid, despite having less than full confidence in the newly appointed American minister there, Daniel Sickles. Sickles had an unsavory past, including the murder of his wife's lover and acquittal on a plea of temporary insanity. But he had redeemed himself during the war and lost a leg at Gettysburg, and his vigorous campaigning for Grant in 1868 helped him win the diplomatic post. Fifteen years earlier, as secretary of the American legation in London, Sickles had assisted in preparing the infamous Ostend Manifesto, asserting that the United States should wrest Cuba from Spain if Spain refused to sell it. This act from the new minister's past added even more weight to the baggage he carried to Madrid.[7]

With the administration's offer of mediation taking shape, Forbes suggested that he return to Madrid and help present the plan to the Spanish government. Eager to get negotiations under way, Fish appointed

Forbes a special confidential agent to be paid from the president's secret contingency fund. In early July, before Grant left Washington for a
round of summer travel, he ordered the preparation of a neutrality proclamation recognizing the Cuban insurgents' belligerency, which could
be issued during his absence if circumstances warranted. Fish pushed
for Spain's speedy acceptance of mediation in order to obviate such a
proclamation.[8]

In early August Fish seized an opportunity to delay the proclamation when complications arose over the fact that East Coast shipbuild-
ers had been contracted to construct gunboats for Spain, apparently for
use against Cuba. Grant was reluctant to see the boats go into Spanish
hands, but a government seizure would be tantamount to a recognition
of Cuban belligerency. Fish argued that such a course would be compa-
rable to that followed by the British in recognizing the belligerency of
the Confederacy, and he warned that the administration should avoid
"doing what Great Britain is very anxious we should do." A temporary
way out appeared when the pro-Cuban Peruvian government protested
the release of the boats on the grounds that Peru was technically still at
war with Spain after their conflict in 1864–1866, and Spain might use the
boats against Peru. In response, Justice and Navy Department officials
took control of the vessels until their intended use could be ascertained.
But Spain protested vigorously, and the Peruvian ruse for detaining the
boats could be sustained for only so long. To avert an administration
decree to release them, which would raise the ire of Cuba sympathizers
in Congress and among the American public, Grant proposed turning
the matter over to the courts under the Neutrality Act of 1818. The administration also leaned on the Peruvians to reach an understanding
with Spain. As expected, a federal district judge ruled that the boats be
released, but the administration had managed to delay this action for
several months. Even so, it did not entirely escape political heat, with
the *New York Herald* charging that it had provided "effective aid to the
Spaniards" while "utterly ignoring the Cubans."[9]

Meanwhile, the execution of the administration's mediation plan
did not unfold as hoped. Without waiting for Sickles, the officer empowered to negotiate, Forbes presumed to do so. Spanish Council president Juan Prim said he would be willing to have the United States mediate, but the insurgents must lay down their arms before negotiations
could proceed. Spain would grant autonomy to Cuba if it paid $150
million, guaranteed by the United States. With his limited experience in
foreign policy, Forbes failed to appreciate the unacceptability of the first

condition without a simultaneous cease-fire by Spanish forces. When Fish asked for an explanation, Forbes simply repeated Prim's position and insisted that the Spaniard wished to negotiate "alone through me." Not surprisingly, Fish was irked by the "indiscreet" Forbes, who, having "blabbed," had complicated Sickles's task.[10]

But Fish had scarcely more confidence in Sickles, whose appointment he considered "a bad one." After the tardy minister arrived in Madrid, Fish urged him to "hasten" the negotiations. When the Spanish Council president asked if his proposal was substantially the same as that presented by Forbes, Sickles replied that it was. Prim then heatedly insisted that Spain would not consider an armistice or take up Cuban independence while the insurgents still bore arms. After a delay of twelve days, Prim presented a counterproposal: (1) the insurgents must lay down their arms, (2) Spain would grant amnesty, (3) the people of Cuba would vote on independence, and (4) if a majority favored independence, Spain would grant it, and Cuba would pay a "satisfactory equivalent guaranteed by the United States." Sickles cabled this development to Fish and headed his report: "President of council authorizes me to state that the good offices of the United States are accepted."[11]

The receipt of Sickles's cable triggered two responses in Fish. First, he ordered the minister to press for Spain's agreement to the US proposal as presented. He dismissed the Spanish proposition that the insurgents lay down their arms. Disordered conditions in Cuba precluded a plebiscite, he said, and besides, the will of the majority was clear.[12] Second, and contradictorily, Fish used Sickles's cable to justify withholding the neutrality proclamation Grant had ordered prepared, on the grounds that the minister had made progress. In mid-August, while traveling in western Pennsylvania, the president warned that Spain planned to "send 20,000 more troops to Cuba to put down, as Americans believe[,] the right of self government." He instructed Fish to issue the proclamation "if Gen. Sickles has not received an entirely satisfactory reply to his proposition to mediate between Spain and the Cubans." This contingent phrase, coupled with Sickles's (overstated) claim that Spain had accepted American good offices, allowed Fish to persuade Grant not to proclaim neutrality at this time. He conveyed his position through Horace Porter, who promptly reported to Fish that "the President[']s views in regard to Cuba . . . coincide exactly with your own."[13]

Grant also moved to quell rumors that he and Fish differed on the issue. On August 21 a *New York Herald* editorial alleged that Fish was the only member of the cabinet who opposed recognition of belligerency and that "in deference to the wish of Mr. Fish the President still post-pones the decisive step." Shortly thereafter, Grant told *Herald* reporter Randolph Keim, "Mr. Fish does not oppose my views on that subject" but "accords with them exactly." The implication was that Grant was in charge and it was not the proper time to issue a proclamation. "The Cubans are hardly yet in a condition of belligerency but matters are rapidly tending that way," he stated. With a veiled reference to the Forbes-Sickles initiative, Grant said, "I am a close student of events and matters are daily tending to a desirable end. It would defeat the aims of the government to state what is now going on but, . . . if the country will only have patience, we may anticipate prudent action at a timely moment."[14]

But the lack of progress in the Madrid talks tried Grant's patience. When the cabinet gathered in Washington on August 31, he wrote out instructions for Fish to send to Sickles, and they contained a new statement of American conditions for mediation: an immediate armistice, Cuban compensation to Spain for public property, protection of Spaniards' person and property if they chose to remain in Cuba, and no guarantee by the United States without congressional approval. Spain had to accept the conditions by September 25 (changed to October 1 in the official cable), or the United States would withdraw its offer. Fish expected Sickles to threaten recognition of the insurgents to leverage Spain's acceptance. Privately, Fish advised the Spanish minister, "It was apparent that Cuba could never again be a valuable or a quiet possession of Spain, & it was better now to part with it, & obtain a valuable equivalent, than to lose it wholly a little later, after expending more of life & of money & obtain nothing." Nonetheless, when rumors of possible US recognition of the insurgents spread through Spain, the Spanish press expressed universal outrage and called for more troops to be sent to Cuba.[15]

While the mediation negotiations limped along in Madrid, the administration scotched a proposal for the United States to buy Cuba. In late August banker August Belmont, a longtime Cuba enthusiast, offered to broker a purchase agreement. Fish responded that such a move was "not within the contemplation" of the administration, and Grant told the secretary, "I do not think it advisable to authorize direct purchase of Cuba by the United States. It is questionable whether a matter of such importance should be considered without the sanction of Congress." Even so, the president shared Fish's frustration at Spain's recalcitrance with Sickles. In a private conversation with Keim, the former general noted that rumors of war were appearing in the foreign press, but he was "not going to be bluffed." "The United States could stand a war" as well as its potential opponent, he said, and even though the navy was "very much reduced," he had "ships enough to begin with." Although Fish would find such an outburst unsettling, at least he no longer had to contend with the Cubans' chief advocate in the cabinet after Rawlins died on September 6.[16]

In Madrid, the Spanish authorities seemed incapable of negotiating coherently or in earnest. Sickles reported that with their shaky government harried by chauvinistic public opinion, the politicians "all try to outdo one another in their devotion to Spanish honor, and in their defiant denunciation of the United States." At the end of September he made one last attempt to persuade the Spanish to accept American mediation. When that failed, the United States withdrew the offer of good offices.[17] Within a few weeks Forbes attempted to inject himself back into the issue by proposing a revised settlement plan, but Grant and Fish refused to endorse it. Sickles told Fish that Prim would like to negotiate but had concluded that doing so "would destroy him."[18]

After the collapse of the mediation attempt, Prussia, at the instance of Spain, inquired whether the United States would accept Prussian good offices as a go-between with Spain. Fish told the Prussian minister that the United States needed no intermediary, but he put the minister's mind at ease by adding that it had no desire to acquire Cuba. The American government did not wish to forgo the customs revenue on Cuban imports or incur the expense of a new dependency. "The people are of a different race & language, unaccustomed to our Institutions or to self government; we would not wish to incorporate them with us." But "under no circumstances," Fish continued, "would we consent that the Island pass into the possession or under the control of any other European Govt." What the United States wanted was "peace & quiet" for Cuba and its independence.[19]

If Spain's trifling with the American offer had irritated Fish, he felt scant sympathy for the Cuban junta. "Instead of trying to gain their independence by fighting on their own soil," he grumbled to George Bancroft, "they rush here by the hundreds & thousands & clamor to send a few Americans or persons of other nationalities to Cuba to fight their battles. . . . Their course & conduct in quitting their Island & trying to get a few others to go there & do their fighting—in constantly, persistently endeavoring to violate our neutrality laws, & to compromise our Government, have excited a feeling of mistrust in their sincerity & in their capacity." In any event, Fish wrote, "All danger of the concession of belligerent rights has vanished." As the new session of

Congress approached, Fish enlisted Sumner to "defend" nonrecognition in the Senate, noting that the Cuban junta's "vigorous onslaught upon the neutrality laws" had "worked out of me nearly all the respect,—and much of the sympathy (& that was very large) I had for them."[20]

As Grant put the finishing touches on his annual message for the opening session of Congress, he dealt at length with the Cuba question. By the time he turned to framing that document in mid-November, he fully agreed with Fish as to recognition. "To this day," he noted in an early draft, "we have no evidence that the governm[en]t of *Free Cuba* has a permanent seat of government, a single port into which to carry prizes; Admiralty, or other courts, to adjudicate prizes or to administer justice, and without all, or some of these requisites I have not felt justified in recognizing belligerency." In the final version, he adopted less pointed language provided by Fish: "The contest has at no time assumed the conditions which amount to a war in the sense of international law, or which would show the existence of a *de facto* political organization of the insurgents sufficient to justify a recognition of belligerency." Grant remained much more sympathetic to the Cubans than Fish was, but he shared some of the secretary's frustrations at the junta's behavior. In a candid moment he told Fish, the Cubans "come here in large numbers & make trouble for us." He called them "inefficient" and said they had "done little for themselves." Yet he had nothing but contempt for Spain's colonial rule, and as a military man, he abhorred the inhumane tactics it employed. He harbored the hope that the Spanish would not "regain the control of the island."[21]

Grant's message placed the Cuban question in the larger context of the Monroe Doctrine and included a strong iteration of the "no-transfer" principle, a cornerstone of American foreign policy. Abjuring any disposition to interfere with existing colonial relationships in the Western Hemisphere, the president said he anticipated a time when European powers would consider it in their best interest to let their colonies go— to let them become "members of the family of nations." Henceforth, he solemnly added, "these dependencies are no longer regarded as subject to transfer from one European power to another. When the present relation of colonies ceases, they are to become independent powers, exercising the right of choice and of self-control in the determination of their future condition and relation with other powers." In his message he also recounted the US efforts at mediation to "put a stop to the bloodshed in Cuba" and reminded Spain that "this nation is its own judge when to accord the rights of belligerency, either to a people struggling to free themselves from a government they believe to be oppressive or to independent nations at war with each other."[22]

This last caveat to Spain had the unintended consequence of giving new hope to leaders of the Cuban junta and their friends in America. In January 1870, at a public meeting at Cooper Union spearheaded by Horace Greeley of the *New York Tribune*, the participants adopted a series of pro-Cuba resolutions, including one favoring the recognition of belligerency. Many blamed Fish for the administration's foot-dragging, but the *New York Sun* went beyond defending the Cuban cause on principle and engaged in severe personal attacks on the secretary. The paper noted that Fish's son-in-law Sidney Webster, a Democrat and a lawyer, had the Spanish government for a client. "The point where the national honor is touched," the *Sun* claimed, lay in "the fact that *the son-in-law of the Secretary of State is the counsel for the Spanish Government, and that the policy of the United States has been changed by the Secretary from an American to a Spanish policy, from a policy favorable to Cuba and freedom to a policy favorable to Spain and slavery*." Under the circumstances, it concluded, either Webster should end his legal services or Fish should resign.[23]

Webster had indeed performed substantial legal work for the Spanish, but his employment had begun long before Fish's appointment. Most of his services entailed assembling evidence against agents of the Cuban junta for violating US neutrality laws, although Webster also appeared in court on the gunboat question. Informally, he had passed on to his father-in-law a rumor regarding Forbes's indiscreet talk about his mission and Belmont's proposal to broker a US purchase of Cuba. He flatly denied any impropriety. "I can say, that I never have advised Mr. Lopez Roberts, directly or indirectly, in respect to any controversy which he had with the State Department."[24]

Although Webster's business connection to Spain opened Fish to criticism, neither he nor Webster nor the president saw anything in the arrangement that would require Fish's exit from the cabinet, which Fish believed was the objective of the *Sun*'s attack. The normally placid secretary labeled editor Charles A. Dana a "Blackguard" who sought "to put pence in his pocket by defamation, & by the robbery of the good name & fame of others. To prove him a slanderer, a libeller, or a liar might not be difficult, but 'cui bono' [to whose benefit]? He is known as such, & the notoriety of a libel or a slander suit would be to him a Godsend, a new sensation, & a new subject for the sale of his paper." Dana had failed in a bid to become collector of customs in New York, one of the most lucrative patronage positions in the entire country. Hence, Fish wrote to a friend, the editor leveled his "assault on me" to "gratify his disappointment and to injure at the same time the President who did not give him the appointment he coveted, & the Republican party which has not recognized him as its leader."[25]

Fish did not need a corrupt relationship through his son-in-law to shape his attitude toward Cuba. He thought that in some ways the leaders of the Cuban junta were their own worst enemies. He was convinced that the free use of bribery by the Cubans with members of Congress and the press explained much of the enthusiasm for their cause. In a newspaper interview, he criticized the mismanagement of the junta, which, instead of using its resources to purchase arms in the United States, which was legal, squandered those resources on filibustering ventures, which were illegal and required suppression by the government under the neutrality laws. Privately he opposed any notion of annexation, believing the Cubans were not "fitted to become citizens of the U.S."[26]

The subject of America's relation to the insurrection dragged on into 1870 and arose during a cabinet meeting in mid-February, during which Grant observed that it "looked as though Congress would very soon determine to grant belligerent rights to Cuba." Fish could scarcely contain his anger. Should the United States take that step, he said, war with Spain would ensue. He grounded this argument on his reading of the Pinckney Treaty of 1795 between the United States and Spain, which explicitly stated that when one of the signatories was a recognized belligerent, it had the right of visit and search on the merchant vessels of the other as a neutral. Fish warned, "Our people will be indignant at the arrest of our vessels, & will resist, or retaliate"—actions likely to escalate into war. Moreover, he argued, without formal recognition, the Cubans could legally purchase munitions in the United States and have them protected on American merchant vessels to within three miles of the Cuban shore. With recognition, the Cubans would lose that legal immunity. Other members of the cabinet were either silent or noncommittal. Grant said simply, "If there come war, we must try & be prepared for it"—no doubt not the response Fish had hoped for.[27]

Fish made the same argument to Senator John Sherman, who had introduced a joint resolution stating that the United States recognized a "state of war" between Spain and its colony Cuba and would "observe strict neutrality." Sherman was chairman of the Senate Finance Committee, and Fish frankly warned him that if his resolution passed, he should be ready to increase the appropriations necessary to fund the army and navy and "prepare bills for the increase of the public debt."[28]

In the House, the Cubans' warmest advocate was Massachusetts congressman Nathaniel Banks, chairman of the Foreign Affairs Committee. He introduced a joint resolution that the president be "instructed to declare and maintain a strictly impartial neutrality." Banks thought that if the administration "loses the opportunity presented by the present condition of Foreign Affairs, it will not stand the opposition of the people." Edwards Pierrepont, who witnessed much of the pro-Cuban agitation in New York, warned the administration that the Democrats were eagerly waiting for it to "blunder" on the issue so that "they can safely attack us as 'friends of Spain and enemies of freedom' and all that sort of thing." But Fish was moved less by possible political repercussions than by legal considerations. "Belligerency is a fact not a sentiment. . . . There must be something of a national organization, some political entity to which 'belligerency' can alone be accorded." The Cubans had no such entity.[29]

Both the Sherman and Banks resolutions went to committee, but indignation over the administration's stance heightened when Congress published State Department correspondence regarding the Cuban question. Citing a "great ocean tide of national feeling," the *New York Tribune* insisted that the question "is no longer the mere property of a Cabinet, to be sat upon by a number of councilors with locked doors. . . . The question has now been delegated to Congress."[30]

With the issue attracting so much attention, the Cubans launched a public relations offensive, issuing a "manifesto to the American people" that claimed the insurgents had an operating government. Members of the junta descended on Washington to lobby the Senate Military Affairs Committee and other congressmen. They also called on Grant, who questioned them closely about conditions in Cuba, acknowledged that they were "confident" about their prospects, but would not commit on the question of recognition.[31]

Five days later he sent Fish up to Capitol Hill, where, according to one account, "Grant himself could not have made a bigger sensation." Appearing before the House Committee on Foreign Affairs, the secretary defended the administration's nonrecognition policy as "the only one that could be sustained by national honesty and fair dealing and a due regard for the *jus gentium*." Although the insurgents had "kept up a state of armed opposition to the Spanish authority on the island, it was not an opposition that could be dignified with a title much higher than that of a guerilla warfare." Critics insisted that Fish was deceiving the president, who "should open his eyes and follow the national will."

But Fish girded for a fight, gathering information uncovered by private detectives about the junta's bribery of congressmen and others. The day after his visit to the Hill, he pushed the attorney general to authorize a grand jury investigation and indictment.[32]

After weeks of relative quiet, the issue burst forth again in late May 1870, when Democrat Daniel Voorhees of Indiana took the House floor to read a news account of death threats against an American diplomat in Cuba. The officer in question, the consul at Santiago, had attempted to gain satisfaction from Spanish authorities regarding two Americans whose seizure Grant had condemned in his annual message. Denouncing Fish, Voorhees said, "the blood of American citizens cries aloud" in "bitter reproaches against him for his imbecility, his sloth, his disregard of the pride and honor and glory and safety of this Republic." Republican Charles Wesley of Vermont responded, charging hypocrisy by Democrats who condemned Spanish attacks on Americans but averted their eyes while hundreds of American citizens were being slaughtered in the former Confederate states. Democrat S. S. Cox and others alleged that Banks was delaying action on the Cuba resolution to avoid imperiling Senate approval of a controversial treaty to annex Santo Domingo, a project in which both Grant and Banks were deeply interested. Banks denied that he was stalling, but several Republicans joined the ranks of his critics, and the pressure for some action by his committee was growing irresistible.[33]

With the pro-Cuba press calling for Fish's head, the secretary was determined that the administration put up a united front, but a tangle with the president nearly precipitated a cabinet crisis. On May 31 Fish presented the cabinet with a draft presidential message on the neutrality question and on West Indian policy generally. Boutwell warned that it might be "regarded as discourteous to the Senate," but the president approved "every word in it except one passage speaking of John Quincy Adams in terms of warm eulogy." (By this time, steady abuse from the Adamses had so irritated Grant that his resentment extended to the dead as well as the living.) When Fish returned the next day, he found that Grant, apparently influenced by Boutwell, was now wavering; he told Fish that he preferred to send the document to Congress as a report from the State Department rather than as a presidential message. But, Fish countered, what was needed was "the President's expression, not the Secretary's," and a report sent that way would imply a difference of opinion between the two. Grant replied that he "approved every word of it" and would say so in a transmittal letter, but his style of writing was so unlike Fish's that if the paper were sent as a presidential message, everyone would see immediately that it was not the work of Grant himself. Fish responded that "the public understood, as a general rule, the Presidents do not write their own messages." But Grant had in fact written much of what had gone to Congress over his name, and he still demurred. Later that day Fish unloaded his feelings to Secretary of the Navy George Robeson: "I do not feel inclined any longer to be made the mark & object of attack of all who want to criticize the foreign policy of the Administration. . . . [I]f the policy I have urged and pursued, be approved by the Pres[iden]t, as I know it is, it is due to me that he assume it, & present it under his own signature, & not leave me to be still longer assailed by those who would not dare assail him."[34]

The next day, June 2, Grant and Fish continued their discussion of the best procedure to follow. Fish complained, "The President is continually quoted & claimed as not in sympathy with the foreign policy of his Administration, & by no act of his before the Public, is the Public disabused." If another secretary of state could pursue a different policy the president preferred, Fish was more than willing to resign. Grant expressed his sincere hope that Fish would stay. He read to the secretary the message he proposed to send with the "report," but Fish claimed it "would be construed as an entire dissent from the policy that had been pursued." Grant wanted to express his "abhorrence" at the butcheries in Cuba, but Fish thought that too much stress on that point would undermine the administration's policy of nonrecognition. As for sending Fish's draft as a presidential message, Grant said he would have to reduce it by two-thirds, leaving out much of the historical background. Fish thought doing so would "destroy the paper." He aimed to trace the evolution of American policy toward the West Indies as "the natural growth & expansion" from a "narrow policy of neutrality under [George] Washington through the subsequent stages," culminating in the no-transfer principle "which has practically exhibited itself in the Treaty for the Annexation of San Domingo, & is to gradually develop into protection or control of the Islands." Again the secretary complained about critics who sought to sow discord between the president and the secretary and soon intended "to open an attack upon the policy of the Administration."[35]

Soon turned out to be the next day, when the *New York Herald* printed a leaked early version of Banks's report on Cuba in an effort to dislodge the report from the Foreign Affairs Committee, along with a recognition resolution. The report showed, the *Herald* editorialized, "to what straits we have permitted a neighboring colony to be driven by our selfish dread of a war with imbecile Spain." Over the next few days Grant labored over Fish's draft to strike an appropriate balance between sympathy for the Cubans and adherence to nonrecognition.[36]

The leaked committee report did not daunt Fish and his allies. Three days later, allegations of bribery against several members of Congress were leaked from the grand jury and appeared in the *New York Evening Post*. The paper also reported that the junta's representatives had tried to win Grant's approval of recognition, but he had refused to endorse anything "antagonistic to the policy which the Administration expected to follow." Several of the congressmen named in the bribery story vehemently denied the charge and called for the permanent expulsion of the *Evening Post*'s reporter, W. Scott Smith, from the press gallery. A hastily concocted committee concluded that although Smith had been naïve in accepting statements made during grand jury testimony as fact, he could keep his press pass. The investigation into the alleged bribery led to no indictments of any legislators, but at a crucial moment the leaks highlighted the suspicion that the Cuban junta was corrupting members of Congress.[37]

The matter of an official statement by the administration reached a head when Indiana representative Godlove Orth and Ben Butler met with Fish on June 10 to urge the sending of a presidential message before the House debate on recognition, scheduled for June 14. They noted that twenty or thirty "quiet members" who could make the difference in a close vote on a resolution might be swayed by Banks's oratory, but if Grant addressed the question, they would "not go against the President's views." The Democrats, meanwhile, would ally with Banks to drive a wedge between the White House and the State Department. As Caleb Cushing put it, there was an "eager desire that the President should speak . . . and absolute conviction that, if he does speak, his voice will be [as] potential as Revelation." Fish spent all of Sunday, June 12, drafting a new message to submit for Grant's consideration.[38]

The next day Fish presented his new, shorter draft to the president and warned of "the danger of disruption in the party." Still Grant hesitated, citing what Fish had all along suspected was his real reason: the fear that pro-Cuban senators might be offended and refuse to support his Santo Domingo annexation treaty. Fish sought to reassure the president. Senators who opposed annexation also opposed Cuban recognition, and of those who supported the treaty, almost none favored recognition. In short, Fish suggested, the president might actually gain favor for Santo Domingo annexation and lose none by withholding recognition of Cuban belligerency. As tinkering with the draft continued, Fish noted that the "President evidently wishes to add something which may show condemnation of Spain, & more of sympathy with Cuba, than w[oul]d be drawn from my draft." Grant considered citing instances of Spanish seizure of American vessels on the high seas, but Fish pointed out that too much stress on "allegations against Spain" for mistreatment of Americans might imply that a declaration of war was called for. He and Robeson suggested that a more general condemnation of Spanish actions could be followed by an expression of hope that Spain would not disregard US protests and by a warning that a future message might threaten action. After another hour's work, the message was complete, and it was sent to Congress the same day, June 13.[39]

The message stated that nothing had changed since the president's annual message six months earlier to warrant recognition of belligerency. The insurgents held no town or city and had no seat of government, no prize courts or seaports where a prize could be taken, no system for collecting revenue, no elections or government outside of the military camps, no manufacturing, and no trade or commerce. Granting belligerency status under such circumstances would amount to "a gratuitous demonstration of moral support to the rebellion." The document cited both sides for "barbarous violation of the rules of civilized nations," but it also stipulated that "fighting, though fierce and protracted, does not alone constitute war." Recognition required the presence of "military forces acting in accordance with the rules and customs of war" and, "above all, a *de facto* political organization of the insurgents" sufficient to constitute a state if left to itself.

In addition, the message noted that American vessels would incur the risks of visit and search if the US government recognized belligerency and proclaimed neutrality. As Grant had insisted, a paragraph was inserted to condemn Spain "executing American citizens without proper trial, and confiscating or embargoing the property of American citizens." He stated, "All proper steps have been taken and are being pressed for the proper reparation of every indignity complained of."

But the message also scored the Cuban junta for using an "apparently plausible demand for a mere recognition of belligerency" as a cover for a scheme to "embroil this Government in complications and possible hostilities with Spain." In light of the controversy over the grand jury leak, the next passage held particular significance: "It is stated on what I have reason to regard as good authority that Cuban bonds have been prepared to a large amount, whose payment is made dependent upon the recognition by the United States of either Cuban belligerency or independence. The object of making their value thus contingent upon the action of this Government is a subject for serious reflection." In place of this last phrase, Fish's draft had charged that the bonds might "in corrupt or designing hands be a premium to efforts towards influencing the opinions which in a popular government are reflected eventually in the action of government." Despite the veiled language adopted, few in Congress or the press could miss the warning that the administration was prepared to remove the gloves to sustain its position.[40]

Grant's message created a sensation. As the clerk read it to the House, a reporter noted, "Banks looked surprised and annoyed, and was quite restless in his seat when it became apparent that the message was nothing less than an attempt at a reply to his own report upon Cuba." Cox of New York jumped to his feet and declared that under the Constitution, presidential messages were limited to providing information, but Grant had presumed to level an "attack" against the report of the Committee on Foreign Affairs. "I would treat it as some of the messages of Andrew Johnson were treated," the Democrat said. "I would lay it on the table without sending it to a committee," that is, ignore it. Banks made a motion to table the message, but under pressure from Republican colleagues, he agreed that it be referred to his committee.[41]

The next day Grant was still "nervous" about the message, worried that some were condemning it as a "veto in advance." He told the cabinet he feared "we made a mistake," but the day's events showed otherwise. In the House, Banks finally presented his resolutions. The first "authorized and instructed" the president to "declare and maintain a strictly impartial neutrality" in "the contest now existing" between the people of Cuba and the Spanish government. The second called for the application of existing US neutrality law. And the third "authorized and requested" the president to remonstrate against the "barbarous manner in which the war in Cuba has been conducted" and to solicit the aid of other governments to try to secure the observance of the laws of war. A minority of the Foreign Affairs Committee produced a report that largely echoed both the president's message and Fish's private strictures against the Cuban junta. After a day of debate, the administration held the upper hand. The House voted 101 to 88 to adopt only Banks's third resolution and to remove the phrase "and requested." Although more than thirty Republicans voted against this essential dismissal of the pro-Cuba movement, the vast majority stood by the administration. This outcome in the House snuffed out any threat of recognition of belligerency in the Senate.[42]

The result sparked jubilation in the administration. Fish's colleagues congratulated him and labeled the proceedings in the House "the greatest triumph the Administration had yet achieved." Fish himself took pride that the episode "has served to concentrate & consolidate the party, & to exhibit a policy, & the capacity of rallying the party." "In a higher view," he added, "it has shown that the Representatives of the Country can rise above the temporary & fervent appeals of a momentary excitement of popular sympathy in support of the obligations of national duties." A few days later the secretary noted that Grant "seemed very well satisfied with the result of the Cuba discussion." When Fish asked if he still had regrets about sending the message, the president replied that although it had sparked "violent & denunciatory" debate, "I like the vote very much." "The measure was right," he later told Fish, "& the whole Country acquiesces in it."[43]

Certainly not the whole country. Banks won praise from many Cuba supporters, including an Illinois Republican who labeled Grant "the apologist of the most inhuman and monstrous tyranny that ever disgraced any age." Such outbursts proved to be the exception, however. "The great Cuban debate is over," stated the *New York Times*, and "the people would never have forgiven" the president "if he had been led astray by those who denounce him for not 'making Cuba free.'" In a striking turnabout, the erstwhile champion of the Cubans, the *New York Herald*, described the House action as "not only a great victory for the sound administrative policy of General Grant, but a most important victory for the republican party itself over the strong and dangerous temptation to go filibustering into Cuba." Moreover, said the *Herald*, the president was "strengthened in Congress as the head and executive embodiment of his party" and "in the general policy of his administration—peace, progress, retrenchment, the lessening of our burden of taxes and the redemption of the public debt." It was not without irony that the Democrats, the party that for decades had exalted Andrew Jackson's executive assertiveness, now lashed out at Grant for interfering with the legislative branch. In the long view, Grant's Cuba message stood as an important milestone in the rehabilitation of presidential influence after the dismal years of Andrew Johnson.[44]

Grant readily acknowledged that he owed Fish a great debt of gratitude. A few weeks later, when he sought to deter the secretary from thoughts of leaving the cabinet, he returned to the subject of Cuba and thanked Fish for his "steadiness & wisdom" in saving him from making serious mistakes on two occasions. One was Fish's withholding of the neutrality proclamation Grant had signed the previous summer. In the other, Grant said, "you led me against my judgment at the time—you almost forced me—in the matter of signing the late Cuban message, and I now see how right it was, and I desire most sincerely to thank you."[45]

Fish could also take satisfaction that administration policy had killed any possibility of an American annexation of Cuba. Nonetheless, he stood by the president and lent his assistance with another project, the annexation of Santo Domingo, that Grant held much closer to his heart. The Santo Domingo issue reached its denouement at about the same time as the Cuban crisis, but it ended far less happily for the president.

9

★ ★ ★ ★ ★

THE GATE TO
THE CARIBBEAN SEA

In the *Alabama* claims and the Cuban insurrection, the Grant administration confronted problems spurred by unavoidable circumstances that
by their nature demanded a response. On another foreign policy question, Grant enunciated a more pointed strategic vision: acquisition of the
Caribbean island nation of the Dominican Republic, commonly referred
to in this era as Santo Domingo. For no other initiative did Grant exhibit
more fervent advocacy, and in no other instance did he encounter more
inflamed opposition. What could have been a rational consideration of
the nation's interest degenerated into a personal conflict between the
president and Charles Sumner—a titanic struggle that ended in the defeat of Grant's dream and contributed to the dissolution of Sumner's
usefulness in the Senate. As the drama unfolded during the first year
and a half of the term, it revealed an extraordinary cast of characters—
some tainted, others suspect, and a few simply bizarre. Whether rightly
or not, Santo Domingo cast a shadow over Grant's administration that
persists to this day.

Santo Domingo occupied the eastern two-thirds of Hispaniola,
the second largest island in the Antilles. Its 21,000 square miles made
it larger than eight states in the Union. The country's rich soil could
potentially yield large quantities of tobacco, coffee, sugar, cacao, and
other commodities for export. Its dense forests held large stands of ma-
hogany, satinwood, and other timbers. Estimates placed the country's

199

population at between 100,000 and 300,000, with the actual number probably closer to the former. The populace included a small group of whites largely of Spanish descent, while the vast majority of inhabitants were black or mixed race.[1]

Ostensibly a republic, Santo Domingo had suffered decades of political instability. After gaining independence from Spain in 1821, the country soon came under the dominance of Haiti, which shared the island with Santo Domingo and had ousted its French masters in 1804. Not until 1844 did the Dominicans defeat the Haitian occupation and create a truly independent nation. But even then the country remained vulnerable to invasion or raids from Haiti and was riven by factions at home, some of which drew on the assistance of Haitian allies. Continued fighting and sham elections led to revolving-door governments. In 1861 Spain retook the country, but in the face of determined Dominican resistance, the Spanish withdrew again in 1865. In the latest upheaval in early 1868, the government of President José Cabral fell to the forces of Buenaventura Báez. Báez had held the presidency three times before, and his grip on the office was hardly less tenuous now, for Cabral and his allies continued an armed opposition. With the treasury empty and enemies in the field, the Báez government gravitated toward seeking outside help in the form of a protectorate or outright annexation, with connection to the United States the most attractive prospect.[2]

The idea of forging such a link had arisen long before the Grant administration. Several times during the 1840s and 1850s the United States had dispatched officers to the Caribbean nation to investigate its economic and strategic potential. Of particular interest was the capacious Bay of Samaná, which overlooked the Atlantic Ocean from a commanding position on the island's eastern coast. In 1854 US Army engineer Captain George McClellan had enthusiastically endorsed the creation of a US naval station. His recommendation did not bear fruit, but feelers for "a more intimate connection" with Santo Domingo resumed after the second ouster of the Spanish. Andrew Johnson's expansionist secretary of state William Seward opened negotiations with the Cabral government for a lease of the bay, which made some progress until Cabral lost power to Báez in 1868. The notion that Samaná Bay might go begging caused some Americans to fear a European intrusion in the hemisphere. In May 1868 Charles Sumner expressed his apprehension to Seward about a possible "movement on the part of the North German Confederation to obtain a naval station in the West Indies."[3]

The Báez government was hardly up and running when it moved

to restart negotiations with the United States. It soon found an eager ally in J. Somers Smith, the American commercial agent (the State Department's principal representative in Santo Domingo), who asked Seward for authority to negotiate an agreement regarding Samaná. The Dominican government also enlisted the services of Joseph W. Fabens, an American businessman and longtime advocate of American investment in Santo Domingo. Closely associated with Fabens was William L. Cazneau, another American émigré who had first gone to Santo Domingo in 1854 on a fact-finding mission for the State Department. With political turmoil seemingly endemic, Santo Domingo's economic potential was largely underdeveloped. As was (and is) typical of entrepreneurs contemplating investment in underdeveloped regions, Fabens and Cazneau asked the Dominican government for various kinds of concessions, from which they naturally expected to profit. One promising venture was their concession to launch a geological and mineralogical survey of the country, for which they would be compensated by title to one-fifth of the public lands surveyed. Secretary Seward congratulated Fabens for securing this project, saying, "It is especially gratifying to see the citizens of the United States take so deep an interest in developing the resources of a sister Republic." The prospects for successful American enterprise in Santo Domingo would grow with closer ties between the two nations, and in the spring of 1868 Fabens gladly agreed to Báez's request that he travel to Washington to push for such a connection.[4]

Although Smith and Fabens shared the same ultimate goal, Smith viewed Fabens warily as a self-seeking adventurer. Nearing the close of his lackluster diplomatic career, Smith apparently feared that Fabens's lobbying in Washington threatened to steal his glory as the broker of American-Dominican union. Smith wrote to Seward that Fabens had no authority to speak for the Dominican government and later claimed that the movement for annexation "all came from me." In November 1868, at Báez's request, Smith sent his own son to Washington to convey a desire for annexation. A delighted Seward inserted into Johnson's last annual message a forthright call for the acquisition of both the Dominican Republic and Haiti, and Báez assured the American president of his government's "ineffable satisfaction at the ideas expressed by Your Excellency." The Dominicans considered raising the American flag and placing themselves "by acclamation" under the government of the United States, but Smith discouraged such a move prior to congressional consideration of the question. Still, he continued to tout the mutual advantages of annexation "*at once.*"[5]

Meanwhile, Fabens, as confidential agent for the Dominicans, worked to enlist support on their behalf. No lone wolf, he counted among his many business contacts steamship magnate and financier C. K. Garrison, as well as Spofford, Tileston, a prominent New York mercantile and financial concern that was launching a steamship line to Santo Domingo and contemplating other enterprises there. In Washington, Fabens cultivated strategic alliances not only with Seward but also with members of Congress, especially Nathaniel Banks, chairman of the House Committee on Foreign Affairs, and his Massachusetts colleague Ben Butler.[6]

Before acting, Banks sought to ascertain President-elect Grant's view. Through intermediary Adam Badeau, Banks stressed "the advantages of the union," but he offered to delay the question until after the inauguration. Badeau reported that the president-elect was "in favor of the proposition" and that "he did not desire its postponement, but preferred that the question should be submitted to Congress without delay." The push for Dominican annexation was well under way in the waning months of the Johnson administration, and Grant would have been perfectly content to have the issue settled before he entered the White House.[7]

In early January 1869 Fabens first pursued the protectorate alternative, revealing to Seward and others the Dominican government's request for such an arrangement. Banks sponsored a resolution in the House authorizing the president to extend protection to both Haiti and the Dominican Republic, but critics charged that the resolution would delegate to the president the congressional power to make war, lead to an entangling alliance, and violate long-standing policy against interfering in other nations' internal affairs. Banks's allies insisted that the resolution was entirely consistent with the Monroe Doctrine, but few rallied to his cause. The House voted overwhelmingly, 126 to 36, to table the resolution.[8]

After this disappointing outcome, Fabens moved on to the alternative plan of pushing for outright annexation, armed with a message from Dominican foreign minister M. M. Gautier that his country was "prepared for the great event." Banks's committee colleague, Indiana representative Godlove Orth, introduced a resolution calling for the annexation of the Dominican Republic as a territory and, after the establishment of a republican government, its eventual admission as a state. But Orth offered no accompanying report explaining annexation's desirability, and without ado the House tabled his resolution by a vote of 110 to 63.[9]

The fate of the two House resolutions exemplified paradoxical attitudes. Although annexation would burden the United States with responsibilities in Santo Domingo far more directly and irrevocably than would protectorate status, many saw annexation as preferable. A protectorate would violate long-standing American practice, but annexation had ample precedent in the history of American expansion. "It is a magnificent island," *Chicago Tribune* proprietor Joseph Medill wrote to Banks, "and in our hands would be worth untold millions to commerce." Still, as the House votes showed, the project faced an uphill fight. The *New York Times* labeled it a "mischievous and absurd" scheme fueled by "private, speculative and even corrupt considerations."[10]

The backers did not lose heart. Two weeks before Seward left office, Banks persuaded him to send Fabens to Santo Domingo on a fact-finding mission to consult with Dominican authorities about annexation. Banks armed Fabens with a letter praising the foresight of President Báez and noting that "Santo Domingo can not fail to be one of the most populous, wealthy and powerful states of the Union." Moreover, he claimed that "sources" (which he did not name) had led him to "believe that the policy upon which this movement is based, has General Grant's concurrence and will constitute a leading feature in the policy of his Administration. Whether or not we succeed now, I have full confidence that we shall succeed hereafter." As he prepared to head back to the island, Fabens told Banks, "I anticipate no difficulty in a speedy and satisfactory solution of the question," and when he returned to Washington a month later, he reported that the "matter [was] fully arranged."[11]

Although the House votes left the Dominican project in limbo, the Johnson administration bequeathed a West Indian legacy of sorts in the form of a treaty with Denmark for the purchase of the island of St. Thomas. At thirty-one square miles, St. Thomas was less than one-hundredth the size of the Dominican Republic. With a price tag of $7.5 million, the Caribbean speck would cost more than the vast territory of Alaska, another Seward acquisition that left many Americans cold. Within a month of the signing of the purchase treaty in October 1867, the hurricane-prone island suffered an earthquake and a tidal wave, which wrecked an American naval vessel and made the place seem like the anti-paradise. Shortly thereafter, the House of Representatives overwhelmingly resolved that "in the present financial condition of the country any further purchases of territory are inexpedient."[12]

The St. Thomas treaty languished in the Senate, but after the election of 1868 the Danes intensified their drive for ratification. They found little support in the Senate or in the new administration. Two months before the inauguration, Sumner informed the Danes that the treaty had no chance. For his part, Grant had scant taste for anything produced by Seward and Johnson. At an early cabinet meeting he was "wholly averse" to endorsing ratification and declared that he did "not like these purchases." For Fish, the only consideration that might incline him toward approval was the possibility that Denmark could sell the island to another power, thus raising security concerns for the United States. But Grant was unmoved. He was content to let the Senate make a decision "without interference from the Administration." After a year's importunities by the Danes, he relented to the extent that he considered advising the Senate that because the United States had negotiated the treaty and Denmark was "a feeble power," ratification would be consistent with American "dignity & power." But at Fish's suggestion, he intimated this view to senators in private rather than by formal message. In March 1870 the Foreign Relations Committee voted unanimously against the treaty, and the time for ratification expired before a vote by the full Senate. Long before the lapse of the St. Thomas treaty, however, Grant had concluded that the country could gain a great deal more at a much lower price by annexing Santo Domingo.[13]

The Dominicans had gained scant support for their project in the waning days of the Johnson administration, and three weeks after Grant's inauguration, Fabens was back in the United States, determined to revive its sagging fortunes. In early April he gave the State Department a report on the natural resources and political and economic condition of the island. Before Fish even had time to read it, he found Fabens in his office, presenting the Dominican government's formal proposal for annexation and admission as a state. Fish gave the plan a frosty reception. His "impressions were against it," he said, and besides, the current special session of the Senate was too short to consider the notion.[14]

The next morning Fabens and Paul Spofford of Spofford, Tileston went to the White House, where, as Fabens put it, the two men "arranged" their "plan of campaign." They apparently met no objection from Grant, for at noon Fabens and Spofford headed up to Capitol Hill, where they held court in the committee room of the Committee on Territories. Throughout the afternoon a succession of senators came by to meet the two-man lobby, including the half-paralyzed but redoubtable Oliver Morton of Indiana, who arrived "in an arm chair borne by 3 black men." The visitors included some of the Senate's leading men—"all wide awake," according to Fabens.[15]

While Fabens and Spofford were singing the praises of Santo Domingo at the Capitol, Fish presented their proposal to the cabinet in a decidedly lower key. He told the president and his colleagues that he was "opposed to considering it at present." Action would have to originate in Congress, Fish said, and no time remained to act before the close of the present short session. After some inconclusive conversation, "the subject was passed by."[16]

Fish's diary entry about this April 6 cabinet meeting was silent as to Grant's attitude, but throughout the spring, others besides Fabens pushed the Dominican project. From Santo Domingo, Smith reported that with few exceptions, annexation was the "general wish of all parties." J. P. O'Sullivan, a longtime acquaintance of Báez and sometime resident of Santo Domingo, hoped to develop economic interests on the island. He took letters of introduction from both Báez and Foreign Minister Gautier to Grant, with whom he talked up the nation's assets. Gautier's letter specifically asked the president to send a representative to Santo Domingo to meet with government leaders. Accompanying O'Sullivan to the White House was California senator Cornelius Cole, another ardent annexationist. Cole dreamed of a canal through Central America that would slash travel time between his state and the East Coast. Acquisition of the Dominican Republic, particularly Samaná Bay, would give the United States a superb vantage point from which to protect the eastern terminus of a canal. Admiral David Porter, the nation's highest ranking naval officer, agreed that Samaná was especially well adapted to the navy's needs.[17]

By the third week of April, Fabens confidently told his partner Cazneau that the president was "very favorably disposed" toward their project, but in fact, Grant would not be rushed. He told Fabens that he could not "look at Sto. Domingo" until after the Senate adjourned, which it did on April 22. Still, the irrepressible Fabens expressed confidence that annexation could be carried when the next session convened in December. But Fabens's own enthusiasm may have falsely fueled his optimism, for he also told Cazneau that Fish was "much interested" and would "cooperate"—an exaggeration of the secretary's attitude at that point, if not a complete fabrication. As late as mid-May, Fish told Edward Thornton that the United States had "no intention whatever of yielding" to the pleas of the Báez government. Although the United States might be willing to "annex countries inhabited by the Anglo-Saxon race and accustomed to self Government, the incorporation of those peopled by the Latin race would be but the beginning of years of conflict and anarchy."[18]

The vehemence of Fish's response suggests that the secretary was blowing off steam about a project for which he initially had little enthusiasm but might have to accept as a loyal member of the administration. As Grant later noted, after hearing from Fabens and others, and "in view of the facts which had been laid before me, and with an earnest desire to maintain the 'Monroe Doctrine,' I believed that I would be derelict in my duty if I did not take measures to ascertain the exact wish of the Government and inhabitants of the Republic of San Domingo in regard to annexation and communicate the information to the people of the United States." He directed Fish to request that the Navy Department send a man-of-war, under the command of "a discreet and intelligent officer," to visit the Dominican Republic and "report upon the condition of affairs." Rather than depending solely on the assertions of Fabens and his allies, "it was thought best," as Fish later put it, "not to act without further information, derived through accurate and trustworthy sources, of which the administration had actual knowledge." Grant and Fish wanted the naval officer to make a comprehensive survey of Dominican political parties and their attitudes toward the United States and other powers, the country's agriculture and commerce, and the government's foreign and domestic debt. Further, they wished to know more about "the extent and character of foreign influence" on the government, as well as how the Dominican people felt about annexation by the United States or the lease of Samaná Bay.[19]

A week earlier the navy had ordered an investigation into whether the bay offered a good position for a coaling station. It now seemed sensible to combine these two missions, and the navy dispatched the USS *Nipsic* under Thomas Selfridge Jr., an Annapolis graduate seasoned by service during the Civil War. But Selfridge's mission ended abruptly in failure. Off the coast of Cuba, the *Nipsic*'s propeller broke off, and the ship limped under sail to Port-au-Prince, Haiti, before heading back to the United States. Selfridge never set foot in the Dominican Republic and had nothing to offer about Dominican affairs.[20]

While the naval mission was in preparation, Fabens encouraged the firm of Spofford, Tileston to offer transportation to American officials on the maiden voyage of its new steamship service to the Caribbean, during which they could examine St. Thomas and especially Santo Domingo. Fabens told Assistant Secretary of State J. C. Bancroft Davis that "an accurate and detailed report of the actual situation of affairs in those islands would be desirable in the present state of the 'Sto Domingo question.'" Not content to rely solely on the navy, the administration decided to send another investigator, Benjamin Hunt, who had spent more than fifteen years in the region.[21]

In the 1840s Hunt had established a mercantile house in Haiti; he soon amassed a considerable fortune and cultivated a deep interest in Caribbean society. In 1858 he retired to Philadelphia, where he pursued his scholarly interest in the tropics. He was an ardent abolitionist, and after the Civil War he championed the rights of African Americans. Hunt had given long and serious study to the benefits of American expansion southward, and particularly its impact on race relations. He had written in 1866 that blacks were particularly "suited" to "facilitate future extension towards the tropics." Because of "their special climatic fitness," he argued, "our people of color must assist" in carrying "thither our enterprise, and with it our laws and institutions." In pursuit of their "own interests and happiness," they could assist in the country's "expansion beyond its present limits; and, soon or late, should the practical assertion of our 'Monroe Doctrine' make it necessary to carry our arms into those latitudes, the late war has shown us where to find soldiers."[22]

Fish considered Hunt "peculiarly well qualified" to investigate Santo Domingo. The secretary instructed him to collect information about the population, including the proportions of whites, Africans, Indians, and "mixtures" of these groups. He also directed Hunt to explore the country's agriculture and extractive industries and to ascertain the extent of its commerce as well as the government's revenue and debt, both domestic and foreign. In addition, Fish asked Hunt to "obtain full and accurate information in regard to the disposition of the government and people of that republic toward the United States, the character of the government, whether it be military or civil, whether it be stable or liable to be overthrown. . . . Inquiry should also be made as to whether any other foreign power may be seeking to obtain possession of any part of that country."[23]

Spofford, Tileston's ship *Tybee* was scheduled to sail in early June. Hunt made preparations to depart and received his instructions dated June 2. But the sixty-one-year-old scholar became seriously ill, and on June 7 he reluctantly wired Fish that he could not make the trip. The next day Fish telegraphed the company that he was going to appoint a replacement for Hunt, but by the time his message arrived, the *Tybee* had already set sail. After the abortive *Nipsic* operation, the collapse of this second fact-finding mission, especially one that would have been conducted by a person of Hunt's expertise, would have enormous consequences.[24]

Fabens was on board the *Tybee*, and after he arrived in Santo Domingo, authorities there asked him to return to Washington and renew their request that the administration send a representative to Santo Domingo to discuss annexation. They also wanted Fabens to reiterate an earlier request for the dispatch of an American warship to help protect the Dominican government from a rebel vessel, the *Telégrafo*, prowling nearby waters. On his return to the United States, Fabens wrote to Fish about the *Telégrafo*, and he wrote to Sumner as well, enclosing a copy of his letter to Fish. Although Fabens's note to Sumner did not mention the annexation project, his call for "one or more of our national vessels" implied the desirability of at least an informal protectorate, which would "give an immense impetus to the peaceful development of the true interests of the Republic." In his reply from Boston, Sumner did not contradict Fabens's view and voiced no opposition to annexation. He merely wrote that he regretted that because Congress was in recess, he could not discuss the question with the secretary of state. Still, he told Fabens, "I beg to assure you of my desire to serve the people for whom you are acting, but you will understand that without access to the doc[umen]ts on file at Washington, I can do little more than send good wishes." *Good wishes.* Sumner's cautious cordiality was in stark contrast to the attitude he would later assume after Grant embraced the Dominican project.[25]

Soon after arriving in New York, Fabens went down to Washington and provided evidence that the *Telégrafo*'s operations posed threats to American merchant vessels, including the *Tybee*. The next day Grant ordered the USS *Seminole* to head to the Caribbean and capture the *Telégrafo* as an illegal ship "interfering with American commerce." On the question of annexation, Fabens was more direct than he had been with Sumner. He gave Fish a letter from Gautier urging the United States to send a commissioner to discuss annexation. "The hour is propitious," Gautier advised, "and the favorable moment should not be lost."[26]

It is not clear when Grant latched on to annexation with his wonted "bulldog grip," but in early July Gautier's message conveyed via Fabens seemed to be saying, "Fish or cut bait." At his meeting with Secretary Fish on July 9, Fabens noted that the *Tybee* would sail again on the seventeenth, and he urged the administration to select a "suitable person" to go to Santo Domingo at that time to make "a true and accurate report

Orville E. Babcock (Library of Congress)

of the present political situation of that island." Fabens hinted that he himself might fill the bill, but Fish would not consider appointing him. On July 10 Spofford, Tileston wrote to Fish again, offering free passage "to any one you may designate should you wish to obtain reliable information about the Island." Grant felt pressured to act and decided to entrust the task to one of his secretaries, Orville Babcock.[27]

As Grant's third selection for the delicate mission, Babcock could hardly be described as the chosen agent of a conspiracy cooked up by Fabens and Cazneau, as some historical accounts would have it. Compared with Hunt, Babcock possessed minimal knowledge of the West Indies. He was not fluent in Spanish. Although Grant had told him that Báez spoke English, he did not, and the two men would require an interpreter. Babcock had never met Fabens or Cazneau; nor, apparently, had he taken much part, if any, in administration discussions about Santo Domingo. Before Grant's decision to send him to the island, Babcock had gone to New York, where he expected to remain for most of the summer. Now he received a telegram calling him back to Washington. Although he possessed neither broad knowledge nor deep intellectual curiosity, the thirty-three-year-old Babcock exhibited a certain savvy in sizing up men and a certain cunning in dealing with them. Given his initial unfamiliarity with the substantive issues of the mission, his chief qualification was his unswerving commitment to serve Grant.[28]

Babcock arrived in Washington on July 13 and learned the nature of his assignment. He told Grant that he should not accept free passage from Spofford, Tileston because "those people having an interest in the steamship company might feel that they had a right to ask me questions, which I should not want to answer." Grant agreed and ordered the State Department to pay for the trip out of the president's secret contingency fund. Babcock's official instructions, signed by Fish, replicated Hunt's almost word for word, except for an additional charge to ascertain the rate of interest on the public debt and the condition of the nation's currency.[29]

Grant also gave Babcock "verbal instructions" that went beyond the charge to investigate Santo Domingo's resources. The administration had received mixed reports regarding the Dominicans' view of annexation. Some accounts said that a number of government officials favored it, but Báez did not. As Grant later put it, "Gen. Babcock was sent to Sto Domingo to ascertain so far as he could the wishes of the Dominican people and Government with respect to annexation to the United States. If he found them favorable he was directed to ascertain the terms on which they desired annexation." Babcock had no authority to negotiate a treaty. He interpreted his orders to mean that he should indicate to Báez that he was open to any suggestion or proposal the Dominican government cared to make, which he would carry back to Grant for his consideration.[30]

With little time to prepare, Babcock headed back to New York for the ship's July 17 departure. Before boarding the *Tybee*, he dropped by the Spofford offices, where he met Fabens for the first time. On the ship he discovered that in addition to Fabens, his fellow passengers included Cornelius Cole and J. P. O'Sullivan, neither of whom he knew. Initially he was skeptical of these men and remained tight-lipped about his mission. He speculated that Cole was traveling to Santo Domingo on "business (?)" and dismissed O'Sullivan as "an adventurer, nothing more," headed to the island "on some RR scheme." After four days at sea, he had a long talk with Fabens and pegged him as "an enthusiast." As the *Tybee* steamed toward Santo Domingo, Babcock noted, "Cannot tell much about that country from these people, too much interest." He eventually warmed to Fabens and Cole but continued to resent the blowhard O'Sullivan for claiming to speak for the administration. On shipboard Babcock talked with several passengers who lived in the country and found that "all speak in favor of the Island." One of them, a merchant of Spanish descent, said the people might initially be skeptical about annexation but "would in a short time all vote for it."[31]

The *Tybee* made an initial stop at Samaná Bay, where an island housed a "splendid coal station." Babcock noted that the people were "all scared" after a recent raid by the rebel ship *Telégrafo*, and he thought that if an American man-of-war were lying in the harbor it could "keep all perfectly quiet here." He judged that the soil on the nearby mountains must be "very fine," given the abundance of corn, cocoa, bananas, and other fruit he saw. "I have no doubt but this island would feed 3 or 4 millions of people if properly cultivated." He initially found the people to be "ignorant but not indolent." After another week, however, he wrote home to his wife that "the people are indolent and ignorant. The best class of people are the American Negroes who have come here from time to time."[32]

On July 27 the *Tybee* hove into the waters off the town of Santo Domingo, the capital. In his diary Babcock jotted down, "See Mc[C]lellan's description"—indicating he had found time to study at least some of the previous reports about Santo Domingo. President Báez was away at Azua, and Babcock was greeted by Gautier, who offered him quarters in the presidential palace. He declined and took a room at the local hotel. He had not been on shore long before Fabens took him to meet Cazneau and Cazneau's wife Jane. Twice during the 1850s Cazneau had conducted investigations similar to Babcock's assignment, and Mrs. Cazneau had written extensively about the West Indies and shared her husband's enthusiasm for annexation. Babcock at first dismissed the Cazneaus as "nice old people from Texas," but before long he was looking forward to escaping his bug-infested hotel to enjoy pleasant evenings with the couple at their plantation house. He was soon "on good terms" with Senator Cole as well and showed him his instructions from Fish, "all in confidence—on his word." The helpful senator volunteered "any assistance" the inexperienced Babcock might like.[33]

Cole and O'Sullivan were so eager for Babcock to start discussions with Báez that they suggested that Babcock and the other Americans take the *Tybee* and pick the president up at Azua, some sixty miles distant. Babcock agreed. Though pleased by the surprise visit, Báez said he would be unable to return with the Americans. He entertained them at dinner, giving Babcock "the seat of honor" on his right. Báez described the rebels as few in number and little more than cattle thieves. He blamed foreign powers for inciting uprisings "to prevent the U.S. from having the island and in hopes of keeping up the discord." Babcock recorded in his diary, "He says he has the kindest feelings for the U.S. and that 'everything is possible.'" But, the visitor sniffed, "This is decidedly Spanish." The presence of others prevented the two men from engaging in substantive conversation.[34]

During the week before the president returned to the capital, Babcock explored the vicinity and was impressed by its agricultural and commercial potential. Relations with his fellow Americans ripened. Cole cultivated his avuncular role, imploring his young friend to "let no chance pass to get the Island" and advising him "to hoist the flag" if the opportunity presented itself. After Babcock's initial wariness of Fabens, the two men grew closer as the essential congruence of their aims became clearer. Fabens showed Babcock "his papers," presumably the correspondence from the Dominican government endorsing annexation. It was Fabens's opinion that "these people will consent to most any reasonable terms," although he thought payment of "an advance" would be necessary. Fabens's "papers," Babcock concluded, revealed "a much more favorable state of affairs than I expected—it looks as if something might be done. Shall know as soon as I see Báez and have a talk with him."[35]

On the downside, Babcock took an instant disliking to commercial agent Smith, whom he considered "perfectly unfit" for his office. Something of a windbag, Smith claimed to be "the originator of the Samaná business," but Babcock saw him as lacking the proper regard for Grant and as "simply a tool of Seward," who had appointed him. Insisting that Báez was "a despot of the worst kind," Smith sympathized with Cabral, the leader of the opposition forces. Cazneau suspected the agent of being a conduit for communication among the rebels. Smith made no secret of the fact that he had granted asylum to some of the Cabralistas and had even charged the State Department for the expense. Babcock thought such asylum put "a premium on revolution" and that Smith had arrogated to "a Consulate what is only granted to a full minister." The State Department agreed and sent Smith a mild rebuke. At the very least, Smith was erratic. In one breath he projected himself as the father of the annexation project, and in the next he questioned "our wanting Sto. Domingo now that we can get Cuba." It should have come as no surprise to Smith that Babcock did not welcome him into his conversations with the Dominican leaders.[36]

Báez returned to the city of Santo Domingo on August 7. On the same day Babcock showed Cazneau "some of my papers" and asked him to serve as his interpreter. Cazneau agreed and informed Babcock about the so-called Hartmont loan, an onerous agreement the destitute Dominican government had entered into with a British firm in May. Under the contract's terms, Hartmont would lend the Dominican Republic £420,000, less a £100,000 commission. At the signing, the firm had given the government an initial payment of £37,000 (for which it expected repayment of £50,000) and promised to furnish the remainder by the end of the year. As a guarantee of repayment, which was to take place over twenty-five years, the government pledged customs revenue, coal and other mines, timber from government forests, and guano deposits. The effective annual interest rate was 18 percent. To raise the funds for the loan to the Dominicans, Hartmont was going to float bonds, primarily in Europe, but if it failed to sell a sufficient number to obtain the full loan amount by December 31, 1869, the deal would be off. Smith had already informed Fish about this loan agreement, and he had also warned Báez of its possible impact on the prospects for annexation. If the loan was executed and annexation went through, the United States could find itself saddled with a large debt. That prospect could kill annexation. Yet, Cazneau warned Babcock, without annexation, the loan to the Dominicans could still be "a dangerous thing for us, for of course when they did not pay the loan, England—as usual—would come in to protect her citizens, and get possession of the Gulf." Cazneau may have invoked these visions of British imperial villainy merely to light a fire under Babcock in the negotiations, but Babcock recorded in his diary, "I have little doubt but such is the scheme."[37]

Substantive discussions between Babcock and Báez began during the second week in August. Babcock called on Cazneau and Fabens for assistance, but not Smith. Babcock laid his cards on the table: He had not come to buy the island, "as such an offer would be an insult." Instead, he had come as a representative of President Grant in response to Báez's communication to the State Department that, as Babcock put it, Santo Domingo "had internal and external troubles, and the union of the two republics would improve both." Báez replied that his country had long been "going backward," and he was convinced it had "no chance but Annexation." When Babcock invited him to present a proposition, Báez said he feared that any proposal he made would be rejected. "I suggested," Babcock recorded in his diary, "that I thought President G. would be able to pay something down, say $100,000—but I would not pledge this—that I was certain that certain munitions of war &c. would be paid also," and that, "as a guarantee," the Dominican government "should cede to us Samaná." Báez asked Babcock to "draw up some notes to submit to him," and he agreed. Thus Babcock, who had started by asking Báez to make a proposal, wound up being the first to put something in writing. In this task Cazneau was happy to lend a hand.[38]

When negotiations resumed, Babcock reiterated that he was authorized simply to transmit any proposition that Báez "might wish to make to President Grant." He gave Báez the "few notes" he and Cazneau had prepared, describing them as "simply ideas not an offer." Báez generally approved of their ideas and suggested that before Babcock made a second trip to Santo Domingo with the text of a formal treaty, he should get assurances from a sufficient number in Congress that it would be ratified. "I assured him," Babcock recorded, "that Genl Grant would not enter into any treaty without weighing the matter well, and feeling assured that it would be approved." When Báez asked about "the shape his proposition must take," Babcock told him that he "wanted something to show Prest Grant, to assure him that Prest Báez would make such & such a treaty." Báez agreed to have Gautier prepare a memorandum. After the meeting, Babcock confidently recorded in his diary, "He seems determined to bring the thing about, it is all he can do now and save his head, or his govt, to better speak . . . but we cannot tell until they put it into writing."[39]

During a lapse in the talks, Babcock set off with Fabens on a five-day tour through the country, an escapade that tightened the relationship between the two men. Along the way, Babcock was struck by the people's lassitude. "They are all Macawber. They seem to think that the Americans will come in and then all will be well." Still, the soil seemed "splendid" and "susceptible of the highest cultivation," needing only an energetic population to bring forth abundance. The travelers hoped to examine the nation's reputed gold mines but had meager luck. Finding only a few women panning for gold, the Americans tried their hand but netted only "a good deal of fun."[40]

Before long, however, Babcock relished the prospects of a more tangible yield. On the fourth day out, the party reached Palenque, a region of sun-drenched savannas extending to beautiful beaches on the southern coast. The next day they returned to Santo Domingo city, and that evening an exhausted Babcock let down his guard in his diary. "I shall be pleased to have the 1000 acres of Palenque promised in case of annexation," he wrote. "It may make my fortune." He did not say who had made the promise, but it was probably not the Dominicans, for in later discussions with Báez, Babcock refused an offer of land from the Dominican government because it might jeopardize American approval of an annexation treaty. It is likely that Fabens made the promise, expecting to give Babcock land he would receive from his company's surveying project. Babcock did not say when the promise was made, but circumstantial evidence suggests that it came after his initial wariness of Fabens; indeed, it may have helped allay that wariness. After Babcock left the island, Fabens wrote to him of his desire to "interest you, in a *material* way, in our Survey Company." Annexation, he wrote, "will prove the bright beginning of a prosperous career for yourself in business life." Neither Babcock's diary entry nor Fabens's letter indicates that any similar promise of land was made to Grant or to any other American official. Nonetheless, Babcock's reference to his prospects for 1,000 acres "in case of annexation" made it clear that the president's confidential agent had acquired a personal financial interest in the success of the annexation project.[41]

Back in Santo Domingo city, Babcock was eager to bring the negotiations to a conclusion. He confronted Báez about the Hartmont loan, and the president insisted he had been desperate for money. Babcock was satisfied that his ploy "had the desired effect of throwing" Báez "onto the defensive." The American then reiterated that he had no offer to make; his purpose was "simply to aid him [Báez] in getting matters into such a shape that I thought it would meet with favor." At this point, Báez complained about an American named Davis Hatch who had been taken prisoner for lending assistance to the rebel forces under Cabral. Babcock "said but little" about Hatch, but before he could steer the conversation back to annexation, Smith arrived.[42]

Smith had come to register a protest about the treatment of Hatch. He claimed the Connecticut man was in Santo Domingo looking after the business interests of American railway magnate Augustus Schell. Hatch, Smith added, had wielded "much influence" as a correspondent for the *New York Times* and was well connected politically in the States. More frank than adroit, Smith claimed that "Hatch had only opposed Báez—not the govt." Báez retorted that Hatch had used his house as "the armory and arsenal for Cabral." Babcock kept quiet, and he and Cazneau left. The Hatch case would surface again in ways that seriously damaged the annexation project.[43]

When talks resumed, Báez tried to ease Babcock's mind about the Hartmont loan, insisting that the deal could be canceled. More important, he said that if the United States would assume the Dominican national debt, "annexation could be made." He put the debt at less than $700,000 but added that he would need a down payment of $100,000 or $150,000 "to enable him to send his generals home and have them set up the cry, 'Vive la America.'" Babcock urged him to put his views in writing, and he would present them to Grant. Later the same day, Báez introduced Babcock to his cabinet. As Babcock recorded the scene, Báez announced "to the Cabinet that I had come here in the capacity of a Special agent to gather information about the country, and he hoped they would all extend to me all the facilities required, and that I could go and talk with them freely." Babcock noted the irony: "Little did he suppose that this was really my mission."[44]

The slow pace of the negotiations tried Babcock's patience. "They act like children," he fumed. Near the end of August, Báez said his government preferred annexation of the whole country rather than the politically risky alienation of just a portion of it by the sale of Samaná. As a precaution, he sought the protection of two American war vessels to cruise in Dominican waters while the annexation question "was being submitted to the people." He and Babcock both thought that landing American troops would be "misconstrued" and was thus out of the question. Báez said, "If the U.S. would send down the advance, and some one with power to treat, that it could all be done in three days." It was a productive meeting, but Babcock noted, "He talked well, but how will he act—quien sabe?"[45]

Two days later Gautier presented Babcock with a draft memorandum of the points Báez had outlined. Compensation for annexation was to be US assumption of the Dominican debt, which Gautier's memorandum now put at $1.5 million. When Babcock objected, Báez "crawfished" and tried to change the subject. Confusion also marked the question of the payment method—that is, whether the United States would pay the debt directly to creditors or give the money to the Dominican government, which would then pay its creditors. Feeling "a little disgusted" by the inconclusive discussion, Babcock later confessed to his diary, "I think they are quite tricky, and I begin to [think] them dishonest." Later in the day the US warship *Tuscarora* arrived in the harbor, a serendipitous event that pleased Báez.[46]

In conversation the next day, Babcock told Báez he would send the *Tuscarora* to pursue the rebel ship *Telégrafo*, provided Báez settled "all my matters"; otherwise, he would send the warship back to the States. "He promised," Babcock noted. Báez raised the question of Davis Hatch, the American being held at Azua, and Babcock told Báez he would "not interfere with Mr. Hatch. I would trust him." (Meanwhile, Babcock had argued for the release of an American sailor who had killed a fellow sailor in a drunken fight.) Later Gautier, accompanied by Cazneau, brought a revised memorandum. He had changed the form somewhat but retained the sum of $1.5 million. Babcock warned that "they had put the figure so high, I was afraid it would defeat the whole matter," but Gautier simply "talked all around the subject again."[47]

On September 2 Gautier informed Babcock that his papers were ready. The same day Babcock spoke with Commander Walter Queen of the *Tuscarora* and "told him what impression I wanted made about the Telegrafo. He seemed to enter into the case." Smith thought the Báez government had exaggerated the threat from the *Telégrafo*, and he spoke with Queen about Hatch's imprisonment, but Babcock told the commander to "pay no attention." The exasperated Smith fired off a letter to Fish complaining that Babcock "has never asked my opinion on the state of this country." Instead "he goes home with impressions derived chiefly from Cazneau and Fabens."[48]

The day before Babcock was scheduled to leave on the *Tybee*, Báez seemed to get cold feet. He communicated to Cazneau "some new idea" about selling Samaná, with the $2 million price to be paid

gradually and "annexation to come afterwards." Babcock told Cazneau to inform Báez that "it was too late and beside[s] his price was
so much that I did not think it would be entertained at all." He concluded that Báez's aim was "simply to get a way to get hold of all of
the money and get off." On September 4 Gautier gave Babcock the
signed memorandum, rushing up with the final papers as the *Tybee*
was about to slip out of the harbor. The amateur diplomat "was glad
to be on my way back, and glad that I had my things in such good
shape." Ten days later he arrived in New York, where he telegraphed
"the old man" and then his wife.[49]

Babcock's diary record of his mission sheds considerable light on
the early phase of the Santo Domingo project. He did not set off as a
partner in some sort of conspiracy to capture and exploit the island nation. Before making his trip, he had barely heard of the principal advocates of annexation. He initially distrusted Fabens but later warmed to
him and also to Cazneau, and he worked closely with them. The push
for annexation originated with the Dominican government, but at the
time Grant selected Babcock for this delicate mission, the president was
leaning toward acceptance. He insisted, however, that the official request for an agreement come not from the United States but from the
Dominicans. Babcock saw it as within his purview to try to influence the
shape of the Dominican offer, but he could not dictate its terms. Indeed,
Báez's refusal to lower the price left him doubtful that the project would
gain approval. Babcock marveled at the country's rich natural resources,
but, imbued with the racial attitudes of his time, he saw those resources
as little more than waste in the hands of the current population.

While Babcock was in Santo Domingo, Grant hungered for information. He eagerly sought to learn Cornelius Cole's impressions of the
island as well as those of reporter Randolph Keim, who had recently
spent several weeks there. Keim had submitted glowing articles on
Santo Domingo to the *New York Herald*. He had left the island a few days
before Babcock arrived, and on his departure, Báez had given him a
letter to Grant once again urging negotiations, which Keim presented to
Grant at Fish's country house on the Hudson in early August. Although
they did not tell him about Babcock's secret mission, Keim concluded
that "a number of influential heads of the government" already favored
the acquisition of Samaná, "if not the whole island of Santo Domingo."
In one of his articles Keim asserted that the Monroe Doctrine must sig-
nify more than just a warning to European nations to stay out of the
Western Hemisphere. Something must be done "to rescue these small

Powers from utter ruin and depopulation. If no foreign government is to be allowed to come in it remains with the United States to assume the responsibility of an effort to reclaim them from the anarchy which now prevails." Grant told Keim he considered this interpretation "the correct doctrine and the sooner this was understood, the better."[50]

But to administration leaders and others, Keim also expressed his disapproval of Fabens and Cazneau, telling a friend he had "ruined" them "at court, so they cannot swindle anymore." Fish, he claimed, "was glad to have a corroboration of his own views in regard to them." Others shared his disdain. Cole told Keim he feared Babcock would "fall into the hands of the Philistines and be influenced by the self-interested motives." In August, when press stories about Babcock's trip (which he described as a pleasure excursion) fed rumors of an annexation project, Bancroft Davis confided to the editor of the *New York Times*, "Babcock, who is a very shrewd and very honest fellow, has gone to St. Domingo for the Govt. to mark, learn, and inwardly digest what he may see there." But, Davis added, "We are beset by a parcel of speculators, among whom is Fabens—to take steps for annexing St. Domingo." Fabens and others had received concessions from Báez, Davis wrote, and "all these people want annexation to give value to their grants. There is no disposition here to go beyond the acquisition of Samaná as a naval station, if it can be got for a moderate sum." It is doubtful that Davis accurately represented Grant's "disposition."[51]

When Babcock returned to Washington in mid-September, Grant was out of town. He laid out the Dominicans' request to Fish, who reported it in a letter to the president. Báez and his cabinet, Fish wrote, "are willing to negotiate for the annexation." Fish's presentation of the case in this manner, with no hint that he was surprised, suggests that he was aware of Grant's verbal instructions to Babcock. He was not "nonplussed by what Babcock told him," as historian Allan Nevins later alleged. The asking price of $1.5 million was the sum the Dominicans considered necessary to defray the national debt, make payments to the army, and cover expenses associated with a plebiscite and the transfer of power. They would turn over all public buildings and installations, the navy, and other government possessions except for property rights in unceded lands, which might be necessary to cover future claims against the Dominican government. The Dominican people would vote on the question of annexation. At the signing of a treaty, the government would expect the United States to provide a down payment of $100,000 in cash and another $50,000 in military supplies. If either country failed to ratify the annexation treaty, this money would be applied to the purchase of Samaná Bay (for $2 million) by an alternative treaty to be negotiated at the same time. Fish informed Grant that the next steamer would leave for Santo Domingo in eight days, on September 25, affording "ample time to send an answer, whether it be of encouragement or otherwise," to the Dominicans.[52]

Fish also told Grant the Dominicans had said they would "arrest" the Hartmont loan "on being assured that their willingness to be annexed is favorably entertained here. Nothing will be done further with that loan until opportunity is had to receive your decision." But Fish was not content to rely solely on the Dominicans' word on this key question. He asked minister John Motley to investigate whether the brokers in London were having any success in selling the Dominican bonds.[53]

Grant returned to Washington on September 22 and heard from Babcock directly. Just at that moment, the Gold Corner conspiracy in New York dominated the administration's attention, and the president could not reach a "definite" judgment about Santo Domingo in time to send his response on the next steamer, which was set to sail the day after Black Friday. Even so, Grant directed Fish to inform Gautier that he approved the "general object" of the offer from the Dominican government, although some of the details "must be varied." Santo Domingo could initially be accepted only as a territory; it would have to await congressional action for admission as a state. In addition, the Hartmont loan must be "cancelled or otherwise withdrawn before any treaty." The president specifically asked Fish to assure the Dominicans that secrecy would be observed and to say that he thought "the general terms will be acceptable to Congress." Grant also ordered Babcock to ask Cazneau to convey the same points to Báez and to assure him that if the rebel vessel *Telégrafo* set sail, an American ship would seize it.[54]

That Grant did not channel these communications through Smith reflected the administration's disenchantment with the commercial agent, which Babcock's enmity for Smith no doubt fueled. The same steamer that took Babcock back to the States carried a letter from Smith to Fish condemning Fabens and Cazneau as "speculators who stand at nothing to bring about their selfish ends"—a statement that could only deepen Babcock's contempt for Smith. More important, one of the confidential memoranda Gautier had thrust into Babcock's hands on the day he departed requested Smith's replacement by someone who would aid in "carrying into effect" annexation. A formal treaty would require the signature of an accredited official clothed with diplomatic status rather than a military officer like Babcock, and the administration soon began casting about for a new commercial agent.[55]

That search gained urgency in early October when Fish heard from Motley that the Dominican bonds had few takers and the Hartmont loan was failing, thus removing an important obstacle to the annexation project. The loan's only potential salvation lay in the revelation of an American intent to annex the country, which would ensure the loan's full repayment (with substantial interest) and thereby enhance the attractiveness of the bonds on the market. Hence, the need for absolute secrecy underscored the importance of finding a compliant and discreet officer to replace Smith as commercial agent. For this delicate position, Grant chose a thirty-three-year-old Union army veteran named Raymond H. J. Perry.[56]

Perry first joined the army in 1858. He served in Sheridan's command during the war and worked as a civilian scout for him in Texas during the first two years of Reconstruction. In the fall of 1869 Perry sought an appointment as US marshal for western Texas. He won endorsements from the leading Republicans in Texas and in his home state of Rhode Island, as well as from Sheridan, who told Grant that Perry was "an active, energetic, and fearless man." Grant informed the attorney general that if a change were to be made in the marshalship, he could do "no better than to take Major Perry." The next day Fish presented to the cabinet a draft annexation treaty, heightening the need to find a replacement for Smith quickly. Perry happened to be in Washington and wrote to Grant, "I am ready to go at an hour's notice to any part of the World alone or in company as you wish; and in any position to serve you. . . . I have taken and can take as desperate chances as any man that lives."[57] Perry also dropped by the White House and left a note for the president, stating, "When you have any rough work to do that requires nerve and activity and a man that will do his duty regardless of anything or anybody I can do it and am ready any time to undertake it."[58]

As it happened, the Texas marshal position had gone to someone else, but Grant was eager to give Perry a job. He told Fish he thought Perry would be "a proper person" to send to Santo Domingo to replace Smith. Thus, in an almost absentminded way, the administration chose Perry for the mission. The former major had a record of hotheadedness in the army, including slapping a superior officer, killing a fellow soldier in what he claimed was self-defense, and shooting three men and cutting more than a dozen others with his saber for refusing to obey orders. Whether Grant and Fish knew about these episodes is not clear, but

General in Chief William Sherman certainly did, for he had signed off on the proceedings of Perry's court-martial in 1865. In October of that year Perry submitted his resignation, but Sheridan immediately converted it to an honorable discharge and hired him as a scout. Recalling his checkered military career, Perry later admitted, "I was at fault myself in some things, if fond[ness] of active life and e[x]citement in the field is a fault and I did not like to be under men that I could not respect."[59]

Whatever Grant and Fish knew of Perry, Perry himself had doubts about his suitability for this new position. While waiting in New York to leave on the *Tybee*, he informed Fish that he would prefer a job that required "nerve, activity, and energy." He wrote, "I am ready to take my life in hand and serve the Government anywhere you wish me. But while our Country is so embarrassed by political, speculating and treacherous men, it does seeme [*sic*] to me that my services, trifling as they are, might be employed to better advantage in the states." Nonetheless, the would-be domestic crusader sailed to Santo Domingo. Soon thereafter he wrote home to his wife, "I want to make some money out of it now as I am here and then return home never again to leave it. . . . I think there is money to be made here and good hard money." The ubiquitous Fabens had been on board the *Tybee*, and he told Perry that he had "a great opportunity for making a rapid fortune." Once on the island, Perry also heard from Cazneau that he could get "a fine plantation." But Perry was "after a reputation not money." He told Báez that if the Dominican government would provide him with 250 mounted men, he would resign as commercial agent, "contract to do all the fighting on the Island," and capture the rebel leaders. Báez rejected this absurd offer. Several months later, one of the Texas politicians who had commended Perry to Grant testified that Perry was made up of "the most combustible materials in a fight" and lacked discretion and judgment "on occasions where such qualities are required."[60]

Given the combustibility of the new commercial agent, trouble within the small American community in Santo Domingo was inevitable. When Perry arrived, he found his countrymen already divided, with "a bitter feeling" existing between Americans who supported Báez and those who backed the rebellion. Moreover, he reported to the administration, those antagonistic groups "have drawn the Government and the Consul [Smith] in opposition to each other." In an abrupt departure from Smith's practice, Perry called an immediate halt to using the consul's office as an asylum for Báez's enemies.[61]

Perry's initial instructions said nothing about the annexation project because the administration was still putting the finishing touches on its policy when he left. Once Motley reported that the Hartmont loan would likely fail, Grant hastened to pursue formal negotiations with the Dominicans. On October 19 Fish presented a draft annexation treaty to the cabinet. Only Postmaster General John Creswell was "thoroughly in favor," while the other members were quietly unenthusiastic. Sitting in as interim secretary of war, Sherman doubted "the influence of the climate on free institutions." Still, the project went forward. A week later, Fish gave Grant a second draft convention for the purchase of Samaná Bay, which he approved.[62]

Grant's plan called for Babcock to return to Santo Domingo with the two draft agreements as the basis for negotiations. The putative treaty of annexation stipulated that the United States would annex the Dominican Republic as a territory for $1.5 million, which the Dominican government would apply to the payment of its public debt. The Dominican government would use unceded lands to pay for any debt in excess of that sum. The treaty required a plebiscite by the Dominican people, and pending that vote, the United States would protect the republic "against foreign interposition, in order that the national expression may be free." In addition, the Dominican Republic would pledge that "after the execution" of the treaty, it would "make no grants or concessions of lands or rights in lands" and "contract no further debts, until Congress shall assume jurisdiction over the territory." For the treaty to take effect, the two nations had to exchange ratifications within four months. The draft treaty made no mention of a down payment. That subject was reserved for an accompanying convention stipulating that the United States would make an initial payment of $150,000 and that, in the event annexation was rejected, it would take possession of Samaná Bay for up to ninety-nine years as security for repayment. The United States would pay an annual rent for Samaná and could "at any time" convert the arrangement to a purchase for $2 million. If the annexation treaty were ratified, it would supersede the lease convention, and the $150,000 would be applied to the purchase price.[63]

On November 6 Fish provided Babcock with sets of instructions for both himself and Perry. Perry's gave him "full powers from the President to conclude" the treaty and convention Fish had drafted. But Fish also advised the agent that it was "the desire of the President that you should confer with General Babcock in every step of these negotiations and be governed by his advice, as he is fully possessed of the views of the President on this subject." More than ten times the length of Perry's instructions, Babcock's orders directed him to "advise" with Perry "unofficially," and they set forth the parameters for negotiations. He was instructed to reiterate the key points that Santo Domingo must first become a territory and that the Hartmont loan must be "cancelled or relinquished" before Perry could sign any agreement. In an auxiliary instruction, however, Fish told Babcock that if the Dominicans could not meet the demand about the loan, the Americans could drop that demand and make the best deal they could, as long as the treaty stipulated that the Dominicans retained responsibility for repaying the loan. In the event of a successful outcome of the negotiations, Babcock should, "as an officer of the army," coordinate with the American naval force in the vicinity to take steps to ensure protection for the popular vote. In essence, the administration's instructions made it clear that Babcock would do the talking and Perry would do the signing.[64]

Babcock soon left for New York, where he prepared to board the USS *Albany* for the trip to Santo Domingo. On November 10 he took two armed men to the US subtreasury on Wall Street and took possession of $100,000 in gold. The *Albany* would also transport $50,000 worth of arms. It set sail later in the day. Accompanying Babcock were General D. B. Sackett, inspector general of the army, whom Grant himself had chosen to serve as interpreter, and General Rufus Ingalls, a friend of Grant's since his West Point days. Ingalls had no assigned role in the negotiations. Having made his mark in the Quartermaster Department during the war, he now served as assistant quartermaster general stationed in New York. On this trip, his task was to investigate "what could be obtained in the island, and its capacities in different ways." Although both Sackett and Ingalls possessed appropriate credentials for their assigned tasks, their selection did nothing to dispel the notion purveyed by the president's critics that he relied too heavily on military men to execute his policies.[65]

The *Albany* arrived at Santo Domingo on November 18, and Babcock promptly handed Perry his commission to negotiate a treaty. He exchanged formal greeting with Báez, who "seemed in good spirit." Babcock wrote to his wife, "The wish for annexation seems to be much stronger than when I left here." Still, "they are Spanish and I shall not trust them. When they put their name to the document I shall know it is all right."[66]

Formal negotiating began on November 19, but when the Dominicans raised questions about some points, Babcock feared "they intend to be tricky." Most important, Gautier expressed anxiety about applying the annexation purchase money to the payment of the Dominicans' public debt. He wanted to add an article to the treaty that would "protect" the Dominican government's ability to pass legislation regarding the mode of paying the debt. Babcock thought the minister was "afraid someone will run off with the money and he will be left in the lurch," but Cazneau said the Dominicans only wanted assurance that they would retain management of their debt. In the end, Cazneau and Báez devised a new article stating that a Dominican commission would apply the purchase money to the debt, and such commission would be "respected and protected by the United States." Otherwise, the two agreements—the treaty of annexation and the convention for the lease of Samaná—differed little in substance from Fish's drafts.[67]

On November 29 both documents were ready to be signed. At the last minute, however, Báez sought a delay so that he could consult the Dominican senate. Article VI of the treaty stated that after its execution, the Dominican government could issue no new concessions of land, and Báez wanted the senate to authorize a land grant to Babcock at Samaná before that provision took effect. The grant would serve, Báez said, as a mark of gratitude to Babcock for dispatching the *Tuscarora* against the *Telégrafo* and for persuading Grant to fire Smith as commercial agent, both of which showed "great kindness on the part of General Babcock." Babcock refused. As Sackett later recalled the scene, Babcock declared, "My God! anything of that kind would ruin the treaty; it would not do!" Babcock recorded in his diary, "I told him how bad it would be and that I must decline it, that as a citizen of the U.S. I should like to go into Business with him, but could not accept a gift now." He did not mention the 1,000 acres in Palenque he had been promised the previous summer.[68]

Perry and Gautier, the official negotiators, proceeded to sign the documents. Perry confessed to feeling some awkwardness in affixing his signature, for he had done "none of the work." "General Babcock," he said, "ought to have the credit as he had had the labor." Over the next three days, the $100,000 in gold and the military stores were unloaded from the *Albany* and taken ashore. Just before he departed, Babcock received a letter from Báez expressing his confidence that Hartmont would not come through with the loan money, but if it did, he would spend none of it and await instructions from Washington. On December 4 the *Albany* set sail for Samaná, where the American flag was raised. Before leaving on December 8, Babcock left two US enlisted men in charge, and American naval vessels were scheduled to stop by from time to time. Fabens gushed in a letter to Secretary Fish that the people waited with "sobs of grateful joy" for "the anticipated blessings of a good government about to be conferred upon them." Perry too assured Fish that "there is a very strong majority in favor of annexation throughout this Island." But the agent also noted, "There are some who are taking a very active part in this matter of annexation who are looking only to their own selfish interest and would jeopardize their flag or friends to gain it."[69]

Babcock arrived in Washington on December 21, and later that day Grant and Fish laid the two agreements before the cabinet. With newspaper rumors abounding, the president gave cabinet members permission to reveal the existence of the lease convention, but he enjoined strict secrecy about the annexation treaty until the Hartmont loan contract expired at the end of the year. Fish also informed American ministers abroad about the agreements. From Berlin, George Bancroft sent his congratulations: "Your achievement is one of the utmost importance & marks an epoch in History." "I think it not certain," the historian added, "that it is best for us to obtain the mastery in the West Indies; but if it is best, you have accomplished it in the simplest and most satisfactory manner."[70]

Grant shared Bancroft's perception of Santo Domingo as the key to controlling the region, but unlike Bancroft, he had no doubt that annexation was necessary to achieve such mastery. In an undated memorandum entitled "Reasons Why San Domingo Should Be Annexed to the United States," the president laid heavy stress on the island's strategic position as "the gate to the Carib[b]ean." It occupied a key point on the route to the Isthmus of Darien, which, with the construction of an interoceanic canal, was "destined at no distant day to be the line of transit of half the commerce of the world." Moreover, the president wrote, Great Britain's possession of "a cordon of islands" in the Caribbean plus outposts in Central and South America required all American coastal trade from the Atlantic Seaboard to ports on the Gulf of Mexico to "pass through foreign waters." Annexing Santo Domingo would provide the United States a base from which to protect that trade. "In case of a Maritime war it would give us a foothold in the West Indies of inestimable value." As matters stood, Santo Domingo was "weak and must go some where for protection. Is the United States willing that she should seek protection from a foreign power? Such a confession would be to abandon our oft-repeated 'Monroe Doctrine.'"

But Grant saw virtues in Santo Domingo beyond its strategic value. In addition to its large stands of timber, the country possessed soil of "unequaled fertility." It could "produce the sugar, coffee, tobacco, chocolate and tropical fruits for a population of 50,000,000 of people. . . . With the acquisition of San Domingo the two great necessities in every family, sugar and coffee, would be cheapened near one half." Whatever Babcock may have told him about the "indolent and ignorant" inhabitants, the president hailed the sparse population as being "in entire sympathy with our institutions," tolerant of "the religious or political views of their neighbors," and "industrious if made to feel that the products of their industry is to be protected." In addition, annexation would enable the United States to deal a death blow to slavery in the institution's last remaining outposts in the Western Hemisphere—Cuba and Brazil. Grant labeled the United States "the largest supporter" of slavery, in that both those countries sent large portions of their exports to America and charged export duties "to support slavery and Monarchy." As an alternative source of these commodities, "San Domingo in the hands of the United States would make slave labor unprofitable and would soon extinguish that hated system of enforced labor" in Cuba and Brazil. And finally, as he continued to wrestle with the problems of domestic Reconstruction, Grant saw the annexation of Santo Domingo as a device to improve the lot of former slaves in the United States. Echoing ideas espoused by Benjamin Hunt, he wrote:

> Caste has no foothold in San Domingo. It is capable of supporting the entire colored population of the United States, should it choose to emigrate. The present difficulty in bringing all parts of the United States to a happy unity and love of country grows out of the prejudice to color. The prejudice is a senseless one, but it exists. The colored man cannot be spared until his place is supplied, but with a refuge like San Domingo, his worth here would soon be discovered, and he would soon receive such recognition as to induce him to stay; or if Providence designed that the two races should not live together he would find a home in the Antilles.[71]

Thus, Grant believed that the annexation of Santo Domingo held tremendous potential to transform life in the United States—economically, politically, and socially—and its relations with the rest of the world. Annexation could stand as the crowning achievement of the president's first term and help him win a second. Initially skeptical about the enterprise, Fish had taken the inchoate memoranda resulting from Babcock's first trip and shaped them into agreements that easily passed muster in the second round of negotiations. All that remained was for Grant to persuade the Senate to approve the momentous step. Santo Domingo's "acquisition is carrying out Manifest destiny," the president wrote at the close of his memorandum. "Can anyone favor rejecting so valuable a gift who voted $7,200,000 for the icebergs of Alasca [*sic*]?"[72]

10

★ ★ ★ ★ ★

THE BATTLE OF
SANTO DOMINGO

Despite Grant's desire to keep the annexation project a secret until December 31, 1869, speculation regarding negotiations with Santo Domingo arose before that date. In late November the press carried reports of Babcock's second trip and his instructions to pursue an annexation agreement. On December 23, two days after Babcock's return and Grant's presentation of the treaty to the cabinet, the *New York Herald* described the negotiations and the agreement in accurate detail. On its editorial page, the *Herald* praised the putative acquisition as a triumph of order "over disorder, industry over idleness," and "a positive good to mankind."[1]

Others, however, appeared less certain. A week later, on December 29, the *Herald* published an authorized article on Charles Sumner's views regarding foreign policy questions. According to the article, "Mr. Sumner thinks we will get all the West India islands sooner than we want them, and that we should neither purchase them nor assist in wresting them from the powers to which they belong. From this it may be inferred that the Senator is opposed to the purchase of St. Thomas, and also to leasing the Bay of Samaná." Grant read newspapers regularly, and it is hard to imagine that the *Herald*'s story about Sumner escaped his notice. Having tangled with the Foreign Relations Committee chairman over the *Alabama* claims, Grant was determined to forestall any resistance to his cherished new project. Although the "interview" with Sumner did

Samaná Bay—a central element in Grant's strategic design for Santo Domingo.
(Library of Congress)

not explicitly mention the annexation of Santo Domingo, Grant decided
to set the senator's mind at ease by giving him a personal preview of
the treaty. The unfulfilled provisions of the Dominicans' Hartmont loan
were set to expire on December 31, thereby relieving the United States of
potential liability for a substantial sum in the event of annexation. With
that exposure averted, Grant felt free to lift the veil of secrecy from the
treaty and move forward with its approval.[2]

Thus the fight for ratification began with an extraordinary show of
deference on the part of the president. One evening a few days after the
Herald's publication of Sumner's views, Grant walked the short distance
across Lafayette Park to Sumner's house on Vermont Avenue with "the
express purpose of consulting with him relative to the treaty." According to Fish, Grant desired to secure Sumner's "favourable consideration
of the project at the earliest possible moment" and thought that "a personal visit, & the communication to him, the *first* outside of his Cabinet,

was proper, & would be received as a suitable recognition of his position & as a mark of confidence."[3]

When Grant arrived, Sumner was entertaining two journalists, John W. Forney and Benjamin Perley Poore, at dinner. At some point George Boutwell joined the group. Sumner offered the president a glass of sherry, which he declined. With little ado, Grant set forth the outlines of the treaty and discussed the strategic and economic advantages he saw in the annexation of Santo Domingo. He tried to stress that he had come out of courtesy to the chairman of the committee that would assume responsibility for the treaty, although he apparently referred to Sumner mistakenly as head of the Judiciary Committee. The senator and his allies later pounced on this error as evidence of Grant's gross ignorance of American governance, while Grant's friends saw it as a mere inadvertence. Sumner later claimed that during the visit Grant "alluded to certain new treaties already negotiated, with regard to which I had no information." But the press had already treated the subject, and Sumner, who read newspapers as avidly as Grant did, must have seen these reports. Moreover, the author of a forthcoming book on Santo Domingo had written to the senator several days earlier, warning him that the Samaná Bay lease was "a swindle." Sumner's later assertion that at the time of Grant's visit he "had no information" about the treaty signified either mendacity or remarkable memory loss. Although accounts by participants in that evening's conversation disagreed in some respects, no one remembered Sumner raising any objection to either the Samaná Bay lease or the annexation treaty.[4]

Instead, according to his own account, Sumner "very soon interrupted" Grant to bring up a patronage case. A few days earlier the senator had received a plea for help from James Ashley, whom Grant had, at Sumner's behest, appointed governor of the Montana Territory but recently dismissed for criticizing the administration. The senator read Ashley's letter aloud and urged his reinstatement. Grant responded with stony silence, and Sumner later admitted that he had taken "too great a liberty with him in my own house." Although claiming that loyalty to a friend had motivated this interruption, he also said, "I was glad of this opportunity of diverting attention from the treaties."[5]

Months later, after relations between Grant and Sumner had completely soured, Sumner told Hamilton Fish that Grant had been drunk that night at his house. Yet it was Sumner and his guests who had been enjoying wine with dinner, and Grant who had declined to join them in a drink. Boutwell told Fish that Sumner's charge was ridiculous, and

Poore later wrote, "Grant was entirely free from alcoholic influence on that occasion, as I told Mr. Sumner again and again afterward."[6]

But the matter of greatest controversy surrounding that conversation was the attitude Sumner exhibited toward the annexation project. Grant insisted that the senator's response signified approbation. Four months later, he told Fish that Sumner "had assured him, in the presence of another person, of his friendship to the Treaty." From this position Grant never wavered. On June 8, 1870, he wrote to Senator Zachariah Chandler that Sumner had spoken of the treaty "in such language as to leave no doubt upon my mind that he would support it." Years later he told Fish that when he explained the treaty to Sumner, "he seemed pleased with it and expressed the desire to see it." Confirming Grant's perception, Boutwell recalled that as Grant was leaving the senator declared, "I expect, Mr. President, to support the measures of your administration." "Most naturally," Boutwell later wrote to Fish, "the President left Mr. Sumner's house with the impression that Mr. Sumner was with him."[7]

Forney's corroboration of Grant's version was even more emphatic. Shortly after the dinner, Forney published an endorsement of the project that, he later averred, reflected Sumner's attitude. He told the senator, "The day after New Year's, my editor called on Babcock and got his data and made an article in favor of the Treaty." Appearing in the *Washington Daily Morning Chronicle* on Monday, January 3, 1870, Forney's editorial noted that the treaty for the acquisition of St. Thomas was still pending but asserted that "a far larger, more fertile and salubrious territory, with a better harbor and unlimited fields for the expenditure of American industry and capital, may be had for a smaller price upon the neighboring island of San Domingo."[8] Forney later told Sumner, "Your action decided my course" in endorsing annexation. He insisted, "I really understood you to be for the Treaty, and . . . but for this, I never would have supported it."[9]

Over time, Sumner offered inconsistent explanations of the fateful encounter at his house. In early June 1870 Forney wrote that Sumner "claims that other information since obtained has shaped his present action" against the treaty, thus implying he had initially supported the treaty but later came to oppose it. Sumner presented a different version in a Senate speech in December 1870 (after the treaty's defeat and the animosity between Grant and the senator had grown flagrant). In this telling, Sumner portrayed himself as never indicating his approval and being circumspectly noncommittal at the dinner. He replayed the scene:

"'Mr. President,' I said, 'I am an Administration man, and whatever you do will always find in me the most careful and candid consideration.'" Sumner declared that his language had been "precise, well-considered, and chosen in advance." How far in advance he did not say. But if this were really the first he had heard of the treaties, as he claimed, how far "in advance" could he have chosen his words? Sumner said the president might have formed the opinion that he would favor the treaty, but Sumner maintained that he had said nothing to justify such a conclusion.[10]

Under questioning from skeptical senators, Sumner added a reason for his reserve. He told his colleagues that "a darling idea of mine, entertained for years, has been a protectorate in the Gulf to be maintained by the great Republic. That idea was in my mind when the President was with me." No one recollected Sumner raising this point at his house. He himself admitted that he had not done so, claiming he wanted to wait until he had read the text of the treaty and the attendant papers to see whether they comported with his protectorate idea. Surely this claim stretches credulity. On that evening Grant was discussing annexation, not a protectorate. And if the president's explanation was not clear, why did Sumner not ask a direct question about his favored alternative? Sumner was willing to confront the president about Ashley, so why not address the possibility of a protectorate—a much more important policy question? Babcock presented the text and papers on Monday, January 3, and Sumner claimed that "the moment I examined the papers . . . I saw clearly that the idea which I had at heart [that is, the protectorate] would not be established by the President's treaties." And yet, astonishingly, the senator raised no objection to Babcock. Indeed, in a letter six months after their meeting, Babcock asserted that Sumner had "volunteered to say that he could not think of doing otherwise than supporting the Administration in this matter," a point the senator repeated when the two met a few days later. Babcock probably exaggerated in his description of those meetings, but when another senator read Babcock's letter during the debate, Sumner made no direct response, suggesting that he could not deny its essential accuracy. Raised only in retrospect, Sumner's point about a protectorate appeared to be an invention designed to explain away his *seemingly* favorable response at the dinner. Taken all together, Sumner's version of events is less plausible than those of the guests at his house, even though their accounts are not in perfect accord. At the very least, upon bidding Sumner good night, Grant had good reason to believe that the senator would come on board.[11]

Under pressure from other senators, Sumner further massaged his version of events. He did not admit saying he would support the treaty, but he acknowledged his error in failing to make his opposition clear right away. Indeed, precisely when and why Sumner's opposition began remained cloudy. As Fish later wrote, when he met Sumner during the period immediately after Grant's evening visit, the senator raised no objection to the annexation treaty. The president officially submitted that treaty and the Samaná lease agreement to the Senate on January 10, 1870; they were then referred to Sumner's committee, where they lay dormant. As committee member James Harlan put it, "I was not able to understand from him [Sumner] what his judgment was for several weeks after that treaty went to committee." On January 15 Grant expressed to Fish his surprise that the annexation treaty had "not attracted as much attention or excitement as he had anticipated." Two weeks later Sumner informed Fish there was no support for the St. Thomas treaty in the Senate, but he omitted any mention of Santo Domingo. Although Sumner had opposed the St. Thomas purchase from the start, he told Fish, "I have a tenderness for Denmark which would make me support it now if there were any reasonable chance for carrying it." This was a remarkable admission in light of the senator's self-proclaimed fastidiousness on foreign policy matters and in light of St. Thomas's price tag, which was five times that for the Dominican Republic. As Wisconsin senator Timothy Howe later recalled, "When the [Dominican] treaty had been in Com. a long time he [Sumner] asked me what I thought of it. I told him frankly I was very sorry it was ever negotiated. But he did not intimate the slightest objection to it." "Mr. Sumner's special error," Boutwell later wrote to Fish, "was that he neglected to return the President's call or in any way to inform the President that he could not support the treaty. . . . I once presented the case to Mr. Sumner very much in this way and he admitted his error in neglecting to return the call of the President."[12]

Some observers concluded that Sumner was waiting for the president to purchase his support by reinstating his friend Ashley. After hearing Sumner's version of the encounter at his house, Howe thought, "He did not intend to commit himself, by a distinct promise to support the treaty, but did mean to commit Grant to the restoration of Ashley by making him believe he w[oul]d support the treaty." Years later Fish charged that Sumner rarely raised the Santo Domingo question with him without "making a request for Mr. Ashley's reappointment." Grant told Fish that Sumner's behavior made it reasonable to "impute such motives to him. I do not, however. Mr. Sumner could never have been bribed but in one way. That would be by flattery." Even so, Sumner remained a persistent opponent of the nomination of Ashley's successor, Benjamin Potts, whose failure to win confirmation would, under the Tenure of Office Act, leave Ashley in place, at least temporarily. In part because of Sumner's obstruction, Potts did not win approval until after the defeat of the Santo Domingo treaty.[13]

Whatever Sumner's root motive, Grant believed the senator planned to kill the treaty by dragging the question out until March 29, 1870, on which date it would expire if not ratified. As the weeks went by, Sumner's purpose grew clearer. A month after Grant had submitted the treaty, Fish confided to George Bancroft that he expected it to fail, not only because of "doubts honestly entertained by many" but also because of "something of jealousy & of smallness of motive operating in certain quarters." By the third week of February, Babcock thought the Dominicans might fear that "they will find themselves where the St. Thomas people are, and by Mr. Sumner's proscess [sic] they will."[14]

Meanwhile, the administration kept its promise to protect the Dominican government while annexation was put to a popular vote. Potential threats to that government came not only from Báez's political enemies but also from Haiti. In January the Dominican opposition leader Cabral lent his assistance to forces rebelling against the Haitian government, resulting in its overthrow, the execution of its pro-Báez president, and the installation of a new president, Nissage Saget, who was sympathetic toward Cabral's insurgency in the neighboring republic. Grant responded instantly. He ordered Rear Admiral Charles Poor to proceed with two warships to Haiti and to inform Saget that the United States "is determined to protect the present Dominican government with all its power." "If the Haytians [sic] attack the Dominicans with their ships," Poor should "destroy or capture them." In addition, Fish advised representatives of the new Haitian government of the United States' displeasure with Haitian aid to enemies of the Dominican government. Poor sailed immediately for Port-au-Prince, where he told Saget that during the pendency of the treaty, any Haitian attack against the Dominicans would be "considered an act of hostility to the flag of the United States, and will provoke hostility in return." Though "displeased," the Haitian authorities signaled their compliance. Before long, Poor headed a fleet of several ships in Dominican waters, and the Báez government was more or less secure.[15]

In early March 1870 word reached the United States that the

Dominican people had voted in favor of annexation, highlighting Sumner's foot-dragging. Finally, he led the Foreign Relations Committee through a hurried investigation, poring over State Department documents as well as reports from army and navy officers who had visited Santo Domingo. The committee took testimony from Babcock and other officers, including Admiral David Porter, who assured Sumner that the United States would encounter "no difficulty in fortifying the harbor" at Samaná Bay. Nonetheless, as Senator Harlan noted, "After exhausting all available sources of knowledge, as it seemed to me, the members of the committee were still in great doubt and came to conclusions reluctantly." Finally, in mid-March Grant acted to smoke Sumner out. Not even bothering to consult Fish, he sent the Senate a sharp message noting that the treaty's deadline was just two weeks away and expressing his "earnest wish that you will not permit it to expire by limitation." The next day the committee voted 5–2 against the annexation treaty, and Sumner reported it adversely to the full Senate. He delayed the adverse report on the Samaná lease agreement for another nine days and did not begin formal debate on the whole question until March 24, just five days before the treaty's expiration.[16]

Two days after the committee vote, Grant rode to Capitol Hill to take personal command of the pro-treaty lobbying. Armed with documents from the State Department, he met senator after senator in the President's Room in the Capitol. Again he emphasized Santo Domingo's material advantages, its strategic value, and its vulnerability to attack by Haiti while it remained independent. According to one press account, he argued that "if the Monroe Doctrine meant that foreign governments should not be allowed to establish themselves on this hemisphere it was the duty of this government to adopt a policy in regard to the petty independencies; otherwise we have no right in justice or humanity to prevent England or France from stepping in and taking the island of St. Domingo or any other island." Grant also said the Dominican people yearned to escape "civil war and domestic disorder"; they were "drawn to us . . . by affection and sympathy on account of our enfranchisement of the colored race here, and repose implicit faith and confidence in our professions of justice and equal rights."[17]

Sumner bristled at Grant's invasion of turf he considered his own. "Must I accept every thing without any exercise of my own judgment?" he wrote to Fish. Purists such as Charles Francis Adams considered Grant's lobbying "deplorable." With no sense of irony, Adams groused that such presidential activism showed Grant's "want of capacity." But the *New York Times* saw the performance differently. "To those sensitive people who are so fastidious that they cannot consent that the President should make a personal effort in behalf of one of his own measures, it may be well to say that when George Washington wanted an appointment confirmed or a measure carried, he went personally to the floor of the Senate, and argued the case with its members."[18]

Still, ratification would be an uphill struggle. Democrats would oppose it, and it enjoyed scant support among New England Republicans, whose territorial ambitions looked northward. Nonetheless, Grant did not feel the need to strike a deal with Sumner. When the senator proposed that the annexation treaty be recommitted to his committee and that the ratification deadline be extended, Grant advised Fish that they could not trust Sumner. "He is an enemy of the treaty; will kill it tomorrow if he can, and only favors delay probably to better secure its defeat. I do not think it good policy to trust the enemies of a measure to manage it for, (and to speak in behalf of), its friends." Grant was confident that "several devoted friends of the treaty" could manage it in the Senate. Two days before debate was set to begin, he and cabinet members were back on Capitol Hill, and that evening he made his case to a gathering of senators at the White House. In the blunt words of the *Herald*'s Washington correspondent, "Had Mr. Sumner been less wrapped up in egotism, the President would have been spared this unpleasant duty of personally appearing before the Senate."[19]

On March 24 Sumner submitted his committee's adverse report on the Samaná lease agreement; he also reported that the committee had voted against the St. Thomas treaty. He then launched into a two-day speech against Santo Domingo annexation. Because the Senate sat in executive session, the proceedings generated no written record, but reports regarding his main points leaked to the press. With annexation, he warned, the United States would be acquiring a country riven by endless strife as well as a huge indeterminate debt, including liabilities associated with the Hartmont loan. Moreover, despite his long record as an abolitionist and a champion of ex-slaves after the war, Sumner denigrated the suitability of the mostly black Dominican populace for inclusion in the American Republic. According to a *New York Herald* report (which may have been too strong in paraphrasing the speech), Sumner described the Dominicans as "a turbulent, treacherous race, indolent and not disposed to make themselves useful to their country or to the world at large." The speech "greatly please[d]" some Republicans such as Connecticut's Joseph Hawley, who told Sumner, "We *don't want any* of those islands just yet, with their mongrel cut-throat races & foreign languages & religion." The irony of Sumner's position was not lost on the *New York Times*: "'To the African,' says this great apostle of human liberty, 'belongs the equatorial belt, and he should enjoy it undisturbed.'"[20]

But the speech disturbed Senator Hiram Revels of Mississippi, the first African American to serve in Congress. Revels told Sumner that he viewed "the question from a Christian standpoint, that is, whether it is not the duty of our powerful, wealthy, and Christian nation, regardless of the trouble and expense which may attend it, to extend the institutions or various means of enlightenment and intellectual, moral and religious elevation with which God has blessed us, to the inhabitants of that Republic, and whether this cannot be done more effectually by annexation than in any other way." But Sumner insisted that the United States could do enough by "a beneficent protectorate without incorporation." Some observers saw raw ego behind his stance. As Nathaniel Banks put it, "He wants probably to show the world that the Senate moves right or left at the wave of his hand." Not surprisingly, the president grew increasingly perturbed and ordered Fish not to communicate any confidential information to Sumner, who was, "'probably without knowing it, unfair & not accurate' in his representation of what he receives from the Dept."[21]

Carl Schurz echoed much of what Sumner said, exhibiting "a very poor opinion of the people" of Santo Domingo. The treaty's chief paladin, Oliver Morton, defended the Dominicans "in their true natures, as a harmless set." Indeed, he argued that the relative sparseness of the population left the fertile and resource-rich country a prime field for American enterprise. Cornelius Cole, who had sailed with Babcock on his first trip, invoked his personal knowledge to educate his colleagues regarding Santo Domingo's economic and strategic advantages. A few days into the debate, the president himself used a press interview to emphasize four central points: (1) annexation would provide the United States with abundant sugar, coffee, and other tropical products; (2) the new free-trade relationship would compel other countries and colonies in the region to remove barriers against American exports; (3) the immense size of the United States necessitated the development of overseas defensive outposts; and (4) such an outpost commanding the Gulf of Mexico would prove invaluable in the event of hostilities with foreign powers.[22]

But Grant's interview appeared the day after the treaty's ratification deadline, by which time he had begun to consider alternatives. One option was to extend the time for ratification of the treaty. Another was to achieve annexation by joint resolution, requiring a simple majority in each house, as had been done with Texas in 1845. Grant also considered sending a new set of commissioners to Santo Domingo to report on the nation's assets and prospects, but in early April he abandoned that idea, fearing it would spur more controversy in the press than it would allay in the Senate. The arrival of representatives from Santo Domingo empowered to negotiate an extension of the deadline gave the administration additional time to marshal its forces in the treaty's behalf.[23] On March 31 Grant submitted to the Senate a treaty with Colombia authorizing the construction of an interoceanic canal across the Isthmus of Panama, thereby underscoring the strategic argument for establishing a US naval station at Samaná Bay.[24]

Meanwhile, during this early phase of the ratification struggle, events in Santo Domingo began to unfold in ways that would jeopardize the treaty's approval. As early as December 1869, in the wake of the treaty signing, commercial agent Raymond Perry had cryptically warned Fish that self-interest underlay the actions of some individuals involved in the project. Initially, Perry himself had expressed a desire to make some "good hard money" during his sojourn, and Fabens and Cazneau had dangled the prospect of riches before his eyes. But when these dreams did not pan out, Perry grew disenchanted and leveled more explicit imputations against the two men in the winter and spring of 1870. On February 20 he wrote to Fish that both were corresponding with Babcock in Washington and that Cazneau, claiming to be an agent of the American government, used the White House envelopes from Babcock "as capital for himself and friends." Perry confided, "I found it necessary to tell this man in presence of President Báez and his Cabinet that he was a 'trickster and a dishonest man.'" He told Fish, "I do not wish to trouble you with any of my private affairs, but when such men as I have mentioned are in correspondence with the Departments, it is time my Govmt should be informed of their characters." Fish showed Perry's letter to Grant on March 18, but the president saw no reason to curtail his lobbying efforts on behalf of the treaty.[25]

At the same time, Perry tried to stay on Babcock's good side, assuring him that "everything is working favorably for annexation." But he also wrote, "You may be sorry to hear that I have had some sharp words with Cazneau. He . . . exhibits your letters to make capital for himself & Fabens. They are not true men, General, they are full of little dirty tricks, and will use or abuse their Gvt. or friends for their own interest."[26]

Perry's letter alarmed Babcock, as did one from Cazneau, who wrote that the commercial agent's lack of "tact, forethought, and experience" was "embarrassing affairs here." He warned, "Perry's want of discretion and self-control" must "not be suffered to check the proper shaping-out of the great business in hand, that is now in the high tide of success." Babcock could not have forgotten the 1,000 acres he had been promised, and he used his diplomatic skills to pacify Perry. He warned the agent that reports of disagreements among the Americans in Santo Domingo were being "used to a disadvantage" by the treaty's opponents. It was important that they all "unite in the great object, viz. securing to our Government the valuable foot hold in the West Indies. . . . I am sure you wish to serve the interest of the President, and will not allow any personal feelings to prejudice you against his wishes." Babcock closed with an admonition that, in his communications, Perry should "not put any private matters with official [ones]—for they have to be shown if the information is used."[27]

But Perry would not be cajoled or commanded. He insisted he had always adhered to a "strict line of duty uninfluenced by influential friends or foes. This has been to serve President Grant and the interest of our Government, to aide [sic] in every possible way the cause of annexation." He continued, "I do not object to any man making money provided it is not done under false pretences and does not effect [sic] the financial interest of our Government." And that is what would happen if Cazneau, Fabens, and Báez got their way, he asserted. Perry closed his reply to Babcock: "I shall never hesitate from any motives of personal prudence to explore any intrigues against my Government which may come to my knowledge." He neglected to mention to Babcock that he had applied to Grant for appointment as US marshal for Santo Domingo in the event of annexation, and that he had listed Báez as one of his "endorcers."[28]

Perry's complaints against Fabens and Cazneau became enmeshed with the case of Davis Hatch, the American businessman detained by the Dominican authorities since the summer of 1869. Hatch was a rival of Fabens and Cazneau in the quest for economic concessions, and he was an ally of José Cabral, Báez's chief political antagonist. In the early 1860s, when Spain temporarily controlled Santo Domingo, Hatch had secured a concession to develop salt mines in Azua province for an American company. After the Dominicans regained their country in 1865, Báez became president and annulled Hatch's grant, but when Cabral seized control from Báez in 1866, he restored it. The grateful American not only tilted toward Cabral's faction within Santo Domingo but also tried to promote a good opinion of Cabral in the United States. He wrote articles for the *New York Times* praising the "virtue, patriotism and intelligence" of the Cabralistas and denouncing Báez as "mystifying, shuffling, intriguing and deceiving." Hatch also wrote letters to friends in Washington denouncing Andrew Johnson's appointment of Báez's friend Cazneau as US commissioner and consul general to the Dominican Republic. On Sumner's motion, the Senate tabled Cazneau's nomination. It was not surprising, then, that after Báez regained power in 1868, he allowed Hatch to resume his business dealings in Azua only on the condition that he lend no aid to factions opposing the government.[29]

Nonetheless, when Cabral mounted a new insurrection in mid-1869, the Báez government suspected Hatch of colluding with the rebels. The authorities arrested him in August and charged him with storing rebel arms and harboring insurgent leaders at his house. Hatch maintained his innocence, although he admitted he had given lodging to some of Cabral's officers and even to Cabral himself. In addition, a US naval commander operating in the Caribbean reported to Washington that Hatch, with no legal standing, had issued a clean bill of health to the rebel ship *Telégrafo*, permitting it to clear the Dominican port of Barrahona, the site of Hatch's home and business. US commercial agent J. Somers Smith interceded with Báez on Hatch's behalf after his arrest, but the Dominican president allowed his trial to go forward, and Babcock, who was present in Santo Domingo at the time, declined to intervene.[30]

Smith apprised Fish of the situation, endorsing Hatch's version of events and laying considerable blame on Babcock for Hatch's continued detention. Several weeks passed before the State Department responded to Smith, at which time it merely expressed the hope that his "representations" to the Dominicans had succeeded. By then, the administration had already decided to replace Smith. In one of his last dispatches, Smith reported that Hatch had been tried, convicted, and sentenced to death, but Báez had granted him a pardon. When Smith's replacement, Perry, arrived in mid-November, he informed Fish that Báez had pardoned Hatch on the condition that he leave the country. The authorities did not release Hatch, however, and he fired off several letters to the new commercial agent, pleading for help.[31]

Failing to get satisfaction from Perry, Hatch turned to Senator Orris Ferry, who happened to be from his hometown of Norwalk, Connecticut. Ferry forwarded a letter from Hatch to the State Department on January 11. Up to that time, Fish had been operating on the information that Hatch had been pardoned, but the next day he sent instructions to Perry to "use your efforts to secure his release." Perry promptly asked the Dominican government to inform him "at once" as to its "intentions." In reporting his action to Fish on February 8, Perry alleged that "Cazneau and Fabiens [sic] have used their influence to keep him [Hatch] where he is, for certain selfish and financial reasons known to themselves, and President Báez is only too willing to be influenced by them." Perry added, "I have *thought* what I have *now written*, for some time, but I supposed it, perhaps, was prejudice." Perry's new candor may have sprung from his chagrin at being left out of the entrepreneurial loop in Santo Domingo. He had asked the Báez government to lease a building in the capital to a friend who wanted to establish a hotel, but the building housed the supreme court, and the government offered an alternative structure. Cazneau wrote to Babcock, "This has not satisfied Major Perry, and he renews his demand for the instant release of Mr. Hatch."[32]

The Dominicans initially pushed back. They reiterated the grounds for Hatch's trial and conviction; they acknowledged his pardon but cited policy reasons for detaining him. Hatch would have gone free, wrote Gautier, "had it not been for the irreconcilable [sic] enmity with which he attacks the government in all of its acts through the newspapers and their agents, inventing calumnies to divert the public mind against annexation." Nonetheless, if Fish insisted on his release, the government would "be very glad to satisfy his wishes." The State Department instructed Perry to demand Hatch's "immediate release," but Perry had already enlisted the help of Admiral Poor, commanding the small fleet of US warships in Dominican waters. Poor advised President Báez that Hatch's prompt release "would exercise a greater influence to his [Báez's] advantage than anything that Hatch or his friends could do, with the aid of the press, to the contrary." This logic—plus, no doubt, the stars on the admiral's tunic—convinced Báez to let Hatch go.[33]

But despite this anticlimactic resolution, the Hatch affair was not over. Convinced that Báez, Fabens, and Cazneau had "persecuted" him, Hatch was determined to get "revenge." Shortly after his release he wrote a scathing letter to Babcock stating that, for countenancing his incarceration, "you ought to have been born in the days of the Inquisition." He charged, "You certainly would not go so far [on] one side of your line of duty as to encourage Mr. Báez in persecuting me, were it not for the hope of some favor—some reward—directly or indirectly." Taking refuge in Havana, Hatch inspired (and probably wrote in part) a story in the *New York World* that censured Babcock's "un-American actions." He also sent a copy of his letter to Babcock to Senator Ferry. The Hatch case would surface again when the battle over ratification of the treaty reached its climax.[34]

After the March 29, 1870, expiration of the ratification deadline, the treaty languished in limbo. In early April Ben Butler tried to get the House to explore the possibility of annexation by joint resolution, but that effort got nowhere. In late April the *New York Times* published a lengthy article touting Santo Domingo as the "Gem of the Antilles." In pursuing ratification, the paper said, Grant was "as persistent in 'fighting it out on this line if it takes all summer,' as he was during the rebellion." About this time Fabens arrived in Washington as the newly appointed minister from the Dominican Republic. Bypassing Fish, he went immediately to the White House to map strategy with Grant, who expressed confidence that the administration stood within striking distance of getting the necessary two-thirds of the Senate on its side. Several days later Fabens and Fish signed a new article extending the ratification deadline to July 1.[35]

Fabens also met with Sumner in a session that lasted four hours. In a report to Báez, the minister claimed that he was "fortunately able to answer many of his [Sumner's] objections to the measure of annexation and to refute certain scandals which malicious persons had conveyed to him." "I have hopes," he chirped, "that he may be induced to sustain the Treaty and if so there is no difficulty in the way of a speedy ratification." In reality, Fabens was sugarcoating Sumner's attitude, for the senator still clung to the idea of a protectorate rather than annexation.[36]

In early May Grant asked Fish to consult with administration senators to develop amendments that would tip the balance toward the treaty's acceptance. He specifically suggested modifications stipulating that public lands were "not to be made liable" for the Dominican debt, calling for the appointment of commissioners to oversee the "application of the purchase money in the liquidation of the public debt," setting priorities for paying the debt held by foreign creditors first, and providing that the United States would "in no event be liable beyond the amount of the purchase money." Fish cast these points into a formal amendment, which Grant approved, and sent it to Michigan senator Jacob Howard. The State Department also instructed Perry to inform Báez of Grant's hope that "with some alterations not very materially affecting the general principles and theory of the Treaty, it may obtain the assent of the Senate."[37]

Besides maneuvering in Washington, the administration sought to win the battle for public opinion. Although Fish still had doubts about the suitability of the Dominican population for American citizenship, he argued that Santo Domingo was "capable of as much production as Cuba." He wrote to influential New Yorker James A. Hamilton, son of Alexander Hamilton, that annexation "would give us what we need, a harbor *outside* our own Coast line—the want of this gave efficiency to the Blockade runners during our late war." Like Grant, Fish portrayed Santo Domingo as "the *key* of the Gulf." Annexation would compel Spain to give up Cuba and its other possessions, spurring an upheaval that would render it all the more difficult for Great Britain to hang on to its Western Hemisphere possessions.[38]

Such reasoning also infused the speeches at a pro-annexation rally in New York organized by Nathaniel Banks and others. Banks described Grant as "greatly interested" in the meeting, and the president was not disappointed. The enthusiastic Cooper Institute crowd unanimously passed resolutions that, in addition to endorsing the strategic argument, expressed "a deep solicitude in whatever affects the welfare and prosperity of commerce." Babcock thanked one of the speakers for the meeting's "decided success."[39]

Still, substantial opposition persisted in the Senate. To the *New York Herald*, the reason seemed clear: a number of senators were paying scant attention to policy concerns and focusing instead on allegations of impropriety connected with the project. "But," the paper editorialized, "is there ever a question of territorial purchase or acquisition without a job—without there being certain parties who will make money from it? The wheels of government in this country would be stopped if we waited till there could be no jobs. It is a great evil, no doubt, but shall we refuse to do a great and good thing in the interest of the country because of some incidental benefit to private parties?"[40]

In the face of discouraging head counts in the Senate, Fish worked to salvage the treaty's chances. He proposed yet another amendment that would give Congress the future option of admitting the territory of Santo Domingo as a state or reestablishing it as a country, either completely independent or as part of a West Indian confederation under American protection. "This proposition," Fish told the president, "would find friends among those who desire the influence of our institutions and our protection to be extended to San Domingo, and to the other islands, but who hesitate upon the question of absorption of tropical possessions." But Grant was wary of any proposal that seemed to originate with the treaty's Senate detractors. Fish assured the president that the amendment had been his own idea and warned that the treaty would "be rejected unless some of its opponents are gained over by some new feature or principle." Grant authorized the secretary to consult Sumner and others about the proposal, but he made few converts.[41]

On May 31 Grant sent the Senate an earnest message noting the extension of the ratification deadline and setting forth once again the economic and strategic arguments in favor of annexation. He asserted that the purchase price was adequate to cover the Dominican debt, and he urged the Senate to devise amendments governing the payment structure along the lines of the modifications he had proposed to Fish. To appeal to the more radical wing of the Republican Party, the president said that annexation and consequent economic development would "give remunerative wages to tens of thousands of laborers not now on the island," and as a result, "Puerto Rico and Cuba will have to abolish slavery, as a measure of self-preservation to retain their laborers." In sum, he touted annexation as "a rapid stride toward that greatness which the intelligence, industry, and enterprise of the citizens of the United States entitle this country to assume among nations."[42]

But the administration's efforts were not helped by Raymond Perry's return to the United States on a leave of absence in late May. Before departing, Perry had fallen into a heated quarrel with Dominican officials. Hearing that the country's consulting senate was considering an application by Cazneau for a large land grant for an immigration project, Perry sent a protest directly to that body, arguing that the concession would violate the pending treaty, which barred any new grants after November 29, the date it had been signed. Gautier vigorously objected to Perry's breach of protocol in addressing the senate directly. Moreover, Gautier claimed that the project grew out of a grant dating back to 1866, and the application concerned only a revision that would allow the creation of immigrant settlements along the Haitian border as a defense measure. As it happened, the Dominican senate rejected the application and Cazneau withdrew it, but Perry persisted in demanding a copy of the papers and accused Gautier of having a financial interest in the project. Finally, the indignant foreign secretary asked Fish to "prevent" Perry's return to Santo Domingo after his leave.[43]

Before he left, Perry also engaged in an angry correspondence with Cazneau, who sent the letters to Fish and complained that Perry's interference seriously jeopardized annexation. By bringing the dispute to Fish's attention, Cazneau betrayed no fear that his project to establish "a line of self-protecting American settlements" along the Haitian border would be seen as some sort of nefarious scheme that he should try to hide. Rather, Cazneau denounced Perry as "a man of reckless and violent impulses" who harbored a "rough contempt for the colored citizens, whom he does not hesitate to surprise with a blow when they displease him." Just before Perry departed, he committed an act that underscored Cazneau's characterization. The agent was supporting an American defendant in a pending lawsuit, and one day in open court he walked up to the plaintiff and slapped him in the face. "Unfortunately," Gautier wrote to Fish, "the man who received the blow is a negro. The painful sensation produced by this occurrence in society here could not well be exaggerated." Gautier renewed his request for Perry's recall.[44]

Still seething when he arrived in Washington, Perry lost no time in telling Fish that Báez had been granting new concessions to Fabens and Cazneau and had been "taking up Government lands" for himself. Moreover, labeling Babcock a "damned rascal," he claimed the general had urged him to assist Fabens and Cazneau in their applications for grants. Should he do so, Babcock allegedly said, Perry "could be a rich man before he left the Island." Perry gave Fish a sheaf of papers that supported his "suspicions," but they contained "no specific fact," and the secretary asked him to put his charges in writing.[45]

Perry also showed copies of his correspondence with Gautier and Cazneau to Sumner. The senator gladly embraced the impulsive young man, whose father later sent him a personal note to "thank you for your friendly course towards my son Raymond in his troubles in the St. Domingo affair." Either Sumner or Perry gave Perry's correspondence to the *New York Herald*, which printed an article that contained lengthy, nearly verbatim passages from the letters. Fish decided to apprise Grant of Perry's charges, especially as they related to Babcock, but Grant had already heard them. Indeed, Perry had seen Grant himself. The president had cut the conversation short before Perry could bring up any allegations against Babcock, but Grant now told Fish that Perry was "running about town, repeating them." The president did not believe Perry's charges, but he nonetheless assured Fish that he had warned "Babcock that if any thing dishonorable or dishonest was proved" against him, "he should answer [for] it with his Commission."[46]

Grant lost no time in fighting Perry's allegations head-on in press interviews. According to the *New York Herald*, "President Grant has implicit confidence in the honor and integrity of General Babcock, and believes that a careful investigation of the charges and of the material upon which they are based will demonstrate that there has been nothing in his conduct in this matter which should justly expose him to adverse criticism." Moreover, Grant stated that any land grants by the Dominican government since the treaty signing "will be treated as null and void by the United States government." Hence, even if it turned out that Báez had given concessions to private speculators, "it cannot in all fairness be used as a sound argument against the ratification of the treaty. It ought not to affect the vote of a single Senator."[47]

Fabens too sought to counteract Perry's stories. He met with Sumner and said he would "cheerfully—cordially—give up everything I have in Santo Domingo, if such an act will remove so much as the obstacle of a hair in the way of ratification of the annexation treaty. *I mean this.*"[48] Sumner was unmoved. Indeed, he later told a *Herald* reporter that Fabens's presence in Washington "added fresh suspicions" regarding the treaty. He claimed that Fabens had told him that Báez had given him "full powers to do just as he pleased" and that Fabens was willing to amend the treaty in any way Sumner might suggest. "All he wanted was to have St. Domingo annexed, and he was not particular about the manner in which it was done."[49]

After their conversation, the livid Fabens exclaimed to Babcock, "If Mr. Sumner (great as he is in his own conceit) really wants to contest with the pen, I can beat him—*easy*. I was educated at Cambridge as well as he, and curious as it may sound, I feel in my very marrow that I can lay him out, in all his fuss and flummery—beautiful." Once Sumner's version of the meeting appeared in the press, Fabens, donning his hat as minister from Santo Domingo, complained to Fish that the senator had "distorted" their conversation "to meet his personal ends." Indeed, Sumner's "form and manner" in discussing the treaty was so bitter as to convince Fabens that "his opposition to its ratification was inspired by personal and not patriotic motives." Sumner "repeatedly asked me to drop this an[nexa]tion scheme and work up a new measure for a protectorate, *offering in that case to vote $5,000,000 for Santo Domingo.* If there has been anything in this whole matter savoring of 'corruption,' if any improper influences have been used to affect the fate of the treaty, the stigma must rest upon Mr. Sumner."[50]

Fish did not hold Fabens in high regard, and it is unclear to what extent he used these allegations of Sumner's "corruption." The secretary did, however, attempt to nullify Perry's charges. After being asked to submit his accusations against Babcock in writing, Perry responded with a letter that made no mention of Babcock's name. Although he had intended to make "a thurough [sic] disclosure," his "reluctance to do or to say any thing that would influence the Senate in opposing the ratification of the treaty and my regard for the reputation of one directly connected with the President has prevented my doing so." Perry supplemented this new solicitude for Babcock's reputation with florid encomia for annexation, apparently designed to shore up his bona fides with the president.[51] He need not have bothered, for his relations with the White House were beyond repair. Fish's reply stated that because Perry had refused to "mention names and facts," the government must regard his charges "as now withdrawn"—just the sort of red flag that set Perry off. He wrote a long letter dated June 7 (but not delivered until June 11), condemning Babcock, Fabens, Cazneau, and Báez. He labeled the draft of his letter to Fish "To Prevaricator," suggesting his feelings about the administration.[52]

Meanwhile, Grant's enemies in the Senate were not content to confine their discussion of the treaty to executive session, where they could score few points among the public. One alternative was to debate the document in open session, but resolutions to do so failed. After Perry circulated his stories, Carl Schurz offered a resolution to direct the Foreign Relations Committee to "inquire into the conduct of certain agents connected with the negotiation of the treaty"—obviously aimed at Babcock. But the Senate narrowly defeated this move, with Vice President Schuyler Colfax casting the tie-breaking vote.[53]

Thus thwarted, the president's opponents turned to the Davis Hatch case. In mid-May Hatch had sent Senator Ferry a petition asking the United States to intervene on his behalf with the Dominican government to help him obtain compensation. He demanded $8,547.12 for lost property and $50,000 for what he had "suffered in person, character, and influence." Although Hatch's fantastic request had no chance, Ferry seized it as an excuse to delve into the Dominican business in general. In presenting the petition on June 8, he not only championed Hatch but also condemned Babcock for working "to keep an innocent citizen in prison." At this, Sumner could not help interjecting that Babcock "ought to be cashiered at once" and his name "struck from the roll of honorable men." Ferry called for an investigation by the Foreign Relations Committee, but other senators argued that putting Sumner in charge would negate "the legal presumption that a man is innocent until proven guilty." Nathaniel Banks described the debate as "violent & vile," noting that "Mr. Sumner attacks Genl Grant as he did Mr. Johnson." The Senate assigned the question to a select committee, but the purpose of the Hatch investigation was clear. As one administration senator put it, "It is simply the Senate undertaking to investigate the conduct of the President for the purpose of affecting action upon a pending treaty."[54]

Vice President Colfax could not pack the select committee solely with administration backers, but he did give them a majority of the seven seats; the minority included Ferry and Schurz. James Nye of Nevada took the gavel as chairman, and Babcock lost no time in sending Nye pointers on how to counter Sumner's "numerous false misstatements." Nye launched hearings immediately. Although the sessions were closed, leaks from all sides provided the press with fairly accurate accounts of the proceedings—which the treaty's opponents were happy to see published. Hatch did not show up, having remained in St. Thomas rather than returning to the United States to push his case personally. In that sense, the hearings were *Hamlet* without Hamlet, but the absence of the erratic Hatch may have worked to the advantage of the treaty opponents, who were less interested in redressing his grievances than in undermining the treaty (and in some cases, Grant's entire presidency). The star witness for the prosecution was Perry. True to form, he showed up in the committee room armed, explaining to the incredulous senators that he never went anywhere without his revolver.[55]

The questions the senators raised in the hearings did not connote an impartial investigation of Hatch's petition; rather, the proceedings were a squaring off of pro- and anti-administration camps. Ferry and Schurz, aided by Democrat George Vickers, did everything in their power to discredit Babcock and the treaty. Michigan's Jacob Howard, chairman Nye, and, to a lesser degree, George Williams of Oregon and Willard Warner of Alabama (all Republicans) took aim at Perry. Perry charged that Babcock had advised him not to intercede with the Dominicans on Hatch's behalf because his release would injure the annexation project. He alleged that Babcock had chided him for protesting the government's issuing of grants in the spring of 1870, claiming that doing so could hurt the treaty's prospects and that such questions could be handled after the treaty's ratification. Perry also asserted that Babcock had told him that he, Babcock, possessed real estate interests with Fabens and Cazneau in Santo Domingo.[56]

Babcock denied all these charges. In reconstructing events during his trips to Santo Domingo, he had the aid of his diary, although he made no mention of its existence to the committee, which could have subpoenaed it. His calm demeanor contrasted with that of the excitable Perry. He frankly admitted that he had not interceded on Hatch's behalf, in large part because he lacked the diplomatic standing to do so. Fish confirmed this point, testifying that Babcock's authority related solely to negotiating the treaty and nothing more. Babcock insisted that he had never told Perry "or anybody else that I did not wish Mr. Hatch released on account of anything he would say or could do as to annexation, because I understood . . . that Mr. Hatch was in favor of annexation of the island of San Domingo." Again Fish weighed in, saying he could not conceive of an American officer asking Perry not to intervene, and adding that such advice would have been a "great indelicacy" and that Babcock's "instructions did not anticipate any case of that kind."[57]

Whatever the parameters of his authority, Babcock considered Hatch guilty of aiding the rebels. He testified he had first heard of Hatch upon receiving a report that a vessel bearing arms for the Cabralistas had been consigned to him. Even more incriminating was evidence that Hatch, without any legal authority, had given clearance papers to the *Telégrafo*, which the United States regarded as a pirate vessel. "I believed Mr. Hatch was guilty of joining the rebellion, and I was not going to have anything to do with the case." According to Babcock's diary, during his first trip to Santo Domingo he had told Báez he would "not interfere with Mr. Hatch" but "would trust" Báez to deal with him. In his testimony, however, he implied that he had gone a bit further. In language that does not appear in his diary, Babcock said that after Hatch's arrest and before his trial, he had told Báez, "Mr. President, you must be certain that you are right in the question of law, if you try Mr. Hatch for any such thing; if you have the proof positive that he has been attempting to overthrow your government, I do not suppose our government will in any way interfere in the case; but you must be very certain that your evidence is entirely correct." During his testimony, Fish presented a lengthy document that cataloged the charges and evidence against Hatch. The committee's majority deemed the judicial process to be in keeping with Dominican practice and therefore not susceptible to complaint by the United States, but the minority denounced it as "a barbarous farce—a transparent act of persecution."[58]

As the treaty's opponents had planned, testimony ranged beyond the Hatch case and dealt with annexation itself, especially the alleged motives of its promoters. Perry declared that he regarded Santo Domingo as "a very valuable acquisition," but he also charged that the self-seeking sponsorship of Fabens, Cazneau, Báez, and Babcock had tainted the project. "Babcock often told me," Perry insisted, "that I must stand by Cazneau and Fabens, and advise with them; that they represented large interests on the island; that he had interests with them." Babcock vehemently denied Perry's charge. Early in the hearings Senator Howard asked Babcock if Báez "or the authorities there" had ever given him a grant of land. Babcock said no and recounted the incident, just before the signing of the treaty, when Báez had offered him a land grant, which he had refused as inappropriate and hazardous to ratification. He did not mention his diary entry stating that he would "be pleased to have the 1000 acres of Palenque promised in case of annexation," a promise apparently made by Fabens. When a committee member asked Babcock to respond to Perry's charge that he had said he "had interests with" Cazneau and Fabens, he insisted, "It is not true. I never had one cent interest with either gentleman on the island." Either Babcock committed perjury or his answer was only technically true at best, either because someone else had promised him the 1,000 acres or because he had not yet actually come into the interest "on the island" while annexation remained unconsummated.[59]

Committee members might have pursued the question of Babcock's "interest" with Fabens, but they did not broach it when he took the stand. Indeed, Schurz vigorously opposed Fabens's testifying at all, most likely because he feared Fabens would sustain Babcock's version of events. Fabens denied virtually all Perry's charges regarding any effort by him, Cazneau, or Babcock to block Hatch's release. Indeed, he said that Cazneau had interceded with Báez to save Hatch's life, and he claimed that Hatch's salt mine concession was still in force. He conceded that Hatch was "very moral and virtuous" in his private life, but at issue was not Hatch's personal character but his "political error," for it was "a great political crime to excite revolution in a country like that."[60]

As the investigation unfolded, Perry worked closely with Schurz, Ferry, Sumner, and other senators, an experience he found heady indeed. In the middle of the hearings he wrote his parents a letter on US Senate stationery: "I have started on a movement in Washington. There is no knowing what is to be the result of it but I am telling the truth from beginning to end and working very hard day and night[;] it is harder work than farming. . . . I have many friends today to help me. I do not like to mention names, untill [sic] we get through with this mysterious affair, old senators and men who know you at home tell me that my course has been a very honorable one and if I carry my point my reputation is made for this world."[61]

Administration senators funneled information about the hearings to Grant, who proved more than willing to help them discredit Perry. At a cabinet meeting he said that "grave charges" had been made against Perry "while in the Army, swindling a Bank in New Orleans, Rape upon a small girl, &c." In his anger, the president may have been repeating unfounded rumors, but Secretary of War William Belknap got the hint, for the War Department quickly dug up the records of Perry's checkered military career and gave them to Senator Warner. Warner entered the material into the committee's record, and he and other committee members raised questions about Perry's shootings and other incidents. Perry defended his actions and insisted that he had "always been honorably discharged from all these complaints made against me."[62]

Administration committee members also pounced on Perry's admission that his communications with the State Department had painted the Dominicans' support for annexation more favorably than the situation warranted. He claimed to have "misrepresented things" out of fear of losing his job, but, he confessed, "I had no business to do so." He admitted in his June 7 report to Fish that he had "very wrongly slightly yielded to the request of Báez and Cazneau, and the wishes of others, and tried to make it appear that there was much enthusiasm on the part of the people." In an official reprimand, Fish told Perry that failing to comply with instructions to report fully to the department and allowing himself "to be seduced into communicating incorrect information" were "cause for censure." Fish also disapproved of Perry ignoring proper channels by communicating directly with the Dominican consulting senate. As the hearings came to a close, Senator Howard entered Fish's reprimand into the record as a final impeachment of Perry's veracity. Shortly thereafter he resigned.[63]

The Hatch hearings changed few senators' minds, but they did illustrate the depth of animosity between the administration and its opponents. Grant was convinced that the investigation had been designed to injure him. It was "strange," he told Fish, "that men cannot allow others to differ with them, without charging corruption as the cause of the difference." He resented insinuations that he stood to profit personally from his policy, and he hesitated, defensively and perhaps naïvely, to impute motives of self-interest to those who served him. In the cabinet, Fish noted, the president referred "warmly & affectionately to Babcock, whose innocence of the charges against him he confidently believes." Grant had earlier warned Babcock that he would lose his commission "if any thing dishonorable or dishonest was proved" against him. His continued expressions of affection suggested either that Babcock had told him about his 1,000-acre prospect and Grant did not consider it "dishonorable or dishonest" or, more likely, that Babcock had succeeded in concealing from the president his own material interest "in case of annexation." After the hearings, the self-satisfied Babcock wrote to Adam Badeau: "Your humble serv[an]t has been *investigated*, since you left, but I think not hurt much. They were after the President and hoped to hitch something onto me—and thus hurt the old man."[64]

The committee's majority and minority reports reflected the senators' aims in the hearings. According to Nye and his allies, the charge that Babcock was "guilty of misconduct" was "totally unfounded, and . . . he conducted himself throughout with perfect honesty and sincerity." Moreover, they declared, "in its negotiation and preparation, the treaty is free from any fraud or unfairness, and . . . the agents employed by the respective governments have all acted with becoming frankness and sincerity." In contrast, the minority report, prepared by Schurz, maintained that "all the influence he [Babcock] used with regard to the Hatch case was invariably directed against the incarcerated man." Furthermore, the minority characterized Babcock's "confidential relations with Mr. Cazneau as most suspicious" and argued that "the only explanation suggesting itself of the efforts made by Cazneau, Báez, and friends, to detain Mr. Hatch in prison, is that Mr. Hatch might, if at liberty, have interfered with 'jobs' in connection with the treaty." Yet Schurz knew that the evidence on that point was limited and inconclusive, and he admitted, "As to the matter of transactions of a corrupt nature connected with the annexation scheme, the committee acquired only incidental information" because its mandate had been limited to the Hatch matter.[65]

Neither report addressed the merits of annexation, and that omission represented a triumph for its opponents. Every comment, every speech, every newspaper report or editorial devoted to the Hatch investigation drew attention away from Grant's portrait of Santo Domingo's advantages. The investigation had succeeded in planting seeds of doubt about the uprightness of the project, which easily took root in this era of heightened suspicion of public misconduct. It made annexation a question of not what was worthwhile but what was worthy.

In the weeks before the final ratification debate in the Senate, Grant mobilized all his forces. "The fight has opened," Babcock wrote, "and he is as much in earnest, as he was in the Wilderness." The president's principal weapon was patronage. As Fish noted, Grant said he wanted "all his friends to use all proper efforts to aid him, that he will not consider those who oppose his policy as entitled to influence in obtaining positions under him, [and] that he will not let those who oppose him 'name Ministers to London,' &c &c." This last point referred to Sumner's sponsorship of Motley, the minister to England, whose days in that post were numbered. Recognizing Sumner as the leader of the opposition to the treaty, Grant sent the Senate a letter in his own hand declaring that, at their meeting at Sumner's house that past winter, the senator had used "such language as to leave no doubt upon my mind that he would support it."[66]

Grant also expected loyalty from his cabinet on the question. He got it from Fish, who, despite his private misgivings about the management of the negotiations, personally lobbied wavering senators. But, Grant complained, Boutwell "opposed" it; Hoar "says nothing in its favor, but sneers at it"; and Cox "does not open his mouth, not a word in favor of it."[67]

Hoar posed other problems for Grant. Several senators expressed dissatisfaction with the attorney general's approach to departmental patronage. Moreover, both Hoar and Boutwell were from Massachusetts, and from the beginning, the attorney general had assured the president that he would willingly step down to alleviate that embarrassment. On June 15 Grant invited Hoar to the White House and requested his resignation, which he submitted immediately. The president particularly wished to propitiate southern senators, and the next day he nominated Amos T. Akerman of Georgia.[68]

Grant felt genuinely conflicted over dismissing Hoar. He saluted him as "able, patriotic, and devoted" and privately extolled him as "a man of great abilities, & learning, & a very charming companion, & true man, & friend." Yet when Fish asked whether Hoar's resignation was connected with the Santo Domingo fight, the president paused and then gave a "peculiar & guarded" reply: "If it was, no one knows it." He frankly admitted, "I have said to Senators & others that I mean to recognize my friends, & those who sustain my policy." Grant expressed his "great regard & affection for Judge Hoar," but, he told Fish, "he has not the capacity of making himself popular with politicians." That comment marked a milestone in Grant's political journey since telling Sherman in 1868 that he had run for president to save the country from "mere trading politicians." After fifteen months in office, he had acquired a fuller understanding of the grim reality of governance in Washington.[69]

Part of that reality was that he could never propitiate obdurate enemies like Sumner, who told Henry Longfellow, "there is much disappointment about the Presdt, who has no experience & little wisdom."

The president returned the contempt. Four days before the treaty was due to expire, Grant told Ohio governor Rutherford Hayes that Sumner was "a man of very little practical sense, puffed-up, and unsound." He branded Schurz "an infidel and atheist; [who] had been a rebel in his own country—as much a rebel against his government as Jeff Davis." When Hayes questioned why the administration wanted Santo Domingo, the president, "in a rapid, brief, but comprehensive way set forth its advantages, [and] described the island, its productions, people etc., etc., in a most capital way." Even so, Grant doubted the treaty could be ratified. Hayes wrote in his diary, "He said he felt 'much embittered' against Sumner for unjust attacks on Major Babcock. Major Babcock could not defend himself; . . . 'I can defend myself, but he is merely a major of engineers with no opportunity to meet a Senator.'"[70]

The same day that he spoke with Hayes, Grant gave Babcock a spirited defense in a letter to Senator Nye. Schurz, possessed by the idea that militarism dominated the administration, had inserted in the committee's minority report a charge that in the preliminary protocol signed with the Dominicans, Babcock had "introduced himself in the official capacity of an 'aide-de-camp to the President of the United States.'" This was not true. The Dominicans had prepared the text of the protocol and employed this designation as a mark of respect for Babcock's former role in the war. Babcock had apparently considered the phrase of no particular significance and had not challenged it. Schurz also noted that the protocol had pledged the president "privately, to use all his influence, in order that the idea of annexing the Dominican Republic to the United States may acquire such a degree of popularity among members of Congress as will be necessary for its accomplishment; and to make no communication to that body until he shall be certain that it will be approved by a majority." With the *Tybee*'s sails about to be unfurled, Babcock had failed to raise an objection to this obviously impossible stipulation, which could have jeopardized the whole project. Schurz denounced the proposed "proceeding" as "utterly unprecedented in the history of this republic" and charged that Babcock must have gone "so far beyond his instructions as to seriously compromise the name of the President." Schurz's rhetorical gambit was clear: either Babcock had violated his instructions or the president himself had sanctioned a great wrong. Deeply angered, Grant did not throw his secretary to the wolves. In his letter to Nye he stoutly maintained that "Gen. Babcock did not exceed my wishes or my verbal instructions." He pointed out that the protocol "was not binding, or intended to be binding upon either government, unless each saw fit to continue the negotiations. . . . Gen. Babcock's conduct throughout meets my entire approval."[71]

By early June, Grant had decided to remove Motley as minister to Great Britain and had begun to canvass senators about a possible successor. Several months earlier, in an unguarded moment, Fish had suggested to Sumner that he could replace Motley. Calling on the senator some time during the winter or early spring, Fish had found him deeply depressed by overwork and his failed marriage; feeling sympathetic, Fish had remarked that time abroad as minister to Britain would do him good. Fortunately, the senator had replied that he would not take the place from his friend Motley, and Fish, realizing his error in making the suggestion, had immediately agreed that Sumner could make a foreign sojourn during the summer recess unburdened by official cares. Neither man said anything about this exchange until after the total collapse of comity between Sumner and the administration, when the senator charged that Fish had tried to bribe him with the English mission to get him to drop his objection to annexation. Fish vehemently denied Sumner's allegation, labeling his overture in early 1870 an "incautious remark of mine, called out by sympathy with a life-long friend, whom I found in deep distress."[72]

But in late June, as the treaty struggle reached its denouement, Senator Simon Cameron and Ben Butler, two of Grant's strongest congressional allies, visited Fish and seriously pushed for Sumner's appointment as minister to England. If Sumner left the Senate, they argued, the treaty could be postponed and carried during the next session of Congress. Even if Sumner declined the appointment, the mere offer would "deprive him of all appeal to sympathy on the score of persecution, or want of recognition," and thus "compel good behavior." The move would help heal divisions within the party and unify it for the 1870 elections.[73]

Fish thought enough of the suggestion to lay it before the cabinet. Grant scoffed at the idea. He would nominate Sumner "on condition that he first resign his seat in the Senate, & with the understanding that he would remove him as soon as the nomination was confirmed." Boutwell advised that if they did consider offering Sumner the appointment, they should first determine whether he would accept it, to avoid putting the president "in S's power by making the offer to be refused, & thrown up at him." Although Fish recorded in his diary that the notion had "at least acquired a lodgment as a question of expediency," Boutwell soon argued against making any change at the legation, and nothing came of the idea of approaching Sumner.[74]

When formal consideration of the treaty began late on the afternoon of June 29, Sumner saw no need to make extended remarks. On June 30, in a last-minute effort to capture doubting senators, Jacob Howard submitted the amendments Grant and Fish had devised to limit US liability for the Dominican debt. All were adopted, but that action proved to be of no consequence. The Senate rejected the treaty, amendments and all, by a vote of 28 to 28, far short of the two-thirds requirement. Sumner and Schurz led a total of nineteen Republicans who voted against the president's treaty.[75]

Postmortem analyses perpetuated the bitterness of the struggle. The pro-administration *New-York Standard* observed that the vote should have represented "the exact and impartial judgment of the Senate," but "other influences interfered." "No administration likes to encounter its friends in an Indian ambush, and this is the position in which it found Mr. Sumner in the San Domingo negotiation," the *Standard* stated. "The President having done him the honor to consult him on this treaty— as though he were in his Cabinet—he should have done the President the honor of announcing the change in his views." The *Daily Advertiser* from Sumner's hometown of Boston, in contrast, thought Grant's forceful marshaling of the resources of the presidency had overstepped the proper bounds of executive behavior. "It has been the course of an honest soldier, firmly convinced that the plan he had adopted was for the national good, and trampling upon all obstacles in the way with a view only to the end, as the same grand soldier marched from the Wilderness to Petersburg six years ago." That sort of leadership, "admirable for the conduct of a campaign in the field, is not properly to be applied to affairs of statesmanship. . . . [I]t is worthwhile to remember that a trait of the ideal soldier quite as commendable as the obstinate advance is the graceful acceptance of an assured defeat."[76]

But Grant did not yet concede that ultimate defeat was assured. Within a week, Fish had signed an agreement with Fabens extending for another year the deadline for exchanging ratifications of the Samaná Bay lease agreement, and the idea of annexation by joint resolution remained alive. Nor was Grant prepared to be gracious to men who had refused to meet him squarely in debating the treaty's merits but instead had assaulted his honor and integrity. For the past year Grant had wanted to fire Motley for his insubordination regarding the *Alabama* claims, but Fish had always persuaded him to leave the minister in place. The day after the treaty vote, Grant insisted that the time had come to name Motley's successor. Again Fish demurred, saying that Motley's behavior had improved since his original offense. He urged the president to allow the minister to remain in office until winter. "That I will not do," Grant shot back. "I will not allow Mr. Sumner to ride over me." Fish observed that he would be striking at Motley, not Sumner, and Grant responded, "It is the same thing." When Fish told him "the Country will not so understand it," Grant replied, "they will when the removal is made." He relented only in allowing Fish to tell Motley that his resignation would be accepted, rather than firing him outright. Grant believed that Sumner had lied to him and that personal animosity, not principle, lay at the heart of the senator's opposition to the treaty. He dismissed Motley not only out of anger but also because he had reached the conclusion that nothing he could do would appease Sumner or secure his support for future administration endeavors.[77]

Motley's dismissal had long been a matter of speculation. Nine months earlier, Fish had written to Sumner that, "under any other Government," Motley's violation of his instructions regarding the *Alabama* claims would have earned him "the most severe censure" or "an immediate recall." At the same time, William Gladstone had concluded that Fish's "slap in the face" in response to the minister's insubordination augured that "Motley will not long remain in England." In mid-May Grant had told Adam Badeau, who was leaving for London to become consul general, that he intended to remove Motley because he considered him "un-American in spirit and not a fitting representative of democracy." Several days before the treaty vote, Sumner himself had heard from his Senate colleague Henry Wilson that Grant had expressed his desire to appoint someone to London who was "more American." Even so, it proved unfortunate for the success of Grant's presidency that, over the months, he had bowed to Fish's pleas to retain the minister. Now, at the moment of supreme frustration after the treaty's defeat, firing Motley would *appear* to be *only* a petulant act of revenge against Sumner. Even Fish's own son-in-law said privately, "Grant is a vulgar bull dog" who "turned Motley out because he is a snob & the friend of Sumner." By seeming to engage in the sort of brutish behavior the senator so readily condemned, Grant handed Sumner an issue that tapped his vast reservoir of self-righteousness. "The treatment of Motley is brutal, cruel, & utterly indefensible," Sumner wailed to Longfellow. "Weary, disappointed, unhappy, I long to leave this place—&, if it were never to return, I think that I should take no lingering look behind."[78]

Motley's reaction was equally emotional. When Benjamin Moran, the secretary at the legation in London, suggested that the dignified response would be to tender his resignation, Motley flew into "a rage and he swore that he would not resign." As the startled Moran wrote in his diary, Motley's "manner and language were violent and undignified, childish and peevish. He swore at the President, damned his countrymen as vulgar and brutal, and wished the damned Govt. might be destroyed." Toying with the idea that he could hang on to his post under the Tenure of Office Act, Motley refused to resign. A shocked Henry Adams, who was visiting the legation, told Moran, "Motley is mad." Even the foreign secretary Lord Granville thought the minister "showed great want of dignity" by his "unreasonable . . . tirades against the President." After waiting four months, Grant finally ordered Fish to remove Motley, but until his departure, he continued "abusing the President and Mr. Fish, calling them brutes in almost every breath." Such was the man Sumner had convinced Grant and Fish to appoint minister to Great Britain. His behavior simply validated Grant's instinctual judgment that Motley lacked the temperament his post required.[79]

Before the session of Congress closed in mid-July, Grant nominated New Jersey Republican Frederick Frelinghuysen, who had recently lost reelection to the Senate, to take Motley's place. Normally confirmation would have been pro forma, but Sumner took the opportunity in executive session to give a two-hour speech, largely ignoring Frelinghuysen and defending Motley. Grant's allies fought back. New Yorker Roscoe Conkling told the Senate that in Motley's first meeting with Lord Clarendon, he had "presented his own position, & not that of his govt," and after that performance, his "recall was only [a] question of time." The Senate approved Frelinghuysen by a vote of 40 to 3, but he never really wanted the position and withdrew two weeks after his confirmation. Nonetheless, the lopsided vote demonstrated that Sumner had no power to save Motley. He told Timothy Howe that Motley's removal was "unequalled in brutality & wrong by any governmental act bearing on office in our history." Howe calmly replied that "when Brooks assaulted a senator [Sumner himself] for words uttered in parliamentary debate he committed a greater wrong than is done to Motley."[80]

To compound Grant's troubles, Hamilton Fish submitted his resignation in early July. Fish had raised the question of leaving on several occasions, but the president "would not listen to it." Lately the two men had differed over policy toward the Cuban revolt, and Fish had never shared the president's enthusiasm for Santo Domingo or Orville Babcock. The secretary felt that he sometimes bore the brunt of public criticism of the administration's foreign policy, and it also seemed that others exercised more influence than he did over appointments in his own department and his own home state. But when Fish handed Grant his resignation letter, the president refused to accept it. He said the secretary's performance was "not only entirely satisfactory to him, but gave satisfaction & confidence to the country." Fish resisted the president's request that he serve until the end of Grant's present term, but "impressed & affected by the earnestness & sincerity of his manner," he agreed to remain until the close of the current Congress in the spring of 1871. When rumors of Fish's possible replacement by Caleb Cushing reached Sumner, the senator rushed to invite Cushing to dinner. "Perhaps you will tell me," he cooed, "if I am to honor you as my chief at the State Depart[ment]."[81]

During the summer and fall, Grant searched for a suitable replacement for Motley who could win confirmation when Congress reconvened. He offered the job to four different senators, all of whom declined, before the fifth, Oliver Morton, accepted. But in mid-October the Democrats won control of the Indiana legislature, giving them the power to choose Morton's successor in the Senate, and he withdrew his acceptance. Ben Butler suggested that appointing Boston reformer Wendell Phillips would win favor among Radicals and "spike all Mr. Sumner's guns." Fish, however, pointed out the absurdity of choosing a man who had referred to the president as a "Dummy at a Minstrel show" and "a restless boy needing constantly to be amused." Grant next offered the post to Conkling, but he too declined, and the issue remained in abeyance until the new congressional session in December.[82]

Meanwhile, Sumner continued to fume. He launched a fruitless war of words with Fish over Motley's initial instructions.[83] He told Fish that dismissing the minister had been the "most grievous personal wrong & irrational thing in the history of the Dep. of State," and "rather than do it, [Fish] should have resigned."[84] He browbeat Bancroft Davis for three-quarters of an hour, "winding up by saying that the removal was 'the most atrocious (in very deep bass) crime in diplomatic history.'" Fish concluded that when Sumner fell into such "outbursts of rhetorical denunciation," he "is not conscious of the extent & violence of his expressions, & is not wholly the master of himself." Fish tactfully observed that "possibly some disappointments embitter him toward the administration," but George Bancroft put it more bluntly: "He suffers from the dire calamity of indulging desires which exceed his powers." Fish encouraged other senators to urge Sumner to moderate his behavior for the good of the party, especially in this congressional election year, but they made no headway. In October Vermont senator Justin Morrill suggested to Grant that Sumner should leave the Foreign Relations Committee because the chairman of that key committee must be on good terms with the administration. Grant agreed. Babcock reported to Zach Chandler of Michigan that Morrill's frustration with Sumner showed "that not all of New England will look upon him as a *Martyr*, if he is set aside. If he can be put aside, it would please the *old man* more than anything in the world." "Outside of the 'mutual admiration society' of the 'Hub,'" Fish said, "nobody seems to think that the recall of a Minister is going to work the destruction of the world."[85]

But Sumner remained implacable. Earlier in the year the administration and the chairman had found common ground in fashioning a successful policy regarding Cuba, but the fight over Santo Domingo, the defeat of the treaty, and the dismissal of Motley engulfed any hope for broader cooperation. Thanks largely to Sumner, the fight had grown personal, and Fish concluded that, "on his own relations with the President, I cannot regard Mr. Sumner as either a reasonable, or a reasoning man." Moreover, despite the failure of the treaty, neither Sumner nor Grant was ready to halt the warfare. As the new session of Congress approached, Grant sought alternative means to promote his annexation project, while Sumner prepared to do everything in his power to punish the president for his supposed great wrong.[86]

11

★ ★ ★ ★ ★

LAUNCHING THE PEACE POLICY

In his effort to secure the annexation of Santo Domingo, Grant gave little evidence that he saw its inhabitants as fundamentally inferior because of their racial or ethnic origins. While many of his opponents (and some of his allies) cast the island's black or mixed-race people as inherently weak or treacherous or naturally suited to inhabit the tropics, Grant saw them as fellow members of the human family, deserving of empathy rather than scorn. He harbored similar feelings toward Native Americans. During his army service in the Far West in the 1850s, he had written to Julia that "the whole race would be harmless and peaceable if they were not put upon by the whites." For years the American government had pursued irregular and capricious warfare in the West, punctuated intermittently by treaties of peace both fragile and transitory. A concurrent civilian policy designed to provide material assistance to the tribes gave as much opportunity for thievery by Indian Bureau agents as it did succor to the suffering Natives. The government's approach angered and alienated the Indians, offered scant protection to settlers moving west, and showed little prospect for lasting success.[1]

After Appomattox, General Grant assumed a central role not only in Reconstruction but also in the management of Indian affairs. Six weeks after Lee's surrender, he dispatched troops to fend off a possible outbreak of hostilities in Minnesota. "It may be," he advised General John Pope, "the Indians require as much protection from the whites as the whites do from the Indians. My own experience has been that but little trouble would have ever been had from them but for the encroachments & influence of bad whites." Over the next four years, the frontier witnessed numerous incidents of violence of varying duration and severity, as well as attempts to forge a policy alternative to war.[2]

During the Johnson administration, sharp differences between the Interior Department, which housed the Bureau of Indian Affairs, and the War Department plagued efforts to fashion a coherent policy. Grant and most military men favored shifting the bureau to the War Department, where it had resided before the creation of the Interior Department in 1849. Grant condemned the exploitation and abuse of Indians by civilian government officials and others, but he did not favor the sort of unbridled armed conquest that military leaders such as Sherman and Sheridan seemed to prefer. "I have always felt," he wrote to Sherman, "that a good part of our difficulties arise from treating all Indians as hostile when any portion of them commit acts that makes a campaign against them necessary." If the War Department could take control of Indian affairs, the next step would be "to deal farely [sic] with the Indians and protect them from encroachments by the Whites."[3]

In early 1867 Grant worked to fashion a comprehensive solution. He relied on the assistance of Colonel Ely S. Parker, a member of his own staff and a full-blooded Seneca, and General John Pope, a longtime advocate of a more humane policy. In separate reports, both Parker and Pope called for the transfer of Indian affairs to the War Department and the elimination of civilian agents, traders, contractors, and the like. This would save considerable expense by substituting career military men, compensated by their regular military pay, for civilian officials, who were usually transient and eager to milk as much from the system as possible. Parker advocated concentrating Indians in a separate territory or territories with a territorial government erected by Congress. He suggested the creation of a board of commissioners to monitor the implementation of Indian policy and to encourage Indians to abandon "their nomadic mode of life" and adopt "agricultural and pastoral pursuits, and the habits and modes of civilized communities." Grant forwarded these recommendations to the Johnson administration through Secretary of War Edwin Stanton.[4]

The proposed changes met opposition in Johnson's cabinet, however, especially from Secretary of the Interior Orville Browning. In the ensuing turf battle, Stanton invited Grant to explain his recommendations at cabinet meetings, where Secretary of the Navy Gideon Welles thought the general came off as "more reasonable than Stanton." Grant also gave the Senate Military Affairs Committee a supporting letter from reformer Henry Whipple, the Episcopal bishop of Minnesota, who denounced rapacious agents and traders and commended Grant for his "firm and decided course in behalf of the poor Indians." Congress did not transfer the Bureau of Indian Affairs, but it did create a mixed—civilian and military—Peace Commission to negotiate new treaties with the Plains Indians and designate new areas for their resettlement. Sherman, who reluctantly accepted a seat on the commission, told Grant, "Somehow we must whip these Indians terribly to make them fear and respect us." But in Grant's opinion, it was "much better to support a Peace commission than a campaign against Indians." The commission signed treaties with various tribes. In an initial report, it called for the lodging of Indian affairs in a separate department and for more humane and honest dealings. But the outbreak of renewed fighting at several points in 1868 negated much of the body's apparent success. Treaties had effected little change, and at its final meeting, with Grant present, the commission advocated the transfer of Indian affairs to the War Department.[5]

In late January 1869 President-elect Grant received a delegation of Quaker leaders interested in the Indian question. He listened sympathetically to their advocacy of a peace policy grounded in religious instruction and the placing of religious practitioners among the Natives. When prospects for congressional action on the bureau's transfer grew dim, he asked the Quakers to suggest individuals he could appoint as agents once he entered the White House. He pledged to support to the fullest extent the Friends' efforts "for the improvement, education, and civilization of the Indians." They responded by supplying a list of men for these posts, applying criteria that emphasized not only religious conviction but also knowledge of farming, managerial skill, and strict financial integrity. Grant submitted their names for appointment soon after assuming office.[6]

In his inaugural address, Grant declared that "proper treatment of the original occupants of the land" deserved "careful study," and he promised to "favor any course toward them which tends to their civilization, christianization and ultimate citizenship."[7] Thus, although Grant sincerely believed that white encroachment lay at the root of the Indian problem, he touted a solution that called for the Indians to abandon their customary ways and embrace white "civilization." As evidence that this was the proper path, he had the success of his own

Ely S. Parker, commissioner of Indian affairs. (National Archives)

aide Parker, who expressed similar views. Hence, the president did not hesitate when he took the bold step of naming Parker as commissioner of Indian affairs. Parker encountered opposition, such as one prejudiced senator who called it "ridiculous" to give the task of civilizing "these wild men of the forest" to "a wild man himself." But Attorney General Hoar determined that Parker, though an Indian, was eligible to hold office, and he won confirmation by a vote of 36 to 12.[8]

Soon after taking office, Grant held the first of many meetings with Indian representatives. The chiefs of the Choctaw, Creek, Cherokee, and Chickasaw nations thanked the president for the sentiments expressed in his inaugural address and offered their help. They suggested that relocating the "wild" Indians near their own settled districts could help pacify them and afford the opportunity to teach them farming and other practical skills. Grant noted that the westward movement of white settlement inevitably led to "difficult" encounters, but he also felt that the "march of civilization" could contribute to pacification. His plans had not yet gelled, he said, but he welcomed any information that would help achieve the Indians' "civilization" and eventual citizenship.[9]

White reformers were eager to put their own impress on the new policy. A week after the Indians' visit, Grant and Interior Secretary J. D. Cox met with a group of Philadelphia philanthropists, including Grant's friend George Stuart. The group's prime mover was William Welsh, a prominent merchant, lay church leader, and Indian rights advocate who urged the creation of a permanent board of Indian commissioners. Both Grant and Cox welcomed the idea of a commission, but Welsh's notions went beyond their expectations. He and his allies persuaded James Harlan, chairman of the Senate's Indian Affairs Committee, to introduce legislation creating a board of commissioners with the power to "supervise and control" the disbursement of appropriations, remove and replace employees on the reservations, regulate trade, and suspend Indian agents and replace them at least temporarily with persons of the board's choosing. Cox objected strenuously. He secured the introduction of a scaled-back proposal limiting the board's jurisdiction to the disbursement of funds and requiring it to conduct its oversight in conjunction with the Interior Department. After considerable debate, Congress appropriated $2 million to enable the president to "maintain the peace" with the Indians, "promote civilization" among them, and "encourage their efforts at self-support." The law authorized the president to appoint a board comprising up to ten commissioners, "who may, under his direction, exercise joint control with the Secretary of the Interior over the disbursement of the appropriations." Parker had proposed a commission composed of both whites and Indians, but Welsh and his allies persuaded Congress to stipulate that the members should be "men eminent for their intelligence and philanthropy, to serve without pecuniary compensation." This made men like themselves the likeliest choices for commissioners and essentially ruled out Indian participation.[10]

Grant signed the law immediately, and he and Cox summoned

Stuart to Washington to advise them in the selection of commissioners. Stuart drew on his wide acquaintance among the nation's philanthropic elite to recommend public-spirited men of substantial wealth who favored reform in the treatment of the Indians. The group represented several religious denominations, and some members had performed eleemosynary service during the war. All but one resided east of the Mississippi River. At its first meeting the board elected Welsh its chairman.[11]

Grant's June 3 executive order outlining the commissioners' duties demonstrated his hesitation in assigning responsibilities legally borne by himself and the Interior Department to persons who owed their positions neither to election nor to Senate confirmation. He laid out regulations to govern matters coming under the "joint supervision" of the commission and the Bureau of Indian Affairs. He authorized the commission to examine the bureau's records, inspect agencies in the Indian country and the goods they purchased, be present at the payment of annuities and the purchase of goods, and advise agents and superintendents "in the performance of their duties." But any suggestions for making changes in agents, policies, or purchasing methods, as well as any complaints against agents, had to be forwarded to the bureau or the Interior Department "for action." Noting that the Treasury Department's "usual modes of accounting" could not be circumvented, the president insisted that "all plans involving the expenditure of public money will be acted upon by the Executive or the Secretary of the Interior, before expenditure is made under the same." He enjoined all officers of the government to cooperate with the commissioners, but to do so "within the limits of such officers' positive instructions from their superiors." Except for a handful of Quakers, Grant had assigned most of the Indian agencies to army officers. While the president was issuing his order to the board, Parker was ordering those army officers to inform the Indians of the government's "pacific intentions" and to prepare their minds to "submit to the inevitable change of their mode of life to pursuits more congenial to a civilized state."[12]

The administration's description of the board's duties disturbed Welsh, who had hoped to arrogate control of Indian policy to himself and his colleagues. Believing that Grant's interpretation of the legislation had reduced the board to "a mere council of advice," Welsh concluded, "I could not act the part of a man if I allowed myself to be emasculated." Two days later he resigned. Cox thought Welsh's notion of a "double headed organization" would lead to "nothing but confusion." He told the board's new chairman, Felix Brunot, that "the best interests of the cause we are at work in would not be promoted by making the Commission *directly* responsible for the control & disbursement of money appropriated by Congress," and Brunot and his colleagues agreed to assume no responsibility for expenditures beyond "general advisory powers." But Welsh did not go quietly. He disliked Parker, whose appointment he decried as "an infatuation heightened by a sentiment in favor of an Indian civilizing his brethren." He accused Parker of insufficient rigor in inspecting shipments of goods to the Indians, implying that Parker had winked at fraud. Cox delivered a sharp rebuke to the ex-chairman, insisting that Parker had acted honestly.[13]

After this shaky start, the Board of Indian Commissioners performed valuable work. By the end of 1869, the board was regularly monitoring purchases and had begun to inspect the various agencies. In their first report the commissioners attributed much of the trouble in Indian country to the rapacity of whites, against whom the government owed the Indians protection. But they made it clear that the long-term solution to the Indian problem lay in the transformation of the Indians and the destruction of their culture. They believed that all the Indians should be gathered onto reservations, where they could be taught agriculture and other productive enterprises and where they could learn the rudiments of representative government. As soon as feasible, land should be allotted severally to them and their tribal relations discouraged. And undergirding it all, the commissioners believed, was instruction in Christianity: "The religion of our blessed Savior is believed to be the most effective agent for the civilization of any people."[14]

Grant's annual message in December 1869 reflected the commissioners' observations, minus the stress on Christianizing the Indians. He noted his selection of Friends as agents on a few reservations but laid greater emphasis on his employment of military men, whose suitability contrasted sharply with that of the typical agent of previous years. Besides the advantage of saving money, he said, "the army officer holds a position for life; the agent, one at the will of the President. The former is personally interested in living in harmony with the Indian and in establishing a permanent peace, to the end that some portion of his life may be spent within the limits of civilized society; the latter has no such personal interest." Grant lamented that the westward movement of settlement did "not harmonize well" with the "aborigines." One or the other had to give way. But "a system which looks to the extinction of a race is too horrible for a nation to adopt without entailing upon itself the wrath of all Christendom and engendering in the citizen a disregard for human life and the rights of others, dangerous to society." The only possible course was placing "all the Indians on large reservations, as rapidly as it can be done, and giving them absolute protection there." In time, they could receive lands in severalty and erect "territorial governments for their protection." In his annual report, Parker sounded a cautionary note, observing that despite a decline in hostilities, several violent outbreaks had marred the new policy's first year. This was all the more reason, Parker said, to hurry the Indians onto reservations. Optimistically, Grant believed that his approach had produced "fair results so far as tried." A few weeks later he told visiting Cherokee and Creek chiefs that his ultimate goal was for Indians to gain "all the rights of citizens" and "cease to be nations and become States."[15]

On the day the new congressional session opened in December, Grant notified the Senate that he had suspended from office forty agents and superintendents who owed their appointments to the old system of patronage. He replaced seven of them with men recommended by the Quakers, whom the Senate promptly confirmed. He assigned all the other positions to army officers. The military personnel did not require Senate approval, but under the Tenure of Office Act, the suspension of the previous agents did. The Senate was unenthusiastic. It dragged its feet on the thirty-three suspensions until the end of the session seven months later, when it restored the appointments of six of the suspended civilians.[16]

The Senate's reluctance to assign the agencies to army officers reflected in part a national outcry following the senseless military slaughter of Indians in northern Montana in late January 1870. This ill-conceived mission to chastise a handful of recreant Piegan Indians turned into a wanton assault on a peaceful village that resulted in the death of 173 Natives, including scores of women and children. Sheridan exacerbated the public outrage by defending the officer responsible. The attack belied the assertion that army officers were ideally equipped to distinguish between good and bad Indians and to protect the former and punish the latter. The incident stopped dead a movement in Congress to shift the Bureau of Indian Affairs to the War Department. But Congress did endorse the peace policy by voting to continue the existence of the Board of Indian Commissioners, although in the future it would "supervise" (not control) the purchase of goods for the Indians.[17]

The peace policy received a boost in early June 1870 when Grant engaged in personal diplomacy in Washington with a delegation of Indians headed by Oglala Sioux leader Red Cloud. Red Cloud had a reputation as a fierce warrior, and his initiation of the meeting marked a hopeful turn in Indian affairs. Also present was his longtime rival, Brule Sioux chief Spotted Tail, who urged the administration to restrain white people from invading the Indians' reservation. Two days later the War Department issued an order to units posted in the West: "When lands are secured to the Indians by treaty against occupation by the whites, the military commanders shall keep intruders off by military force if necessary."[18]

In preliminary discussions with Cox and Parker, Red Cloud complained that the government had not kept its promises, and he requested the delivery of promised rations and arms for hunting game. Cox said the administration was pushing for a substantial appropriation from Congress to ensure that the Indians received adequate rations. On the arms question, however, he noted the fears of whites in the West and said the Indians had to provide solid promises of peace before the government could provide any weapons. When the Indians met Grant, Red Cloud reiterated his earlier requests and also asked that the government abandon Fort Fetterman, which occupied a key point on the Bozeman Trail and was central to the military's operations. Grant emphasized his commitment to a lasting peace but refused to close the fort, noting that it was necessary not only to control "badly disposed" Indians but also "to keep the whites off of the Indian reservation." Additionally, it served as a base of supplies. The president promised to see that the government faithfully carried out appropriations and other laws, and he urged the Indians "to go to farming and raising cattle as soon as possible, and thus thereby greatly add to their comforts." Grant told them he had instructed the secretary of the interior to "supply all their wants, and see that justice was done them," a statement that, according to a report of the Board of Indian Commissioners, "produced great satisfaction."[19]

Nonetheless, Red Cloud appeared downcast at a follow-up meeting with Cox, and the secretary tried to assure him of the government's good intentions. Praising Parker's assimilation to the white man's world, Cox declared, "We will be brethren to you in the same way if you follow his good example and learn our civilization." Choctaw leader and diplomat Peter Pitchlynn put the advice to the Indians more starkly: "You must adopt the white people's ways if you want to preserve yourselves. You cannot be Sioux always unless you do so. If you fight the whites they will kill you all." Red Cloud understood and never again led Sioux warriors into battle against the government.[20]

Grant and Cox could not keep their promises without action by

Congress, but the Indian appropriations bill had been stalled for months. On the last scheduled day of the session, Grant, Cox, Parker, and commission secretary Vincent Colyer were on Capitol Hill pushing for an agreement between the House and the Senate. The president wrote a special message on the spot, warning that "without such appropriation Indian hostilities are sure to ensue, and with them suffering, loss of life, and expenditures vast as compared with the amount asked for." When Grant threatened the legislators with a special session, they extended the session a few hours and appropriated the money.[21]

But before adjourning, Congress also passed the army appropriations bill, which included a provision making it unlawful for military personnel to hold civilian office, on pain of dismissal from the army. This move had been pushed by some members of Congress who bridled at the loss of their patronage influence in staffing the Indian agencies. During the recent fight over the Santo Domingo treaty, Grant had shown his willingness to lavish patronage on senators and congressmen to achieve his ends, but he drew the line at the Indian agencies, positions he considered too sensitive to be left to hack political appointees. This new legislation barring army officers from these posts heightened the attractiveness of religion-based appointments.[22]

Soon after Congress adjourned, the president asked religious denominations in addition to the Friends to recommend nominees to replace the army officers. He continued to receive old-style patronage recommendations for these positions, but he insisted that he would appoint no individual who had not received an endorsement from a religious group. When Congress convened for the third session of the Forty-First Congress in December 1870, he submitted the names of the new appointees, most of whom the Senate confirmed en masse. In his annual message he pledged that the government would demand strict accountability from the new agents, whose responsibility it was to "watch over" the Indians and "aid them as missionaries, to Christianize and civilize the Indian, and to train him in the arts of peace."[23]

Both Parker and the Board of Indian Commissioners hailed the new approach as "wise and humane," and Cox declared that "a peaceful policy appeals with great power even to the wildest savage." Nonetheless, the new system experienced problems. Jealousy plagued the distribution of agencies. With a graspingness worthy of spoils-hungry politicians, missionary groups fought for the privilege of making appointments. Antagonism between Catholics and Protestants further tainted the scramble. In addition, the groups had trouble finding worthy and capable persons who were willing to make the enormous sacrifice required for the arduous work at desolate outposts in the West. In a few instances the agents' abysmal pay drove them to engage in the same sort of dishonest practices their political predecessors had followed.[24]

Moreover, ill will marred relations among the program's managers in Washington. The Board of Indian Commissioners, still determined to dominate Indian policy, gave credence to rumors alleging misfeasance by Parker in the letting of contracts. The animus against Parker was fed by William Welsh, who pursued a vendetta against the commissioner and finally succeeded in spurring a congressional investigation. Allowing Welsh to play lead prosecutor in its hearings, the House Appropriations Committee concluded that management of the Bureau of Indian Affairs showed "irregularities, neglect, and incompetency, and, in some instances, a departure from the express provisions of law." But it also found no evidence of "fraud or corruption" on Parker's part or "any pecuniary or personal advantages sought or derived by the Commissioner, or any one connected with his Bureau." Nevertheless, the committee sponsored legislation that required the bureau to submit payments for goods and services to the Board of Indian Commissioners for "examination, revisal, and approval," with the final determination resting with the secretary of the interior. When irregular procedures continued into the spring of 1871, the board raised a howl, and Cox's successor as interior secretary, Columbus Delano, insisted that Parker send the board the required vouchers. Believing the new law deprived him of his "proper responsibilities" and made him "simply . . . a clerk" to the board, Parker resigned. Grant could no longer protect his friend from the political heat, but in accepting his resignation, he praised Parker's management of the bureau as being in "entire harmony with my policy, which I hope will tend to the civilization of the Indian race." Parker's place went to noted statistician and reformer Francis A. Walker.[25]

The legislation that confirmed the board's power to audit the commissioner contained another provision abolishing the so-called treaty system, which had governed Indian-government relations for decades. Although the government would honor existing treaties, it would no longer recognize any Indian group as "an independent nation, tribe, or power with whom the United States may contract by treaty." The law in part reflected the House of Representatives' resentment at being forced to approve appropriations contracted by the executive branch and the Senate through treaties negotiated without House participation. Although the government would continue to make less formal agreements with tribes, the provision ended the practice of treating an internal population as a "sovereign" entity equivalent to the nation of the United States.[26]

Grant welcomed the change. As a general, he had suspected that sometimes the Indians launched military operations to force new treaties under which the government would give them new annuity payments and arms. But the abolition of the treaty system also comported with Grant's more sympathetic policy as president. He told Congress that the government could not hold whites "blameless" for past hostilities, and it was time to try a new policy that treated the Indians as "wards of the nation," for "they can not be regarded in any other light than as wards." And yet, for all the sympathy embodied in Grant's approach, the administration's new policy rested on the belief that peace in the West and survival of the Indians could be achieved only by a radical transformation in their mode of living. "I entertain the confident hope," the president declared in his second annual message in December 1870, "that the policy now pursued will in a few years bring all the Indians upon reservations, where they will live in houses, and have schoolhouses and churches, and will be pursuing peaceful and self-sustaining avocations, and where they may be visited by the law-abiding white man with the same impunity that he now visits the civilized white settlements."[27]

Like many Americans of the nineteenth century, Grant subscribed to the faith that the United States marched in the vanguard of progress. In the clash of cultures in the West, he believed, the Indians stood on the wrong side of history. The key to their survival lay in forfeiting their "backward" ways. Just as the thralldom of slavery had wrought stagnation in the South, the Indians' retrograde communalism stood as an obstacle in the path to their advancement. Hence, Grant favored the eventual division of tribal lands in severalty and believed that the key to the Indians' success was "to cultivate the soil" and "to perform productive labor of various kinds." He understood the Indians' resistance to suggestions that they abandon a culture that exalted hunting and warlike virtues for a settled life of striving. He may have appreciated the irony of such advice coming from him—a man who had failed at farming before the war and about whom John Rawlins had said in 1866, "he knows how to do nothing but fight" and "would fail in other positions." Grant, of course, had proved Rawlins wrong, and he remained confident of the ultimate realization of his vision for the Indians. "When I said, 'Let us have peace,' I meant it," he told a reporter in the spring of 1871. "I want peace on the Plains as everywhere else." "I have lived with the Indians and I know them thoroughly. They can be civilized and made friends of the republic." But "you can't thrash people so that they will love you"; you must "make enemies friends by kindness."[28]

After two years in office, Grant could look back with a degree of satisfaction at the noble experiment he had launched. Yet as matters turned out, persistent antagonism on the frontier would demonstrate how difficult it was to transform white and Indian enemies into friends.

12

★ ★ ★ ★ ★

REFORM AND REVOLT

A key objective of President Grant's peace policy was to improve the personnel in the Indian service and move beyond what J. D. Cox called "the old regime when agencies were given as political prizes to partizans." Within the first year of the administration, something like a merit system began to emerge in other areas as well. In the Patent Office, an agency that placed a premium on technical expertise, the commissioner implemented a program of competitive examinations adapted "to the work to be done," and the office selected personnel from a list ranked by test scores. The Census Bureau remodeled its existing examination to fit the skills sought in its employees, and the Treasury Department took similar steps.[1]

But such efforts represented an entering wedge rather than a radical reworking of federal practices. The spoils system remained alive and well. For decades, presidents had received and acted on advice from congressmen and senators in making appointments. Despite its potential for abuse, this cumbersome mechanism had a grounding in logic. Especially in selecting nominees for the thousands of federal offices scattered around the country, members of Congress knew better than the administration in Washington the character of the applicants and the needs of their localities. As Grant later put it, "In a country as vast as ours the advice of Congressmen as to persons to be appointed is useful, and generally for the best interests of the country." Of course, like his predecessors, Grant also quickly grasped the utility of patronage in securing congressional backing for his policies.[2]

Abuses had inhered in the system for decades. During the 1860s, however, the great increase in the bureaucracy raised concerns about whether this clumsy method of hiring could meet the needs of a modernizing society. In addition, Andrew Johnson's extensive use of removals and replacements in his fight with the Republican Congress gave concrete examples of abuse that reformers could cite to rally support for a wholesale restructuring. Years before Grant took office, bills had appeared in the legislative hopper to institute system-wide competitive examinations and other changes.[3]

And yet, while Grant was building his administration, many men who had been or would become prominent in the civil service reform movement seemed to put their scruples on hold as they joined the scramble to obtain offices for themselves or their friends. As matters turned out, their frustrated ambitions fueled their determination for reform. Charles Sumner, who had submitted a reform bill as early as 1864, badgered Grant and Hamilton Fish for diplomatic appointments, but he never seemed satisfied with the success he achieved. When Henry Adams failed to secure berths in Washington for his friends, he scolded Grant for carrying the nefarious patronage system "to a point beyond anything that had been reached before." When reformer Charles Eliot Norton did not receive a coveted diplomatic appointment, he decried "Grant's surrender" to the politicians. Norton was representative of the country's "best men"—those who believed that their intellectual training, high principles, and understanding of government ideally fitted them for government appointments, without having to endure the odious business of politicking. They soon discovered that the new president felt no need to bow to their sense of entitlement. As a result, in the words of Ari Hoogenboom, the foremost historian of the civil service reform movement, many reformers "recognized the evils of the spoils system only after it thwarted their ambitions."[4]

No one exhibited this mingling of resentment and reform more than Carl Schurz. Having migrated from Germany in 1852, Schurz had settled in Wisconsin, where his work as a Republican politician won him appointment as minister to Spain by Abraham Lincoln. In 1862 he returned to fight in the war, after which he took up journalism and in 1867 moved to St. Louis. In 1868 he stumped for Grant among his fellow German Americans, an important voting bloc. Despite his brief residence in

Carl Schurz. (Library of Congress)

Missouri, after the November victory Schurz sought election to the US Senate by the state legislature.[5]

Even before Grant took office, Schurz began his quest for patronage. When one of his opponents for the senatorial seat claimed to have an inside track with the president-elect, Schurz beseeched the general's political adviser Elihu Washburne to give him "a lift" and help him convince his fellow Missourians that, as senator, he would be a key player in the distribution of offices. *I do want to win*," he wrote. "I presume I too may have a little influence with the incoming Administration, at least it would seem somewhat natural that I should have. *And I should like to have that understood.*" Ignoring Schurz's presumption, Washburne acknowledged the "great value" of his recent campaign work but added, "Genl Grant should guard himself vigilantly against mixing up in these Senatorial contests." This rebuff notwithstanding, Schurz won the nomination of the Republican legislative caucus by a slim majority, and he went on to win election to the Senate.[6]

Soon after arriving in Washington, Schurz began a round of visits to the president and cabinet secretaries looking for jobs for his friends, especially German Americans. He scored some successes, but he did not find a particularly warm welcome at the White House. When he pushed a candidate for the St. Louis post office, he discovered that Grant had already filled the position. He must have bristled when the president told him, "Why, Mr. Schurz, I know Missouri a great deal better than you do." (Grant had actually lived in Missouri three times longer than Schurz had.) On one occasion Schurz cloaked his frustration by writing to Fish in mock despair that "the hue of health has left my cheeks" because three failed candidates for consulships were hounding him "like ghostly apparitions." In response, Fish said the would-be diplomats should "thank" Schurz and be "glad that they escaped the chance of being themselves beheaded because some future Schurz wants their places for his friends." Fish matched the senator in japery but made his point. It did not take Schurz long to realize that he wielded marginal influence. "I have worked very hard for my friends," he told an associate. "The utter absurdity of our system of appointment to office has this time so glaringly demonstrated itself that even the dullest patriots begin to open their eyes to the necessity of reform. I have taken a solemn vow to pitch in for it next winter."[7]

When Congress convened in December 1869, Schurz followed through on his vow, submitting a bill that called for the creation of a civil service board to administer examinations that would govern the selection of most federal appointees. The proposal met a chilly reception in the Senate, where opponents blocked its consideration on the floor. In the House, Rhode Island congressman Thomas Jenckes, a longtime advocate of reform, sponsored a similar bill. Jenckes privately claimed that Grant supported his measure, but the president gave no sign of that in his first annual message, and Jenckes's bill got no further than Schurz's. Opponents, including many Republicans, condemned the measure as undemocratic. The proposed exams, they said, would lead to "a privileged class" by taking the power of recommendation away from the people's elected representatives and giving it to an elite board responsible to no one. One Republican warned that the scheme "would fill the Departments with educated incompetency, while force and capacity for the real duties of office would be ignored." Others noted that it would hurt the employment prospects of disabled Union veterans. John Bingham, principal framer of the Fourteenth Amendment, decried the bill as unconstitutional for depriving the president and department heads of their appointment powers. Jenckes's bill went back to committee before Congress adjourned in mid-July 1870.[8]

In the Senate, Lyman Trumbull of Illinois proposed a bill that would have barred members of Congress from making recommendations and the president and department heads from conferring nominations based on such recommendations. But Jacob Howard of Michigan asserted that the president "must rely on some one or some set of persons to give him proper information," and "there are no persons to whom he can so safely apply for advice respecting the fitness of candidates for office as members of the two Houses of Congress." Trumbull's bill got nowhere before the adjournment.[9]

Within the administration the most vocal advocate for reforming the civil service was Secretary of the Interior Jacob Cox. In a series of controversies that sprang largely from the secretary's own imagination, Cox squared off against Grant in ways that made him the darling of civil service reformers and nourished their suspicions of the president's attitude toward the issue. Never fully comfortable in the cabinet, Cox eventually left under circumstances he tried to spin to his own advantage.

Initially Cox showed some acceptance of traditional practices, telling a senator that in filling positions he felt bound to give preference to persons "who are in full sympathy with the Republican party, including many soldiers who served during the war." Yet the longer he dealt with patronage, the more disenchanted he became. He devoted the peroration of his first annual report in December 1869 to a plea for a thorough reworking of the system: replacing politically driven "rotation in office" with long-term tenure in subordinate positions, "making capacity and integrity the sole tests of the fitness of the applicant, and throwing competition open to all." By the summer of 1870, Cox had reached the disquieting conclusion that because "the Executive in ordinary times has comparatively little control of measures, or influence in framing a policy," an administration had little chance of achieving its objectives except through "the use of patronage, which is in itself corruption." Indeed, Cox had begun to see advantages in the ministerial system of England, where cabinet members could influence policy as advocates speaking from their seats in Parliament. There was no chance the United States would adopt a parliamentary system or abandon the separation of powers that Americans saw as essential to restraining government. Hence, Cox decided to "set my face like a flint in the direction of the Civil Service Reform."[10]

In general, Grant acquiesced in Cox's program, but without great enthusiasm. In one notable instance, however, the president did intervene to reverse an appointment decision by Cox. At the behest of Michigan's senators, Grant reinstated an experienced Indian agent in the state, W. H. Brockway, whom Cox had replaced with an appointee from another state recommended by a religious organization. Grant admitted to Cox that he had been motivated in part by a desire to please the senators, but he also told the secretary that because Brockway was a Methodist minister, "the new rule adopted will not be violated by his appointment." This intervention was a rare occurrence during Cox's tenure. Indeed, Grant told other cabinet members that he "appreciated" Cox's "thorough integrity" and thought the Interior Department was "better administered by him than ever before."[11]

After instituting competitive examinations, Cox moved to protect departmental employees from party committees seeking to "assess" their earnings. His notion flew in the face of a time-honored practice whereby officeholders were expected to remit about 1 percent of their salaries to help underwrite political campaign expenses. Matters reached a head during the 1870 midterm elections. When the Republican congressional campaign committee asked the secretary for a roster of Interior Department employees, he reluctantly complied and insisted that the committee emphasize to the clerks that their contributions were entirely voluntary, because "any compulsory assessment would be a political immorality." When state party committees made similar requests, Cox declined to provide the information.[12]

Cox's opposition to assessments pleased civil service reformers, but regular Republicans considered it treachery. A few weeks before the bellwether October elections in 1870, Michigan senator Zachariah Chandler traveled to Washington and told Fish he was "concerned at the effect produced by Sec. Cox'[s] letter about collecting money for the Election." Agreeing that the problem threatened, "very seriously, the chances of Republican Success," Fish promptly wrote to Grant, who was in New

York, about "the difficulties" and "the views of Senator Chandler (in which I concur) as to the importance & the possibility of overcoming them, & of obtaining, as we hope, a triumph this Autumn, which, very probably, will settle the next Presidential Election." But even though Fish cast the matter as potentially affecting the president's own reelection, Grant did not issue an order countermanding Cox's position; nor did he openly embrace it. He decided to leave the matter between Cox and the political committees. Although other cabinet secretaries did not follow Cox in discouraging assessments, the president let his order stand.[13]

Interior Department personnel may have appreciated Cox's ban on assessments, but neither they nor the political committees liked another change he instituted. Breaking with practice, Cox stipulated that clerks in Washington could return to their home districts to vote only if they subtracted the missed time from their annual leave allotment. Other departments routinely granted such leaves without penalty. (This was before absentee voting.) In this era of razor-thin margins in swing states, even a handful of votes could make a difference. When Grant returned to Washington in early October, Cox was away, and the president told Assistant Secretary W. T. Otto it would be a good idea if all the departments followed a uniform practice. Otto assured Grant that he would inform the clerks that the Interior Department would permit them to take election leaves with no loss of pay or annual leave time.[14]

Otto may have telegraphed the results of this meeting to Cox, for on the same day, October 3, Cox wrote to the president and resigned as secretary of the interior. In his letter Cox noted that his views regarding civil service reform had brought him "more or less into collision with the plans of some of our active political managers, and my sense of duty has obliged me to oppose some of their methods of action through the Department." Cox did not, however, claim that the president had failed to support him or his civil service measures; indeed, he made no mention at all of Grant's attitude on the question. Rather, he stated that because his reform efforts had roused "opposition which it may not be for the interest of your Administration to provoke," he deemed it his "duty" to resign. Cox also referred to the precarious state of his personal finances, which he had discussed with Grant on earlier occasions. His "original acceptance of the position" had been an "interference with plans of life formed" long before, and "a return to my private business . . . will only be carrying out what I have most desired to do."[15]

Yet Cox immediately ascribed his abrupt departure to a disagreement with Grant over civil service reform. He told friends that if Grant had responded to his comments on reform with some show of support, he would have withdrawn his resignation. But Grant did not see Cox's letter as an invitation to discuss the matter of civil service. Responding on the same day he received it, October 5, he accepted Cox's resignation, effective when the secretary finished his annual report at the end of October. Like Cox's letter, Grant's reply said nothing about how the president felt about civil service. Horace Porter thought Grant should have seized the opportunity and "squelch[ed] Cox's insinuations," but the president's "good nature again prevailed." In his response Grant showed solicitude for Cox's need to shore up his family's economic situation. He thanked the secretary for his "zeal and ability" in office and expressed the hope that "in the new sphere you have pointed out for yourself . . . you may fully realize your brightest expectations."[16]

If Grant was not particularly sorry to see Cox go, it was not because of the secretary's civil service views. Rather, it was because of his behavior, bordering on insubordination, in connection with another matter—the so-called McGarrahan claim. The issue, which had been a minor irritant in official Washington for years, involved a dispute over a tract of land in California containing a lucrative quicksilver mine. The New Idria Mining Company had worked the mine for several years and claimed ownership under federal preemption legislation passed in 1866. In 1857, however, William McGarrahan had purchased interest in the tract, known as Panoche Grande, from a Mexican citizen named Gomez, whose claim rested on a land grant issued by the Mexican government in 1844, before California became part of the United States. Although the registration of Gomez's original grant had been flawed and incomplete, McGarrahan insisted that in equity it was valid, and for nearly a decade he had tried to win recognition of his claim. He had pushed his case in the courts, in the Land Office housed in the Interior Department, and in Congress, where he sought a private act upholding his claim. Some observers considered his claim bogus at best and possibly fraudulent, but in the Congress before Grant took office, the House passed a bill recognizing McGarrahan's right to the land. Major Republican leaders were situated on either side of that vote—a configuration that amply illustrated the difficulty of sorting out the complicated issue. The Senate took no action on the bill, and the question carried over to the Forty-First Congress, which took office with Grant.[17]

In the executive branch, adjudication of questions related to land grants rested with the Interior Department's Land Office, and the New

Idria Company was eager to obtain a ruling in its favor. But early in the administration, Grant decided that the Interior Department should take no action until after Congress had disposed of the question. In the summer of 1870 the House Judiciary Committee voted 7 to 3 against McGarrahan, but because the committee had not made an official report before Congress adjourned in mid-July, the question carried over to the next session set to convene in December. Nonetheless, in August, in a letter highly prejudicial against McGarrahan's position, Cox ordered the commissioner of the Land Office to proceed to evaluate New Idria's request for a patent.[18] Cox had not consulted the president, who learned of the move from a friend representing McGarrahan. Grant had no opinion as to the case's merits, but with regard to the procedure for its adjudication, he clarified his position in a gentle reminder to the secretary:

> I understand that you have appointed one day this week to hear arguments in the McGarrahan case. That is well enough because if Congress should fail to settle that case we may have it to do, and the sooner we know all the points of it the better. However[,] as the matter has been taken in hand by Congress before the incoming of this administration, and as so much fraud is charged, and believed to exist, on both sides, I am not willing that my name should be signed to a patent for either party until Congress has either decided or declared their inability to do so.[19]

Grant was more attuned than Cox to congressional sensibilities, and he recognized that neither side in the question stood blameless. Cox, however, interpreted Grant's letter as a personal affront and gave a tart response that shocked the president. On the status of the claim in Congress, Cox said, "you must have been misinformed." He asserted that Congress had "no peculiar jurisdiction of the subject" and that, according to an opinion by the attorney general, either party had a "right to insist upon a hearing & decision" in the Interior Department. Cox characterized McGarrahan as "a fraudulent claimant" guilty of "unscrupulous" conduct and "unblushing knavery," thereby implying that Grant's position aided a nefarious scheme. In a burst of hyperbole, the secretary warned the president that "no question more gravely affecting the dignity of the Executive & its independence will be likely to arise during your administration." "I can make no compromise," he stated, "& if I fail to secure to the fullest extent your approval of my course, I must beg you to relieve me at once from duties which without your support I shall utterly fail in." Cut "severely" by this remark, Grant was tempted to ask for the secretary's resignation at once, but in fact he made no response at all. Cox had begun his August 23 letter with the statement that he had informed the appropriate official of the president's determination not to sign a patent prematurely, and Grant apparently took that statement as sufficient compliance to forgo dismissing Cox.[20]

Six weeks later, however, the issue reared again. On October 4, the day before Grant received Cox's unexpected letter of resignation, Boutwell shocked the president at a cabinet meeting by commenting that the secretary of the interior had issued a patent to the New Idria Company. As Fish noted, "The President, with much animation & more feeling than I almost ever saw him exhibit," stated that if the story were true, "I shall have a new Secretary of the Interior within an hour after learning the fact." Neither Cox nor Otto was present, and Grant reminded the group of his determination to defer an executive decision until after Congress had concluded its consideration. He retrieved the secretary's August letter from a drawer and read aloud the offensive passage. Fish observed, "He evidently has been much disturbed." Little wonder, then, that when Cox's resignation arrived the next day, Grant made no effort to induce him to stay. This was an extraordinary turn of events: Cox had submitted his resignation purportedly for one set of reasons, related to his perception that Grant had not supported him on civil service reform, while Grant had decided to accept the secretary's departure in large part for another set of reasons, related to his perception of Cox's insubordination on the McGarrahan question.[21]

Even before his departure was officially announced, Cox quietly began to cultivate his image as a martyr for civil service reform. In private correspondence he alleged that Grant had succumbed to "efforts of the intriguers" and had "made a break in the system of Indian appointments," but the only evidence he could cite was the sole case of the Indian agent in Michigan, who Grant contended still met the peace policy's qualifications. On the question of assessments and election leaves, Cox implied that Grant had become the captive of Chandler and Pennsylvania senator Simon Cameron. Reform journals and others soon picked up the theme. *Harper's Weekly* blamed Cox's departure on "the pressure of those who believe that the civil service of the country should be organized upon the lowest party considerations."[22]

Grant struck back at the insinuations that he had opposed Cox's reform activities. At the White House he intimated to reporters that Cox had resigned for private reasons—that he had a growing family and wanted to return to his law practice to shore up his finances. Grant did not invent these assertions about the secretary's aims, for Cox himself had cited them. According to Fish, when he suggested that Cox be appointed to replace Motley, Grant replied, "Cox would not accept, has told him his plans, speaks of his age, & the size of his family &c." Grant told reporters that he and Cox had no dispute related to public policy, although he mentioned in passing their disagreement about the McGarrahan question but noted that Cox had come around. He flatly denied that he had allowed Chandler or Cameron to exercise "dictation or interference" in departmental affairs. But news accounts that focused on Cox's personal financial motives for leaving only fueled the ex-secretary's anger, and friends egged him on. James Garfield urged him to "exhibit the cause of your resignation" as "a clear case of surrender on the part of the President to the political vermin which infest the government." At the end of October, Cox gave reporters copies of his letter of resignation and Grant's reply. He also distributed copies of his earlier letters to political committees regarding assessments, thereby implying that he and the president had parted ways on that matter, which was not the case. At the same time, Henry Adams arranged with Cox to write an article on civil service reform for the *North American Review*.[23]

Publication of the letters fulfilled Cox's aim to dramatize his sacrifice on the altar of reform. A gathering of Yale professors saluted his determination to resign "when you found yourself obstructed in prosecuting the great reformation to which you had committed yourself." Although the president's allies saw Cox as "a suspicious creature" and a traitor, many shared Massachusetts senator Henry Wilson's fear that the correspondence not only would be "damaging to us beyond measure" in the impending midterm elections but also would "be disastrous [sic] in the future."[24]

Grant hesitated to do anything that could further injure Republican prospects, but he and his aides again mounted a defense. They began to suggest more forcefully that in the McGarrahan business, as the *New York Herald* put it, "Mr. Cox's skirts are not so clear as his friends would like to make the public believe." After the election, the administration released the text of the August letters between Grant and Cox on the claim issue. The White House hoped the president's letter warning about fraud "on both sides" would portray him as a judicious steward of the public interest and that Cox's vehement denunciation of McGarrahan would reveal him as too determined—perhaps suspiciously so— to uphold the New Idria claim. Indeed, future Supreme Court justice

John Marshall Harlan thought "Cox's letter to the President about that claim betrays too much *zeal*."[25]

Cox wrote voluminous private letters defending himself, and he fed anti-Grant information to reporters. But seasoned political friends eventually advised him to keep quiet. Garfield warned that the impression that Cox had wanted to leave the cabinet and welcomed "a difficulty" with Grant was gaining currency. Although Cox still maintained that Grant had released the McGarrahan letters as part of an assault on his integrity, he began to see the vulnerability of his position. "I am willing to 'let there be peace' so far as the public relations are concerned," he told Garfield. That course seemed even wiser when Garfield reported that some observers in Washington were concluding that Cox's August letter "showed you an advocate of the New Idria Company." Hence, when Congress revisited the claim question in early 1871, Cox decided to avoid testifying rather than give "temptation to meddlers to revive the controversies with the President."After an investigation by the Judiciary Committee, the House of Representatives passed a resolution calling for the correction of a mutilation of the Interior Department's land records several years earlier. Although this action did not directly recognize the legality of McGarrahan's claim, it suggested the claim's validity and implied a censure of Cox's management of the case. Cox asked Garfield to line up senators against the resolution, and the Senate ultimately failed to act before the adjournment of the Forty-First Congress. Meanwhile, Cox the civil service reformer also asked Garfield to use his patronage influence to get an appointment for one of his former law apprentices as postmaster at Warren, Ohio.[26]

Hamilton Fish made an effort to reconcile his two friends, but the ex-secretary remained convinced that the president followed "a rule or ruin policy." In the wake of their struggle, Cox insisted that Grant had "ruined himself." That was hardly true, but the protracted controversy had a lasting impact and contributed to the tainting of Grant's historical reputation. Allan Nevins, while noting that Cox acted "tactlessly," portrayed the secretary's "decapitation" as "singularly shabby." Cox himself did what he could to promote that impression. Twenty-five years after leaving the cabinet he wrote about Grant, "It seems impossible to defend his integrity except at the sacrifice of all intelligence." A few months after resigning, Cox was working closely with disenchanted Republicans to deny his former chief a second term.[27]

Among the earliest champions of the anti-Grant movement was Carl Schurz, whose relations with the president grew increasingly hostile during the Missouri elections of 1870. Despite winning appointments for several of his friends, Schurz could not help feeling that the administration tilted toward his factional enemies. In the spring he favored passage of a bill for voting rights enforcement but suggested he did not trust the president's use of military power. He also charged that the annexation of Santo Domingo could lead to "an almost fatal exercise of arbitrary power, and possibly to acts of military usurpation." After the rejection of the treaty, Schurz hastened to assure the president that he had not attacked him personally—only confirming Grant's conviction of his insincerity.[28]

Back in Missouri, Schurz headed a so-called liberal Republican faction that opposed the Grant regulars and advocated the reenfranchisement of former Confederates. At the Republican state convention, party regulars refused to adopt Schurz's platform plank on the issue, and he and his allies promptly bolted. The liberals held their own convention and nominated B. Gratz Brown for governor. The regular Republicans renominated Governor Joseph McClurg and adopted a platform that saluted the president's administration, while the Democrats decided to throw their support to Brown in the hope of defeating McClurg.[29]

The revolt did not take Grant by surprise, for he had seen the lay of the land during a recent visit to St. Louis. The telegraph had hardly stopped clacking with news of the dueling conventions when he jumped into action, cleansing the state's federal patronage of anti-administration influence. Schurz had begun to drift away from the defense of blacks' rights, and Grant saw the Missouri revolt, especially the liberals' willingness to coalesce with the Democrats, as a threat to Republican Reconstruction policy. "They intend," Grant wrote to a St. Louis friend, "nothing more nor less than the overthrow of the party which saved the country from disruption, and the transfer of controll [sic] to the men who strove for disruption." Striking back at the senator, he gave the new position of appraiser of merchandise at the port of St. Louis to a noted advocate of blacks' rights, Isaac F. Shepard, whom he described as "a staunch Republican, and one of the first officers with me willing to take command of a Colored regiment." Schurz insisted to Grant that "true Republicans" supported his movement.[30]

On Election Day, Missourians voted handily to reenfranchise ex-rebels and overturn the exclusionary system of test oaths. Thanks to Democratic votes, the liberal Republican Brown won a landslide victory.

In other contests, however, the results confirmed Grant's prediction that Democrats would be the big winners. They won 77 of the 138 seats in the new state house of representatives, while the liberals took 21. Brown claimed a victory for "true Republican principles," but the error of that analysis became starkly clear when the new legislature voted to give a US Senate seat to Frank Blair, the Democrats' racist, fire-eating nominee for vice president in 1868. It was a bitter moment indeed for Schurz when he introduced his new colleague in the well of the Senate.[31]

Republican divisions also hurt the party in New York, where the two Republican senators, Roscoe Conkling and Reuben Fenton, battled for dominance. Grant was eager to build an effective organization in the Empire State, where he hoped to exchange his narrow loss in 1868 for victory in 1872. Early in his term he had given the collectorship of the port of New York, the most powerful and lucrative patronage post in the country, to businessman Moses Grinnell, who had raised campaign funds in 1868 but was not identified with either faction. Grinnell turned out to be less than adept at both the governmental and the political aspects of his job. By the late spring of 1870, Grant was thinking of replacing him with Thomas Murphy, a former state senator and accomplished wire-puller. Although the thought of tapping the aggressive, ill-educated Irish upstart shocked the bluestocking Fish, in midsummer Grant decided to move Grinnell into the lesser position of naval officer, in place of a Fenton Republican, and appoint Murphy collector. In the Senate, Conkling championed Murphy while Fenton attacked him. The ensuing two-man brawl reached a climax when Conkling answered Fenton's charges of corruption against Murphy by threatening to reveal court records showing that Fenton himself had once had a brush with the law for allegedly stealing a large sum of money. One senator described the scene in the chamber as "tragic." The Senate confirmed Murphy by a vote of 48 to 3. Not only had the president's man prevailed, but Grant had found in Conkling a political lieutenant with combat skills worthy of Sherman or Sheridan.[32]

Although the ideological dimension of the administration's resistance to Schurz's revolt in Missouri was more transparent, the New York fight was more than a struggle over power for power's sake. As an increasingly pragmatic political leader, Grant realized that he could accomplish none of his policy objectives without power, and he saw reinvigorating the New York organization as central to retaining and exercising power. He left the new collector on his own, but as Horace Porter wrote to Murphy, the president expected him to "distribute the patronage of your office as to render the most efficient service to the country, and the cause of the Administration." Still, Grant paid a price for the appointment. The embittered Fenton would enlist in the anti-Grant movement in 1872. More important, by embracing Murphy, Grant handed "reformers" a weapon to wield against him. In the words of the *New York Times*, "The President is rendering it a task of increasing difficulty to defend him against enemies into whose hands he is constantly playing."[33]

The anxiety suggested by the *Times* seemed to be borne out by the Republicans' November 1870 defeat in New York. Rigorous enforcement of new federal election laws helped reduce fraudulent voting engineered by the Tweed machine, but the Democrats still won the municipal elections and carried their state ticket to victory. The customhouse changes had not cured Republican divisions, and Murphy had not been in office long enough to perfect an organization that could outmaneuver Tammany Hall, a hard task for any Republican chieftain.[34]

In contests elsewhere in 1870, the Democrats made gains that were not unusual for a midterm election. In the House of Representatives, around thirty seats shifted from the Republicans to the Democrats. Even so, in the Forty-Second Congress, Republicans still held 56 percent of House seats and 76 percent of those in the Senate. Moreover, well over half the Democrats' gains occurred in the former slave states, a result of their determination to undo Reconstruction's protections of black voters by fair means or foul. Those gains bolstered arguments for stiffer regulatory measures by the federal government, but they also suggested that the GOP would need to place greater emphasis on key northern states in future presidential elections. A third of the party's House losses occurred in the key swing states of New York, Pennsylvania, and Indiana. Taken together, these three states held 43 percent of the electoral votes needed for a majority in the Electoral College in 1872.[35]

Although the Republicans' foremost advocate of civil service reform, Thomas Jenckes, lost his bid for reelection, "reformers" sought to cast the general outcome in 1870 as proof that the party must move in their direction. The *Nation* urged the party to pass "a good measure of Civil Service reform" to "enable it to recover." So-called revenue reformers, who considered the previous summer's tariff reductions inadequate, also took heart, hosting a dinner in New York to celebrate "the triumph of Revenue Reform principles in the recent Congressional Elections." Representatives from both groups gathered at a conference in New York to tout the importance of linking the two movements. "All our people are in high spirits," wrote E. L. Godkin. "The Lord is delivering the politicians into our hands."[36]

Not quite. The administration and its friends did not regard the election as a devastating blow. They took comfort that, as Fish put it, "We shall have a majority quite large enough in the next Congress." And Babcock reported to Zach Chandler that "the President feels well, and withall [sic], I think more than pleased. It is a great vindication, and he will not forget his friends."[37]

Even so, as Grant contemplated being on the ballot himself in two years, he saw a need to unify the party, and he soon offered more overt espousal of civil service reform as a way to build bridges to the disaffected. He had been deeply wounded by Cox's accusations on the subject. Even before the election, James H. Wilson had advised the White House that Cox should be "promptly counteracted, not by newspaper publications, but by the adoption of an active policy in favor of Civil Service reform," which would earn the president plaudits "as a great statesman & civil magistrate." As Grant prepared to submit his annual message a few weeks after the election, he consulted with Senator Lyman Trumbull, a leading advocate of reform. Trumbull later reported to Cox, "If left to himself I think Gen. Grant would condemn the present system of appointments & the assessment of officials for political purposes as strongly as any one; but I fear his anxiety for a re-election may cause him to yield his better judgment in order to gratify unprincipled demagogues who for selfish purposes always hang round the footstool of power."[38] Trumbull's doubts proved unjustified, for Grant followed through in his message. "Always favoring practical reforms," he wrote:

> I respectfully call your attention to one abuse of long standing which I would like to see remedied by this Congress. It is a reform in the civil service of the country. . . . There is no duty which so much embarrasses the Executive and heads of Departments as that of appointments, nor is there any such arduous and thankless labor imposed on Senators and Representatives as that of finding places for constituents. The present system does not secure the best men, and often not even fit men, for public place. The elevation and purification of the civil service of the Government will be hailed with approval by the whole people of the United States.[39]

In a single stroke Grant became the most prominent advocate of civil service reform in the nation. "His words," said the *New York Times*, "elevate the subject above the low level of every-day partisanship, and commend it to the favor of every man who has the honor and efficiency of the Government at heart." Not surprisingly, the embittered Cox insisted that Grant's "prompt acceptance of the Civil Service Reform" after the election was simply part of a larger "unscrupulous stratagem to retrieve his position with the public at my expense." But for Henry Adams, it was "something to have got to the mark on Civil Service," although he still saw "a long fight before us." The *Nation*, which was often harshly critical of Grant, conceded that he had written "frankly and heartily." George William Curtis, a champion of reform as well as a friend of the administration, expressed his great relief in the pages of *Harper's Weekly*: "If the Republican party will say amen to this distinct and emphatic declaration of the President, it has the opportunity opened to it of instantly awakening the most enthusiastic sympathy of the most intelligent and, in many senses, the best part of the country."[40]

As Curtis's comment suggested, Grant wanted Congress to play a part in developing a detailed reform program, thus giving senators and representatives a stake in its success. The usual cast of reformers responded by reviving their bills, but once again the devotees of the established system of patronage blocked these measures. On the last day of the session, March 3, 1871, Congress threw the problem back to Grant in the form of a rider to an appropriations act. It authorized the president to appoint a commission to investigate the question and assist him in preparing rules and regulations governing appointments. Rushed through at the last moment, the measure, though watered down, represented a momentous step. "We rejoice," said *Harper's Weekly*, "that the Republican party, upon the suggestion of a Republican President, has thus begun one of the most vital and valuable of reforms."[41]

Grant's new luster as a civil service reformer dimmed a month later when he dismissed Moses Grinnell as naval officer in New York. This marked another round in Grant's ongoing feud with Senator Fenton and followed a scathing report engineered by Fenton that accused collector Murphy of patronage abuses at the customhouse. But the president soon retook the high ground with his selections for the new civil service commission. At its head he placed Curtis, whose reform credentials were beyond question. Representing the western perspective was Joseph Medill of the *Chicago Tribune*. Grant also chose three government officials, E. B. Elliott, David C. Cox, and Joseph H. Blackfan, who represented departments that had already instituted some improvements: Treasury, Interior, and Post Office. Rounding out the group were Alexander Cattell of New Jersey, who had just left the Senate, and Dawson Walker, a judge from Georgia. Even the *Nation* conceded that these "excellent" appointments demonstrated that Grant "really meant what he said" in his annual message and left "no doubt of his sincerity." Soon after its appointment in June the commission started its work, which would continue for the next half year.[42]

Unlike civil service reformers, revenue reformers could take little solace from the president's 1870 annual message. Six weeks previously, Fish had recorded a conversation in which Grant said that "he is not half as much of a protectionist now as he was a year ago, but . . . 'Free trade' is impracticable, [and] would ruin the country if attempted." Pragmatism, not dogmatism, drove the president's ideas about fiscal policy. With undisguised impatience he declared in his message, "Revenue reform has not been defined by any of its advocates to my knowledge, but seems to be accepted as something which is to supply every man's wants without any cost or effort on his part." Taxes had already declined by $80 million. If revenue reform meant eliminating tariffs altogether and relying solely on "directly taxing the people, then I am against revenue reform." If it should lead to a failure to collect sufficient revenue to meet government expenses and pay the public debt and veterans' pensions, "then I am still more opposed to such kind of revenue reform." He conceded that the nation's returning fiscal health might permit the reduction of customs duties on some items, but he counseled caution, for "the necessities of the country compel us to collect revenue from our imports" to ensure adequate revenue. And—most distressing to free traders and other opponents of protectionism—he asserted, "Such a tariff, so far as it acts as an encouragement to home production, affords employment to labor at living wages, in contrast to the pauper labor of the Old World, and also in the development of home resources."[43]

The *New York Tribune*, the country's premier protectionist newspaper, hailed Grant for opposing "destruction either of Revenue or Protection." But from his professorial perch at Harvard College, Henry Adams told Cox that this section of the message was "in the style of a very ignorant collegian. It is to be regretted that the President does not know what Revenue Reform means, but I think we shall teach him as much as he will be able to learn before long." But in the ensuing congressional session, Republicans took their lessons from Grant, not Adams. Bills for tariff reduction got nowhere. Indeed, Pennsylvania protectionist William Kelley persuaded the House to pass a resolution favoring the repeal of the *internal* revenue system as soon as it could be done safely, thus suggesting the perpetuation of protective customs duties as the indispensable source of government revenue.[44]

The section of Grant's annual message in December 1870 that sparked the most controversy involved not a domestic issue but his attempt to revive the project for the annexation of Santo Domingo. In no sense did the president interpret the dip in Republican strength in the recent elections as signifying disapproval of his Caribbean policy. At great length he reiterated the strategic, economic, and humanitarian arguments for annexation he had made numerous times before. Unless the United States acted now, he warned, a European nation would step in, "and then will be seen the folly of our rejecting so great a prize." "So convinced am I of the advantages to flow from the acquisition of San Domingo, and of the great disadvantages—I might almost say calamities—to flow from nonacquisition, that I believe the subject has only to be investigated to be approved." He urged Congress to authorize him to appoint a commission to negotiate a new agreement.[45]

In short order Senator Oliver Morton offered to introduce a resolution to carry out Grant's wishes. The president asked Fish to work with Morton, and the State Department fashioned a resolution for the appointment of a commission to investigate the resources, political conditions, and debt structure of the Dominican Republic and whether its people desired annexation. Once the commission reported, the president would either initiate negotiations for annexation or submit the report to Congress, allowing it to pursue annexation in the manner it thought best. At a conference at the White House, Morton suggested eliminating the phrase regarding negotiations and simply stating that the president would submit the commission's report to Congress. Morton introduced the resolution in that form. Grant also met with House Foreign Affairs chairman Nathaniel Banks, who favored a commission to negotiate a treaty.[46]

Charles Sumner, meanwhile, returned to Washington for the new session with his battle armor strapped on. In November he had given a press interview in which he claimed, "A friend of mine, who has been down there, says that the whole coast of the Bay of Samaná is staked off into lots and marked 'Cazneau' and 'Babcock' and 'Baez' and that one or two particularly large ones are marked 'Grant.'" Sumner conceded that this was "most likely" done without Grant's knowledge, but he gave no sign that he doubted such hearsay or questioned whether the alleged plotters would be so absurdly indiscreet. (Although Babcock thought he had some land coming—at Palenque, not Samaná, and from private parties, not the government—no evidence suggests that Grant did. Sumner's "friend" apparently massaged suspicion into fable.) In the Senate, Sumner proposed a resolution requesting that the administration furnish all papers and correspondence related to the previous attempt to acquire Santo Domingo. Grant's allies blocked Sumner's resolution until after the Senate had approved Morton's, and the State Department delayed sending the requested material until after the resolution calling for the commission had cleared the House. Sumner's rage was further stoked by a letter from Motley insisting that the Senate's rejection of the Dominican treaty had been the "only cause" of Grant's "outrage upon me." Nor did Sumner appreciate a letter from Frederick Douglass saying that if Santo Domingo "honestly wishes to come to us, I now see no reason against the policy of receiving her." The Massachusetts senator thus entered the debate on the Morton resolution determined to scorch the administration.[47]

Sumner launched his attack on December 21, 1870, in a marathon session that lasted until 6:35 the next morning. But his tirade was as much character suicide as assassination, for at every turn he met members of his own party by whom, according to one congressman, he was "badly kicked & cuffed around."[48] In his opening round Sumner melodramatically intoned that Morton's resolution (which merely called for a commission) represented "a new step in a measure of violence" that "commits Congress to a dance of blood." He claimed that American warships in waters near the island posed a threat to Haiti, but Timothy Howe argued that an American naval presence represented the "mildest step" toward the very kind of protectorate that Sumner himself claimed to favor.

Sumner declared that Grant's message had referred nine times to acquiring "San Domingo"—the name by which the entire island was often designated—implying that he meant to take over Haiti as well as the Dominican Republic. Several senators scoffed at Sumner's disingenuous twisting of the president's inadvertent phraseology into a policy of conquest. "No sane man," said Conkling, could listen to this talk of "nine menaces" without seeing it as a "mutilation of language, well nigh affronting commonsense." Sumner spent a considerable amount of time trying to clarify his statements regarding his discussion of the treaty with Grant the previous winter, but his antagonists charged him with inconsistency if not fabrication. Whatever Sumner claimed to have said about his position that night, said Vermont's George Edmunds, what mattered was "the fact that he did suffer the President to go away from his house under the impression, of which the Senator himself was cognizant, that he was friendly to that proposition when he was not."

Sumner even referred to allegations in the press that Grant was so angry he would have "demand[ed] satisfaction" from the senator if he had not been president and that Babcock had talked of "personal violence." Sumner resorted to one of his favorite tropes, reliving his fight against the spread of slavery in the 1850s, including his savage beating at the hands of Preston Brooks on the Senate floor. "This whole measure of annexation," he declared, "and the spirit with which it is pressed, find a parallel in the Kansas and Nebraska bill, and in the Lecompton constitution, by which it was sought to subject a distant territory to slavery . . . and now we witness the same things—violence in a distant island, as there was violence in Kansas; also the same presidential appliances; and, shall I add, the same menace of personal assault?" Sumner seemed not to have pondered the degree to which such wild comparisons cheapened the heroic fight for racial justice he had waged in the 1850s and continued to wage in the postwar years. Conkling charged that Sumner's aim was simply to have his story about personal threats "winged with the feathers of the Associated Press" around the country. Moreover, with no sense of irony, Sumner reiterated his racialist argument against annexation: "The island of San Domingo, situated in tropical waters and occupied by another race, never can become a permanent possession of the United States. . . . Already by a higher statute is that island set apart to the colored race," and it was wrong "to remove them from the sphere in which they have been placed by Providence."

It was an extraordinary performance. Edmunds, who had voted against the annexation treaty in July, observed with sadness that Sumner "has demonstrated to the Senate and to his own friends that the worst enemy he has in North America today is himself." More ominously, Conkling asserted that "the Committee on Foreign Relations should not be composed of those who have added insult to injury, and arrayed themselves not only in opposition to the Administration, but so arrayed themselves in manner and in substance as to make it impossible for the Administration to confer, as it has a right to do, with all the committees of this body." After the all-night session, the Senate passed Morton's resolution by a vote of 32 to 9, and the House followed suit.[49]

Within days Sumner published an edited version of his speech under the title *Naboth's Vineyard*. He inserted new passages to bolster his position and, except for a few scattered exchanges, excised the speeches of senators who had challenged him.[50] Not surprisingly, Sumner's political allies rushed to congratulate him. "The great body of the people are with you," wrote James Ashley, and despite "the wild schemes of Morton & Conkling, and the still wilder threats of the President, . . . the end will be a triumph for you." Frederick Douglass had been present at the speech and complimented Sumner on its "force and effect," but he also told the senator that he could see no "good reason for degrading Grant in the eyes of the American people," and he particularly thought Sumner "did wrong" to associate the president's name with the "infamous names of Pierce, Buchanan, and Johnson." But analogizing his present fight with his past crusades lay at the heart of Sumner's purpose. "I am in the midst of a struggle as in the olden time for the down-trodden," he wrote to a friend. "The same pressure now as against Kansas!"[51]

In the administration's view, however, the Massachusetts senator showed increasing signs of derangement. "Sumner is crazy," Fish told Boutwell, "a monomaniac upon all matters relating to his own importance & his relations toward the President." Boutwell recounted a recent conversation in which the senator had alluded to "charges against the President of a nature so outrageous & violent" that Boutwell refused to repeat them to Fish. Solicitor General Benjamin Bristow thought Sumner had "acted the bear" in the debate and that throwing him "overboard" would not hurt the Republican Party, at least in the West. "He is too vain to be useful in any party."[52]

In any event, Congress had created the Santo Domingo commission. E. R. Hoar thought it was "merely to let the administration down 'easy,'" but Grant saw it as the only way to keep the project alive. He appointed three men of impeccable reputation to lead the investigation: Benjamin Wade, who had served three terms in the Senate and had stood alongside Sumner in the forefront of the Radical wing of the Republican Party; Andrew D. White, a reformer and historian and first president of Cornell University; and Methodist bishop Matthew Simpson, a prominent church leader and advocate of Radical Reconstruction. When Simpson declined, Grant turned to Samuel Gridley Howe of Boston, an education reformer and philanthropist and Sumner's good friend. As Secretary of the Navy George Robeson put it, if Howe "concurs in a favorable report it will disarm Sumner, & his immediate advocates—if he disagrees it will be accepted as Sumner's view." Fish thought the selections presented "the most emphatic rebuke to those who attempted to question the sincerity of the President's motives or the integrity of those who were intrusted with his confidence." They would "disarm much of the clamor which would-be-dictators of the foreign policy of the government have aroused." Indeed, Sumner conceded privately that Grant had chosen "good commissioners, instead of partizans."[53]

The appointments did not require Senate confirmation, and the commissioners set off immediately. Accompanying them was a staff of nineteen, including Frederick Douglass, who served as an assistant secretary, and nine scientists, including botanists, naturalists, geologists, mineralogists, and zoologists. The USS *Tennessee* also transported ten journalists. The president told Rutherford Hayes that if the commissioners "reported unfavorably, that would end the matter; if favorably, then he hoped annexation would take place." Grant had been stung by rumors of land being staked out for him in Samaná, and he privately requested the commissioners to examine all available records pertinent to such allegations and, if they found any truth in them, to "expose me to the American people." The group arrived at Samaná Bay on January 23 and pursued their work for nearly two months.[54]

Whatever the commission might report, Sumner had no intention of changing his mind, and he continued to fight the administration on another front as well. Motley had finally vacated his post in December. In his last dispatch to Fish he defended his performance at length and denied violating his instructions regarding the *Alabama* claims. He also referred to rumors "that I have been removed from the post of minister to England because of the opposition made by an eminent Senator who honors me with his friendship to the ratification of the San Domingo treaty." (In writing "San Domingo," Motley employed the same language Grant had used in his message and Sumner had decried as a "menace" to Haiti.) Motley informed Sumner of the substance of his dispatch and asked him to publicize it.[55]

When Fish received Motley's "End of Mission" dispatch, he immediately caught on to the game and set to work preparing a response. This took the form of a dispatch to Motley's temporary replacement in London, chargé d'affaires Benjamin Moran. When Fish finished his draft, Vice President Schuyler Colfax thought it might be "too severe," but Grant said he did not want "a word changed in the whole paper." The State Department arranged for the immediate press publication of the documents. In his dispatch, Fish repeated the evidence of Motley's insubordination and noted that the president had decided to dismiss him long before the defeat of the Dominican treaty. Motley was "entirely mistaken" in ascribing the administration's "loss in confidence" in him to Sumner's opposition to the treaty. "Men are apt," wrote Fish, "to attribute the causes of their own failures or their own misfortunes to others than themselves; and to claim association or seek a partnership with real or imaginary greatness, with which to divide their sorrows or their mistakes." Many other senators, the secretary noted, had opposed the treaty but "continued to enjoy the undiminished confidence and the friendship of the President—than whom no man living is more tolerant of honest and manly differences of opinion . . . or would look with more scorn and contempt upon one who uses the words and the assurances of friendship to cover a secret and determined purpose of hostility." That this last phrase referred to Sumner's performance at his after-dinner meeting with Grant few readers could fail to understand.[56]

The documents created a sensation, but Sumner made no immediate comment. Privately he called the administration's course "disgusting" and urged Motley to make some reply. Motley, however, "wish[ed] never to come before the public again, for the amusement of my enemies," although in London he went "around talking in the most violent bitter manner." Among the president's supporters, publication of the correspondence sparked jubilation. "Your vindication of the action of the administration is complete," Washburne wrote to Fish. "People never sympathize with a man who goes bawling about because he has been turned out of office." As for the still pending issue of the *Alabama* claims, Thurlow Weed told Fish, "You have done much to relieve the whole question from embarrassment. The English Government and People will see that the views and action of this Administration in reference to the question, have been enlightened and conciliatory."[57]

Grant and Fish were indeed much concerned about the *Alabama* question. On the very day the Motley correspondence went to the Senate, Fish had the first of several meetings with Sir John Rose, the unofficial envoy sent to Washington by the British to seek a basis for restarting negotiations. Within a week, the two men had reached general concurrence that the two countries should submit the question to a commission comprising representatives from each. But Fish argued that at the outset of negotiations, Great Britain should admit its liability for the claims. Rose objected, and Fish proposed an alternative formula whereby Britain would admit liability regarding the *Alabama*'s depredations and the two sides would submit the claims related to the other British-built Confederate vessels to arbitration. Although Rose still demurred about admitting liability for the *Alabama*, Fish submitted this formula to the president and cabinet. Grant initially objected that British negotiators would be inflexibly committed to instructions from their government, but Fish convinced him that British willingness to participate in talks in Washington signaled their commitment to reaching a settlement. Grant and the cabinet approved the formula, though with the "express under-standing" that along with losses inflicted by the other ships, "the question of liability for any consequential damages should be referred to the decision of some tribunal" of arbitration. This stipulation indicated the American aim for an adjudication of indirect claims against Great Britain. Fish also moved to secure the endorsement of senators, especially members of the Foreign Relations Committee, and within a few days, a majority of them were on board. But both Fish and Rose knew that the chairman had the capacity and perhaps the inclination to wreck their efforts.[58]

Grant initially opposed consulting Sumner at all, but Fish convinced him of the importance of demonstrating "respect" for the committee. Yet when Fish asked Sumner what he should say to Rose, the senator "declaim[ed]" rather than responding. Before getting back to Fish, Sumner conferred directly with Rose, who concluded that the senator had no "other motive than a vindication of himself, and the purpose of keeping the solution of the question in his own hands."[59]

When the senator sent Fish a memorandum two days after their meeting, Fish could scarcely contain his anger. Sumner accepted the principle of formal negotiations, but only as long as the "terms of submission" left "no reasonable doubt of a favorable result." Fish dismissed this condition, observing that it meant "the alleged cause of difference must be abandoned before a settlement is attempted!" The "greatest trouble," Sumner argued, was the threat of Fenianism "excited by the proximity of the British flag in Canada." He therefore concluded, "The withdrawal of the British flag cannot be abandoned as a condition or preliminary of such a settlement as is now proposed. To make the settlement complete the withdrawal should be from this hemisphere, including Provinces & islands." Astonished, Fish wondered if Sumner could seriously be suggesting that settlement of the *Alabama* question depended on Britain's leaving Trinidad, Barbados, and the Falklands. In his curt reply, Fish ignored the territory question altogether.[60]

Fish read Sumner's memorandum to the cabinet on January 20, but the president took no immediate action. That evening the secretary dined at the home of Robert Schenck, who had recently been confirmed to succeed Motley in London. Sumner was present and refused to speak to either Fish or the assistant secretary, J. C. Bancroft Davis—treatment that Sumner himself later described as "the cold shoulder." Schenck took

Fish aside and repeated what Sumner had told him—that is, that the publication of Fish's dispatch to Moran regarding Motley had released the senator from "all restraints of the confidences of private correspondence & conversation" with Fish. In addition, Sumner was spreading the word that he possessed some letters from Fish that "would disclose something." "What he refers to," Fish wrote in his diary, "I cannot imagine. Poor fellow! He is crazy." But more was at stake than Sumner's mental health. Although he may have thought he wielded some sort of controlling threat, such behavior simply confirmed Fish's growing belief that he could not trust Sumner to conduct business that concerned his committee and the Department of State. After the dinner at Schenck's, Rose wrote to Lord Granville that he had "seen gentlemen in the confidence of the President and of the Committee on Foreign Affairs, and I find the idea is entertained of removing Mr. Sumner from that Committee."[61]

Concluding that Sumner meant mischief, Grant ordered Fish to inform Rose "at once" that the United States would "accept their proposal for a Commission to settle all the questions." Fish told Rose the next day that the administration would spare no effort "to secure a favorable result, even if it involved a conflict with the Chairman of the Committee on Foreign Relations." But Fish stated strenuously that the United States expected the formal negotiations to yield some British admission of liability. If the British understood that "no settlement can be made without very large concessions on the part of G. B. with respect to the Alabama claims," and that the United States would "expect British Commissioners to be confidentially instructed in this sense," then the United States would accept the British proposal for a joint commission. This formulation worked. Speaking through Thornton, the British government formally proposed a Joint High Commission to consider the Canadian fisheries question and other issues between the two countries, and the American government agreed to participate if the commission considered the *Alabama* claims as well. The British acceded. The exchange of official letters gave no hint of concern about the "territorial cessions" Sumner had proposed as a preliminary condition.[62]

If Sumner's aim had been to derail formal negotiations, he failed. Nonetheless, as Foreign Relations chairman, he could still throw formidable, perhaps fatal, obstacles in the way of any treaty that might emerge from the Joint High Commission, as he had done with the Johnson-Clarendon Convention in 1869. As Grant put it, Sumner had been "on the warpath ever since" the Santo Domingo treaty was submitted to the

Senate, and he was "perfectly rabbid [*sic*] since the removal of Motley."
"Sumner is malicious," Fish confided to Weed. "He has (I am told) de-
clared that no settlement with Great Britain & no determination in the
Foreign Affairs of the country shall be made by Grant's Administration.
He cannot control & wishes to defeat. . . . [H]is vanity and conceit have
overturned his judgment, which never was of the best."[63]

Fish's anxiety was justified. As Sumner plotted strategy, he decided
to revive the argument that the queen's proclamation recognizing the
Confederates as belligerents was "an essential point in our case" and
that the American commissioners should demand that it be submitted
to arbitration. Grant and Fish had rejected this notion from the beginning, but Sumner entertained "no idea of abandoning the question on
the Proclamation."[64]

The senator also sharpened his knives for a renewed attack on
Grant's Dominican policy, in anticipation of the report of the investigative commission. In particular, he considered condemning Grant's order
that sent naval vessels to Dominican waters to afford protection during
the annexation plebiscite. Sumner polled constitutional and legal scholars on what he considered the move's illegality, but he found little support. Chief Justice Chase rejected Sumner's position and indicated his
belief that the United States had legitimately exercised "a kind of naval
protectorate" over "the small American states." Richard Henry Dana, an
expert on international law, opposed annexation but informed the senator that "after signing a treaty of cession and while its adoption is pending," each side has a right to protect "the subject matter," that is, the
country to be ceded. Nonetheless, Sumner insisted that Grant had committed "an act of war." He showed his petulance by refusing to report
out of his committee the nomination of Grant's brother-in-law Michael
Cramer, a Methodist minister and experienced diplomat, to be minister
to Denmark. After two months, the administration's friends pried the
nomination loose by a discharge resolution, which Sumner decried as a
"censure" of his committee. He stormed out of the chamber, and Cramer
won confirmation without dissent.[65]

Exhausted by his feverish efforts to assemble a case against Santo
Domingo, Sumner suffered a near collapse in mid-February 1871. His
doctor diagnosed it as a severe attack of angina pectoris, which had
plagued him for years, but Sumner circulated stories that traced the
flare-up to wounds received in his 1856 beating. Friends urged him
to forgo or postpone a speech on the Dominican issue for the sake of
his health, but he plowed ahead, turning to former commercial agent

Raymond Perry and former detainee Davis Hatch for information he hoped would incriminate the administration.[66]

For weeks, administration figures expressed mounting alarm about Sumner. "His assaults upon the President are simply scandalous," Fish wrote. "He picks up any falsehood against the Pres. & gives it utterance in his ponderous rhetoric." Sumner told his Senate colleague Henry Wilson that both Grant and Babcock had threatened him with physical assault. Fish wrote to Washburne, "He exhibits what I believe is a very common incident to insanity, & an equally unfailing sign of it, a constant apprehension of designs to inflict personal violence on him. . . . His friends should subject him to 'treatment'—that I think is the term they use in connection with the insane." Sumner's fears of assault were baseless, of course, but whatever the validity of Fish's armchair diagnosis, the administration and the senator had reached an impasse. Sumner did not intend to retreat, and Fish worried that "he is at work in advance endeavoring to prevent any settlement of the English questions."[67]

By the time the first session of the Forty-Second Congress convened in early March 1871, the administration had concluded that Sumner ought to be stripped of his chairmanship. At the beginning of each new Congress, the Senate elected its committees de novo. Typically, most committee members were carried over from the previous Congress, but no senator held a proprietary right to a seat on a particular committee. Fish took the lead in working with Timothy Howe, chairman of the Senate's Committee on Committees, to argue the administration's case that the head of the Foreign Relations Committee should not "be a person who has publicly assailed & vilified the Pres[iden]t & openly announced that he held no relations with him."[68]

Howe's committee recommended not returning Sumner to the Foreign Relations Committee—not even as a member—and suggested making him chairman of a new Committee on Privileges and Elections instead. Sumner refused to accept the new assignment, and a bitter debate ensued. His allies claimed that even though the Foreign Relations chairman had broken off "personal relations" with the president and the secretary of state, he was perfectly able and willing to continue "official relations." But Howe asserted that "the head of that committee should be on speaking terms, at all events, with those officers, in order to discharge all his duties to the people of the United States." Alleging that Grant was trying to force Sumner's removal because of his opposition to Santo Domingo, Schurz argued that Republicans should "consider whether they are quite ready to sacrifice their cause to the whims of one single man." George Edmunds retorted that the party faced a far greater threat from men like Schurz, who believed that "every motive which is not exactly the motive that suits him is dishonest." James Nye put the matter bluntly: "We cannot remove the President of the United States; we cannot remove the Secretary of State; but we can change the head of a committee to make the operations of our foreign relations harmonious and pleasant to all." Preliminary procedural votes revealed deep divisions among Republicans. In the end, however, the Senate approved the committees by a vote of 33 to 9, although Sumner and his friends had either exited or refused to vote.[69]

Grant denied asking that "any particular person" be put on a committee. "All that I have asked is that the Chairman of the Committee on Foreign Relations might be some one with whom the Secretary of State and myself might confer and advise. This I deemed due to the Country in view of the very important questions, which, of necessity, must come before it." Whatever Grant's precise role, Sumner's removal marked an extraordinary exercise of executive power and demonstrated the strength of Grant's influence in Congress. "In bold relief," said the *New York Herald*, "it brings out General Grant in a new character—as the recognized head of the republican party. . . . He rises from the subordinate position of Andrew Johnson to the commanding attitude of Andrew Jackson." Still, the administration's victory came at the price of deeper ill will among men who sympathized with Sumner or opposed the president's foreign policy or resented the resurgence of executive power after the struggle with Johnson. George William Curtis, who generally supported Grant, commiserated with the senator: "Six years ago the Senate was unwilling that the President should remove his Cabinet advisers at his pleasure. Now it is willing that he should name the heads of its Committees! It is a fall in which we all fall down."[70]

Sumner relished the martyr's role, calling the "proceedings against me . . . the natural culmination of the brutality to Motley." In a newspaper interview he again attacked Grant's Santo Domingo policy, accusing the president of usurping Congress's war power. When the reporter asked Sumner if he thought Grant saw the "matter as a violation of the constitution," the senator exploded: "He? What does Grant know? He doesn't know anything, sir. . . . He is not a man capable of understanding principles or of grasping anything in a comprehensive way. He does not understand the primary elements of the constitutional requirements for war. All he knows is how to execute. Put him on a horse and he'll blunder along somehow in the field. There's where his vocation ends."[71]

Such outbursts only convinced Fish that Sumner was "crazy upon an entire class of matters" and so blinded by his "love of adulation" that "in his quarrels he is incapable of seeing the truth." Privately Fish cited yet another reason for removing Sumner—his failure during the recent session of Congress to report out of his committee ten treaties that Grant had sent to the Senate. Fish leaked this information to friendly journalists, insisting that Sumner had purposely "obstructed the public business," which by itself was "more than sufficient to justify his *removal* from the Chairmanship."[72]

Four days after the Senate vote on committees, Republicans in New Hampshire suffered a narrow defeat in state and congressional elections. Sumner's friends portrayed the setback as a protest against the senator's treatment, but in fact the result was extremely close; indeed, the Democratic candidate for governor failed to win a majority and required election by the legislature. The true lesson for Republicans from the New Hampshire election, said the *New York Herald*, was that "a party without a head is like an army without a general, and that the republican party must stand by General Grant or go to pieces."[73]

But Sumner was determined to ride the wave of supposed popular indignation. In late March the Santo Domingo commission returned to the United States amid rumors that its report would endorse annexation. Indeed, a week after landing on the island, Wade had concluded, "All that Grant said about it is true & all that Sumner said is false." A month later he advised the president, "Annexation will be the crowning glory of your Administration; for God's and humanity's sake do not give it up."[74]

To steal a march on the commission, Sumner took to the Senate floor on March 27 to deliver a blistering attack, elaborating the points in his recent interview. Focusing on the presence of US naval vessels in the island's waters, he charged that "the President has seized the war powers carefully guarded by the Constitution" and "employed them to trample on the independence and equal rights of two nations"—Santo Domingo and the "Black Republic" of Haiti. In one breath he decried the annexation treaty as a contract obtained from the Dominicans "under duress," and in another he claimed that the president had sent Babcock to "answer the cry" of "the unscrupulous usurper" Báez, who was bent on "the sale of his country." Sumner reserved particular vitriol for Babcock, failing to mention that Babcock had been Grant's third. choice for the mission, tapped only after Caribbean expert Benjamin Hunt withdrew because of illness. Grant compounded all these wrongs, said Sumner, by presuming to violate his proper relationship with the Senate: "Presidential visits to the Capitol, with appeals to Senators, have been followed by assemblies at the Executive Mansion, also with appeals to Senators; and who can measure the pressure of all kinds by himself or agents, especially through the appointing power, all to secure the consummation of this scheme." That Grant and Sumner had starkly different notions of what it meant to be presidential, Grant would readily admit.[75]

Sumner had his speech printed in advance, and the administration was prepared to respond. George Robeson said the president had a "constitutional power to negotiate treaties," and the Báez government was legitimate, "both *de facto* and *de jure*." The two countries had arrived at two treaties, one for annexation and another for the lease of Samaná Bay; the latter was still pending and thus represented a material interest of the United States. The United States had "not fired a shot nor landed a man in hostile attitude on the island," but Robeson insisted that it was "the plain duty of the Executive to protect, if need be, the integrity of this constitutionally acquired interest, so that the subject of the negotiation might remain intact." To protect "the thing contracted for" was "certainly not to make war, or to take part in the conflict of a country, nor to coerce, nor to attempt to coerce any Power."[76]

Administration senators underscored these points. Timothy Howe declared that the president was as duty bound to protect the country's contracted interest as he was "to protect any portion of the possessions of the United States." Moreover, Howe argued, nations must not only "be good" but also "do good" to the extent of their ability. Under the Monroe Doctrine, the United States had "as much right to intervene for the peace of Dominica" as the Monroe administration "had to intervene against the Powers of Europe and for the peace of the Spanish colonies in South America." Oliver Morton asserted that the United States had a right to protect its interest in Samaná from Haiti, just as it would have had a right to stop England from interfering in negotiations with Russia for Alaska, which Sumner had fervently supported. Sumner's real purpose, Morton said, was "not to argue the impropriety of the acquisition" but "to fix a crime upon the President."[77]

In the course of his speech, Sumner projected himself as dedicating "the efforts of my life" to doing "what I can for the protection and elevation of the African race." But at bottom, he feared that Grant was eclipsing his reputation as blacks' foremost champion. Just four days before Sumner spoke, the president and the attorney general had gone to Capitol Hill to discuss rampant lawlessness in the South and to present a message "urgently recommend[ing]" new legislation to strengthen Grant's authority to fight the Ku Klux Klan. The next day he issued a proclamation commanding armed bands in South Carolina to disperse, preparatory to sending troops. His actions, said the *New York Herald*, showed "broad statesmanship." But Sumner diverged from the printed text of his speech to mock Grant's sincerity and liken his Dominican policy to crimes in the South: "It is difficult to see how we can condemn with proper, whole-hearted reprobation, our own domestic Ku Klux with its fearful outrages while the President puts himself at the head of a powerful and costly Ku Klux operating abroad. . . . I speak now against the Ku Klux on the coast of St. Domingo of which the President is the head, and I speak also for the African race which the President has trampled down." Senators stood aghast. "Has 'judgment fled to brutish beasts'; and have 'men lost their reason?'" Howe exclaimed. "No man need tell me," said Morton, "that he is the friend of liberty, the friend of the colored man, if he spends his time and his talents for the purpose of putting this Government into the hands of the Democratic party."[78]

Sumner's Santo Domingo speech pleased his friends such as William Lloyd Garrison, who said its "legitimate corollary is the impeachment of the President." But whether he had burnished his image among African Americans was open to question. From Tennessee one person wrote, "We Colored People owe you evrything, . . . but your speech give great rejoiceing among the Democrats. . . .We fear that in your great love for the Inhabitants of San domgo and your interest in there behalf, that the well fare of the Colored Race in our own Country is over looked, for you must know that if the Democratic Party triumphs in the Presidential election in 72 that our Condition will be any thing but justice & right." Speaking for mainline Republicans, Congressman G. W. Hazleton told the leader of the party in Wisconsin that Sumner's "wanton, wicked, and unjustifiable attack" appealed primarily to a group of senators who "are mad because they cannot control Gen. Grant and so they propose to crush him." It also pleased the Democrats, who "at once ordered the speech by the thousands for a campaign document."[79]

Some of those copies no doubt wound up in Connecticut, an evenly divided state that held state and congressional elections one week after Sumner spoke. Many observers believed the Democrats' victory in New Hampshire had emboldened white terrorists in the South, in part prompting Grant's anti-Klan message and proclamation. Thus, said the *New York Times*, "the result of the election in Connecticut on Monday next will be regarded in some measure as determining whether the command of the President shall be obeyed, or set aside through weakness." Desperate Connecticut Republicans asked Sumner for campaign help, but he refused to join in a display of unity. Even so, the Republicans won the governorship and carried three of four congressional seats. "It is a bitter pill" for Sumner, said Howe, but administration supporters were "jubilant." The *Boston Daily Advertiser* called the Connecticut result "a vindication of the republican party from the damaging blows" inflicted by Sumner. After the GOP did well in other state and municipal elections, an elated Boutwell told Fish that Sumner's Santo Domingo speech "has not produced a crack in the Republican party. No one thinks or cares about it."[80]

Two days after the Connecticut election, Grant scored another victory of sorts when he sent Congress the report of the Santo Domingo commission. With occasional flights of hyperbole, the commission presented an otherwise straightforward account of the island nation's assets: a capacious harbor for trade and security, fertile soil, "vast and various" resources, a healthful climate, a manageable debt, and people who, though uneducated, were educable and "good and faithful laborers." Moreover, the commissioners asserted, "by the inevitable laws of trade," the development of Santo Domingo as a powerful state "would make slave labor in the neighboring islands unprofitable, and by the spread of its ideas render the whole slave and caste system odious." As for rumors that American officials had received concessions or land grants from the government during negotiation of the 1869 treaty, the commissioners declared that "no pains were spared to ascertain the exact truth," and they concluded that "no such grant or concession was made in any way in connection with the negotiation or preparation of the treaty."[81]

Grant's message conveying the report was a masterstroke. He did not reiterate his arguments for annexation, noting simply that the report "sustains all that I have said heretofore." Instead he detailed the origin and unfolding of the annexation project. In the spring of 1869 he had received from an "agent of President Báez" (no doubt Fabens) a proposition for the annexation of the Dominican Republic, together with a description of the nation's assets and the observation that if the United States were not interested, the Dominicans would look elsewhere. Citing his "earnest desire to maintain the 'Monroe Doctrine,'" Grant said he would have been "derelict in my duty" and "charged with a flagrant neglect of the public interests" if he had failed to investigate the country. In addition, he would have been accused of "utter disregard of the welfare of a down-trodden race praying for the blessings of a free and strong government, and for protection in the enjoyment of the fruits of their own industry. Those opponents of annexation who have heretofore professed to be preeminently the friends of the rights of man I believed would be my most violent assailants if I neglected so clear a duty." No one could mistake this reference to Sumner.

The president said he had sent Babcock to Santo Domingo "not to secure or hasten annexation" but to examine the country and the attitude of the people and government (although Babcock's record of his trip indicated that he believed he was to pursue annexation). The Senate's rejection of the annexation treaty "only indicate[d] a difference of opinion between two coordinate Departments of the Government," but because that rejection occurred "simultaneously with charges openly made of corruption on the part of the President, or those employed by him," the "honor of the nation" demanded an investigation. The commission's report, he insisted, "fully vindicates the purity of the motives and action of those who represented the United States in the negotiation."

Grant declared that he would offer no further "personal solicitude" but would leave the question to Congress and to the American people—"that tribunal whose convictions so seldom err, and against whose will I have no policy to enforce." In closing, he took a final swipe at Sumner, Schurz, and others who had maligned his integrity:

> No man could hope to perform duties so delicate and responsible as pertain to the presidential office without sometimes incurring the hostility of those who deem their opinions and wishes treated with insufficient consideration; and he who undertakes to conduct the affairs of a great government as a faithful public servant, if sustained by the approval of his own conscience, may rely with confidence upon the candor and intelligence of a free people, whose best interests he has striven to subserve, and can bear with patience the censure of disappointed men.[82]

Speaking for Grant's supporters, the *New York Times* observed that the "eminently judicious" message would sustain "the belief of any honest citizen in the purity of motive and integrity of conduct on the part of the President." It "contrasts finely with the brutal temper exhibited by Sumner's speech," Timothy Howe wrote. "And the merit of the message is, it is genuine. There is nothing pharasaical [*sic*] or Pecksniffian about

Grant. He puts on no amiability for public occasions." West Point professors William Bartlett and Dennis Hart Mahan supported annexation as a boon to the nation's defense, and they hailed the "masterly message" as a "moral triumph for the President & disaster to the miserable faction that have so much abused him." Grant had drafted the message himself, but it pleased Fish; the secretary had never been as enthusiastic about annexation as his chief, and he welcomed its fading from prominence as a disturbing element in the nation's foreign relations. The White House ordered a large quantity of copies of Grant's message, including a German edition for the edification of Schurz's special constituency. Even if annexation was beyond resuscitation, the administration was satisfied that, as Horace Porter put it, in a political sense "the San Domingo report and message worked wonders."[83]

Those wonders did not extend to Sumner. "Never has our country been so much demoralized by Presidential influence as now," he wrote to Garrison. "The Senate & the people are subjugated." Sumner had already prepared yet another speech, this one excoriating Fish for his "assault" against him in the Motley correspondence, but friends talked him out of making such a statement. Still, he distributed copies secretly, thus giving the secretary no opportunity to reply. Edward Pierce, one of Sumner's closest confidants, frankly told him that Grant's Santo Domingo "explanatory message was a shrewd movement and enabled him to recover himself." Moreover, Pierce wrote, "the mass of men are indifferent to what becomes of a *negro* country and government"; they regarded the Dominican question as "not very important, and one that ought not to make any breaches in the Republican party. Therefore they will take no ground against the President's course." He advised Sumner that the best thing to do was to "avail yourself of all opportunities to support actively all party measures that you think right" in order to dispel "the charges of 'disappointment'—'sympathy with the Democrats' &c." But Sumner would not be reconciled. "There is a *dementia* in the Republican party," he told Schurz. "We must save it."[84]

The strong endorsement of the president's message suggested that many judged his decision to cease pushing for annexation as more statesmanlike than Sumner's tirades. It stanched the loss of support for the administration on the Dominican question, and the reaction demonstrated Grant's hold on a major portion of the Republican Party. "The tone of public sentiment is wonderfully changed," Howe wrote. Three weeks after the message, Pierce conceded that "Grant would be renominated for election if a Convention were now to be held." But that high regard did not rest solely, nor perhaps even primarily, on the well-received message, for the spring of 1871 witnessed executive action on two other fronts that enhanced the president's standing: the defense of blacks' rights in the South and progress toward settlement of the *Alabama* claims.[85]

13

★ ★ ★ ★ ★

WAR AT HOME

In the spirit of his campaign invocation, "Let Us Have Peace," President Grant had entertained hopes for a relatively speedy end to Reconstruction. He had eased the readmission of the last of the former Confederate states, pressed for ratification of the Fifteenth Amendment, and endorsed enforcement legislation to uphold the right to vote. Yet continuing recalcitrance by southern whites demonstrated the need for more action. In his annual message in December 1870 Grant observed that "violence and intimidation" had marred the recent elections in several states and reversed "the verdict of the people." He reiterated his commitment to "a pure, untrammeled ballot, where every man entitled to cast a vote may do so, just once at each election, without fear of molestation or proscription on account of his political faith, nativity, or color."[1]

Republicans in Congress shared the president's concern. Early in the session Oliver Morton sponsored a resolution requesting the president to provide any information he had about activities of the Ku Klux Klan and similar organizations in North Carolina, especially "murders and outrages for political purpose" committed by such groups.[2]

Grant responded in two reports. The first provided information from War Department field officers about violence not just in North Carolina but in the South in general. The twenty printed pages of abstracts cataloging murders and other outrages extending back several years presented a dismal picture of persistent lawlessness. In a second report on January 17, 1871, the president focused on North Carolina, forwarding from Governor W. W. Holden a large body of correspondence, testimony, and other documents. Holden charged that an "organized conspiracy is in existence in every county of the State" and "unless active measures are taken the lives of its loyal citizens are no longer safe, and their liberties a[re] a thing of the past." At this time, Grant also held a well-publicized meeting with national representatives of the Union League and vowed that the mission of the Republican Party would not be finished until the free exercise of the franchise was secured for all.[3]

Morton moved to refer both of Grant's reports to a select committee, which would also conduct its own investigation of affairs in the South. In short order the Senate voted to create the committee, and John Scott of Pennsylvania, an administration loyalist, became its chairman.[4]

While Republicans felt growing alarm about the violation of voting rights, they rejected calls for a blanket amnesty that would remove the Fourteenth Amendment's ban on officeholding by former Confederate leaders. Congress did, however, regularly pass private acts releasing certain individuals, such as former generals and other high officials, from these so-called disabilities if they took an oath of future loyalty. In early 1871 Congress removed a political barrier for lower-level former Confederates as well. An 1862 law, still on the books, mandated that all individuals, including lifelong unionists as well as ex-Confederates, who were elected or appointed to office under the US government must take a so-called test oath, swearing to both past and future loyalty. Former Confederates obviously could not take such an oath. In early February Congress passed a bill stating that ex-Confederates not covered by the Fourteenth Amendment could enter office upon swearing only to future loyalty. This legislation troubled Grant, for rather than simply repealing the 1862 test oath altogether, it left that provision in place for everyone except these Confederate classes. "By this law," the president told Congress, "the soldier who fought and bled for his country is to swear to his loyalty before assuming official functions, while the general who commanded hosts for the overthrow of his Government is admitted to place without it. I cannot affix my name to a law which discriminates against the upholder of his Government." Yet Grant did not believe it was "wise policy to keep from office by an oath those who are not disqualified by the Constitution, and who are the choice of legal voters," and he let the bill become law without his signature. The 1862 test oath was not repealed in toto until 1884.[5]

While the Senate's select committee pursued its investigation of the South, Congress turned again to election fraud in northern cities. Grant's comment in his annual message about casting a ballot "just once" reflected Republicans' anger at their opponents' persistent use of repeat voting and other fraudulent techniques, particularly in New York, despite the regulations created by the legislation of 1870. Republicans now moved to tighten those procedures with a bill spelling out the duties and powers of federal election supervisors and deputy US marshals in cities with populations greater than 20,000. Supervisors would be authorized to observe registration and voting and to participate in the counting of ballots, and deputy marshals would not only keep the peace at the polls but also arrest violators of federal laws and take them to court.[6]

As Democrats pointed out, this bill would apply not only to New York but also to nearly seventy other cities. It would, they charged, consolidate "power in a great central Government." Noting that "Caesar made himself master of all the elections," Representative Daniel Voorhees warned of "the grim, silent, taciturn man of action, whose opinions are never uttered in advance, and whose purposes are enveloped in constant mystery. . . . He can command troops; and therefore he wants to command them. He loves power; and the control of an army at the ballot-box is a certain means of obtaining and retaining power." Republicans, of course, saw a different threat to liberty. As Representative Burton Cook put it, "In so far as the popular will fails to be fairly expressed and fairly embodied in forms of law our Government becomes the meanest, basest despotism that ever cursed the earth. . . . The question, stripped of all gloss, is simply this: shall this country be governed by a majority of its citizens, or by the repeaters of the cities." The bill passed by large partisan majorities, and Grant signed it into law on February 28, 1871.[7]

While Grant and Congress perfected the structure to combat election fraud in northern cities, reports of terrorism in the South reached a crescendo. In North Carolina, Governor Holden faced an impeachment trial largely because of his aggressive efforts to put down the Klan. In mid-February South Carolina governor Robert Scott sent the president a plea from the state legislature for federal protection against "barbarous" violence that state authorities were powerless to quell. At a cabinet meeting Grant read a report from that state's constable recounting murders and whippings in several counties. He decided to send federal troops from Texas to South Carolina.[8]

The new Forty-Second Congress convened on March 4, 1871, on the heels of the expiring Forty-First. Many legislators, including Speaker James G. Blaine, contemplated a quick adjournment until the regular session in December, but Grant wanted the House and Senate to stay long enough to deal with the southern crisis. Although high-tariff legislators feared an extended session would open the way for measures that cut rates, Grant would not be deterred. He wrote to Blaine and cited the "deplorable state of affairs existing in some portions of the South demanding the immediate attention of Congress. If the attention of Congress can be confined to the single subject of providing means for the protection of life and property in those Sections of the Country where the present civil authority fails to secure that end, I feel that we should have such legislation." That evening Governor Scott wired the president that "an actual state of war exists" in two South Carolina counties, and Grant dispatched additional troops.[9]

Although Sumner's removal from the Foreign Relations Committee was distracting Washington's attention at the moment, evidence of turbulence in the South mounted. On March 10 the Senate select committee reported its findings that the Ku Klux Klan operated as a political organization in North Carolina in the interest of the Democratic or Conservative Party and carried "out its purpose by murders, whippings, intimidations, and violence." Although "many hundreds, if not thousands" of Klan members had participated in the mayhem, "not one has yet been convicted in the whole State." The committee's Democratic minority dismissed these findings as exaggerated and warned that federal action would result in "the total destruction of the autonomy of State governments." Yet even General Sherman, no great friend of Reconstruction, observed that "Union People" in the South "are hustled, branded and even killed," and "any Southern Citizen may kill or abuse a Negro or Union Man with as much safety as one of our Frontiersmen may kill an Indian." Shortly after Scott's group reported, Congress created a special committee comprising members from both houses to conduct an investigation of the entire South.[10]

The immediate problem for the Grant administration was South Carolina. In a meeting at the White House, Grant assured the state's Republican officials that contingents of both infantry and cavalry were on their way. "If two regiments will not do it, ten shall be sent there, and kept there, too, if necessary, as long as this Administration is in power." It had become clear, however, that the expanding southern crisis re-quired the administration to move beyond ad hoc responses and seek a clearer definition by Congress of the executive's power to act.[11]

Initially Congress made little progress toward resolving the question. Ben Butler maneuvered an anti-Klan bill through an underattended House Republican caucus in mid-March, yet when he attempted to introduce it on the floor the next day, he encountered opposition not only from Democrats but also from Republicans, including Blaine, who favored an early adjournment. They combined to pass a resolution creating a House investigating committee and delaying the matter until the December session. On March 20 Butler was able to introduce his bill, but there was little chance of its consideration, let alone passage. Prospects for action seemed equally dim at the other end of the Capitol.[12]

While Congress dawdled, Grant decided to intervene. On the morning of March 23 he huddled with Senator Morton in the Red Room at the White House, and in the afternoon he, Attorney General Akerman, and other cabinet members headed to Capitol Hill to consult with legislators. The more the president heard, the more convinced he became that he must push Congress to act. Not unlike those critical times during the war when he had surveyed a situation and then dashed off orders to subordinates, he sat down at his table in the President's Room at the Capitol and drafted a brief and pointed message. He aimed to leave little doubt as to the necessity of and constitutional justification for action. Citing the "proof" in the Scott committee report, he declared, "A condition of affairs now exists in some of the States of the Union rendering life and property insecure and the carrying of the mails and the collection of the revenue dangerous." The disturbances clearly exceeded the capacity of the states to control, but, Grant said, it was not clear "that the power of the Executive of the United States, acting within the limits of existing laws, is sufficient for present emergencies. . . . Therefore I urgently recommend such legislation as in the judgment of Congress shall effectually secure life, liberty, and property and the enforcement of law in all parts of the United States." Acknowledging the extraordinary character these emergency powers might take, he suggested it might be "expedient" to limit their duration to the end of the next session of Congress. As one congressman in the room later recalled, the president wrote the message "without pause or correction, and as rapidly as his pen could fly over the paper." The *New York Tribune* called it "an appeal to arms" whose "palpable effect" was "promptly to unite the Republicans who have been wrangling over this question."[13]

Grant followed up with action in South Carolina, ordering the attorney general to prepare a proclamation to underpin the dispatch of troops. Akerman presented his draft at a cabinet meeting on March 24,

Grant accepted it, and the document went out the same day. In it, the president cited the constitutional obligation of the federal government to protect the states from domestic violence. He noted that in South Carolina "combinations of armed men" were "committing acts of violence" of such magnitude as to "render the power of the State and its officers unequal to the task of protecting life and property and securing public order." Under the law, he observed, in such cases the president had the authority to employ the militia or the armed forces of the United States "necessary for the purpose of suppressing such insurrection or of causing the laws to be duly executed." As required by statute, preparatory to his use of troops, his proclamation commanded the "unlawful combinations" of "insurgents" to "disperse and retire peaceably" within twenty days. The *New York Times* applauded the proclamation as the "logical consequence" of Grant's promise in his inaugural address to protect citizens in "every portion of our common country."[14]

While the proclamation provided the legal justification for the use of troops, House Republicans responded promptly to Grant's message, introducing a bill to expand his authority. It declared that a state's inability or unwillingness to protect its citizens constituted a denial of equal protection of the law, as mandated by the Fourteenth Amendment, and it empowered the president to employ the armed forces to secure such constitutional protection. Further, the bill authorized the president to suspend the writ of habeas corpus and institute martial law in locations where the violent disruption of normal processes prevented the conviction of offenders and the preservation of peace.[15]

The bill occasioned intense debate. Democrats warned of centralization, the destruction of the states, and unchecked military despotism. Ohioan Philadelph Van Trump denounced Grant as "a mere military chieftain, unlearned in the civil policy of the government," for whom "no violation of the Constitution, however palpable, no assumption of power, however outrageous, is deemed too great a sacrifice in extending and strengthening the executive power in his hands." A small group of Republicans opposed the bill, none more vociferously than Carl Schurz, who saw the habeas corpus provision as "a pretext for placing the highest privilege of an American citizen at the mercy of the Executive." Most Republicans rejected such scaremongering and were willing to trust the president with new powers to meet the emergency. George Hoar scoffed at those who "fear the exercise of power in the day-light by the President of the United States," while "they would leave undisturbed at midnight, in the darkness, these demons of the mask."[16]

After his initial message and visit to the Capitol, Grant kept a relatively low profile. But two days after the bill passed the House, he attended an enthusiastic Republican rally in Washington engineered by Morton and Vice President Schuyler Colfax. "After our differences," John W. Forney told the cheering crowd, "it was inspiring to see the Republican majority of the House marching up in solid phalanx at last . . . under the inspiration of the recent message of the President." Colfax declared that the great issue of the day was the "reign of terror" in the South, "which your President intends to put down whenever the law-making power of the country puts the necessary power into his hands."[17]

The measure carried by a largely partisan vote in each house, and Grant signed it immediately on April 20. In its final version, the Act to Enforce the Provisions of the Fourteenth Amendment, or Ku Klux Klan Act, outlawed conspiracy to overthrow or oppose the authority of the government or to deprive persons of their constitutional rights or to interfere with officials protecting persons' rights. It made violators liable to both criminal prosecution and civil action. In cases in which domestic violence or unlawful conspiracies deprived persons of their rights and the states either refused or failed to afford protection, the president could employ the militia or the army and navy to do so. The final act omitted mention of martial law, but it did empower the president to suspend the writ of habeas corpus in carefully defined areas where unlawful combinations had overthrown or "set at defiance" the constituted authorities. This provision would terminate at the end of the next regular session of Congress. The law represented an extraordinary expansion of national executive authority to defend individuals' constitutional rights. The *New York Herald* labeled it a "tyrannical and un-American measure" that the president "will not, out of deference to public opinion, enforce."[18]

Grant soon proved the *Herald* wrong. Canceling a planned trip to California, he again called on Akerman to draft a proclamation. Issued on May 3, the document drew the country's attention to the new law's provisions and admonished "all persons to abstain from committing any of the acts" it prohibited. "I will not hesitate to exhaust the powers thus vested in the Executive whenever and wherever it shall become necessary to do so for the purpose of securing to all citizens of the United States the peaceful enjoyment of the rights guaranteed to them by the Constitution and laws." Grant and Secretary of War William Belknap alerted army troops in the South to assist federal civilian

Attorney General Amos T. Akerman. (Library of Congress)

authorities in executing the enforcement legislation. In the case of South Carolina, where violence was most pronounced, the president told Belknap to order troops "in all cases to arrest and break up disguised night marauders."[19]

The administration's new energy in assaulting the Klan won praise from longtime defenders of African Americans. The old abolition leader Gerrit Smith hailed the president as *the most prominent upholder* of the Republican Party's *great moral ideas*. Smith told Charles Sumner, "We must have either him or some abominable Ku Klux Democrat for our next President." But Sumner still insisted that Grant was "the lowest Presid[en]t, whether intellectually or morally, we have ever had." "At the proper time," he wrote to Smith, "I shall appeal to the colored voters to reject him." "Do not," he added, "charge me with personal feelings." On the Democratic side, some party leaders, especially in the North, sought to distance themselves from the disturbances in the South. They touted a so-called New Departure by which their party declared acceptance of the postwar constitutional amendments and support for equal rights "without distinction of race, color or condition." Republicans, including Grant, doubted their sincerity. The president told a reporter, "If the democracy succeeded, the southern leaders, who are still hostile to the Union of the States, and, in that view, enemies of the republic, would gain possession of the government and before long annul, so far as they could, the acts of the republican party." Sincere or not, the New Departure had scant effect in diminishing Klan activity.[20]

Akerman jumped into the work of enforcement with a will. He harbored few illusions about the magnitude of the task, for he knew that many white southerners "hate the negro because he has ceased to be a slave and has been promoted to be a citizen and voter." He thought "nothing is more idle than to attempt to conciliate by kindness that portion of the southern people who are still malcontent," but he hoped the federal government could "command their respect by the exercise of its power." Under his prodding and that of Solicitor General Benjamin Bristow, federal attorneys in the field issued hundreds of new indictments and secured many convictions. Army troops sometimes aided in making arrests, but with only 5,000 men on duty in the entire South, they were hardly ubiquitous, and their effectiveness was limited. Lack of funds and personnel also hampered the prosecutorial effort. So too did Klan intimidation of juries. Prosecution success rates varied from state to state, depending on the capacity or energy of federal officials and the intensity of local Klan participation. Prosecution did not always follow indictment, but even in those cases, federal investigations and arrests exposed the terrorism to public scrutiny.[21]

Klan resistance to restraint by judicial process raged most flagrantly in South Carolina, where white conservatives recoiled against the Republican government voted into office by the state's black majority. Murders and other outrages mounted, despite Grant's proclamations in March and May. In late June Senator Scott met with the president before heading off with two other members of the congressional joint committee to investigate conditions in the state. They remained for more than three weeks, taking testimony that confirmed Scott's worst fears. After returning north he passed the evidence on to Grant, suggesting that it might be time to let the Carolinians know that "the limit of endurance has been reached" and invoke the Ku Klux Klan Act. On September 1 the president read Scott's letter to the cabinet and referred to the attorney general the question of whether to suspend the writ of habeas corpus. To ascertain the necessity of doing so, he sent Akerman down south to assess the situation firsthand.[22]

Leaving in mid-September, Akerman traveled to Georgia and North Carolina but spent most of his time in South Carolina. He soon concluded, "I doubt whether from the beginning of the world until now, a community, nominally civilized, has been so fully under the domination of systematic and organized depravity." Grant also did some investigating of his own during a tour of the Midwest to show the administration flag in states that were holding elections. In Kentucky he met with John Marshall Harlan, the Republican candidate for governor, who frankly told him how difficult it was for federal officials to prosecute the Klan with their paucity of funds. In Dayton, Ohio, Grant met with Akerman, who reported on the desperate situation in South Carolina. Grant ordered him to prepare the warning and proclamation necessary to suspend the writ. Akerman drafted the documents and sent them to Bristow in Washington; he then headed back to South Carolina to assist with the prosecutions.[23]

While Akerman was off battling lawlessness in the South, he became the victim of treachery in Washington. For some time, Bristow had bridled at playing second fiddle to the attorney general, whose competence as a lawyer he denigrated behind his back. Bristow considered resigning as solicitor general or, alternatively, trying to take Akerman's place. When Grant spoke with Harlan, who was Bristow's former law partner, the Kentuckian listened carefully for any indication of "a present purpose to make a change in his household." Grant gave no such sign, but Harlan assured Bristow, "You can obtain at his hands almost any promotion whenever an opportunity presents." Another Kentucky friend advised Bristow that Akerman's exertions could "ruin the best administration the country has ever seen." Bristow did not defend his chief but instead spread the word that Akerman was "doing no good" in South Carolina.[24]

When Grant returned to Washington, Bristow told him that Akerman "was altogether *too small* for the place in every particular, that he was ridiculed by the Court & the profession generally and that he was a *dead weight* on the administration, . . . & that there was absolutely no hope of improvement under A." The president was shocked. Although Akerman had not quite met his expectations, Grant "expressed great surprise that he had failed as disastrously" as Bristow alleged. Moreover, the president said the justices had said nothing critical of the attorney general. Indeed, Grant called Akerman "an earnest man & thoroughly honest," and he was "quite troubled" by the idea of turning him out on allegations of "want of capacity." Bristow made a feint to offer his own resignation, but Grant would not hear of it. "Of course," Bristow told Harlan, "if I ever had any chance for the succession (as some of my friends here seem to think) I have 'knocked my own fat in the fire.'" He thought former Oregon senator George H. Williams might get the job. Harlan advised him to urge Grant not to tell others what Bristow had said about Akerman.[25]

While these intrigues unfolded, the fight against the Klan proceeded. On October 12 Grant issued a preliminary proclamation giving the perpetrators of unlawful conspiracies in nine South Carolina counties five days to cease their assaults on the constitutional rights of "certain portions and classes of people," and ordering them to deliver their arms and disguises to federal authorities. When no noticeable response ensued, he followed through with a suspension of the writ of habeas corpus. The president was traveling in New England at the time, and Akerman was still in South Carolina, so Grant ordered Bristow to prepare the proclamation. Dated October 17, the document repeated the strictures of the warning, noted the conspirators' failure to cease what amounted to rebellion, and suspended the privileges of the writ for all persons arrested in violation of the April 20 act "during the continuance of such rebellion." Bristow acted dutifully but not enthusiastically. After "modestly entering my protest," he told Harlan, he presented a draft that adhered closely to the terms of the specific legislation, and he advised the president that the suspension could not be applied to cases unrelated to the act. Bristow hoped the proclamation would "stop the operations of the infernal Ku Klux," but he confessed to Harlan, "I don't like the precedent." His attitude suggested that it was Akerman's vigor in pursuing the Klan as much as his supposed incompetence that drove Bristow's machinations against the attorney general.[26]

Grant's warning and proclamation were in some measure overshadowed by the horrific stories that filled the newspapers after the Great Chicago Fire began on October 7. While the conflagration raged, the president ordered Sheridan to "render all the aid you can" in the form of army equipment and supplies to "relieve sufferings from the great calamity." At the request of citizens, he sent four companies of troops to the city to help maintain order and protect lives and property. But Grant drew the ire of Illinois governor John Palmer, an erstwhile Democrat who had been elected as a Republican in 1868 and was now drifting into the anti-Grant Liberal Republican movement. Palmer complained to the president about the federal actions and insisted that state authorities were "abundantly able to protect every interest of the people." Grant responded that he meant no disrespect to the state officials' capacity but simply aimed "to benefit a people struck by a calamity greater than had ever befallen a community, of the same number, before in this country." But Palmer would accept no explanation. He insisted that Grant had issued the orders "without reflection" and had violated the Constitution and the laws. Grant gave up trying to assuage Palmer. When Congress reconvened, he supported legislation to expedite the reconstruction of government buildings in the city and to underwrite relief in the form of temporary exclusion from tariff and internal tax levies.[27]

Meanwhile, Akerman spent nearly three weeks in South Carolina. Armed with the new proclamation and assisted by federal troops, he and the state's US marshal arrested more than 470 members of the Klan. Hundreds more fled, and as Akerman tersely put it, "flight was confession." Those who absconded tended to be the more well-to-do leaders of the organization, while the men arrested were largely from the poorer class, many of whom resented being abandoned to face fines and imprisonment. As Akerman indicated to a news reporter, the resulting indignation "is just what is desired. It breaks up the order by arraying the rank and file against the leaders." But the prosecutorial effort proved painfully slow. Within a month, five defendants had been tried and convicted, and another twenty-five had pleaded guilty. Despite the difficulty of securing convictions, the administration had accomplished a great deal in checking the Klan as an organization, but terrorism was far from permanently defeated. Akerman "rejoiced at the suppression of Ku Kluxery even in one neighborhood" but decried the "perversion of moral sentiment among the Southern whites which bodes ill to that part of the country for this generation. Without a thorough moral renovation, society there for many years will be—I can hardly bring myself to say savage, but certainly very far from Christian."[28]

Akerman returned to Washington and reported at length to the cabinet on October 31. Grant said that if state authorities could not protect lives and property, he was prepared to do so with all the power Congress had given him. Akerman provided him with statistics about Klan prosecutions, which Grant cited in his annual message in a lengthy account of the federal struggle in South Carolina. In a gesture of sectional conciliation—and not unmindful of the approaching presidential election in 1872—Grant used his message to suggest that the time had come to consider relieving all but the top ex-Confederates from the Fourteenth Amendment's ban on officeholding. Still, he lamented that the "condition of the Southern States" was "not such as all true patriotic citizens would like to see." For their own good, he urged southerners to cease the "social ostracism" and the "personal violence or threats" that discouraged northerners and "much-needed capital" from going south to aid in the region's recovery.[29]

During Akerman's absence, Bristow continued his campaign to have his boss ousted. A week after Akerman returned to the department, Bristow concluded that either he or the attorney general must go. Fish was no champion of Akerman and found his reports to the cabinet nearly unendurable. At one meeting, he noted, Akerman had the Ku Klux Klan "'on the brain'—he tells a number of stories—one of a fellow being castrated—with terribly minute & tedious details of each case. It has got to be a bore to listen twice a week to this same thing."[30]

In early December the press began to speculate about Akerman's possible departure. The *New York Herald* alleged that other cabinet members considered him "quite self-opinionated, tenacious of his own views and rather disagreeable in considering those of others." But such charges likely reflected the *Herald*'s own animus against Akerman's aggressive southern policy. Other press reports claimed that Supreme Court justices had complained to Grant that Akerman was "hardly competent" for his position. When the speculation turned to possible successors, the *Herald* reported a concerted movement on behalf of Bristow, who, according to the paper's Washington correspondent, "has been the real Attorney General." Some forty or fifty members of Congress, mostly from the South, had reportedly asked for the Kentuckian's appointment. Their effort failed, however, for Grant tapped George H. Williams for the post. In the end, although he did not choose Bristow to replace Akerman, the president did succumb to the whispering campaign Bristow had begun. When he asked for Akerman's resignation, Grant could not mask his chagrin. "My personal regard for you is such that I could not bring myself to saying what I here say through the medium of a letter. Nothing but a consideration for public sentiment could induce me to indite this." He offered Akerman his choice of federal judgeships in Florida or Texas or a diplomatic post, all of which he declined. In a follow-up letter, Grant crossed his fingers and told Akerman, "I can refer with pride to the uniform harmony which . . . has constantly existed, not only between us but also between yourself and Colleagues in the Cabinet." Some observers speculated that Grant was bowing to railroad interests that disliked some of the attorney general's rulings, but Akerman himself thought Grant's decision reflected, in part at least, a growing concern over diminishing support among northerners for a forceful policy in the South. "Even such atrocities as Ku Kluxery," he wrote to a friend, "do not hold their attention, as long and as earnestly, as we should expect."[31]

As usual when considering the nomination of a former colleague, senators confirmed Williams immediately. With Bristow's ambition for promotion now foreclosed, he tried to resign as solicitor general, but Grant convinced him to stay. Although Bristow suffered some negative publicity for his apparent self-promotion, his political advisers assured him that he remained well positioned for the future. James Harrison "Harry" Wilson wrote that the post of solicitor general afforded him "a commanding position and reputation throughout the country," and Harlan expressed his "hope that the withdrawal of your resignation will prove to have been the best thing you could have done." Bristow kept his bona fides with the president intact. He stayed on for another year before resigning. In 1874 he returned to the administration as secretary of the treasury—one of the most fateful appointments Grant ever made.[32]

Williams had been an occasional confidant of Grant since the early days of Reconstruction, when, as a senator, he had advised the general in his clashes with Andrew Johnson. A stalwart administration man, Williams had defended Grant's interests as a member of the Senate's Santo Domingo investigating committee. When Williams lost his Senate seat, the president briefly considered naming him to replace Motley, but both he and Fish concluded that Williams was "hardly big enough for the place." They did, however, select him to serve on the Joint High Commission to negotiate the *Alabama* claims with Great Britain. As the first cabinet member from the West Coast, Williams was politically helpful to the president in that region. In Washington, however, he encountered some criticism because of the activities of his young and striking second wife, considered by many too assertive in her social pretensions and by some too loose in her morals. As Wilson put it to Bristow, Williams "sectionally may strengthen the administration, sexually also for all I know, & if half that has been said, is true!"[33]

But on the all-important southern question, Williams was sound. As a senator he had helped frame some of the key Reconstruction legislation and had backed Johnson's impeachment. The day after his confirmation, he told a Washington crowd that he favored "using the whole power of the country in the most vigorous and effective manner to crush out every conspiracy against the peace of society and the safety of the unoffending citizens." For his part, Akerman tried to accept the change as having nothing more than "a personal bearing." "The President, I am sure," he wrote hopefully to a friend, "is resolute in his determination to protect the friends of the Government at the South." Indeed, although Williams faced the same budgetary constraints that had hampered Akerman, the new attorney general increased the pace of prosecutions during the ensuing year. He promised to wield all the government power at his command to "subdue and repress" the "passions of hatred and revenge" that plagued the South. Time would show, however, how far the administration stood from vanquishing those passions and finally defeating the new guerrilla rebellion.[34]

14

★ ★ ★ ★ ★

PEACE ABROAD

In the spring of 1871, while the Grant administration and Congress forged the tools to fight the Ku Klux Klan, negotiations proceeded to resolve the *Alabama* claims and other pending issues with Great Britain. During January Hamilton Fish and John Rose reached an informal agreement sanctioned by both governments to submit all the questions to a Joint High Commission comprising representatives of the two nations who would pursue formal talks in Washington. Fish knew that he was "dealing with 'perfidious Albion,'" but he—and the American public—welcomed a movement toward settling the vexing issues. Rose's American banking partner, New York Republican Levi Morton, assured Grant that a successful outcome would afford him as much "lasting fame as the Military events of the past."[1]

In selecting the American commissioners, Grant and the cabinet considered legal prowess, though not necessarily familiarity with the issues in dispute. Fish would head the group, joined by Robert Schenck, the new minister to London; former attorney general Rockwood Hoar; and George Williams, who would later become attorney general. Fish suggested the importance of including a Democrat, and Grant settled on seventy-eight-year-old Justice Samuel Nelson, who had expertise in maritime law and, as a member of the Supreme Court, would likely refrain from being overtly political. Assistant Secretary of State J. C. Bancroft Davis would serve as secretary to the American commissioners.

Fish suggested George Bemis as a possible assistant secretary, but when Boutwell observed that Bemis "will do whatever Sumner wants," Grant rejected him outright. Sumner tried to get the nominations of the commissioners referred to the Foreign Relations Committee (which he then still chaired), but the Senate blocked this maneuver and approved the nominees.[2]

The British selected a strong set of commissioners with international experience deeper than that of the Americans. Edward Thornton's long familiarity with the issues plus his close acquaintance with Fish made him indispensable. Heading the group was Earl de Grey and Ripon, Lord President of the Privy Council in William Gladstone's Liberal government. Stafford Northcote, a leading member of Parliament, represented the opposing Conservative Party. John MacDonald, prime minister of the Dominion of Canada, spoke for Canadian interests. Gladstone also tapped Montague Bernard, an Oxford professor of international law who had just published a book upholding Britain's professed neutrality during the Civil War. For secretary, the British chose Lord Tenterden, who had written the British memorandum roundly criticizing Fish's position in his September 25, 1869, instruction to Motley.[3]

On February 25, 1871, Grant hosted an official welcome for the British commissioners. Thornton reported to foreign secretary Lord Granville, "The President was most friendly and cordial in his manner to Lord de Grey, and conversed with him for nearly an hour, and I have reason to believe that his Lordship made a very good impression on the President." Northcote, who was not present for that initial greeting, met Grant a few days later and concluded, "Never was there a man who set one less at one's ease, or impressed one less with an idea of dignity." Like others who mistook Grant's shyness with strangers for something vaguely sinister, Northcote thought he "looked as if he had been caught picking a pocket and was afraid of a row." But the Englishman found the president "a little more conversable" and "in better spirits" the next time they met—the same day the Senate's Committee on Committees axed Sumner from Foreign Relations. As for the Massachusetts senator, Northcote saw "a touch of wildness in his eye which suggests the possibility that he may go out of his mind. It is said that he is now haunted with the idea that somebody is dogging him and meaning to attack him." During the Britons' months-long sojourn, Americans in and out of government treated them to a rich social life, including a champagne-fueled, hoked-up fox hunt during which Northcote claimed he had "never suffered so much from suppressed laughter."[4]

The visitors were on their best behavior with Sumner, who, notwithstanding the loss of his chairmanship shortly after their arrival, still had potential to spark "a great deal of bad feeling" in America about a prospective agreement. "He is very anxious to stand well with England," Northcote observed, "but, on the other hand, he would dearly like to have a slap at Grant." No believer that domestic politics stopped at the waterline, Sumner spoke openly to the British diplomats in a manner "very caustic on the President." After one dinner with the senator, Northcote confided to his diary, "Never did the world produce so vain a man as our friend Sumner." But, bowing to Sumner's amour propre, the British commissioners accepted the bounty of his table and cellar and attended appreciatively to his effusions of wisdom. "I think he is much pleased at being still recognised as a power," Northcote wrote. The stroking paid off. Sumner assured Henry Longfellow that the commissioners "are pleasant, refined, cultured—& I like them, as is my wont with such people."[5]

Although Fish kept Sumner at arm's length, he drew on the expertise of another administration critic, Charles Francis Adams, who, as minister to Great Britain between 1861 and 1868, had gained frontline experience with the *Alabama* issue. Adams thought that, as one held in "public estimation as an accomplished statesman," he ought to have been chosen as one of the American commissioners. When Bancroft Davis asked his opinion of the preliminary statement of the American position, Adams was cheered by "the recognition of my existence." But he soon dismissed the request as an effort "to cover up the conduct of the President" toward him. "It is not for me to intrude upon an arrangement of a commission which intentionally left me out. Indeed the condition of the government is such as not to make it desirable to be in any way associated with it."[6]

In managing the negotiations, Grant did not stand over Fish and dictate details, but he did monitor the talks, and the commissioners consulted him about essentials. The British commissioners, in contrast, felt the heavy hand of their government despite its being 3,000 miles away. Communications passed between them and London either by seaborne dispatches, which took about two weeks to arrive, or by highly expensive telegrams via the Atlantic cable, which offered greater speed but whose brevity sacrificed clarity. More than once the government's attempts to prescribe specific language exasperated the British commissioners, who had a better understanding of what was necessary to secure the Americans' acquiescence. The negotiations lasted nine weeks.

"It is very hard work," Hoar observed, "something like playing chess or fencing for several hours a day, with all your faculties on the stretch."[7]

At the first substantive session on March 4, the commissioners agreed to focus most of their attention on three paramount questions: the *Alabama* claims, American access to inshore Canadian fishing grounds, and the water boundary between British Columbia and the United States at the San Juan Islands in the Pacific Northwest. In addition, the agenda included navigation of the St. Lawrence River and Lake Michigan, various trade issues between the United States and Canada, and access to canals near their border. The British also sought to raise the question of claims against the United States growing out of the Fenian raids into Canada, but Fish objected that such claims did not fall within the purview of the commission, and they were eventually dropped. Over the weeks, the commission alternated its focus on the various issues rather than dealing with them seriatim, largely because of the lag in communications with the government in London.[8]

The *Alabama* claims proved to be the thorniest issue. At the outset, Grant and Fish had a clear set of goals. Most fundamentally, they expected Great Britain to pay an indemnity for the losses Americans had suffered because of the British government's action, or inaction, during the war. This would require the commission to generate a set of principles governing a neutral nation's responsibilities, rules by which to measure the extent of Britain's culpability. Moreover, even if the British did not admit wrongdoing, they should make some suitable expression of regret. The failed Johnson-Clarendon Convention had lacked such an expression, a chief reason why Americans found it unacceptable. Fish had outlined these basic goals as early as the summer of 1869 in conversations with John Rose, and he and his colleagues now pursued them with resolve.[9]

When the *Alabama* talks began on March 8, Fish outlined the American grievances. He charged that Great Britain had "failed in the proper performance of her duties under the International Law" in allowing the *Alabama* and other cruisers "to be constructed, fitted out, armed, or equipped" within British jurisdiction before going into Confederate service. The American claims reflected the direct losses caused by the depredations of these ships, as well as the cost of pursuing and capturing them. Significantly, Fish also cited indirect costs incurred owing to the transfer of a large portion of the American merchant fleet to the British flag, increased charges for commercial marine insurance, and the prolongation of the war, which added enormously to the government's expense in subduing the rebellion. He estimated that the direct claims exceeded $14 million. "At the present," he added, "we present no estimate of the indirect losses, but without prejudice to the right to indemnification on their account." To "yield" these indirect losses, he advised the British commissioners, "would be a very large concession" on the part of the United States.[10]

Fish suggested two ways to settle the direct claims. The "easiest and most practical mode" would be for Great Britain to recognize the principles of international law, "as we have presented them," and pay a lump sum that the United States would distribute to the claimants. The alternative would be to submit the claims to "a proper tribunal" for adjudication according to the principles of international law, "as we have submitted them," to determine the liability of each cruiser and the amount of loss sustained, plus interest. Fish then outlined four principles that the United States regarded as applicable. First, "any great maritime power" is "bound to use active diligence in order to prevent the construction, fitting out, arming, equipping or augmenting the force within its jurisdiction, of any vessel whereby war is intended to be carried on upon the ocean against a power with which it is at peace." Second, when such a vessel escapes, the power must use "like diligence to arrest and detain her when she comes again within its jurisdiction." Third, the power "is further bound to instruct its naval forces, in all parts of the globe, to arrest and detain vessels so escaping, wherever found on the high seas." Fourth, any power failing to observe these rules is to be held responsible for the losses such vessels inflict.[11]

The American commissioners regarded these principles as existing law, but the British argued that they were not in force at the time of the alleged acts during the war. They proposed submitting the question of the relevant principles as well as the claims to an arbitrator. They were willing, however, to have the present commission consider revisions to existing international law for the future. Fish responded that Britain's recent revisions of its Foreign Enlistment Act to conform to international law amounted to an admission that its former statutes, in effect at the time of the actions under scrutiny, did "not enable Great Britain properly to perform her international obligations," including its prevention of the departure of vessels like the *Alabama*. The United States would not consent to submit the question to arbitration "unless the principles of international law, by which the arbitration was to be guided, were first clearly laid down."[12]

At the next session, de Grey offered a substitute for the American declaration of principles. Although his paper contained only two state-ments, which were much watered-down versions of Fish's, it nonethe-less signified tacit acceptance of the idea of instructions to guide an ar-bitration, precisely what Fish and Grant had aimed for. Lord Granville balked, however, at including the word *construction* in the list of prohib-ited activities related to a putative war vessel, and Fish advised his col-leagues that the term *construction* "might be abandoned if words clearly expressing the same idea were substituted." He devised the phrase "adapted . . . to warlike use," which the Americans believed subsumed *construction*. The British accepted this change, and it remained in the final version of the treaty.[13]

Jousting over the language in the statement of international prin-ciples continued off and on for the next five weeks. The British would not admit that these principles represented rules in effect during the war, but they did agree that "in deciding the questions between the two countries . . . the Arbitrators should assume that Her Majesty's Gov-ernment had undertaken to act upon the principles set forth in these rules." By this locution, the British saved a bit of face, and the Americans ensured that the rules devised by the commission would apply. Hence, both sides recognized the critical importance of carefully defining the parameters for arbitration. The Americans hoped for a definition of "un-neutral behavior" that was broad enough to cover Britain's objection-able performance in relation to the *Alabama* and the other vessels, while the British labored to keep it narrow. But the British also insisted, and the Americans readily agreed, that the rules they devised should apply to future relations between the two nations. This consideration imposed an element of restraint on both sides. The Americans believed that the United States would more likely be a neutral than a belligerent in future wars, and in such conflicts the United States would want the restrictions on neutrals to be narrowly defined. Conversely, the British favored a broader definition to protect themselves from the depredations of future American-built *Alabama*s. At one point in the negotiations, Grant cau-tioned that the proposed neutrality rules should not be "more stringent than the U.S. w[oul]d like to have them in the future."[14]

The statement of principles in the final treaty appeared in con-voluted language that resulted from the efforts at compromise. First, a neutral government was bound to use "due diligence to prevent the fitting out, arming, or equipping, within its jurisdiction," of any vessel it had reason to believe was intended "to carry on war against a Power with which it is at peace"; also, it was to use "like diligence" to prevent such a vessel's departure to carry on war, "such vessel having been specially adapted, in whole or in part, within such jurisdiction, to warlike use." Second, a neutral government must not permit either belligerent to use its ports or waters as a base of operations against the other, to refurbish military supplies or arms, or to recruit men. Third, the neutral was bound to use "due diligence" over its ports and waters and all persons within its jurisdiction to prevent "any violation of the foregoing obligations and duties." After the commissioners had completed their work on these articles, Fish presented them to Grant and the cabinet, who offered "a unanimous expression of extreme satisfaction."[15]

While work on the neutrality principles neared completion, Fish raised the question of a British expression of regret. The British proposed that the treaty preamble "express, in a friendly spirit, the regret felt by Her Majesty's Government for the escape, under whatever circumstances, of the Alabama and other vessels from British ports, and for the depredations committed by those vessels." Grant was "much pleased" with the statement, and it went into the treaty. But Granville also instructed his commissioners that it was "essential not to admit 'liability.'" After some heated discussion, the Americans agreed to the insertion of a reference to "the speedy settlement of such claims which are not admitted by Her Majesty's Government." In reality, the phrase was more face-saving for the British than dispositive of the issues, given the fact of the arbitration itself plus the British expression of regret, which amounted to a confession of wrongdoing by their government.[16]

Of greater practical consequence was the issue of which claims would be submitted for arbitration. During Fish's talks with Rose in the lead-up to the Joint High Commission, Grant and the cabinet had stated that "the question of liability for any consequential damages should be referred to the decision of some tribunal." In his opening statement on March 8, Fish had referred to the whole panoply of possible claims, direct and indirect. He knew the British would balk at an explicit reference to indirect claims, but in framing the statement regarding the arbitrators' purview, he sought language broad enough and vague enough to allow the Americans to assert that it subsumed such claims. Conversely, de Grey favored language limiting the claims to those growing out of the depredations of the vessels. In general, however, he favored vague verbiage so that Britain could claim the arbitrators had no power to investigate indirect claims because the treaty gave them no specific authority to do so. As Fish's earlier wrangles with Sumner had shown, he did not put much stock in the indirect claims, but he recognized that the submission of such claims by the United States, followed by their rejection by the arbitrators, would benefit America as a neutral in the future. In a private meeting of the American commissioners, Fish said, "It was pretty well agreed that there were some claims which would not be allowed by the arbitrators," but it was "best to have them passed upon." Fish told the British that the Americans' "earnest desire was to arrive at a conclusive settlement of all questions between the two countries," and he "doubted whether the mere reference" to arbitrators of only the direct claims "would appease the popular mind in the United States."[17]

The missteps that marked Granville's attempted long-distance management showed tellingly in the consideration of this issue. After the commission had essentially completed the preamble, Granville inexplicably proposed the insertion of a passage indicating that the arbitrators would "investigate all complaints and all claims on the part of the United States." The British commissioners strongly objected to the word *complaints*. "We have been fighting for several days against the often-renewed proposals from the United States' Commissioners to insert this word in the reference," they cabled Granville. "It would, we fear, afford an opening for asking for compensation for the recognition of belligerent rights, &c . . . [and] we have thought it our duty to keep out any expressions which might render such proceeding possible." Nonetheless, the treaty as signed stipulated that the purpose of the arbitration was "to remove and adjust all complaints and claims on the part of the United States" and that the arbitrators should "examine and decide all questions that shall be laid before them." Such language gave the United States ample leeway in determining what claims to submit to the arbitrators. The British offered amendments to limit the scope of the reference, but Fish and his colleagues resisted. The British backed down, and the Americans concluded that the treaty's terms did not bar the United States from submitting indirect claims.[18]

When the commission turned to framing the arbitration procedure, the British called for a single arbitrator who was the head of state of a country friendly to both nations. The Americans favored a tribunal composed of lawyers with expertise in international questions. The Americans carried the day, and the treaty called for a tribunal of five members, one chosen by the United States, one chosen by Great Britain, and one each chosen by the king of Italy, the president of the Swiss Confederation, and the emperor of Brazil. The tribunal would convene in Geneva, Switzerland, and the three neutrality principles set forth in the treaty would govern its deliberations. After determining Britain's liability, the arbitrators could either award a lump sum to be paid to the United States or leave the assignment of damages to a board of assessors. The generous timetable for the exchange of arguments meant that a final decision was at least a year away.[19]

The second contentious item on the commission's agenda, the Canadian inshore fisheries, was long standing and intertwined with trade relations between the United States and its British northern neighbor. The Americans' principal goal was to regain fishing privileges for New Englanders in Canadian waters approximating the rights they had enjoyed under the Marcy-Elgin Reciprocity Treaty of 1854. The United States had abrogated that treaty in 1866, largely because its reciprocity stipulations, plus new Canadian tariffs on American manufactures, had tilted the export-import balance substantially in Canada's favor. Grant's administration was barely under way when the Canadians, through the British, began to push for negotiations to reinstate as much of the reciprocity arrangement as possible. The president stood adamantly opposed, however, and publicly declared that "the advantages of such a treaty would be wholly in favor of the British producer." Except for a few individuals engaged in trade, he said, "no citizen of the United States would be benefited by reciprocity." Fish had resisted Thornton's efforts to start trade negotiations, and in reaction, Dominion authorities instituted draconian measures against American fishermen by enforcing restrictions set forth in the Anglo-American Convention of 1818. In some ways, these aggressive acts aroused Grant's ire more than the abstract question of neutrals' rights in the *Alabama* dispute. At one cabinet meeting he insisted "very earnestly" that he would "not admit" Canada's interpretation of the 1818 treaty and exclaimed that he wished Congress would declare war against Great Britain. Having let off steam, he directed the secretary of the navy to dispatch a vessel to the region to protect American fishing boats and advise their captains of their legitimate rights. But this precaution had little impact, and during the 1870 fishing season, the Canadians seized 400 American vessels. Fish kept up a steady drumbeat of protest to Thornton, and in his annual message Grant denounced the "vexatious treatment" of "the hardy fishermen of the United States." Thus, going into the deliberations of the Joint High Commission, Fish wanted to settle the question expeditiously before the beginning of the 1871 fishing season.[20]

Grant and Fish were interested in regaining access to the fisheries less for their "commercial value," which they considered negligible, than for "political" considerations—"to avoid the danger of collisions" between Canadians and American fishermen that might precipitate a wider conflict. But the British commissioners found themselves under unrelenting pressure from their Canadian colleague, John MacDonald, who thought the only equitable trade-off for the fisheries was an "enlarged commercial intercourse." In the opening discussion, de Grey proposed a new reciprocity treaty, which the Americans dismissed out of hand. Undaunted, MacDonald suggested a revival of the Treaty of 1854, perhaps with adjustments and ancillary provisions, such as free navigation on the St. Lawrence River. Again Fish said no, and the commissioners discussed alternatives, including free trade in a small number of commodities or the American payment of a gross sum for access to the inshore fisheries.[21]

The discussion dragged on for weeks, largely because of MacDonald's recalcitrance. "Our duel is a triangular one," Northcote complained in his diary, "and Canada gives us as much trouble sometimes as do the United States." At various times Fish and his colleagues offered different combinations of a lump-sum payment (at one point, $1 million) plus trade concessions in exchange for the fisheries, but MacDonald repeatedly raised objections. An exasperated de Grey wrote to Granville that the Canadians thought they could "bully the Americans into giving way and seem indifferent to the risk they run by such a policy." At the end of March, the Americans proposed that, in exchange for the fisheries, Canadian coal, salt, fish, fish oil, and firewood would be admitted into the United States duty-free, and after July 1, 1874, timber and lumber would be included as well. Once again, MacDonald objected.[22]

American producers opposed the admission of these commodities duty-free, and the administration was reluctant to give up the substantial revenue they yielded. Hence, Fish was delighted when the British rejected the American offer. De Grey again raised the possibility of a monetary payment for the fisheries, and Fish suggested submitting the question of the amount to arbitration. Grant approved the plan, but once again, the Canadians objected. By now, however, Gladstone regarded the Canadians as "rampantly unreasonable." Granville cabled the British commissioners that the American proposal "ought to be accepted by Canada rather than leave the question unsettled," though he did urge them to try to obtain the free admission of fish. In fact, the Americans had already offered free fish, but they modified their proposal to reduce the payment for the inshore fisheries by the value of the duty-free admission of Canadian fish. The commission adopted this formula. Only the Canadians were displeased, but MacDonald did not block this solution.[23]

The treaty as signed granted Americans permission to fish in the coastal waters of Canada and gave equivalent rights to Canadians in American waters. It called for the importation of fish and fish oil from each country to the other free of customs duties. Further, it mandated the appointment of a three-member commission to determine the monetary compensation due to Britain from the United States. The agreement would last for at least ten years, after which either party could give two years' notice of termination. (Although under this treaty Americans again entered Canadian waters to catch fish, the fisheries provisions eventually turned sour. Wrangling over the appointment of the commission delayed its action until after the Grant administration had ended. In November 1877 the Halifax Commission awarded Great Britain $5.5 million, a sum the United States considered excessive. Americans also believed that British authorities failed to pay adequate compensation when local Canadians violently interfered with American fishing operations. The United States gave notice that it intended to terminate the agreement effective July 1, 1885.)[24]

The Joint High Commission devoted several sessions to the third major issue—the dispute over the water boundary between the United States and Vancouver Island, which was part of British Columbia. Like the fisheries, this issue had a long history. The Treaty of 1846, designed to settle the long-festering dispute over the boundary through Oregon country, vaguely stated that the line ran from the forty-ninth parallel off the mainland "to the middle of the channel which separates the continent from Vancouver's Island; and thence southerly through the middle of the said channel." Because of an imperfect understanding of the area's geography, the designation "middle" proved imprecise. In subsequent discussions, the United States claimed that the boundary ran through the Haro Channel, which was close to Vancouver, and the British claimed it ran through the Rosario Channel, which was closer to the US mainland. The main point at stake was the possession of San Juan and ancillary islands lying between the Haro and Rosario Channels. San Juan's strategic location gave it obvious military significance.[25]

In taking up the subject, the British commissioners favored submitting the boundary to arbitration, but Fish and his colleagues disagreed. The Americans' vehemence reflected in part their belief that the British had misled US representatives at a crucial point in the creation of the 1846 treaty. The Americans charged that, after telling the American minister that they would accept the Haro Channel as the boundary, the British later insisted that the treaty provision placing the line through the "center" of the waters referred to the Rosario Channel. De Grey accused Fish of maligning the "integrity and good faith" of the British government, but he then adopted a stratagem of delay that amounted to extortion. "The United States' Commission are unreasonable about San Juan," he cabled Granville. "We think that the best mode of bringing them to reason will be to go on with the discussion of the other questions until we approach the point of settlement, and then to tell them that if they are obstinate about San Juan we cannot settle upon any of the points, and the whole negotiation must therefore fall to the ground." Granville approved.[26]

The next month saw little movement on the question. Finally, Fish told Grant that the commissioners' inability to achieve a negotiated settlement would probably necessitate a submission to arbitration. The president was "strongly disinclined" to accept that course, but Fish felt reasonably confident that a tribunal would find for the Americans. The key, he believed, was to demand the right to submit the past diplomatic correspondence that included convincing evidence for the US position regarding the Haro Channel. Grant said he would accede to arbitration as "a last resort," although he would have preferred to deal with the question in a separate treaty. Fish noted, however, that the British insisted on packaging all the issues into a single treaty. The cabinet agreed that if all other questions were "satisfactorily disposed of," the United States "could afford" to refer the San Juan question to arbitration.[27]

Thus, the Britons' delaying tactic to force arbitration worked, but in the end, the Americans had the last laugh. The United States insisted that each party be allowed to submit as evidence "such documents, official correspondence and other official or public statements" necessary to support its case. In addition, the Americans demanded that the arbitrator must choose either the Haro Channel or the Rosario Channel. When de Grey asked why a third, middle course would not be acceptable, Fish flatly declared that the United States wanted "a decision—not a compromise." The British assented to both these demands. Fish's adamancy paid off. In the fall of 1872 the designated arbitrator, Emperor William of Germany, accepted the American evidence and drew the boundary along the Haro Channel.[28]

Interspersed among discussions of the three central issues, sessions of the commission dealt with various less compelling questions. Some of these matters Fish called "small potatoes," but others generated important trade-offs in the settlement of the larger issues. The treaty granted citizens of the United States free navigation of the St. Lawrence River and gave British subjects the same privilege on three rivers through the Alaska territory. British subjects gained free navigation of Lake Michigan for a minimum of ten years. Each side also granted citizens of the other country access to canals near their border on the same terms enjoyed by its own citizens. Similarly, the citizens of each could ship goods in bond through the territory of the other without paying customs duties. In addition, the treaty established a commission to adjudicate claims growing out of the Civil War (other than the *Alabama* claims) that citizens of each side had against the other. All told, the 478 British claims, related mostly to the military seizure or destruction of property, amounted to $60 million. The 19 American claims totaled less than $1 million, and the majority grew out of a cross-border Confederate raid on St. Albans, Vermont. In 1873 the claims commission rejected all the American claims and recognized only a fraction of the British claims, for a total award of $1,929,819.[29]

At a meeting on May 2, the cabinet considered the virtually complete treaty, and Grant authorized Fish and his colleagues to affix their signatures. The commissioners gathered for the ceremony at the State Department on May 8. The president was out of town and could not attend. De Grey thanked Fish "most cordially for what you have done; without your efforts no treaty could have been agreed to." Less graciously, MacDonald took pen in hand and said to the secretary in a half whisper, "Well, here go the Fisheries." Fish replied that Canada "got a good equivalent," but MacDonald insisted, "No, we give them away." Northcote called the treaty "fair & honorable," although Great Britain had conceded "much more than he thought she would be induced to do, & very much more than she could have done two years ago." As the nervous young State Department clerk prepared the papers for sealing, Tenterden dropped "quantities of burning sealing-wax on his fingers," Northcote noted. "The poor man was so much excited that he burst into tears at the conclusion of the affair." Still, in "great good spirit," the commissioners toasted their achievement with strawberries and ice cream.[30]

The administration now faced the trial of maneuvering the treaty through the Senate. Grant called a special session for May 10 and immediately submitted the treaty for ratification. He told president pro tem Henry Anthony he hoped the Foreign Relations Committee would "not keep it long under consideration." Even before the treaty was signed, Grant and Fish had begun lobbying, meeting with the new Foreign Relations chairman Simon Cameron and other committee members. The British commissioners lent their aid to the campaign. Tenterden and Montague Bernard traveled to New York, where they urged key merchants to rally Senate support for the treaty, while de Grey and Northcote buttonholed senators in Washington.[31]

The text of the treaty became publicly known almost immediately through an unauthorized printing in the *New York Tribune*. Senators wasted valuable time trading allegations about the source of the leak until Grant intervened, urging them to suspend the investigation and get on with their deliberations. The publication of the details aided the fight, for the treaty won popular acclaim. The *New York Herald* hailed the negotiation as "one of the most interesting and important political events of the nineteenth century" and said, "the enlightened and peace-loving people of this great republic will accept this treaty with something of the faith of St. Paul." The only significant discordant voice came from Massachusetts fishermen, who feared the impact of free Canadian fish, but they lacked the heft to sink the agreement.[32]

The treaty's champions paid much closer heed to another Massachusetts interest—the state's senior senator. Sumner found himself in a quandary. When he pumped lawyer George Bemis for arguments he might make, Bemis called the agreement "an *ignominious surrender of everything valuable*." But the treaty contained too much of what Sumner himself had advocated for him to adopt Bemis's extreme position. Francis Bird, the senator's political lieutenant, warned that "the general judgment of the country is earnestly in favor" of the agreement. Echoing Grant's 1868 campaign slogan, he advised Sumner, "Let us have peace." Sumner hesitated to give a blanket endorsement to Grant and Fish's achievement, yet he did not want to disappoint his friends, the British commissioners. Northcote found him "very friendly," although Sumner had also stated, "If it is attempted to force" the treaty "through as a measure of the Administration, the Democrats 'and some others' [himself, obviously] will be forced to criticise it." If not a measure of the administration, what else could it be? Sumner spoke of possible amendments, but he also told the British that the more he read the treaty, "the better he liked it." On May 19 he gave a long speech in executive session that, according to the *New York Herald*, amounted "very much" to a "restatement" of his *Alabama* speech in April 1869, including the assertion that Britain's "great wrong" had been according premature recognition to the Confederacy. But this new speech lacked the impact of the senator's former effort, and in open session Sumner distanced himself from the *Herald*'s account, which he labeled "a pure invention." Sumner spoke for four hours, and as Northcote observed, "The first three and a half were spent in giving a history of the world, and showing how much more he knew than anybody else, and the last half hour in discussing the three rules in the Treaty which he approved, and then [he] sat down without moving any amendments. This looks very well."[33]

Those "three rules" stipulating the duties of neutrals caused the most contention. Lyman Trumbull and others thought the second rule barring belligerents from using neutral ports to augment their arms or military supplies might be misconstrued to limit neutral nations' right to sell arms in the regular course of commerce. They believed an amendment might be necessary to avert such an interpretation. From the beginning, however, Grant had made it clear to Cameron and others that he wanted no amendments because such changes would have the dangerous effect of reopening negotiations, and "there is no telling when the matter will end." Fish told Trumbull that any amendment to the treaty, "however trivial, will probably inevitably destroy it entirely." Thornton thought an exchange of notes between himself and Fish could clarify the intent of the second rule, but Fish considered it inappropriate for them to interpret the treaty. Instead, he thought the Senate should make the point in a resolution that could be submitted to the British for approval. He and Thornton drafted a pair of resolutions, which Fish passed on to Cameron to introduce at the appropriate moment.[34]

At the next session after Sumner's speech, Garrett Davis, a Kentucky Democrat who fervently opposed the treaty, offered an amendment to strike out Article 6, the very heart of the *Alabama* section containing the three rules governing neutrals. Some Democrats had previously endorsed the treaty, and national party chairman August Belmont had argued that supporting it served "not only the best interests of the country but the welfare of the Democratic party." But now that the treaty's passage was assured, the Democrats caucused and decided they could display opposition to it after all, without hurting the national interest. The treaty's backers handily defeated Davis's amendment, but Democrats proposed a series of other amendments to key provisions, any one of which would have killed the treaty. None had a chance of passage, but Democrats could tell their Irish American constituents that they had done their best to scuttle an agreement with the hated Great Britain. Across the aisle, Sumner offered three amendments to tighten the provisions governing the relations of belligerents and neutrals, but he had promised de Grey he would "not press them to a division." The Senate rejected all three. Sumner thus had the satisfaction of trying to do "something for the improvement of Intern[ational] Law," without unduly offending the British commissioners.[35]

On May 24, after a thirteen-hour session, the Senate voted 50 to 12 to approve the treaty. Two Democrats bucked their caucus and joined forty-eight Republicans voting in favor of the agreement. The opponents consisted of ten Democrats plus the scalawag Republican J. Rodman West of Louisiana and the unpredictable Republican William Sprague of Rhode Island. The Republicans who voted yes included Sumner and several other critics of the administration: Carl Schurz, Reuben Fenton, and Thomas Tipton of Nebraska.[36]

Immediately after the vote, Cameron offered the two explanatory resolutions drafted by Fish and Thornton at the behest of Trumbull and others. One stated that the second rule in Article 6 did not prohibit "any exportation from the neutral country of arms or other military supplies in the ordinary course of commerce." The other requested the president to submit this understanding to the British and obtain their assent. Grant and Fish saw little need for these resolutions, and now their allies played obstructionists, using various parliamentary measures to inhibit their adoption. When the Senate adjourned its special session on May 26, the resolutions died. The administration had won ratification of the Treaty of Washington unencumbered by amendments or senatorial interpretation. Grant and Fish signed the document immediately and dispatched it to England.[37]

A few days later the president gave a press interview touting the treaty as a signal triumph and predicting its speedy ratification by the British. He rejected criticism that the two governments had rushed the negotiations with insufficient consideration:

> The facts are that every article of the treaty was submitted to me after it was adopted by the Commission and approved by me; and that each article was in the same way submitted to the British Cabinet. . . . The point aimed at was not merely a pecuniary satisfaction for our losses by the Alabama and other cruisers from British ports, but the settlement of an irritating and disturbing question likely any day to bring the two nations into armed conflict. My aim was by this treaty to secure peace through justice, and I believe I have succeeded.

The same was true of the fisheries question, which of late had required each side to dispatch naval vessels to prevent flagrant conflict between private citizens. "I don't attach much importance to the pecuniary consideration one way or the other," Grant said. "The pith of the thing is the avoidance of war. . . . There were so many questions between us and England demanding settlement that war seemed the only alternative. It is well, sir, that war has been avoided. I prefer the treaty to war."[38]

Americans saw the treaty as a triumph. "The statesman who averts war," wrote Thurlow Weed, "renders better service than the soldier who carries his country safely through one." The *New York Evening Post*, no friend of the administration, hailed the "wise and just agreement" as "one of the most important documents in our political history." A week after the Senate vote, even the dour Charles Francis Adams admitted that he thought "better of the settlement every day," although he added that Grant was "still a mystery" whose "associations do not improve." Despite his yes vote, Sumner remained disturbed. "We have lost where we should not," he wrote to Bemis. Sumner berated Bemis as "responsible" for the outcome because he had refused to write about the issue, and he now urged the lawyer to prepare a brief "going over all the points, not forgetting Hasty Belligerence"—an argument the treaty had ignored but Sumner fancied would go before the arbitrators.[39]

From London, Adam Badeau reported, "The English evidently think that they have got the worst of it, but that it is as good as they deserved, and much better than no treaty at all." The British asked for a joint statement that the second rule would not prohibit arms sales in ordinary commerce, but again Fish refused to affix his name to an interpretation of the treaty. He suggested that when the two powers presented the three rules to other maritime powers and invited their adherence, as the treaty called for, they could include that observation regarding the second rule. Queen Victoria signed the treaty, and ratifications were exchanged in London on June 17, Bunker Hill Day. The president proclaimed the treaty in effect on July 4.[40]

A week later, while sojourning at his summer residence in Long Branch, New Jersey, Grant received a visit from Fish, who handed him his resignation. The question had been on Fish's mind for months, and he had raised it with the president soon after the ratification vote. In earlier conversations, Grant had called up all his persuasive powers to talk Fish out of leaving. But now a bout of ill health, no doubt linked to the months of hard negotiations, spurred the secretary to offer his resignation again, this time in writing. Again Grant expressed his deep regret, but he could not convince Fish to stay beyond the convening of Congress in early December. This would give him time to find a replacement.[41]

But Grant's heart was not in the quest. In August he hit upon the novel idea of asking Vice President Schuyler Colfax to head the State Department and thus "give up a higher for a lower, and harder, position." Colfax declined. In November Grant suggested three New Yorkers who might do: Cornell University president Andrew White, George William Curtis, and lawyer Edwards Pierrepont. But Grant thought White lacked political standing, and he did not like Curtis; Fish thought Pierrepont was unsuitable. By early December, the president still had not settled on a replacement. He again pleaded with Fish to stay, saying that members of Congress had assured him they would give Fish anything he "might wish in the way of organization or otherwise" in the department. Grant also coordinated a lobbying campaign that culminated in a letter signed by Colfax and nearly all the Republican senators urging Fish to remain. At last he relented. "I cannot express to you what a great gratification it affords me," Grant said. "You . . . have inaugurated a policy in our relations with other Powers which gives promise of the avoidance of embarrassing questions in the future, as well as having disposed of some of the most difficult & threatening questions of the past."[42]

Missing from the list of Fish's senatorial endorsers were administration critics such as Sumner, Schurz, Fenton, Trumbull, and Tipton. Schurz told Fish he would have signed the letter but chose not to link arms with senators friendly to the administration. Sumner, meanwhile, had been confidentially distributing printed copies of his undelivered speech in which he railed against Fish's "strange and unnatural conduct toward me."[43]

During the summer and fall of 1871, as Fish was easing toward what he expected to be his exit, he assumed a new boldness in countering efforts to renew entanglements in Santo Domingo. Grant had more or less disposed of the issue in his April 5 message accompanying the commission's report to Congress, but at a June 16 meeting the cabinet considered a request from the Dominican government for aid to maintain itself, especially against Haitian-backed rebels. Grant also presented a letter from Samuel Howe, a member of the former US investigating commission who was now involved in the Samaná Bay Company, a commercial venture. Howe urged a renewal of the unratified agreement for the lease of Samaná, the pendency of which would justify continued naval protection. But Fish argued that any obligation to provide such protection had ended. The lease agreement had expired because the July 1870 agreement to renew it had never been sent to the Senate for approval. Still, cabinet members expressed sympathy for the Dominicans and discussed ways to aid them. Grant proposed that the lease convention be revived as a way to "give moral support—protection," although he had told Howe the Dominicans could expect no rent money without approval by Congress. He suggested that Fish renegotiate a renewal with Joseph Fabens, who was again in Washington, but Fish demurred, denying that Fabens had any authority to represent Santo Domingo. The president ordered negotiations to proceed in Santo Domingo through the American commercial agent Fisher Ames.[44]

The next day Fish and Boutwell agreed that any renewal of the naval "protection would expose the President to much criticism & censure from all in the Republican party who wish to find fault with him." Fish dutifully ordered Ames to conduct the talks, but he said the lease agreement must stipulate that American protection would begin only after ratification, not during its pendency. The Dominicans refused to sign the agreement in that form and insisted on renewing it unchanged. Fish took this demand to Grant, who "very promptly" decided to "drop the whole matter, and leave the whole question for Congress & the People." "Thus," Fish recorded with satisfaction, "a troublesome, vexatious & unnecessary question is, as I trust, finally got rid of." Grant ordered the Navy Department to cease all protection of Santo Domingo and to discontinue possession of Samaná Bay.[45]

When it came time to prepare the president's annual message for December 1871, Fish urged the insertion of a statement explicitly laying the Dominican question to rest. Grant promised to "introduce a few words" on the subject, but in fact he did not do so. With the presidential election looming on the horizon, he thought it best to let that dog slumber. Even so, he would never abandon his conviction that the United States should annex the Dominican Republic. The controversy surrounding his project had taken a heavy toll on his political standing and would forever cast a shadow on his historical reputation. Nonetheless, until the day he died, Grant remained convinced that the annexation of Santo Domingo would not only yield large economic benefits but also help avert "a conflict between races" by offering African Americans a refuge from ill treatment or leverage to secure a better life at home.[46]

After ratification of the Treaty of Washington, some of the rumors about Fish's possible resignation included speculation that he might be sent to Geneva as the American arbitrator in the *Alabama* case. Charles Sumner reacted predictably: "Is there a single point in our case which he understands?" He need not have worried; Fish had no interest in the job. When Fish heard (and doubted) that Sumner himself might want the position, he remarked that the senator was "not likely to be troubled with the refusal." Selection of the agent who would prepare and manage the American case was much easier; Grant immediately tapped Bancroft Davis for that assignment. True to form, Sumner expressed "despair" at the appointment of Davis, calling him a "rotten egg" who lacked "ability & character."[47]

In choosing the arbitrator, Grant and Fish took several weeks and mulled over many names. As with all appointments, political considerations had some bearing. Early on, Grant suggested Oliver Morton, one of the president's strongest allies in the Senate. But Fish alleged that both his peers and the country had a "want of confidence" in Morton, and he alluded to "his reputation for looseness of morals" (a common insinuation against the paraplegic senator). From the beginning, Fish and Davis favored Charles Francis Adams, but Grant "decidedly" objected to the patriarch of the contemptuous and contemptible Adams family. He said he "would rather appoint an out-&-out democrat" or possibly the noted lawyer Richard Henry Dana. Boutwell also opposed Adams, a rival in Massachusetts politics. But Fish believed they should "disregard all question of politics." Because the success of the administration's "treaty would be judged in a large degree" by the tribunal's decision, they "needed the ablest & most efficient man in the Country, one who had both National and foreign reputation." Moreover, Fish told the president, with Adams as arbitrator, "should the judgment fall short of popular expectation, it must be admitted that you sent the man of all others most familiar with the Case, and any responsibility for failure to obtain all that the most sanguine may have claimed, will in the public estimation be taken from the Administration—while on the contrary, if the judgment be what we hope, you will have not only the credit of obtaining it, but the additional claim of magnanimity, in having selected an Arbitrator, not politically or personally identified with your Administration." Nonetheless, Grant replied, "I confess to a repugnance to the appointment of an Adams."[48]

If Grant had had access to Adams's diary in this period, his repugnance would have found ample justification. When the press carried rumors that the former minister was under consideration, Adams felt certain he had no chance because "mediocrity is the keynote of the Administration." Even though he considered the Treaty of Washington a "wise" settlement, he refused to attend a Boston rally celebrating it because "I cannot but remember the pointed manner in which I was ex-cluded from any share in it." But in early August Grant offered Adams the position of arbitrator and thus showed his capacity to rise above his sense of personal and political grievance for the sake of the public good. Adams accepted but showed his incapacity to rise above his sense of personal and political entitlement. When the press praised his appoint-ment, he confided to his diary, "I receive it all as a flattering testimonial of the estimation in which I stand before the people, which I am free to say I think I deserve." Nor did his selection for this important mission silence his criticism of the president. When he stopped in London on the way to Geneva, an American diplomat could not help noticing that Adams and his family "have a poor opinion of Gen'l Grant and all his surroundings."[49]

Meanwhile, Davis began to prepare the American case. He fed sec-tions to Fish, who commended the agent's "mastication of Earl Johnny" —Lord John Russell, Britain's foreign secretary during the war. Davis also sent drafts to some of the nation's leading lawyers, including Rock-wood Hoar, Democratic senator Thomas F. Bayard, and Adams. Adams told Davis the paper "could have little effect upon my own judgment" because "I am already so familiar with all the facts upon which it must ultimately rest." At an event in Boston, Adams crossed paths with the president, who asked if he did not find Davis's case "very able." Adams agreed but could not resist recording in his diary that Grant "was living under a perpetual consciousness that he was in a position to which he is not equal by his education or tastes. Yet this is the best the people can do."[50]

Throughout the long struggle for a settlement of the *Alabama* claims, the administration had pursued three central goals: some "expressions of regret" by the British, "a competent indemnity" for the damages Amer-icans had suffered, and "some agreement as to the laws of neutrality for the future." The Treaty of Washington included Britain's statement of regret and created the Geneva tribunal to determine indemnity. The treaty also outlined three fundamental rules to guide a neutral country's behavior in time of war. But the United States wanted the arbitrators to take an additional step in defining the relations between neutrals and belligerents: to issue a decision declaring legally groundless the sort of indirect claims Sumner had invoked in his 1869 speech. The administra-tion's aim was not to get in another slap at Sumner but to create a legal precedent to protect a neutral United States from any such claims in the future. As Fish put it, "To us, who are generally neutrals, with a very extended line of coast, a small navy, *no* police—& a very adventurous population, it would not be unfavourable to our future interests, should the Tribunal decide that a neutral is not liable in pecuniary damages for the indirect consequences of an accidental or unintentional breach of its neutral obligations." Hence, in the last chapter of the American case, Davis cited American losses due to "the transfer of the American commercial marine to the British flag," the "enhanced payments of insurance," and "the prolongation of the war," which required additional costs to suppress the rebellion. Compared with the rest of the elaborate case focusing on direct claims, Davis's discussion of these points was almost negligible. But it was sufficient to put the indirect claims on the table, where the administration hoped the arbitrators would not hesitate to sweep them away. The United States expected no payment for these claims; securing the future, not recouping the past, lay at the heart of the administration's purpose.[51]

The arbitration tribunal convened at Geneva in mid-December 1871. Besides Adams, its members included Alexander Cockburn, chief justice of England; James Stampfli of Switzerland; Count Frederick Sclopis of Italy; and Viscount d'Itajuba, the Brazilian minister to France. Sclopis became the tribunal's president. The agents of the two principals submitted their written cases, and the tribunal adjourned for six months. After the exchange of documents, the administration heard nothing official from the British government for more than six weeks.[52]

In the interim, however, the British press raised a howl about the American case, especially the "monstrous and incredible demands" represented by the indirect claims. Many Britons still bristled at the threats embodied in Sumner's speech and now convinced themselves that they would soon be paying hundreds of millions of pounds as an indemnity to the United States for half of the "prolonged" Civil War. "There has probably never been an instance in which the influence of newspapers in moulding opinion has been more effective or more general," American minister Robert Schenck wrote to Fish. The Americans feared the British government was using the country's press as well as diplomatic intrigue to turn Continental opinion against the US position in order to prejudice the European arbitrators and Itajuba against the American case. Schenck and Davis, who was in Paris, mounted a counteroffensive through the European press and American diplomats. Davis also had to work on the attitude of William Evarts, whom Grant had reluctantly appointed one of the American counsel and who was now suggesting that Grant might be forced to decide whether to withdraw the indirect claims. Davis assured Fish that he would be "vigilant to prevent any trap from being laid for either you or the President."[53]

In early 1872 the British government asserted that under the Treaty of Washington, it was "not within the province" of the tribunal to "decide upon the claims for indirect losses and injuries." This denial of jurisdiction opened a controversy that lasted for several months and occasioned some of the most difficult diplomacy associated with the *Alabama* question. In Washington, Thornton repeated the denial in a tense meeting with Fish, who made "a gesture of vexation" and asked, "Well then is all our work of last year to go for nothing? . . . [W]e can never withdraw any part of the Claim, [we] are content to let the Tribunal pass upon it, & reject the claim for indirect damages & we will accept the decision without complaint, but we will never allow G[reat] B[ritain] or any other power to dictate to us what form our Complaint shall take, or what claims we shall think proper to advance." Unless Britain's attitude changed, he said, the arbitration would collapse. Fish told Schenck the indirect claims had been part of the *Alabama* question from the beginning, and "to have omitted them would have created mistrust, & raised an outcry against the 'case' in this country, which would have presented us before the Tribunal & the world, as divided among ourselves, & have weakened our moral position in view of the arbitration."[54]

Thornton, however, saw raw politics at work. He wrote to Granville, "The President has been accused by a portion of the Democratic party of having sacrificed the interests of his country; he will now enter upon the approaching Election with an assertion which will not fail to have its effect upon this impulsive people, unfounded though it may be—that the Treaty was so advantageous to the U.S. that H.M. Govt proposes to withdraw from it." Fish acknowledged to Thornton that omitting the indirect claims would have sparked "an outcry from the people," but he reiterated his central point that the United States expected those claims to be rejected. He said that while Davis was preparing the case, he himself had inserted the words "in equity" in reference to the indirect claims to indicate that he did not believe "there was any right *in law* to make such claims." Fish told Thornton that when discussing the case with the American counsel, he had admitted the claims could not be supported by law and had even joked with Evarts that he might invoke them simply "as bars 'on which the spread eagle might perch.'" Most important, however, although the United States would not aggressively defend the claims, withdrawing them would defeat the administration's larger purpose in having them discredited. From Paris, Davis sent the reassuring word that Adams was "all right" and agreed that the question "should be determined by the Arbitrators."[55]

The attitude of the British press sparked a popular outcry in the United States, which Grant sought to allay. In a press interview he minimized the possibility of war but insisted that once the United States had made its case, the tribunal should decide the issue on its merits. He noted that the British had made claims for the repayment of a Confederate government loan before the mixed claims commission created by the Treaty of Washington for non-*Alabama* issues. Such claims clearly lay outside the purview of the commission, and in fact, the Fourteenth Amendment barred the payment of any such debt. Nonetheless, the president said, the United States had shown "no excitement" at this "outrage upon our national honor," and Britain ought to deal with the *Alabama* case with the same equanimity.[56] Grant and other Americans thought the British ministry's intransigence in part reflected its own political insecurity. Under severe questioning from the opposition in Parliament, Gladstone had declared that "a nation must be taken to be insane" to admit "claims of this character," and Grant told a reporter that the United States "cannot be used as an instrument in the hands of any foreign Ministry to shield itself against embarrassments arising from local political divisions."[57]

At a lengthy cabinet meeting on February 6, all members agreed that the United States should withdraw no part of its case. During the discussion, a clerk arrived with Schenck's telegram conveying the text of Granville's note denying the admissibility of the indirect claims. While the talk swirled around him, the president took out a piece of paper and wrote the substance of a response: "This Govt. sees no reason for a change of its presentation of claims against the British Govt. It is for the Geneva Commissioners to decide what claims are valid under the Treaty and to determine the amount of awards."[58]

Fish took this kernel provided by Grant and composed a formal response to Granville. He consulted with Adams, who was back in the States briefly. Adams agreed that "the construction put by us upon the terms of the Treaty is the just one." He clearly wished to aid the American cause, but he could not escape his deep contempt for Grant. In a meeting with Adams and Fish, Grant said that if Great Britain should boycott the arbitration, "letters should be written to all the powers having arbitrators to say that we expected them to proceed in their labors just the same as if she made an appearance." Adams found this idea "preposterous," but he kept silent and later wrote in his diary how glad he was to have avoided being secretary of state and to have "been spared the trial of educating such an ignoramus." Yet three months later, as the crisis dragged on and Britain did threaten to boycott, Adams told Evarts, "my [sic] idea had been, to endeavor to go on with the arbitration so far as to make decisions on the various issues"—precisely the "preposterous" idea Grant had suggested.[59]

Grant thought Fish's response to Granville "splendid" and urged him to run it by key members of Congress before sending it off. The February 27 dispatch to Schenck offered a detailed rebuttal of Granville's assertions. Fish avowed that Grant would not have sanctioned the Treaty of Washington if he believed it excluded "any class" of claims. The issue pertained not merely to the present circumstances but also to "questions of public law which the interest of both Governments requires should be definitely settled." Fish noted that the treaty had established the tribunal to adjust "all complaints and claims on the part of the United States." (This was the very phrase that Granville had insisted be inserted, despite the British commissioners' warning that it would be used to justify the Americans' submission of indirect claims.) Fish insisted that these claims had been part of the dispute from the beginning, that during meetings of the Joint High Commission the British had "never asked us to withdraw" them, and that the final treaty did not exclude them. Reiterating that the United States never expected "an extravagant measure of damages," he closed with the hope that the indirect claims would present "no obstacle to deprive the world of the example of advanced civilization presented by two powerful States exhibiting the supremacy of Law and of reason over passions, and deferring their own judgments to the calm interpretation of a disinterested and discriminating Tribunal."[60]

Fish relayed the points of his dispatch to Davis and added his private observation that "Bull has made an ass of himself" and "jeopards the whole Treaty." As a possible way out, Fish proposed setting a maximum and minimum award to the United States, but Grant resisted that idea. Schenck suggested the United States might offer to withdraw the indirect claims if Great Britain would accept the American interpretation of the San Juan boundary under the Treaty of 1846. Grant warmed to this notion, but the British rejected it. Schenck concluded that Gladstone had "so committed himself, at the opening of the session of Parliament, to an extreme position" that he thwarted "every step towards accommodation."[61]

Granville's response on March 20 proposed no course of action other than the US withdrawal of the indirect claims. He made two points: (1) the treaty did not treat such claims as included among those to go before arbitration, and (2) such claims, if found valid in any war, would work a tremendous hardship on a neutral party. The United States disagreed with the first point, which Granville's note failed to substantiate. On the second point, Granville asked (he thought, rhetorically), "Are the Government and people of the United States themselves prepared to undertake the obligation of paying to an aggrieved belligerent the expenses of the prolongation of the war, if, when the United States are neutral, they can be shown to have permitted the infringement of any one, or part of any one, of the three Rules through a want of due diligence on the part of their executive officers?" To this question Grant and Fish would answer with a resounding "No!" Securing the arbitrators' condemnation of such claims now and for the future was the whole point of demanding their adjudication.[62]

With the arbitration seemingly in jeopardy, Adams asked Fish whether it made any sense for him to return to Geneva. Fish urged him to go. "The President thinks that if the Arbitration is to fail, it must fail through the action of Great Britain, and that this Government must maintain its readiness and expectation to proceed with the 'Case.'" A hopeful sign occurred when the British submitted their countercase by the mid-April deadline, which Fish thought would "make it more difficult for England to back out." Even so, they reserved their right to object to the indirect claims.[63]

As the controversy dragged on, some Americans pushed for a withdrawal of the indirect claims and criticized Fish for submitting them. New York banker Levi P. Morton and his British partner John Rose, who were concerned about marketing US government bonds in England, urged the administration to yield on the claims question, but Grant and Fish rejected the advice of these and other "Amateur Diplomatists." Fish told Morton, "We cannot consent that Great Britain [shall] construe the Treaty both for herself & for us." Believing "the bankers, bond dealers, & the commercial interests generally" to be motivated only by "the patriotism of the pocket," Fish resisted "the intermeddling of volunteer parties, who in their anxiety, whether in the interest of their financial or commercial enterprises, have labored to decry & denounce the position of this Government." The administration got Foreign Affairs Committee chairman Nathaniel Banks to throttle a House resolution in favor of waiving the claims. Although Grant had entertained some doubts about the advisability of submitting the indirect claims, when the *New York*

Herald alleged that he and Fish disagreed on the issue, the president sent word to publisher James Gordon Bennett that such rumors were not only false but also injurious to the country's interests.[64]

Fish characterized Granville's March 20 note as filled with "uncandid pettifogging and prevarication." His April 16 instructions to Schenck presented a lengthy history of the indirect claims, the assertion of which dated back to 1862. But Fish himself prevaricated when he asserted that during the Treaty of Washington negotiations, the British commissioners had made no "dissent or remonstrance" against the admissibility of the indirect claims. Records show that on more than one occasion, they resisted language implying the inclusion of such claims. In the end, however, as Fish noted, the treaty empowered the arbitrators to examine "all *complaints and claims*," with "no limitation to their discretion and no restriction to any class or description of claims." Offering no defense of the substance of the indirect claims in law, he again assured the British, "Should that august Tribunal decide that a State is not liable for the indirect or consequential results of an accidental or unintentional violation of its neutral obligations, the United States will unhesitatingly accept the decision."[65]

Informally, the administration labored to bring this last point to the arbitrators' attention. In a conversation with the Italian minister in Washington, Luigi Corti, Fish repeated the statement word for word, expecting Corti to pass it along to his countryman Sclopis, the tribunal president. Grant dispatched Boutwell to Boston to ask Adams, who was about to sail for Europe, to communicate the point to the British arbitrator and members of the London government and "thus relieve them from the apprehension of an adverse award." Afterward, Boutwell reported that he thought Adams's "impressions were in entire accord with the suggestion." In his diary Adams wrote, "I am not quite sure that I should be made the mule to carry so heavy a burden, on their account. But fear of responsibility is not one of my defects."[66]

In Geneva, meanwhile, Davis and the agent for the British case, Lord Tenterden, feared the imminent collapse of the arbitration, and Davis floated an idea that might break the impasse. It was clear that the two sides could reach "no political settlement of the question," but "a result might be reached through the joint action of the Counsel in agreeing" that the indirect claims fell outside the legal parameters of the lawsuit pending before the tribunal. Davis posited that President Grant "could not of his own accord refuse to present any claim that was within the terms of the Treaty. The validity of the claim is a question for the arbitrators, not for him. But he will certainly be justified in accepting in the conduct of the law suit the opinion of his counsel upon the law. Would not the British Cabinet be so as well?" Tenterden warmed to Davis's idea but massaged it in a crucial way. Instead of having the lawyers initiate the process, Tenterden thought it would be better "to have the arbitrators come together of their own motion before" the beginning of oral presentations, "for the avowed purpose of relieving the two governments by consideration in advance of argument . . . of the question of the liability of Great Britain for the indirect damages." Davis agreed. The United States could thus avoid withdrawing the indirect claims, but if the arbitrators stated "what their impressions are," this would, in effect, constitute a decision that both sides could accept. Davis reported the idea to Fish and observed that such things were "often done by legal tribunals." At the time, both Tenterden and Davis wondered about the practicability of such a course, but in fact, they had hit upon the scheme that would break the logjam two months later.[67]

Before hearing from Davis, Fish had come up with a "crude idea" similar to the one pondered by the two agents. If Britain agreed never to make indirect claims against a neutral United States, the two nations could agree to submit the present claims to the arbitrators as an "abstract question"; this would "get them out of the Case" and set the stage for "future relations between the two Govts." The president approved Fish's plan but told him that Britain should initiate the proposal, which the United States would then accept. Fish proceeded on that basis. But Granville's response proved unsatisfactory. Working with Schenck, the foreign secretary devised a formula that would include a statement by the United States that "the Arbitrators are not to have regard" for the indirect claims. Fish rejected this as tantamount to a virtual "'withdrawal' to which *under no circumstances* can the U.S. agree." At this point, Adams arrived in London and let Granville know that when the arbitrators convened, he would be willing to propose a procedure "formally to decline or even to disapprove the entertainment of" the indirect claims. This echoed the idea contemplated by Davis and Tenterden in Geneva. Gladstone saw its possibilities and scribbled in his diary, "Mr. Adams—proposed overtures to Arbitrators. Within limits, not disapproved."[68]

This development was, however, unknown in Washington, where Grant and Fish, frustrated by Granville's unwillingness to accept Fish's plan, adopted a new tack. Grant called Republican members of the congressional foreign affairs committees to a meeting at the State Department, and he and Fish proposed telling the British that the United States would entertain a British proposal to frame a supplementary article to the treaty to exclude indirect claims. With Gladstone's opponents in Parliament threatening to scuttle the arbitration altogether, the ministry agreed to frame such an article. But over the next month, the two sides could not agree on its wording, especially regarding a neutral party's liability for indirect claims in the future. At bottom, Fish saw Britain's objections to the American version as "unsubstantial, not to say frivolous." By early June, it had become clear that no accommodation would emerge before the June 15 deadline for the two sides to present their arguments in Geneva. Fearing "the probable failure of the 'Washington Treaty,'" Grant considered sending Congress a message underscoring the point that the United States had submitted the indirect claims to establish "a principle for our protection when we may be the neutral." Such a message would highlight "the concessions made by this Govt. to secure the benefits of a treaty equally honorable and advantageous to the two countries directly interested in the treaty, and, as an example, to the civilized world."[69]

With no consensus on a supplementary article in sight, the British pushed for a joint request for an adjournment of the tribunal, allowing more time for the two sides to work out their differences, but the administration refused to join such a request. When the tribunal convened on June 15, Davis filed the American argument, but Lord Tenterden withheld the British argument and asked for an adjournment of eight months. The prospect of a long delay appealed to none of the parties in Geneva, who recessed for a few days to contemplate the next move.[70]

Adams saw that, given the circumstances, some way had to be found that would permit the arbitrators to "decide upon rejecting the whole question of the indirect claims." Davis and Tenterden had reached the same conclusion two months earlier, but they believed the arbitrators had to appear to take the initiative in devising such a solution. Adams initially asked Davis to see whether the British legal team would be willing to proceed immediately with adjudication of the *direct* claims. They refused, but Roundell Palmer, a noted lawyer advising the British in Geneva, suggested that the arbitrators could and should issue a decision on the indirect claims. Even though it would technically be extrajudicial, the British would regard such a decision as "binding" *if both sides assented to it*. This was the breakthrough all had been hoping for—a mechanism that excluded the indirect claims from the arbitration per se but also provided the decision the United States desired. The next step was to prepare an acceptable statement of the decision that could be entered into the record. Adams drafted one for the arbitrators to issue, but it "greatly disappointed" Davis, so he and the American and British lawyers completely reworked the paper. It fell to Adams to present the proposal to his fellow arbitrators, and as he went into an evening meeting with his colleagues, Davis showed up at the door "and put into my hands the final draught as agreed upon by the lawyers." After a lengthy discussion, the members of the tribunal approved. Some contemporary observers and later historians hailed Adams as the savior of the tribunal, but Davis, Tenterden, and Palmer deserve the real credit. As Adams himself observed, "Much of the result arrived at was due to the ready cooperation of all parties, which needed only the hint to set them in motion. The only share that fell to me was the responsibility for making overtures."[71]

On June 19 Count Sclopis read the paper as the decision of the tribunal. The arbitrators observed that the months-long adjournment proposed by the British might end up "making this arbitration wholly abortive." That being the case, they said:

> The arbitrators think it right to state that, after the most careful perusal of all that has been urged on the part of the Government of the United States in respect of these claims, they have arrived, individually and collectively, at the conclusion that these claims do not constitute, upon the principles of international law applicable to such cases, good foundation for an award of compensation or computation of damages between nations, and should, upon such principles, be wholly excluded from the consideration of the tribunal in making its award.[72]

Davis immediately cabled the tribunal's opinion to Fish, who forwarded it to Long Branch for Grant's instructions. Fish told the president that he considered the statement "an honorable solution." As "a virtual Judgment upon the Admissibility of the indirect claims," it amounted to "the practical attainment of what we have contended for." After hearing from Grant, Fish instructed Davis that the president now regarded the issue of the indirect claims "as adjudicated and disposed of." The arbitrators' opinion, he added, "is the attainment of the end which this Government had in view in the putting forth of those claims. We had no desire for a pecuniary award, but desired an expression of the Tribunal as to the liability of a neutral for claims of that character. The President, therefore, . . . accepts their declaration as determinative of their judgment upon the important question of public law upon which he had

Uncle Sam: "The question is now settled, and I am not liable for indirect damages in [the] future." (*Harper's Weekly*, July 27, 1872)

felt it his duty to seek the expression of their opinion." After both sides registered their acceptance of the statement, the British filed their argument, and Davis cabled Fish, "Arbitration goes on."[73]

The delicate dance over the indirect claims took place against the backdrop of the 1872 election campaign, and the opposition press pounced on the tribunal's decision as a failure for the American side.

The *New York Tribune* called it "purely an English victory," with "nothing decided for the future." But Fish insisted, "It was [in] our interest to have precisely the decision we have," and he published his correspondence with Davis to prove that this was America's aim all along. Grant told a newspaper interviewer, "The triumph has been all ours, and a great and important triumph it is. We have got the whole question just where we wanted it and solved as we wished it to be. . . . It is of greater importance to the United States than to any other country in the world that the rights and duties of neutrals shall be distinctly ascertained and definitely settled, and settled precisely as they have just been." On the stump, Senator Roscoe Conkling hailed the administration's success as "the greatest event of diplomacy in our history."[74]

The tribunal took less time to adjudicate the direct claims than the two governments had needed to resolve the issue of the indirect ones. In the course of their deliberations, the arbitrators dismissed the charges related to the *Georgia*, for which they found insufficient evidence to hold England culpable. This came as no surprise to Grant, who confessed to Fish that he "would not wonder if the whole case, except the Alabama, went against us. Would we not be better off if it did? We do not want to be bound by to[o] strict rules as neutrals." Clearly, Grant considered establishing the rights and prerogatives of a neutral United States of much greater significance than gaining a sum of money from the British. Even so, the tribunal held Great Britain liable for the depredations committed by the *Alabama*, *Florida*, and *Shenandoah*. On September 14 the arbitrators announced the award of $15.5 million to be paid by Britain to the United States.[75]

This successful conclusion elicited wide approval in the United States. In the words of the *New York Times*, "If any Administration ever deserved an acknowledgment of their good faith in seeking the interest of the whole country, without selfish bias of any kind, that Administration is General Grant's in the *Alabama* matter." Grant himself, the press reported, regarded the tribunal's award as not simply a matter of "dollars and cents, but the preservation of amity between England and this country, with full and firm maintenance of our national dignity. These points have been achieved. . . . We are now at peace with the world, and peace is the synonym of prosperity." The president's reference to prosperity was more than political fustian in the middle of his reelection campaign. Clear heads on both sides of the Atlantic had long feared the immense damage that war could work on the intertwined economic interests of the two nations. Although they would experience other diplomatic clashes in the ensuing decades, the Treaty of Washington and the Geneva Arbitration represented milestones in the developing rapprochement that would crest in the twentieth century.[76]

At the time, however, many Britons bridled at the arbitrators' decision. "They generally regard it as a verdict of Guilty on all the charges," Benjamin Moran observed, "and feel angry with us for having proved to a disinterested Tribunal that they were Confederates of the rebels in trying to destroy the U.S. during the war, while claiming credit for pretended neutrality. Still, they are glad that the vexatious question is settled." Schenck wrote to Secretary Fish, "It is a new experience for Great Britain to find a government which has compelled her to not only make an apologetic expression of regret for her wrong doing, but to respond in damages for the injuries committed." Yet, he added, "out of all this settlement—when the soreness has had time to heal—you will see there is to come great good feeling & respect of this people towards us. They can't help but admire us—& at bottom are generally fond & proud of us—but Oh! how jealous of our growth & strength."[77]

Predictably, the *New York Tribune* labeled the outcome at Geneva a failure and insisted that the "trifling sum" of the award "is positively all we have gained." The paper's proprietor, Horace Greeley, was currently engaged in a desperate campaign to replace Grant in the White House. In a strange turn of events, Greeley had won the nomination of the so-called Liberal Republicans, a faction of persons within the party who, for a variety of reasons, had developed a deep antipathy for the president. So intense was their hostility that they could not accord Grant any credit for any success—not even the Geneva Arbitration—that might counter their efforts to portray his administration as failed and corrupt. The Liberals had convinced themselves that a second term for Grant posed a grave threat to the nation, but as the election returns showed two months later, the majority of Americans rejected their jaundiced view and stood by the president.[78]

15

★ ★ ★ ★ ★

VINDICATION

Soon after the completion of the Treaty of Washington, the administration's signature achievement, a Republican officeholder wrote to Bancroft Davis that it would constitute "the best electioneering document of the day," removing "all threatening storm-clouds" on the political horizon. In the months after its ratification, Grant himself thought, "We have a very promising chance of securing a loyal Administration of the government" in the next year's presidential election. Although he claimed "no patent right to the office" and said it would "be a happy day for me when I am out of political life," few Americans, either friends or enemies, doubted that he desired a second term. Certainly the main issue that had drawn him into his first candidacy, the problem of the South, remained central and unsettled. He wrote to Adam Badeau in November 1871, "I do feel a deep interest in the republican party keeping controll [sic] of affairs until the results of the war are acquiesced in by all political parties. When that is accomplished we can afford to quarrel about minor matters." Quarreling had, of course, marked much of his time in office, and Grant was not one to walk away from a fight. As he later recalled, 1872 was the only year he truly desired to run for president. Having endured years of "the bitterness of political and personal opponents," he was eager to find out "how the country felt."[1]

The bitterness intensified as a new round of president making approached. For some, revolt within the Republican Party had begun when they failed to win patronage influence with the president, but after two and a half years, the factionalism reflected differences over policy as well. Some conservatives, who increasingly took on the label of Liberal Republicans, denounced Grant for what they considered to be militaristic centralization in his approach to the South and called for amnesty for all ex-Confederates. Some thought he had given insufficient support for a reduced tariff. Others doubted that he would faithfully implement the reform measures being crafted by the Civil Service Commission.

But the opposition to Grant also bore a cultural dimension. The elite reformers who liked to regard themselves as the nation's "best men" believed the president was, at his core, "vulgar-minded" and "ill bred." One Liberal complained, "He seems to have forgotten our principles and the *men* who made him what he is." As the *New York Herald* observed, just as the "political aristocracy of all parties" had shown a deep disdain for the rough-hewn westerners Abraham Lincoln and Andrew Jackson, "we find the same objections from the same high and mighty classes applied to the plain and unpretending General Grant." And yet, the objections that "are pleaded most earnestly against General Grant, touching his common habits and manners of life, and ways of thought and action, and his ignorance of books and precedents, and of refined statesmanship and diplomacy, are really his strongest recommendations with the masses of the people, because he is of them and for them, and because they sympathize with him as their representative against those pretentious political nabobs who affect to look down upon the unlettered masses with pity or contempt." In 1868 Americans had seen little in Grant beyond the great general who had saved the Union, and they elected him. Now they saw much more and beheld a man much like themselves: steady, unflashy, commonsensical, and patriotic. "In talking with the common people," one Illinois Liberal reported to Lyman Trumbull, "I find [them] generally for Grant." That popular fealty posed a huge obstacle to the Liberal project to unseat the president.[2]

During the long stretch when Congress was out of session from spring to fall 1871, Liberals around the country began to discuss strategy for the coming election year. They could not simply rely on the Democratic Party to defeat Grant's reelection, because that party lacked, as J. D. Cox put it, "the moral elements necessary for a healthy and reformatory organization." Instead, Liberals should draw the "reform" element from both parties into a "third movement," as Carl Schurz called it, to defeat both Grant and the Democrats. Schurz hoped to transfer to the national stage the success achieved by the Liberal Republicans of Missouri in 1870 by cultivating "a very large number of Southerners" who "detest Grant" but "care nothing about the Democratic party." In September 1871 he told a large audience in Nashville that the best way for southerners to throw off the "monarchical police state" commanded by Grant was to unite with the Liberal Republicans. Similarly, revenue reformers such as Amasa Walker favored "a new arrangement of parties" that would reject Republican protectionism and advocate "sound economic issues."[3]

Some Liberals harbored the belief that they could seize the Republican Party apparatus from the Grant men. Their experience at New York's state convention in late September 1871 taught them how futile that hope was, when administration loyalists led by Roscoe Conkling crushed a movement headed by *Tribune* editor Horace Greeley and anti-administration senator Reuben Fenton. The demoralized Fenton-Greeley contingent had no choice but to walk out. Despite crescendoing criticism from both Liberals and Democrats, Grant remained popular, as evinced by Republican victories in the fall 1871 off-year elections. In the key states of Ohio and Pennsylvania, where Republicans heartily endorsed the national administration, the party posted solid wins in October, with substantial gains over the previous year. In New York, the Republicans outpolled the Democrats by 19,000 votes and won a two-thirds majority in each house of the legislature. Although the outcome reflected a popular revulsion against Tammany Hall and boss William Tweed, Hamilton Fish concluded that it "enures nevertheless to the benefit of the Republican Party. I think there can no longer be any question of the success of that party in the next presidential election. The country needs at least four more years of Republican rule, & I think will secure it."[4]

These Republican victories made Grant less willing to propitiate his Republican adversaries. "I have never done ought to give offence to Mr. Sumner, Mr. Schurz, the Springfield Republican people, the Cincinnati Commercial people, nor Mr. Greeley," he said. "Yet they have all attacked me without mercy." As Fish noted, Grant affirmed that if Sumner would "retract & apologise for the slanders he has uttered against him in the Senate, in his own house, in Street Cars, & other public Conveyances, at Dinners & other entertainments & elsewhere, as publicly, openly & in the same manner in which he has uttered these slanders he [the president] would listen to proposals for reconciliation." But Grant thought Sumner "has not the manlyness ever to admit an error. I feel a greater contempt for him than for any other man in the Senate." Similarly, he saw Schurz as an ungrateful man, "a disorganize[r] by nature and one who can render much greater service to the party he does not belong to than the one he pretends to have attachment for."[5]

Still, the president was open to taking steps to allay criticism of his administration. Shortly after the New York election, he accepted the resignation of Thomas Murphy, the political operative he had appointed customs collector. Murphy had done his part in securing the party's victory, but mounting accusations of malfeasance and mismanagement made his departure inevitable. To take his place Grant selected Chester A. Arthur, another Conkling ally but an efficient and honest administrator. Liberals damned the president for appointing Murphy in the first place, but other observers thought that affairs at one federal facility, albeit an important one, had few consequences in the national political landscape. John Bigelow, former editor of the *New York Times* and no great admirer of Grant, wrote to Whitelaw Reid, Greeley's assistant at the *Tribune*:

> I do not believe the people of the U.S. will ask for a change of President this time. With all his ineptiae, Grant has proved the best President the country has had in our time, and the people I think have more faith in him and in his patriotism than in any President, certainly since . Jackson if not since Monroe. His faithful collection of the revenue and its application to the payment of our debts touches the pockets & pride of every American and make them as indifferent out[side] of N.Y. to your indictment of Murphy as a duck to rain. His settlement of the English difficulties has been a masterpiece of diplomacy second to nothing in our diplomatic history.

Given such achievements, Bigelow told Reid, it was "almost idle to talk" of Grant's supposed "weakness for presents, for the society and hospitality of rich men, of a taste for horses and their jockeys, whiskey & cigars. A few weaknesses do not injure a President in the eyes of the people."[6]

Grant used his annual message in December 1871 to tout the administration's accomplishments on the eve of the election year. He highlighted the Treaty of Washington and the prosecution of the Klan. Although the disturbances in Cuba continued, the United States enjoyed "friendly" relations with foreign powers. During the previous twelve months the administration had reduced the national debt by $86 million and lowered the interest rate on government bonds. "The past year has, under a wise Providence, been one of general prosperity to the nation."

In mapping a program for the coming year, the president proposed much that was reminiscent of the Liberals' agenda. He called for abolishing internal taxes on all sources except alcohol and tobacco; more important, he favored reducing the tariff "in such a manner as to afford the greatest relief to the greatest number." He advocated removing customs duties on some raw materials not produced in the United States and reducing other levies to the extent they could be cut "without disturbing home production or reducing the wages of American labor." On the question of amnesty for former Confederates, he called for removal of the officeholding disqualifications of the Fourteenth Amendment, excluding only the "great criminals" of the rebellion. On civil service reform, he again advocated an end to the system of congressional recommendations for applicants, and he promised that the Civil Service Commission's program would get "a fair trial." Further, he called for a government-owned telegraph system and greater protection for immigrants entering the country. Even the *New York Tribune* conceded, "On the whole, we find much more to approve than to condemn in this message, and believe that it will be favorably regarded by a large majority of the American people."[7]

Even so, as reformer David A. Wells avowed, the president's critics intended to pursue "a continued & desperate effort to break down Grant & his administration." Early in the congressional session, Charles Sumner introduced a resolution for a constitutional amendment to limit presidents to a single term. The change would not affect Grant, but no one could mistake the senator's animus. He couched the proposal as essential to civil service reform, asserting that a president limited to one term would not be tempted to use patronage to garner support for reelection. But Conkling argued that the notion sprang not from an impulse to improve the civil service but from disappointment over the failure to control it: "Nine tenths of the warfare upon the President, in the ranks of his party, has proceeded from disaffection over patronage." Conkling further asserted that the proposal was not only undemocratic but also illogical, for it ignored "the truth that men are encouraged in good, and deterred from evil, by making their fate contingent on their conduct." Sumner's one-term resolution died aborning.[8]

More ominously for Grant's reelection prospects, Lyman Trumbull, who harbored presidential ambitions of his own, spearheaded a movement in the Senate to create a Committee on Investigation and Retrenchment to examine operations in the executive branch. But Conkling and other administration allies were not caught napping. They secured a friendly majority among the committee's members and maneuvered to limit its scope.[9]

The committee soon focused on the New York customhouse, where the chief complaint concerned the so-called general order business, the carting and storing of imported goods before their owners paid customs duties. Under Murphy's management, a company headed by George K. Leet had established a near monopoly on this business, and merchants complained that it charged exorbitant rates. Leet had served in a minor position on Grant's staff after the Vicksburg campaign. Early in his administration the president had offered to appoint the thirty-three-year-old Leet collector of internal revenue at New Orleans, but he decided to go into private business in New York instead. In March 1869 Grant gave him a letter of introduction to merchant Moses Grinnell, who was about to become collector of customs. Leet used Grant's letter—essentially abusing the president's friendly gesture—to persuade Grinnell to grant him a portion of the general order business. Grinnell did not do so until after Leet had secured the services of the firm of F. M. Bixby, which had several years' experience running such operations. Bixby paid Leet $5,000 per annum for using his influence to gain the assignment. After Bixby refused Leet's plea for a larger retainer, Leet considered seeking a government position in the customhouse, but Grant adamantly refused to endorse him. He then decided to go into the general order business himself with a partner, Wilbur Stocking. Murphy succeeded Grinnell as collector in July 1870 and sent increasing business to Leet's firm, which became a highly lucrative enterprise.[10]

The Senate committee examined Leet's general order business and Murphy's management of the customhouse in minute detail. Leet gave unabashed testimony about his ambition to gain control of the general order business, but the anti-administration members of the committee were hard-pressed to find credible evidence that he had done so through any nefarious influence from the White House. Indeed, Leet had been in business less than a year when complaints from merchants moved Grant to advise Murphy, "There is so much noise, and talk, and scandal" about Leet "on account of his being with me during the war" that "I think I had better stop that, and I think that young man had better leave." Murphy put the president off by saying that most of the clamor came from steamship lines that wanted the general order business for themselves. Six months later, Murphy himself was out of a job.[11]

The political motive of the investigation's prime movers seemed clear when Horace Greeley took the stand. He confessed that he knew next to nothing about the business of the customhouse, but he complained of "a grave abuse by custom-house officers patrolling our State to control its politics." Ample evidence showed that Murphy had selected and used customs employees in the interest of the Republican Party and the president, but such practices dated from long before Grant's or Murphy's tenure. Greeley also testified that he had an impression that Grant's secretaries, Horace Porter and Orville Babcock, were "silent partners" with Leet and were "making large sums of money" out of the business, although he conceded, "I know no facts to prove it." Porter and Babcock vehemently denied Greeley's allegations, and the administration planted a story in the *New York Herald* stating that the president had full confidence in them. Moreover, Grant said Secretary of War John A. Rawlins had asked him to write the letter of introduction for Leet and that he himself had known Leet "only in a general way." Grant labeled Leet's arrangement with Bixby "an infamous transaction" and said he was sorry Murphy had not removed Leet, as he had requested.[12]

With state elections looming in New Hampshire and Connecticut, party officials urged Grant to take steps to change the general order business "without any delay." In fact, reform was already under way. The president ordered Attorney General George Williams and Treasury Secretary George Boutwell to initiate prosecutions in New York against all persons, officials or not, who had admitted to paying or receiving bribes. By mid-February 1872, Grant and Boutwell had determined to discontinue or modify the system. Boutwell ordered new collector Chester Arthur to initiate reforms at the customhouse according to "the President's wish that the work shall be so arranged and conducted as to give the largest facilities to merchants with the least possible cost." In mid-March Arthur promulgated new rules that included lower storage charges based on a scale recommended by the Chamber of Commerce. Most important, he issued a new list of warehouse companies that would handle the general order business; conspicuously absent was the firm of Leet and Stocking. The new rules were implemented, said the *New York Tribune*, "to the great relief of the merchants of the city."[13]

The Senate committee did not issue its official report until June. Not unexpectedly, the Republican majority exonerated Grant, Porter, and Babcock of wrongdoing and concluded that "no 'monstrous abuse' has been discovered in connection with 'the general-order business,' unless it be the misrepresentation, not to say mendacity, which has been piled upon it." Equally predictably, the minority report labeled Leet and Stocking's business a monopoly "grossly exacting and oppressive to the merchants of New York." But the "real responsibility," they said, lay with Grant, for "improper administration of the appointing power" and failure in his constitutional duty to execute the laws faithfully. But even the committee Democrats admitted that Arthur had "commenced reforms which promise to be valuable and enduring." Their report did not appear until after Grant's renomination, and it had little impact on the general election campaign.[14]

While the customhouse investigation inched forward, Charles Sumner and Carl Schurz launched yet another attempt to derail Grant's reelection prospects. On February 12, 1872, Sumner introduced a resolution calling for a special committee to investigate whether the administration had violated neutrality during the Franco-Prussian War by selling arms to France. Specifically, they alleged that in late 1870, after the War Department refused to sell weapons to Remington Arms because the firm was an agent for France, Remington used a third party, Thomas Richardson, to purchase arms that eventually wound up in French hands. During the war Grant had been committed to strict neutrality, and in January 1871 he had suspended all sales of government arms to avoid any surreptitious sales to either France or Prussia. The president had taken that step after Schurz himself had complained about such sales, and yet a year later, during the debate over Sumner's resolution, Schurz insisted he had heard of the Remington-Richardson transaction only in the past few weeks. The timing of the resolution to investigate alleged pro-French actions nearly a year after the end of the war suggested an overriding political motive—particularly an attempt to turn Schurz's fellow German Americans against the administration. Supporters of the administration labeled the charge not only bogus but also damaging to American interests: it could prove an irritant to Kaiser Wilhelm, who was currently arbitrating the San Juan boundary dispute, and it could also undermine the American position on neutrality in the Geneva Arbitration. After several weeks of investigation, the special committee, dominated by administration senators, concluded that War Department officials had "proceeded in the full belief that they were acting in strict conformity with the law" and that "the manner of sale, at the worst, was a mere error or irregularity in the details of the execution of an undoubted power." The committee acquitted the president of any willful unneutral action, and the issue soon fizzled. As editor Samuel Bowles wrote to Schurz, "Clearly you are making no impression upon the country at large."[15]

The assaults in Congress against the administration during the winter and spring of 1872 had scant effect on Grant's renomination prospects. Indeed, they wound up demonstrating the great depth of his support among congressional Republicans. Outside of Washington, the effort to create a viable national Liberal Republican organization had difficulty getting traction. In early January, Iowa Liberals claimed a victory when administration senator James Harlan lost reelection, but his defeat was largely due to intrastate factionalism, and Horace Porter described the victor, Representative William B. Allison, as "one of our intimate friends here." Ohio witnessed an effort to replace Senator John Sherman with J. D. Cox, a move that, David Wells told Cox, "would make Grant's nomination even doubtfuller." The plan called for a handful of Liberal legislators to vote with the Democrats to elect Cox, but an insufficient number of Democrats agreed to back him, and the scheme collapsed. Moreover, in early spring elections in New Hampshire and Connecticut, Republican tickets defeated Democrats in contests widely regarded as referenda on the administration. "In this result," said the *New York Times*, "Schurz and the rest of the 'sore-heads' may find an accurate measure of their influence." But for the Liberals, of course, taking the presidency from Grant was the main goal, and they could point to these election outcomes as evidence of the Democrats' inability to accomplish that end and hence the need for a new organization. In January a state convention in Missouri called on Republicans who favored reform to meet in a "national mass convention" at Cincinnati on May 1.[16]

Grant's allies monitored the development of the Liberal movement closely. Principal responsibility for organizing the Republican presidential campaign lay with national party secretary William Chandler. Beginning in March, he wrote to state party officials asking about political conditions and particularly the strength of the Liberal movement. Most of the responses minimized the impact of the revolt. Reports from three states indicated exceptions to the general party optimism: Missouri, the birthplace of the revolt; Louisiana, where intense factionalism divided the party; and Illinois, the home of at least two aspirants for the presidency, Lyman Trumbull and Justice David Davis. The Davis candidacy was hardly a sign of strength for the Liberals, however. On February 22 a national convention of the Labor Reform Party nominated Davis for the White House on a platform calling for a paper currency, taxation of government bonds, an eight-hour workday, and government control of the railroads and telegraph. "What fellowship can we have with the absurdities of that sham Labor Reform platform," Cox asked Wells, "& how can its candidate be a proper one for us?"[17]

The Labor platform also called for a nonpartisan civil service, but Grant had already acted on that front. On December 19, 1871, the president promulgated the rules devised by the Civil Service Commission he had appointed six months earlier. Grant was not enthusiastic about instituting competitive examinations for admission to the service, and he bristled at critics who "think it preposterous in me to give appointments to persons who I ever knew and particularly to those who feel any personal friendship for me." He also insisted on retaining the executive's power to remove officers. Nonetheless, over the course of the commission's work, he had met several times with its chairman, George William Curtis, to help move the project along. When the president released the rules that would take effect on January 1, 1872, he promised they would be "faithfully executed" and asked "for all the strength which Congress can give me to enable me to carry out the reforms."[18]

The rules called for a fundamental reordering of the federal personnel system. Most positions would be classified into grades, with entry into the service limited to the lowest grade. Appointees would be selected from among the top three performers on a public competitive examination. Vacancies above the entry level would be filled by examinations among applicants from other grades, or public examinations if no one in the service was qualified. Most officials would serve on probation for the first six months. Individuals whose jobs involved handling money would require approval by their immediate supervisors responsible for the funds. To conduct the examinations and organize the system, the president would appoint a three-person board of examiners for each department. The rules did not apply to department heads, assistant secretaries, judicial personnel, ambassadors, and other higher-level officials. Besides replacing political influence with a merit-based system for most appointments, the rules barred the levying or payment of "any assessment of money for political purposes, under the form of voluntary contributions or otherwise." The commission would continue as the newly named Civil Service Advisory Board.[19]

No president had ever gone so far to elevate the civil service, but the reformers generally refused to give Grant credit for taking that step. The Missouri Liberal convention issued a platform that said nothing about his new rules and instead denounced "the shameless abuse of Government patronage for control of conventions and elections." James A. Garfield told Cox that the administration's civil service policy was "absurd" in light of the customhouse allegations. And yet Garfield admitted that "the great body of Grant's superserviceable friends" in Congress—the men who supposedly benefited from the spoils system—"are furious against the Civil Service Report."[20]

Indeed, regular Republicans who customarily stood in the president's corner launched a blistering attack against the reform plan. They condemned it for favoring the educated rich over the "sons of the poor, in violation of the most essential principle of republican institutions," and they warned that "no examination can test the moral character and moral qualities" of applicants. They also argued that when the people elected a party representing a particular policy, the executive should appoint to office "friends of that policy." One party worker bluntly stated the political consequences in a letter to the president: "If there is to be no reward, or hope of reward for *services* rendered and *money* expended— by appointment to some official position, do you, or can any one suppose, that this *necessary labor* and *money* will come to the Party freely or in any other manner?" Even members of the cabinet spoke of the "impracticable character" of the reforms. Williams suggested asking for an appropriation for the examining boards in order to throw "upon Congress the decision whether they will carry out the proposed scheme." After much wrangling, Congress whittled a $100,000 request down to a $25,000 appropriation.[21]

Although Grant shared the critics' skepticism about certain elements of the plan, he told Curtis that he was "undisturbed" by the attacks in Congress. "It is my intention that Civil Service reform shall have a fair trial," he wrote to advisory board member Joseph Medill. "The great defect in the past custom is that Executive patronage had come to be regarded as the property of individuals of the party in power. The choice of Federal officers has been limited to those seeking office. A true reform will leave the offices to seek the man." In mid-April he instituted a more detailed version of the rules to be "enforced as rapidly as the proper arrangements can be made." Assessments were "forbidden," he declared, and "honesty and efficiency, not political activity, will determine the tenure of office." Speaking for the Liberals, the *New York Tribune* insisted that Grant was simply making an "appearance of keeping up Civil Service Reform."[22]

At this point, the Liberal Republican convention in Cincinnati was just two weeks away, and the scramble for the presidential nomination remained ongoing. Schurz was ineligible because he was not a natural-born citizen. Many Liberals favored Charles Francis Adams, the American arbitrator in Geneva. The son and grandson of presidents, a two-term congressman and former minister to Great Britain, Adams had an impeccable reputation for which no one had a higher regard than himself. An Anti-Mason turned Whig turned Free-Soiler turned Republican, he had no sense of commitment to party. His opposition to Sumner in Massachusetts politics and his disapproval of Radical Reconstruction appealed to Democrats, whose backing many Liberals considered indispensable to victory.[23]

Through the spring, however, Adams refused to angle for delegates and even declined to discuss issues. His sons gingerly stepped into the breach, with John Quincy telling Wells that his father's "political opinions are substantially in accord with the Missouri platform." But Wells and other leading Liberals felt that "inference was not enough." Wells wrote to Adams directly to solicit his views, and he naïvely asked whether Adams would "allow any one or all of us combined to speak for you"—that is, negotiate—at the Cincinnati convention. Adams wrote back that he would give no authority for anyone to speak for him. He claimed he did not want the nomination but would consider it if "the call upon me were an unequivocal one, based upon confidence in my character earned in public life, and a belief that I could carry out in practice the principles which I professed. . . . But if I am to be negotiated for and have assurances given that I am honest, you will be so kind as to draw me out of that crowd." When Adams's letter appeared in newspapers, it made him seem less inclined to lay down his plow than to poke his would-be followers in the eye. He remained the front-runner but had handed his rivals a weapon to use against him.[24]

Other candidates included Trumbull, who had pushed investigation of the administration. Sponsor of the Civil Rights Act of 1866, Trumbull had since soured on Reconstruction. He had voted to acquit Andrew Johnson, opposed the Ku Klux Klan Act, and favored universal amnesty to allow white leaders to take control of the South. He had positioned himself as a crusader for civil service reform and against corruption, and he thought Liberals should emphasize these issues over the tariff, about which they could reach no consensus. He fiercely contested with David Davis for support in Illinois, but outside that state, Trumbull showed greater strength.[25]

Governor B. Gratz Brown of Missouri attracted followers around the country, especially in the South, but Schurz had never forgiven him for supporting the election of his cousin, Democrat Frank Blair, to the Senate. Rumors that Schurz favored Adams intensified Brown's ill will toward the German interloper, who overshadowed him in Missouri politics.[26]

Also on the list of candidates was Horace Greeley, whose impulse for self-promotion was as unblushing as Adams's was discreet. As editor of the nation's premier Republican newspaper, Greeley had been an early supporter of the administration; Grant had cultivated his friendship and had even considered appointing him minister to England. But the relationship soured after Greeley sided with Reuben Fenton in the factional fights in New York. On patronage questions, the president came to regard applicants advocated by Greeley as "fawning, deceitful and dishonest men." At bottom, Grant thought, "Mr. Greeley is simply a disappointed man at not being estimated by others at the same value he places upon himself. He is a genious [sic] without common sense . . . , and I have come to doubt his intentions." For his part, Greeley nursed a visceral contempt for Grant. "I want a candidate," he told a friend, "who can get on with less liquor if such can be had—to say nothing of Tobacco."[27]

The national circulation of the *Tribune* gave Greeley wider name recognition than other candidates. In 1871 he enhanced his visibility with a speaking tour through the South, where he emphasized sectional reconciliation and universal amnesty. But Greeley's erratic personality and his embrace over the years of various isms left many Liberals doubting his electability. Revenue reformers who favored a reduced tariff recoiled against his long-standing protectionism. Two months before the convention, Greeley told a friend that if the new party opposed protection, "*that* I can't go, even though it would make me president." And yet a few weeks later, in a move intended to curry favor with the reformers, he affixed his signature to the New York call for the convention, which stated that "Federal taxation should be imposed for revenue, and so adjusted as to make the burden upon the industry of the country as light as possible." When Cox heard that "Greeley and his friends are trying to force the Cincinnati Convention to a non-committal policy on the tariff question," he warned Wells, "If we do not declare squarely for Revenue Reform I believe failure at the elections will await us." Unable to coalesce behind a particular candidate before the convention, Liberals also disagreed about what the new party should emphasize beyond personal attacks against Grant, whether it be civil service reform, anti-corruption, sectional reconciliation, or revenue reform.[28]

While the Liberals floundered, Grant capitalized on his incumbency. Besides monitoring the American case in Geneva and implementing civil service reform, he acted "presidential" in other ways. In January and again in April he met with delegations of African Americans to signal his support for pending legislation calling for equal access to public accommodations; in May he followed with a public letter endorsing "any effort to secure for all our people, of whatever race, nativity, or color, the exercise of those rights to which every citizen should be entitled." Congress, however, failed to pass the supplementary civil rights bill before the session ended, in part because of opposition by Trumbull and other Liberals. In March the president struck a blow for conservation by signing legislation creating Yellowstone National Park. In addition, he issued a proclamation reinforcing his previous order that a congressional mandate limiting work by government laborers to eight hours a day should entail no reduction in the workers' earnings.[29]

At the same time, Grant resisted becoming embroiled in the intense Republican factionalism in Louisiana between the forces of Governor Henry Clay Warmoth and those associated with federal officeholders in the state, most prominently New Orleans customs collector James F. Casey (who was Julia Grant's brother-in-law). When the state legislature convened in January, both factions claimed legal supremacy, but the president flatly denied each side's request for military support to establish control. Given that undue "militarism" was one of the Liberals' persistent charges against him, Grant refused to declare martial law in New Orleans and instead ordered US troops to limit their actions to preserving the peace. Unable to "see any justification for Executive interference," he urged Congress to send an investigating committee to the state. The president thought the testimony showed that, despite being an "efficient and honest" officer, Casey had lost the public's confidence and should be removed. But after considerable protest from Louisiana citizens convinced him that firing Casey would be tilting toward the opposing faction, he allowed the collector to retain his post.[30]

While trying to stay out of the Louisiana infighting, Grant signaled that he was not backing away from fighting terrorist activity in the South. He widened the command responsibility of Major Lewis Merrill, who had played a leading role in the fight against the Ku Klux Klan in South Carolina the previous fall. In April the president sent Congress a message justifying his declaration of martial law in that action. His purpose, he said, had been to suppress the Klan, which "by force and terror" aimed "to prevent all political action not in accord" with that group and "reduce the colored people to a condition closely akin to that of slavery."[31]

In early March Grant welcomed a ten-person "embassy" from Japan on a largely ceremonial visit. In formally receiving the delegates, the president took care to note that "the improvement of the commercial relations between our respective countries . . . cannot fail to strengthen the bonds which unite us." Prospects for increased trade also spurred Grant to appoint a government commission to study the merits of various proposed routes for a canal linking the Atlantic and Pacific Oceans. Many Liberals favored such a project, but they and Grant still disagreed on revenue legislation regarding trade. The president told a gathering of industrialists at the White House that although he favored eliminating tariffs on commodities not produced in the United States, "a reduction of the duties on articles that we could manufacture had but one tendency, viz., that of depressing industry and injuring the working classes and reducing them to a condition of the pauper labor of Europe."[32]

While Grant was pursuing his duties in the winter and spring of 1872, Republican conventions in state after state chose delegates who were committed to him. Even Greeley told his managing editor to lighten up on the president because "a good many of our subscribers are Grant men, and we must not irritate them needlessly." In mid-April the president's candidacy received the blessing of Henry Ward Beecher, who gave a rousing speech in Brooklyn, declaring, "There has never been a better administrator. . . . [U]nder General Grant we shall have a prosperity that shall be the admiration of all the world." A week later, emphasis on the nation's prosperity marked several speeches at a huge rally at Cooper Union, where party leaders praised the president's financial policies, his handling of the South, his Indian policy, his embrace of civil service reform, and his negotiation and implementation of the Treaty of Washington. All these speakers conceded some problems in the previous three years but insisted that the Republican Party could clean house with no help from the renegade Liberals.[33]

Indeed, when the delegates gathered for the Liberal Republican convention in early May, it became clear that the Liberals' own house could use some scrubbing. According to Samuel Bowles, the meeting included not only "the theoretical reformer" but also "the disappointed place-seeker and the corrupt intriguer. There were good men who were not wise, and there were wise men who were not good." Because official delegates for each state were chosen from among persons who had simply showed up, seasoned wire-pullers for Greeley captured nearly all of New York's large bloc of seats, leaving only three for revenue reformers. Moreover, Greeley made it clear that if the convention advocated a reduced tariff, he would withhold the *Tribune*'s support for its nominee. He advocated instead a plank that consigned the tariff question to the judgment of Congress, essentially excising it as an issue in the presidential campaign. After long debate, revenue reformers on the resolutions committee accepted this formulation, in large part because they were confident that the convention would select a nominee who shared their views.[34]

The platform, adopted on the third day, opened with a scathing indictment of Grant. It alleged that the president had "openly used the powers and opportunities of his high office for the promotion of personal ends . . . kept notoriously corrupt and unworthy men in places of power and responsibility . . . used the public service of the Government as a machinery of partisan and personal influence . . . [and] shown himself deplorably unequal to the tasks imposed upon him by the necessities of the country, and culpably careless of the responsibilities of his high office." On questions related to Reconstruction, the platform embraced the "equality of all men" and the Reconstruction Amendments, but with an eye to white southern voters, it also favored universal amnesty for ex-Confederates and supported "local self-government" over "centralized power" and "the supremacy of the civil over the military authority." It endorsed civil service reform but offered no specific remedy beyond a one-term limit for presidents. It ignored the reforms Grant and the Civil Service Commission had instituted. The platform remitted the tariff issue "to the people in their Congress districts, and to the decision of Congress thereon, wholly free of Executive interference or dictation." On other financial matters, the document upheld the public credit, denounced repudiation, and called for a speedy return to specie payments. It also favored "full reward" for Union soldiers and opposed further land grants to railroads. Much of the platform reflected standard Republican doctrine, but it completely ignored Grant's popular achievements such as the Indian peace policy and the Treaty of Washington.[35]

After the convention adopted the platform, chairman Carl Schurz immediately moved on to balloting for the presidential nominee, allowing no formal speeches for the candidates. The previous day, Schurz's rousing keynote address, calling on the delegates to put aside "State pride" and nominate a "statesman" of "superior intelligence," fed rumors that he favored Adams over his fellow Missourian Brown. Determined to strike back, Brown boarded a train for Cincinnati, where he began canvassing for Greeley. He had help from Frank Blair, who spread the word that Democrats would support a ticket of Greeley and Brown.[36]

When the balloting began on May 3, Adams held a healthy lead, with two-thirds of the votes needed to win, followed by Greeley, Trumbull, Brown, Davis, and Andrew Curtin of Pennsylvania, with a handful of votes for Chief Justice Salmon Chase. Before Schurz could announce the result, however, Brown took the platform and withdrew his name from contention. As J. D. Cox noted, Brown then gave "a brief, but passionate & excited harangue in favor of Greeley." Afterward, the New Yorker gained considerable strength, while Adams suffered from the failure of the Massachusetts delegation to unite behind him and from the active opposition of Sumner's ally F. W. Bird. On the fourth ballot, Greeley trailed Adams by just twenty-eight votes, but on the next tally, Adams's lead grew to fifty-one. At this moment of crisis, Greeley's lieutenant Whitelaw Reid and other New Yorkers streamed across the convention floor, manufacturing a loud if specious pro-Greeley demonstration, and amid a flurry of vote changes, Greeley went over the top on the sixth ballot. When someone offered the customary motion to make the nomination unanimous, Schurz heard a chorus of nays and declared it defeated. The convention chose Brown for vice president.[37]

The outcome at Cincinnati stunned the founders of the Liberal movement, which Cox said had been "defiled by its enemies." Schurz complained to Greeley himself that his nomination "was a successful piece of political huckstering" that left the Liberal movement "stripped of its moral power." "After what I saw of the men and observed as to the measures taken to nominate Greeley," Edward Atkinson said, "I feel bound to oppose his election to the utmost. I should feel safer with Grant by far." Four thousand miles away in Geneva, Adams wrote that Greeley's nomination "completely oversets all the calculations of the original authors of the convention—for success with such a candidate is out of the question. . . . The governing party will of course exult a good deal."[38]

Exult the Grant men did. Greeley's nomination, said Hamilton Fish, lowered "the standard . . . for public position near to that which elevated a Roman Emperor's horse to a Roman Consulate." Wisconsin congressman G. W. Hazleton reported to his state chairman, "The great mass of the republican party was never more compact, and never more eager for a fight than it is today," while the Democrats "are completely bewildered with reference to the best plan for beating Grant." The president himself confided to Elihu Washburne that "no one is satisfied but Greeley himself. . . . His nomination has had a good effect however. It has apparently harmonized the [Republican] party by getting out of it the 'sore-heads' and knaves who made all the trouble because they could not controll."[39]

But the sorest sorehead of them all, Charles Sumner, had not rushed to join the Liberal Republican movement. For months he had held back, largely because he thought Liberals such as Schurz had abandoned his principal concern: the advancement of African Americans' rights. Nor had he relished embracing a party that seemed poised to nominate his Massachusetts rival Adams. Bird had played on Sumner's vanity, urging him to issue a "bill of indictment" against the administration that might result in his own nomination. But Sumner did not bite. He could not shake the feeling that the new organization could never be anything more than an adjunct to the hated Democrats, nor could he abandon the belief that his own political future lay with the Republican Party.[40]

Hence, after Greeley's nomination, Sumner argued that the coming campaign should "be *personal* & not *political*." Such a campaign would allow him to retain his Republican Party bona fides and still attack its nominee. Privately he believed that "Greeley is not our model, but he is much better than Grant." "There will be no party issue," he told a friend, "no question between the two parties, Republican and Democratic—but simply a personal issue between Greeley & Grant—between the two G's—the *great* G & the little g. On such an issue can a good Republican hesitate? Is not the pen mightier than the sword?" Sumner urged Reid to use the *New York Tribune* to show "the unfitness of our military chief" and expose "the pretensions of Genl. Grant as a civilian." Liberals pressed him to make a speech, but Sumner hesitated, pleading that it was best to wait and see whether the Republican convention might select a nominee who could unite the party, "which Grant cannot." A few days before the Republicans convened, however, Sumner changed course by 180 degrees, taking to the Senate floor with a blistering assault that he hoped would deliver a knockout blow to the president's renomination.[41]

Entitling his speech "Republicanism vs. Grantism," Sumner fulminated for four hours against the president's alleged capture and betrayal of the Republican Party, while portraying himself as "one of the straitest of the sect." He reiterated his charge that Grant had abused military power to menace Santo Domingo's neighbor, the "Black Republic" of Haiti, thereby "treading under foot the Constitution." Whereas most Liberals denounced Grant's aggressive intervention in the South, Sumner saw his actions on behalf of African Americans as inadequate and reflecting a lack of "any true sympathy" for them. Grant's recent endorsement of the civil rights bill, he said, had been a "meaningless juggle of words, entirely worthy of the days of slavery." Sumner accused Grant of nepotism but spent vastly more time expounding on the history of nepotism beginning with the fifteenth-century popes than uncovering actual cases of Grant's relatives holding federal offices. The senator accused Grant of "gift-taking," apparently referring to the houses he had received in recognition of his military service, but he could cite no instance since Grant's inauguration as president. He criticized the president for surrounding himself with an "illegal military ring" at the White House and for appointing cabinet members "having small relations with the Republican party."

In delivering his scattershot indictment, Sumner's rage blinded him to its contradictions. On the one hand, he accused Grant of laziness, incompetence, and detachment—treating the presidential office "as little more than a plaything . . . where palace cars, fast horses, and sea-side loiterings figure more than duties." On the other hand, he denounced the president for being too domineering and intrusive—for exercising "autocratic pretension," making the Republican Party "the instrument of *one man and his personal will*," and exhibiting a "Caesarism or *personalism*, abhorrent to republican institutions." In a passage that perhaps revealed the true root of Sumner's animus, he castigated the president essentially for exercising independent judgment and disagreeing with men like himself: Grant, he said, "insists upon quarreling until he has become the great presidential quarreler, with more quarrels than all other Presidents together, all begun and continued by himself." Although Sumner had initiated many of these fights, he declared that "a president has no right to quarrel with anybody." Sumner's sympathetic biographer describes this speech as one of his "poorest efforts, clearly reflecting prolonged . . . mental and emotional strain." With an eye toward the delegates about to gather in Philadelphia, the senator threw down the gauntlet: "Can Republicans without departing from all obligations, whether of party or patriotism, recognize our ambitious Caesar as a proper representative?"[42]

Republicans gave their answer in Philadelphia in early June. Speaker after speaker at the national convention denounced Sumner not just for his opposition to the president but also for his apostasy from the party's faith. One delegate asserted that Sumner's recent "abuse and calumny" would give "Grant more sympathy and votes than Mr. Sumner dreamed of." Accentuating the positive, the Republican orators praised the president for reducing the nation's debt and the burden of taxation, bringing greenbacks closer to par with gold, launching the Indian peace policy, and maintaining peace abroad.

But the central theme of the convention oratory focused on Grant's continuing efforts to secure the gains achieved by the Civil War, emancipation, and Reconstruction. The crowd gave a thunderous welcome to seventy-five-year-old Gerrit Smith, the famed abolitionist and longtime friend of Sumner, who called on the nation to give the president a second term to "crush out Ku-Kluxism and save the negro and the few white men who defend the negro from the bloody, fearful, and terrible vengeance threatened against them. . . . [W]e must have Grant a few years longer in the Presidency, because the anti-slavery battle is not yet fought out." Several other speakers echoed Smith, including four men of color. William H. Grey of Arkansas declared, "Had it not been for the passage of the Ku-Klux law and the man at the helm who had the nerve to execute it, that organization would be to-day in full venom in that section of the country. . . . The black people stand solid together. They know intuitively who is their friend."[43]

The delegates stood together as well. The next day, June 6, Illinois put Grant's name before the convention, setting off "a perfect wilderness of hats, caps, and handkerchiefs waved to and fro in a surging mass." In short order the convention voted unanimously for the president's renomination. At the White House, Orville Babcock handed a telegram to Grant, who read its good tidings and gave it back without a word. To avoid well-wishers, the president immediately got into his buggy and took a long, solitary drive through Washington's outskirts. When he returned, he accepted the congratulations of a few senators and expressed his gratification at the convention's unanimity, which, as a reporter paraphrased his sentiment, "showed that the vile slanders uttered against him found no believers among his friends." The expected result caused little disruption at the White House, where the staff paid closer attention to the contest for the second spot on the ticket.[44]

Nearly two years before the convention, in September 1870, Vice President Schuyler Colfax had announced that he would not seek renomination, largely for personal financial reasons. In the interim, some observers had looked to Colfax as a potential presidential nominee who could bridge the divide between Liberals and regulars in the party. In November 1871 the president accepted Colfax's denial of any complicity in such a movement, which Grant ascribed to "people intent upon creating jealousy between us." By the beginning of 1872, Colfax had reconsidered his earlier withdrawal for vice president, and his friends launched a campaign to secure his renomination. By then, however, thoughts of running with Grant had occurred to other men, most prominently Senator Henry Wilson of Massachusetts.[45]

The Republican ticket for 1872. (Library of Congress)

Grant refrained from exerting any overt influence in the vice presidential contest, a stance that bespoke little real attachment to Colfax. On the eve of the balloting in Philadelphia, press reports alleged that Grant preferred Wilson. As the senator's supporters noted, Grant and Colfax were both westerners, whereas Wilson's nomination would give the ticket strength from New England, as well as register a rebuke to Sumner. A relatively poor man who had started life as a cobbler, Wilson was popular with labor. Moreover, his ardent abolitionism and support for Radical Reconstruction would wear well in a campaign that was shaping up to emphasize sectional issues. Voting on the first ballot had the two leading candidates seesawing back and forth until near the end, when Wilson pulled ahead but was still a dozen votes shy of victory. Several states scrambled for recognition to change their votes, and Wilson went over the top. Colfax wired the convention that he would "cheerfully" support the ticket: "Men are nothing, principles everything." Grant diplomatically told a reporter that the idea "seems to have been to have the two candidates from different sections of the country. Otherwise there is no preference between the two men. Personally I have a great affection for both Wilson and Colfax."[46]

In large measure, the convention platform reaffirmed much of the doctrine Grant had been espousing in office. It upheld the recent constitutional amendments; called for "complete liberty and exact equality in the enjoyment of all civil, political, and public rights"; insisted on suppression of the Klan; and approved of amnesty for former rebels. The platform advocated "peace with all nations" and condemned British attempts to interfere with former subjects from Ireland who were now American citizens. It opposed further grants to railroads but endorsed measures to encourage American commerce and shipbuilding. It favored pensions for disabled Union veterans. On civil service, the delegates swallowed hard and called for going beyond reform by executive action and passing "laws which shall abolish the evils of patronage." The platform saluted Grant's reduction of the national debt and interest rates, and it called for the speedy resumption of specie payments. Horace Greeley himself might have run on the tariff plank, which stated that "revenue, except so much as may be derived from a tax upon tobacco and liquors, should be raised by duties upon importations, the details of which should be so adjusted as to aid in securing remunerative wages to labor, and to promote the industries, prosperity, and growth of the whole country." In addition, the platform stated that the admission of women "to wider fields of usefulness is viewed with satisfaction, and the honest demand of any class of citizens for additional rights should be treated with respectful consideration."[47]

The latter plank represented a recognition of women's increasing role in American political discourse. In addition to demanding the right to vote, many women favored other reforms such as temperance. In May a convention of the new Equal Rights Party nominated Victoria Woodhull for president. But Woodhull's advocacy of free love and her party's call for socialistic reform repelled many reform-minded women to whom the Republicans' outreach had greater appeal. Matilda Joslyn Gage, chairwoman of the executive committee of the National Woman Suffrage Association, expressed gratitude to the GOP "for its opening the door to us as it did at Phila[delphia]." Henry Blackwell, the reformist proprietor of the *Woman's Journal*, favored "throw[ing] our *united force* of women speakers into the field" behind Grant. "*Mr. Greeley is the most conspicuous opponent of Woman's political equality*," he said, while "Gen. Grant and his wife, on the contrary, are Woman Suffragists." Blackwell may have overstated the Grants' position, but William Chandler cheerfully used party funds to subsidize campaign speeches by Gage, Susan B. Anthony, Lucy Stone, and others.[48]

With Grant and Greeley now in the field, Democrats could no longer delay setting a course. Many stood aghast at the nomination of Greeley, who for decades had savaged the Democratic Party in the *Tribune*. The question now was whether to endorse him or to nominate a Democrat at their own convention in Baltimore. Cox and other revenue reformers opposed to Greeley pushed for an alternative ticket of Adams and Ohio Democrat William Groesbeck, but these efforts were a sideshow compared with the Greeleyites' aggressive wooing of Democrats.[49]

Whitelaw Reid, Greeley's right-hand man, said the Democrats must decide "whether they will ride in the wagon or follow at its tail." Realizing that he and his allies must work especially hard to make their candidate palatable to southern Democrats, Reid did not hesitate to use thinly veiled racist appeals. He warned a Georgia newspaper editor that Grant was likely to win "the negro vote," which was "largely controlled by secret societies the organization of which was now in the hands of the office-holders." Greeley's election, he promised, would be "of immense service" to the South. The *Tribune* issued a pamphlet touting Greeley's views on amnesty and Reconstruction, and Reid encouraged the highlighting of any information that would "make the northern democracy comprehend that the South is unanimous" for the Liberal candidate. In mid-June the Indiana Democratic convention came out for Greeley, and

Democrats around the country increasingly agreed that they had no viable alternative. On July 10 the national convention nominated Greeley and adopted the Cincinnati platform verbatim.[50]

When the Republican convention committee notified Grant of his nomination, he responded with genuine feeling: "It is certainly gratifying to me to learn that, after holding office for three years—never having before held a political office, and never having been a candidate for nomination—I have been indorsed by my former supporters. This is something I cannot forget." His official acceptance letter was brief and undetailed. He promised "the same zeal and devotion to the good of the whole people" that he had previously shown. "Past experience," he added, "may guide me in avoiding mistakes inevitable with novices in all professions and in all occupations." He would aim to bequeath to his successor "a country at peace within its own borders, at peace with outside nations, with a credit at home and abroad, and without embarrassing questions to threaten its future prosperity." He closed with his "desire to see a speedy healing of all bitterness of feeling between sections, parties or races of citizens, and the time when the title of citizen carries with it all the protection and privileges to the humblest that it does to the most exalted."[51]

Greeley wrote a longer letter that essentially reiterated the planks of the Liberal Republican platform. He called for "a real and not merely a simulated reform in the civil service," to be attained chiefly by a one-term limit for presidents. He continued to evade the tariff question by labeling it "the people's immediate business" to be handled by Congress. But most of all, he emphasized sectional reconciliation, again recognizing that he had to win support from white southern Democrats to have any chance at winning the White House. He favored maintaining "the political rights and franchises" acquired by African Americans after the war, but he devoted more emphasis and space to solicitude for the prompt restoration of such rights supposedly lost by ex-Confederates. In a letter accepting the Democratic nomination, Greeley stated, "Having done what I could for the complete emancipation of blacks, I now insist on the full enfranchisement of all my white countrymen." He promised a policy aimed "at local self government, and not at centralization." He ignored the violence perpetrated in the South by the Klan and similar groups and insisted that each state be "left free to enforce the rights and promote the well-being of its inhabitants." Less concerned about peace between the races than about harmony between the sections, Greeley declared that the people of the North and South should "clasp hands across the bloody chasm which has too long divided them."[52]

The two acceptance letters set the tone for the campaign that followed. The prominence of sectional issues derived in part from the settlement or diminution of others. On the civil service question, Greeley had never been much of a reformer, Grant had already launched a system to replace patronage with a merit system, and the average American had never shown much interest in the issue anyway. In May and June Grant signed compromise tariff legislation that lowered the customs duties by an average of 10 percent and expanded the duty-free list, thereby undercutting an issue that had already been rendered anomalous by Greeley's disagreement with the revenue reformers. Congress also allowed the unpopular income tax to expire. The country was relatively prosperous, and Greeley could not charge the incumbent with hard times. The Liberal/Democratic candidate and his supporters sought to make much of Grant's alleged shortcomings as an administrator, but Greeley's sometimes bizarre behavior and his past association with machine politicians in New York vitiated such arguments. Amnesty had been one of Greeley's main goals, but two days after transmitting his acceptance letter, Grant signed a bill that removed officeholding disqualifications from all but a small number of ex-Confederates. With all these political issues substantially neutralized, the campaign largely came down to competing views on how to resolve the lingering southern question—how to fashion the correct relationship between the national and state governments and, especially, how to ensure the rights of the newly enfranchised African Americans. Grant espoused justice for all citizens and envisioned a continuing federal government role to guarantee it. Greeley, in contrast, emphasized reconciliation between the sections, with the traditional white ruling class again taking control in the South.[53]

No one found this contrast more distressing than Sumner. Greeley's position contravened all that Sumner stood for on the issue, but the senator could not overcome his hatred of Grant, despite the pleas of many of his longtime associates in the abolition movement. "If Horace Greeley is President," Lydia Marie Child warned him, "the Democratic Party . . . and the Rebels will exert all their cunning to undo every good thing the Republican Party has done." Frederick Douglass wrote, "You cannot give up your relation to those who have looked to you as their political Redeemer. You cannot give up the almost dumb millions to whom you have been mind and voice during a quarter of a century." Such entreaties only angered Sumner and fueled his determination to speak out. He denied harboring any personal dislike for Grant and claimed it was the president's "utterly heartless & insensate conduct" toward Haiti that made him "indignant, as when Kansas was assailed, the case being as bad as that of Kansas."[54]

In a published letter to a group of black voters, Sumner embraced Greeley and adopted in toto his plea for reconciliation. He pointed to Greeley's early abolitionism and falsely claimed that Grant had never "at any time shown any sympathy with the colored race, but rather indifference if not aversion." For menacing the black republic, Grant "deserved impeachment for high crimes and misdemeanors, rather than a renomination." Sumner even implied that blacks' assertiveness was partly to blame for their troubles in the South: "I am sure it cannot be best for the colored people to band together in a hostile camp, provoking antagonism and keeping alive the separation of the races." Moreover, he tacitly adopted white southerners' indictment of the Reconstruction regimes in lecturing his black correspondents that "while justly careful of your own rights, you cannot be indifferent to the blessings of good government." Whereas Sumner had previously equated any disagreement with him on sectional and racial issues as a reincarnation of the old debate over slavery, he now insisted, "I am against fanning ancient flames into continued life." The nomination of an abolitionist by the Democrats and especially by southerners, he argued, demonstrated their "willingness to associate the rights of their colored fellow-citizens with that reconciliation of which Horace Greeley was an early representative."[55]

Greeley thanked the senator for his "noble letter," but Douglass countered with a statement warning African Americans against "the insidious and dangerous advice and counsel of Mr. Sumner." With Greeley, Douglass said, "we would enter upon a sea of trouble," but "with Grant, our security is unquestionable; our happiness will be made lasting." Grant himself told a reporter that on the question of defending blacks' rights, he was perfectly willing to have his actions judged next to Sumner's words. He charged that the senator's mismanagement of civil rights legislation showed that he was not "such a good friend to the black man as he professed." As for himself, the president conceded that he had not been an original abolitionist but had favored emancipation as a war measure. He believed that, once free, African Americans should have the ballot to "make the gift complete" and give them "full possession of the rights of freemen." In a letter to Washburne, Grant concluded, "Poor old Sumner is sick from neglect and the consciousness that he is not all of the republican party. . . . If he is not crazy his mind is at least so effected as to disqualify him for the proper discharge of his duties as Senator." E. R. Hoar agreed: "Sumner is simply insane, and would satisfy himself with the safety of restoring the whole of Buchanan's Cabinet, with Jeff. Davis at the head of it, if he saw no other way to impress upon mankind the fearful consequences of displacing a Chairman of the Committee on Foreign Relations."[56]

Sumner's letter appeared on the eve of the August 1 state election in North Carolina, which the two sides hotly contested as an indicator of their relative strength in the national campaign. Although the GOP candidate for governor eked out a win over his opponent by a margin of less than 1 percent, Tar Heel Republicans hailed the "glorious" victory over "the combined forces of Ku Klux Conservatives, Democracy, and Greeley." From the White House, Babcock reported to Badeau, "North Carolina is all right after all the liberal lies. . . . What a splendid party we shall have with all that *scum* taken off." In September, victories in Vermont and Maine added to the Republicans' momentum.[57]

No one worked harder for victory in these states or in the nation at large than party secretary William Chandler. Winking at the new civil service regulations, he superintended the assessment of officeholders and government contractors for contributions. He monitored party work in the states and distributed pro-administration newspapers. The national committee dispatched speakers across the country and mailed voters millions of pamphlets such as *U. S. Grant and the Colored People*, *Grant's Amnesty Record*, and *The Financial Record of President Grant's Administration*. Chandler reported his activities to the president and also recommended appointments that would help carry individual states.[58]

Chandler and the national committee did all they could to encourage a movement among Democrats who could not swallow Greeley, including compiling a list of Democrats willing to speak for Grant and Wilson. They also furnished material aid to disgruntled Democrats who organized a national convention in Louisville on September 3 to select a straight-out Democratic ticket. Chandler told Grant, "The moral effect of a democratic bolt, great or small, cannot fail to give us many votes of the rank and file." The convention nominated Charles O'Conor, a prominent New York lawyer who had helped prosecute the Tweed Ring. O'Conor declined to run but publicly avowed his "inexpressible aversion" to Greeley's election and wound up with more than 20,000 votes. In New York, the Republicans reached out to the opposition party by nominating Democrat John A. Dix for governor. Grant himself urged the famous former general to accept, assuring him that his nomination signified that "victory and reform had been inaugurated in the state."[59]

Following political etiquette, Grant did not openly campaign. He told Roscoe Conkling that only two previous candidates had personally campaigned, "and both of them were public speakers, and both were beaten. I am no speaker and don't want to be beaten." In June he attended commencement ceremonies at Harvard University, where he was awarded an honorary doctor of laws degree, commending not only his military service but also his "strengthening the national credit, lightening the public burdens, reforming the civil service," and settling "grave disputes" with Great Britain. He spent the summer at Long Branch, except for a few brief, ostensibly nonpolitical trips. At Newark, New Jersey, he touched on the tariff issue, telling a gathering at an industrial exhibition that the city's "manufacturers have an influence opposed to the importation of foreign manufactures." In the fall, the favorable outcomes of the Geneva and San Juan arbitrations added luster to his record. "We are now at peace with the world," he told reporters, "and peace is the synonym of prosperity." When the press carried rumors that he planned to alter his Indian policy, he issued a public letter stating that "if any change is made, it must be on the side of the civilization and Christianization of the Indian. I do not believe our Creator ever placed the different races of men on this earth with the view of having the stronger exert all its energies in exterminating the weaker."[60]

Grant knew that a personal animus against himself, more than antipathy toward his policies, drove many of his adversaries. In August he told a reporter, "The asperities of an election campaign will give my political opponents and my personal enemies an opportunity and an excuse to say all that can be said against me," and "that opportunity I do not grudge them." He was anxious not only to see "whether the republican party, whose choice I again happen to be, is to have its policy sustained or not." He also wanted to "know whether the majority of my fellow citizens were willing to aid my enemies in fastening slanders upon me." "The severest test I have had to undergo," he confided to a friend, "has been slanderous and false abuse with hands and tongue tied. I do hope this mode of warfare will end soon."[61]

Part of that warfare amounted to a whispering campaign alleging that Grant abused alcohol after becoming president. That he served and partook of wine in the White House is easily documented, but scandalmongers were determined to paint the worst picture. Liberal Republican congressman George Julian of Indiana told his constituents that he had "seen Grant drunk on the streets since he has been Pres[iden]t." According to another story, "President Grant was so drunk at Rawlins' funeral that Mrs. Rawlins noticed it." Grant, of course, could not respond, but others did. Fish told correspondents that while "I have been much with him, at all hours of the day and night, . . . I have never seen him in the most remote degree under any excitement from wine or drink of any kind . . . [and] his use of wine is as moderate and proper as that of a gentleman need be." Henry Wilson, a teetotaler who regretted that the president drank at all, issued a public statement that he had seen Grant hundreds of times "in his camp, in his family, at his own table, at the table of others, at home and abroad, and I have never seen him under the influence of liquors." The allegations against Grant lost much of their sting amid press accounts of public intoxication by Liberal vice presidential nominee Brown.[62]

Whitelaw Reid thought a presidential candidate should "keep his mouth absolutely shut from beginning to end," but Greeley relished a public role. Despite much ridicule, he broke with tradition and undertook a speaking tour through Pennsylvania, Ohio, and Indiana before their October state elections. He touched on financial issues and leveled charges of corruption against the administration, but he mainly focused on calls for sectional reconciliation. Although he favored suppressing southern "lawlessness and violence" with "a strong hand," much of what he said carried an unmistakable racial message to white voters. In May he had delivered a stern lecture to an African American audience, asserting that blacks "are inclined to lean on and expect help from other races, beyond what is reasonable and beyond what is wholesome." On the stump, he blamed Republicans for continuing sectional rancor and declared that "the first of all questions is the emancipation of all the White men of the country, so that they shall enjoy equal rights with the Black men of the country. That is the question on which I stand as a candidate." Despite Greeley's previous record as a champion of African Americans, his handling of racial questions during the campaign led Democrat Horatio Seymour to conclude that it had been "wise to put him up . . . as he can be made of use in driving negroes out of office."[63]

Greeley hoped the October elections would boost his chances in November, but the Grant Republicans won them handily. After these victories, Grant likened the Liberal Republicans to the prairie wolves of the West, where two could make enough racket to sound like a hundred. Leaders on both sides had little doubt about November. Grant sent Washburne a state-by-state prediction that turned out to be remarkably accurate, illustrating his grasp of the nation's political profile. Greeley, in contrast, failed to recover from the blow dealt him by the early elections. The grave illness of his wife caused him to suspend his campaign activities, and her death on October 30 sent him into deep despair. A week before the election, Reid observed that Greeley suffered "mental aberration" and his mind was "seriously unbalanced."[64]

Grant trounced Greeley. He racked up 55.6 percent of the popular vote, achieving the largest margin of victory since 1828. As Greeley's own paper put it, "There is scarcely a parallel to the completeness of the rout." Greeley won only six states, all in the former slave South; Grant took the rest of the South, with the exception of Arkansas and Louisiana. Those two states witnessed such outrageous disturbances at election time that Congress refused to receive their electoral votes—auguring the persistence of the troublesome southern question during the president's second term. Grant received 286 electoral votes. Before the electors could cast their votes, Greeley broke down completely, was placed in a "private lunatic asylum," and died on November 29. The president attended his funeral. Three Georgia electors cast their votes for Greeley, while his sixty-three other electors scattered their votes among Brown and others. The election returns confirmed Grant's widespread popularity but also showed that Greeley had been an ineffectual and even repulsive challenger. Some Democrats just stayed home, and in several states, Greeley's totals showed a marked decline over the Democratic vote in 1868. The Democracy lived to fight another day, however, while the outcome pulverized the Liberal Republican Party. Over time, its members slinked back to the Republicans or drifted to the Democrats.[65]

In the crowd at the White House on election night, Admiral David Porter noted that Grant "bore the result in his usual quiet way, but no doubt his heart was glad." To the degree that the contest had been a referendum on sectional and racial issues, African Americans and their white allies believed they had grounds to take heart. Soon after the election, the president received the congratulations of a group of blacks and avowed, "I wish that every man in the United States would stand in all respects alike. It must come. A ticket on a railroad or other conveyance should entitle you to all that it does other men." To the degree that the election was a personal contest, as Sumner and others had tried to make it, the Republican victory was sweet. "The whole fight against you by this 'Unholy Alliance' has been a warfare of scandalous falsehood & personal abuse," Robert Schenck wrote to the president, and the victory "will serve as a crushing, demolishing blow to a most unprincipled coalition, & serve as a lesson for the future against the employment of infamous slander & fraud." At his second inaugural, Grant told his countrymen that from the beginning of the war through his second election, "I have been the subject of abuse and slander scarcely ever equaled in political history, which to-day I feel that I can afford to disregard in view of your verdict, which I gratefully accept as my vindication."[66]

But as events of the second term would show, neither the opponents of Reconstruction nor Grant's personal enemies were willing to lay down their arms.

16

★ ★ ★ ★ ★

SECOND TERM WOES

Reelected presidents have often found their second terms more troubling than their first. Grant proved to be no exception. Despite the aura of triumph that surrounded his victory, he confronted a host of difficulties in the years afterward. Disorder in the South persisted as whites fought to regain control of government and society. Within a year the national economy collapsed into a deep and pervasive depression that outlasted Grant's presidency. Men around the president betrayed his trust, and his critics gave no letup in their excoriation. Although Grant's first term had hardly been free of troubles, they accelerated during his second term and did much to stain his presidency's historical image.

In the short term, however, Grant used his fourth annual message to underscore the successes his campaign had emphasized. Thanks to the outcomes of the Geneva and San Juan arbitrations, for the first time in the nation's history, it had no boundary dispute with Great Britain. Both the national debt and taxation had been reduced, and the economy stood on a sound basis. Grant called for moving toward specie payments, "having due regard for the interests of the debtor class and the vicissitudes of trade and commerce." Noting that internal improvements had been "carried on with energy and economy," he favored further support for enterprises to reduce the cost of transporting products from the interior to the seaboard for export. He also recommended study of the feasibility of a government telegraph. His Indian policy, he claimed, "has been as successful as its most ardent friends anticipated within so short a time."

Grant expressed regret at the continued fighting in Cuba, which he attributed in part to the perpetuation of slavery on the island. He called for legislation to prevent or at least discourage American citizens from owning or dealing in slaves there. As for race relations at home, he deplored the crimes of "reckless and lawless men" in the South and expressed satisfaction that "the prosecution and punishment of many of these persons have tended greatly to the repression of such disorders." He was open to requests for pardons of those convicted but warned, "Any action thereon is not to be construed as indicating any change in my determination to enforce with vigor" the laws against "conspiracies and combinations" that "disturb the peace of the country."

Grant's skepticism about elements of the civil service reform program was evident in an early draft of his message. He feared that competitive examinations did not lead to the "greatest efficiency" and could result in the appointment of "enemies of the Administration to the exclusion of its friends." Instead, he favored a "thorough examination" of an appointee *after* selection. As for promotions, he thought that "no examining board, strangers to the parties appearing before them, can any more determine the fittest man for advancement than they can go into a business establishment and inform the proprietor, by a mental examination of his employees, who are the fittest men for advancement there. With a proper selection of heads of departments the most worthy promotions can be made by selection." But in the final version of the message he left these ideas out. Instead, Grant promised his "earnest endeavor" to apply the rules devised by the Civil Service Commission, noting, however, that only the "direct action of Congress" could make them binding on his successors.[1]

Despite personal misgivings, Grant struck a blow for civil service reform in a wrangle over the Philadelphia postmastership. Soon after his reelection he met with a delegation of Pennsylvania Republicans who favored the appointment of merchant and party stalwart George Truman, not only to reward the state's services in the recent victory but also to unify the state party. Grant refused their request. In keeping with the civil service rules, he decided to promote an official within the post office. The Pennsylvanians groused, but reformers were pleased. As one wrote to Grant, "I have never known an act [to] give such universal satisfaction to all good men of both parties, as this. . . . I feel more proud of our President, and more confident of national reform now than ever before."[2]

U. S. Grant: "I am determined to enforce those regulations." (*Harper's Weekly*, December 7, 1872)

On the same day Grant met with the Pennsylvania group, he accepted the resignation of Solicitor General Benjamin Bristow, who was leaving government service to become a railroad executive. To replace him, Grant selected William Phillips, a North Carolina lawyer who had prosecuted the Klan. By Phillips's appointment, said the *New York Times*, "President Grant has given the country one more proof that civil service reform with him is something more than a pretense." On Bristow's departure, Grant expressed genuine regret and saluted his "zeal and ability." But even though Bristow thanked the president for his "personal and official kindness," privately he harbored less friendly thoughts. "I fear he has not profited much by the lessons which a wise man would draw from the late campaign," Bristow confided to John Harlan. "He is flattered by a set of sycophants & servers into the belief that his personal strengths won the fight; and it has not entered his head that there is any considerable dissatisfaction with the make-up of his Administration." Still, Bristow told Harlan, "my opinion is that he means to avail himself of the grand opportunity that now lies before him to make a great name for himself and to do great good for the country."[3]

At this juncture Grant had an even more important place to fill than Bristow's: a seat on the Supreme Court occasioned by the resignation of Samuel Nelson. Bristow claimed that several of the justices thought Grant should appoint him, but the president had already decided on New Yorker Ward Hunt, an eight-year veteran of the state court of appeals. No one could claim that Hunt was a brilliant jurist, but he had earned a good reputation as a lawyer and a judge. As a longtime friend of Conkling, he easily passed political muster. Fish told the cabinet that Hunt had "joined the Republican party on its first formation & has been unwavering." Shortly after Congress convened in early December for its three-month short session, the Senate confirmed Hunt's nomination.[4]

Even before his second inauguration, the southern question returned to the forefront of Grant's concern, largely because of disputes growing out of the 1872 elections. In Alabama the Republican candidate had won the governorship, but both parties claimed a majority in the legislature and had organized competing bodies. In December Grant and the cabinet approved a solution proposed by Attorney General George Williams, whereby each party would control one house. This proved acceptable to the parties in the state.[5]

Louisiana, however, was much more problematic. In the 1872 election, Republican senator William Kellogg had run for governor against John McEnery, the candidate backed by a coalition of Democrats and dissident Republicans led by retiring governor Henry Clay Warmoth, who had thrown in with the Liberals and Greeley. In a fair election, Kellogg likely would have won, but both sides claimed victory. A volley of fraud allegations, as well as complex legal maneuvering, rendered the outcome deeply obscure. The Kellogg forces turned to US district judge E. H. Durell for help. A Lincoln appointee who in 1867 had ordered the seating of African Americans on federal juries, Durell issued orders sustaining Kellogg's position. In Washington a few days later, Williams advised the president and the cabinet that there could "be no doubt but that the Republicans cast a majority of votes in the late Election" and that the Kellogg legislature was "properly organized according to law & in compliance with the Constitution." That legislature had impeached and suspended Warmoth, and Williams recommended the recognition of Lieutenant Governor P. B. S. Pinchback, an ally of Warmoth's enemies, as acting governor. Pinchback thus became the nation's first black state chief executive. Grant may have inclined toward the Kellogg party anyway, but Durell's official pronouncement left him little choice. The administration ordered the federal marshal to enforce the judge's orders, employing US troops as needed.[6]

The Warmoth-McEnery forces refused to concede, however, and organized their own legislature. They dispatched a delegation to Washington to ask the president to send Supreme Court justice Joseph Bradley and circuit judge William Woods to New Orleans to review Durell's orders. Grant said he had no authority to do so, and he also refused to send a panel of three eminent individuals to investigate the election. "It would," he said, "be dangerous for the President to set the precedent of interfering with the decisions of Courts." The delegation having failed, McEnery proceeded to take the oath of office, and Kellogg's backers inaugurated him as well. Although Grant ordered the War Department to allow the Warmoth-McEnery party to organize a government (though not to legislate), pending the ultimate decision of the courts, Williams advised the federal marshal that the administration's recognition of the Kellogg government "is final, and will be adhered to, unless Congress otherwise provides."[7]

Indeed, Grant was eager to have Congress weigh in, but the Republicans were fragmented. In the House, some argued that Louisiana's muddle was a state problem to be handled by state courts. Others saw a federal role based on the Constitution's clause guaranteeing each state a republican form of government. In the end, the House did no more than authorize further study. In the Senate, a committee investigation uncovered widespread fraud in the election, but its members could not agree on a response. Some advocated recognizing Kellogg, while others favored McEnery. Wisconsin's Matt Carpenter sponsored a bill for a new election in the state.[8]

For some time, Grant had been planning a spring goodwill tour through several southern states, including Louisiana. By late February, however, with no satisfactory resolution of Louisiana's troubles in sight, he canceled the trip. He had received several letters indicating that "evil disposed persons" might be "inclined to do harm" to him. Mrs. Grant told Fish that she was "much averse to the President's undertaking the trip," and the cabinet agreed that he should abandon the idea. Instead, he traveled up Capitol Hill to press senators and representatives to coalesce behind some policy, and the next day he sent a special message urging action.[9]

In his February 25, 1873, message, Grant attributed the origin of the "grave complications" in Louisiana to an attempt by election officials controlled by the Warmoth faction (which he did not name) to defeat "the will of a majority." He noted the state supreme court's recognition of the Kellogg faction's election officials and their decision, but he also observed that the recent Senate investigation had revealed so much fraud as to render the election's true outcome doubtful. He therefore urged Congress to devise some "practical way of removing these difficulties by legislation." "I am extremely anxious to avoid any appearance of undue interference in State affairs," he declared, but unless Congress acted, "I shall feel obliged, as far as I can by the exercise of legitimate authority, to put an end to the unhappy controversy which disturbs the peace and prostrates the business of Louisiana, by the recognition and support of that government which is recognized and upheld by the courts of the State"—that is, the Kellogg government.[10]

If Grant hoped to convince Congress to share responsibility with him for fashioning a Louisiana policy, Kellogg's congressional supporters saw the president's message as an incentive to take no action. Oliver Morton described McEnery as an "enemy of the colored people" and argued that Congress should "let the whole business alone" and leave Kellogg in power. The Indiana senator assured Grant that Kellogg headed a legal government and insisted that "the President can do nothing else than recognize the existing government." When Carpenter's bill for a new election came before the Senate, it failed by a vote of 18 to 20. Congress approved no alternative, and Grant stood by Kellogg.[11]

The divisions in Congress over Louisiana reflected broader troubles in the legislature. The lame-duck session of the Forty-Second Congress between the 1872 election and the president's second inauguration demonstrated that Grant's notions of proper government action were much broader than the cramped ideas of many Republicans and nearly all Democrats. Farmers' Granges and other groups had begun to complain bitterly about monopoly control and other abuses by railroads, and Grant saw a possibility for relief in the form of government aid for the construction of alternative modes of transport. But Congress would not go beyond the standard "rivers and harbors" bill, which contained nothing on the scale of the transportation projects Grant envisioned. A Senate committee reported favorably on the advisability of creating a system of postal telegraphy, but no legislation resulted. In a special message, Grant took aim at the practice of polygamy in the Utah territory and asked Congress to close loopholes in the rules governing prosecution against it. The Senate passed a bill, but it died in the House. Congress even dragged its feet on passing legislation to give effect to the fisheries provisions of the Treaty of Washington. Believing that the nation's honor was at stake, Grant made two trips to the Capitol to push the measure and sent a special message urging action in advance of the approaching fishing season. At last, the bill passed the House, and the Senate followed suit two days later.[12]

The legislative lassitude derived in part from the unfolding Crédit Mobilier scandal, which, as one administration official complained, occupied Congress "to the exclusion of everything else." Several years earlier the directors of the Union Pacific Railroad had constituted another company, Crédit Mobilier, to build the railroad's line. Financed by government bonds, the project promised large returns. One of the directors, Representative Oakes Ames of Massachusetts, sold small amounts of the company's stock at bargain prices to some of his associates in Congress, including a few major leaders such as James Garfield, Henry Dawes, and William Kelley. According to press accusations, these transactions were designed to avert an investigation of the company's suspect methods. Ames may have believed he was cultivating friendly attitudes toward the enterprise, but historian Mark Summers, the leading authority on corruption in that period, argues that the recipients of the low-cost stock "were likely innocent of having taken a bribe. Nothing was promised, nothing delivered." The shares were purchases, not gifts; for most of the legislators, the returns amounted to relatively little; and none of them (except Ames) served on the Pacific Railroad Committee, the obvious place to thwart any snooping. But with the public's sensitivity to any insinuation of "corruption," congressional leaders sought to limit the damage and quickly created a special committee to investigate. Some of the accused congressmen issued flat denials, and others tergiversated, but altogether, their performances seemed to confirm the popular notion that so much smoke must mean fire. The committee condemned the fraudulent Crédit Mobilier–Union Pacific relationship, but the House's final action, merely censuring Ames and one colleague, hardly quelled the indignation.[13]

Although these stock transactions occurred before the Grant administration took office and had no direct relationship to it, the involvement of Vice President Schuyler Colfax (who was Speaker of the House at the time) and his successor Henry Wilson proved an embarrassment. Wilson more or less cleared himself with a marginally plausible story that a broker had purchased the stock in Wilson's wife's name, and Wilson had demanded its immediate return. Colfax offered a weak and inconsistent defense that left his credibility in tatters, along with his political career. A motion in the House to instruct the Judiciary Committee to investigate possible impeachment narrowly lost, 105 to 109. Saddened by this turn of events, Grant wrote to the vice president, "I am as satisfied now as I have ever been, of your integrity, patriotism and freedom from the charges imputed as if I knew of my own knowledge your innocence." Grant permitted the distraught Colfax to publish his letter, illustrating his capacity for magnanimity. Still, many agreed with Bristow that if the president "could have been deprived temporarily of the power to wield his pen about the time he wrote the Colfax letter, it would have been better for his reputation."[14]

As the short session wore on, the scandal took its toll. "Little beyond the Appropriations bills seems *really* to engage attention," Fish lamented. "Almost every man on our side of the House that the party has been in the habit of looking up to is smooched," said Bancroft Davis. "This must demoralize the Republicans in the next House, and leave Grant without a strong party that he can depend upon."[15]

Congress did not help matters when it passed legislation raising government salaries. For some time, observers in and out of government had remarked on the inadequate compensation of officials in Washington. The president's pay, $25,000 per year, had not risen since George Washington's day, but its purchasing power had fallen to a quarter of what it had been then. Although the White House had a domestic staff, the president bore the expenses of living and entertaining there. Since taking office, Grant had dipped into his private funds or borrowed money to make up for his insufficient salary. Other officials fared even worse. The salaries of cabinet members ($8,000) and members of Congress ($5,000) were considerably more than the wages of the average American, but they fell short of what most such men could earn in private life. Moreover, congressmen were faced with extraordinary expenses, including maintaining a second residence in Washington, where rents had increased 25 percent since the war. Their expenses rose even higher in January when Grant signed legislation abolishing the franking privilege.[16]

As a remedy, Ben Butler introduced a bill to raise the president's salary to $50,000 and that of cabinet members to $10,000. Supreme Court justices' salaries would also increase. For members of Congress, Butler proposed raising salaries to $8,000 and replacing the standard mileage allotment with reimbursement for actual travel expenses. The project to increase executive and judicial pay met general approval, but Butler's proposal for a congressional pay raise sparked a firestorm, largely because it included a provision that would make it retroactive for the current Congress that was about to expire. The House at first rejected the plan, but Butler maneuvered it into the general appropriations bill, putting the new pay for Congress members at $7,500 but retaining the retroactive feature. The spending bill, with Butler's amendment, passed during the last hours of the session. Grant would get his deserved raise, though it was tainted by Butler's misbegotten scheme.[17]

The Republican Party paid a heavy political price for the so-called Salary Grab. From Paris, Elihu Washburne wrote that Congress was "simply a gang of thieves. . . . What a pity the President did not veto the salary steal." But blocking the general appropriations bill to kill the salary rider would have left all three branches of the government unfunded and would have required Grant to call the new Forty-Third Congress into special session to begin the appropriations process all over again. A veto was thus out of the question, but that conclusion did little to stem the political damage. An early test came in the spring election in Connecticut, where Congressman Henry Starkweather found that "the feeling brought out against Congress by the 'Salary Steal,' as it is called, is very bitter, and some of our best Republicans will refuse to vote." Starkweather had voted against Butler's bill and managed to hang on to his seat by a reduced vote, but the Republican candidate for governor lost by a sizable margin.[18]

The lame-duck session of the Forty-Second Congress poisoned public confidence not only in that institution but also in government generally. "I sometimes fear that public virtue has utterly died out in the country," wrote Washburne. Episodes like the Crédit Mobilier scandal and the Salary Grab undermined support for perfectly legitimate government activity and turned citizens against useful aids to enterprise, such as land grants to railroads and steamship subsidies to revive the merchant marine. Moreover, at the very time these dramatic events were unfolding in Congress, Mark Twain and Charles Dudley Warner were racing to finish their novel *The Gilded Age: A Tale of Today*, satirizing what seemed to be rampant corruption and misrule. In the book, Crédit Mobilier ringleader Oakes Ames appears as Mr. Fairoaks, and revelations that Kansas senator Samuel Pomeroy tried (unsuccessfully) to bribe his way to reelection inspired the portrait of the corrupt Senator Abner Dilworthy. Later observers seized on the title of Twain and Warner's pasquinade of one particular moment as a label for the entire period and carelessly equated the "Grant Era" with the "Gilded Age." But some contemporary observers drew finer distinctions and saw Grant and his administration's agenda as victims of congressional misbehavior. It was hard, Fish lamented, to rely on "half-hearted professing supporters (suffering under the cloud of impending suspicion) to carry the measures of a Government." "Congress and the party it represents have forfeited public confidence," the *New York Herald* editorialized on the morning of Grant's second inauguration, "but the people still trust and honor the soldier President and look to him to redeem the national character from the stain left upon it by their dishonored representatives."[19]

Grant used his second inaugural address on March 4, 1873, to point his countrymen's vision to a higher plane. Noting that when he entered office the nation was still suffering from "the effects of a great internal revolution," he cited his four years' "effort to restore harmony, public credit, commerce, and all the arts of peace and progress." "It is my firm conviction," he added, "that the civilized world is tending toward republicanism, or government by the people through their chosen representatives, and that our own great Republic is destined to be the guiding star to all others." In a veiled response to critics who had accused him of militarism, he said, "Under our Republic we support an army less than that of any European power of any standing." To those who had criticized his absences from Washington, he asserted, "The theory of government changes with general progress"; with the advent of the telegraph and railroad, "all parts of a continent are made contiguous for all purposes of government."

In addition, Grant sought to convey the message that sectional harmony and defense of blacks' rights need not be incompatible, and he especially appealed to white Americans to rise above their racial prejudices:

> The effects of the late civil strife have been to free the slave and make him a citizen. Yet he is not possessed of the civil rights which citizenship should carry with it. This is wrong, and should be corrected. To this correction, I stand committed, so far as Executive influence can avail.

Social equality is not a subject to be legislated upon, nor shall I ask
that anything be done to advance the social status of the colored man,
except to give him a fair chance to develop what there is good in him,
give him access to the schools, and when he travels let him feel assured
that his conduct will regulate the treatment and fare he will receive.

Perhaps crossing his fingers, the president said that the former rebellious states "are now happily rehabilitated." He added, "No executive
control is exercised in any one of them that would not be exercised in
any other State under like circumstances."

Grant stated that he still believed the annexation of Santo Domingo
would have been in the "best interest" of the United States and of the
Dominicans, but he had not pushed it since the rejection of the treaty.
He dismissed the idea that governments became "weakened and destroyed" when they extended their territory. "Commerce, education,
and rapid transit" aided by the telegraph and the railroad had "changed
all this." In a flight of fancy, he added, "Rather do I believe that our
Great Maker is preparing the World, in His own good time, to become
one nation, speaking one language, and when armies and navies will be
no longer required."

The president touched briefly on several policies and goals he had
long favored: specie resumption, internal improvements to enhance
commerce, revival of the merchant marine, encouragement of manufacturing, and elevation of labor. He gave special attention to the plight
of the Indians, posing a stark choice between "the benign influences of
education and civilization" and "wars of extermination" that "are de-
moralizing and wicked":

> Our superiority of strength and advantages of civilization should
> make us lenient toward the Indian. The wrong inflicted upon him
> should be taken into account and the balance placed to his credit. The
> moral view of the question should be considered and the question
> asked, Can not the Indian be made a useful and productive member
> of society by proper teaching and treatment? If the effort is made in
> good faith, we will stand better before the civilized nations of the
> earth and in our own consciences for having made it.

In a more tepid passage, Grant said his efforts in behalf of civil service reform "shall be continued to the best of my judgment. The spirit of
the rules adopted will be maintained."[20]

Reaction to the second inaugural address followed the partisan lines that had hardened during the 1872 campaign. The *New York Tribune* called the speech "the utterance of a man of the best intentions profoundly desirous to govern wisely and justly, and profoundly ignorant of the means by which good government is secured." The *Washington National Republican*, in contrast, hailed it as "a broad, comprehensive summary of the needs of the present and of the future." But Grant's expansive notions about government action to meet those needs did not sit well with many observers, including some of his supporters. The *New York Times* took issue with "his belief that the National Government ought to do sundry things usually committed to individual enterprise." "In a man of less perfect self-restraint, and less complete subordination to what he clearly discerns to be the common sense of the people, such opinions might be dangerous."[21]

Whatever Grant's fellow Americans thought of his inaugural address, the onrush of events soon captured public attention and challenged many of his policies. The next day an outbreak of fighting in New Orleans belied his roseate assertion that the southern states were "happily rehabilitated." Militia units of Democratic gubernatorial claimant John McEnery, aided by a mob of several hundred, stormed police stations in the city, including the arsenal in an old colonial building known as the Cabildo. Grant ordered US forces on the scene to "prevent any violent interference with the state Government." The pro-Kellogg metropolitan police fought back and, with the salutary presence of US troops, forced the mob to disperse. The Kellogg police arrested several members of the McEnery legislature, effectively shutting down that faction's pretended state government.[22]

Although the "Battle of the Cabildo" was brief, it illustrated the persistent defiance of the South's white supremacists. They were determined to retake control and looked forward to the time when northern public opinion would no longer sustain federal intervention on behalf of blacks' rights. The *New York Tribune* helped hasten that day when, in late March 1873, it launched a series of openly racist articles by James Pike, condemning the Reconstruction government of the "prostrate state" of South Carolina. Pike had explored South Carolina firsthand, but as his biographer notes, his "desire to damn Grant and the Radicals led him to distort his own findings." Although his articles bore a patina of journalistic impartiality, they betrayed his extreme racism. Pike described black legislators as "the dregs of the population habilitated in the robes of their intelligent predecessors, and asserting over them the rule of ignorance and corruption." This portrait powerfully affected northern attitudes. The *Tribune* expressed the hope that with the South's future in the hands of its young white men, "the day of redemption is not far distant."[23]

Two weeks after the publication of Pike's first article, white supremacists in Louisiana perpetrated one of the worst instances of violence during the Reconstruction era. The drama unfolded in the remote town of Colfax in Grant Parish, situated about 220 miles northwest of New Orleans. Although Governor Kellogg had unhorsed McEnery's forces in New Orleans, the Democrat's adherents in the countryside remained determined to retake local governments. For weeks, Grant Parish had witnessed rising tension between rival claimants for parish offices. The crisis came on Easter Sunday, April 13, when upwards of 100 blacks who were holed up in the makeshift courthouse in Colfax were set upon by about 140 whites led by the Democratic would-be sheriff, C. C. Nash. After the two sides exchanged shots for a few hours, the whites set the courthouse ablaze. As most of the blacks fled, whites mowed them down. Nash and his men took three or four dozen prisoners but later shot these captives as well, killing three-quarters of them. All told, scores of blacks lost their lives. Two deputy US marshals, whom Kellogg had sent to arrest the Democratic pretenders to office, did not arrive until two days later, when they discovered the ghastly carnage.[24]

When the news reached Washington, Grant was preparing for an extended tour of the West. Although he maintained contact via telegraph, he relied heavily on his cabinet officers in Washington to frame the administration's response. The Justice Department dispatched an undercover agent who mingled among whites in Grant Parish and gathered an abundance of incriminating material. Eventually the government brought indictments against ninety-eight alleged perpetrators, tried nine, and convicted three. Appeals in the case ultimately led to the Supreme Court's decision in *United States v. Cruikshank* (1876), which profoundly affected the course of Reconstruction. In the immediate wake of the massacre, whites threatened violence in other parts of the state, and the War Department and army commanders on the scene dispatched troops to the affected areas. When Grant returned to Washington, he met with Attorney General Williams, approved his "aggressive movement," and vowed to "sustain everything done to preserve law and order in Louisiana, even to the limit of the federal forces." An inflammatory speech in New Orleans by Wisconsin senator Matt Carpenter, who had denied the Kellogg government's legitimacy and called for a new election, encouraged the governor's enemies and heightened tensions in the state, leading Kellogg to step up his calls for federal help. Grant responded on May 22 with a strongly worded proclamation reminiscent of the one he had issued before suspending the writ of habeas corpus in South Carolina.[25]

In his proclamation, Grant noted that the judicial authorities of Louisiana had upheld Kellogg and his associates as the legal officeholders in the state and that Congress, "by refusing to take any action," had "tacitly recognized" them as well. Citing both the Constitution's guarantee clause and federal legislation, he asserted his power to use the armed forces to suppress insurrection and protect the state's citizens from domestic violence. He enjoined the disorderly persons to disperse and return to their homes. Grant made it clear that he would use force to keep Kellogg in power, and a shaky peace ensued. But he had not convinced the McEnery forces of Kellogg's legitimacy. Although direct challenges to the governor subsided, guerrilla warfare continued in rural areas, and Kellogg's opponents simply waited for a more opportune moment to strike.[26]

Around the time of the Colfax massacre, another violent episode involving the Modoc Indians weakened support for Grant's peace policy, which was already tenuous in the minds of many. The Modocs were a small tribe whose ancestral home lay around Lake Tule, near the Oregon-California border. To please ranchers who coveted the tribe's grasslands, the government had struck a treaty with the Modocs in 1864 that called for their relocation to a reservation twenty-five miles north. Forced to share this reservation with another, more numerous tribe, the Modocs grew dissatisfied. Before long, one of their leaders, Kintpuash—called Captain Jack by whites—led a contingent of Modocs back to their home. Grant's superintendent of Indian affairs for Oregon, Albert Meacham, sympathized with the Modocs and persuaded them to go back to the reservation, but they soon returned to Lake Tule. Finally, in November 1872, the army moved against them, opening what became known as the Modoc War. The army did not have an easy time, despite its vastly superior numbers. After several weeks, Grant and Secretary of the Interior Columbus Delano appointed a negotiating team headed by Meacham and including General Edward Canby, commander of the army's Department of the Columbia. On orders from Washington, Canby ceased hostile operations pending the talks, but impatient Modoc leaders pushed Kintpuash to a desperate act. At a negotiation session on April 11, 1873, he suddenly arose and murdered Canby and another white. Meacham, partly scalped, lived to recount the horror.[27]

Canby's brutal murder stirred his comrades' wrath. Sherman wired General Alvin Gillem, commander of US forces at the scene, and told him that, in light of the "perfidy" of the Modocs, the president had authorized him to order Gillem to respond with an "attack so strong and persistent that their fate may be commensurate with their crime. You will be fully justified in their utter extermination." Opponents of the peace policy hailed Sherman's telegram. But supporters urged Grant not to let the Modoc episode become an excuse for ending the humanitarian policy. The president, of course, could not sanction Sherman's call for extermination and instead adopted a balanced approach. He told a reporter, "The peace policy, which has been abused and condemned, strictly provides for the stern punishment of Indians when circumstances warrant it; but innocent tribes should not be visited with punishment on account of the treachery of some particular one, nor should the peace policy entire be pronounced against for failure in this singular instance."[28]

With the support of the administration and the public at large, the army struck decisively, and the outnumbered Modocs soon surrendered. In July a military commission tried Captain Jack and five others, who had no legal counsel and little understanding of the proceedings. All were convicted and sentenced to death. Before approving the executions, however, Grant ordered a panel in Washington to review the court-martial. Although the panel found no irregularities in the proceedings, the president commuted the sentences of two men who had been subordinates to life in prison. In October, Captain Jack and three others were executed. The remaining Modocs, numbering fewer than 200, were relocated several hundred miles eastward; their tribal relations were broken up, and their members were distributed among other Indians. Grant hoped the public would view the episode as the exception that proved the rule regarding the viability of his peace policy. Even so, the horrific Modoc affair nourished growing skepticism about that policy's ultimate success.[29]

The onset of Grant's second term brought a blow to yet another of his important policy initiatives when, two weeks after the inauguration, a disagreement with George Curtis led to his resignation as chairman of the Civil Service Commission. Grant had maintained a good working relationship with the commission since its creation and had occasionally met with the body to discuss further elaboration of the rules. In late January 1873 the president nominated James Benedict to be surveyor of customs in New York. Benedict had been a deputy in the office, and his promotion was entirely in keeping with the rules. But he failed to pass muster with Republican Party leaders in the state. His prospects for Senate confirmation soon became dim, and Grant withdrew his name to spare him a rejection. In an attempt to reconcile party regulars and reformers, Grant appointed a three-person committee consisting of Curtis, customs collector Chester Arthur, and anti–Tweed Ring reformer Jackson Schultz to advise him as to a new nominee for surveyor. Just at this time, Curtis suffered a month-long illness, and the ad hoc committee never met to deliberate. Finally, Grant turned to someone whose abilities he knew firsthand and nominated George Sharpe, then serving as US marshal for the southern district of New York. A graduate of Rutgers who had studied law at Yale, Sharpe had served on Grant's staff in the army. As marshal, he had conducted a census in his district that helped defeat election frauds perpetrated by the Tweed Ring. A committed Republican, Sharpe had, despite holding an important federal office, worked hard for Grant's reelection.[30]

Sharpe's nomination shocked Curtis, who took Grant's failure to consult him while he was ill as a personal affront. He wrote (or inspired) an anonymous letter to the *New York Tribune* asserting, "Men do not willingly consent to be thus publicly—shall I say snubbed? or would a stronger word be more appropriate?" Curtis informed Grant that he was resigning as commissioner because "the circumstances under which several important appointments have been recently made seem to me to show an abandonment both of the spirit and letter of the Civil Service regulations." In a terse reply, Grant said, "I regret your resignation, especially the grounds upon which you base it, but must accept it."[31]

Curtis's departure gave the administration a black eye, and reformers pounced. The *Nation* observed that Grant "does not understand what civil-service reform or reform of any kind means." In fact, Grant well understood the place of civil service reform in American politics, and he knew that to inch the new system forward, he could not go too far beyond what the regular politicians, who dominated Congress, were willing to accept. The president had misgivings, but he understood that his own position lay between two groups that not merely espoused irreconcilable views but also held each other in deep contempt. Over the years, he had taken abuse from both sides, though much more from the reformers than from the politicians. Nonetheless, he stuck by his commitment to reform. Two weeks after Curtis left, commission member Joseph Medill resigned to serve as mayor of Chicago, and Grant assured him that "the spirit of the rules adopted will be maintained."[32]

Grant demonstrated his continuing support through the new members he appointed. To replace Medill he chose former Ohio congressman Samuel Shellabarger, a strong advocate of civil service reform. For Curtis's position he selected New Yorker Dorman Eaton, who had battled the Tweed Ring and others. Like many of his fellow reformers who disclaimed ambition while craving office, Eaton pushed himself forward for Curtis's job and used his connections to help him get it. As soon as he heard of the chairman's resignation, Eaton wrote three letters in four days to his former law partner, J. C. Bancroft Davis, to signal his availability. "You know," he told Davis, "I am not an office seeker & would not do any compromising thing to get the high place. But if the president chooses to place me on the Civil Service Board, I think I should find some satisfaction in discharging the duties there in a way he would approve." Eaton even managed to sit near Grant at a dinner in New York to further his cause. Davis advocated Eaton, and he secured the nomination. Afterward, Eaton wrote that his "unsolicited appointment" demonstrated "the sincerity, independence, & honor of the president."[33]

Such self-promotion notwithstanding, Eaton, like Grant, had a clearer appreciation of the political difficulties attending the reform effort than did immediatists like Curtis and E. L. Godkin. He emphasized the importance of cultivating more favorable public opinion based on "a sensible & cautious administration of the rules." Grant told Eaton and Shellabarger that "the greatest evil" in the patronage system was "the interference of members of Congress in the dictation of appointments." In late May 1873 he organized the first of several meetings between the newly constituted board and the cabinet, resulting in a new set of rules that Grant promulgated on August 5. These rules stipulated that a recommendation letter from a congressman or senator, unless specifically requested by an appointing officer, should have no more weight than one from a private individual. Moreover, recommendations from whatever source must be in writing. The rules also disallowed firing an officeholder merely to open a place for someone else. Grant promised that the new rules would be "enforced as rapidly as the proper arrangements can be made." Even Godkin's *Nation* conceded, "All the proposed regulations must be admitted to be useful, and calculated to give greater strength and sincerity to the reform."[34]

Less than two months after Curtis's resignation came news of the death of Chief Justice Salmon P. Chase, presenting the president with the single most important appointment decision of his entire eight years. Grant shed no tears over Chase's passing. Infected with an almost pathological ambition for the presidency, the chief justice had yearned—and angled—for a nomination against Grant in 1868 and again in 1872, despite ill health. His behavior as presiding judge at the Johnson impeachment trial had subverted the Republicans' case; his opinion in the *Legal Tender Cases*, Grant believed, had jeopardized the administration's financial policy and threatened the nation's economy; and on southern issues, Chase had drifted toward the Democrats. Upon his death, Fish drafted the customary presidential announcement, which Bancroft Davis submitted to the president for his approval. Grant read it and then took out a pencil and replaced the phrase "eminent purity and usefulness" with "long public service." He also bridled at another of Fish's passages: "Fidelity of purpose, earnestness of conviction, ability of the highest order, broad philanthropy, untiring industry and devotion to the public good, marked the life of the late Chief Justice." The president struck out this entire sentence and told Davis, "I can't quite go that." The excision was a petty act, but Grant saw little reason to unduly exalt in death a man whose official behavior had, he believed, largely forfeited his countrymen's respect.[35]

In one sense, Grant would have been delighted if the chief justice had outlived his administration, for he dreaded being "badgered by applicants & their friends." George Boutwell thought the president should "give the country a thorough and tried republican," arguing, "if we believe in our principles we should see to it that they are sustained by the courts rather than the principles of our enemies." Grant agreed, but finding the right person would not be easy. Fortunately, he had ample time to look because both Congress and the Court would be out of session for several months.[36]

Chase's body was barely cold before the press began speculating about his replacement, and aspirants started a frantic game of musical chairs to get his seat on the bench. New York lawyer Edwards Pierrepont had long coveted a Washington appointment and suggested himself, but Grant did not consider him big enough for the place. Associate Justice Noah Swayne hatched a plan whereby he would move up to chief justice and Grant would tap Bristow for his vacated seat. Despite his respect for both men, Grant was cool to the idea, not least because he feared the sixty-eight-year-old Swayne would leave the post before the end of his administration and force him to go through the whole process again. The president gave less thought than the newspapers did to the idea of appointing former attorney general E. Rockwood Hoar and none at all to William Evarts, who had served on the Geneva legal team but had also defended Johnson at his impeachment trial. Julia Grant later claimed that she was an early supporter of Roscoe Conkling. By the end of July, the president's former secretary Horace Porter was telling friends that New Yorker Conkling was the man. Nonetheless, Grant would not be rushed. In September the nation suffered a major economic crisis that demanded his attention, and he decided to let the Court matter gestate until nearer the time when Congress convened.[37]

Before that economic crisis struck, Grant could console himself that, despite the sea of troubles besetting his second term, at least the nation was enjoying substantial prosperity. Three years of good harvests and reasonable prices for farmers, good wages and nearly full employment for labor, and high returns on investments for businessmen had fostered a sense of contentment that helped Grant win a second term. In his latest annual message he had congratulated Americans for being blessed with "a general prosperity vouchsafed to but few peoples."[38]

Since taking office, Grant and Boutwell had followed a policy to keep the economy, especially the money market, on an even keel. Even so, Boutwell was one of the cabinet's more controversial figures. While most political leaders called for a speedy return to specie payments, Boutwell, with Grant's blessing, wished to avoid rushing toward that goal prematurely. Instead, he favored a policy of "growing up" to resumption, that is, delaying an official return to specie payments until such time as business and trade had expanded enough to increase the demand for currency and bring greenbacks up to par with gold. Boutwell understood that, along the way, various circumstances could cause disturbances in the money market. He believed the Treasury Department, in the absence of any other effective agency, should act like a central bank to counteract those disturbances. On such occasions he would use surplus funds to buy government bonds and thus infuse the economy with needed cash. "A degree of flexibility in the volume of the currency is essential," Boutwell maintained. "This is a necessary work, and inasmuch as it cannot be confided to the banks, where, but in the Treasury Department, can the power be reposed?" Such forward-looking notions scandalized orthodox economic thinkers, such as Senate

Finance Committee chairman John Sherman, who held sway in the Republican Party.[39]

Sherman and other conservatives took particular exception to the Treasury's issuing $5 million in greenbacks during the harvest season in the weeks before the 1872 election. In Boutwell's absence, but with his approval, Assistant Secretary William Richardson conducted the transaction. He used notes from what he and Boutwell called the Treasury's "reserve"—the $44 million in greenbacks that represented the difference between the maximum authorized by wartime legislation ($400 million) and the amount in circulation when Congress halted contraction of the paper currency in 1868 ($356 million). Boutwell defended the $5 million infusion as not only legal but also necessary for "the relief of the business of the country." But Sherman disagreed and launched a Finance Committee investigation. Within a week, a majority of the committee had denied the Treasury's authority to take such action and warned that issuance of the whole $44 million would disturb the value of property and contracts. Two Republicans on the committee upheld the secretary's power to issue the notes "to meet any emergency or exigency in the money-market or trade of the country." But Sherman proceeded to offer a resolution declaring that the Treasury had no power under existing law to conduct such operations. Although the resolution had no chance of passage, the press reported that Grant was "insulted" by this attempt to "encroach on the Executive duties and rights." Administration allies denounced the "meddlesome intrusion" as "a direct insult to the Chief Magistrate," showing that "some Senators have not divested themselves of the arbitrary power which they assumed at the close of the war, in derogation of the Constitution."[40]

Although Sherman's resolution died, the controversy discouraged the Treasury from issuing any more greenbacks from the reserve. In mid-March the press reported Richardson's belief that it would take "a very extraordinary emergency" to induce the Treasury to "expand for the relief of the market." "He believes," said the *New York Herald*, "with the President, that the only way to make bad legislation disagreeable is by enforcing it. The Senate Finance Committee made issue with the Treasury Department for increasing the greenback circulation last fall, and if any hardship should follow from a strict observance of the views expressed in the resolution of the Senate it will not be the fault of the Treasury Department."[41]

Richardson found himself in a delicate spot, for he was looking to take over the top Treasury job from Boutwell. At the beginning of his second term, Grant had renominated his cabinet in order to stop the importunities of prospective applicants who thought he might be contemplating changes. All were promptly confirmed. The one exception was Boutwell, who had taken advantage of Henry Wilson's accession to the vice presidency to move into his Senate seat. In accepting Boutwell's resignation, the president commended him for having "admirably conducted" the nation's financial policy. He expressed the hope that his successor's policy "may be as successful as yours has been, and that no departure from it will be made except such as experience and change of circumstances may make necessary."[42]

Designating a new secretary proved problematic. Many in New York City had hoped that Fish might also resign, opening the way for a representative of the nation's commercial and financial capital to head the Treasury Department. But once again, Grant convinced Fish to stay. Richardson, a graduate of Harvard College and Harvard Law School, had arrived in Washington as Boutwell's protégé from Massachusetts early in the administration. Unlike his chief, he had no previous experience with governmental finance. Indeed, not expecting to stay long, Richardson had retained his lifetime appointment as a probate judge in Massachusetts. But now he was eager to be secretary. Although he had learned much in four years, his candidacy for promotion got a tepid response, even within the administration.[43]

The president initially thought of tapping Richardson for an interim appointment and then transferring another cabinet member permanently to Treasury. But when Boutwell and Fish got wind that Grant might give the job to Columbus Delano, they blanched. John Sherman's enmity for Delano stood in the way, and rumors were floating around Washington that Delano's son, who worked in the Interior Department, was connected with shady dealings. Boutwell argued for Richardson's appointment but confessed to Fish that he would rather see the position go to Attorney General Williams. Richardson begged Fish to intercede on his behalf. He acknowledged that his connection with the issuance of the $5 million in greenbacks counted against him, but he told Fish, perhaps threateningly, that it had not been his idea; "he had done it as a party measure and had borne all the censure and odium of it, and thought he was entitled to recognition and consideration for his services." In addition, Richardson reported that he had been offered a job as head of an American banking house in Paris. He could, he pleaded, resign the Treasury post almost immediately after being appointed, having gained cachet for the banking job. With remarkable restraint at such blatant self-serving, Fish replied that because of the Crédit Mobilier, Salary Grab, and other recent scandals, the Republican Party was "on the defensive and care should be taken to avoid any further subjects of attack."[44]

Finally, Grant decided to appoint Richardson temporarily, believing that he was competent to perform the duties of secretary, especially the negotiations for a new bond issue, which might take several months. Equally important, Grant thought "his nomination would indicate to the country an adherence to the financial policy which had been established and would thereby quiet expectations and efforts towards a change in that policy." Richardson's name went to the Senate with the other cabinet members, and all were sworn in on March 18. Three days later, by way of vindication, Richardson reported to the cabinet that during the half decade since Sherman and others insisted that Congress had frozen the greenback level, the quantity in circulation had in fact "constantly fluctuated sometimes to the amount of several millions in the course of two days." Although Richardson settled into his new job, turmoil in the economy would soon test his—and Grant's—mettle.[45]

As if Grant's second term were not troubled enough, in early July 1873, four months after his inauguration, the *New York Herald* launched a series of articles warning Americans that the president was maneuvering to win a third nomination and election. Congress had left Washington in March, Grant and most of the cabinet had scattered to their various summer retreats, and political news had momentarily dried up. To boost sales, the paper's brash publisher, James Gordon Bennett Jr., pushed the phantasm of Grant's imperial aspirations in scores of articles under double-leaded headlines accusing him of "CAESARISM." The president "is as completely master as was ever Jefferson, Jackson, or Lincoln," claimed the *Herald*. His allies were allegedly scheming for a third term, "which to our mind affects our Republic as gravely as the Republic of Rome was affected when Julius Caesar was offered the crown by subservient Senators. . . . We must meet Caesarism now, not by postponing this question out of deference to the feelings of General Grant, but by meeting it, discussing it, and searching public opinion." Other journals responded, but more often out of wonder than any anxiety for the nation's safety. "The bugbear called 'Caesarism' is rather a sneer than an argument," said *Harper's Weekly*. "Shall we, then, go into hysterics in advance?"[46]

The president largely ignored the tempest stirred up by the *Herald*.

But a month later, the paper itself printed a conversation in which Grant disclaimed any inclination to manage the country's politics to retain power for himself. "The execution of the duties of the office of President," he said, is "quite as much as one man can attend to, and a good deal more than I find agreeable." "Let me see," he went on. "This is August—March to August is five months, and now the newspapers are anxious to know if I am to serve a third term when the second is hardly begun. The way Congress has treated all of my recommendations doesn't make me appear either influential or dangerous." Perhaps only half jokingly he added, "If the newspapers want to know whether I will be renominated why don't they quiz the party that elected me?" Grant's allies scoffed at the Caesarism taunt. As Oliver Morton put it, "He did not save the Republic to destroy it afterwards."[47]

Nonetheless, the *Herald* continued its crusade until mid-September, when a panic struck Wall Street. At that moment of crisis, Americans who craved rather than feared resolute strength in their government turned to see how the Grant administration would react.

17

★ ★ ★ ★ ★

CRISES DOMESTIC AND
FOREIGN

In the years after the Civil War the American economy exhibited phenomenal growth as an integrated capitalist system burgeoned. Although the South lagged behind, during the five years prior to 1873, the economy hummed along at a prosperous clip, marked by substantial railroad building, expanding manufactures, and increased agricultural production. Linking the various elements together was a monetary system comprising coin, greenbacks, national bank notes, and government securities—mainly bonds representing the war debt of more than $2 billion. Debt pervaded the private sector as well, for many of the new enterprises, especially railroad construction, proceeded on borrowed money. As the debate over Boutwell's greenback operations had shown, orthodox economic thinking assigned a limited role to government. Most mainline politicians thought its principal responsibility in managing the money supply was to ensure a "sound" currency and otherwise keep its hands off. George Bancroft beseeched his nephew J. C. Bancroft Davis in June 1873, "Pray use your influence *not* to let one dollar more of paper money be issued; & to get back to the currency of the Constitution as soon as possible." The aptness of such orthodoxy for the new age of capital met its first great test in the financial panic that struck in September 1873.[1]

Prior to September, confidence in continued good times persisted for most of the summer. Few observers saw much to worry about when

419

the Brooklyn Trust Company could not meet its obligations and closed its doors in July. Although the firm's loss had little wider impact, its failure proved symptomatic of a larger problem. This bank, like many others, had overextended itself in financing railroad construction, much of which pushed into areas where only marginal demand existed. Although such investment bespoke confidence, the return on railroad securities came slowly. Many financial institutions sacrificed credit flexibility by converting much of their liquid capital into fixed railroad capital with an uncertain payoff. For some time, American banks had been placing a large portion of their railroad bonds with European investors, but a panic on the Vienna stock exchange in May drastically curtailed the overseas market for those securities. American banks struggled to carry more of the bonds themselves, severely straining their own credit.[2]

These developments made little impression, however, and did not occasion an immediate response from the government. Secretary of the Treasury William Richardson expected the usual tightening of the money market during the fall harvest season and had used gold sales during the summer to raise $14 million to help relieve the strain through the purchase of government bonds. In late August Richardson wrote to Grant at Long Branch, noting that he considered this accumulation sufficient "to keep the currency balance strong, preparatory to the autumn business." The secretary had also made a comparison of the country's commerce during the present year with that during previous years and reported that he was "very much pleased at the favorable exhibit." Exports had increased dramatically, the Treasury's coin holdings had increased, and the government was running a budget surplus. "The Department and the Department business are very quiet," he assured the president.[3]

The quiet did not last. In early September money grew tight, bank reserves in New York fell, and two more institutions that were heavily invested in railroads failed. On September 17 stocks on the New York exchange took a tumble, and the next day disaster struck. The highly respected banking house of Jay Cooke and Company, heavily encumbered by Northern Pacific securities that it could not unload, collapsed and closed its doors. The storied institution had gained its reputation largely from marketing government bonds during the war. Shuttering its offices crippled confidence in banks generally, and panic reverberated across the land. People scrambled to withdraw their deposits and hoarded their cash, adding to the currency stringency. In Cincinnati, John Sherman "saw men going around the city almost crazy with fright, bankers, wealthy men, because they said they had their money tied up in New York." The New York Clearing House devised a plan whereby banks could help endangered institutions by sharing their currency reserves. To halt the implosion of stock prices, the stock exchange closed for ten days.[4]

While bankers and other interests struggled to save themselves, calls for government assistance poured in. "Relief must come immediately," former customs collector Thomas Murphy pleaded, "or hundreds if not thousands of our best men will be ruined." Grant was attending a veterans' reunion in Pittsburgh when Cooke collapsed. He kept in touch with Richardson by telegraph, and late on September 19 Grant ordered the secretary to buy $10 million in bonds. Richardson acted immediately, using greenbacks he had accumulated during the summer to assist the fall crop movement. Hamilton Fish, deeply conservative on money matters, fretted that Richardson would give in to the clamor and "be weak enough to interpose" in the crisis. "By all means," he wired his colleague, "I trust you will not issue more greenbacks. Such is the desire of the soundest thinking people."[5]

Two days after the Cooke collapse, Grant headed to New York, not only to demonstrate his concern but also to outline the limits of what the government could do. On Sunday, September 21, he and Richardson found themselves besieged by bankers and others praying for further action. Several argued that the Treasury should issue $20 million to strapped banks from the greenback reserve in exchange for clearinghouse certificates or, alternatively, place funds in the banks as federal depositories, which could distribute the money at their discretion. Grant and Richardson rejected both these loan propositions as inexpedient and illegal. They reminded the group that in the last session of Congress a majority of the Senate Finance Committee had declared that the president had no legal authority to use the reserve for such a purpose. Grant indicated, however, that the reserve could be tapped in the event of a shortage of regular revenue to pay the government's own bills. He aimed to have the government do what it could to ease the crisis, but any action must conform to the law, and he could not sanction the New Yorkers' loan proposals. Before the meeting closed, the bankers asked Grant and Richardson to visit the subtreasury the next day to observe the situation. Grant agreed, but Richardson convinced him of the inadvisability of putting in an appearance on Wall Street, and the two left for Washington.[6]

Fish assured Richardson that everyone except stock speculators

Uncle Sam: "Look out, boys, they say he's a Caesar (seizer)." (*Harper's Weekly*, October 11, 1873)

hoped "that you will adhere to the policy of non-expansion. It may be a severe remedy, but severe cases require severe remedies." The Republican *New York Times* echoed that view: "The idea that there is a duty imposed upon the President, or on the Government, as it is generally put, to protect the public against the consequences of even such an extraordinary event as the panic, is not an idea consistent with the principles of our Government."[7]

Nonetheless, back in the capital, Grant and Richardson sent another $20 million in greenbacks to New York and ordered the assistant treasurer to buy all government bonds offered. Richardson later claimed that "the currency paid out of the Treasury for bonds did much to strengthen many savings banks, and to prevent panic among their numerous depositors." Yet, he noted, "it became evident that the amount [of bonds] offering for purchase was increasing to an extent beyond the power of the Treasury to accept." He advised Grant that he did not think it "well to undertake to furnish from the Treasury all the money that frenzied people may call for." With the president's assent he stopped the purchases on September 24. Still, Grant made no apology for the bond purchases that had already occurred. In a press interview he defended the action as "not so much real as moral." The banks had "become stampeded." "Had not the Treasury seemed to aid them in some way, the fright would have become more general and the consequence to the country more fatal."[8]

Not all members of the cabinet shared Fish's flinty conservatism. Columbus Delano, a former Ohio congressman who was sensitive to distress in the West, urged "a very wide expansion and general inflation." Orville Babcock, who had heard the complaints of businessmen with Grant and Richardson in New York, backed up Delano. Grant himself was not convinced that the administration was doing all it could to ease the crisis. Only with "great difficulty," Fish said, could Richardson and Williams "restrain" the president and persuade him to issue a balanced statement of policy.[9]

On September 27 Grant did so in a public letter to two New York businessmen. He asserted that "the first thing needed to relieve this condition" was a restoration of "confidence on the part of the people." The government was "willing to take all legal measures at its command," but he called for the "active co-operation of the banks and moneyed associations." With the money the Treasury had already paid out to purchase bonds, coupled with the banks' withdrawal of large deposits from the Treasury, he considered the banks "now strong enough to adopt a liberal policy on their part, and by a generous system of discounts, to sustain the business interests of the country." Should the banks do their part, he added, the $44 million in reserve funds would serve as a fallback, available to "meet the demands of the public necessity as the circumstances of the country may require." In the meantime, the Treasury would make a small infusion through an early disbursement of the November interest payments on its bonds.[10]

The "public necessity" arrived shortly, for the impact of the panic soon affected the government's own balance sheet. Revenue receipts lagged in October, and the price of gold had fallen so low that the Treasury could not easily sell from its stocks to raise currency. Any failure to meet the government's obligations would have wreaked havoc with its credit. Hence, Richardson started tapping the greenback reserve to pay the government's normal expenses and other debts. Although he had refused to sanction using the reserve for the purposes proposed by the New York bankers, Richardson defended the present action as perfectly legal, despite the Senate Finance Committee's attitude the previous winter. "Where would the government be now," he asked one reporter, "if Senator Sherman's theory had been carried out?" Nonetheless, the conservatives in the cabinet warned against going too far. To allay the anxieties of hard-money interests, Richardson agreed to issue a statement that he would take greenbacks from the reserve to meet only the necessary expenses of the government. By early January, the reissue of the notes amounted to $26 million, more than half the reserve.[11]

Inevitably, the panic sent a temblor across the political landscape. Ten days before Cooke fell, the Republicans in Maine carried a state election by a large majority, prompting the *New York Times* to assert, "The Democratic party is breaking up." But reports of the Democracy's demise proved greatly exaggerated. Six weeks after the panic began, Oliver Morton wrote, "Men are everywhere being thrown out of employment; wages are reduced; . . . men who have money will neither lend it nor invest it nor deposit it in the banks. The political consequences are as immediate & direct as any other. One of them was the loss of Ohio [in October], & there was a very greatly reduced majority in Iowa, with a very fair prospect now of losing New York & Virginia next week." The Republicans did indeed lose New York and Virginia, as well as the governorship in normally reliable Wisconsin. "The bulk of the people will follow their instinct in such matters," the *Times* now said, "and their instinct leads them just now to believe the Democratic cry that the Republican Party is responsible for the panic."[12]

The political turmoil intensified the pressure on the administration. Buffeted by currency expansionists and by hard-money enthusiasts, Grant made pronouncements that showed his views remained inchoate—a state of mind that was not unusual, given the primitive economic thinking of the time. Men like Fish believed that government should do virtually nothing and simply let the supposed natural economic laws take their course until the country righted itself. Grant had no training and little experience in economic matters, but his instincts told him the government should try to ameliorate the nation's troubles. He lamented the monetary system's lack of "elasticity"; indeed, he took some consolation that the panic might at least "lead to legislation to relieve the want of elasticity." In the short term, he again admonished bankers to cooperate. "Cannot the Bank Presidents," he wrote to John Williams, president of New York's Metropolitan Bank, "be brought together and resolve to aid each other, and the business interests generally?" Williams took the president's letter to a meeting of the New York Clearing House Association, where the assembled bankers, many of whom favored more active government intervention in the form of relief from the reserve, were unimpressed. They merely thanked the president for his "best wishes" and said they would act in the "spirit" of his recommendation.[13]

For the longer term, Grant was open to considering structural changes in the monetary system to ease its rigidity. Postmaster General John A. J. Creswell argued for the creation of a postal savings bank system, which could help avert panics of the type just endured. Grant saw merit in the idea until Fish and most other cabinet members labeled it impracticable. Grant also believed that "beneficial effects" would flow from the increased circulation of silver that the Bonanza mines of the West had begun to produce in "almost unlimited amounts." Silver's potential impact was constrained, however, by a law Congress had passed in February 1873, stopping the coinage of the standard silver dollar. Boutwell had feared that a flood of cheap silver dollars coined from ore produced by the new mines would drive gold out of circulation and wreck the administration's plans for specie resumption. The Coinage Act of 1873 thus omitted the silver dollar from the list of coins to be minted, and very few people noticed its absence at the time of the law's passage. It is not clear how well Grant appreciated the implications of the omission when he signed it. In any event, in the wake of the panic, he focused on smaller silver coins, of which he believed the country could absorb some $200 million to $300 million. In late October Richardson started a modest program of exchanging silver coins for fractional currency and paying small government debts with these coins. It was clear, however, that such a plan was not going to cure the nation's economic ills.[14]

In searching for ways to give elasticity to the currency, Grant spoke favorably of the so-called 3.65 percent interconvertible bond, which had attracted support from soft-money Republicans such as Ben Butler and Pennsylvania congressman William Kelley. Several weeks after the panic, Kelley met with Grant and Richardson to push the proposal. Under the plan, the interest rate on government bonds would be set low enough so that in tight-money times, people would cash in the bonds for greenbacks, which they could invest commercially at higher interest rates, thereby increasing the money supply. Conversely, when money was abundant and commercial interest rates low, people would exchange their plentiful greenbacks for government bonds, thereby shrinking the money supply. At a November 7 cabinet meeting, Grant suggested it would be "advisable to authorize" the plan. But Fish and other hard-money members considered it inflationist, and Grant abandoned the idea. At the same meeting, the cabinet considered ways to increase the emission of national banknotes but reached no conclusion. With the economy suffering from unprecedented turmoil (and with the Federal Reserve forty years away), no obvious tools were at hand to allay the crisis. Fish wrote in his diary that, after discussing various strategies, "a general expression of opinion was made that some plan should be considered, adopted, and presented as an Administration measure."[15]

The presentation of such a plan would have to wait until the president's annual message, however, for the *Virginius* affair, which started a few weeks after Cooke's collapse, plunged the administration into a crisis with Spain. Since Grant's definitive June 1870 statement against recognition of the Cuban rebels as belligerents, relations with Spain had dragged along at a low to medium level of irritation. Fish steadily pressured Spain for reform in the island and an end to its brutal tactics in warfare. He also complained about the Spanish expropriation of American private property and the seizure of American citizens on charges of filibustering or running arms. Governments came and went in Spain, including the abdication of the king and the creation of a shaky republic in early 1873, but no essential changes in its Cuba policies resulted. Fish noted that in the weeks leading up to each of Grant's December annual messages, the Spanish stepped up their promises of reform, offering "buttered parsnips" but failing to deliver. No ministry presiding over the loss of Cuba could expect to survive in power, and any apparent truckling to the United States could prove almost as dangerous. When Spain insisted that it could not negotiate a settlement with the Cubans until they laid down their arms, Fish had a straightforward answer: "Redress wrongs and resistance will cease."[16]

The United States pushed for the abolition of slavery in Cuba, not only for humanitarian reasons but also to undermine wealthy planters' support for Spanish control. In the fall of 1872 the Spanish minister in Washington, José Polo de Bernabé, heard rumors that the cabinet was considering calling for a higher tariff against Cuban commodities to pressure Spain. To avert that move, the Spanish abolished slavery in nearby Puerto Rico as a step toward action in Cuba. The impact was limited, however, for Puerto Rico had only 50,000 slaves, while Cuba had ten times that number. Polo also raised the far-fetched idea of the US government guaranteeing Spain's payment for the emancipation of slaves, which Grant rejected out of hand.[17]

While the administration dealt with the Spanish, it remained wary of a resurgence of congressional support for the Cubans. On February 3, 1873, Nathaniel Banks introduced a watered-down measure calling for the president to "promote a just and permanent peace between the people of Cuba and the Spanish Government." But Grant spoke with leaders on Capitol Hill to "prevent precipitate legislation," and Banks's resolution never emerged from committee.[18]

Nonetheless, by August 1873, Grant's frustration with the stalemate led him to suggest that recognition of the Cubans might give them a "moral advantage." Fish argued that such a step would open the way for the Spanish to search American vessels, which would lead to complaints, then "excitement," then war. Delano thought the solution was US acquisition of the island. When Grant rejected that idea, Delano, in a veiled but tactless reference to Santo Domingo, said, "Burnt child dreads the fire." The irritated president denied the connection and insisted that annexation "is not desirable, but independence is."[19]

Still, he worried that if the monarchists succeeded in regaining control in Spain, a new king in need of money might borrow from other European powers, using Cuba as collateral. Those nations would then have a vested interest in supporting Spain's fight against the insurgents. In late October the cabinet again discussed recognition, but Fish insisted that conceding belligerent rights would be a "falsification of every principle of public law" and of everything the United States "had said with respect to the recognition of the belligerency of [the] Confederates." No new policy emerged, but Fish took the precaution of ordering the new US consul general Henry Hall, who was about to leave for Havana, to report on the status of the insurgency and how recognition might affect the rebels, the Spanish authorities, American citizens and property, and "American commerce generally."[20]

Hall had barely unpacked his bags when he learned that, near the British colony of Jamaica, a Spanish warship had captured the steamer *Virginius,* flying the American flag and carrying arms and men to the insurgents. He cabled the State Department immediately, as did Daniel Sickles, the American minister in Madrid, who persuaded the Spanish leaders to tell the captain-general in Cuba to await orders before inflicting any punishment on the crew. The activity of the *Virginius* came as no surprise, for its record of assistance to the rebels was well known. On Friday, November 7, Fish was reporting the capture to the cabinet when a messenger interrupted with news that four men from the ship, including an American, had been executed. During the discussion, Grant passed a note to Fish: "Would it not be well to telegraph Sickles that the summary infliction of the death penalty upon the prisoners taken from the Virginius will necessarily attract much attention in this country, and will be regarded as an inhuman act, not in accordance with the spirit of the Civilization of the Nineteenth Century?" Fish embodied this sentiment in his instructions to Sickles, which also cited the need for further investigation and "most ample reparation" in the event of the wrongful killing of an American. Fish told Polo the situation was "grave," but the minister expressed doubt that the *Virginius* had been "properly carrying the American flag."[21]

The news of the deaths ignited indignation among Americans. The pro-Cuba press called for swift action against the Spanish, and the Cuban junta played on American sympathies. The day after news of the killings reached the United States, Bancroft Davis was on a train to New York when he was accosted by Frederick Dent, Grant's brother-in-law. Dent, speaking in a loud, drunken voice, demanded, "What are you going to do with the Virginius?" Dent had eavesdropped on the previous day's cabinet meeting and bellowed to Davis, "I hope we shall n't stand this. I want to be sent down there with my battery." Davis reported the incident to Fish. "What a nasty crew to have about one!" Fish wrote back. "Drunken—stupid—lying—venal—brainless. Oh! that 'Somebody' [Grant] were rid of such surroundings."[22]

When the cabinet met again on November 11, Fish had received Hall's report on conditions in Cuba, and the president and the secretaries determined that nothing had changed to justify recognition. They also concluded that war was "not desirable, but might be within the contingencies." Indeed, the group discussed the readiness of the army and navy. Belknap had not yet given orders for the transfer of troops, but Robeson had one or more ships ready to go to sea. The next day he ordered the USS *Kansas* to Cuban waters. The same day, news reached Washington that the Spanish had executed dozens more prisoners off the ship, including the captain. Fish immediately cabled Sickles to protest the act as "brutal, barbarous, and an outrage upon the age." On November 14 Grant and Fish sent Spain an ultimatum demanding the "restoration" of the *Virginius*, the release of the remaining prisoners, a salute to the American flag in the Cuban port of Santiago, and punishment of the officials responsible for the ship's capture and the executions. If Spain refused "satisfactory reparation" within twelve days (by November 26), Sickles was instructed to close the legation and leave Madrid.[23]

After laying this diplomatic groundwork, the cabinet discussed possible military action. The group acknowledged constitutional and statutory strictures forbidding "the Executive branch of the Government to do acts amounting to war," but they nonetheless proceeded with military preparations. Grant ordered Robeson to concentrate all the available naval vessels at Key West, Florida, and he and Fish assured the navy secretary that if he exhausted his budget, "Congress would not hesitate to sanction his action even in excess of appropriation and of law." Fish found the idea of war with Spain abhorrent, but he saw both political and diplomatic utility in a bit of saber rattling. When Edwards Pierrepont warned him of war fever in New York, Fish replied, "The Administration does not need the stimulus of public meetings—it is 'fired up' & you will see Monitors & vessels of war moving to the Antilles, as fast as they can be put to sea. We appreciate that a certain class of negotiations are best conducted by a nation with its full armor on its back, and *we are in thorough earnest*."[24]

Spain's initial response to the American ultimatum was procrastination, indicating its intention to make reparations if the facts warranted. At a cabinet meeting on November 18, Fish thought this earnest of compliance was sufficient to delay Sickles's departure from Madrid, if need be, to avoid "resorting to the extreme measures of war." But Grant favored keeping the pressure on. He dismissed Spain's assurances as "only the same sort of procrastination to which we have been accustomed. . . . [T]here would be time enough before the 26th to decide whether to extend the time." Matters were not helped by the hotheaded

Sickles's venomous relations with Spanish officials, and the administration welcomed Spain's request to have the negotiations shifted to Washington.[25]

The foot-dragging persisted, however. Polo proposed arbitration, which Grant promptly refused because the dispute involved a "question of National honor and indignity to the flag." Sickles thought the Spanish were stalling so that they could send more troops and ships to Cuba, but the Spaniards said they were trying to determine the provenance of the *Virginius*, which they claimed was not under American ownership at the time it was seized. Fish believed it made little difference if the Spanish officials who had perpetrated the acts thought the ship was American. Nonetheless, he asked New York collector of customs Chester Arthur to ascertain the vessel's history. Fish was eager to get the ship and the survivors released before Congress convened in early December, lest the crisis provide ammunition for those who advocated recognition of Cuba or, worse, armed intervention. Letters from would-be volunteers piled up on Grant's desk. As one White House visitor observed, "There were several from old rebel soldiers offering their services. The threat of war alone seems to have awakened a regard for the old flag."[26]

Although Grant analyzed the military situation in Cuba with Sheridan and other army leaders, a diplomatic settlement remained the administration's objective. Finally, on November 27 (Thanksgiving), Fish and Polo outlined a solution, and Grant weighed in on the final details. The two diplomats signed a formal protocol two days later. Under the terms of the agreement, Spain would release the *Virginius* and the surviving captives to the United States immediately. If it were determined that the ship had been flying the American flag legally, Spain would offer the appropriate salute by December 25. If it turned out that the display of the flag was illegal, the United States would forgo the salute, and Spain would issue a disclaimer of any intent to commit an indignity to it. In the latter case, the United States would initiate legal proceedings against those responsible for the illegal claim of American registry. Spain would investigate and punish the officials responsible for the incident.[27]

To prolong the irritation, the Spanish, claiming to fear popular fury in Cuba, asked whether they could surrender the *Virginius* to an American ship outside of Cuban waters, perhaps in Spain or Puerto Rico, or to the consul of a third power. Grant rejected this idea but said that the handover in an American port might be acceptable. Yet he was eager to get the issue settled. In an outburst to the cabinet, he suggested telling the Spanish that they had three days to deliver the ship, or he would turn the matter over to Congress with a recommendation for reprisals, a recognition of Cuba's independence, and a temporary suspension of the neutrality acts. After venting, he decided to let Fish continue to push for an expeditious surrender of the ship. Grant truly wished to avoid conflict, as did most people in the government and the country, although he was amused at the pusillanimity of some in Congress. At a subsequent cabinet meeting he joked, "If Spain were to send a fleet into the harbor of New York, and bombard the city, the Senate might pass a resolution of regret that they had had cause for so doing, and offer to pay them for the expense of coming over and doing it." Finally, the Spanish delivered the ship to an American vessel at one of Cuba's lesser ports on December 16. The next day Attorney General Williams issued a finding that the ship had been owned by Cubans and was not entitled to fly the American flag. No salute took place, and Polo wrote to Fish that "no intention to insult it ever could or ever did exist." In an ironic twist, on its way to New York the *Virginius* encountered a fierce storm and sank. It took another year of diplomatic pressure to get Spain to pay an indemnity of $80,000 for the American lives lost.[28]

In reporting the affair to Congress, Grant portrayed Spain's surrender of the ship and survivors as "an admission of the principles upon which our demands had been founded." Most Americans accepted that bit of hyperbole out of gratitude that the crisis had not led to hostilities. Despite the initial fever, skepticism about the ship's legal status, coupled with worries about the cratering domestic economy, had turned most people against going to war. As Fish put it, the country had averted "an *unnecessary* war undertaken for a dishonest vessel." The nation generally applauded the administration. Whitelaw Reid, who had done all he could to replace Grant with Horace Greeley, saluted the administration's performance as "just, sagacious & dignified—worthy, every way, of a nation strong enough to protect its flag anywhere, but too strong to make war hastily, or on other than imperative grounds." Although sympathy for the Cubans persisted, many Americans had concluded that the lessons of Reconstruction militated against any entanglement with the island. Betraying his racist-tinged disenchantment with the administration's southern policy, Bancroft Davis wrote, "We certainly do not want war, and still less a million more negroes who can't read or write, and who are voters, with two and perhaps four seats in the Senate."[29]

The administration's general satisfaction did not extend to Sickles, who had pushed for an aggressive response to Spain. In Fish's opinion, Sickles saw warmongering by the press "as evidence of the popular sentiment" and "was preparing his sword and epaulettes to be at the head of the movement." Humiliated by the transfer of negotiations to Washington, Sickles offered his resignation after the signing of the protocol, but Grant and Fish refused, not wishing to cause any disruption before the final consummation. A few days after delivery of the ship, Sickles again submitted his resignation, and Grant promptly accepted it. Delighted to have this disturbing element removed from the nation's relations with Spain, Fish recommended Caleb Cushing as an ideal replacement. Cushing had served as counsel at the Geneva Arbitration, and Fish regarded him as a "thorough Spanish Scholar." Grant thought his nomination was "the best that could be made." He named Cushing in early January 1874, and he won quick confirmation.[30]

Before Cushing could take up his duties in Madrid, however, he got caught up in Grant's search for a new chief justice. After Chase's death in May 1873, the president had let the matter ride during the summer and early fall while neither Congress nor the Supreme Court was in session. Although lawyers, politicians, and the press suggested a host of eminent judges and attorneys, Grant decided to go with his original inclination, and on November 8 he offered the job to Roscoe Conkling. Over the months, the New York senator's name had figured in the speculation about Chase's successor but had not sparked much enthusiasm. Still, friend and foe alike saw him as a man of undoubted ability and energy. Even the skeptical James Garfield thought he would make "an able Chief Justice" if he would "forego all political ambitions." But there was the rub. Conkling was politics incarnate, totally committed to the fortunes of the Republican Party and the current presidential administration. That commitment no doubt informed Grant's decision. But the president's choice also testified to his appreciation of the fundamental political character of the Court and his understanding that on the great issues growing out of the war, Conkling as chief justice would have been the un-Chase. But even though Conkling's acumen won respect in some circles, his influence came from forceful advocacy rather than judiciousness, and few would have ascribed to him a judge's temperament. Abandoning the overt political wars for the relative detachment of the bench would have been an enormous wrench. Believing "I would be forever gnawing my chains," Conkling declined.[31]

Once his first choice had turned him down, Grant was willing to listen to the suggestions of others. Horace Porter urged him to appoint George Williams as chief justice and to make Benjamin Bristow attorney general. Porter told Bristow, "I got Babcock and some of our other friends to work most vigorously and everything possible has been done in that direction." At a cabinet meeting on Friday, November 28, a consensus emerged behind Williams's appointment, but the president was not quite comfortable with that choice. On Sunday he asked whether Fish would accept the chief justiceship. The secretary declined, whereupon Grant raised the idea of appointing seventy-three-year-old Cushing; he would not remain in the job long, but his appointment could "bridge over the embarrassment of making a selection." The next day, Monday, Grant proposed Cushing at a specially called cabinet meeting. The secretaries were unenthusiastic. With Williams sitting at the table, several pointed out that this would "pass over a conclusion reached last Friday to appoint Williams," and Fish objected to using Cushing to fill such an important office on a provisional basis. Finally, Grant decided to send Williams's name to the Senate, along with Bristow's for attorney general.[32]

If Williams chafed at his treatment in the cabinet, the public reaction to the two nominations must have compounded his mortification. Bristow received warm praise. Kentucky Democrat J. W. Stevenson, a member of the Judiciary Committee, assured him, "Your selection meets with universal approval & Republicans & Democrats alike commend it as one most fit & eminent to be made." But, Stevenson added, "it is impossible at this time *to say*, whether Williams will be confirmed or not." The press generally found Williams lacking in both ability and experience. Even Assistant Attorney General C. H. Hill conceded that his boss's nomination met "universal disapprobation" and was "a bitter pill to the lawyers in the Senate." Only with great difficulty did Conkling convince his fellow members of the Judiciary Committee to report the nomination to the floor, where sharp debate ensued and action was postponed. "It is distinctly understood that the President makes it a matter of party fealty," Hill reported to Bristow. "The pressure from the White House is tremendous."[33]

But many senators felt even greater pressure from their own houses. Part of Williams's problem was his wife, for whom many in Washington society felt nothing but disdain. With a personal career bordering on the salacious before she married Williams (her third husband), Kate Williams had deeply offended other capital wives by her social pretensions, including extravagant entertainments at their Rhode Island Avenue mansion. She had particularly provoked senators' spouses by insisting that, as a cabinet wife, she occupied a higher social standing. Hill wrote to Bristow, "The fair sex are to a man (or to a woman) opposed to the appointment and of course under such circumstances exert great influence." Rumors oozed through Washington that Mrs. Williams had used her feminine wiles to advance her husband's prospects and that she had "'screwed' her husband into the Attorney Generalship." One reporter wrote to the *New York Sun*'s Charles Dana that Williams claimed that *"his wife* knew of Grant's purpose to nominate him [as chief justice] on Saturday night [and] that he did not learn it till Monday morning. . . . One of the shrewdest of the old Senators said yesterday in conversation about this appointment—'Mrs. W. has the most profitable c—t that has been brought to Washington in my day.'" The reporter erred or lied about the timing of Williams's knowledge of his appointment, for Fish's diary demonstrates that the attorney general was present when the cabinet discussed his prospective nomination on *Friday*, November 28. Nonetheless, the president's enemies were prepared to believe the worst. "It seems Mrs. Williams drives this nomination after her own fashion," Democratic senator Thomas Bayard of Delaware wrote to Manton Marble of the *New York World*, "and sad . . . it is to have the avenues to the higher seats of justice soiled and stained by such acts."[34]

Williams's position did not improve. Indeed, his chances of confirmation had grown so perilous that Bristow withdrew from consideration as attorney general on December 22. Although the Judiciary Committee had reported Williams's nomination to the floor, it continued to investigate allegations against him. One of the star witnesses against him was his former Democratic Senate colleague from Oregon, James Nesmith. Horace Porter bristled that "the Judiciary Committee is sitting listening to every idle story, every lie told by political opponents, who arrive every day to feed the fight. . . . He is quiet and dignified through it all; but it looks more like the political fight of ward politicians than a contest over the confirmation of a Chief Justice of the United States."[35]

The committee heard testimony that, a week after his nomination, Williams had fired a district attorney in Oregon who was pursuing an election fraud investigation that threatened to smirch Senator John Mitchell. Mitchell, of course, was one of the men who would decide the fate of Williams's nomination. Worse, the committee uncovered evidence of spending irregularities in the Justice Department. Most damaging, Williams had drawn on the contingent fund to purchase, at his wife's instance, a landaulet carriage and two horses and to pay the wages of two liverymen. Conkling took the allegations to the president, who discussed them with Fish. Grant said that he did not think Williams had "done anything corrupt or illegal but that there had been indiscreet things done." In addition to the carriage, he noted that during the panic, when the banks were not paying private checks, Williams had used government funds to meet household expenses. Williams claimed he had made all this good, but Grant thought "this appropriation of Government funds was unjustifiable," and Williams "would probably not be confirmed."[36]

The Williamses fought back. Against the advice of his colleagues, Williams sent a detailed explanation of his personal and family finances to the committee. It did not help. Chairman George Edmunds thought that rather than exculpating Williams, the facts showed "negligence and carelessness, and great indiscretion." Mrs. Williams tried intimidation, threatening to ruin others if her husband's nomination failed. She peddled a story to Fish's wife that money from the Justice Department's Secret Service fund had been used to secure Conkling's reelection. Grant himself flatly denied this allegation, stating that "the only use of that fund for any election purposes" had been to defray the expenses of voter registration in New York City under the terms of the Enforcement Acts of 1871. This was "perfectly legitimate," he insisted, and he "stood prepared to justify it."[37]

Nonetheless, with matters going from bad to worse, Grant journeyed to Capitol Hill for a discussion with the Judiciary Committee. Edmunds and the others laid out all the allegations and evidence. When the president still hesitated, the senators advised him that he "owed it to himself, to Judge Williams, to the Republican party, to the Senate and to the Country to withdraw the nomination." Relenting, Grant concluded that Williams "ought to relieve" him of the onus and ask that his nomination be withdrawn. The president commissioned Fish to relay the message and suggested that Williams attribute his request to disintegrating support in the Senate. Williams showed some defiance, but he complied. In his letter to the president he insisted that he had performed all his duties "with clean hands and an upright purpose," but "the floodgates of calumny in all directions have been opened upon me." Trusting that time would lead to vindication, he asked the president to withdraw his name, and Grant did so the next day. Refusing to give further notice to the charges against the attorney general, the president allowed him to keep his job. At a cabinet meeting the next day, Williams made a statement that, according to Fish, left "the impression that although he may have been indiscreet, he had not been intentionally wrong."[38]

Pressed to settle the question, Grant returned to the time-buying option of nominating Cushing and sent his name to the Senate on January 9, 1874. Within four days the nomination imploded. Although some objected to Cushing's advanced age, others found him politically unacceptable. A prominent pro-southern northern Democrat before the war, he had opposed the Wilmot Proviso, enforced the Fugitive Slave Act as attorney general, pushed the Kansas-Nebraska bill, and upheld the *Dred Scott* decision. He had, however, done an about-face during the war, rallying to the Union cause. He had also served Grant and Fish as an informal adviser and as counsel at Geneva and consulted on foreign policy with Sumner. Indeed, the Massachusetts senator believed that Cushing's interpretations on the bench would be as "large & strong— as my own—for Human Rights & sustained by learning & ability." But other Republicans could not forget Cushing's prewar record. "Never trust a convert," Wendell Phillips warned Sumner. Justice David Davis also lobbied against the "old scoundrel." In the Senate, Cushing's most ardent opponent was Aaron Sargent of California, who had crossed political swords with him in their mutual hometown of Newburyport, Massachusetts, years before. To Sargent's delight, a smoking gun was uncovered in the War Department's Confederate archives in the form of a letter Cushing had written in March 1861 to Jefferson Davis. In this otherwise innocuous letter of introduction written for a former employee before the firing on Fort Sumter, Cushing commented that events had "overthrown the American Union," and he referred to the "Confederate States" as a "country." After Sargent revealed this letter to his colleagues, Grant told the Senate that "information has reached me which induces me to withdraw" Cushing's name.[39]

"Shaken & demoralized," the president took up the question once again. Fish pushed his favorite candidate Rockwood Hoar. Grant respected the former attorney general, but Hoar had recently stated that, in his opinion, Congress lacked the constitutional authority to issue paper currency as legal tender. Grant could not afford to appoint a justice whose ideas ran counter to the administration's monetary policy. Bristow renewed the suggestion of appointing a chief from within the Court, perhaps with the ulterior motive of opening an associate justice slot for himself, but the idea of an internal appointment was dead. Through intermediaries, Grant again inquired if Conkling would take the post, and again he said no. Grant finally decided to offer the position to Morrison R. Waite of Ohio. Not widely regarded as standing in the front ranks of American lawyers, Waite had nonetheless turned up on several persons' short lists, largely because of his able service on the legal team at Geneva. No skeletons skulked in his closet. Hoar spoke for many when he wrote to Jacob Cox, "How relieved and comfortable we all feel in your Ohio neighbor, a worthy, upright, faithful, laborious and respectable gentleman; of thorough education, legal training and fair ability." In the Senate, Sumner, who thought too little was known about Waite's views, delayed the confirmation so that he could give a speech on the ideal attributes of a chief justice. Nonetheless, Waite won approval, 63 to 0, with Sumner not voting.[40]

After seven agonizing weeks, what Fish called "a hard parturition" had finally yielded a competent if not brilliant chief justice. Fish looked back at the opposition leveled against Williams as "very unjust & ungenerous." He decried the "tendency now in the Press & in the Public (debauched thereunto by the Press) to invade private life, to find objections to public men." Despite the trying circumstances, Timothy Howe and others close to Grant thought he had shown "thorough and steadfast good sense" and in the end could find "no better man." Still, the tortuous process confirmed some critics' low opinion of Grant's capacity. "What a pity it is that our poor President has not some one to guide him," Hill moaned to Bristow. "Heaven only knows where he will land the party." Seething over his perceived ill treatment, Bristow complained that some people thought Grant had nominated him for attorney general only to strengthen Williams's chances "with a certain class of senators." He feared that the withdrawal of his name gave the impression that "it was only intended from the first to make a useful tool of me for some 'other fellow's' benefit, or that it was discovered that I was unfit for the office." Nonetheless, despite the ambitious Kentuckian's concern for his own reputation, he would soon find that the president had no intention of barring him from the national stage.[41]

When the first session of the Forty-Third Congress convened in December 1873, the Court question drew far less attention than the economic troubles stemming from the panic two months earlier. Over the next several months, Congress struggled with the currency issue, trying to find a legislative formula that would strike a balance between two irreconcilable blocs—those who favored inflation to ease the burdens of debtors and others suffering from the collapse, and those who adhered to orthodox hard-money principles, which the creditor class favored. Through the winter and spring, Grant played a central role in influencing legislation, and his evolving views placed him firmly in the latter camp.

The president began to work on his annual message in mid-November. In framing the financial section, he consulted with members of Congress as well as the cabinet. Garfield found that Grant's "discussion of the financial situation shows more study and reflection than I have known him to give any other document; though I fear he will recommend something that amounts to an inflation of the currency." The congressman's fears were not altogether unjustified.[42]

On fiscal matters, Grant's message urged Congress to observe "great economy," especially since tax revenues were likely to fall. He recommended cuts in public works spending and greater vigilance in weeding out fraudulent claims stemming from the war. In the longer term, to avert the passage of unnecessary spending bills, he advocated constitutional amendments to permit a line-item veto, to bar logrolling legislation in the final twenty-four hours of a congressional session, and to limit bills in special sessions to the subjects for which the president had called them. These proposals went nowhere. Although Grant's calls for frugality obviously left no room for countercyclical spending to stimulate the economy, he did sympathize with people suffering from the effects of the depression. Perhaps remembering his own struggles in the 1850s, he discussed with the cabinet the draconian provisions of federal bankruptcy legislation passed in 1867. In his message he advocated excising a provision of that law permitting creditor-induced "involuntary bankruptcy on account of the suspension of payment." Congress complied, negating that section in a general revision of the bankruptcy laws.[43]

As for monetary policy, Grant said, "We can never have permanent prosperity until a specie basis is reached," but he also noted that "sufficient currency is required to keep all the industries of the country employed." He called for legislation to achieve a more even distribution of money, which tended to gravitate toward interest-paying national banks in the East, and for the formation of clearinghouses to facilitate the movement of money to understocked institutions. He warned against "undue inflation," which would afford only "temporary relief," but he argued that "elasticity to our circulating medium . . . and just enough of it to transact the legitimate business of the country and to keep all industries employed, is what is most to be desired." How to achieve that elasticity and a "sufficient currency" was the key question. Most of the suggested plans, he said, "look to me more like inflation," and in a vaguely worded passage, he now rejected the interconvertible bond notion he had toyed with earlier. As an alternative, he offered an idea the cabinet had discussed—that in times of stringency, the secretary of the treasury be authorized to issue additional banknotes to national banks, up to a fixed percentage of their normal issue, upon the banks' depositing government bonds with the Treasury.

Although Grant did not embrace inflation, he asserted that the economy had suffered considerable contraction. In actual terms, the circulation of greenbacks had declined $63 million because that quantity of notes had been deposited in banks to replace government bonds withdrawn or retired in the last four and a half years. More important, the nation had experienced a substantial "comparative contraction of the currency" relative to the large increase in population and acceleration of economic activity, including vast growth in manufacturing, railroad building, and agricultural production. As many an inflationist had argued, Grant believed that the volume of currency had not kept pace with this development. Realizing that such talk might alarm orthodox thinkers, he concluded this section of his message with the hope "that the best method may be arrived at to secure such an elasticity of the currency as will keep employed all the industries of the country and prevent such an inflation as will put off indefinitely the resumption of specie payments, an object so devoutly to be wished for by all, and by none more earnestly than the class of people most directly interested— those who 'earn their bread by the sweat of their brow.'"[44]

In language sometimes less than crystalline, Grant identified the dilemma confronting policymakers: how to adjust the money supply to meet the needs of an economy that was faltering in the near term but burgeoning in the long term, and at the same time avoid inflating the currency to the point of jeopardizing a return to specie payments. "The President has bestowed more labor on this message than any other that he has ever written," Garfield observed. "There are some crudities in his financial discussions but on the whole it is a pretty good message."[45]

Richardson's Treasury Department report echoed Grant's suggestion of temporary increases in the issuance of national banknotes during times of stringency. He claimed that his infusion of currency through bond purchases in the wake of the panic had strengthened many banks and "checked the general alarm to some extent," but he conceded that the "loss of confidence" was so pervasive that no amount of currency could avert a disruption of business. He also said, "It ought not to be the business of the Treasury Department to increase and diminish the amount of legal-tender notes from time to time, according to the condition of the money market, and for the sole purpose of affecting that market." Yet he did acknowledge some flexibility in using the reserve. He rejected the conservatives' notion that the 1868 law ending green-back contraction had set the maximum circulation at $356 million. Rather, that was the minimum. The wartime laws creating the currency had set the maximum at $400 million, leaving $44 million available for reissue to meet the "ordinary demands" on the Treasury during revenue shortfalls. Indeed, by mid-January, Richardson had reissued $26 million of the reserve, for a total circulation of $382 million.[46]

Members of Congress agreed with the president that legislative action was imperative, but the scores of proposals they dropped in the hopper represented all points on the spectrum, from the rigidly hard money to the wildly inflationary. Legislators would need time to sort them out, but meanwhile, they gave attention to another priority: repeal of the Salary Grab enacted the previous year. After the GOP's dismal showing in the 1873 elections, Republicans believed their "*water-logged*" party "must pump out and tack ship, or we can't win." Some members of Congress had refused their back pay. Their eagerness now to pass a repeal bill led Senator John Logan to quip that members of the House "all seem to be patriots and will I think take no pay whatever for their services." In January Congress passed a bill repealing its members' raises, both retrospective and prospective. But it left in place the new salaries for the president and the Supreme Court justices, which a general consensus had approved. As usual, however, inveterate Grant haters saw the worst. "The salary grab is repealed," wrote Gideon Welles, "but Grant the chief grabber is left with the plunder."[47]

In the weeks after Grant's message, the nation looked to Capitol Hill for action on the economic crisis. But after two months Fish wrote, "Congress is 'dragging its slow length along,' *talking* economy, & wasting time in the talk." Both parties were divided on the issue, largely along sectional lines. Members from the West and the South generally favored inflation, and those from the Northeast opposed it. Grant found that his own supporters disagreed on the issue. Lobbyists for interest groups of all stripes prowled the corridors, urging this or that measure. In late February a turn in the debate indicated that inflationists might secure an unacceptable bill, leading Grant to draft a preemptive special message. In it he argued for "immediate, permanent, unrepealable steps toward resumption." To raise the funds necessary to begin specie payments, he envisioned reduced expenditures and increased internal taxes on whiskey and tobacco, a repeal of the 10 percent reduction in general tariff rates implemented in 1872, and a reinstitution of the customs duties on coffee and tea. He also recommended free banking legislation, including "such provisions as to prohibit an increase of legal tenders."[48]

Clearly Grant was moving away from the balanced approach of his annual message and toward the views espoused by northeastern conservatives. Massachusetts congressman George Hoar recalled a conversation in which the "deeply moved" president expressed "his dislike of irredeemable currency" and argued that the "greatest sufferers" from a delay in the return to specie payments were workers and the poor who, unlike speculators, had no cushion to protect them from currency fluctuations. Grant was prepared to intervene in the legislative process, and when he presented his draft message to the cabinet, the secretaries generally acquiesced in its views. Yet several of them doubted the "expediency or necessity" or even the "propriety" of the president's making "specific recommendations" to Congress. Less fastidious about interbranch etiquette, Grant had, of course, submitted policy recommendations in the past, but this issue's political divisiveness gave him pause. He agreed to withhold the message, await the action of the legislature, and, if necessary, present his views in a veto. A month later Garfield found him "very much distressed at the course of Congress" and urged him to submit his special message. But Grant was sensitive to the charge of attempting "a veto in advance of legislation as an unbecoming threat by the Executive," and he desisted.[49]

After five months of maneuvering, on April 14, 1874, Congress passed what had come to be known as the Inflation Bill. Compared with many other measures it had considered, the final bill was relatively simple, though still controversial. It set the greenback maximum at $400 million, thereby legitimating the $26 million from the "reserve" the Treasury had already emitted and allowing for the issuance of $18 million more. Further, it authorized the Treasury to issue $46 million in additional national banknotes, raising their maximum to $400 million as well. The bill also included revisions in the national banks' reserve requirements. Although this last provision may have offset some if not all of the apparent increase in the money supply, in the ongoing arguments, friend and foe alike asserted that the bill would live up to its name and inflate the currency.[50]

All eyes turned to Grant, who came under enormous pressure from both sides. Labor and agricultural groups urged him to sign the bill. Groups of businessmen and bankers in New York and Boston dispatched delegations to Washington to lobby for a veto. With his own natural sympathies for the "great sufferers" at the hands of speculators, Grant was particularly irritated by a Boston manufacturer who tactlessly decried the greenbacks as an illegitimate currency and implied that Grant had packed the Supreme Court to have them upheld. The president angrily insisted that "the war could not have been successfully carried on without them." He told another delegation that if he "ever could be in favor of inflation, it would be from the effects of such arguments as that gentleman advocated against it." Still, he spent nearly the full ten days allowed by the Constitution mulling what course to take.[51]

Incentives existed for accepting the bill. It was not overly expansionist. Approving it could avert a more inflationary measure and help lay the vexing money question to rest. And a veto could cripple the Republican Party in the West in the 1874 congressional elections and result in an unbridled inflationist majority. Grant's initial inclination was to sign the bill but also to submit an explanatory message to "soothe the East." He prepared a draft that characterized the measure as "a compromise between the advocates of the two financial extremes, and as a final settlement of the question." He wrote that it was "not expansive as claimed" and that raising the greenback limit to $400 million would simply "legalize what has already been frequently done." The section related to banking, he asserted, would lead to a more even distribution of currency. Failure to approve the bill, moreover, would simply prolong the financial dispute, during which "trade and commerce would remain paralized [sic]."[52]

As Grant later recalled, after writing this message, "I read it over, and said to myself: 'What is the good of all this? You do not believe it. You know it is not true.'" Casting aside his "fallacious and untenable" arguments, he drafted a veto message and presented it to the cabinet. The three westerners in the group—Delano, Williams, and Belknap—plus Robeson of New Jersey, all opposed the veto, largely on political grounds, while Fish and Creswell endorsed it and Richardson "acquiescently approved." The expansionist Delano argued that vetoes were unpopular unless they rested on constitutional grounds, but Fish countered that "the good faith of the nation was above the Constitution," and Grant said, "That is so." When Delano and others warned of backlash against Republicans in the West, Fish answered that the "whole honest sentiment of the country irrespective of party would sustain" a veto. Despite the cabinet's division, the president signed the veto message. "I shall be more censured & abused for this than for any [other] act of my life; but I am convinced that I am right." Grant's toying with acceptance of the bill had again pushed Fish to the brink of resigning, but the president's final determination to veto it, coupled with the troubling positions of other secretaries, led Fish to shelve his resignation once more.[53]

In his message, Grant decried the bill's call for additional paper circulation as "a departure from true principle of finance, national interest, [and] national obligations to creditors." The bill, he said, ran counter to pledges by both political parties, his own pronouncements, and previous congressional enactments, including the Public Credit Act, the first law he had signed, which he quoted in full. The $44 million reserve, he said, could be used only in emergencies when government revenues fell below expenditures. Specie resumption remained his great goal, and to achieve it, he recommended higher taxes to accumulate gold in the Treasury. "I am not," he declared, "a believer in any artificial method of making paper money equal to coin." He admitted that he had been "disposed to give great weight" to the sectional maldistribution of banknote circulation but observed that those states below their quota of notes still had $29 million available. "When this is all taken up," he concluded, "or when specie payments are fully restored or are in rapid process of restoration, will be the time to consider the question of 'more currency.'"[54]

Kept secret until it was presented to Congress, the message struck like a bolt of lightning. Senators and representatives gathered in knots to assess its implications, and one reporter noted a common remark that "this veto was the most important political event since the close of the war. The inflationists all assert that Grant has committed political suicide and stabbed the party to death, and the 'hard money men' hold with equal emphasis that he has covered himself with glory and saved the party." From his post in Russia, US minister Marshall Jewell observed that the veto would "dispel the illusion which has so long had possession of the public mind that Grant is run by anybody." Connecticut congressman Joseph Hawley dashed off a note to the president: "So long as we have a history you will be remembered as having saved the nation's life, but in the coming centuries there will be historians who will claim that in saving our national honor you have done the cause of republican government even a greater service." Feelings on the other side ran just as deep. Reporters noted that as inflationist John Logan listened to the message in the Senate chamber, "his face was almost black with apparent rage." Two weeks later he was still fuming: "Grant thinks he has done the greatest thing since the days of Jackson, he is being flattered all the time by the aristocrats of the country until no one can tell what he contemplates. I begin to feel that our country will not last long under Republican rule of this kind."[55]

The cabinet readily acknowledged Grant's leadership on the issue. Fish told a New York friend, "You must give the President the undivided credit for what he did. Never did a man more conscientiously reach his conclusions than he did in the matter of that Bill, & this in the face of the very strongest & most persistent influences brought to bear upon him. . . . He has a wonderful amount of good sense, & when left alone is very apt to follow it, & to 'fight it out on that line.'" Grant knew that many party friends who had stood with him on Reconstruction issues and against the Liberal Republicans would be "permanently embittered" by the veto. But, he told Garfield, he "could not help it"; the more he studied the bill, the more convinced be became of its "dangerous character." Garfield thought that ultimately the politics would run in the president's favor: "General Grant is one of the luckiest of men. For twenty years no President has had so fine an opportunity to stay the current of popular delusion and mischief. He has done it manfully . . . [and] the more thoughtful men of all sections will rejoice."[56]

In the short term, however, Grant's veto changed few minds in Congress, where members kept an eye on the upcoming fall elections. In an attempt to override the veto in the Senate, no one from either side changed his vote, and the inflationists fell far short of the necessary two-thirds. Still undaunted, they sought to infuse inflationary elements into a House bill to institute free banking, and again the battle raged between hard- and soft-money forces. Again Grant stepped in. When he heard reports that some legislators were misrepresenting his position, he met with the chairmen of the House and Senate financial committees and other leaders to set them straight. He also publicized his views in a memorandum to Senator John P. Jones of Nevada, which appeared in newspapers on June 6.[57]

The Jones memorandum placed Grant even more solidly in the hard-money camp. He recommended repeal of the clause in the 1862 act that had made greenbacks legal tender so that henceforth all contracts, including those for wages, would be based on coin. This move would "correct our notions of values" and make the specie dollar "the only dollar known as the measure of equivalents." Further, he called for the resumption of specie payments on July 1, 1876, and for all redeemed greenbacks to be canceled and destroyed. Such legislation, he argued, would "work less hardship to the debtor interest, than is likely to come from putting off the day of final reckoning. It must be borne in mind too, that the creditor interest had its day of disadvantage also when our present financial system was brought in by the supreme needs of the nation" during the war. In addition, he recommended the withdrawal of all paper money in denominations below $10 and their replacement by coin. To accumulate specie needed for redemption, he called for the issuance of bonds and increased taxes if necessary.[58]

The memorandum pleased hard-money advocates, who encouraged Grant to urge Jones to embody his views in a new bill. But if the senator saw the memorandum as useful in forestalling inflationist legislation, he doubted the time was ripe for the severe measures the president endorsed. Similarly, Speaker James G. Blaine, fretting over the fall elections, warned that the enactment of Grant's proposals "would be ruinous to the Republican party and the country." After an extended effort, Fish convinced Grant of "the impolicy of introducing any bill."[59]

Even so, the president's memorandum to Jones put Congress on notice that his veto stamp lay ready at hand. With an eye down Pennsylvania Avenue, legislators wrangled for two more weeks and finally passed a modest compromise bill. It legalized Richardson's use of the $26 million from the greenback reserve, but it also set the maximum for greenbacks at $382 million and stipulated that "no part thereof shall be held or used as a reserve." The bill relieved national banks from holding reserves against their note circulation, other than a 5 percent redemption fund kept in the Treasury. Gone was any reference to free banking, although the bill called for the redistribution of up to $55 million in national banknotes from states with an excess to those with inadequate amounts. Congress passed the bill on June 20, and Grant signed it.[60]

Although this act accomplished little and left key questions unsettled, the protracted debates of the winter and spring of 1874 turned out to be the high-water mark for inflation sentiment in the Republican Party, though it by no means disappeared. In controlling that tide, no one was more effective than Grant, who acted as a powerful legislative leader. Although he did not succeed in obtaining his proposals, he used the veto of the Inflation Bill, the Jones memorandum, and a continuing veto threat to defeat unacceptable measures and influence the shape of legislation. "People who take Gen. Grant for a simpleton don't quite know the kind of man they have to deal with," said the *New York Times*. "He is now the only prominent man in the Republican Party who is making any headway." According to Marshall Jewell, "Genl Grant never exhibited more courage and good sense than he has shown in regard to these late financial measures. It looks to me as tho he had saved our party and commands the situation." Even so, the party's prospects for the fall elections were anything but cheering. The depression persisted.

Republicans still disagreed about the currency, and the party's congressional campaign committee could do little more than promise voters that "when Republicans discover the true way they will pursue it."[61]

Grant's legislative influence in the currency fight was all the more impressive given that during much of the session, Richardson stood under a cloud of scandal. The allegations involved certain moiety contracts whereby the Treasury Department engaged private contractors to aid in the collection of delinquent taxes, for which the contractors received exorbitant fees. During his tenure as secretary, George Boutwell had eliminated these agreements, but Ben Butler had slipped a provision into an 1872 bill allowing for three such contracts in the future. Two of them bore little fruit, but the third, which was given to John Sanborn, a Butler ally, became a bonanza. Under the original agreement (signed by Richardson as assistant secretary) and three additions, Sanborn was authorized to pursue several individuals and corporations for supposedly evading taxes. Both Boutwell and Richardson (as secretary) ordered internal revenue officials to cooperate and give Sanborn access to tax records. All told, his aggressive methods yielded $427,000 in supposedly delinquent taxes, from which he received half, or $213,500. Sanborn claimed that he paid out "probably $160,000" to others who had assisted him, but it was rumored that some of the money went to Butler.[62]

The House Ways and Means Committee launched an investigation, and in his testimony, Richardson did himself no favors. He disclaimed virtually all knowledge of the affair, insisting he had not consulted with Sanborn and, as a matter of routine, had merely signed contracts and orders prepared by his subordinates. But Sanborn testified that he had met with the secretary half a dozen times regarding the contracts and that Richardson had known exactly what he was signing. Richardson tried to shift responsibility to the department's solicitor, who in turn insisted that he had been following orders from the secretary. As Fish noted, "The Sanborn business has a *very, very* awkward look." It was hard to escape the conclusion that Richardson was either a liar or negligent to the point of incompetence. Grant decided that the secretary should leave the cabinet, although Ways and Means chairman Henry Dawes asked the president to defer action until the committee made its report. That report, issued in early May 1874, condemned the moiety system and asserted that most or all of the taxes Sanborn had gathered would have been collected by internal revenue officials "in the ordinary discharge of their duty," without his huge commission. The committee members found "nothing impeaching the integrity" of Boutwell or Richardson or indicating "corrupt motives" by either man. But they asserted that Richardson, his assistant secretary, and the department's solicitor all "deserve severe condemnation for the manner in which they have permitted this law to be administered." Before the end of the session, Congress abolished the moiety system.[63]

The report put the last nail in Richardson's coffin, although he delayed his resignation to give the president time to find a replacement. Vice President Henry Wilson argued that E. R. Hoar could restore an aura of responsibility to the department, but Grant wanted someone from outside New England, where politics was "covered with 'Butlerism' or Anti 'Butlerism.'" Delano, who had once served eighteen months in the Treasury Department as internal revenue commissioner, craved the top job. Grant considered him, perhaps as a sop to inflationist sentiment, but hard-money men opposed him, and Conkling reported that evidence reflecting on Delano's integrity made his confirmation impossible. More in keeping with the ideas expressed in his Inflation Bill veto, the president decided he should select a treasury secretary who was unmistakably committed to conservative monetary views. On the heels of the Ways and Means report, he offered the job to Elihu Washburne, known for his rugged honesty and hard-money zeal. But Washburne declined.[64]

Among those who followed these developments closely was Benjamin Bristow. The former solicitor general was ambitious, but, imagining that he had been ill treated when nominated for attorney general, he was ambivalent about rejoining the administration. During the time Delano was under consideration, Grant sent an emissary to ask Bristow if he would accept Delano's place as head of the Interior Department, but the Kentuckian coquetted. He refused to answer until "distinctly" appointed, and then he planned to say no. (At the same time, he gossiped to John Marshall Harlan that Grant had been drunk on a recent trip to Philadelphia.) But after Washburne declined the post, Bristow's friends began pushing him for treasury secretary. In mid-May Grant suggested to Horace Porter that Richardson seemed to be rebounding in public opinion, but Porter told the president he "was never more mistaken in his life, and that with such a weight he could never swim ashore." Porter said that appointing Bristow would meet no opposition and obviate "taking an untried man into the Cabinet." In addition, Bristow's warm support for the Inflation Bill veto had impressed the president. Finally, Grant worked out an arrangement whereby he would name Richardson to a vacancy on the court of claims and nominate Bristow as treasury secretary. After the cabinet gave unanimous approval, the president submitted both nominations on the same day. Only afterward did he have a conversation with Bristow about his appointment. Bristow easily won confirmation in the Senate without a division, while Richardson's court appointment passed by a vote of 27 (all Republicans) to 20 (16 Democrats and 4 Republicans).[65]

Bristow liked to portray himself as not particularly ambitious, but this was the second cabinet seat he had been willing, if not eager, to accept in the past six months. From the beginning, his political associates regarded his sojourn in the Treasury as the "preparatory heat" for the presidential race in 1876. "Your location is right," wrote David Davis, "and there is no one in the Republican ranks likely to be candidates who will command the same confidence." Harry Wilson urged the new secretary to make reform his watchword in the Treasury and the springboard for his political advancement. "The only way to save the Republican party is to punish rascality and introduce *reform*," Wilson wrote. Bristow embraced the advice. "Your suggestion about the mode of preserving the Republican party meets my hearty approval, and . . . I mean to carry it out." He tapped Wilson's brother Bluford as solicitor of the Treasury Department. Before long, the younger Wilson proved himself not only an able public officer but also an energetic political lieutenant.[66]

Within three months, however, Bristow's contentious nature had begun to resurface, and he was telling Harlan that he regretted taking the job. The work overwhelmed him, and he found himself involved in a nasty tangle with Secretary of the Navy George Robeson. At issue was the appointment of a financial agent to handle the marketing of a new bond issue in London. Robeson favored former senator A. G. Cattell, who had performed a similar task under Richardson. Robeson hoped to win election to the Senate from New Jersey and thought Cattell's appointment would remove a potential rival. Others endorsed Cattell as well, and fastidious Vermont senator George Edmunds described him as "very capable and upright." But Bristow refused to make the appointment. Not only did he tell Grant that a Treasury employee could handle the negotiation, but he also tried to undercut Robeson's influence by complaining to the president about the Navy Department's management of its accounts. He alleged that the department had too close a relationship with the banking house of former treasury secretary Hugh McCulloch. This was sure to be a red flag to Grant, who disliked McCulloch "more than any living American" because of McCulloch's treatment of him during the Johnson administration. Robeson complained angrily to Bristow for going behind his back to the president, but Bristow ultimately selected John Bigelow, head of the Treasury Department's Loan Division, for the London job. Grant warned Bristow about an episode of drunkenness by Bigelow on a previous assignment, but he accepted the secretary's decision and acquiesced in Bigelow's posting.[67]

While these events unfolded, Bristow's political advisers urged him to keep cool. "You must not get impatient with your present surroundings," Harlan wrote. "No man ever had such an opportunity as you now have for achieving all that you could wish in the way of power and fame." Harry Wilson advised him to "capture" his colleagues "by the use of honey and brains instead of choler and pepper sauce." The ambitious Wilson was eager to be appointed minister to Russia, and he persuaded Bristow to plead his case. The position had opened up when Grant appointed Marshall Jewell, the former minister, to replace John Creswell as postmaster general, who had resigned to return to private pursuits. But Fish objected to Wilson, and Grant appointed an experienced diplomat instead. Still, Bristow could take satisfaction that the president held him in high regard. In late October 1874 a friend told him that in conversation Grant had been "very outspoken in praise of you. He said that you were among the few public men that he had seen who could say no, and stand by it under every pressure." Eventually, however, Bristow's ambition and solipsism would bring his relationship with the president to grief.[68]

But for now, at least, Bristow stood as the cabinet's respected representative of the South. Grant had long honored the Kentuckian for his bravery at the head of a Union regiment and for his prosecution of the Klan in the administration's early days. Bristow still believed that the "lawlessness & violence against the Negroes must be stopped at all hazard." After years of a steady erosion of Reconstruction, Grant needed all the help he could get in his continuing struggle to strike a workable balance between the defense of civil rights and the cultivation of sectional reconciliation. As his second term wore on, that task grew only more difficult.[69]

18

★ ★ ★ ★ ★

RECONSTRUCTION UNDER SIEGE

The Panic of 1873 not only devastated the nation's economy. It also undermined the Republicans' drive for a successful Reconstruction. As economic distress struck countless Americans, Grant and Republican leaders found it increasingly difficult to persuade northern whites frightened for their own futures to support the cause of racial justice. In the South, the former slaves, already at the lowest rung of society, saw their lives grow ever more desperate.[1]

Moreover, a few months before the panic, the Supreme Court's decision in the famous *Slaughter-House Cases* threatened prospects for mounting any new civil rights initiatives or even sustaining the progress already made. Although the cases involved the regulation of butchers in New Orleans and did not deal directly with the freed people, it bore grave implications for the federal protection of civil rights. Drawing on traditional notions of federalism, the Court maintained that despite the Fourteenth Amendment, most privileges and immunities enjoyed by citizens remained under the jurisdiction of the state governments and were not "placed under the special care of the Federal government." The decision delighted white southerners and dismayed Republicans.[2]

Grant thought Congress should respond by passing additional legislation. In his December 1873 annual message he called for "the enactment of a law to better secure the civil rights which freedom should secure, but has not effectually secured, to the enfranchised slave." On the same day, Charles Sumner reintroduced his supplementary civil rights bill, which mandated equal access to public accommodations, common carriers, places of amusement, public cemeteries, and public schools and barred racial discrimination in jury selection. Sumner had long advocated such a measure, and a few days later a similar bill was introduced in the House. In mid-December Grant met with delegates from the National Colored Convention and argued that enfranchisement and equal rights should have come automatically with emancipation. "It is unfortunate that any enactment is necessary to secure such rights, but existing prejudice seems to have rendered it necessary. I hope the present Congress will give the relief you seek." But "if such a bill is defeated," he added, "it will probably be because an extreme measure is urged by some person who claims to be a particular friend of the colored man."[3]

"Some person," of course, was Sumner, and as in past debates over his bill, the schools provision was the main sticking point. As a longtime trustee of the Peabody Education Fund, Grant strongly supported education for blacks and whites in the South. But he shared fund leaders' doubts about moving directly to mixed schools. Though fully committed to racial equality before the law, he hesitated to put children on the front lines in the fight to achieve "social" equality. Moreover, recognizing the ingrained prejudice throughout the country, Grant feared the impact of such a move on Republican prospects in the coming midterm congressional elections. Consideration of the bill occurred first in the House, where Ben Butler reported it from the Judiciary Committee. Soon after debate started, Grant and the Peabody Fund's general agent conferred with Butler, and the president advised him it would be "unwise to attempt to force mixed schools upon the South." Butler got the message. Expressing concern for "what on the whole is best for the white and the colored child," he moved immediately to have his bill referred again to committee, and it did not emerge for the remainder of the session.[4]

In the Senate, Sumner's bill lay dormant for months. Before it emerged from committee, the sixty-three-year-old senator's long-standing heart disease finally overtook him, and he died on March 11. The ensuing obsequies rivaled those accorded Abraham Lincoln, and African Americans were prominent among the mourners. Grant and the entire cabinet attended the Senate funeral. In the words of one reporter, the president's face bore an "expressionless look," and "it was impossible to discover by the movement of a muscle throughout the ceremonies any sign of emotion."[5]

Controversy did not die with Sumner. Three years earlier, in the wake of his failure to win reappointment as Foreign Relations chairman, he had written a violent anti-administration speech. His friends persuaded him not to deliver it, but he distributed it privately in printed form. Less than a month after his death, this "suppressed" speech, dwelling mostly on the dismissal of Motley and the Santo Domingo issue, appeared in the *New York Tribune*. Although men of all political faiths had sincerely honored the great services of the dead statesman, reading this philippic from the grave soured many. When Sumner died, Timothy Howe had spoken of a "sentiment of common brotherhood towards him." Now, said Howe, "the speech will indelibly stain Mr. Sumner's memory." Hamilton Fish, the target of much of Sumner's venom, thought "the meanness of printing & circulating privately an attack which he dared not make openly, & leaving it to be published after the grave has protected its author from a reply, is characteristic."[6]

Nonetheless, Sumner's Republican colleagues in the Senate concluded that passing his civil rights bill would be a fitting memorial. Democrats argued that the *Slaughter-House* decision implied that any such legislation would be unconstitutional, but Republicans argued for a more expansive view of rights guaranteed by the Fourteenth Amendment. Although the schools question drew fire, the Senate passed the bill with that section intact on May 23, 1874, by a partisan vote. Despite Butler's efforts to win consideration in the House, the session closed with no action, and the bill was carried over to the next session in the fall.[7]

Grant favored civil rights legislation, but he increasingly reckoned that many of the Republicans who had come into power in the southern states were not ideal instruments to achieve a successful Reconstruction or to lend much help to the Republican Party. Several months earlier he had begun an effort to conciliate moderate whites through patronage. His aim, Fish explained to one ex-Confederate, was to appoint southerners "in whom, both North & South, the country will have & have had confidence" and to get rid of officeholders "who have not satisfied the expectation of those among whom they were to exercise their functions." The latter type had helped foster unacceptable governments that not only stymied conciliation but also sullied the party. At a gathering of Republican leaders at the White House in mid-January 1874, Grant declared that it was time for the GOP to "unload" its "dead weight. . . . This nursing of monstrosities has nearly exhausted the life of the party. I am done with them, and they will have to take care of themselves."[8]

No state proved more frustrating than Louisiana, which was still fractured after the disputed election of 1872. Grant's proclamation in May 1873 threatening the use of troops had resulted in an uneasy peace at best, and white Democrats' hatred of the government of Governor William Kellogg continued to smolder. Grant had based his recognition of Kellogg on a decision by federal judge E. H. Durell, but impeachment proceedings against Durell on trumped-up charges of drunkenness and malfeasance vitiated the authority of the judge's order. Meanwhile, Wisconsin senator Matt Carpenter, who was essentially in league with Kellogg's enemies in the Warmoth-McEnery faction, proposed to reintroduce his bill calling for a new election. Grant was so disgusted with Kellogg that he toyed with the idea of supporting Carpenter's bill. "I am tired of this nonsense," he told the White House gathering. "Let Louisiana take care of herself."[9]

Grant's exasperation alarmed party leaders, who thought a new election "would be absolutely and certainly fatal to the loyal men of the state." William Chandler warned the president that it would "be impossible under any proposed auspices to get the full Republican vote to the polls and to prevent illegal democratic votes." Louisiana Republicans also protested against a new election. At bottom, the situation left Grant no good choice. In late January 1874 he and Attorney General Williams prepared a draft message on the subject, but he eventually accepted the cabinet's advice against submitting it to Congress. Thus, by official silence, the president tacitly continued the administration's recognition of the Kellogg regime. After sporadic debate, Carpenter's bill for a new election died.[10]

Matters in Texas proved more amenable to Grant's new inclination to steer clear of southern "monstrosities." There, the issue involved a dispute over the state election in November 1873, during which Republican governor Edmund Davis lost his bid for reelection by nearly a two-to-one margin, and Republicans across the board fell. Davis was willing to bow to the inevitable, but when state party leaders brought suit in state supreme court based on a technical violation of a newly passed election law, the Republican judges invalidated the election. With Democrats threatening to take control of the government anyway, Davis turned to Grant for help. Without hesitation the president refused to send troops. Grant reminded Davis that the governor himself had approved the election law and that both parties had conducted their campaigns under that law in good faith. "Would it not be prudent, as well as right," he asked the governor, "to yield to the verdict of the people as expressed by their ballots?" Davis promptly resigned, three months before the expiration of his term, and turned the government over to his Democratic opponent. Texas Republicans felt abandoned, but Grant could see no alternative. "Fortunately for the country," said the *New York Times*, "President Grant has acted sensibly in the Texas matter."[11]

Texas was a cakewalk compared with Arkansas, where the political tangle rivaled that in Louisiana. Again Grant tried to avoid overt intervention. Once more, the issue stemmed from a disputed election—in this case, the 1872 contest for governor between Elisha Baxter, the regular Republican candidate, and Joseph Brooks, a Liberal Republican backed also by Democrats. Baxter eked out an apparent victory, which the legislature confirmed early in 1873. But in the ensuing months the new governor appointed Democrats as well as Republicans to office; he favored ending the disenfranchisement of ex-Confederates, was opposed to state aid for railroads, and took other positions that led many Republicans to switch their support to Brooks. Conversely, many Liberal Republicans and Democrats moved into Baxter's camp. These switches notwithstanding, in September 1873 Grant signaled his willingness to protect Baxter from forcible ouster.[12]

By the following spring, however, the so-called Brooks-Baxter war threatened to grow hot. The Arkansas Republicans secured a court order declaring Brooks the governor and staged an armed coup against Baxter. Both sides pleaded with Grant for help, but initially he would do no more than order federal forces in the state to remain neutral and preserve the peace. He urged the two sides to negotiate a settlement and promised to give such an agreement "all the assistance and protection" he legally could. But several weeks passed with no progress. Grant and Williams suggested that Baxter and Brooks convene the legislature, including members who supported each man, to decide the gubernatorial question. But negotiations proved fruitless, and Grant and Williams felt compelled to fall back on the original legislative confirmation of Baxter's election. Williams delivered an opinion upholding the General Assembly's constitutional authority to make a decision, and Grant issued a proclamation recognizing Baxter as governor. Citing calls from Baxter and the legislature for protection under the Constitution's guarantee clause, the president ordered "all turbulent and disorderly persons," that is, Brooks's followers, to disperse. The coup was over, and Brooks relinquished the statehouse to Baxter. Grant and Williams believed that Brooks had actually received a majority in the election, but they felt they had no authority to go against the determination made by the legislature. Baxter solidified his relations with the Democrats, and as later events would show, the outcome of the administration's action marked the effective end of Reconstruction in Arkansas.[13]

Among the most effective arguments leveled by white southerners against the Reconstruction governments was that they were saturated with corruption. The propertied classes in particular portrayed themselves as victims of reckless and self-serving tax and spending policies pursued by the Republican regimes. Although the charges were generally exaggerated, enough thievery, inexperience, and incompetence existed in some states to lend plausibility to the imputation of corruption. For Grant, whose increasingly conservative monetary policy reflected his desire for acceptance by the solidly respectable classes, the allegations of corruption in the South became a source of embarrassment.

Nonetheless, the president believed that recalcitrant southern whites bore considerable responsibility for the supposed misgovernment. In March 1874 he met with a delegation representing the South Carolina Taxpayers Association and the Charleston Chamber of Commerce. The group railed against the state government for extravagance and labeled its tax system a "monstrous oppression . . . administered by those who own a mere fraction of the property of the State." The White House visitors made little headway with the president. He frankly told them "that they had been among the advocates of State Sovereignty, which had brought on the war, and he did not see how they could appeal to Congress or the Executive to interpose between them and their State legislature." Moreover, "after the war the North had been disposed to treat them with great kindness, but . . . their attitude of resistance had forced Congress and the Government and the North into legislation and Amendments to the Constitution which they had been very reluctant to adopt." The president would do no more than express his hope that the South Carolinians "might soon find the relief they desired."[14]

While Grant struggled with the currency question and southern troubles in the winter and spring of 1874, the civil service issue required him to continue his balancing act between reformers and spoilsmen. In his annual message in December 1873 he cited the system of rules he and the Civil Service Board had put into place, but he repeated his call for legislation to give the reforms the sanction and cooperation of Congress. In a draft of his message, he called it "a matter of great embarrassment to the Executive to resist the importunities of New Members of Congress to make changes,—sometimes of the entire federal patronage in their districts—many times on no higher grounds than the failure of the office holders to favor the nomination of the member elect, although there is no complaint of lack of support after the nomination." Not wishing to irritate legislators, he ultimately left this passage out and suggested that Congress create a committee to work with the Civil Service Board to frame regulations that would have the approval of both branches. "Proper rules," he argued, "will protect Congress, as well as the Executive, from much needless persecution." Both chambers appointed such committees, but the selection of members, especially Ben Butler in the House, hardly signaled a congressional embrace of reform.[15]

Moreover, Grant's appointment of William A. Simmons to be the collector of customs in Boston, the most powerful patronage post in New England, raised questions about the sincerity of his own commitment to reform. Reformers protested fervently, primarily because, while holding federal office, Simmons had been an active political ally of Butler. Simmons also drew the ire of Butler's Republican factional opponents, including George Boutwell. Still, Grant refused to withdraw Simmons's name unless his opponents could demonstrate that he was unfit. Withdrawing the nomination simply because of factional objections would constitute an "injustice." In the Senate, Grant's allies defended Simmons's character, against which, they said, his opponents had made no case. Grant's wishes prevailed over the usual dictates of senatorial courtesy, and the nomination carried by a vote of 30 to 16.[16]

The new congressional committees on civil service showed little disposition to enact real reform. Indeed, the House committee gave serious consideration to a bill that would shift the selection of large classes of appointees from the president to members of Congress and eliminate competitive examinations, which congressmen particularly disliked. The bill clearly violated the Constitution and never emerged from committee. Both Grant and civil service commissioner Dorman Eaton conceded that it was "impracticable" to apply the principle of competitive examinations to officers requiring Senate confirmation, but this concession did not assuage the congressional spoilsmen. Congress had kept the Civil Service Board on a starvation diet for years, and the push was on to take away the last crumbs. In mid-April 1874 Grant submitted a temperate special message asking merely for an appropriation equal to the previous year's amount, $25,000, to "continue the work in its present form." But Congress refused, and Butler even tried to force the board to return whatever funds it had left over from earlier appropriations. Although that attack failed, the Civil Service Board was forced to limp along on the $10,000 it had remaining in its account.[17]

These tribulations in the spring of 1874 were momentarily relieved by the White House wedding of eighteen-year-old Nellie Grant in late May. But even though the occasion was a brilliant social event, it hardly gave unalloyed joy to the bride's father. The groom was an Englishman, Algernon Sartoris, whom Nellie had met two years earlier. Grant had doubts about the marriage from the beginning. Upon learning of the couple's engagement, he had written to Sartoris's father to inquire about Algernon's "habits, character and prospects" and his "business qualifications." Grant hoped that Sartoris would become a US citizen and live with Nellie in America, but that was not to be. On May 21, while the Marine Band played the "Wedding March," the president escorted the bride into the East Room, wearing his "usual stolid expression." During the ceremony he averted his tear-filled eyes and "looked steadfastly at the floor." Hamilton Fish and British minister Edward Thornton signed the marriage certificate as the official witnesses, thereby giving the affair a dollop of diplomatic symbolism. But Grant could expect no political dividend. James Garfield probably spoke for many Americans when he grumbled in his diary, "I think the girl makes a great mistake in marrying an Englishman." (Grant's initial wariness was borne out. Sartoris drank to excess and proved unfaithful. The couple split, and Sartoris died at age forty-two in 1893.)[18]

In the summer of 1874 the administration's attention again turned to the South, where, despite the administration's conciliatory overtures, conservative whites grew increasingly defiant. Indeed, Grant's seeming reluctance to intervene may have emboldened them. In Louisiana, Governor Kellogg retained office by the grace of Grant's recognition, but conservatives formed so-called White Leagues to force Republicans out of local office, by violence if necessary. These terrorist groups found encouragement in an opinion issued by Justice Joseph Bradley in the criminal case growing out of the April 1873 Colfax massacre. In federal circuit court, Bradley upheld the appeal of three murderers who had been convicted under the Enforcement Acts. Bradley concluded that the Fourteenth Amendment authorized Congress to legislate regarding action by states but not action by individuals, as had occurred at Colfax. His opinion would thus invalidate portions of the Enforcement Acts. But the district judge impaneled with Bradley disagreed, and their difference of opinion sent the case to the Supreme Court for final adjudication. In the meantime, Kellogg complained to Attorney General Williams that Bradley's opinion, on top of the administration's apparent aversion to intervention, had convinced the terrorists of their immunity from federal action and made them even more audacious.[19]

In July Grant turned down the Mississippi governor's request for troops to ward off violence at the pending city election in Vicksburg on the grounds that the situation did not meet the constitutional justification for such federal action. As the summer wore on, however, reports of actual violence in several states made him more amenable to intervention. From Arkansas, Oliver Morton wrote that conservative whites throughout the South had mounted "a most formidable, aggressive, and hostile movement against the colored people and white Republicans." From east Texas a local judge wrote to the president, "This country is in a state of perfect anarchy!" In late August John Marshall Harlan told new treasury secretary Benjamin Bristow that "the recent slaughter in Tennessee" was part of a larger plan "to force the colored people South into the Democratic ranks, or drive them from the polls." A few days later, White Leaguers at Coushatta, Louisiana, killed six white Republican parish officials and at least three blacks as well. By September, the reign of terror had ousted Republican governments in eight of the state's parishes.[20]

On September 1 Williams traveled to Long Branch to report on the situation to Grant, who was ready to act "decisively and promptly." The president wrote (and published) a letter to Secretary of War William Belknap denouncing the "recent atrocities" as demonstrating "a disregard for law, civil rights and personal protection that ought not to be tolerated in any civilized government." With local authorities seemingly powerless, he said, it was "the duty of the government to give all the aid for the protection of life and civil rights legally authorized." Grant and Williams drafted a circular order to US marshals and attorneys directing them "to proceed with all possible energy and despatch to detect, expose, arrest, and punish the perpetrators of those crimes, and to . . . spare no effort or necessary expense." The president ordered Belknap to consult with Williams about the placement of troops. Grant denied any intention to interfere with pending elections, and the order to Justice Department officials cited the specific laws under which they were to act. "My hope," the president told reporters, "is that the moral effect of the presence of troops in some localities may render their active use unnecessary."[21]

The White Leaguers in Louisiana tested Grant's resolve almost immediately. On September 14 they staged a coup in New Orleans that left more than thirty people dead. They overthrew Kellogg's government and installed as acting governor the Democratic claimant to the lieutenant governor's office until "governor" John McEnery could arrive. The early information Grant received from New Orleans was scanty, but according to one reporter, "It sounded to him very like the first war news of 1861." He resolved to halt any new contagion of rebellion. The next day he issued a proclamation giving the insurgents five days to disperse. On September 16 the cabinet met twice to devise strategy. Postmaster General Marshall Jewell observed that the president was "cool and collected and thoroughly determined."[22]

Even so, the situation offered a prime example of the administration's frustrations in trying to direct a successful Reconstruction policy from Washington while saddled with state politicians who were unequal to the task. Kellogg counted among his supporters the collector of customs at New Orleans, Grant's brother-in-law James F. Casey, but that did not stop the president from scoffing at the governor's "weakness and imbecility." Jewell thought Kellogg was "a first class cuss but there's no getting rid of him." Grant raised the question of calling a special session of Congress to frame a broad-based policy, but Fish and others pointed out that the fall midterm election campaign was well under way and members would not take kindly to being called away from their districts. Jewell and Bristow contended that "a majority of the wealth, intelligence & business interest" favored the Democrat McEnery, and Bristow even suggested that Grant revoke his proclamation. But Grant said he "would never make it up as long as there's an insurgent pretender in the chair." Fish also argued that recognizing the insurrectionary government would encourage "lawlessness & usurpation" and "the violent overthrow of existing Governments." Grant gave no quarter. He ordered additional troops and alerted naval vessels at Key West to be ready to sail to New Orleans. He also ordered that "under no circumstances" was the military in New Orleans to recognize the usurpers. At the end of the five days, he warned, "Such action will be taken as the emergency may require." McEnery quickly saw the futility of further defiance and relinquished the government to Kellogg.[23]

Grant won praise for peacefully quelling the incipient rebellion, but he had not weakened white conservatives' determination to regain power or solved the problem of ineffective and questionable Republican regimes. As Jewell put it, "How to back the Government without backing these worthless reprobates is a question the Cabinet is trying to solve." By the fall of 1874, Democrats had regained control in all but four southern states: Louisiana, South Carolina, Florida, and Mississippi. With state after state falling into Democratic hands, the quest for a solution was growing ever more desperate and ever more futile.[24]

Whether Hamilton Fish would take part in that quest was also growing more doubtful. In the midst of the New Orleans crisis, Fish had left Washington for his summer home on the Hudson. Soon after his arrival, he received a request from the White House to prepare a commission for the appointment of one of Belknap's relatives as minister to Ecuador. Fish suspected Orville Babcock of engineering this appointment, which he regarded as the last straw after a long history of interference by Babcock and others in the affairs of the State Department. "I am tired of this sort of thing," he exploded in his diary. "I fear that the President has the 'third term' in his mind." The next day Fish sent his resignation to the president. He cited unspecified "recent events" that led him to believe his influence as head of the State Department was "overshadowed by others" and his "continuance in office is no longer useful."[25]

Circumstances prevented the two men from conferring until October 24. When they sat down to talk, Grant was "really . . . at a loss" as to Fish's reasons for leaving and asked him to stay. Fish proceeded to unload. He complained of interference by Babcock and others in making appointments. He alleged that someone in the White House had urged the *Washington National Republican* to criticize his policy regarding Cuba, which, he reminded the president, was the administration's policy. He cited the War Department's commissioning of two officers to convey a ceremonial gift of arms to the emperor of Japan, with no notice to the State Department. Either he had lost Grant's confidence, he said, or the president was allowing the State Department to be "ruled & controlled by outside, irregular, & incompetent influences." Fish insisted that Babcock was not "a safe Counsellor to the President in matters pertaining to my Department," and he "could no longer submit to interference & meddling either by him or by the other Departments."[26]

Grant admitted "that things had occurred, which should not have been allowed." He insisted, however, that "they had in every instance been the result entirely of thoughtlessness & without the slightest idea of interfering with the appropriate duties" of the State Department or "any want of respect" for Fish. When the secretary said he could stay only with a guarantee of no further interference, Grant promised "there would be no recurrence of any cause of complaint." Upon this assurance the secretary withdrew his resignation. Part of Fish's annoyance reflected his sense of punctilio, but he also had little tolerance for the staff system Grant had brought with him from the army. As he had written privately, he thought Babcock was "spoiled by his position" and lacked "consideration for the official responsibilities & proper authority (official) of civilians." And yet, even though he was well aware of suspicions regarding Babcock's honesty, Fish raised no such questions with the president. Protection of his turf rather than ethical considerations lay at the root of his disgruntlement in 1874, and he accepted Grant's assurance that there would be no further trespassing.[27]

Fish's threat to leave compounded Grant's anxiety about the approaching midterm elections. The administration's southern policy, coupled with the Republicans' push for additional civil rights legislation, left the party little hope for maintaining, let alone expanding, Republican representation from the South. Some northern Republicans staunchly defended these policies to their constituents, but Liberals such as Carl Schurz preached that after giving black men the right to vote, it was "much wiser and safer" to "leave all else to the gradual progress of public opinion." Grant's middle-of-the-road approach to civil service hardly pleased reformers and did nothing to spark enthusiasm among regular Republicans. The Crédit Mobilier scandal, the Salary Grab, and the Sanborn contract, despite being relatively minor incidents and in some cases tainting both parties, fed a widespread sense that the party in power was hopelessly corrupt. By the same token, the Democrats held the Republicans accountable for the nation's economic collapse and the depression, which was well into its second year. And the currency issue left the GOP badly divided. Northeastern Republicans defended the president's hard-money pronouncements, but those in the inflationist West faced a hard fight against soft-money Democrats and new independent parties touting greenback expansion.[28]

Grant's enemies tried to make him the issue in the midterm campaign, blaming him for the nation's troubles and accusing him of jockeying to get himself reelected in 1876. Just as the *New York Herald* had trumpeted "Caesarism" in the slow news summer of 1873, a "third term" scare in 1874 was largely an invention of the press. In the summer and fall the *Herald* published numerous articles decrying Grant's supposedly limitless ambition. Whitelaw Reid, who aimed to make the *New York Tribune* "an eyesore to Grant," believed that the third term issue "might give the Liberals their opportunity." Journalist and former diplomat John Bigelow spent July and August researching the "historical authority" for the two term tradition for an article designed "to give Grant's third term pretensions their *coup de grace*." In mid-September Reid published Bigelow's piece, covering eight columns in the *Tribune*. Both Bigelow and Reid pushed for an anti–third term resolution at the New York Republican convention. But largely under the influence of administration forces led by Conkling, the state convention was silent on the issue and instead adopted a plank that hailed Grant's administration as "distinguished by achievements in domestic and foreign policy unsurpassed in the history of the country."[29]

In large measure, the press's harping on the third term bogeyman revealed less about Grant's ambition than about his stature in the nation. His opponents' alarm illustrated his strength. Seemingly all he had to do was ask, and he could lead the country into imperial ruin. Whether or not men like Reid actually believed that Grant craved another term as president, their overheated, preemptive campaign implied that they thought he had enough national appeal to win another term or at least sufficient support to capture a third nomination. In mid-October the *Herald* published what purported to be interviews on the subject with members of Congress. If the paper sought to discredit the idea of a third term, its effort backfired, for it reported a substantial proportion of members in each house "favorable" to it. The journalists' pumped-up anxiety about a third term, whether real or feigned, did not represent the president's rejection by the American people. Instead, the plausibility of a third term scenario reflected a tacit recognition of Grant's continued ascendancy in the American political landscape. As the 1874 election campaign neared its end, Bigelow wailed, "I am astonished to find how strong is the feeling in favor of continuing Grant in power, and how many are ready to elect our President for life."[30]

As usual, Grant played no overt part in the fall campaign, but as in years past, he took a "nonpolitical" trip through the West in October, which brought him into contact with welcoming crowds along the way. On a brief tour through the Indian Territory, he highlighted one of his more popular policies, making short speeches to groups from the Cherokee, Choctaw, and Creek nations. "While I hold my present position," he declared, "I shall endeavor to see that you are protected in the enjoyment of your personal and civil rights." He praised the Indians for their accomplishments in farming and stock raising. "With industry and a proper observance of the laws of the country and the rights of others, you cannot fail to become prosperous and useful citizens." At Springfield, Illinois, Grant delivered a short address at the dedication of the

Lincoln monument, where he saluted the martyred president's courage and unselfishness in the struggle to preserve the nation's free government. Lincoln, he said, remained "the same staunch, unyielding servant of the people," despite the "obloquy, personal abuse and hate" critics had leveled against him "without restraint through the press, upon the stump and in private circles." Grant had fashioned these remarks carefully, and the implicit parallel with his own persecution could not have been inadvertent.[31]

The returns from the October elections confirmed Republicans' worst fears. They suffered substantial losses in the key states of Indiana and Ohio. In both, the money question loomed large, and in Ohio, a breakaway temperance movement also hurt the party. Still, the *Herald* and other papers continued to toll the third term tocsin and tried to make the nonissue a test for Republican leaders, demanding that they reveal whether or not they favored it. This clamor alarmed the old abolitionist Gerrit Smith, who publicly condemned it as a "trap" to divert attention from "the really sole issue which is before the country": whether the Democratic Party, "the murderous enemy of the black man," should be allowed back into power. The pressure for an anti–third term pronouncement focused on New York governor John A. Dix, who was locked in a fierce contest for reelection. In a speech at Cooper Union, Dix ignored the matter, but under questioning he said he opposed a third term and thought that when the "proper time" arrived, Grant would "express his desire to be relieved from the cares of office."[32]

Shortly after the October elections, Harry Wilson, who favored Bristow for 1876, told the treasury secretary that the losses "ought to serve as a lesson to the President, and induce him to permit an authoritative declaration against a third term." Without such a declaration, New York would go Democratic in November, Wilson warned, and "then it will no longer be a question of a third term, but of what democrat we shall have as a successor to the second term." Bristow took the hint and tried to enlist Fish and Jewell to help maneuver Grant into a declination. At the next cabinet meeting, Bristow urged the president to publicly disavow any intention to run again, noting that he could cite Dix's comment as the reason for making such a statement. But Grant did not bite. As Fish noted in his diary, "The President said that the whole thing was too absurd to be talked of, that it had been started by the New York Herald as one of its sensations and for the purpose of personal annoyance to him. That it had been dead for nearly a year but had been lately revived by the Sun, Tribune and Democratic press. That he had never given it a thought or spoken of it except in ridicule and contempt and he was not disposed now to do otherwise than he had done." Fish said the issue was "working disastrously" in New York, but the president stood his ground against issuing a formal statement, although he did authorize the secretaries to repeat "anything he had said on the subject."[33]

The next morning the *National Republican* carried a leaked account of the cabinet meeting, stating that Grant "did not think it would comport with his dignity as President of the United States to make a statement on this question in response to the clamors of the newspapers." "These expressions of the President," the paper added, "were heartily indorsed by the members of the Cabinet." Fish, Bristow, and Jewell were convinced that the leak had come from Grant himself and were disturbed by what they considered a mischaracterization of their views. They decided it would be "unbecoming" to say anything in print, but they considered themselves free to tell people "individually" that they had "not expressed any assent." This refusal by the secretaries to accept Grant's explanation bespoke a lack of trust for the president, which was compounded by their willingness to talk behind his back. Grant's relationship with Fish, tested but solid, could survive such behavior. The relative neophytes in the cabinet, Bristow and Jewell, stood on shakier ground. The friction over the third term question augured increasingly strained relations down the road.[34]

Dix lost the New York governorship to Democrat Samuel Tilden, and the Republicans also lost the state assembly and a US Senate seat. Across the country in 1874, as Fish put it, a "Tornado" swept Republicans from office. For the first time since before the war, the Democrats won a majority in the US House of Representatives. Republicans saw their seats dwindle to just 103, compared with 182 for the Democrats and 8 won by independents. Democratic resurgence in the South caused a 60 percent drop in Republican representation from that region. Republicans lost nearly as heavily in the Midwest, where inflationism loomed large. In New England, where Republicans tended to endorse Grant's monetary views, their losses were fewer but still substantial. The GOP retained a solid hold on the Senate, but among the class of senators chosen for the new term beginning in 1875, fourteen were Democrats and eleven were Republicans.[35]

Bigelow gleefully told Reid that the elections spelled the end of "Grant & the Third Term abomination." But the degree to which the allegation of Grant's ambition affected the outcome is unknowable. It likely did so less as an issue in itself than as a convenient handle for voters who were already alienated from the Republican Party because of hard times, southern troubles, and scandal. Even so, cabinet members who had most feared the impact of the third term cry held Grant accountable for the party's loss. Jewell complained that the president had not "really appreciated the importance of the Republican party." "The verdict rendered at the late elections," he wrote to Bancroft Davis, "is not that the people are dissatisfied with Republicans, and Republican ideas, but that they are greatly dissatisfied with a Republican administration." At the same time, with stunning two-facedness, Jewell sent Grant's old mentor Elihu Washburne a sugary letter describing the president as "so honest and outspoken that he lacks as a politician, of course, but it is his honesty that makes the public believe in him."[36]

Bristow's reaction mirrored Jewell's. He wrote to a Kentucky associate, "I do not believe there has been any general change of political conviction in the minds of the people, but there has been a restless feeling under existing rule and a disposition to have a change. . . . I feel very confident that with good management and the introduction of proper reforms, the Republicans can yet carry the country in 1876." Within weeks, Butler was warning Fish that he suspected "two Presidential aspirants in the Cabinet, Jewell & Bristow." Neither would "be true to the President," and both were "constantly advertising themselves in the papers by declarations of great intended reforms which turn out to be small things." Bristow was not yet admitting that he hoped to head the ticket in 1876, but his aide, treasury solicitor Bluford Wilson, told his brother Harry that if the secretary championed reform, "before another year he would be the strongest man in the party, and able to take a nomination or dictate one at his pleasure."[37]

For his part, after the 1874 election defeat, Grant was determined to present a strong front in his annual message at the opening of the lame-duck session in December. Three issues stood out: the depressed economy, civil service reform, and the South. Violence during the recent election campaign lent particular urgency to the southern question. Giving vent to his anger, the president drafted fiery passages for his message that Fish considered better suited for "a heated Congressional debate or a rough newspaper article." Grant moderated his remarks, but they still rang with passion and reflected his frustration at the intractable problem of Reconstruction.[38]

The president condemned the "violence and intimidation" that White Leagues and similar groups had perpetrated before the election

—stockpiling arms and conducting "military drills with menacing demonstrations." Most egregious, "murders enough were committed to spread terror among those whose political action was to be suppressed." In the face of this terrorism, Grant upheld the use of troops and justified "interference by Federal authority" under the Fifteenth Amendment and the 1870 Enforcement Act. Indeed, if the amendment and law did not warrant such interference, "then they are without meaning, force, or effect, and the whole scheme of colored enfranchisement is worse than mockery and little better than a crime." Acknowledging that some people exaggerated the outrages and others belittled them, Grant thought Americans should be focusing on "a correct survey" of conditions and "rebuking wrong and aiding the proper authorities in punishing it." He dismissed white southerners' protests about "negro rule" as "a most delusive cry." To be sure, southerners in some states had "most trying governments to live under." "But," he asked, "can they proclaim themselves entirely irresponsible for this condition? They can not. Violence has been rampant in some localities, and has either been justified or denied by those who could have prevented it." He warned southerners that any "theory" under which they need not fear further federal interference was "a great mistake." Although he regretted adding "one jot or tittle to Executive duties or powers," he vowed to enforce the Constitution and laws "with rigor." For a lasting solution, Grant urged, "Treat the negro as a citizen and a voter, as he is and must remain, and soon parties will be divided, not on the color line, but on principle. Then we shall have no complaint of sectional interference." Events soon showed the pertinence—and the futility—of such advice.[39]

On the very day Congress listened to the reading of the president's message, racial violence in Vicksburg, Mississippi, left as many as a dozen African Americans dead. Later that night white raiders entered blacks' homes and killed many more. The state legislature called for help, and Grant responded with a proclamation against the "insurgents," preparatory to sending additional troops to the state. He also asked Sheridan to visit Vicksburg and New Orleans to "ascertain the true condition of affairs" and authorized him to assume command of the Military Division of the South. Sheridan started his tour within a few days and arrived in New Orleans in the midst of an incident that profoundly undermined the already waning northern will to back federal intervention.[40]

Louisiana had been in a state of turmoil since the November election. The situation so alarmed observers in Washington that the House of Representatives dispatched a subcommittee of its Committee on the Condition of the South to investigate. As in past years, terrorist groups backing the Democrats had intimidated black and white Republican voters, and after the election, Governor Kellogg's Republican allies on the Returning Board reversed results allegedly gained by such tactics. The board's action reduced a supposed Democratic majority in the next Louisiana house of representatives to a tie, leaving the house itself to determine contests for the five remaining seats. In late December Attorney General Williams told the cabinet he had heard that the Democrats intended to insist on taking the offices they considered rightfully theirs. Grant suggested that "in case of trouble," it might be necessary to place the state under martial guard. Williams expressed doubt about the statutory authority to do so, but events in New Orleans soon took over.[41]

On January 4, 1875, members of the Louisiana house of representatives gathered for an organizational meeting. On the initial roll call by the clerk of the previous house, fifty-two Republicans and fifty Democrats responded. One of the Democrats immediately nominated Louis Wiltz for speaker and conducted a voice vote that was unrecognized by the clerk. Wiltz seized the gavel and organized the house for the Democrats. Several Republicans protested, scuffles ensued, and some members drew pistols or knives. Wiltz quickly called in the local commander of US troops, Colonel Phillipe Regis De Trobriand, who restored order with a few words. The Democrats then awarded the five contested seats to their colleagues and claimed the majority. The Republican members sought help from Kellogg, who asked De Trobriand to return to the house and remove "all persons not returned as legal members." With a squad of troops, the colonel escorted the five Democratic claimants out. When most of their legally elected party colleagues also filed out in protest, the Republicans claimed the majority, elected their own speaker, and organized the house.[42]

Sheridan arrived in New Orleans later that night and reported to Belknap that "a spirit of defiance to all lawful authority" pervaded the city and state. The general saw the root of the trouble in the terrorism committed by the White Leagues and similar groups. He suggested that Congress or the president declare them "banditti" subject to trial by military commission. Belknap did not specifically endorse this proposal, but in response to Sheridan's several telegrams, he wired, "The President and all of us have full confidence in and thoroughly approve your course." In a follow-up telegram, Belknap assured Sheridan that "the President and Cabinet confide in your wisdom, and rest in the belief that all acts of yours have been and will be judicious." In an effort to clarify the confused reports coming out of New Orleans, the administration gave copies of the telegrams to the press.[43]

The supposed intrusion of the military in a state legislature startled the nation, and the publication of Sheridan's telegraphic exchange with Belknap exacerbated the shock. Few events were more damaging to the cause of Reconstruction or Grant's efforts to sustain it. Massachusetts congressman Henry Dawes wrote that many of his colleagues were "amazed and dumfounded" at the administration's "stupidity and blindness." Releasing and approving Sheridan's "banditti" dispatch were "blunders equaled only by the crime of dispersing a Legislature at the point of the bayonet." Longtime supporters of African Americans such as Wendell Phillips urged the administration to support Sheridan "promptly and vigorously," but the more prevalent reaction was protest expressed in meetings in several cities. Although the president had not ordered De Trobriand's removal of the Democrats, critics said it confirmed all their allegations about Grant's desire to establish a military despotism on the ruins of the Republic. Those calling for a protest meeting in New York claimed, erroneously, that federal troops "acting under orders from the President" had "broken into and dispersed" the legislature, thus committing a "crime" and a "marked attack upon the rights of American citizenship." Although Republicans as well as Democrats attended these meetings, such overheated rhetoric convinced administration allies that it was "preposterous" to call the protests "a *non-partisan* movement." "The whole object of this meeting," Edwards Pierrepont told Grant, "is to break down the administration and build the opposition upon its ruins." Heated disagreements also broke out in Congress. Carl Schurz warned that "the lawlessness of power is becoming far more dangerous to all than the lawlessness of the mob." George Edmunds defended the administration's use of "the power of government to protect defenseless and innocent men against an organized conspiracy to deprive them of liberty, and of life, and of right."[44]

Belknap's published dispatches complicated the administration's efforts to deal with the crisis. Fish, Jewell, and Bristow insisted that they were not included in the "all of us" that Belknap said had approved Sheridan's course. But Grant "very warmly defended the telegrams and said they did not express more than approval of Sheridan's acts" rather than his recommendation. Fish condemned De Trobriand's action as "an outrage upon the independence of the State Legislature." Jewell agreed, but Bristow took a more nuanced approach. While he did not approve of the military action in the legislature, he believed the "great mass" of whites were "disloyal & prepared to screen and justify murder of the blacks & persecution of political opponents." Williams argued that the administration could justify the intrusion in the legislature by "treating the Military as a 'Posse Comitatus' called in to maintain the peace." Grant agreed, adding that the troops could be regarded as such because they were in the state "in pursuance of a call made in accordance with the Constitution." But Fish insisted that the army could never be regarded as a posse comitatus. The administration should "disclaim and denounce" De Trobriand's action and "withdraw" from Belknap's "expression of confidence" in Sheridan. But Grant said he would "certainly not denounce it" and would not "censure" Sheridan. The president asked Williams to draft a message to Congress that would "recapitulate the events which he thought would show the necessity of what had occurred."[45]

The need for care in framing this message grew more urgent with the return of the congressional subcommittee investigating the Louisiana election. The three congressmen happened to be present when De Trobriand removed the Democrats from the legislature, and they confirmed Sheridan's version of events. But rumor had it that their report would claim that virtually no intimidation had occurred during the 1874 election, that the Returning Board had wrongly awarded seats to Republicans in districts that Democrats had legitimately won, and that the five expelled members were entitled to their places. Bristow saw a "whitewash" coming, and Grant was angry that Speaker Blaine had not taken his advice about the membership of the committee, which included a Democrat and two Republicans who were not friendly to the administration. Despite the subcommittee's apparent unanimity, Grant remained "determined under no circumstances to apologize for anything that had been done" by the military at New Orleans. He asked Belknap to have Sheridan submit an account of the "political murders" in Louisiana since 1866, which he intended to incorporate into his message.[46]

Once he had a complete draft, Grant presented it to several Republican senators to lay the groundwork for an endorsement by Congress. One of them, Timothy Howe, wrote to a friend, "The *great* man in this crisis is the President. You ought to see him. Just as much excited as your door posts would be if a fever and ague patient entered the house. I saw him with some six or eight of the ablest men in the Senate in consultation on his message. Every paragraph was scrutinized. No single suggestion was made that he did not instantly see the whole force of."[47]

At the outset of his January 13 message, the president decried the "lawlessness, turbulence, and bloodshed" that had characterized political affairs in Louisiana since the beginning of Reconstruction. The current trouble stemmed from the contested election of 1872. Relying heavily on Williams's draft, Grant gave a detailed account of the administration's legalistic response to that dispute based on the Fifteenth Amendment and the Enforcement Acts. "A shameful and undisguised conspiracy," he said, had engaged in "the most glaring frauds and forgeries" against Kellogg and the Republicans, and the election turned out to be "a gigantic fraud" with "no reliable returns of its result." Nonetheless, the US courts, acting conformably with the Constitution and statutes, had determined Kellogg's victory, which a Senate investigating committee had also upheld. On balance, Grant had concluded that Kellogg had "more right" than his competitor to recognition as governor. Although Grant had asked Congress to review the question of the 1872 election, it had done nothing, and "its inaction has produced great evil."

In gruesome detail, Grant recounted the "butchery of citizens" at Colfax, Coushatta, and elsewhere in the state, marked by a "bloodthirstiness and barbarity . . . hardly surpassed by any acts of savage warfare." With bitter irony he noted, "Fierce denunciations ring through the country about office holding and election matters in Louisiana, while every one of the Colfax miscreants goes unwhipped of justice, and no way can be found in this boasted land of civilization and Christianity to punish the perpetrators of this bloody and monstrous crime."

As for the legislative elections of 1874, Grant said he had "no evidence" that the Returning Board had not operated according to law; therefore the persons they designated as elected were entitled to their seats. On January 4 "the Democratic minority of the house undertook to seize its organization by fraud and violence." The president acknowledged that military interference in a legislature "is repugnant to our ideas of government," but in this case, circumstances seemed "to exempt the military from any intentional wrong." The troops had received no orders from Washington to take such action. They had been "placed in Louisiana to prevent domestic violence and aid in the enforcement of the State laws," and they "may well have supposed that it was their duty to act when called upon by the governor for that purpose." More important, their presence "prevented bloodshed and the loss of life," and in the end, "nobody was disturbed by the military who had a legal right at that time to occupy a seat in the legislature." In passages he added to Williams's draft, Grant particularly excused Sheridan, who "never

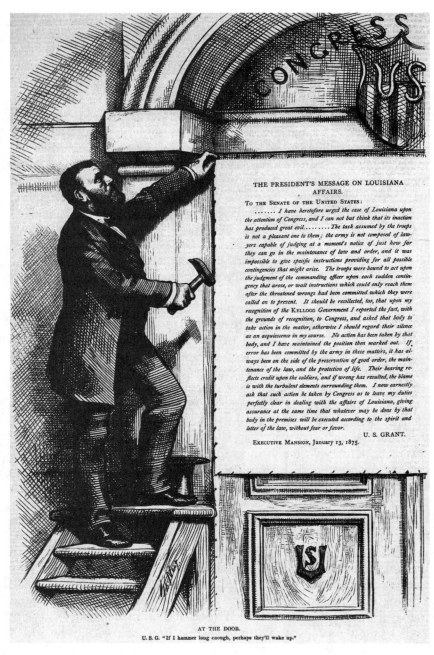

THE PRESIDENT'S MESSAGE ON LOUISIANA
AFFAIRS.

To THE SENATE OF THE UNITED STATES:

.... I have heretofore urged the case of Louisiana upon
the attention of Congress, and I can not but think that its inaction
has produced great evil......... The task assumed by the troops
is not a pleasant one to them; the army is not composed of lawyers capable of judging at a moment's notice of just how far
they can go in the maintenance of law and order, and it was
impossible to give specific instructions providing for all possible
contingencies that might arise. The troops were bound to act upon
the judgment of the commanding officer upon each sudden contingency that arose, or wait instructions which could only reach them
after the threatened wrongs had been committed which they were
called on to prevent. It should be recollected, too, that upon my
recognition of the KELLOGG Government I reported the fact, with
the grounds of recognition, to Congress, and asked that body to
take action in the matter, otherwise I should regard their silence
as an acquiescence in my course. No action has been taken by that
body, and I have maintained the position then marked out. If
error has been committed by the army in these matters, it has always been on the side of the preservation of good order, the maintenance of the law, and the protection of life. Their bearing reflects credit upon the soldiers, and if wrong has resulted, the blame
is with the turbulent elements surrounding them. I now earnestly
ask that such action be taken by Congress as to leave my duties
perfectly clear in dealing with the affairs of Louisiana, giving
assurance at the same time that whatever may be done by that
body in the premises will be executed according to the spirit and
letter of the law, without fear or favor.

U. S. GRANT.

EXECUTIVE MANSION, January 13, 1875.

AT THE DOOR.

U. S. G. "If I hammer long enough, perhaps they'll wake up."

U. S. Grant: "If I hammer long enough, perhaps they'll wake up." (*Harper's Weekly*, January 30, 1875) proposed to do an illegal act." In framing his "banditti" dispatch, the general had been influenced by "the utterly lawless condition of society surrounding him." The president asserted that "nothing would give me greater pleasure than to see reconciliation and tranquility everywhere prevail, and thereby remove all necessity for the presence of troops." But, he warned, "neither Ku Klux Klans, White Leagues, nor any other association using arms and violence to execute their unlawful purposes can be permitted in that way to govern any part of this country."[48]

In the entire history of Reconstruction, Grant's Louisiana message stands out as an eloquent affirmation of the federal government's constitutional duty and moral obligation to defend justice. Republicans distressed about the political impact of the New Orleans crisis welcomed it as a much-needed tonic. "The Republican party has been scared to death," Howe wrote. "But the color is coming back." Grant got a great boost the next day when the *New York Times* published a long analysis of the New Orleans incident by eminent lawyer E. W. Stoughton, who asserted that because only "lawfully returned" members could "participate in the organization of a legislative body," Grant's upholding of De Trobriand's action sustained an "inflexible" rule "indispensable to the existence of every representative assembly, and, indeed, to representative governments." E. R. Hoar told the president, "The Republican party and the Country owe you a debt of gratitude." From the opposing perspective, John Bigelow complained to Samuel Tilden that "Grant has pretty effectually succeeded in identifying his party with his Louisiana policy."[49]

Still, Bigelow and others doubted that Republicans could remain unified for long. The publication of the House subcommittee's report two days after Grant's message provided fodder for skeptics. Protest meetings continued, driven by administration opponents eager to exploit the crisis to discredit executive intervention in the South once and for all. A gathering in Boston's Faneuil Hall organized primarily by Charles Francis Adams passed resolutions declaring that "the sword" must "be the supporter and not the destroyer of civil liberty" and warning that "illegal violence, with whatever pretences it may be covered, and whatever object it may pursue, must inevitably end at last in the arbitrary and despotic government of a single person."[50]

Grant's message, as stirring as it was, did not chart a new course or frame a permanent settlement to the Louisiana question. Rather, he aimed to prod Congress to take such action "as to leave my duties perfectly clear in dealing with the affairs of Louisiana." In the Senate, men of both parties endlessly replayed the events of January 4 in minute detail, but the avalanche of words produced no action. Republicans defended the administration's course but seemed incapable of framing a concrete policy for dealing with Louisiana.[51]

The House proved more responsive. The Republicans sent the other members of the Committee on the Condition of the South to Louisiana essentially to redo the botched investigation of the original subcommittee. The committee's leaders, George F. Hoar and William A. Wheeler, also hoped they could work out a compromise to resolve the Louisiana impasse and eliminate the state's troubles from the national discourse. House Radicals, meanwhile, pushed for two new measures—one to strengthen federal enforcement of voting rights, and another to enhance the protection of other civil rights. With little time before the lame-duck session was scheduled to end on March 3, these men realized this might be their last opportunity to enact legislation to undergird the party's Reconstruction goals. Led by Ben Butler, they pushed the civil rights issue first, believing it was more likely to spur Republican unity, which they could then marshal to pass an enforcement measure. The House had yet to act on Sumner's civil rights bill, which the Senate had passed during the previous session. When Butler brought the bill before the House, Democrats invoked every parliamentary roadblock at their disposal. Once again, the schools provision proved to be the main hang-up. Finally, a consensus emerged among Republicans to remove that provision, and the bill passed on February 4. Because it differed from the Senate version, the bill would have to go before that body again.[52]

Although some Liberal Republicans sided with the Democrats against the bill, the sense of unity and purpose sparked by Grant's message helped rally the Republicans on civil rights. As the bill neared passage, Henry Dawes wrote to Samuel Bowles, "Party lines in both Houses have straightened up wonderfully since this Louisiana fight, and both parties have resolved to stand or die in the old attitude toward the South. Party intensity runs higher than at any time since the war. Nobody will step out a hair."[53]

Unfortunately, within days the Brooks-Baxter war reignited in Arkansas, and Grant's response vitiated much of the administration's renewed credibility. In the spring of 1874 Grant had recognized Elisha Baxter as governor of the state over Joseph Brooks. Before that official recognition, however, Baxter and the Democratic legislature had called for a state convention to write a new constitution they could use to solidify Democratic control of the state. In the fall elections conducted by the Baxter government, the new constitution prevailed, as did the Democratic candidate for governor, Augustus Garland, and Baxter relinquished his office to Garland. Republicans cried foul, insisting that both the constitution and the election were illegitimate on the grounds that Baxter had cheated Brooks out of the governorship in 1872. As an illegitimate claimant to office, they said, Baxter had had no authority to convene the legislature to call the constitutional convention. After Grant's May 1874 proclamation recognizing Baxter as governor, the House of Representatives had created a select committee to investigate the situation in Arkansas. Headed by Vermont Republican Luke Poland, the committee considered these new developments within its purview.[54]

For months, the administration had monitored the trouble in Arkansas. After Garland's putative election, Grant took no immediate action, but in his December annual message, the president noted that the new constitution had come into being in a manner not in accord with the rules for amendment contained in the 1868 constitution, and the convention had set a new election to be held "in a manner contrary to the then existing laws of the State." As the weeks passed, his skepticism about the legitimacy of the new constitution and the Garland government grew. Nor could he take much comfort when Garland told him that if a White League existed in the state, "I do not know it." In late January the president went up to Capitol Hill to press his views, emphasizing that Congress ought to take action to avert the kind of incident that had occurred in New Orleans. He met with the investigating committee but was disappointed to find Poland and others leaning toward recognition of the Garland regime. The next day, when he reported the conversation to the cabinet, Fish described the president as "very warm and decided in his language and apparent determination," but the cabinet reached no conclusion at this January 22 meeting.[55]

Two weeks later, the Poland committee issued a report upholding the new Arkansas constitution and Garland. Even though the creation of the new document diverged from the amendment method prescribed in the old constitution, the committee concluded that the people of the state had a right to make their own constitution, and the new one was "republican in form." The committee could find no grounds "to say the General Government can, or ought to, interfere; and no amount of irregularity in the processes by which this state of things was brought about furnish[es] just reason for doing so." The latter clause implied a blanket injunction against federal intervention to uphold processes established by the state constitutions created under Reconstruction. The committee submitted its report on Saturday, February 6; on Monday, Grant, without consulting the cabinet, responded with a short, sharply worded message.[56]

Even though Grant had originally believed that Brooks received a majority of votes in the 1872 election, he had recognized Baxter in his May 1874 proclamation because the state legislature had done so. Now the president returned to his initial conclusion that Brooks had rightfully been elected governor in 1872. He asserted that "all the testimony" sustained that view, and he sent along with his message a mélange of documents that, he implied, contained such proof. Brooks had been "unlawfully deprived" of his office, and his enemies had used "violence, intimidation, and revolutionary proceedings" to overthrow the constitution of 1868 and create a new constitution and government. Such "proceedings, if permitted to stand, practically ignore all rights of minorities in all the States." In preparing his message, Grant had considered recommending that the new government and constitution be declared "nugatory and void" and Brooks declared the "lawful governor." But he backed away from that position and instead questioned whether Congress ought to recognize "a precedent so dangerous to the stability of State government, if not of the National Government also." He "earnestly" asked Congress to "take definite action in this matter to relieve the Executive from acting upon questions which should be decided by the legislative branch."[57]

The vagueness of Grant's reference to "all the testimony" and his apparent failure to consult with the attorney general resulted in a message that lacked the legal acuity and rhetorical impact of his Louisiana message. To many, the Arkansas statement seemed like an inexplicable flip-flop, and some suspected the worst kind of motives. Fish thought the president had been led into "a grievous error," and he and Bristow speculated that Grant had given in to influence by Arkansas' Republican senators, who had had a falling out with Baxter over his refusal to support a railroad bond bill. John Harlan warned that if the president removed Garland by force, "the Republican party will go under never to rise again."[58]

But in fact, Grant had raised an important question about whether enemies of Reconstruction might use similar purportedly constitutional means to overthrow established governments in the future. "What is there," he asked, "to prevent each of the States recently admitted to Federal relations on certain conditions changing their constitutions and violating their pledges if this action in Arkansas is acquiesced in?" As it turned out, most Republicans proved unwilling to join the president in opposing such methods and instead saw them as consistent with the people's fundamental right to form their own government. Illinois congressman J. D. Ward, the sole dissenter on the Poland committee, stood by Grant and warned that if Congress sanctioned the "grand machinery of fraud" used in Arkansas, there would be "no stability to government, no rights to minorities left." But his was a lone voice. Most Republicans accepted the fait accompli in Arkansas.[59]

Grant had no intention of going beyond what Congress or public opinion would sanction. Two weeks after his message he told Bristow, "Brooks & his friends are going to insist that I shall overthrow the Garland Government in case Congress takes no action in the Ark[ansas] matter, but I cannot do that." If Congress approved the Poland report or did nothing, he said, "I will at once recognize Garland & sustain him." Bristow admitted that he had been "a good deal disturbed" by the message; he now asked Grant if he, Bristow, could pass on to others what the president had said about recognizing Garland. Grant said he preferred that Bristow not repeat it. He added that his "only purpose" in issuing the message "was to get Congress to take hold of the whole southern question & settle it." Again, Bristow asked permission to repeat the president's views, and again Grant demurred. Nonetheless, the secretary broke the president's confidence the next day. Suspecting that Grant had some "method" in mind, he recounted the conversation to Harlan and said he thought Grant aimed to "quiet me."[60]

Bristow also reported the conversation to Fish, but he added a detail guaranteed to stoke the secretary of state's suspicions of the White House. Bristow noted that during his conversation with Grant, Babcock had come into the room, as "he always does[;] he never allows me to be with the President without coming into the room." Whereas Bristow told Harlan that twice the president had asked him not to repeat his views, Bristow told Fish that Grant initially had "no objection" to his doing so, "but Babcock interposed and said that he thought that nothing should be said, that it was necessary to be bold and take decided ground, and not enter upon explanation or disclaimer. . . . [T]hereupon the President withdrew his assent and said that he did not wish anything said about it." Bristow also told Fish that he was convinced that Babcock and Secretary of the Interior Columbus Delano were conspiring against him.[61]

The Senate took no action on Grant's Arkansas message. In the House, members engaged in a short but acrimonious debate on the Poland report. Despite Ward's defense of Grant's position, the prevailing opinion was that the federal government could not indefinitely freeze the constitutions created during congressional Reconstruction. On a vote to approve the report, 80 Republicans stood with Ward, but 65 joined the Democrats, and the report carried by a vote of 150 to 81. A week later, Grant recognized Garland's government.[62]

The Arkansas imbroglio underscored the need for a speedy settlement of the Louisiana issue. The House Committee on the Condition of the South had spent several weeks in the state, not only reinvestigating the tortured election of 1874 but also trying to broker an agreement between the warring factions. This latter task fell largely to committee member William Wheeler, a New York Republican highly regarded for his negotiating skills. The essentials of a deal had emerged by the time chairman George Hoar presented the committee's findings to the House in late February. The report cited the endemic political violence in the state, including incidents that took place in 1874. It accused the Returning Board of erroneously seating some Republican representatives, but it also condemned the attempted usurpation of the legislature by the Democrats. The committee declined to pass judgment on the legality of De Trobriand's action but acknowledged that it had prevented bloodshed. To effect a settlement, Hoar submitted resolutions recognizing Kellogg as governor until the end of his term and urging the Louisiana house to redress the Returning Board's mistakes and give representatives their rightful seats. By a party-line vote the US House of Representatives approved the resolutions, opening the way for implementation of the so-called Wheeler adjustment, whereby Kellogg kept his job, the Democrats took control of the house, and the Republicans retained their majority in the state senate. By taking no action, the US Senate tacitly accepted this outcome. Senate Republicans did, however, pass a resolution approving Grant's action "in protecting the government in Louisiana" and the people against domestic violence, as well as "enforcing the laws of the United States in that State."[63]

Many Republicans viewed the Louisiana and Arkansas crises as object lessons in the intractability of the southern problem and as warnings against future intervention. Others, however, thought these events highlighted the need to provide the president with additional weapons to protect elections and the right to vote. Grant's allies fashioned a bill that would close lacunae in existing enforcement legislation. It would prohibit discrimination in voter registration, bar intimidation with firearms at polling places, and outlaw conspiracy to overthrow the government or interfere with the execution of laws. Most important, the measure would once again empower the president to suspend the writ of habeas corpus. But the bill's sponsors encountered resistance in the Republican caucus, and Grant did not make it a legislative priority. Although his Louisiana message had helped galvanize House Republicans to pass the civil rights bill, the Louisiana and Arkansas troubles had the opposite effect on the enforcement measure. After prolonged debate, the bill's backers agreed to restrict the habeas corpus provision to Louisiana, Mississippi, Arkansas, and Alabama and to mandate its expiration after two years. The House passed the bill in this form four days before the end of the session by a vote of 135 to 114, with 32 Republicans voting against it. In the Senate it did not go beyond a second reading. With Democrats poised to take over in the next House, the prospect of strengthening the president's hand with new enforcement legislation came to an end.[64]

In the last days of the session, the Senate did take up the civil rights bill. Democrats tried to attach amendments that would necessitate sending it back to the House, thus killing it, but the Republicans thwarted them. Although Schurz and other Liberal Republicans opposed the measure, it passed by a vote of 38 to 26. On March 1 Grant signed the bill, which became the last major piece of civil rights legislation enacted before the mid-twentieth century. The Civil Rights Act of 1875 barred discrimination by race in public accommodations, inns, public conveyances, theaters, and other places of amusement and in the selection of juries. The impact of the law was slight, however, and its judicial emasculation began almost immediately. Three weeks after Grant signed the act, a federal circuit judge instructed a jury in Memphis that the law represented an "almost grotesque exercise of national authority" in violation of the Constitution, which did not assign such matters to the federal government but reserved them to the states. In addition, despite the act's seemingly sweeping provisions, blacks found that it provided little protection, for it could work no fundamental change in racial attitudes. "What we want just now," said the *New York Tribune*, "is something to quiet the inordinate hopes of the more ignorant negroes as well as the foolish fears of the ignorant whites." In 1883 the Supreme Court declared the Civil Rights Act unconstitutional.[65]

The final adjournment of the Forty-Third Congress on March 3, 1875, closed a chapter in the devolution of Reconstruction. The turbulence and controversy of the past several months signaled how difficult it would be for Grant or anyone else to rally northern public opinion to a robust defense of African Americans' rights or the few remaining Republican regimes in the South. Edwards Pierrepont, who would soon join the administration, told Fish, "The temper of the Nation is now *conservative* and desires peace, union and active enterprise and industry all over the country." The nation "wants repose and yearns for a revival of its productive industries and of healthy trade."[66]

Those concerns were not new, of course; indeed, they had been uppermost in most people's minds since the panic. While Grant and Congress had wrestled with the southern question during the short session, they had also struggled to fashion an economic policy that could help the country turn the corner and put it on the road to recovery.

19

★ ★ ★ ★ ★

SOUND MONEY, CROOKED WHISKEY

In addition to the southern question, President Grant highlighted two other important issues in his annual message in December 1874: civil service reform and economic policy. The latter question had grown ever more urgent as the country remained crippled by depression. In the wake of the November election losses, press rumors had cast Grant as ready to back away from his conservative money views, but he "very indignantly repelled this idea." He authorized Fish and Bristow to say that, on the contrary, he felt "strengthened in the opinions expressed in his Veto message." Conservatives were "glad to know," as one told Bristow, "that the President still stands by the 'Hard money' part of his record."[1]

Yet, in preparing his annual message, Grant did consider a spending proposal that alarmed Bristow and other orthodox Republicans. In an early draft, he endorsed an extensive program of transportation projects that would "serve directly to give employment to many thousands of hands, and indirectly to the employment of other tens of thousand[s]." In the previous session, a Senate committee had advocated such a program, consisting primarily of dredging rivers and building canals to counteract price gouging by railroads. In the summer the Republican campaign committee had endorsed the idea. But the proposition shocked fiscal conservatives, who saw "economy and retrenchment" as "the true remedy" for the economy's woes. Bristow and House

Appropriations chairman James A. Garfield worked to keep the president from adopting the "foolish notion that it was necessary to make large appropriations on public works to give employment to laborers." In the final version of his message, Grant cited Congress's investigation of "cheap transportation" but made only an indirect reference to the "many interests that might be fostered to the great profit of both labor and capital." In his Treasury report, Bristow called for "rigid economy in the public expenditures" and warned that "lavish outlay of money by the Government leads to corresponding habits of extravagance among the people." Later generations of economists, of course, would regard Grant's original prescription for a stimulus as more suited to the country's needs than the pinched notions of the fiscal hard-liners.[2]

On the currency issue, however, Grant readily said what conservatives wanted to hear. He told Congress that until it passed legislation for a return to specie payments, the country could expect "no prosperous and permanent revival of business and industries." To ensure the policy's success, Congress should repeal the greenback legal-tender clause as it applied to future debts, empower the Treasury to borrow gold to redeem notes, and provide sufficient revenue to "sustain permanent redemption." On the last point he favored the restoration of a tariff on tea and coffee and a 10 cent per gallon increase in the internal whiskey tax. He called for a general adjustment of the tariff to increase the revenue, but he also wanted to eliminate duties on raw materials not produced in the United States. To address fears of contraction, he argued that with resumption, Congress could safely authorize free banking—that is, remove limits on banknote issues, a step that was "essential" to "give proper elasticity to the currency." In his report, Bristow elaborated the president's proposals, although he said little about "elasticity" and instead emphasized "stability," a quality that "attaches only to coin."[3]

Despite deep differences, Republicans in Congress saw the need to coalesce behind some financial policy before the close of the lame-duck session and the loss of power to the Democrats in the House. Hard-money Republicans such as Henry Dawes welcomed the administration's pronouncements as "an unmistakable voice com[ing] to our aid from high authority, demanding an affirmative and an aggressive policy toward these Treasury notes." Soft-money Republicans in the House sought to steal attention from the president's recommendations by bringing up an expansionist interconvertible bond bill left over from the previous session. But Democrat S. S. Cox stated what most Republicans already understood: "You know that the President will veto it if you pass it." The bond bill sank out of sight, and the scene of operations shifted to the Senate, where a movement for compromise was fast taking hold.[4]

In the upper chamber the Republican caucus appointed an eleven-member committee to draft an acceptable measure. Headed by John Sherman, the committee represented all points on the spectrum, from hard-liner George Edmunds to soft-money champion Oliver Morton. Although the wide divergence led to wrangling in the committee, cooler heads understood that at stake was not only the policy question but also the future of the Republican Party.[5]

At a party caucus on December 19, Sherman's committee submitted a compromise measure for the resumption of specie payments. The bill's first two sections were relatively minor, calling for the redemption of fractional paper currency (denominations of less than a dollar) with silver coins and the abolition of the charge the government levied for converting gold bullion into coin. The last section—the heart of the bill—drew on Grant's recommendations. It called for free banking coupled with a reduction in the greenback circulation equal to 80 percent of new banknotes issues; the reduction would continue until greenbacks reached a new maximum of $300 million. Most important, this section also stipulated that the Treasury would redeem greenbacks in gold beginning on January 1, 1879. To accumulate specie to meet redemption needs, the Treasury could use regular revenue or sell bonds. After a lengthy discussion, the caucus endorsed the committee's bill without changes. Bristow kept in touch with the committee and reported its work to Grant.[6]

Sherman presented the bill on Monday, December 21, and the Senate passed it the next day by a party vote of 32 to 14. A delighted Grant wrote to a friend, "I feel very confident for the future of our country and party." The House recessed for the holidays before considering the bill on January 7, 1875. In the interim, the January 4 incident in the Louisiana legislature had placed a premium on minimizing points of contention among Republicans. Sponsors quickly forestalled debate as well as amendments, and the resumption bill carried by a vote of 136 to 98, again largely along party lines.[7]

Grant could rightly claim credit for spurring the legislators on with his annual message, but he was not quite satisfied with the Resumption Act as passed. He signed it, but on January 14 he also submitted a message pointing out to Congress further steps that were "essential to make this law effective." First, to increase gold revenues for redemption, he recommended restoring tariff duties on tea and coffee and repealing the 10 percent horizontal reduction in rates enacted in 1872. Second, mindful that some thought four years was too long to wait for resumption, he called for an immediate redemption of greenbacks in gold, beginning with a premium of 10 percent that would gradually decline to zero on the prescribed resumption day of January 1, 1879. Third, to accommodate the increased production of fractional silver coins required by the law, he recommended the creation of another mint.[8]

Congress took no action on the latter two suggestions, but it did respond to Grant's call for increased taxation. Tax writers on the Hill asked the administration for specific recommendations. At a cabinet meeting, Bristow reported that customs duties had been steadily declining, and the group decided to reiterate Grant's tariff recommendations. In addition, they accepted a suggestion by Secretary of the Interior Columbus Delano, who had previously served as commissioner of internal revenue, to recommend a hike in tobacco taxes from 20 cents to 24 cents per pound. Delano also advocated raising the tax on whiskey from 70 cents to $1 per gallon. Both Grant and Bristow doubted that this tax could be collected at such a high rate. Instead of paying it, distillers would bribe government officials to falsify their production reports. But Belknap, who had once been an internal revenue collector, argued that the government could collect the higher tax, and the current commissioner, J. W. Douglass, apparently agreed. Although the recommendation went forward, events soon demonstrated the prescience of Grant and Bristow's doubts.[9]

These proposals met opposition from congressmen wary of endorsing any tax increases. The House passed a measure incorporating many of the administration's suggestions, but at midnight on March 1, forty-eight hours before the adjournment, the Senate voted to table the bill by a vote of 30 to 29. The next day several senators asked Grant for help. He adjourned a cabinet meeting early and headed up Capitol Hill to pressure wavering Republicans. That evening the Senate revived the bill and passed it, 30 to 29. It repealed the 10 percent horizontal tariff reduction and increased customs duties on several other items as well. It also raised the tax on distilled spirits from 70 cents to 90 cents per gallon and the tax on tobacco from 20 to 24 cents. "Some timid Republicans were unwilling to vote increased taxes," Timothy Howe wrote. "But the President saved us again. There never was such a President in the White House. One so absolutely fearless."[10]

Although Grant was willing to see the funding for resumption come substantially from increased tariff duties, the administration also struck a minor blow for freer trade in the negotiation of reciprocity with Hawaii. The idea had been discussed for years, and Fish had started formal negotiations with Hawaiian representatives in November 1874. Grant pushed the project, which was aided by a state visit from King Kalakaua. By the end of January, a treaty was complete. The most vocal opponent was free trader and liberal reformer David Wells, whom Grant had eased out as special commissioner of the revenue early in the administration. Fish assured the Hawaiian delegates that Wells was simply "a conceited, ill natured person, disappointed & angry not to have received more of recognition from the Administration." The Senate ratified the pact, 50 to 12. It included a provision that barred Hawaii from granting any port or harbor to any other foreign power, an important check on British expansionism. Under the treaty's operation, Hawaii prospered economically and became increasingly linked to the United States before final annexation in 1898.[11]

Although Congress raised taxes, it took no action on Grant's suggestion for an accelerated greenback redemption. Few legislators of any stripe desired to reopen that divisive question or disturb the compromise the Specie Resumption Act represented. What hard-money forces got from the law was no inflation and a definite date for resumption, plus immediate redemption of fractional currency in silver. What inflationists got was no contraction. In practice, however, the soft-money backers did not get even that. In mandating a reduction of greenbacks equal to 80 percent of the new banknotes issued, the act did not specify whether the 80 percent should be computed on the net or gross issuance of bank circulation. Grant decided to use the latter figure, so that even if more national banknotes were withdrawn than new ones issued, the Treasury would still calculate the 80 percent greenback withdrawal on the newly issued notes. As a result, the overall paper currency, greenbacks plus banknotes, declined by more than $15 million by November 1, 1875.[12]

Grant's prominent role in the passage of the Specie Resumption Act marked the progression in his thinking on the money question since the Panic of 1873. In his annual message two months after the Wall Street collapse, he flirted with inflationist notions in asserting that the nation suffered from a currency deficiency. But by late February 1874, he had begun to resist the blandishments of some of his closest political allies who had enlisted in the inflation movement. He struggled over his decision when Congress presented him with the Inflation Bill, but he wound up issuing a ringing veto, followed by the rigidly hard-money Jones memorandum. Eager for a settlement of the vexatious problem after the 1874 election disaster, he joined in fashioning the resumption law and ancillary legislation. Although the act was not everything the president desired, his advocacy marked a defeat for inflationists and helped shift the Republican Party's center of gravity toward the hard-money side.

With an eye to the party's future, Republicans in the lame-duck session had labored over the resumption compromise as a way to neutralize the divisive money question. On civil service, the majority of Republicans proved much less willing to erect permanent undergirding for reform. During the previous session in the spring of 1874, Congress had refused Grant's request for funding for the Civil Service Board, but he did not give up. In the fall, soon after taking office as postmaster general, Marshall Jewell noted, "I am running the Department strictly within the rules of the civil service. I found the President meant business by it, and really wanted to have it carried out." In his December annual message, Grant laid his cards on the table for the lame-duck Republican Congress.[13]

He said the administration had observed the rules as best it could, given "the opposition with which they meet." The result had "tended to the elevation of the service." Nonetheless, it was "impracticable to maintain them without direct and positive support of Congress." He had made that point many times before, but now he underscored an additional obstacle to making the improvements work: civil service reformers who were too quick to find fault when the rules were "apparently" departed from. These reformers claimed that the administration violated the rules whenever it removed an officeholder against whom no specific charges had been filed or whenever it retained those against whom charges had been "made by irresponsible persons." "Under these circumstances, therefore, I announce that if Congress adjourns without positive legislation on the subject of 'civil service reform,' I will regard such action as a disapproval of the system, and will abandon it, except so far as to require examinations for certain employees, to determine their fitness. Competitive examinations will be abandoned."[14]

To no one's surprise, Congress failed to renew the Civil Service Board's funding. A few days after the session closed in March 1875, Grant informed cabinet members that they should consider the reform he had established by executive order as abandoned. They should abolish the departmental examining boards and return to making appointments in accordance with standing law. The *New York Herald* claimed that Grant's reform had been a "specious pretense" from the beginning. But such censure failed to take into account Grant's genuine discomfort when faced with the odious task of fielding congressional recommendations and selecting winners and losers among office seekers. More charitably, *Harper's Weekly* stated, "The President honestly wished to do something to diminish the appalling and threatening mischief of the system of appointment by mere political influence," but he lacked the "kind of perception and resolution which can alone accomplish results." But in fact, Grant had perceived the issue's limited popular appeal. Even Carl Schurz later observed that when the president abandoned the rules, "the people generally accepted the event with cool indifference."[15]

Publicly, Civil Service Board chairman Dorman Eaton indicated that he understood the president's difficulties. In a speech, he called the abandonment of reform "a needless and unjustifiable surrender." But he also said that "the greater responsibility for the disaster rests upon Congress and the party managers." Indeed, he added:

> The President is entitled to justice, which will award him no small praise. He was the first President who had the moral courage and the disinterestedness to attempt the overthrow of the spoils system, and he was the last of the great forces of his party to leave the field. He sustained the contest amid the most outrageous aspersions of his motives, and faithfully repulsed the solicitations of friends and partisans beyond the example of any of the late Presidents.

Privately, however, Eaton told quite another story. After stewing a few months, he exploded in a letter to Bancroft Davis:

> The Civil Service Rules were doing much good, the President was very cordial, & my relations to him and with the members of the cabinet were frank & agreeable. . . . Had the President maintained his position or *his honor*, the new system would have slowly & steadily won its way with no further serious collision. But, *all of a sudden*, the *third* term question became critical. The President was convinced (as I believe by Conkling) that the rules would be in his way. The President *ignominiously* surrendered to his ambition. I saw he was no longer as frank as before. The message in which he tried to shift the responsibility upon Congress was prepared without notice to any member of the Com[mit]tee. In short, the President was not unselfish

> & faithful enough for the occasion. . . . The President gained nothing, not even *a chance* of a 3d term. The country was disgraced & his great & just fame was tarnished. The Republican [Party] earned nothing but discredit by repudiating the noblest work in which it has engaged since the war.

"I think I know these facts, though *I have written them to no one* before," Eaton told Davis. Actually, he offered only assertions, not facts; like many who disagreed with Grant in this period, he ascribed the president's actions to furtive angling for a third term.[16]

Eaton's duplicity exemplified the two-facedness of many of Grant's opponents who donned the livery of reform. As his annual message illustrated, Grant felt that civil service reformers had not given him credit for the efforts he had made. His sense of ill treatment at the hands of reformers deepened with time, and he grew less circumspect in showing it. Shortly after leaving office, he described civil service reform as simply another kind of place hunting—"to reform this man out and the other man into office." Two years after he left the White House, while on a world tour, he told a reporter he had given the reform "an honest and fair trial." But, he added, "there is a good deal of cant about civil service reform," and "many of those who talk civil service reform in public are the most persistent in seeking offices for their friends." No one in the government, he believed, favored reform more than the president, who bore the brunt of the "vexations and cares" of patronage. But reform must rest "entirely with Congress," whose members must be willing to forgo seeking offices for their friends. Patronage was not "corruption," he maintained. Instead, it was "a condition of our representative form of government," an instrument the president used "to get along with Congress, have the government go smoothly, and secure wholesome legislation."[17]

Grant's efforts to deal with the South, civil service, and specie resumption in late 1874 and 1875 proceeded against a backdrop of growing troubles in his official family. Only the thinnest cloak of civility covered the backbiting that pervaded the cabinet and the president's staff. In the space of a few months, two cabinet secretaries would be forced to resign, and others would sense the insecurity of their positions.

Attorney General George Williams had managed to hang on to his job after the forced withdrawal of his nomination as chief justice, but his standing in Washington, and that of his wife, was not secure. Kate

Williams's relations with the other cabinet wives had become so strained that Julia Grant received her "in a cold and distant manner" during a reception for King Kalakaua in December 1874 and tried to exclude her from the New Year's reception at the White House. Grant thought a solution might be to let Mrs. Williams try her hand at the tsar's court by appointing her husband minister to Russia. But Fish pointed out that evidence of Williams's mismanagement of the Justice Department was surfacing and would raise censure during a nomination fight. Similar allegations had scuttled Williams's bid to be chief justice, and Grant dropped the idea of the Russian appointment.[18]

But the president had not counted on the wounded vanity of Kate Williams. As she had in the earlier case, she defended herself by slurring others in the government, this time by sending a series of anonymous letters to cabinet secretaries, members of their families, and even Julia Grant. In early March 1875 Belknap asked Treasury Department solicitor Bluford Wilson to investigate some unsigned letters he had received accusing him of skimming money from French arms sales. Aided by the Secret Service under his authority, Wilson determined that Mrs. Williams had written the letters, probably with the assistance of the former chief of the Secret Service, H. C. Whitley. Whitley had resigned under pressure from Wilson several months earlier, and he shared Kate Williams's desire for revenge. In apprising his brother Harry of the investigation, Wilson implied that the letters included intimations of sexual misconduct. He "had uncovered material for a national scandal that would make that of the Eatons [in Andrew Jackson's time] respectable in comparison and which if made public would cover the administration with a cloud of infamy. The President has sinned against light in keeping the Williams' [sic] in his Cabinet and society and the public would not spare him in the face of the infamous exposure." Wilson described a letter to Mrs. Grant as "the meanest of the series" and a "startling contribution to the pile of filth."[19]

The solicitor plotted strategy with Belknap, Babcock, former private secretary Horace Porter, and Secretary of the Navy George Robeson, who had also received letters. All agreed that the attorney general had to go. Babcock proposed making the case for Williams's dismissal on the basis of his financial misdealings, as several members of Congress had suggested. But Wilson insisted that the president be told the whole story, including the letters. Babcock next suggested using Whitley to threaten Mrs. Williams with imprisonment for her part in the Justice Department peculations and thereby ensure her silence about other matters. Again

Wilson demurred, privately speculating that Babcock wanted to keep Whitley quiet about misdeeds Babcock himself had committed. Bristow seconded his lieutenant's firmness and urged Grant to fire Williams.[20]

Shortly after the meetings with Wilson and the others, Babcock apprised Grant of the letters. Equally damaging to Williams, Roscoe Conkling told the president that the chief clerk of the Justice Department was passing information regarding the attorney general's malfeasance to a Democratic organization known as the Manhattan Club. Bristow also gave Grant "very alarming" information regarding transactions in New York. The stories reached a critical mass, and the president asked Williams for his resignation. Grant told Fish "that he had a high respect for Williams but feared that he had been entrapped, or that transactions had passed through his hands without his notice, for which he could not fail to be held officially responsible, of a very deplorable nature." To relieve the president of any hesitation he might be feeling, Fish recounted a "startling" story he had heard in New York, claiming that Mrs. Williams had secured a $30,000 bribe from the firm of Pratt & Boyd to get the Justice Department to drop a suit against the company.[21]

To replace Williams, Grant chose Edwards Pierrepont, the former federal district attorney for New York. Having long yearned for high office, he accepted with alacrity. In making the selection, Grant told Fish he wanted "a person whose character and ability would give assurance of no occasion for the Democratic Party in the next house of challenging the administration of the Department." The president was also eager "to avoid an investigation of the past." For that purpose, Pierrepont seemed ideally suited. Two months earlier he had warned Bristow that the Democrats' "whole game" was to use investigations to "break down the Republicans by any means fair or foul." Republicans, he said, should "not be led into rash and foolish measures to prove their virtue" or be "fooled or taunted into playing into the hands of the enemy."[22]

But Bristow and his friends read the political tea leaves differently. The secretary argued "that the best & only way for Grant to help the party is to unload his Administration of the dead weight." No one celebrated Williams's departure more than Bluford Wilson, who told his brother that when he left the Treasury Department, "I'll take some scalps with me. I have already an Attorney General, and a private secretary or two, with some minor trophies, would add to the value of the collection." After disagreeing with Grant's Arkansas policy, Bristow had thought seriously about resigning, but the Wilsons and others had urged him to stay. "The chief reason in my mind for your retention of your present office,"

Secretary of the Treasury Benjamin H. Bristow. (Library of Congress)

wrote John Harlan, "is because I believe that by so doing you may make yourself President in 1876." Harlan thought Bristow would have particular strength with the Liberals—the very men who were Grant's implacable foes. But Porter also urged Bristow to stay and claimed that Grant favored the secretary as his successor. "Of course I believe just as much or as little of all this as I like," Bristow told Harlan.[23]

Bristow repeatedly told friends of his discomfort in the cabinet and with public life generally. But in mid-March 1875 he and his wife discussed the situation with Bluford Wilson, who went away with "the distinct understanding" that "without any avowed purpose to put himself in the hands of his friends," Bristow "would nevertheless accept all the responsibilities that may fairly follow his continuance in public life." Wilson was "highly gratified," and Harry Wilson thought it was time to begin "arranging a plan of campaign." The treasury secretary received encouragement from Garfield, and in late March he conferred with E. W. Stoughton, A. T. Stewart, E. D. Morgan, and others in New York and Philadelphia and found them "talking me up for the presidency." To Harlan, Bristow pooh-poohed such talk as "absurd" and "injudicious," but he did not ask his friends to stop their quiet canvassing. The prospect of becoming president had found lodgment in his psyche and could not help but color his actions in the months ahead.[24]

Bristow was eager to see Columbus Delano leave with Williams, not only because he considered the interior secretary corrupt but also because he was sure that Delano was plotting to drive him out of the cabinet. "He is a very mean dog," Bristow wrote to a friend, "and deserves the execration of every honest man." In mid-December 1874 Assistant Interior Secretary Benjamin Cowen told Bristow that Delano was engaging in "intrigues" against him; he also alleged that Delano and especially his son John, former chief clerk to his father, were involved in nefarious land office schemes in the West. A few months later Bristow enlisted an old army friend, Frank Wolcott, to secretly delve into Delano's dealings. Wolcott soon hit pay dirt in conversations with L. C. Stevens, a disgruntled clerk in the Federal Land Office in Cheyenne. Stevens reported that the surveyor general for Wyoming Territory, Silas Reed, had been letting contracts for surveys of public lands to deputy surveyors who agreed to share their large profits with silent partners who did no work and rarely put up any money for the projects. Among those receiving such unearned proceeds was John Delano. Wolcott wrote to Bristow that Secretary Delano had "knowledge of the whole transaction," and unless he resigned before the next Congress met, the scandal would furnish the Democrats with enough ammunition to "blow our side clear out of the water." Wolcott persuaded Stevens to send documentary evidence to Bristow, who received it in early April. Believing the material would sink Delano, Bristow promptly gave it to Grant.[25]

Among the papers was a canceled bank draft for a payment to John Delano from one of the silent-partner contracts. In addition, Stevens's cover letter to Bristow asserted that he had seen a letter from Columbus Delano thanking surveyor general Reed for helping his son. Although the silent-partner contracts were technically legal, they amounted to schemes to bilk the government. To intimates, Grant confessed he was "shocked" and "grieved" over the fall of Delano, for whom he had "great affection." He told Fish the charges against John Delano were "undoubtedly true," but the interior secretary had "managed the Department 'Elegantly' and whatever wrongs may have been done were without his knowledge."[26]

Grant believed that, to some degree, the trouble simply reflected "personal differences between the Secretaries of the Interior & of the Treasury." Still, Delano would have to go. At the end of April the president opened discussions with cabinet members about a replacement, although he did not relish taking action based on the word of Stevens, whom he regarded as a "spy." Moreover, the press had begun to carry rumors of Delano's imminent departure for complicity in corruption, and Grant thought that if Delano resigned now, "it would be retreating under fire and be accepted as an admission of the charges." The secretary remained in place another five months.[27]

Delano was the third member of the cabinet (after Amos Akerman and Williams) whose departure had been engineered by Bristow. He bristled at the delay, however, and complained to Grant that Delano had "a fixed & deliberate purpose to involve me in a personal quarrel with a view to create a diversion from charges that have been publicly made & with which I have had nothing whatever to do." Bristow, of course, had a great deal to do with those charges. Delano fought back, leaking purported cabinet discussions during which most of his colleagues allegedly said they wanted him to stay. Twice during the summer Bristow submitted his own resignation, which Grant refused. Finally, in October Grant appointed former Michigan senator Zachariah Chandler to head the Interior Department. During the struggle, Bristow's advisers never allowed him to lose sight of where his own political interests lay. Harry Wilson thought Bristow was "destined to be our Candidate next year," and "if he were to go out now he'd have nothing to stand upon." Bluford Wilson told the secretary that the key to victory in 1876 was to "leave nothing for the opposition to investigate, and to this end Delano must be made to go." Bristow understood. "I believe the way to insure success in 1876," he told a Kentucky friend, "is to purge the party of all rogues that have fastened themselves upon us and to satisfy the people that we mean to have honest government."[28]

Clearing "rogues" out of the cabinet necessarily entailed manipulation behind the scenes, but in the spring of 1875 Bristow directed another anti-corruption drama that put him more squarely in the political spotlight. This was the fight against the notorious Whiskey Ring. The conspiracy, whose origins dated years before the Grant administration, involved collusion by distillers with Treasury officials to evade internal revenue taxes. The scheme tended to flourish when taxes on alcohol were relatively high, as the distillers reckoned it cost less to bribe revenue officials than to pay what they considered exorbitant levies. The ring received a boost in early March 1875 when Congress raised the tax on whiskey from 70 cents per gallon to 90 cents. Grant had called for a more modest 10 cent increase in his 1874 annual message, and he and Bristow had warned that setting the rate too high would invite evasion. Nonetheless, Congress had set its sights on raising money for specie resumption and chose the higher rate.[29]

Before 1875, efforts to uncover and demolish the ring had met little success, in part because ring members who held office in Washington alerted their allies around the country whenever investigators were about to descend. As early as November 1872, three revenue agents conducting an investigation of distilleries in St. Louis, a central locus of the ring, found substantial irregularities, but one of the agents fell prey to bribery. That agent submitted a whitewashing report that Commissioner of Internal Revenue J. W. Douglass accepted. Another agent, Homer Yaryan, pressed Douglass to take action against the ring, but according to later testimony by Yaryan, Douglass hesitated, pleading that its leaders claimed to have the protection of influence at the White House. In December 1874 Bristow convinced the commissioner to send a new team of investigators to St. Louis, but at the last minute, Orville Babcock secretly persuaded Douglass to revoke the order. The next month Yaryan proposed a plan to send agents to surreptitiously monitor how much whiskey distillers produced, which could then be compared with revenue bureau records showing the amount of whiskey taxed. But Douglass rejected Yaryan's idea on the grounds that he was developing a different plan of action.[30]

Douglass's plan called for the transfer of supervisors of internal revenue between several cities. These officials oversaw the government's revenue collection operations. Douglass thought that instructing the reassigned supervisors to be especially vigilant against lawbreakers in their new locations would go far toward dismantling the ring. Grant had discussed such a transfer with Douglass several months earlier and had approved it in principle. When Bristow's suspicions of fraud grew, the president, independent of Douglass, suggested a transfer order to the secretary. Although Douglass's proposal would have shifted several individuals, his primary aim was to switch John McDonald, headquartered in St. Louis, with the supervisor at Philadelphia, Alexander Tutton. Douglass believed McDonald was one of the ringleaders, but McDonald's friendly relations with Grant made a frontal assault problematic. Hence, the commissioner conceived the transfer as a flank attack to break up McDonald's corrupt operation. Unfortunately, Douglass gave scant thought to the willingness of other supervisors to pull up stakes and relocate to unfamiliar cities. In particular, Tutton, a longtime resident of Philadelphia, strongly objected to being forced to drag his family "out there" to St. Louis for six months or a year. Moreover, Tutton told Grant that even though the transfer scheme might compel the ring to suspend operations, it would have ample time to cover up past transgressions and thus deprive the government of evidence to win convictions. Grant later testified, "I resisted all efforts to have the order revoked until I became convinced that it should be revoked or suspended in the interest of detecting frauds that had already been committed." He suspended the transfer order on February 4, 1875.[31]

Instead of the transfer plan, Tutton suggested an undercover surveillance similar to the one conceived by Yaryan. Yaryan himself laid his idea before Bristow and Bluford Wilson, whose interest was piqued by his intimation that Babcock might be involved in the ring. If that were true, Babcock would have a vested interest in keeping McDonald in St. Louis. In fact, Babcock did argue against the transfer of supervisors and in favor of sending investigators, though not undercover, as Yaryan proposed, but "open and above board." On February 3 an associate of McDonald's in St. Louis wired Babcock, "We have official information that the enemy weakens. Push things." The next day Grant suspended the transfer order. Within a few days, internal revenue agent John Joyce, a McDonald ally from Missouri, was in Washington and reported that the transfer "order [was] busted forever." Joyce boasted to McDonald that Bristow and Douglass had "both tried to poison Grant, but he won['t] drive in their wagon worth a d—n." That reassurance proved premature.[32]

Bristow and Wilson soon concluded that Douglass was a weak reed, lacking the will or the stamina to fight the ring. They tried to maneuver Harry Wilson into the commissioner post, but Grant refused. Although Bluford convinced himself that Babcock opposed Harry because he would target the whiskey thieves, Grant would have been hard-pressed to justify giving two top jobs in the Treasury Department to two brothers. Without Harry's help, Bristow and Bluford decided to circumvent the commissioner altogether and launch a covert investigation, as Yaryan had suggested.[33]

In mounting this effort, they received help from political journalists eager to strike a blow against Grant. These included George Fishback, proprietor of the *St. Louis Democrat*, and Washington correspondent Henry Van Ness Boynton. Boynton had been gunning for Grant at least since the imbroglio with Jacob Cox early in the administration, and he soon allied himself with the Wilson brothers in pushing Bristow for the presidency. Early in February 1875 Fishback offered to put Bristow in touch with an individual who could secretly monitor activity at the St. Louis distilleries. Bristow and Wilson jumped at the offer. They circumvented normal Treasury channels and communicated by coded messages sent through Fishback and Boynton. Wilson superintended the stealth campaign and added other agents, including Yaryan, to monitor the distillers in St. Louis and other cities. Evidence quickly mounted of an elaborate scheme involving distillers and revenue officials. Fraudulent activity took various forms: shipping whiskey labeled as vinegar, listing the whiskey at lower proof, or simply using the government's revenue stamps multiple times. The cheating cost the government millions of dollars in tax revenue.[34]

In mid-April 1875 Bristow gave the president an outline of these findings. Shortly thereafter Grant left for Massachusetts to attend the centennial commemoration of the battles of Lexington and Concord. Several cabinet secretaries (not including Bristow) joined him at this important celebratory event. While the president was away, John McDonald showed up in Washington and complained to Wilson and Bristow about their sending investigators into his district without his knowledge. When they showed him the evidence against him, he broke down and pleaded for an opportunity to assist in the investigation. They refused. When Grant returned, he agreed to see McDonald but gave him no more satisfaction than had the Treasury officials. McDonald handed the president his resignation on April 23 and returned to St. Louis. After Grant's return, Bristow gave him a full account of the ring's operations. Concluding that evidence of "the most outrageous frauds" had been "lying under the Commissioner's nose unexamined" for months, he urged the president to fire Douglass. Grant acted immediately, giving the post not to Harry Wilson but to former senator Daniel Pratt of Indiana.[35]

Without waiting for Pratt to take his position, Bristow and Wilson designed a series of raids against distilleries around the country. On Friday, May 7, they laid their plan before Grant, who, according to Wilson, responded in a manner "in the highest degree creditable." He was particularly disturbed that McDonald, whom he had considered a friend, "had grievously betrayed, not only that friendship, but the public." The president fully endorsed the planned raids, and he also "indicated an entire willingness to co-operate with the Secretary of the Treasury in such changes as might be necessary" in the personnel of the Internal Revenue Service. Later that day instructions went out to groups of agents to be ready to pounce on Monday, May 10.[36]

Babcock got wind of the movement afoot and on May 7 sent two letters of caution to McDonald, one signed with his own name and the other with a pseudonym. Apparently fearful of what might be revealed about himself, Babcock urged McDonald to keep quiet. Hinting that he could secure McDonald's protection, Babcock wrote, "Your friend is doing the best he can. You can, I believe, rely upon him." McDonald interpreted "friend" as "President Grant." It is not clear whether Babcock knew that Grant felt "grievously betrayed" by McDonald, as he had told Bristow earlier in the day. But if he did, he lied to McDonald about the president's willingness to help. Babcock also told McDonald he had heard rumors that some lower officials and whiskey men in St. Louis might turn state's evidence. He warned that if "some of the gaugers and distillers want to squeal, . . . *they will not be allowed to turn informers and then go free themselves.*" Babcock's fear of squealers was justified. The raids were barely under way when Bristow wrote to John Harlan that he had heard "from a number of persons in St. Louis offering to tell all about the frauds if I will relieve them from prosecution, but as yet I have made no agreement with anybody and do not propose to do so unless it becomes absolutely necessary to reach high officials." How high he did not say.[37]

The raids in St. Louis, Chicago, Milwaukee, and elsewhere proved a smashing success. On the first day they netted sixteen distilleries and as many rectifying houses. Agents soon arrested hundreds of people. The campaign won praise in the press and added new luster to Bristow's image as a reform crusader, which he did not discourage. "You have doubtless seen by the papers that I have got myself into an ugly fight," he wrote to E. W. Stoughton. "The matter has not been at all exaggerated in the prints." To ensure competent management of the prosecutions, both Grant and Bristow wanted new blood in some of the district attorneys' offices. In selecting these new lawyers, the president ordered Pierrepont to "consult with the Secty. of the Treasury, who has been investigating these matters." A crucial point was St. Louis. Grant had decided that the federal attorney there had to be replaced, even though several leading Republicans defended him. At the suggestion of Harry Wilson and Belknap, Bristow recommended David Dyer. Although the postmaster at St. Louis warned Grant that Dyer had flirted with Missouri's Liberals, he got the job. Dyer soon wrote to Harry Wilson, "The *Knife* will be used freely until the last dishonest official head falls in the basket. In *this* rests the hope of the republican party."[38]

Within a month, Dyer had secured several indictments, including bills against McDonald and Joyce. In apprising Grant, Bristow warned that the St. Louis frauds might "reach much further than we have supposed." As Dyer prepared his cases, he uncovered telegrams between ring members in St. Louis and parties in Washington, and he sent copies to Bristow and Wilson. Among the correspondents was William Avery, chief clerk of the Treasury Department who had previously been chief clerk in the internal revenue office. Avery's complicity would account for the forewarning the ring had received whenever the Treasury contemplated dispatching investigators. Under Dyer's guidance, the grand jury indicted Avery. One telegram found by the prosecutors stood out. Sent to McDonald on December 13, 1874, it stated, "I succeeded. They will not go. I will write you." It was signed "Sylph." Dyer suspected Avery of sending the wire, but Bristow obtained the original order blank from the telegraph company's Washington office. The handwriting showed beyond a doubt that its author was Orville Babcock. This message would explain Douglass's abrupt cancellation of the investigatory expedition Bristow had asked him to send to St. Louis in December. Stunned, the secretary told a friend, "In my efforts to destroy the corrupt whisky ring, I have come across one branch of the subject which I do not know just how to deal with."[39]

Bristow did not rush to inform the president. At a cabinet meeting on July 21, he read the telegrams, including those signed "Sylph." Twice he stated that they were not in Avery's handwriting. He waited for someone to ask whose handwriting it was, but the question never came up, and he did not volunteer Babcock's name. A few days later, Bristow revealed Babcock's connection with the "Sylph" telegram to

Fish, who noted that his colleague appeared "very much worried and threatens to resign."[40]

Yet three days later, Bristow skipped another opportunity to inform Grant. On July 29 the president forwarded a letter he had received from W. D. W. Barnard of Missouri, reciting various rumors surrounding the St. Louis cases. Among other things, Barnard alleged that Dyer disliked Grant and that the attorney for McDonald and Joyce was claiming that the president "could not give them up, or Babcock was lost." Grant sent the letter to Bristow "to the end that if it throws any light upon new parties to summons as witnesses they may [be] brought out." Giving Bristow the Barnard letter rather than suppressing it suggests that Grant was hardly engaging in any sort of cover-up. Bristow could have used the letter's mention of Babcock's name as an opening to tell the president about the "Sylph" evidence. He did not. Instead, he used Grant's endorsement on the letter to dispel press rumors that the president did not support his fight against the ring. Grant wrote on the letter: "Let no guilty man escape if it can be avoided. Be specially vigilant—or instruct those engaged in the prosecutions of frauds to be—agains[t] all who insinuate that they have high influence to protect, or to protect them. No personal consideration should stand in the way of performing a public duty." Publicizing this endorsement would lock Grant into supporting Bristow's course in the likely event Babcock were indicted. Bristow asked Grant for permission to publish the July 29 endorsement, and Grant consented. It appeared publicly in mid-August.[41]

Meanwhile, Bristow and Wilson were revealing the "Sylph" story to several others, including the prosecution team in St. Louis; Fish, Pierrepont, and Jewell from the cabinet; and Harry Wilson as well. These men urged Bristow to take the matter to Grant, although Bluford Wilson convinced him to question Babcock first. Babcock admitted writing the "Sylph" message but denied that it had any relation to the whiskey conspiracy. Bristow frankly told Babcock that he intended to inform the president, and he warned that a new grand jury in St. Louis would likely indict Babcock when it convened in November. Bristow had heard that Babcock might be able to obtain a position with the New York Elevated Railroad, and he asked Horace Porter, Babcock's stout defender, to advise his friend to resign, but Porter refused. It seemed clear to Bristow that Babcock's friends thought that if he were indicted he would have a better chance for acquittal if he remained a secretary in the White House.[42]

In early September Bristow traveled to the president's summer home at Long Branch with a letter of resignation in his pocket. He finally laid out the "Sylph" story but failed to convince Grant of Babcock's complicity in the Whiskey Ring. The president thought the mysterious telegram stating "They will not go" probably referred to the revocation of the order transferring the supervisors, but Bristow noted that this occurred nearly two months *after* the telegram had been sent. Bristow's decision to resign surprised Grant, and he resolutely opposed it. As Bristow reported to Harlan, "He said my resignation now would be accepted by the country as evidence of a disagreement between us on the whisky matters & would damage both him & the party greatly." Demonstrating their agreement on the whiskey matter had been Bristow's purpose in publishing Grant's endorsement on the Barnard letter, but now the secretary bridled when Grant expressed the same wish for congruence. "Every objection to my resignation related to his own good & not to *mine*. But this is the old, old story. I feel that I am wasting the best years & energies of my life for the benefit of others who will care nothing for me *after* it is all over."[43]

A few weeks later, Grant set off on an extended tour that took him as far west as Salt Lake City. He planned to spend several days in St. Louis to attend to personal business related to his farm. Babcock traveled with him. While they were in St. Louis, Bluford Wilson wrote special instructions to John Henderson, the associate counsel with Dyer. Henderson, a former Republican senator who had voted to acquit Andrew Johnson, harbored no fondness for Grant. Wilson ordered him to use secret agents to watch the defendants McDonald and Joyce—especially "their associations, movements, and plans with reference to the charge of conspiracy"—during the next ten days, precisely when Grant would be in St. Louis. He adjured Henderson to "neglect no fair precaution to reach the very bottom or *top* of the conspiracy in its ramifications." When later accused of trying to add a presidential scalp to his collection, Wilson claimed that his aim in using spies had been to catch Babcock, not Grant, consorting with the defendants.[44]

As Justice and Treasury officials planned their prosecution strategies, they gave careful consideration to the question of bargaining with lesser defendants to turn state's evidence against bigger game. In mid-October Bristow sent a gingerly worded instruction through Wilson to the prosecutors in St. Louis, advising them to make no offers "unless important ends are to be gained in other cases." "I would ask no agreement in advance . . . unless, on hearing the statement of the party in open court, it should be deemed proper to use him as a witness against a greater offender. The conviction and punishment of corrupt and guilty officials are of first importance, and all things proper to this end should be used." In practice, the prosecutors took this as license to give breaks to distillers and lesser government employees who confessed in order to secure their testimony against higher public officers. Clearly, Babcock was in Bristow's sights. A week after his general instruction, he and Pierrepont urged Dyer to be on the lookout for any new evidence that would substantiate the private secretary's guilt. But the attorney general cautioned Dyer that any indictment of Babcock must rest on irrefutable evidence, for "if we acted upon insufficient proof, an unnecessary scandal would be brought upon the administration and upon the country." Much to the administration's relief, Dyer and his associates found no additional evidence warranting an indictment of Babcock before the fall off-year elections.[45]

Although few states held elections in 1875, politicians watched them for signs of the public mood on the eve of the presidential contest. How would voters react to the intractable southern question as represented by the crises in Louisiana and Arkansas, Congress's refusal to fund civil service reform, the continued economic depression, increased taxes, the persistence of ugly warfare in Cuba, and scandal tainting several federal departments? Even the president's peace policy for Native Americans lost some of its luster as Indians resisted the adoption of "white" ways and concentration on reservations, and whites grew less patient with gentle treatment of the "savages."

In the southern plains, the peace policy required war. A rivalry over buffalo herds precipitated fighting between white hunters and Indians, who had grown restless on the reservations. In what came to be known as the Red River War of 1874–1875, Grant authorized Sheridan to engage the recalcitrant tribes and force them back onto reservations. Sheridan aimed to pursue a similar approach in the northern plains, but Grant hoped to avert open warfare there. He entered into direct negotiations with Spotted Tail and other Sioux leaders, and in exchange for $25,000 in goods, they agreed to give up their buffalo hunting rights in Nebraska. The president urged them to do all they could toward "preparing yourselves for the life of white men." But the Indian question grew more complex with the discovery of gold in the Black Hills, which lay within the Great Sioux Reservation. Although existing treaties barred the incursion of white settlers, keeping them out proved difficult. Grant tried to buy the region from the Sioux, but those negotiations failed, and in

November the government finally halted military resistance to miners' entry. Inevitably, further conflict would burst forth in 1876.[46]

Meanwhile, allegations of corruption at the Indian agencies under Columbus Delano's leadership of the Interior Department further undercut the president's policy. Grant himself complained to Delano about "laxity" in the delivery of supplies. In July Yale paleontologist O. C. Marsh issued a sensational, detailed allegation that the government was providing inferior goods, especially food, to the Red Cloud Agency. Grant and the Board of Indian Commissioners appointed a special investigative commission, which found many of Marsh's allegations ill-founded or overblown. But the commission did substantiate the existence of fraud, thus adding to the president's justification for accepting Delano's resignation. Despite these problems, the president told a group of concerned ministers at the White House in early November that "he did not regard the peace policy a failure, and that it . . . would not be abandoned while he occupied that place." Indeed, "it was his hope that during his administration it would become so firmly established as to be the necessary policy of his successors."[47]

On the political front in 1875, Indian affairs had less impact than the administration's other burdens. In early March Republicans eked out a narrow victory in New Hampshire, but the next month in the swing state of Connecticut, the Democrats won the governorship, a majority in the legislature, and three out of four congressional seats. Marshall Jewell ascribed the loss of his home state to the "stand still" in the economy. Not unexpectedly, administration critics cast the outcome as a referendum against a third term. According to Jewell, that issue "was used mainly by those wanting an excuse for leaving the party," but many loyal Republicans who were nervous about the upcoming contests in the fall and in 1876 began to distance themselves from the idea. Bristow thought "the President is really meditating a third term," and after the Connecticut loss, the party convention in Bristow's home state of Kentucky sought to kill the idea by minimizing it. The Kentucky Republican platform labeled the charge "an absurd device" created by Democrats "to disrupt the Republican party and produce a division between it and the President." Grant told Bristow the resolution was "the most sensible thing he had ever seen on the subject." True to form, Bristow tried to pin the president down by asking his permission to publish the comment, but Grant said he was saying nothing publicly about the question.[48]

Yet pressure for a statement mounted. In late May Pennsylvania Republicans praised the administration but labeled the two term limit "the unwritten law of the Republic" and declared themselves "unalterably opposed to the election to the presidency of any person for a third term." Once Grant read that plank in the state party platform, he acted. He "scratched off" a response in the form of a public letter and invited several cabinet members (but not Bristow or Jewell) to look it over. Although they suggested several changes, he insisted on retaining a passage upholding the constitutionality of a third term.[49]

Directing his letter to the chairman of the Pennsylvania convention, Grant attributed the clamor to a portion of the press that was "hostile to the Republican party and particularly so to the Administration." He had thought it beneath his dignity to respond until the Pennsylvania convention, with an element of party authority, raised the question. He said he had not originally sought the presidency, and but for the call of duty, he would have preferred to keep his position in the army. As for a third term, he said, "I do not want it any more than I did the first." But the idea of limiting a president's term, he insisted, "can only come up fairly in the shape of a proposition to amend the Constitution," and until "such an amendment is adopted the people cannot be restricted in their choice by resolution further than they are now restricted, as to age, nativity, &c. It may happen in the future history of the country that to change an Executive because he has been eight years in office will prove unfortunate, if not disastrous." He added that it was "preposterous" to suppose that a president could force his own reelection or renomination. If the letter thus far offered little balm for those who claimed to fear a third term, he closed, "I am not, nor have I ever been, a candidate for a renomination. I would not accept a nomination if it were tendered, unless it should come under such circumstances as to make it an imperative duty, circumstances not likely to arise."[50]

The president had not consulted Julia Grant, who relished White House life and would have objected to throwing away a chance to stay. But had he thrown it away? The letter left the door open enough to admit multiple interpretations. George Bancroft told Bancroft Davis that Grant "did not mean to be taken at his word, but to stop the resolves of conventions, & bide his time and his luck." "But," Bancroft added, "the party pretty unanimously takes him at his word." Still, the *New York Herald* claimed the letter left Caesarism "as a political issue more potent than ever" because it contained nothing to prevent Grant's *accepting* a third term. Fish thought the Democrats were "reluctant to accept anything that may prevent their still harping on" the question. No group regretted the president's letter more than African Americans. "He has been the shelter and savior of my people in the hour of supreme danger," wrote Frederick Douglass, "and naturally enough we feel great concern as to who is to come in his stead."[51]

Two days after Grant's letter appeared, the Ohio Republican convention praised him as a "capable and judicious statesman" but also hailed "Washington's example in retiring at the close of a second presidential term," calling this "a fundamental rule in the unwritten law of the republic." Buckeye Republicans faced a hard fight in trying to unseat incumbent Democratic governor William Allen, who appealed strongly to inflationist sentiment. The GOP nominated former governor Rutherford Hayes. Observers saw Ohio as a bellwether for 1876, and the central issue in the 1875 campaign was the money question. The Democrats called for abandoning the Resumption Act, abolishing national banks, and making greenbacks the only paper currency. Republicans damned their opponents' "wretched and dishonest scheme." GOP speakers flocked to the state, and the party flooded it with sound money literature.[52]

Such efforts were costly. At the risk of further damaging his reputation as a civil service reformer, Grant sanctioned an assessment on federal employees. When a fund-raising committee circular seeking contributions of 1 percent of officeholders' salaries raised eyebrows in the cabinet, Grant said he fully approved of soliciting money through "voluntary" contributions, with no compulsion or threat of dismissal, "for the laudible [sic] purpose of maintaining the organization of the republican party." As he explained, "Money is necessary for this purpose, to buy & distribute documents, print tickets, send speakers into the field, &c. and I do not see that any parties are more directly interested in this than the office holders whose places yieald [sic] them a compensation of more than $1000 pr. annum. I understand it is to be distributed to none others." Zachariah Chandler, who designed the circular, told Bristow, "The President not only approves what the Committee is doing, *but the manner* of doing it."[53]

Early in the campaign, Grant was not quite as anxious about Ohio as other Republican leaders were, but as the fight wore on, he grew more concerned about securing a victory. As in past years, he traveled extensively during the fall, including stops in Ohio, although he generally steered clear of the speaker's stand. The one notable exception occurred at a soldiers' reunion in Des Moines, Iowa, where he tangentially addressed an issue that was roiling the Ohio campaign: the question of public support for religious schools.[54]

That spring, Ohio's Democratic legislature had passed a law mandating that the state provide inmates of prisons and state hospitals access to religious instruction in their own faiths. Republican campaigners capitalized on Protestants' prejudice and charged that the Democrats would next try to give public education funds to Catholic parochial schools. "Of course we make the financial discussion prominent," former governor Edward Noyes noted, "but the Catholic issue, of a division of the School fund, is the one which will give us our great gains." Grant said nothing publicly about the issue when he passed through Ohio, but he did raise it in a speech to a reunion of the Army of the Tennessee in Des Moines. After the usual encomia to his comrades' bravery in preserving the Union, Grant called for northerners and southerners to stand together "as brothers" with "a common heritage" to resist new enemies "threatening the perpetuity of free republican institutions." Insisting that he was not engaging in "partizan politics," he eased into the school issue:

> In a republic like ours where the citizen is the sov[e]reign and the official the servant, where no power is exercised except by the will of the people, it is important that the sovereign—the people—should possess intelligence. The free school is the promoter of that intelligence which is to preserve us as a free nation. If we are to have another contest in the near future of our national existence I predict that the dividing line will not be Mason & Dixon[']s but between patriotism, & intelligence on the one side & superstition, ambition & ignorance on the other. . . . Encourage free schools and resolve that not one dollar of money appropriated to their support no matter how raised, shall be appropriated to the support of any sectarian school.

At various points in his life, Grant had bristled privately at what he considered religious communicants' thralldom to a domineering clergy, but he did not specifically mention Catholicism in his speech. Still, Catholic journals decried the president's seeming exploitation of religious bigotry. Many other publications, however, praised his speech, and Grant hardly stood alone among Republican politicians on this issue. Garfield worried that the church posed a threat to "modern civilization," and Blaine insisted that public schools must be kept "free from sectarian interference or domination."[55]

In addition to the school issue, Grant's speech emphasized sectional reconciliation and thus reflected another theme in the Republican campaign—a de-emphasis of the southern question. The crises in Louisiana and Arkansas had soured many northerners on further intervention in defense of blacks' rights. Hayes thought, "As to southern affairs, 'the let-alone policy' seems now to be the true course." In the cabinet, no one subscribed to that view more fervently than Pierrepont, whose Justice Department would necessarily stand at the center of any new interventions. He opposed taking any action in the South that could disturb northern public opinion and jeopardize victory in Ohio, which he considered central to Republican chances in 1876. Early in the summer the attorney general commissioned Ohio lawyer Alphonso Taft to go to Long Branch and, without telling Grant that Pierrepont had sent him, stress to the president "the great importance of carrying Ohio." Pierrepont's priorities were soon tested by disturbances in Mississippi. He worried that federal intervention there could repulse northern support for the party. In order to thwart such action, Pierrepont misled the president as to the true state of affairs.[56]

Like Ohio, Mississippi held a state election in 1875. In early September, White Line paramilitary groups determined to regain the state for the Democrats launched a campaign of violence that left more than thirty people dead. Governor Adelbert Ames, a carpetbagger, lacked sufficient manpower to deal with the crisis and asked Grant to use troops under the proclamation he had issued the previous December against "insurgents" in Mississippi. But Pierrepont advised the president that the proclamation was no longer in effect. Nonetheless, Grant, who was not in Washington at the time, ordered the adjutant general to instruct the local US Army commander in the state to assist Ames, if the attorney general considered such action "entirely legal." Again Pierrepont dragged his feet, ordering that the troops be put on alert but not moved into action. Governor Ames asked Grant to issue a new proclamation under the Constitution's clause guaranteeing each state "a republican form of government," the standard justification for intervention. Grant forwarded this request to Pierrepont.[57]

The attorney general asked the State Department to prepare the official document, but he also did all he could to ensure the proclamation would never be issued. He asked Ames to be more specific about the insufficiency of the state militia, but before the governor could respond, Pierrepont wired Grant on September 10 that he had issued no proclamation and activated no troops because, "from the information received," he considered "the war in Mississippi over." At the same time, he told reporters that the situation did not warrant intervention, and as evidence he displayed a copy of a telegram from the Democratic chairman of Mississippi stating that there were "no disturbances in this state" and that sending federal troops would simply "increase the distrust of the people" in Ames's government. The next day Ames replied to Pierrepont that calling out the state militia, which consisted largely of blacks, would give rise to "a war of races," which everyone wanted to avoid. He insisted that the Constitution's guarantee clause left the president no room for discretion and that his request for help could "not well be refused." Still, Pierrepont resisted. He told Grant that the guarantee clause did not apply unless actual attempted action by state forces proved inadequate, and he sent the president a raft of telegrams from Mississippians claiming that the state was peaceful. Moreover, Pierrepont took the extraordinary step of sharing his opinions with the press before making his official recommendation to Grant. By doing so, he narrowed the political boundaries of the president's options.[58]

When Grant received the attorney general's report on September 13, he described himself as "somewhat perplexed to know what directions to give in the matter." He instructed Pierrepont to send him the new proclamation for his signature and to keep it ready in case the need arose. Should it become necessary to act, he wrote, "I shall instruct the commander of the forces to have no child's play. If there is a necessity for Military interference there is justice in such interference as to deter evil doers." In the meantime, the attorney general should urge Ames to "strengthen his position by exhausting his own resources in restoring order before he receives Govt. Aid." Grant conceded that "the whole public are tired out with these annual, autumnal outbreaks in the South," but he noted that "there is so much unwholesome lying done by the press and people in regard to the cause & extent of these breaches of the peace that the great majority are ready now to condemn any interference on the part of the Government." Even so, he told Pierrepont, "I do not see how we are to evade the call of the Governor, if made strictly within the Constitution and Acts of Congress thereunder." If the question of intervention were simply a matter of executive discretion rather than constitutional mandate, he wrote, then the guarantee clause would become "a dead letter," and the decision would be reduced to a political question. "The so-called liberal and opposition press would then become the power to determine when, or whether, troops should be used for the maintenance of a republican form of Government." Fully cognizant of his constitutional responsibility, Grant had not rejected the possibility of military intervention in Mississippi.[59]

And yet, in framing his response to Ames, the attorney general quoted selectively from Grant's dispatch and distorted its tone and tenor. Pierrepont quoted Grant's comment about "autumnal outbreaks" and the majority's condemnation of interference, but he omitted any reference to the president's attribution of such attitudes to "unwholesome lying" by the press. Pierrepont's draft of his letter to Ames stated that he had sent Grant a proclamation that would be issued "if you [Ames] say so," but Pierrepont struck that statement from the final letter. He also left out Grant's agreement with Ames's view regarding the mandate embodied in the guarantee clause. Instead, Pierrepont added his own interpretation that the Constitution stipulated that a governor should, if possible, first consult the state legislature, and he faulted Ames for not doing so. He further lectured the governor (a Medal of Honor recipient during the war) that Mississippi's Republicans should "have the courage and the manhood to *fight* for their rights." If Ames proved unable to suppress the "bloody ruffians" by "*all the means at your command*," then "the President will swiftly aid you in crushing these lawless traitors to human rights." In short, the attorney general seemed to be telling Ames: lead your forces to slaughter, and then the federal government will step in.[60]

Pierrepont apparently hoped that the bold promise of help offered at the end of his letter would deter the Mississippi White Liners and obviate federal military intervention. When Bristow, Jewell, and a small group of Mississippi politicians in Washington urged him to publish his letter to Ames, Pierrepont sought Grant's permission, noting that "they all say it will produce quiet." Significantly, he added, "No proclamation issued." Grant consented, and Pierrepont gave the letter to reporters, further circumscribing the president's options. The attorney general's stratagem succeeded. "The policy of the Administration in this matter has been changed," gloated the *New York Tribune*. "Even the President is slowly learning the temper of the people on the question of military intervention." Grant had in fact stood ready to intervene with "no child's play," but the comments from his September 13 dispatch, as selected and manipulated by Pierrepont, have come down through history, erroneously, as evidence of his supposed abandonment of the forceful defense of Reconstruction. As for the proclamation the president had signed to justify intervention, Pierrepont withheld it and tucked it away in his private papers, where it remains to this day.[61]

Left to his own devices, Ames tried to recruit a mixed-race militia but found that "the Republicans are paralyzed through fear and will not act." The White Liners forbore overt violence so as not to provoke federal intervention, but Ames suspected they would wait until just before the election, when it would be too late for a presidential proclamation to do any good. He asked Grant to at least send him a detective to infiltrate the White Line organization and divine its plans, and the president ordered Pierrepont to do so. Instead of an experienced investigator, however, Pierrepont sent his longtime friend George Chase and asked him not only to ascertain "the true condition of affairs" but also, "if possible, to quiet the political excitement in that State." At the attorney general's behest, therefore, Chase was less a detective than a conciliator. He soon worked out an agreement whereby the Democrats promised a peaceful election and Ames disbanded the two militia units he had cobbled together. Ames gleefully told Pierrepont that he expected "peace, order and a fair election," and the attorney general shared the good news with Grant and the cabinet.[62]

While the peace negotiations were pending in Mississippi, Pierrepont's northern strategy began to pay off. Ohioans went to the polls in mid-October and narrowly elected Hayes. Chase later told Hayes that "Judge Pierrepont alone prevented Federal interference in Mississippi," and Hayes was convinced that the attorney general had done him "great good" in his campaign. After Ohio was safe, Pierrepont affected a tougher stance in his communications with Ames, telling the governor that if the Democrats broke their agreement, "everything is ready at the tick of the telegraph" to dispatch federal troops. But the White Liners bided their time, engaging in an escalating campaign of terror and intimidation that required little actual killing to be effective—a strategy that became known as the Mississippi Plan. Even Chase called for troops on the eve of the election, but it was too late. Blacks stayed away from the polls, and the Democrats won in a landslide, thereby ending Reconstruction in yet another southern state.[63]

But many Republicans thought that Mississippi, which would cast only eight electoral votes in 1876, was a small price to pay for the swing state of Ohio with its twenty-two electoral votes. The trade-off marked one more step in the Republican Party's subordination of the southern question to other issues. Although the relative impact of the money question and the school controversy in Ohio remained indeterminate, party leaders saw financial issues assuming primacy in the nation's politics over questions of section and civil rights. The GOP did well across the North in 1875, winning the governor's race in Pennsylvania and a majority in the legislature in New York. After the November victories, President Grant told serenading Republicans at the White House,

"While the Republican majorities were not great, they were sufficient to accomplish the purpose. The 'rag baby' has been entirely suppressed, and the people now know what kind of money they are to have in the future, and I think we have an assurance that the Republicans will control this Government for at least four years longer."[64]

No one rejoiced more than Pierrepont. "Nothing but folly or divine providence can prevent Republican success in '76," he wrote to Bancroft Davis. Alas for Republican prospects—and for President Grant's reputation—folly or divine providence was about to intervene. The day after the election, the grand jury in St. Louis issued new indictments, and the Whiskey Ring returned to center stage.[65]

20

★ ★ ★ ★ ★

THE PRESIDENT UNDER FIRE

The Republican victories in 1875 sparked renewed speculation that Grant might break with tradition and run again for president, but unfolding events soon made such talk idle. The day after the November election, the grand jury investigating the Whiskey Ring in St. Louis indicted a prominent Republican newspaper publisher and a former internal revenue collector. At the same time, prosecutors prepared to try John McDonald and former Treasury Department chief clerk William Avery. Further indictments loomed. The renewed war on crooked whiskey not only smothered third term speculation but also intensified friction within Grant's official household. Equally important, the Whiskey Ring scandal and other allegations of wrongdoing leveled by the president's opponents killed his chances of squiring a policy agenda to a successful conclusion. Indeed, Grant spent his last eighteen months in the White House as a president under fire.[1]

Although the impetus to defeat the Whiskey Ring came from within the administration, Democrats aimed to make that fight the beginning of a general political assault. In early December 1875 their party took control of the House of Representatives for the first time since before the Civil War. Embracing the party's small-government notions, the Democrats showed no intention of sanctioning anything Grant or their Republican colleagues might propose. With twenty-one southerners chairing committees, one wag observed, "It is the first time Lee's army ever took Washington." Certainly the forward thrust of Reconstruction was dead. Obstruction was the Democrats' goal, but they aimed not just to block but to blacken. "Our fellows in Congress," a Maine Democrat argued, should "wade into the opposition, expose their corruption, *investigate*, shake out their dirty linen before the people, keep them defending, keep them at it constantly." One of their first acts was to pass a resolution declaring that the two term tradition had become "a part of our republican system of government, and that any departure from this time-honored custom would be unwise, unpatriotic, and fraught with peril to our free institutions." The vote was 233 to 18. The fact that more than 60 percent of the Republican representatives voted in favor of the resolution added to its sting. Of the six African American representatives who voted, all opposed it.[2]

Despite the dim prospects, Grant greeted the opening session with the longest annual message of his presidency. To a large extent he traversed familiar territory. Notwithstanding the still depressed economy, he invoked a raft of statistics to put the best face on the nation's material progress during its first century. He called for legislation to undergird specie resumption, recommended reduced expenditures, and advocated the restoration of tariff rates on tea and coffee and the reduction of others, especially on raw materials. He asked Congress to outlaw the "flagrant" crime of polygamy in Utah and the importation of Chinese women for immoral purposes. He claimed continued "satisfactory and encouraging results" from his peace policy but urged the passage of measures to deal with troubles growing out of the discovery of gold in the Black Hills on the Sioux reservation. His chief pronouncement about foreign affairs, pushed by Fish, was the continued nonrecognition of Cuban belligerency.

Acknowledging that political maneuvering would dominate the session, Grant challenged the Democrats by reprising the defense of nonsectarian education he had outlined in his Des Moines speech. He called for a constitutional amendment to require the states to establish and maintain free public schools; to forbid the teaching of "religious, atheistic, or pagan tenets" in them; and to prohibit the granting of public school funds "for the benefit or aid, directly or indirectly, of any religious sect or denomination." The proposal also stipulated that public schools must be accessible to all children "irrespective of sex, color, birthplace, or religions." Nowhere else in the message did the president say anything about the South, and although he did not specifically discuss mixed schools, the reference to "color" lent moral support to efforts in the southern states to educate both races. His reference to "birthplace," moreover, connoted the inclusion of immigrant children. In addition, arguing that civic instruction was essential to republicanism, he advocated making education "compulsory" and barring "all persons who can not read and write from becoming voters after the year 1890." Anti-Catholic Protestants found much to like in the school funding proposal, but Grant also suggested that the exemption from property taxes be ended for most ecclesiastical property, except for church buildings and cemeteries. In the cabinet, Grant had argued that "the exemption of so large an amount of property from taxation threw an unjust burden upon others and should be restricted."[3]

The property tax suggestion went nowhere, but Congress did give some attention to the president's school proposal. Early in the session James G. Blaine introduced a shorter version of the amendment that simply banned the use of public money for sectarian schools. It passed the House near the end of the session in August. But a revised version failed narrowly in the Senate, and the proposal died. Little else that Grant had proposed in his message made it through the Forty-Fourth Congress. Obstruction and investigation, not legislation, drove the House of Representatives.[4]

By the time Grant issued his message in early December 1875, Orville Babcock's legal situation had grown perilous. Two days after the November election, the Associated Press reported that new indictments in St. Louis included ones against Babcock and the president's brother Orvil Grant. Prosecutors quickly scotched those rumors, and Benjamin Bristow confided to John Harlan that Orvil Grant had nothing to do with the Whiskey Ring. But Babcock was another story. "So far as I am advised," Bristow wrote on November 7, "there is not *sufficient* proof before the grand jury to convict him, though there is enough to cast grave suspicions on him, and whether indicted or not the next House of Representatives through an investigating committee can & will make a great deal of it." As the stakes rose, Bristow contemned yet another of his colleagues—Edwards Pierrepont. "I am perfectly sure he is utterly unscrupulous & treacherous, and while he professes to cooperate with me in pursuing and punishing fraud he will secretly do what he can to save the exposure of certain parties and to destroy me. . . . I am surrounded by treachery & hatred at every point." Bristow again thought of resigning, but Harlan warned him that his "great future" would "be imperiled if you should quit your post voluntarily when the war upon the whiskey ring is raging."[5]

When the Associated Press report appeared, Horace Porter rushed to Washington to counsel Babcock. The two of them convinced Pierrepont to send solicitor Bluford Wilson to St. Louis to advise the prosecutors not to indict Babcock "except upon the clearest and fullest testimony." Technically, Wilson worked for the Justice Department, and Bristow thought Pierrepont was trying to prevent "an 'improper' indictment against Babcock & thus stop the scandal." But Wilson played along, dutifully went to St. Louis, and assured the attorney general, "We have nothing to fear from hasty or ill advised action." He failed to report that, in preparing their cases against others, district attorney David Dyer and associate counsel John Henderson were "still dragging" for evidence against Babcock.[6]

A worried Babcock sought Porter's help in shielding himself behind the president. Porter obtained a copy of the letter Wilson had written to Henderson instructing him to have detectives tail the conspirators McDonald and Joyce while Grant and Babcock were in St. Louis. Inserted into the passage urging Henderson "to reach the very bottom or *top* of the conspiracy" were the letters "W. H.," apparently referring to the White House. Porter confronted Wilson with this copy and accused him of setting spies on the president. The solicitor promptly showed Porter the original in his letterbook, demonstrating that the "W. H." had been inserted in the copy by some unknown hand. Porter accepted that explanation. Wilson later testified that he then asked Porter for his interpretation of Babcock's December 13, 1874, "Sylph" telegram that assured the conspirators, "They will not go." Porter brushed aside the telegram's contents as concerning "some parties who were going out to St. Louis on bridge business." Instead, he focused on the signature, which he claimed referred to a "lewd woman" with whom Grant had had "intimate relations" and who was blackmailing him. Porter's clear implication was that the investigators should drop the telegram from their inquiry to avoid embarrassing the president. In later testimony, Porter flatly denied Wilson's version of their conversation. He recalled telling the solicitor that, according to Babcock, "Sylph" derived from a joking comment made by McDonald about a "handsome woman, but rather large in size," whom they had seen in St. Louis. But the notion that Wilson would invent Porter's "lewd woman" interpretation scarcely seems credible, and Wilson remained convinced that Porter concocted the explanation to deter the investigation. If that was the case, Porter was willing to risk the president's good name to save Babcock's neck.[7]

McDonald's trial began on November 15. On the same day, Bristow had an amicable meeting with Grant and reported that nothing new had surfaced that was damaging to Babcock. Wilson, meanwhile, was pumping the St. Louis prosecutors for any new evidence against Babcock that might come to light during the McDonald trial. They soon found a smoking gun—a telegram Babcock sent to John Joyce on December 5, 1874, in which he reported he had not found "that anyone has gone or is going." Babcock was apparently referring to the question of whether the Treasury Department had recently ordered any investigators to St. Louis. He had signed this dispatch not with "Sylph" but with his own name.[8]

Wilson rushed a copy to Bristow, who, with Pierrepont, presented the new evidence to the president. According to Wilson, Grant "took lofty ground in relation to the matter." While he expressed the hope that Babcock's "innocence would yet become apparent, he nevertheless said with firmness and emphasis that if he was guilty he hoped he would be prosecuted to the bitter end. As for himself, he expressed no fears that his name would be smirched, while he felt that it was perhaps true, that his confidence had been most grievously betrayed." The group then showed the dispatch to Babcock, "who was unable to recall the circumstances under which it was sent, but insisted that in any event it could not relate to any criminal transaction, between himself and the person to whom it was addressed."[9]

The jury convicted McDonald on November 22. Avery's trial began the next day, and soon thereafter the prosecutors sent Bristow, Wilson, and Pierrepont another parcel of telegrams incriminating the president's private secretary. All were from Joyce to Babcock. The most damaging, dated December 3, 1874, asked, "Has Secretary or commissioner ordered anyone here?" This provided the context for Babcock's December 5 telegram assuring Joyce that he had not discovered that "anyone" was headed to St. Louis. Henderson submitted these dispatches at Avery's trial, but Avery's lawyer objected that Henderson was simply aiming "to make a drive at the Executive Mansion." Henderson insisted that the telegrams did "not in the least implicate the President of the United States" but showed that he had been "grossly deceived and imposed upon by men who professed to be his friends, here and in Washington." The judge admitted the telegrams, which appeared in press reports of the proceedings. Henderson and his colleagues confided to Wilson that "none of us believe" Grant was "implicated in the ring in any way," but if his private secretary was indicted, they would pursue "the prosecution of Babcock as an inevitable duty."[10]

Bristow and Pierrepont showed the new telegrams to Grant, who asked Babcock for an explanation. Babcock tried to link them to the appointment of an internal revenue official in St. Louis and to the transfer of supervisors contemplated in December 1874. Pierrepont later testified that this "seemed to be a satisfactory explanation to the President." But the attorney general and Bristow frankly told Babcock that if he was innocent, he should go to St. Louis and make his explanation. Grant agreed. The attorney general even helped Babcock draft a telegram to Dyer demanding to testify. But the district attorney replied that the evidence portion of Avery's trial had ended. With Babcock's indictment now only a matter of time, Pierrepont and Bristow wired Dyer, "Proceed with caution. Be sure of your ground. Protect the innocent, but prosecute the guilty."[11]

Growing desperate, Babcock invoked his status as an army officer and demanded that the president convene a military court of inquiry to consider his case. At a special meeting of the cabinet, Grant said he thought that Babcock was innocent, "that he had been given no chance to explain the telegrams sent; that if indicted he would have no chance before a court; that he [had] thought [of] a Court of Inquiry, but before deciding the matter, he would like to have the views of the members of the Cabinet." Belknap said that Babcock's request for what would be a "searching" investigation implied his innocence, but if the evidence warranted a trial, the case would go to a court-martial. Fish said he doubted that a military inquiry could unearth more facts than a civilian court or provide Babcock any greater opportunity to present his side. Marshall Jewell and Zachary Chandler favored the military court. Bristow declined to give an opinion. Pierrepont warned that it might look as if Grant were shifting the case from a civilian to a military court because of his "personal feeling for Babcock." He suggested a delay, but the next day the president announced that he would grant Babcock's request. He ordered Belknap to create a court comprising generals Phil Sheridan, Alfred Terry, and Winfield Hancock, the last a known Democrat. Only after the president had made his decision did Bristow say that in his "judgment the effect of a Court of Inquiry would be very disastrous to the Adm[inistration] as it would seem like interfering with the action of the Civil Court." Pierrepont said he would tell the prosecutors not to suspend their criminal proceedings against Babcock, for any seeming interference with the civilian court would "be ruinous to Babcock, the President and the Administration." Grant ordered the attorney general to direct the prosecutors to provide the military court "with any documents and facts which they might require." This Dyer and his associates refused to do.[12]

If Grant saw the military inquiry as a reasonable approach, he considered Dyer's withholding of evidence a "great outrage" that tended to confirm tales he had heard from Babcock's friends that the prosecutors were out to get the president. Babcock's fellow private secretary Levi Luckey had been called to St. Louis as a witness in the Avery trial. While there, he said, "parties came to me & told me of a great many things on the part of Dyer & Henderson & also of officers of the Treasury which looked like treason to the President." Grant said Luckey's report "coincided with other information" he had received. At the same time, Horace Porter showed Grant his copy of Wilson's September "bottom or *top*" letter to Henderson. The idea that Wilson had set spies on him made such a "painful impression" on the president that he demanded an explanation. Wilson insisted that "*top*" referred to revenue officials and Babcock "but never under any circumstances the President of the United States." He cited Grant's injunction to "let no guilty man escape," at which Grant interjected that he had meant Babcock. Wilson claimed he had given the prosecutors "the strictest instructions against hasty, ill-advised or vengeful action." He also conveyed Porter's "lewd woman" interpretation of "Sylph," which Grant dismissed with "a contemptuous gesture." Grant accepted Wilson's explanation of his behavior, but he still defended Babcock's innocence and remained bitter against Dyer and Henderson.[13]

Grant's mistrust of Henderson exploded after reports that the lawyer had criticized the president during his summation at the Avery trial. In referring to Grant's decision to halt the transfer of revenue supervisors in February 1875, Henderson said, "What right has the President to interfere with the honest discharge of the duties of a Secretary of the Treasury? None whatever. What right has he to interfere with the discharge of the duties of Commissioner Douglass? None. The law tells Douglass what to do." Besides betraying a strained notion of the chief executive's role in his own administration, Henderson's comment implied that Grant had acted according to some nefarious design. Henderson's fellow prosecutors rushed to his defense, as did Wilson. But Grant labeled him "a personal enemy," and Pierrepont ordered Dyer to dismiss Henderson immediately for his "outrage upon professional propriety." Although Bristow joined in the cabinet's umbrage, with characteristic solipsism he believed the matter had been trumped up to "get me into a row on a *side issue* to get rid of me." "The P believes thoroughly in Babcock's innocence," he groused to Harlan, "& doesn't hesitate to say so. It is very certain that I am in bad odor."[14]

To replace Henderson, Pierrepont authorized Dyer to secure "the most able and efficient counsel you can find, without regard to politics." In a second telegram he sent a specific request from Grant to hire noted Missouri lawyer Samuel Glover. Glover declined, and on the basis of Pierrepont's first telegram, Dyer considered himself authorized to make the selection. He chose James Brodhead, a close friend. Brodhead was a political ally of the rabid Democrat Frank Blair, and news reports called him "as hostile to the administration as Henderson." Dyer offered the post and Brodhead accepted it before the administration had a chance to object. Grant thought of blocking the appointment, but Pierrepont warned that doing so would "do mischief" politically. Moreover, he said, "If we reject Broadhead [*sic*], there is danger that it will re-act against Gen. Babcock and deprive him of any fair trial" if people "think the action here is to shield him." Dyer regretted Henderson's departure, but he succeeded in painting Grant into a corner in the choice of his successor.[15]

On December 9 the grand jury indicted Babcock for conspiring with others to defraud the government of tax revenue on a million gallons of whiskey. Babcock asked Grant to dismiss the military inquiry, since he now had "a means of vindication" in federal court. Among the grand jurors, no one had fought against the indictment more vigorously than Elias Fox, a former Republican state chairman and a friend of both Grant and Babcock. Dyer was convinced that Fox relayed information from the grand jury to the president, a charge Fox vehemently denied. The same day as Babcock's indictment, the grand jurors, likely at Fox's behest, sent a public letter to Grant thanking him for the "moral support" embodied in his injunction "Let no guilty man escape." They saluted his "wisdom, patriotism and independence . . . in directing the measures necessary for detecting and correcting the gigantic frauds which have so lately preyed upon the public revenues." This paean to the president could hardly mask the public relations disaster of Babcock's indictment.[16]

Hard on the heels of Henderson's outburst in court, Babcock's indictment convinced Grant that Treasury officials and prosecutors had him in their sights too. C. S. Bell, who had done some snooping for Babcock during Avery's trial, told Grant the indictment was meant to "blacken" Babcock "for the purpose of striking a blow at the President, because he was so near to him." His suspicions thus confirmed, Grant put Bell on the public payroll so that he could go to St. Louis and infiltrate the district attorney's office in the run-up to Babcock's trial. "I want to know all that is going on," Bell recalled Grant telling him; "if General Babcock is innocent I do not want him persecuted; if he is guilty I want him punished. I want you to report *facts*." But Grant's chief interest was in divining the prosecution's strategy, for he had already made up his mind about Babcock's innocence. A few days after seeing Bell, Grant wrote to Babcock's wife that he expected "his full vindication":

> I have the fullest confidence in his integrity, and of his innocence of the charges now made against him. After the intimate and confidential relations that have existed between him and myself for near fourteen years—during the whole of which time he has been one of my most confidential Aides & private Sec.—I do not believe it possible that I can be deceived. It is scarcely possible that he could, if so disposed, be guilty of the crime now charged against him without at least having created a suspicion in my mind. I have had no such suspicion heretofore nor have I now.
>
> His services to the government, in every capacity where he has been employed, have been so valuable, and rendered with such a view to its good that it precludes the theory of his conspiring against it now.
>
> My confidence in Gen. Babcock is the same now [that] it was when we were together in the field contending against the known enemies of the government.

The note was vintage Grant: unquestioning loyalty to one he considered a steadfast friend, and gentle solicitude for an anxious spouse. As for Bell, before leaving Washington he became convinced of Babcock's guilt after Babcock urged him to steal all the evidence against him so that it could be destroyed. Failing in his efforts to see Grant again, Bell went to St. Louis, where he offered to assist the prosecutors. He soon lost his job.[17]

Angered by rumors that the prosecutors were contemplating indictments of members of his own family, Grant called Wilson in on Christmas Day for another dressing-down. Wilson denied the rumors. But whether or not Treasury officials and prosecutors were out to get Grant, they clearly aimed to break up the president's staff system represented by Babcock and his fellow secretaries. As Wilson put it, both

Bristow and Jewell thought "the kitchen cabinet should be abolished and its influence abrogated."[18]

Bristow's allies also saw the whiskey fight as an opportunity to boost his presidential prospects for 1876, although he himself remained aloof from the scramble. As early as May 1875, in the wake of the initial distillery raids, Bluford Wilson had told a Treasury Department investigator that "Mr. Bristow was to be the next President," and Wilson was "very positive . . . in his instruction that Mr. Bristow was the right man to go for." Ten days after Babcock's indictment, Bristow's new clerk, A. E. Willson, told Harlan the time had come for the movement to take "definite shape and system" and to highlight the secretary's "resolute performance of the duties in hand" as the way to "strengthen the popular confidence that will carry him on." Indeed, presidential politicking proceeded in tandem with the prosecutorial effort. In meetings with the supervisor of internal revenue in Chicago, Wilson not only discussed legal strategy against the ring but also took heart that the supervisor would "leave no stone unturned to advance the Secretary's interest in Illinois, Wisconsin & Michigan." Wilson reported to his brother that Dyer could "manage Henderson and the latter will doubtless control Missouri which I have counted as certain for Bristow, as it will be if Henderson can be kept straight."[19]

Meanwhile, Babcock's indictment spurred his St. Louis lawyers into action. Their correspondence with him leaves little doubt of Babcock's complicity in the Whiskey Ring. Their first concern was not assembling evidence that demonstrated their client's innocence but suppressing evidence that showed his guilt. The lawyers obtained assurances from both McDonald and Joyce that they would not testify against Babcock. In particular, Babcock feared the uncovering of incriminating letters he had sent to the two conspirators. Joyce was happy to give the letters in his possession to the defense lawyers, and at one point Mrs. Joyce even sewed some into her skirt to avoid their detection by government detectives. McDonald was less forthcoming with his cache of letters, apparently hoping to use them as leverage when it came time to ask for a pardon. But McDonald did conspire with lawyer Chester Krum in inventing a bogus explanation of Babcock's December 13, 1874, "Sylph" telegram stating, "They will not go." They came up with the idea of saying it referred to two individuals planning a trip to St. Louis in connection with an appointment. "If we can engineer an explanation of this description, it will work well," Krum wrote to Babcock. "But we cannot advance anything of the sort, unless we can maintain the theory unshaken." This idea did not pan out, but Krum was willing to suborn witnesses if necessary: "I hope to connect with a witness for the Govt. and assure him that his lines will fall in pleasanter places if he aids us."[20]

In January 1876 Grant was inundated with reports that prosecutors were granting light punishments to distillers and low-level officials who agreed to turn state's evidence against higher government officers. He considered this practice "perfectly atrocious." In a tense meeting with Wilson, he asked about the prospective testimony of an internal revenue gauger named Abijah Everest. Wilson said that Everest would claim that Joyce had asked him to mail a letter containing $500 to Babcock. Grant expressed his concern that Everest had been granted immunity. "When I said let no guilty man escape, I meant it, and not that nine men should escape, and one be convicted." Grant apparently revealed Everest's story to Babcock, for later that evening, Babcock made "a very prompt and emphatic denial" to Wilson. In several meetings with Pierrepont, the president complained about the plea bargaining and urged him to stop it. Although the attorney general thought the reports about these efforts had been exaggerated, he wrote a circular to the prosecutors, more tangential than direct, cautioning them to see "that no guilty one who has been proved guilty, or confessed himself guilty, has been suffered to escape punishment." In St. Louis, Dyer intended to keep the attorney general's order a secret, to avoid scaring off potential witnesses. But Babcock wanted to do just that. He obtained a copy of the circular from Grant's office and leaked it to the press. "They were trying to drown me, trying to destroy me," Babcock later told Pierrepont, "and I had a right to protect myself."[21]

Bristow feared the public would see Pierrepont's circular as an attempt to "fetter" Babcock's trial, and its publication compounded his morbid sense of isolation. He told Harlan that Grant "constantly talks to others about me as his enemy" and "shows by his manner that he is brim full of wrath against me." On Sunday, February 6, two days before the opening of the trial, Bristow careened toward a nervous breakdown. According to his clerk A. E. Willson, "Col. Bristow's illness which has an apoplectic tendency and is the result of the nervous strain and excitement of the past ten days became almost alarming. He was discouraged, disheartened and as he expressed it unmanned." Willson reported to Harlan, "What has hurt Bristow worst of all & most disheartened him is the final conviction that Grant himself is in the Ring and knows all about [it]." Why Bristow had reached that conclusion Willson did not say, nor did he cite any evidence. Moreover, Bristow was not so psychologically undone that he could not discuss the presidential race with several men, including Bluford Wilson, that same day. Later in the afternoon he called on Fish to bemoan his "painful" position in the cabinet and reiterated his desire to resign. With no sense of the contradiction, he claimed that a rumor of "a disagreement between him and the President" was "without foundation, although the President's manner was *cold*, distrustful and at times offensive, and severe in his insinuations and his remarks." Bristow denounced Pierrepont's circular order and denied that he himself had ever given "any special instructions" to the prosecutors, failing to note that less than two weeks earlier he had signaled his approval of the plea bargaining in a letter to an official in Chicago. Bristow also brought up the presidential nomination and asked for Fish's advice. Fish tried to "sooth[e] him," suggesting that Grant was "naturally sensitive" about the prosecutions because of his friendship with Babcock. He advised Bristow to stay in his post until after the party's national convention. Resignation might result in his nomination on an independent ticket, but it "would defeat his chances of nomination as the regular candidate of the Party."[22]

Nonetheless, by the next day Bristow had pulled himself together, and he went to see Grant and renewed his offer to resign. Grant asked him to stay until after the trial. Bluford Wilson described this meeting as "kindly throughout," showing that the president was either "a consummate dissembler" or "entirely satisfied with Bristow's course." Even so, Wilson told his brother Harry, "Bristow and I are marked for slaughter as soon as Babcock's trial is over." With the circular order, he believed, the "champion snake" Pierrepont "has gone back on us completely," while Porter and others "have carried the President against us and will hound us both into disgrace and oblivion if possible."[23]

The start of the trial on February 8 raised tensions even higher. Federal circuit judge John Dillon, a Grant appointee, presided, joined by district judge Samuel Treat. Babcock's St. Louis lawyers yielded management of his defense to a crack team that included former attorney general George Williams; Emory Storrs, one of the nation's leading criminal lawyers; and John K. Porter, a former New York appeals court judge. They earnestly hoped that Grant would testify, and Horace Porter told the president that if he gave his personal testimony, rather than a deposition, "*an honorable acquittal will absolutely follow.*"[24]

On the trial's opening day, Grant laid the question of his testifying before the cabinet. The prosecutors had subpoenaed virtually everyone on the White House staff. "The President manifested a great deal of excitement," Fish noted, "and complained that they had taken from him his Secretaries & clerks, his Messengers, & doorkeepers; that the prosecution was aimed at himself, & that they were putting him on trial; that he was as confident as he lived of Babcock's innocence, referred to his long association with him, the entire confidence he had in him, and that he knew he was not guilty; that were he guilty it would be an instance of the greatest ingratitude and tre[a]chery that ever was." The cabinet opposed his going to St. Louis, and Grant decided to submit a deposition.[25]

Grant gave his testimony in his White House office, with Chief Justice Morrison Waite presiding. Special counsel Lucien Eaton represented the prosecution, and William Cook represented Babcock. Bristow and Pierrepont were also in the room. Because the defense had called the president to testify, Cook led off the questioning. Grant said he had long felt "great confidence" in Babcock's integrity and efficiency and had learned nothing to shake that confidence. Babcock had never tried to influence him to halt the investigation and had never spoken to him regarding the order transferring revenue supervisors. Babcock's explanations of the various supposedly incriminating telegrams "seemed to me to clear up all grounds of suspicion against him," Grant said. "Have you," Cook asked, "ever seen anything in the conduct of General Babcock, or has he ever said anything to you which indicated to your mind that he was in any way interested in or connected with the whiskey ring at St. Louis or elsewhere?" "Never," Grant answered.[26]

Eaton's questioning did much to confirm Grant's suspicion that he too was on trial. Dyer wanted Eaton to "show on cross-examination that the President had no knowledge of the secret correspondence of Babcock with Joyce and McDonald." This would demonstrate that Babcock could have participated in the conspiracy without Grant's knowledge, but this approach necessarily entailed questions that focused on what the president knew and when he knew it. Dyer urged Eaton to "let no matter of delicacy stand in the way of a full and complete examination." Several of Eaton's questions cast suspicion on Grant's original appointment of McDonald as supervisor. Did he know that McDonald was ignorant and barely able to sign his name? Grant said that he knew McDonald was illiterate. Did Grant recall that his own good friend C. W. Ford had described McDonald as a "bad egg," that several members of Congress had opposed his appointment, or that an affidavit had been filed against him at the Treasury Department? Grant denied knowing or said he could not recall. In fact, McDonald had had several positive recommenders, including General Sherman, but Eaton tried to create the impression that despite the many objections to McDonald, Grant had given a central place to a key player in the ring. Eaton read several of the telltale telegrams and asked whether the president knew of them at the time they were sent. He said he had no recollection of having knowledge of them at that time. Grant had earlier mentioned being under political pressure to suspend the order transferring the supervisors, but when Eaton asked him which congressmen had asked him to do so, he declined to give names. In conclusion, Eaton stated, "Now I suppose, Mr. President, that the substance of your testimony is—what we all know to be true—that if there has been any misconduct on the part of Gen. Babcock, it has not come to your knowledge." He replied, "Yes, sir; that is true."[27]

The session did nothing to assuage Grant's bunker mentality. Afterward, he exploded to Fish that the trial was "a prosecution aimed at himself not Babcock [and] that the Secretary of the Treasury had become possessed with the idea of the complicity of the President." He complained that detectives had watched him in St. Louis and that "all sorts of small devises were being resorted to to annoy him, and hold him up to public condemnation." Grant spoke "very bitterly of Bluford Wilson who he said was manipulating and controlling these movements." As soon as the trial was over, he said, Bristow should leave the cabinet. Meanwhile, Wilson told Dyer that Bristow "repudiates" Pierrepont's circular cautioning against excessive plea agreements to gain testimony by low-level accomplices.[28]

In presenting their case against Babcock, the prosecutors did put accomplices on the stand. On the third day they called Abijah Everest, who, one reporter said, looked like "the kind of man who would say a prayer while stabbing you in the heart." Everest said Joyce had asked him to mail two letters to Washington, each containing $500—one addressed to Babcock and the other to Avery. Under cross-examination, however, he admitted that he had seen Joyce slip a $500 bill into only one of the envelopes, and he could not tell which one. The prosecutors hoped the various telegrams passing among the principals would demonstrate Babcock's connection to the ring. Regarding the "Sylph" telegram, however, the defense submitted several clearly innocent, mostly politically related items of communication between Babcock and Joyce to demonstrate that there was no reason to presume that the "Sylph" telegram referred to a potential investigation of the ring. More important, the defense convinced the judges to exclude the December 5,

1874, telegram ("I cannot hear that anyone has gone or is going") signed with Babcock's name, on the grounds that, in the absence of the original order form, there was no proof that Babcock himself had sent it.[29]

In addition to winning the exclusion of this dispatch, the defense explained other telegrams by arguing that McDonald and Joyce had used various stratagems to gull Babcock into sending them vaguely worded messages they could wave under the noses of fainthearted distillers to demonstrate their influence and protection in Washington. This scenario portrayed Babcock as a dupe rather than a conspirator. The lawyers also argued that the ring's real source of warnings regarding potential investigations was John Hoge, a revenue agent who, after an earlier investigation, had accepted a bribe from the ring to falsely report to the Internal Revenue Bureau. They labeled the two $500 bills allegedly sent to Babcock and Avery a "damnable trick," arguing that Joyce intended for Everest to relate the episode to the distillers as evidence of Joyce's supposed pull with the administration. To complete their picture of Joyce's charade, the defense called a St. Louis letter carrier who testified that Joyce had persuaded him to retrieve the letters from the box where Everest had deposited them. The prosecutors thought of impeaching this witness but gave up the idea when they realized the Republican postmaster of St. Louis could produce plenty of the letter carrier's colleagues willing to swear to his reputation for veracity. The defense rounded out its case with several character witnesses, including Sherman, and Grant's deposition.[30]

In their summations, the prosecutors returned to the December 1874 telegrams. They noted Joyce's December 3 dispatch asking if either the secretary or the commissioner planned to send anyone—that is, any investigators—to St. Louis. But because the court had excluded Babcock's December 5 telegram from evidence, defense attorney Storrs acted as if it did not exist and asserted—untruthfully—that Babcock had never answered Joyce. The press carried the text of the December 5 telegram, but the sequestered jury did not see it. The prosecutors also pointed to the "Sylph" telegram of December 13, but the defense insisted that McDonald, who had been in Washington, had already informed his colleagues that the proposed investigation had been called off, obviating any need for Babcock to do so. According to Storrs, Babcock did not prevent the investigation, and his "Sylph" telegram was "idle or worthless." Storrs's colleague John Porter attributed the prosecutors' "earnest zeal" to "their avowed hostility to President Grant." Dyer had the last opportunity to speak, and his colleagues, fearful that he would rise to this bait, urged

Bluford Wilson to rein him in. Wilson promptly wired Dyer to be "temperate in all allusions to the President," and he was.[31]

After the "most painful day" of being "abused, maligned and misrepresented," Babcock returned to his hotel room and "gave way to tears." He wrote his wife a letter that focused not on his innocence but on what the judge and jury would do. He was "not sanguine." "If I am to be ruined," he wrote, "we must bear it." Like anxious defendants from time immemorial, he prayed, "God grant that I may be spared and be a good Christian all the remainder of my life."[32]

The next morning Judge Dillon gave the court's instruction to the jury. In large part he presented an evenhanded recap of the evidence, although he echoed the defense's statement that Joyce's December 3 telegram "was not answered." Moreover, he observed that no testimony nor any documentary evidence directly implicated the defendant in the conspiracy. That left only circumstantial evidence. Under settled judicial practice, circumstantial evidence could establish complicity, but the bar was necessarily higher than for direct proof. "If the evidence can be reconciled either with the theory of innocence or of guilt, the law requires the jury to give the accused the benefit of the doubt, and to adopt the former." Under Missouri law, a defendant could be neither compelled nor permitted to testify; therefore, "the law clothes the defendant with a presumption of innocence, which attends and protects him until it is overcome by testimony which proves his guilt beyond a reasonable doubt—*beyond a reasonable doubt*—which means that the evidence of his guilt, as charged, must be clear, positive and abiding, fully satisfying the minds and consciences of the jury." The instruction was all the defense could have hoped for. Dyer was so disillusioned that he did not even bother to return to the court to hear the jury's verdict. After just two and a half hours of deliberation, the jury pronounced Babcock not guilty.[33]

The verdict won general approval, in part because it averted a great embarrassment to the nation. Even the *New York Tribune* acknowledged that the "country is to be congratulated" because it "would have been an almost intolerable mortification to every patriotic American if the private secretary of the President of the United States had been found guilty of conspiracy to defraud the revenue." Still, despite his acquittal, the evidence against Babcock known to the public left his reputation beyond repair. Even before the verdict, Grant had advised Fish that he intended to tell Babcock "it was better for himself and necessary for the President" that he leave the White House. Fish argued against dismissing Bristow, pointing out that doing so would simply give him the "popularity of martyrdom" and probably the Republican presidential nomination as well. Grant agreed, and relations between the two men grew less tense. Bristow had been on the brink of resignation, but he now breathed a sigh of relief that "the storm has blown over."[34]

But for Grant, the storms continued, and his anger had not really subsided. He was enraged when Henderson submitted a bill for $26,000 (equal to more than half the president's annual salary). He thought of refusing to pay the lawyer "one cent" and considered firing Dyer outright, but the cabinet counseled caution. The Democrats, hardly willing to let the scandal fade, immediately created a special committee in the House to investigate the whiskey frauds. Moreover, Babcock proved reluctant to depart. He returned from St. Louis with a sense of triumph and took up his old desk in the room next to the president's office. When Grant seemed reluctant to push him out, Fish reminded the president that he needed no resignation because Babcock was merely an army officer detailed to the White House for no set term. In Babcock's absence, the president had tapped his son, Ulysses Jr., to stand in as private secretary, and on March 3 he made the appointment permanent. Grant believed that with a family member in this sensitive post, anyone could see that an assault on his secretary would be an assault on himself. Grant would have liked Babcock to vacate his position as superintendent of public buildings in Washington as well, but he told Fish that that appointment was in the hands of the Army Corps of Engineers, and Babcock stayed. In the ongoing improvement and beautification of the capital, Babcock had in fact compiled an impressive record, though it was not free of controversy, owing to the questionable methods of the city's chief developer and territorial governor Alexander Shepherd. Six weeks after Babcock left the White House, Treasury Department officials secured another indictment against him in a bizarre case related to machinations among the city's political factions, but he was again acquitted.[35]

While Babcock's trial unfolded in St. Louis, another scandal engulfed Robert Schenck, minister to Great Britain. Early in his tenure, Schenck, as a stockholder and paid director of the Emma Silver Mine Company in Utah, had allowed his name to be used in advertising the firm's shares in London. When reports of the connection appeared in the press in late 1871, Grant and Fish ordered Schenck to resign his membership on the board. He complied, although he kept his resignation quiet until he could unload his stock. Schenck assured Fish that he had paid for the shares "dollar for dollar" but later admitted that he had purchased them through a highly advantageous loan from one of the company's stock vendors. When the failing company ceased paying dividends in 1873, intimations reached Grant that the stockholders were going to accuse Schenck and other company leaders of enticing them into purchasing worthless stock in a bogus enterprise. The president and Fish considered alerting the minister about these allegations, but after further thought, they decided to say nothing so that they would be able to distance the administration from Schenck if the rumors grew into a public concern.[36]

Schenck had performed admirably during the negotiation of the Treaty of Washington and the Geneva Arbitration, and Grant and Fish were loath to throw him overboard. But with the Democrats in control of the House, it was only a matter of time before his indiscretions would face scrutiny. The crisis came while Babcock was in the dock. To forestall an investigation, Grant demanded that Schenck step down, but a delay in communications gave the Foreign Affairs Committee time to organize and launch its inquiry. Schenck asked to stay on until it was over, but Grant "promptly and earnestly" said, "No! we have scandals enough without assuming any more." The committee proceeded with its hearings. Even though the final report found Schenck "not guilty of a fraud or of any fraudulent intention," it condemned his connection with the mining company as "ill-advised, unfortunate, and incompatible with the duties of his official position." Fish persuaded the committee chairman to elide direct censure of the administration, but the affair put one more blot on the White House.[37]

A week after Babcock's acquittal in St. Louis, and three days after the House authorized the Schenck inquiry, yet another spectacular scandal struck, this time within the cabinet. For weeks the House Committee on Expenditures in the War Department had been combing through the department's operations for signs of malfeasance. The most sensational discovery was evidence of bribery involving the secretary of war himself, William Belknap.

The story originated in 1870 when Belknap's wife Carrie suggested to a friend, Caleb Marsh, that she could arrange his appointment to a lucrative position as post trader at one of the western forts. Upon learning that a position at Fort Sill, Indian Territory, was about to open up, Marsh considered applying for it. But the incumbent, John Evans, wished to remain at his post and was willing to pay to do so. The two men struck a deal whereby Evans would keep the job if he handed over $12,000 per year, which Marsh would split with the Belknaps. Belknap accepted the arrangement and signed a receipt for his first quarterly installment of

$1,500 in November 1870. Although Belknap later claimed the money was related to his wife's personal finances, the payments continued after her death in December and after Belknap's marriage to her sister Amanda three years later. The arrangement drew some attention in 1872 in connection with complaints about high prices at trading posts, but Belknap deflected inquiry by instituting new regulations and lower prices. Privately, he and Marsh agreed to a 50 percent reduction in the payments from Evans. Once Belknap married Amanda, the payments helped fund their lavish lifestyle.[38]

When the *New York Herald* published allegations about the scheme in February 1876, Democrats on the Expenditures Committee smelled blood. They wired Marsh, who was living in New York, and asked him to come to Washington. He arrived in the capital, but instead of reporting to the committee, he went to the Belknaps' house. Mrs. Belknap urged him to say that the money was hers and that he was serving as her banker, but Marsh refused to lie. He thought about leaving the country, but when he was subpoenaed he returned to Washington. Meeting in secret, the Democratic members of the committee took Marsh's sworn testimony on February 29. The next day they included the Republicans when they invited Belknap to review the evidence and examine Marsh. With Belknap standing by in tears, his lawyer read a proposal whereby the secretary would confess if the committee would agree to leave his wife out of the matter. At a meeting that evening, the committee voted unanimously to reject Belknap's proposal and agreed to meet the next morning at 10:30 to initiate impeachment proceedings.[39]

Inevitably, Secretary of the Treasury Benjamin Bristow stepped into the crisis. After the evening meeting, a Republican committee member, Lyman Bass, scurried to the secretary's house and told him the story. Here was another chance for Bristow to tell the president how rotten his administration was. The next morning, March 2, Bristow went to the White House and cryptically told Grant that the committee had discovered something bad and advised him to send for Bass if he wanted to know what it was. Under questioning from Grant, Bristow named Belknap but declined to give details. He urged the president to talk to Bass before seeing anyone else. Dumfounded by Bristow's mysterious intimations, Grant sent a messenger to ask the congressman to come at noon. Moments after Bristow departed, Belknap arrived, scarcely able to speak and leaning on Zachary Chandler for support. His incoherence hardly clarified the matter for the president, whom he begged to accept his resignation. Grant did so immediately, handing Belknap a letter

WASHINGTON, D. C.—INTERVIEW, AT THE WHITE HOUSE, BETWEEN PRESIDENT GRANT AND
SECRETARY BELKNAP.

Interview at the White House between President Grant and Secretary Belknap.
(*Frank Leslie's Illustrated Newspaper*, March 18, 1876)

accepting his resignation at 10:20, ten minutes before the House committee was to meet.[40]

At a cabinet meeting the next day, Grant admitted that he had not fully understood the gravity of Belknap's resignation or "that acceptance was not a matter of course." The cabinet discussed whether a public officer had the right to terminate his tenure in that way. In a letter to Harlan the day after the meeting, Bristow claimed he had gone to the White House the morning before Belknap quit "to prevent the President from falling into the error of accepting the resignation." This was at best a distortion and at worst a lie. Bristow's own reconstruction of the conversation indicated that he had merely advised Grant to see Bass before anyone else. Moreover, when the cabinet discussed the question of an officer's right to resign, Fish recorded, "Pierrepont & Bristow seemed to think that he had such right." Reduced to its essence, the question was: could an officer evade impeachment by resignation? It was debatable, but the press lashed the president for acting hastily, allegedly to rescue Belknap. Bristow did nothing to counteract that criticism. Grant felt a fondness for Belknap and his wife and shrank from believing them dishonest. Nonetheless, he directed Pierrepont "to examine the law with a view to consider what action could be taken against the late Secretary, either criminal, or civil."[41]

Despite his sympathy for the Belknaps, Grant did not exhibit the same solicitude he had shown Babcock, in part, no doubt, because he was less inclined to view the legal actions against Belknap as an attack on himself. For his part, Belknap felt abandoned. He wrote to his sister, "My resignation which was made to save the President from the abuse which might follow, and which, if I do say it, was a magnanimous act, is tortured into a *confession* now by those who are so anxious to convict." The attorney general put detectives on Belknap for fear he might flee, but Belknap said Pierrepont did so "to glorify himself" and "thus strike a down man." As for Bristow, Belknap fumed, "He is the Arch-Conspirator who has struck one by one of the Cabinet & is after the President himself."[42]

Belknap received little pity from his immediate subordinate, General in Chief William Sherman. Over the years, Sherman had grown increasingly frustrated as Belknap assumed much of the authority over the army that had formerly belonged to the general. He saw Belknap's fall as the predictable result of a law passed early in the administration that had taken the authority to appoint post traders from army officers and placed it in the War Department. "Congress ought to be indicted, not Belknap," Sherman complained. "They took from me certain power and conferred it on him as a legitimate source of profit or patronage, and because he used it as they had a right to suppose he would, they hold up their hands in holy horror and cry Shame!" As a result of the scandal, Grant moved to redress the skewed balance of authority between the general and the secretary. Sherman, who had shifted his headquarters to St. Louis two years earlier, moved back to Washington.[43]

Prospects for better treatment by a new secretary of war eased Sherman's return. The day after Belknap resigned, Grant and the cabinet took up the question of a replacement. Bristow had promised Harry Wilson he would push him for the appointment—an absurd notion, given Grant's animosity for Bluford. During the cabinet discussion, Bristow broke his promise and instead recommended E. R. Hoar, equally unlikely to get the job. Grant first offered it to Senator Lot Morrill of Maine, who declined, privately telling Fish that he was "not in harmony with the personal surroundings of the President." The cabinet considered several names and finally settled on Alphonso Taft, a distinguished Ohio lawyer. The former state court judge had gained some public notice for a dissenting opinion upholding the Cincinnati school board's ban on Bible reading in the schools, a position that squared with Grant's support for nonsectarian public education. With little connection to Washington, Taft had scant familiarity with military affairs, making him more than willing to restore Sherman's leadership role. He easily won Senate confirmation and occupied the secretary's chair nine days after Belknap left.[44]

By then, Belknap found himself facing two trials: impeachment and criminal prosecution. The House inched forward with impeachment, concluding that resignation did not relieve the ex-secretary of liability to trial by the Senate. After a lengthy debate in the Senate over whether its jurisdiction extended to a former official, the trial began on July 6. Marsh was the star witness, although most of what he said echoed his previous committee testimony. On August 1 thirty-seven senators voted to convict Belknap—well over half, but five short of the required two-thirds. Of the twenty-five who voted against conviction, twenty-three said they had done so because of a lack of jurisdiction. Belknap convinced himself that these men considered him innocent but were simply "afraid of popular clamor." "Whatever the papers may say," he insisted, "the result is an acquittal—it exonerates me as fully as if I had a thousand votes."[45]

While the congressional proceedings unfolded, the administration prepared to move against Belknap in federal court. Shortly after Belknap's resignation, Pierrepont asked the Expenditures Committee for its evidence, which he intended to present to a federal grand jury. But the Democratic House voted to reject his subpoena. The case also led to social awkwardness in Washington. The cabinet secretaries admonished a tearful Julia Grant not to be seen with Mrs. Belknap, but Belknap was pleased that the "Grants treat us with exceeding kindness." At the end of March, Pierrepont asked the president and the cabinet if he should proceed toward an indictment. Grant hesitated, but Fish argued that although the evidence was insufficient to convict, "the Administration owed it to itself and the country to press the indictment." But even though Grant directed the attorney general to proceed, the court case against Belknap remained in abeyance until after the impeachment verdict. By then, the 1876 presidential campaign was in full swing, and Republicans had no desire to see the matter stirred up before the election. Finally, in January 1877, Belknap's lawyer asked the Justice Department for a dismissal. The administration turned the matter over to the district attorney, who replied that "a long, expensive and laborious trial" would likely end in a hung jury. Grant accepted that judgment. "In view of the long suffering of the accused," he ordered the case dismissed three weeks before he left office.[46]

The cascading scandals inevitably raised questions about Grant's ability to judge men's character—the trait that had served him so well during the war. Enemies saw incompetence or complicity, but Fish later cited "the abuse of his confidence" by selfish, designing men. Grant's Methodist minister excused him on the grounds that "he was of such personal integrity and uprightness that he refused to believe it possible that other men were not influenced by his own high motives." Six years after leaving office, Grant himself claimed, "I have never felt the slightest concern for myself through all the abuse that has been heaped upon me. I was of course much annoyed that such things could happen as did while I was the Executive of the Nation. I was probably too unsuspecting."[47]

Certainly, the revelations of the winter and spring of 1876 distressed Republican Party leaders. "The news from Washington has sickened me, and I am ashamed of my party," Henry Dawes wrote after Belknap resigned. "I can't tell what is next." The Democrats were determined there would be plenty more. Beyond the legitimate search for scoundrels in the government, they proved relentless in their efforts to embarrass if not harass the administration. The House Military Affairs Committee demanded a list of all army officers detailed for civilian service, with a view to possibly banning such duty—a clear assault on Grant's staff system. The War Department prepared the list, but the cabinet changed the designation of these assignments from working for the president to working for the commander in chief of the army.[48]

The Democrats also rammed through a bill to lower the president's salary to $25,000 per year again, although the change would not apply to Grant. He promptly vetoed it out of "duty to my successors" and to the "dignity" of the office. On another front, the House Democrats demanded that Grant catalog and explain his absences from "the seat of Government" and establish whether the performance of his official duties while outside of Washington conformed to law. He flatly refused to answer. Instead he sent a message, drafted by Fish, that defended the president's right to conduct business elsewhere and pointed out the utility of the telegraph and railroads for doing so. In addition, he provided a detailed account of the "hundreds upon hundreds" of official acts his predecessors had performed while away from the capital. The response provided a needed boost to Republican morale and exposed the Democrats' pettiness. Perhaps, said the *New York Tribune*, congressmen "could themselves serve the country quite as well as they now do if they were to stay at home and send their speeches to Washington over the wires."[49]

Still, despite Grant's vigorous defense of the prerogatives and dignity of his office, the mood in the administration remained one of frustration and anger. "The House is as unpleasant and as ugly and ignorant as it is possible to be," wrote Assistant Secretary of State John Cadwalader. "They do nothing for us, and make us all the trouble they can." The drama played out against the backdrop of the coming presidential campaign. The Democrats' determination to end their long exile from power fueled their efforts to paint the administration's record as black as possible. Among the Republicans, the erstwhile Liberals aimed to nourish disenchantment with the administration, seize control of the party, and demand the nomination of a man of their choosing. Grant was not a candidate, but in a variety of ways, his administration would be center stage as the presidential election of 1876 unfolded.[50]

21

★ ★ ★ ★ ★

SECURING THE SUCCESSION

After accepting the Republican presidential nomination in 1868, Grant confided to Sherman that he had agreed to run to save the country from "mere trading politicians." Eight years later, as he began his last year in office, Grant himself had become a thorough politician. He had lobbied on Capitol Hill, twisted arms at the White House, wielded patronage, fashioned policies, enlisted a cadre of legislative lieutenants, and done much to set the nation's agenda. He had won a landslide reelection, but he had also battled a host of enemies. He had become committed to the Republican Party, convinced that its fortunes and those of the nation stood inextricably entwined. So believing, he took a keen interest in the protracted struggle to choose his successor—an intense drama that did not reach its climax until hours before he handed over the keys to the White House. That unfolding drama both reflected and influenced the shape of Grant's reputation as president.[1]

The vexations Grant had found in the presidency did not deter a large field of candidates hoping to win the office. For the first time since 1860, the Republican Party faced a wide-open convention. The odds-on favorite was popular Maine congressman James G. Blaine. Blaine had served six years as Speaker of the House, winning respect on both sides of the aisle for his evenhanded management. But the Crédit Mobilier scandal had tinged his reputation, and revelations in the spring of other apparent misdeeds deepened suspicions about his character. Senator

Oliver Morton had earned Republican reverence for his Herculean efforts on behalf of the Union cause as governor of Indiana, and he enjoyed respect as an ardent champion of African Americans' rights. Generally a stalwart ally of the administration, he had offended conservatives by his support of the Inflation Bill. Moreover, a stroke in 1865 had left his legs paralyzed, and despite his vigor in the Senate, his candidacy suffered from prejudice against electing a "cripple." Morton's chief rival for support among pro-administration Republicans was Roscoe Conkling. No one stood by the president more effectively in Congress, in private conclave, or on the public platform. Yet the supremely arrogant Conkling showed a disdain for lesser mortals in the Republican Party. He and Blaine hated each other uncordially, and if either man were nominated, he faced probable knifing by the other's friends in the election. A few states backed favorite sons to leverage their convention bargaining power. Governor Rutherford Hayes rose somewhat above favorite-son status by virtue of his vote-getting ability in unpredictable Ohio and his innocence of recent party infighting.

The other major candidate was Benjamin Bristow. Soon after he became secretary of the treasury in June 1874, his political allies Bluford and Harry Wilson and John Marshall Harlan had begun a long-march campaign to position Bristow as the party's noblest crusader for cleansing government. These men, especially the Wilson brothers, had ambitions of their own. Harry had hankered after numerous positions under Grant and hoped for greater appreciation of his talents by President Bristow. Bluford thought he might run for Congress in a Bristow campaign or, even better, become attorney general in a Bristow cabinet. As solicitor of the treasury, he spent much of his time advancing his chief's political fortunes.[2]

Key to the Bristow strategy was winning the endorsement of Liberal Republicans. Having seen their organization disintegrate after the Greeley fiasco, the Liberals deliberated how best to exert their influence in the coming contest. As early as February, the Wilsons and Bristow began negotiating with them. Bluford told twenty-five-year-old Henry Cabot Lodge that if the Liberals supported Bristow at the Republican convention, the secretary would, in the event he lost, be willing to take second place on an independent ticket behind Charles Francis Adams. Henry Adams considered his father out of the running and pushed for an independent nomination of Bristow regardless of what the Republicans might do. Bristow himself told Lodge that if the Republican Party "did not come up to his principles," he would "leave it." Each camp was obviously using the other, but the two agreed that denigrating Grant was central to their campaign. They believed, as Horace White put it, "the public mind is feverish enough on the subject of administrative rascalities" that the Liberals could "terrify the party" into backing their candidate.[3]

Carl Schurz spearheaded the Liberals' anti-administration campaign. He advised Bristow that "the party machine men would surely prevent the nomination of a true reformer for the Presidency, unless they were made very clearly to understand that they cannot do so with impunity." He organized a meeting of some 200 sympathizers to issue that warning to the Republicans, and Bristow gave his blessing. Bristow's actions convinced California senator Newton Booth that "the presidential disease has broken out all over him," and he warned the meeting organizers that "the American people resent any attempt of the 'elect' to teach them what they ought to do." Nonetheless, they plowed ahead. The gathering's closing statement drafted by Schurz did not name Grant, but its animus was clear: Americans felt a "burning shame" at "the shocking evidence of the demoralization and corruption of the present," especially "the employment of the Government service as a machinery for personal and party ends." "To reestablish the moral character of the Government by thorough reform," the country must select a presidential candidate "whose name is already a watchword of reform" and one who "deserved not only the confidence of honest men, but also the fear and hatred of the thieves." The address did not mention Bristow by name, but no one could mistake the reference.[4]

The Liberals also encouraged the Democrats in the House to persist in their investigations and thus generate "fuel to keep the fire going." But many were opposed to subjecting Grant to impeachment, which would distract attention from other investigations and provide the president a forum to defend himself. Better to keep the fight in the political arena. "The November election," Charles Nordhoff wrote, "impeaches him & will condemn him."[5]

The Committee on Naval Affairs obliged with a months-long examination of Secretary George Robeson's management of the Navy Department. The principal charge was that Robeson had accepted payments from E. G. Cattell, a contract broker who served as liaison between naval suppliers and the department. Early in the secret phase of the investigation, Fish had heard reports that the committee chairman aimed to "have the Head of the Navy Department in a worse fix than Belknap." Robeson insisted the allegations were false, and the public phase of the investigation took months. The committee subpoenaed Robeson's bank accounts, which showed that he had made substantial deposits during his tenure as secretary. But even the Democratic majority of the committee concluded, "Any direct or positive proof to connect Mr. Robeson with the reception of any of the money corruptly received by E. G. Cattell from contractors is wanting." The Republican minority claimed the evidence indicated that "the Secretary is in receipt, from various legitimate and proper sources, of an income amply sufficient to account for all his actual deposits and balances" and that he had committed "no fraud, corruption, or willful violation of the law." In view of the inconclusive evidence and the complexity of the legal issues involved, the Democratic members concluded not to recommend impeachment but instead passed that question off to the Judiciary Committee, where it remained in abeyance when the session closed. As one correspondent reported, "It seems now to be determined to let the charges rest suspended over the head of Mr. Robeson until next winter, which means that they are to be used as political capital in the fall campaign."[6]

The Democrats also hoped to make political capital out of an investigation conducted by the Committee on Expenditures in the Justice Department. Specifically, the committee examined disbursements totaling $34,000 paid by attorneys general Amos Akerman and George Williams out of the department's Secret Service appropriation to John Davenport, the chief federal supervisor of elections in New York City. The implication was that the money amounted to a political slush fund, but both Williams and Davenport testified that the supervisor had used it to create an elaborate registration system to combat the fraudulent voting rampant in the Tweed era. Congress had established the supervisor system for large cities under the Enforcement Act of February 1871, and Davenport had launched a crusade to purge New York's voter rolls of those not duly registered or eligible. Williams testified that the president had authorized the funds, and Grant made no bones about the fact that he intended the money to be used "in accordance with the law to prevent frauds in election." Nonetheless, as the Democrats intended, the hearings sparked a sensation. The *New York Herald* professed great shock that the hearings had revealed "the President to have been the author of a raid upon the Treasury" to create a "corruption fund." Once again, however, the committee Democrats were forced to conclude that the evidence did not sustain any charge of criminal culpability. Indeed, their chief recommendation was not that anyone be impeached or indicted for breaking the law but that all the election laws passed during

Reconstruction be repealed, the enforcement appropriations eliminated, and the corps of election supervisors abolished. The Democrats' real complaint was not that the law had been violated but that it had been effective. No action resulted, and Davenport kept his job, serving in administrations of both parties until 1894.[7]

After Babcock's acquittal, the House Democrats were determined not to let the Whiskey Ring scandal die. They created an investigating committee that held hearings all spring and summer, fueling Grant's feelings of persecution. After a week of hearings, the press reported the president had fallen ill because of "severe mental anxiety." He particularly bridled at the testimony of John Henderson, who reiterated his earlier criticism of Grant for reversing the order transferring the revenue supervisors. If the president could dictate the action of a subordinate officer, he said, "the President of this country is a mere monarch." Henderson's testimony reinforced Grant's suspicions of Bristow and Bluford Wilson, who, he believed, had used a detective to "abstract papers important to the defense of Babcock, and to create prejudice against" himself. His indignation heightened in late April when Wilson peremptorily fired revenue agent W. B. Moore for offering admittedly hearsay evidence incriminating Homer Yaryan, the chief agent who had worked closely with Treasury officials and prosecutors against Babcock.[8]

In the cause of "investigation," the normally parsimonious Democrats threw off their penny-pinching ways. By one estimate, some thirty committees conducted inquiries, each requiring money to hire a clerk and a stenographer, pay witness fees and expenses, and publish hundreds of copies of reports, some of which exceeded a thousand pages. Not content with the scalps of men such as Babcock and Belknap, they even tried, unsuccessfully, to pin accusations on Bristow, Fish, and Jewell. From Paris, an American diplomat wrote home, "The fury of 'investigation' in Washington has reached such a stage that it is something like the days of the French Revolution when it was enough to cry 'suspect'—& the man was ruined."[9]

In this poisoned atmosphere, Grant and the administration had scant hope of working with their opponents on matters of public policy. The Democrats dragged their feet on appropriations bills, hoping to cut expenditures to the bone and slash the number of offices. Grant and Fish even encountered opposition to a bill to implement the terms of the 1875 reciprocity treaty with Hawaii. Southern Democrats in the House predicted damage to domestic rice and sugar producers and warned of any scheme that might lead to the annexation of territory with "inferior" inhabitants. Joined by northern protectionists, they came close to defeating the bill, which later passed more handily in the Senate. Grant was encouraged by the report of a commission he had appointed to study the optimal location for a canal through Central America. The commission advocated building it in Nicaragua, but the president and Fish thought it best not to submit the report to Congress but to begin negotiations for a treaty. Grant ideally envisioned a neutral canal open to all nations willing to unite behind the project by treaty. But Fish was unable to bring negotiations with Nicaragua to a successful conclusion before the administration ended.[10]

In the area of civil rights, Grant could expect no assistance from the House Democrats, whose caucus bowed to dominant southern members. During a debate over amnesty for ex-rebels, many southern Democrats even offered an unseemly defense of Jefferson Davis and the Confederacy. In March white southerners took heart when the Supreme Court's decision in *United States v. Cruikshank* invalidated the indictments of the perpetrators of the Colfax massacre on the grounds that the protections afforded by the Fourteenth Amendment applied to state action, not acts by individuals. On the same day, in *United States v. Reese*, the Court offered a narrow reading of the Fifteenth Amendment and the Enforcement Act and overturned a conviction in a voting rights case. Disturbed by these developments, Grant used a conversation with a black congressman, Jeremiah Haralson of Alabama, to publicize his intention "to do all in his power to encourage and protect the colored people." Like other Republicans, Grant believed the Democrats' retrograde attitudes would make the southern question an important issue in the election campaign, and he discussed with Haralson who would make the strongest Republican candidate for the region.[11]

Publicly, Grant maintained neutrality in the nomination race, although rumor had it that he was privately advocating Conkling. In mid-April Pierrepont told Fish that the New York senator was "low spirited and dissatisfied" because he had received no endorsement from the administration, despite having "invariably maintained all its measures." Nonetheless, a few weeks later Bristow complained to John Harlan that "the whole force of the Administration is to be exerted to force Conkling's nomination." Hardly the "whole force," of course, since Bluford Wilson and his minions in the Treasury were earnestly working for Bristow. After his presidency, Grant recalled that he had never thought Conkling had much of a chance, and "any one, except Mr. Bristow, would have been satisfactory to me." He said his personal favorite had been Fish, who had also caught the eye of a few Liberals. Grant said that, unbeknownst to Fish, he had written a letter of endorsement to be laid before a deadlocked convention, but the right moment never came. If Grant did write such a letter, it never surfaced at the convention. Fish was the sentimental favorite among his associates in the State Department, but the secretary himself was certain that if Conkling failed, which was likely, the senator would block the nomination of any other New Yorker.[12]

A key element in Grant's supposed campaign for Conkling was the appointment of J. Donald Cameron as secretary of war. The move, it was said, was designed to win Conkling the support of Pennsylvania, where Cameron's father, Senator Simon Cameron, dominated the Republican organization. But as the convention balloting would show, Conkling received not a single vote from the Pennsylvania delegation.[13]

Instead, Cameron's appointment came as part of a larger shift in assignments. After Robert Schenck's disgrace, Grant had offered an olive branch to the Liberal wing of the party by nominating renowned Boston lawyer Richard Henry Dana to be minister to England. But Dana's nomination was soon savaged by a fellow lawyer who accused him of plagiarism and by Ben Butler, against whom Dana had once run for Congress. Fish decried the opposition as one more example of "the encroachments which the two branches of the legislature have made on the Constitutional prerogatives & powers of the Executive." After Dana's rejection, the position in England remained open until Grant's cabinet reordering in late May, when he gave it to Edwards Pierrepont. The attorney general had long hoped for the London post, and Grant was no doubt pleased to get rid of the baggage Pierrepont carried for supposedly doing the president's bidding in the Whiskey Ring prosecutions. To replace Pierrepont, Grant shifted Alphonso Taft from the War Department to the Justice Department, a place more suited to his tastes and talents. Cameron, Pierrepont, and Taft all won easy confirmation.[14]

But Bristow and his allies were convinced that Cameron's appointment fit into a larger plan to undermine his presidential campaign. Throughout the spring the treasury secretary bombarded Harlan with letters insisting, "Every power of the administration is being used against me. . . . The politicians everywhere are putting their heads together to kill me off." He was certain that other campaigns had hired detectives to "cook up stories on me."[15]

Certainly Bristow had made enemies, but to some degree his suspicions reflected the negative character of the campaign his own men were conducting against his rivals. As early as February, Grant told Fish that Bristow was "being pushed along by too large a number of ze[a]-lous young friends." Republican national secretary William Chandler thought "the bigoted, intolerant advocacy of Bristow only tends to his defeat." A month before the convention, Fish warned his colleague that other candidates were charging his friends with "inspiring the assaults upon them," and Bristow conceded that the Wilsons and others "might have been imprudent." Nine days before the delegates convened, Bristow told the president that he intended to resign, and the two men agreed not to reveal his plan until after the convention. By remaining in the cabinet until after the nomination, the secretary protected himself from more open criticism by the president's friends, and by allowing Bristow to stay, Grant avoided making him a martyr.[16]

The delegates who gathered in Cincinnati knew the Democrats would take their cue from the House majority and make "reform" a cornerstone of their campaign. Hence, the Republican platform treated the administration gingerly. One section said the party held "all public officers to a rigid responsibility" and called for the "speedy, thorough, and unsparing" punishment of violators of official trusts. The final plank contained only tepid praise for the president: "The national administration merits commendation for its honorable work in the management of domestic and foreign affairs; and President Grant deserves the continued hearty gratitude of the American people, for his patriotism and his eminent services in war and peace." And yet the platform also endorsed several policies and proposals with which Grant was closely associated: specie resumption, a tariff adjusted to the needs of the economy, barring the use of public school funds for sectarian education, outlawing polygamy, generous military pensions, and, most important, a peaceful South where all citizens could enjoy their rights unmolested. Questions of race and section predominated in the document, which gave notice that the southern question would hold sway in the coming campaign.[17]

In the nominating speeches, advocates for Bristow highlighted his identification with reform, sometimes employing language that repelled the administration's allies. "No rings, no cliques, no combinations of personal interest against the interest of all the people; no personal government," declared George Curtis. Richard Henry Dana spoke of "a great cloud over the Administration" and said, "The body politic is laboring under a severe and dangerous disease." Such rhetoric won Bristow few friends. In the balloting he started in third place; he rose to second on three ballots but never garnered half as many votes as

542

front-runner Blaine. The delegates who wanted to stop Blaine turned not to Bristow but to Hayes, who had no factional enemies. Harlan and the Kentuckians and most other Bristow delegates joined to give Hayes a narrow victory over Blaine on the seventh ballot. Grant immediately telegraphed the nominee: "I congratulate you and feel the greatest assurance that you will occupy my present position from the Fourth of March next."[18]

The next day Bristow submitted his resignation, effective three days hence on June 20. Bluford Wilson also resigned. Grant later vented his feelings to Fish, describing Bristow as "treacherous in the Cabinet." As Fish wrote in his diary, Grant "said Bristow's nature was one of intense selfishness and ambition and of extreme Jealousy and suspicion, and that from the time he entered the Cabinet he had set his eye on the Presidency with a distrust and hostility to himself (the President) and to every member of the Cabinet." When Fish noted that Bristow had always been "kind and friendly" to him, "The President replied yes: not because he loved you any better than the others, but because he feared you. . . . [H]e feared to differ with you on account of your general character and sought to appear in harmony with you before the public but would have turned upon you as quick as the others but for that cause."[19]

Convinced of Bristow's perfidy, Grant acted on his own suspicions to rid the Treasury Department of men who had done Bristow's bidding. In seeking a new secretary, Grant told Fish he wanted someone who "would be willing to make all the changes" he wanted in the department. He chose Maine's Lot Morrill, longtime chairman of the Senate Appropriations Committee. Even before Morrill took office, however, Grant dismissed Wilson's ally, chief revenue agent Homer Yaryan, who had been particularly aggressive against Babcock. The president also reinstated W. B. Moore, the agent Wilson had fired after he testified against Yaryan to the Whiskey Ring committee. Grant's avowed aim was to "correct an injustice" done to Moore, "a faithful officer" and a disabled Union veteran. In accepting Yaryan's resignation, internal revenue commissioner D. D. Pratt saluted his "intelligence, judgment, zeal and integrity." Shortly after Pratt's letter appeared in the newspapers, Grant fired him as well.[20]

Grant may have thought he was evening the score with men who had trifled with his reputation, but they did not surrender. Yaryan went before the committee and insisted that Grant lacked sympathy for the prosecutions. Bluford Wilson proved to be the Democrats' star witness. He too cultivated the impression that Grant had given scant support to the Treasury's investigations, and he repeated Horace Porter's "Sylph" theory, alleging Grant's relations with a "lewd woman." Even Bristow thought Wilson went "too far in giving his testimony." The former secretary himself appeared briefly before the committee but refused to answer substantive questions, claiming executive privilege. Privately, he said that Grant "has all along been willing to wink at dishonesty & corruption if indeed he has not actually enjoyed the fruits of it." Grant maintained his innocence and thought Bristow refused to testify in order to nourish the impression that the president had something to hide. He called Bristow's bluff with a letter, which he published, releasing Bristow and all present and former cabinet members to "answer all questions asked" by the committee. Still Bristow refused. Behind the scenes, he and his allies circulated the rumor that Grant was "drinking heavily." The hearings left Grant all the more bitter against his erstwhile subordinates. At the close of the congressional session in mid-August, he told an interviewer he had always been "impelled by proper motives" and was "willing to leave the whole matter to the judgment of the country."[21]

The congressional session had dragged on into August not only because of the myriad investigations but also because of a prolonged fight over appropriations. Although both parties espoused retrenchment, the Democrats were determined to make deeper spending cuts than the Republicans were willing to accept. With the prospects for legislation bleak, a government shutdown loomed. Two weeks before the beginning of the new fiscal year on July 1, Grant sent a special message warning of "the evils which would result from nonaction of Congress." He suggested that if the two houses could not agree on appropriations bills by June 30, they should pass a continuing resolution to maintain spending at the current level until regular bills passed. He even provided the text for such a resolution. Congress complied, but the ongoing stalemate required the passage of five temporary extensions before the regular appropriations won approval.[22]

The main sticking point was the Democrats' aim to shrink funding for regular operations of the government, in large part by cutting positions and reducing salaries of government clerks, postal workers, and other employees. As the crisis unfolded, the cabinet deliberated over what the executive branch could do in the event of a failure to approve funding. In one meeting Jewell insisted that, in the event of a shutdown, he would run his department "law or no law." When the president remarked that "we must act under the law," Jewell repeated that he "would go on the same unless ordered to the contrary." Self-righteous and prone to tell tales out of school, Jewell had managed to alienate both Grant and Bristow over the past few months. Now Grant thought Jewell's latest outburst was a threat to throw the blame on the president for any stoppage of the mails. A few days later, when the president ordered cabinet members to notify their workers that without appropriations, "no power existed to pay them," Jewell replied that he could "not see how any order [to subordinates] was required." Grant's fuse was already short because of the investigations, and a week later, when Jewell challenged him regarding some appointments, the president told Fish he "could stand his annoyance no longer." He asked for Jewell's resignation and in his place promoted James N. Tyner, the second assistant postmaster general and a close ally of Oliver Morton. Later, in an unguarded moment, Grant told an interviewer he had grown "very tired of Mr. Jewell generally at the Cabinet meetings" and did not "like his way of doing the business intrusted to him."[23]

Facing the grim duty of implementing a reduction in force, Grant ordered the department heads to protect first the jobs of Union veterans and their widows and dependents. When an inadequate sundry civil appropriations bill came to his desk, he seriously considered a veto but affixed his signature to halt the stalemate. Even so, he chastised the House for a measure seriously "defective in what it omits" and cited several bureaus and divisions whose business would suffer. "To appropriate and to execute are corresponding obligations and duties," he lectured. "I deem it a duty to show where the responsibility belongs for whatever embarrassments may arise in the execution of the trust confided to me." In the case of the consular and diplomatic appropriations bill, the House inserted a directive that certain officers should be notified "to close their offices." Grant refused to bow to this attempt to "invade the constitutional rights of the Executive."[24]

Besides their willingness to fund investigations, the one exception to the Democrats' vaunted frugality was the rivers and harbors bill, which set spending for internal improvements. Having been largely frozen out of this largesse for more than a decade, Democratic House members stuffed the bill with projects for their districts. They used logrolling to entice senators to go along. Grant, however, balked. He signed the bill to secure funding for the undertakings he approved, but as for those he considered "purely private or local," he said, "under no circumstances will I allow expenditures upon works not clearly national." His refusal represented the first major impoundment of funds by a president since

Thomas Jefferson's time, and it was the last until Franklin Roosevelt's. He won praise for exercising "practical retrenchment" and taking "care that no public money goes out to 'improve' worthless ditches and pools."[25]

One of the few instances in which Grant received cooperation from Congress came at the end of the session, when legislators appropriated $1.6 million to add 2,500 cavalrymen to US forces engaging the Indians in the West. The measure came a month after the shocking news of the annihilation of much of George Custer's Seventh Cavalry at the Battle of Little Big Horn in late June.[26]

Grant had not abandoned the goals of his peace policy, but two circumstances complicated their achievement. The discovery of gold in the Black Hills region of the Sioux reservation spurred the movement of white miners into the area, in contravention of the 1868 treaty that designated the Sioux lands as inviolate. In addition, several hunting bands led by Sitting Bull, Crazy Horse, and other warriors proved reluctant to settle on the reservation, and their hunting forays inevitably led to clashes with whites. At a meeting with Sheridan in November 1875, Grant agreed that the army would no longer enforce the ban against the miners' entry into the territory, and he authorized military action to force the "hostiles" onto the reservation. Sheridan immediately devised plans for a winter offensive, but significant fighting did not get under way until the spring of 1876. The general envisioned a convergence of three columns of troops against the Indians in the Big Horn Valley, with Custer leading one of the columns westward from Fort Abraham Lincoln in the Dakota Territory.[27]

Before the campaign got started, however, Custer was summoned to appear before the House committee investigating Belknap. The contempt the two men felt for each other was common knowledge. At the hearings, the colonel did his best to besmirch the secretary, and he did not care if the taint extended to Grant. Indeed, Custer repeated rumors that the president's brother Orvil had a stake in the post tradership business. Custer's performance outraged the president, who had long disliked the army's golden-haired prima donna for his self-promotion.[28]

Shortly after Custer's testimony, Grant ordered that he be excluded from the expedition against the recalcitrant Sioux. A public outcry and intercession by Sheridan and department commander Alfred Terry got Custer restored to the mission, but merely as head of his regiment, not as commander of a column. Nonetheless, once the campaign was under

way, Custer, who was technically under Terry's command, was determined to "cut loose" and engage in independent action. He neglected
to coordinate with other sections of Terry's column, shifted several companies of the Seventh Cavalry against an Indian force of indeterminate
size, and met an ignominious defeat and death at Little Big Horn, along
with more than 250 men in his regiment. The disaster rallied the nation to embrace a military solution to the Indian problem in the West,
and Grant found himself swamped with offers from volunteers eager
to avenge Custer's loss. He stuck with the regular army and welcomed
Congress's quick authorization of the 2,500 new cavalrymen.[29]

Grant shed no tears for Custer. When an interviewer asked whether
the fiasco was "a disgraceful defeat of our troops," he responded, "I
regard Custer's massacre as a sacrifice of troops, brought on by Custer
himself, that was wholly unnecessary." He accepted the need for renewed fighting, however. The onset of winter inured to the benefit of
the better-equipped bluecoats. One by one, the nonagency tribes succumbed, and by spring 1877, the war was essentially over.[30]

The renewed warfare and its grimness moved some to condemn
Grant's peace policy as a failure, but the president refused to accept its
defeat or relinquish its long-term goals. The stinginess of Congress in
appropriating sufficient funds to meet the Indians' needs, he believed,
had helped bring on the new fighting. In the midst of the uproar over
Custer's defeat, he took counsel with Bishop Henry Whipple, a leading
advocate for better treatment of the Indians. Whipple recommended relocating the Sioux to the presumably more fertile land of the Indian Territory, dividing the land in severalty for Indians to engage in agriculture,
and creating an Indian government with a Native police force. Grant
endorsed Whipple's views, and Congress authorized the president to
appoint a commission to negotiate a new agreement with the Sioux. But
Congress stipulated that no further subsistence would be paid to any recalcitrant Sioux war bands, and none to the Sioux generally unless they
relinquished the Black Hills to the United States and allowed whites
access to the region through their reservation. Grant appointed Whipple and others to the commission, which in September and October got
several tribes to accept an agreement.[31]

In his December 1876 annual message, Grant urged Congress to approve the agreement. He noted that his "humane" policy had achieved
peace throughout most of the West, except for the Black Hills region. He
explained:

Hostilities there have grown out of the avarice of the white man, who has violated our treaty stipulations in his search for gold. The question might be asked why the Government has not enforced obedience to the terms of the treaty prohibiting the occupation of the Black Hills region by whites. The answer is simple: The first immigrants to the Black Hills were removed by troops, but rumors of rich discoveries of gold took into that region increased numbers. Gold has actually been found in paying quantity, and an effort to remove the miners would only result in the desertion of the bulk of the troops that might be sent there to remove them.

The new agreement would eliminate "all difficulty in this matter." Three days before Grant left office, Congress approved the pact.[32]

Although Grant failed to fully realize his dreams of a remodeled Indian culture, and although his notion of bending the Indians to white ways offends modern sensibilities, he could look back with pride at the peace policy he had fashioned. "On the eve of your retirement from office," wrote a group of Indian delegates in Washington, "we desire to express our appreciation of the course you have pursued towards our people while President of the United States—At all times just and humane you have not failed to manifest an earnest wish for their advancement in the arts and pursuits of civilized life, a conscientious regard for their rights and the full purpose to enforce in their behalf, the obligations of the United States."[33]

Whatever success Grant may have attained with his Indian policy, it played virtually no role in the 1876 campaign. Neither party's platform mentioned it. Instead, the Democrats painted a dire picture of the country's condition and larded their platform with numerous paragraphs beginning, "Reform is necessary. . . ." Their nominee for president, Samuel Tilden, despite his reputation as a political wire-puller par excellence, had assumed the mantle of reform as governor of New York and had frequently slammed the national administration. The speaker who placed his name in nomination declared that the "great issue" was "the question of administrative reform." The Democrats aimed to make the election a referendum on Grant's eight years in office.[34]

For their part, the Republicans insisted that they could be trusted to root out wrongdoing, and they emphasized the purity of Rutherford Hayes's record. A few disaffected Republicans like Bristow concluded that Grant was so benighted and self-absorbed that "*he is going to defeat*

Hayes if he can do it. At any rate he is determined that Hayes shall not be elected as a *Reformer*." To suppose that Grant could find vindication in Hayes's defeat bespoke Bristow's alienation more clearly than Grant's political perversity. A loss by Hayes would inevitably be laid at Grant's door. Three days after the nomination, the president told a crowd of celebrators, "I know Governor Hayes personally, and I can surrender with unfeigned pleasure my present position to him, as I believe I shall do."[35]

In preparing his acceptance letter, Hayes understood the delicacy of his task—to revive the active support of the party's Liberal element while not alienating the organization men who were still loyal to Grant. Like Grant, he called for a speedy return to specie payments. As Grant had done, Hayes endorsed a constitutional amendment barring public funds for sectarian schools. On the South, he took a balanced approach. He favored efforts to pacify the region and give it "the blessings of honest and capable local government," thereby suggesting a return to home rule by whites. But he also insisted that such government must "protect all classes of citizens in their political and private rights," as guaranteed by "all parts of the Constitution . . . the parts that are new [that is, the Thirteenth, Fourteenth, and Fifteenth Amendments] no less than the parts that are old." The reference to local government gave the whiff of a suggestion that Grant had erred in propping up Reconstruction regimes. On civil service reform, Hayes's rhetoric resonated with Grant's pronouncements, but he went even further. Arguing that a president eager for reelection was tempted to abuse the patronage to build support, Hayes promised to serve no more than one term. Few could miss the contrast with Grant's alleged yearnings for a third term.[36]

Inevitably, word reached Hayes that the comment displeased Grant, and the nominee rushed to assure the president that he meant no "reflection on you." Grant saw no point in jeopardizing a Republican victory over the issue: "I am not aware of any feeling personal to myself on account of your allusion to your determination not to be a candidate" for a second term. "You say distinctly what course you will take, without condemning what the people have done on seven distinct occasions—re-elect the incumbent." He assured Hayes, "You will have my hearty support."[37]

Although the proprieties of his position as well as his reluctance to speechify kept Grant from the campaign trail, he and others in the administration threw their weight behind the Republican cause. At the risk of offending civil service reformers, the president heeded party managers in matters of patronage and told one officeholder whose resignation he requested that it was "in the interest of Republican success." Secretary of the Interior Zachariah Chandler became chairman of the Republican National Committee and had the president's blessing in levying campaign assessments on federal employees. Postmaster General James Tyner took an active part in his home state of Indiana, which included distributing funds to secure the vote of the state's "large floating population." In addition, under the Enforcement Act of 1871, the Justice Department supplied nearly $300,000 to hire more than 16,000 special deputy marshals and election supervisors in New York and elsewhere. Grant also had a hand in defining the central campaign issue for the Republicans: the southern question.[38]

Each of the two parties suffered too much internal division to make the currency question a winning issue, and the school question never gained much traction. "Hard times" favored the party not in power, but the Democrats' negative notions about government left them short on plausible solutions. The Democrats shouted for "reform," but Hayes's reputation for probity helped muffle that chant, and the Democrats themselves still bore the stigma of the Tweed Ring. It quickly became apparent to Republicans that the best strategy to divert attention from economic depression and allegations of corruption was to focus on southern white recalcitrance and African American rights. As if on cue, an outburst of racial violence in Hamburg, South Carolina, dramatically thrust the issue to the fore.

On July 8, the very day Hayes issued his letter of acceptance, a minor altercation between blacks and whites in Hamburg escalated into a white mob attack that left at least half a dozen blacks dead. Grant denounced the massacre as "cruel, bloodthirsty, wanton, [and] unprovoked"—a repetition of the kind of violence that had marred elections in other southern states, particularly Louisiana and Mississippi. The latter state, he said, "is governed today by officials chosen through fraud and violence, such as would scarcely be accredited to savages, much less to a civilized and christian people." South Carolina's Republican governor, D. H. Chamberlain, sought federal help and traveled to Washington to meet with Grant, Secretary of War Cameron, and Attorney General Taft, who helped him frame his request. In a response released to Congress and the public, Grant declared that whites in some states seemed to believe they had "the right to Kill negroes and republicans without fear of punishment, and without loss of caste or reputation." Only "the Great Ruler of the Universe" could know the "final remedy" for such deep-seated hatred. But, he said, government was a "failure" if it did not protect citizens' "life, property and all guaranteed civil rights," of which "in this country the greatest is an untrammelled ballot." The president did not send help immediately but promised to provide, if necessary, "every aid for which I can find law, or constitutional power."[39]

Republicans lost no time in tying the renewed racial violence to their opponents, and the Democrats struggled to neutralize the issue. Tilden included a paragraph in his letter of acceptance promising to protect all citizens, "whatever their former condition, in every political and personal right." Advising Tilden that the Republicans were using the Hamburg massacre to highlight the threat to blacks' rights, New York Democrat Scott Lord spearheaded passage of a House resolution calling for "certain, condign, and effectual punishment" of anyone resorting to violence to prevent "the free exercise of the right of suffrage in any State." By such efforts, the Democrats admitted the Republicans' argument and validated the GOP's concentration on the southern question. "Our main issue must be," Hayes advised party speakers, "*it is not safe to allow the Rebellion to come into power.*"[40]

Grant agreed. He told an interviewer that if the Democrats gained control of the presidency and both houses of Congress, they would bankrupt the nation by allowing "millions and millions" in southern claims for damaged property and pensions for former Confederates. "There would even be danger that the claims for the value of slaves would be considered and paid." While traveling in Pennsylvania the president told an audience of blacks that, "to the extent of the power vested in him, it was his purpose to see that every man of every race and condition should have the privilege of voting his sentiments without violation or intimidation. When this was secured, we would then, and only then, deserve to be called a free Republic."[41]

Using the Lord resolution as justification, the administration ordered Sherman to ready all available troops to protect "all citizens, without distinction of race, color or political opinion, in the exercise of the right to vote as guaranteed by the fifteenth amendment." The Justice Department also outlined the circumstances under which US marshals could call on the military's assistance. The troops stationed in the eleven states of the former Confederacy numbered fewer than 7,000 and could hardly police the thousands of polling places throughout the region, but they could be moved to hot spots. A Washington correspondent noted that Grant's order, spurred by Lord's resolution, "puzzled the Democrats exceedingly to know how to denounce it."[42]

And yet, by 1876, white Democrats in most of the South had

succeeded in creating such an atmosphere of intimidation that they needed little overt violence to convince many African Americans to forgo exercising their political rights. Under the constitutional mandate to ensure that the laws be faithfully executed, Grant did order some troop movements, the most notable occurring in South Carolina. For weeks he had been receiving informal reports that the state's Democrats were using so-called rifle clubs to terrorize and even murder their political opponents. Finally, after Governor Chamberlain informed Grant that he lacked sufficient means to suppress "insurrection and domestic violence," the president issued a proclamation ordering the lawless "insurgents" to disperse. He also instructed Sherman to transfer "all the available force" to South Carolina to "sustain" the proclamation. The renewed intervention risked alienating northern Liberals from the Republican cause, but Grant told a reporter that "overwhelming" evidence showed "a state of affairs in South Carolina which demanded imperatively the official action which I have taken." With the arrival of several hundred troops, the violence subsided, but the white supremacists had already accomplished the work of intimidation.[43]

The outcome of the election on November 7 killed any hope Grant may have entertained for an orderly transition of power. With 185 electoral votes necessary to win, the immediate result showed Tilden with 184—mostly from the southern states, but also from the swing states of New York, Indiana, Connecticut, and New Jersey. Hayes had won 165 electors from the North and the West. Both sides claimed the 20 remaining votes: 19 from Florida, Louisiana, and South Carolina, where the outcome of balloting remained in dispute, and 1 vote from Oregon, which was being contested on a technicality. Hayes had clearly carried Oregon, but the Democrats tried to disqualify one of his electors on the grounds that he held a federal office. The uncertainty in the presidential election immediately gave rise to tense and complicated maneuvering that lasted until the day before the winner took the oath of office. Although Grant initially suspected that Tilden had prevailed, he hoped Hayes would triumph in the end. During the ensuing crisis, his primary goals were to maintain the peace and secure an outcome that would meet the obligations of the Constitution and the laws, as well as win substantial acceptance in the country. Any attempt to seat Hayes forcibly would backfire and do lasting damage not only to the Republican Party but also to the nation.[44]

The task of determining the outcome in the three disputed southern states lay with returning boards empowered not only to compile the official count but also to reject any fraudulent returns. Florida, Louisiana, and South Carolina were the last former Confederate states still in GOP hands, and because Republicans dominated their returning boards, Democrats feared foul play. In the aftermath of the election, Democratic national chairman Abram Hewitt and President Grant dispatched leaders of their respective parties to the state capitals to observe the boards' work. The president also ordered Sherman to make troops available to maintain peace and ensure that the boards were "unmolested in the performance of their duties." "No man worthy of the office of President," he declared, "would be willing to hold it if 'counted in' or placed there by any fraud." At Fish's suggestion, Grant concluded his published order to Sherman: "Either party can afford to be disappointed in the result but the Country cannot afford to have the result tainted by the suspicion of illegal or false returns." When the president took the precaution of increasing the garrison in Washington by a few hundred troops, inveterate Grant haters such as Confederate general Gideon Pillow cried that he aimed to block the election, upend the Constitution, and make himself "the absolute ruler of a Government of *force*." Although others criticized the move less dramatically, Grant stood by his intention to quell disorder from whatever source. "If Buchanan were President," he told associates, "we might have war."[45]

The viability of Grant's efforts to keep the peace depended in large part on his maintaining a position of absolute impartiality. In late November he ordered federal troops to uphold Governor Chamberlain, whose term had not yet expired. But the two parties were also contending for control of South Carolina's legislature, and Chamberlain sparked a heated cabinet debate when he asked to use federal troops to help the Republicans organize the new state house by ousting Democrats who had not been approved by the returning board. Cameron called the situation "war and revolution," but Grant interrupted him, saying, "Decidedly no! no! it is no such thing. . . . [T]he question of organization of the Legislature belongs to the State to settle and not to the general government." He ordered Colonel Thomas Ruger, the commander in Columbia, to "have nothing to do with it." Still smarting from the public reaction when troops had entered the Louisiana legislature in 1875, he told Ruger, "I want to avoid anything like an unlawful use of the Military and I believe it would be regarded with disfavor if they were used in taking men claiming seats out of the legislative hall."[46]

The same day Grant sent these orders, he agreed to meet with

Hewitt, who was anxious for a clarification of the president's intentions. The Democratic national chairman began with honeyed remarks about Grant's great service to the nation and the Democrats' disposition to "do him full justice." Grant would have found the latter point laughable had he not felt so unfairly assaulted by his critics. As Hewitt noted, "The President replied that the present House of Representatives had not given evidence of a desire to do him justice" and "had raked up petty accusations against him." Hewitt told Grant that "it rested wholly with him whether the present complication should result in war, or in a peaceful solution." Grant replied that "if there was to be any fighting, he certainly would not begin it." He would "maintain order" but "would not provoke any collision by the use of mere power, where it was not his duty to employ it."

On the presidential question, Grant asserted that Hayes had carried South Carolina and Florida. In confidence, he admitted to Hewitt that Tilden had apparently received a small majority in Louisiana, but the official count rested with the returning board, which, he admitted, was "in very bad odor with the public." Hewitt asserted that if Louisiana's votes were thrown out altogether, Tilden would either have a majority of the remaining electors or be elected by the House. Without accepting Hewitt's claim, Grant stated that he "did not expect there would be any serious trouble; that a solution would be reached, that would, in the main, be satisfactory to the people." If Tilden prevailed, he would be inaugurated quietly. Grant emphasized, however, that it was not "for him to decide the question, but it was the duty of Congress under the Constitution; that his duty would be to see that their decision was carried into effect."[47]

The substance of this conversation appeared in the newspapers, much to Grant's annoyance. He assured Chamberlain, "I never authorized the chairman of the democratic national committee to give forth my views to determine the political action in any state." In a press interview he noted the irony: "The same party that perpetrated frauds in some of the Southern States for Tilden complain[s] of frauds in Florida, Louisiana, and South Carolina, but if there had been no frauds in Mississippi, North Carolina and Arkansas these states would have gone for Hayes," giving him a clear victory. And the president reminded his countrymen of the larger context: "Governor Hayes represented the party which in the late election carried all but four of the States which furnished the means for suppressing the rebellion; and Governor Tilden carried all but three of those which sought to destroy the Union."[48]

This spirit informed Grant's preparation of his annual message delivered on December 5. In an early draft he cited the "singular spectacle" of "nearly a solid section of the country supporting one candidate when it is clear that with an untrammeled, protected freedom of franchise to all legal voters the result would have been far different." "Intimidation and assassination," he wrote, had produced this result. After a contentious cabinet meeting, Fish convinced Grant that this apparently partisan departure from the wonted "high tone" of an annual message would cause more harm than good. The president struck the section, but he did point out the need for Congress to enact greater safeguards for presidential elections and devise methods to remedy the kind of crisis the nation now faced.[49]

That crisis appeared in sharp outline on December 6—the day electors were supposed to send their votes to Congress. In the disputed states, the returning boards had ruled for Hayes, thus confirming the Democrats' fears. Rather than acquiesce, they as well as the Republicans submitted slates of electoral votes. Now what? The Constitution vaguely stated that at a joint session of Congress, the president of the Senate was to "open all the certificates and the votes shall then be counted." It was unclear whether the Senate president should do the counting. Since Vice President Henry Wilson had died in 1875, Republican Thomas Ferry of Michigan occupied that position, and many Republicans thought he alone should tally the votes. Democrats insisted that because a joint session of Congress was required, both houses must participate in the count. If that process ended with neither candidate receiving a majority, the election would go to the House, whose Democratic majority would choose Tilden. For the Republicans, it was vital that the full electoral vote be counted—with all the disputed votes going to Hayes. But even if the Democrats resorted to trickery or fraud to frustrate a full electoral vote and thus send the decision to the House, the question remained whether they could sustain their "victory" against the Republican Senate, the Republican-dominated Supreme Court, and the Republican president in command of the military. Although some GOP senators considered a count by Ferry legally suspect and politically dangerous, if no viable alternative appeared before inauguration day, a count by the Senate president would be the Republicans' ultimate deliverance. As an impasse loomed, the two houses appointed special committees to search for a solution.[50]

Hayes favored a count by Ferry, as did Oliver Morton and Hayes's fellow Ohioans James A. Garfield and John Sherman. But Roscoe

Conkling opposed it. The New York senator had never gotten over losing the nomination to Hayes. Tilden's representatives quietly cultivated Conkling's friendship, and he began making patronage deals with the new Democratic governor who had succeeded Tilden. Many reform Republicans also objected to a count by Ferry. Carl Schurz advocated submitting the question to an impartial body such as the Supreme Court, and he warned Hayes not to be misled by "an unscrupulous set of politicians bound to maintain themselves in power." Schurz craved a post in the new cabinet and freely advised Hayes about other appointments he should make. Petulantly—or obtusely—Schurz recommended Benjamin Bristow, Marshall Jewell, Jacob Cox, John Henderson, and Daniel Pratt, all of whom had been dismissed or had vacated their posts after disagreements with Grant. Revanche as much as reform stirred Carl Schurz's blood.[51]

Rumors that Hayes might stock his administration with Grant's antagonists naturally disturbed the president. Garfield warned Hayes of "the very great importance of having the President cordially with us to the end of his term," and Sherman advised "extreme deference to his opinions." At Sherman's request, Taft traveled to Columbus to explain Grant's concerns, and Hayes sent him back to Washington with a letter to the president expressing his "admiration and gratitude" for his course both "before and since the election." Hayes also wrote that he thought he and Grant were "generally agreed" on the cabinet question, although he would make no announcements until after the count was completed. Grant welcomed this assurance.[52]

Hayes followed up by sending his intimate adviser James Comly to Washington to visit the president in early January. Comly assured Grant "there was not one chance in a million" that Hayes "would appoint Bristow to a Cabinet position, in view of the fact that he had made himself so personally obnoxious to the President and so large a section of the Republican party." Comly reported to Hayes that Grant was "much gratified." He noted, "*At this point in the conversation he drew the friendly cigars from his pocket* and tendered one to me as he settled down to a quiet smoke and a confidential talk. . . . The President went all through the secret history of the Bristow connection with the Cabinet, and gave me the proofs of such duplicity and treachery on Bristow's part as were astounding." In a separate meeting, Garfield and Hayes's own congressman told Comly that Bristow "would be the worst man in the country to take into a new Cabinet. He had created such intense animosities that his presence in a Cabinet now would be almost fatal to the success of any Administration." Comly also asked Grant about Conkling's attitude toward the electoral count. The president said that although he had not seen much of the senator lately, he thought Conkling believed that Hayes had won, but he was "puzzled" about the proper constitutional mode for declaring the result. Grant also indicated that he had no influence over Conkling.[53]

While the crisis dragged on into mid-January, Grant stuck to his policy of preserving the peace without tilting toward either contestant vying for control of the governments in South Carolina and Louisiana. That proved more difficult in the latter state, where the two rival claimants for the governorship, Republican Stephen Packard and Democrat Francis Nicholls, each took the oath of office. Grant denied recognition to either one, whereupon Nicholls used force to replace five judges on the state supreme court with his own appointees. Their first job would be to rule his government legitimate. The returning board had actually found for Packard, and when the cabinet in Washington discussed the dueling governments, Fish noted, "A general coincidence of opinion seemed to exist, that whenever it became necessary to recognize one or the other, that the Packard one was that which must be recognized." Still, Grant noted that he would not express an opinion while Congress was examining the question. Two days later, on January 14, he wired General C. C. Augur, the US commander in New Orleans, outlining the administration's position and noting the legal precedence of the returning board's decision over any pronouncements by Nicholls's "illegal" supreme court. At that point, the administration was not opting for either government but, Grant stated, "should there be a necessity for the recognition of either, it must be Packard." This telegram to Augur caused an uproar, not only among Nicholls's partisans but also among Democrats across the nation. Notorious lobbyist Sam Ward snipped to Tilden that "Grant was in Whiskey when he sent that dispatch." The misinterpretation of his position annoyed the president, who told the cabinet he had "certainly not" intended for the commander to accord recognition to Packard. He instructed the military to stand by his orders to merely keep the peace and tilt neither way.[54]

Grant's exasperation burst forth in a conversation with Fish the next day. Though he rarely slept poorly, he was losing sleep over the Louisiana mess and "expressed great anxiety" for "relief from the pressure brought to bear on him." The "men attempting to rule Louisiana," he said, showed "extreme incapacity" and "had simply gone there to hold office." Across the South, white conservatives had spurned the plea of his first inaugural address to approach the problems of Reconstruction "calmly, without prejudice, hate, or sectional pride." The situation had grown so bad that he now thought the Fifteenth Amendment had been "a mistake, that it had done the negro no good, and had been a hindrance to the South, and by no means a political advantage to the North." As for Louisiana, although under current advices he regarded the Packard government as technically the legal one, the returning board's operations were "surrounded with difficulty and suspicion." He considered submitting the question of recognition to Congress, but Fish thought doing so might raise constitutional questions about the relative authority of the branches. Grant also believed that several senators, including Conkling, would not sustain the Senate president's power to count the electoral votes. Although he "most earnestly desired the declaration of Gov. Hayes as President," he feared that if Hayes assumed power with the votes of two or three states questionable, "he would be much crippled in power." Worse, however, if Tilden became president, "he would be unable to satisfy the expectations of the South," and white southerners, freed from any fear of military intervention, would grow even more defiant of the federal government.[55]

The president thus kept his fingers crossed that the congressional committees studying the problem would find a workable solution. As George Edmunds put it, what was needed for the vote count was "a method that leaves the result uncertain, although the steps be clear." On January 18 Edmunds submitted a bill to create an Electoral Commission comprising five members from the Senate, five from the House, and five from the Supreme Court. The ten congressional members would include five Republicans and five Democrats. Four of the justices would be chosen ostensibly according to geography, but they would also be balanced between the parties. These four would choose the fifth justice, most likely independent David Davis. The bill appealed to Democrats, who thought it revived Tilden's chances. Many Republicans opposed it, however, and Hayes thought Grant ought to use a veto, if necessary, to thwart it. But Grant lobbied for the bill, telling members of Congress that without "some tribunal whose decision both political parties would accept, . . . we would have anarchy and possibly bloodshed." The election of Justice Davis to the Senate from Illinois, leaving only Republicans to fill the commission's fifth judicial slot, eased the minds of some Republicans, and the bill passed. An exultant Grant thanked Congress for providing "an orderly means of decision of a gravely exciting question," but the *New York Herald* observed, "The relation of the President to the bill seems more particularly worthy of commendation than that of any other man."[56]

The administration had no official role to play in the Electoral Commission, but Grant seized the occasion of a congressional inquiry into troop movements during the election to submit a voluminous report detailing violations of political rights in several states. He said the evidence "left no doubt whatever in my mind" that intimidation and violence had required federal intervention and had "undoubtedly contributed to the defeat of the election law" in the three disputed states and also in Mississippi, Alabama, and Georgia. Such evidence could bolster the Republicans' argument to the commission that the returning boards were justified in excluding counts where serious disruption had occurred.[57]

Although the electoral crisis engrossed official Washington and the country, Grant made an effort to draw attention to financial matters. With a month left in his term, he submitted a special message calling for legislation to accelerate the resumption of specie payments. He suggested a new bond issue to reduce the legal-tender notes in circulation and thus bring the paper currency closer to par with gold. But continuing divisions over the money issue, as well as obsession with the electoral crisis, prevented Congress from acting on the president's proposal.[58]

Grant also found that despite his efforts to follow a nonpartisan path in the election's aftermath, his political enemies continued to snipe at him personally. In late November the *New York Sun* published a long front-page article rehashing the Whiskey Ring allegations under the headline, "Grant Dishonored." The story included a "missing link" that supposedly connected the president to the ring. This link was a note Grant had allegedly sent to William Avery, advising him that ringleaders John Joyce and John McDonald were "reliable and trustworthy" and telling the treasury clerk to "let them have the information they seek"— that is, notice of possible investigations by department agents. Grant immediately denounced the note as a fabrication. Even anti-Grant journalist Henry Boynton told Bristow it was "a flat forgery" and labeled the *Sun* article "one of [editor Charles A.] Dana's worst fiascos."[59]

A more tangible residuum of the whiskey scandal involved pardons for some of the men convicted of complicity in the ring. During the summer of 1876, Grant had issued pardons to a handful of participants, generally on the recommendation of the prosecutors and the Justice Department. That fall Taft argued for the release of Avery, and Grant pardoned him in November.[60]

Joyce and McDonald found less favor. Soon after their convictions, the two conspirators began threatening to make damaging revelations unless they were pardoned. Joyce wrote to Orville Babcock, "McDonald and myself have stood like rocks in mid ocean to break the waves that raged high and fearful against yourself and the President. . . . Will such pluck and fortitude as ours be ignored?" Through his lawyer Chester Krum, the semiliterate McDonald claimed, "I have got sufficient in my Hands to convince the world that it is not mean feelings or spite & I say once for all I must Have Liberty or a fite." Krum told Babcock he knew of nothing in McDonald's possession that could "hurt the President or any one else," but he warned that the former supervisor "might possibly create a disagreeable controversy." Krum suggested that "McD's threats be taken as those of a sick man, whose patience has been sorely tried." The threats made little impression on Grant, and Taft opposed his plea for release. But fourteen months in a cell had ruined McDonald's health. He told Krum, "My Hed is all broke out & I blead all the time from the bowles." Former prosecutor David Dyer endorsed a pardon, and five weeks before leaving office, the president granted one, citing "painful and dangerous maladies" threatening McDonald's life. Still smarting from what he considered the former treasury secretary's betrayal, Grant told Babcock that he considered "McDonald a better man than Bristow." He had little regard for Joyce, however. He approved a few other Whiskey Ring pardons in the last days of his term, but not for Joyce. Taft presented a favorable recommendation, but the president objected, and Joyce remained behind bars.[61]

Babcock served as a back-channel conduit between the Missouri convicts and the administration. Babcock himself, of course, needed no pardon, but his future hardly seemed rosy. With Grant's term about to end, he could not expect to retain his position as superintendent of public buildings in Washington. Still, both the president and Mrs. Grant welcomed him at the White House, and Grant listened attentively when Babcock offered advice on such matters as dismissing the case against Belknap. The president still felt solicitude for his longtime aide. Before leaving office, he arranged for Babcock to enter the Light House Service, thus allowing him to remain on the government payroll. In severing their official relations, Grant saluted Babcock's "integrity and great efficiency" and thanked him for his "faithful and efficient service as private Sec. for more than six years."[62]

While Babcock settled his future, he and others in Washington were spellbound by the unfolding drama of what he termed the "National Returning Board." When the Electoral Commission began its work, Joseph Bradley took the fifth justice's seat. Bradley gave the Republicans an eight-to-seven edge on the commission, whose determinations would stand unless they were rejected by both houses of Congress voting separately. On February 9, by a vote of 8 to 7, the commission decided Florida for Hayes, setting a pattern it would follow to the end. After it also gave Hayes Louisiana, the most problematic state, Grant assured the Ohioan that the result was "virtually determined" and invited him to stay at the White House before the inauguration. But the Democrats cried foul. Some in the House thought they could stop the count and avert Hayes's election by employing dilatory tactics to block the House's receipt of the commission's reports. More responsible party members, however, argued that in light of the Democrats' strong vote in favor of creating the commission, they could not honorably derail its operation. After the commission awarded Oregon's vote to Hayes, obstructionist Democrats in the House, including a preponderance of southerners, moved on February 24 for an immediate adjournment to block receipt of the report. But Speaker Samuel Randall, a Pennsylvanian, ruled against such "dilatory" motions, and the House voted to reject delay by a substantial margin. Grant followed these proceedings closely. The next day he told a reporter that because those who "sought unnecessarily to postpone the count met with a very decisive rebuke," he expected the selection of a president in time for the scheduled inaugural.[63]

While Tilden's prospects faded, southerners looked after their own interests. Some threatened to obstruct the presidential count to extort assurances from Hayes that he would remove federal troops and thus allow the seating of Nicholls in Louisiana and Democrat Wade Hampton in South Carolina. (A ruling of the Florida supreme court had already awarded that state's offices to the Democrats.) Leading the southern negotiators was Edward Burke, who represented Nicholls, although his efforts could benefit South Carolina's Democrats as well. In truth, Burke and his associates had scant leverage, given that Senator Ferry could finish the count himself at any time and thwart the Democratic obstructionism. Moreover, Hayes had already indicated in his letter of acceptance his intention to favor "local government" in the South, on the condition that Democrats agreed to uphold the new constitutional amendments. His representatives in Washington agreed to speak with the southerners, not to procure Hayes's victory but to wring from them promises to respect blacks' rights.[64]

Grant took no direct part in these negotiations, but his commitment to maintain peace ultimately aided Hayes's cause. He resisted calls to recognize Packard and Chamberlain. In an interview published on February 26 he said, "The entire people are tired of the military being employed to sustain a State Government. If a Republican State Government cannot sustain itself, then it will have to give way." But, he said, "it would be improper for me to fix a Southern policy for my successor and thus embarrass him." This statement strengthened the Ohioans' position in their talks with the southerners, for it gave to them the bargaining chips of recognition and the disposition of troops. In a conversation with Burke the same day, the president reiterated his position about recognition and even conceded that Louisiana's "most influential elements" backed Nicholls. But he warned of possible federal interference if Nicholls, "carried away by the possession of power," committed "violent excesses." Indeed, a few days earlier, Grant had ordered federal troops in South Carolina to disband mounted rifle clubs that were organizing a parade. Burke was pleased to hear that Grant planned no recognition of Packard, but the president's neutrality, his decision to leave troops in place, his avowed intention to put down any hint of Democratic violence, and his determination to launch no "policy that might embarrass his successor" left the southern spokesmen no alternative but to meet the Ohioans' demand that they make specific promises regarding constitutional protections for African Americans. They did so, and the count moved inexorably forward.[65]

On March 1 Packard asked Grant to recognize and support his government, but the president steadfastly adhered to neutrality. Through his secretary C. C. Sniffen, Grant replied that during his remaining days in office, troops would "not be used to establish or to pull down either claimant for control of the State," although troops would "hereafter, as in the past, protect life and property from mob violence, when the state authorities fail." When General Augur in New Orleans sought clarification, the administration's response during its hectic closing hours was muddled. Grant wrote to Secretary of War Cameron that Augur should no longer require Packard and Nicholls "to observe the status in quo [sic]," and the general should "limit his orders to the mere preservation of peace in case of riot." Sherman, however, ordered Augur to use his "counsels" to "prevent any material change in the attitude of the contending parties till the new Administration can be fairly installed,

HARPER'S WEEKLY.

A JOURNAL OF CIVILIZATION

Vol. XXI.—No. 1056.]   NEW YORK, SATURDAY, MARCH 24, 1877.   [WITH A SUPPLEMENT. PRICE TEN CENTS.

Entered according to Act of Congress, in the Year 1877, by Harper & Brothers, in the Office of the Librarian of Congress, at Washington.

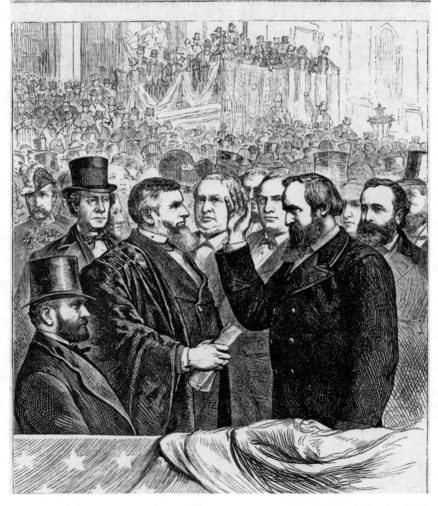

President Grant witnesses the public inauguration of his successor, Rutherford B. Hayes. (*Harper's Weekly*, March 24, 1877)

and give the subject mature reflection." By the time Sherman sent his reply to Augur, Congress had at last completed the presidential count— at 4:10 on the morning of March 2—and declared Hayes the winner. Despite the last-minute confusion, Grant had succeeded in avoiding recognition, maintaining neutrality, and preserving the peace. He thus could bequeath to Hayes the issue of recognition and the deployment of troops in Louisiana and South Carolina.[66]

Hayes arrived in Washington midmorning on March 2. Grant's term would officially end at noon on March 4, but because that was a Sunday, the inauguration was set for March 5. Grant persuaded Hayes to take the oath of office privately, before a dinner at the White House on the evening of March 3. On Monday, March 5, Grant escorted his successor to the east front of the Capitol, where Hayes took the oath again before a crowd of 30,000. No one could have been more relieved at the peaceful outcome of the crisis than the retiring president. Julia Grant hosted a luncheon for the new first family, after which the Grants departed for a brief stay at the home of Hamilton Fish. "No American," wrote James A. Garfield, "has carried greater fame out of the White House than this silent man who leaves it today."[67]

22

★ ★ ★ ★ ★

THIRD TERM DREAMS

The "silent man" whom Garfield saw exit the White House on March 5, 1877, had no intention of leaving the interpretation of his legacy to others. The electoral crisis gave no time for a formal "farewell address," but Grant used his final annual message to Congress in December 1876 to place his construction on the preceding eight years. He opened with one of the most remarkable passages in all presidential communication:

> It was my fortune, or misfortune, to be called to the office of Chief Executive without any previous political training. From the age of 17 I had never witnessed the excitement attending a Presidential campaign but twice antecedent to my own candidacy, and at but one of them was I eligible as a voter.
>
> Under such circumstances it is but reasonable to suppose that errors of judgment must have occurred. Even had they not, differences of opinion between the Executive, bound by an oath to the strict performance of his duties, and writers and debaters must have arisen. It is not necessarily evidence of blunder on the part of the Executive because there are these differences of views. Mistakes have been made, as all can see and I admit, but it seems to me oftener in the selections made of the assistants appointed to aid in carrying out the various duties of administering the Government—in nearly every case selected without a personal acquaintance with the appointee, but

upon recommendations of the representatives chosen directly by the people. It is impossible, where so many trusts are to be allotted, that the right parties should be chosen in every instance. History shows that no Administration from the time of Washington to the present has been free from these mistakes. But I leave comparisons to history, claiming only that I have acted in every instance from a conscientious desire to do what was right, constitutional, within the law, and for the very best interests of the whole people. Failures have been errors of judgment, not of intent.

With this apologia, Grant tacitly conceded that his administration had not unfolded as the American people had expected. He cited his original naïveté, but few could forget that he had soon become a willing and often effective player in the political arena and thus bore a large responsibility for both the successes and the shortcomings of his two terms. More to the point was his condemnation of the noxious political atmosphere, poisoned by his unrelenting critics. From the beginning, antagonists had leveled personal abuse against him and had indeed twisted differences over policy into evidence of moral turpitude on his part. Less convincingly, the president attempted to shift some of the blame for mistakes to his subordinates and to the members of Congress who had recommended their appointment. The exculpatory passage did little to change the judgment of his contemporary assailants. As the *New York Times* put it, "The President should have known his enemies better than to suppose that they can be appeased by a confession of inexperience or a plea of good intentions."[1]

After these opening remarks, Grant turned his attention to specific issues. He said that because of the wrangling between Congress and Andrew Johnson, the work of Reconstruction had "virtually commenced" with his own administration. The essential question was "whether the control of the Government should be thrown immediately into the hands of those who had so recently and persistently tried to destroy it, or whether the victors should continue to have an equal voice with them in this control." Grant asserted that Reconstruction was "the work of the legislative branch" and that his "province was wholly in approving their acts." He thus forbore citing the several instances of his own ardent efforts, both in rhetoric and through action, to guarantee freedom and equality for the former slaves. Grant well knew that the unrelenting recalcitrance of southern whites had largely thwarted his aims, but in the midst of the electoral crisis, Hamilton Fish had persuaded him to delete references to "intimidation and assassination," to avoid exacerbating tensions. Grant thus missed the chance to highlight some of his administration's noblest moments in defense of the right.[2]

More forthrightly, he claimed success in stabilizing the nation's finances. Taxes had been reduced, as had the national debt and the interest rate on government bonds. The achievement of a favorable balance of trade helped move the nation toward the scheduled return to specie payments. But he ignored the Panic of 1873 and the persisting depression—a silent acquiescence in the conservative view that, beyond maintaining a sound currency and frugality in expenditure, government could do little to restore prosperity or ameliorate distress. Indeed, he reported that the administration planned to impound half the appropriation Congress had made for internal improvements. Grant defended his Indian policy as "humane," but he lamented that the greed of the white man perpetuated hostilities in portions of the West. He cited the labors of various commissions growing out of the Geneva Arbitration, but he failed to seize the opportunity to extol the Treaty of Washington, the signal foreign policy triumph of his administration.

At the end of his message, Grant offered a long passage rehearsing his greatest disappointment—the rejection of the annexation of Santo Domingo. "If my views had been concurred in," he said, "the country would be in a more prosperous condition to-day, both politically and financially." Again he spoke of the island nation's resources, its market for American products, the prospect of increased trade with no tariff barriers, the impact of such trade in undercutting slavery in Cuba and Brazil, and the prospect of Santo Domingo as a haven for African Americans that would make "the negro 'master of the situation,' by enabling him to demand his rights at home on pain of finding them elsewhere." In a draft of the message, Grant had stated, "The subject has not been understood and hence ignorant abuse has been heaped upon the Administration," but in the final version he simply said that he did not aim to renew his recommendation for annexation but "to vindicate my previous action in regard to it."

He closed with the observation that after his "official life" terminated, "it is not probable that public affairs will ever again receive attention from me further than as a citizen of the Republic, always taking a deep interest in the honor, integrity, and prosperity of the whole land."[3] *Not probable.* That phrase gave friend and foe alike something to ponder.

On Grant's last day in office, a generous editorial in the *New York Herald* saluted the retiring president for his "robustness of intellect and force of character." "It is safe to assume that President Grant will not suffer in the estimation of posterity by the extreme license of partisan libels during the period while he has held office." Compared to successes such as the *Alabama* settlement and the Inflation Bill veto, the paper predicted, the "occasional bad appointments" and other negative aspects of his presidency would "be thought trivial enough, if thought of at all."[4]

Such was not to be. Immediately, Hayes took steps to distance himself from his predecessor's supposed failings. His inaugural address called for "radical" civil service reform and a constitutional amendment setting the presidential term at six years and "forbidding a reelection." Now the *Herald* hailed "the Anti-Caesarism of President Hayes" and bashed Grant for using patronage to secure a second term (and perhaps a third). Hayes honored Grant's wish that no cabinet post go to Benjamin Bristow, but he made other appointments that were nearly as offensive. He gave the State Department to William Evarts, a leader in the public protests against Grant's Louisiana policy, and the Interior Department to Carl Schurz. Such appointments made the former president "very blue and much disgusted," and he even went to the Capitol to urge Republicans to defeat Schurz's confirmation. Several leading senators shared his disappointment, but eventually Schurz, Evarts, and Hayes's other nominees won Senate approval. The turn of events delighted Grant's enemies. "God bless you all!" Edward Pierce, Charles Sumner's executor, wrote to Schurz. "Would that the dear Sumner could have lived to see this day!"[5]

But Grant was determined to separate himself—literally—from the savagery of politics by indulging his passion for travel. In mid-May he and Julia set off for a European trip that eventually took them around the world. Somewhat to his surprise, he found that his private travels bore a very public aspect. In effect, he became a superb goodwill ambassador for the United States. Across the globe, leaders and their people, who knew little and cared less about the petty infighting of American politicians, hailed him as one of the foremost military commanders of all time and as a former president of the great Republic. He enjoyed the adulation but insisted that the warm expressions of respect were accorded "not to me, but to the country from which I hail." With the possible exception of John Quincy Adams's seventeen years in the House of Representatives, Grant's world tour constituted the most important public service of any ex-president in the nineteenth century.[6]

In response to public salutes, the distinguished traveler gave speech after speech. Although he never became fully comfortable addressing crowds, he grew more adept and less timid. Grant touched on a range of topics. In Britain he dwelled on the emergent friendship of the two great English-speaking nations, linked as they were by "one kindred, one blood, one language, and one civilization." He thanked the people of Manchester for supporting the North during the Civil War. To groups of workers he affirmed his conviction that "labour dishonors no man." Describing himself as a man of peace, not war, he recalled that he had pushed for a lasting settlement of the *Alabama* question. He said he had always opposed the indirect claims "because I feared the future consequences of such a demand. In any future arbitration we would have been placed at a great disadvantage by its allowance." He endorsed the general idea of arbitration of international disputes and envisioned a time when "the nations of the earth will agree upon some sort of congress, which shall take cognizance of international questions of difficulty, and whose decisions will be as binding as the decision of our Supreme Court is binding on us."[7]

In East Asia, Grant tried his hand at mediation when the Chinese government urged him to intercede on its behalf and persuade Japan to enter negotiations regarding the two countries' conflicting claims to the Ryukyu Islands. He agreed to help and, without taking sides, pressed the Japanese to meet the Chinese in a spirit of magnanimity. He also warned that the conflict played into the hands of Europe's imperialist powers. The two nations agreed to initiate talks, but they eventually broke down, and Japan took control of the islands.[8] Grant's sojourn in China and Japan piqued not only his fascination with the two exotic nations but also his solicitude for their welfare in a changing world. In Tokyo he observed, "The course of the average Minister, Consul & merchant in this country & China towards the native is much like the course of the former slave owner towards the freedman wh[en] the latter attempts to think for himself in matters of choice of candidates." Unless Western policies changed, he predicted "a terrible calamity."[9]

As Grant gained a broader understanding of the world, many Americans acquired a new appreciation of his ability and strengths. In the eyes of many, not since the war had he appeared so commanding or capable. A naval officer on one of the vessels transporting Grant's party wrote home complaining of the "annoyance & trouble" of carrying "the great ring-master about the mediterranean," but he soon changed his mind. "My opinion of old USG has changed wonderfully," he reported. "Chock full of information & good ideas[,] . . . Grant knows what it costs to make a yard of cotton [in the] south or in Providence—the bushels of grain exported for years—the fluctuations of exchange—the Army & Navy ration to an ounce & all such information & he is *never* wrong about a figure or a date." Methodist leader John Newman told a Chicago newspaper that, upon his return, Grant would "be the best informed man in America upon the manners, institutions, geography, topography, populations, and, above all, the resources of all the peoples of the globe. This nation has never appreciated the intellectual greatness of the man. His mind is not one of ratiocination, but of intuition. He grasps a thing instantly and unerringly." After encountering Grant in Paris, Mississippi senator Blanche K. Bruce told reporters that the public now saw him as "both a wiser and greater man than when he was President."[10]

Nonetheless, Grant soon found that old political animosities dogged his steps. When John Motley died, the ex-minister's eulogists seized the occasion to strike at Grant again. In the *New York Tribune*, George Smalley wrote that Grant's dismissal of Motley had been "frivolous" and an "insult" and that Motley "was never quite the same man . . . ; it may be said to have killed him."[11]

Livid at Smalley's "charge of slow murder," the former president struck back. In an interview with *New York Herald* reporter John Russell Young, Grant explained that he had dismissed Motley for violating his instructions regarding the *Alabama* dispute. He would have fired the minister immediately but had held off at the request of Secretary Fish. He recounted that the fate of the Treaty of Washington had been rendered doubtful after Sumner, as Foreign Relations chairman, had failed to carry on his committee's routine business, including squiring other treaties to approval. Grant denied responsibility for Sumner's removal but admitted being "glad when I heard that he was put off." He observed, "I may be blamed for my opposition to Mr. Sumner's tactics, but I was not guided so much by reason of his personal hatred of myself as I was by a desire to protect our national interests in diplomatic affairs."[12]

The attacks and Grant's response sparked a months-long controversy between his friends and enemies, replaying many of the quarrels that had marked his presidency. Grant himself took part in press interviews. Denying that the mere fact of Sumner's opposition to Santo Domingo was at the root of their quarrel, he noted that he had gotten on well with other senators who had opposed the annexation treaty "as vehemently but not as abusively as Mr. Sumner. It is one thing to oppose the measures of an Executive and another to express that opposition in terms of contumely and attributing the basest motives, as were attributed to me, in the St. Domingo business." Sumner, he said, "was dogmatic, opinionated, infallible in his own estimation—the be all and do all in any matter in which he took part; of a temper that made business with him almost impossible."[13]

While the war of words raged over the old administration, Grant grew disenchanted with the new one. In the summer of 1877 workers struck several railroad lines, and Hayes dispatched federal troops to a number of localities. Grant accepted Hayes's action but thought the press exaggerated the threat. "One thing has struck me as a little queer," he confided to a friend:

> During my two terms of office the whole Democratic press, and the morbidly honest and "reformatory" portion of the Republican press, thought it horrible to keep U.S. troops stationed in the Southern States, and when they were called upon to protect the lives of negroes—as much citizens under the Constitution as if their skins were white—the country was scarcely large enough to hold the sound of indignation belched forth by them for some years. Now however, there is no hesitation about exhausting the whole power of the government to suppress a strike on the slightest intimation that danger threatens.

When white southern leaders reneged on their promises to Hayes to protect blacks' rights, many Republican leaders blamed Hayes's lenient policies for the disintegration of the party's southern wing. Grant shared their dismay.[14]

After the Democrats won both houses of Congress in the midterm elections of 1878 and sought to repeal civil rights enforcement legislation signed by Grant, his skepticism about Hayes's lenient southern policy intensified. He thought the "conciliation" was "all on one side," and he lamented the unintended consequences of granting black suffrage. It had simply given forty votes in the Electoral College to "the old slave-holders," who "keep those votes, but disfranchise the negroes. That is one of the gravest mistakes in the policy of reconstruction." In retrospect, he thought it would have been better to hold the formerly rebellious states under "military rule" for as much as ten years, or until they "showed a willingness to come into the Union, not on their own terms but upon ours." Such an occupation "would have avoided the scandals of the State governments, saved money, and enabled the Northern merchants, farmers, and laboring men to reorganize society in the South." But that was not done, and the government should allow no turning back. "Suffrage once given can never be taken away, and all that remains for us now is to make good that gift by protecting those who have received it."[15]

Grant also saw Hayes's approach to civil service as wrongheaded. Hayes did not reinstate the reforms launched by Grant, but he did try to curtail the influence of officeholders in politics, and he pursued an appointment policy that worked against many Grant Republicans. Fish wrote to Grant that the "lick spittle press" praised Hayes's "Reforms" as "improvements over the Corrupt ways of the last Administration," and Grant wrote back that the reformers Hayes listened to were "great humbugs." But the main problem was that Hayes was throwing away one of the key sources of a president's effectiveness. Hayes "exercises but little influence with the legislation," Grant said, largely because of "the Utopian ideas he got, *from reformers*, of running a government without a party." A prime example was the Bland-Allison Act passed in February 1878, calling for the remonetization of silver. In Grant's opinion, "The country, and country's credit, has not received so severe a blow since the attempt of the Southern states to secede." Grant was "supremely disgusted" that Hayes wielded so little influence that he could not stop the bill—not even with a veto.[16]

Almost from the beginning, Republicans repelled by Hayes's policies began to advocate a return to Grant as the surest way to restore vigorous leadership to the party and the country. Initially, Grant poohpoohed the idea. After sixteen straight years of arduous public service, he did not miss employment. Observing Hayes's "trials," he said, made him "feel more than ever the relief of being again a *Sov[e]reign*," or simply a voting citizen. But the more Hayes's "trials" seemed to be of his own doing, the more Grant worried about the nation's future. "It looks to me," he wrote in the spring of 1878, "that unless the North rallies by 1880 the Government will be in the hands of those who tried so hard fourteen—seventeen—years ago to destroy it." Denying any inclination to resume the "harness," he warned that in the next election the North— the Republicans—must "bury the last remnant of secession proclivities, and put in the Executive chair a firm and steady hand, free from Utopian ideas [of] purifying the party electing him out of existence."[17]

To Grant and his friends, Hayes's approach to civil service reform simply favored one faction over another, especially after the president moved to oust Chester Arthur as collector of customs in New York. In driving "this wedge of discord" into the party, Fish wrote to Grant, Hayes had bowed to "the most embittered hostility, of the most disappointed of the 'Liberals' toward 'Grant' & 'Grantism.'" In reaction,

Grant's friends were now "more numerous today, than when you left," and many Republicans, even some erstwhile critics, harbored hopes for a "restoration." By mid-1878, one Liberal journalist wrote that "the country just now seems crazy about Grant," and something must be done "to kill the rising Grant party."[18]

Publicly, Grant remained cool to a return to politics, but many believed the outcome of the midterm elections in 1878 enhanced his prospects for a presidential run two years later. The fall campaign witnessed renewed violence and intimidation in parts of the South, but despite the warnings of Stalwarts—as Republicans who favored Grant came to be called—Hayes did little to change his lenient policy. The failure of that policy to charm southern whites was clear when the Republicans won only three of seventy-three national House seats in the former Confederate states and lost every southern Senate seat contested that year. Outside the South, the Republicans did much better in states where they emphasized the currency issue. But for the upcoming national campaign, it was unclear whether the money issue or the southern question would predominate. Grant's record positioned him well to run on either. He thought the 1878 results in the North "put the republican party right for /80. Providence seems to direct that something should be done just in time to save the party of progress and national unity & equality."[19]

But Ulysses Grant had never been one to leave anything to Providence. Although the idea of running again for the presidency had a slow gestation, as early as February 1879, his traveling companion and informal publicist John Russell Young concluded that Grant had decided to try. Writing to a friend, Young said he had spent much time on shipboard with Grant "looking out on the waves, and *scheming for a third term*!!!! You never knew such a schemer as the Gen. He sits up for hours and hours, late and schemes." Two months later in Singapore, British colonial governor Archibald Anson asked Grant about his chances of being elected president again. The general replied, "Were the elections going to take place this year, I think I should have a fair chance, but as they do not, I cannot be sure of the stability of public sentiment."[20]

If Grant was scheming, part of his strategy was to continue to disavow any ambition for a return to power. "I am not a candidate for any office," he wrote to Adam Badeau just before leaving Japan for home, "nor would I hold one that required any maneuvering or sacrifice to obtain." But he soon found that others were more than willing to do the maneuvering for him. At the fore stood key leaders of the Republican Stalwarts: Roscoe Conkling, Illinois senator John Logan, and national party chairman J. Donald Cameron. When Grant arrived in California in September 1879, he received a warm welcome rivaling those he had encountered abroad. In the ensuing weeks he made a triumphal journey across the nation. In a speech at the annual reunion of the Army of the Tennessee in Chicago, he projected the image of a seasoned statesman who had seen firsthand how other countries regarded the United States—that is, as "one of the first powers in all that goes to make up a great nationality." "Let us be true to ourselves," he said, "avoid all bitterness and ill-feeling, either on the part of sections or parties toward each other . . . and we need have no fear for the future of maintaining the standing that we have taken among the nations." "The Grant boom soars," Massachusetts senator Henry Dawes wrote in mid-December. "If it doesn't subside soon, it will sweep the Republican party and the country the *devil* knows where."[21]

Despite his lofty rhetoric about unity, Grant knew that many Republicans opposed his candidacy. Hayes wrote in his diary that even though the former president was the "general popular favorite," many "thoughtful men" opposed the idea of a third term, and "many more fear a return to the unfortunate methods and men of General Grant's former Administrations." Nonetheless, at Grant's behest, Hayes traveled to Philadelphia for a secret meeting with his predecessor on the day after Christmas. Grant handled the visit with tact and finesse. As Hayes recalled, the two men "went over all the questions—the Third Term &c &c &c. . . . All that he said was so judicious, patriotic, and free from self seeking that it was calculated to make a most favorable impression." Grant could not have expected an endorsement from Hayes, but in the ensuing preconvention campaign, the president remained officially neutral, despite the candidacy of his own treasury secretary, John Sherman.[22]

Grant had returned to the United States nine months before the Republican National Convention was scheduled to meet, too early to ride the initial popular enthusiasm to a nomination. In late January 1880 he left again on a trip to Cuba and Mexico and once more garnered press attention. In February he wrote to Elihu Washburne, "I am not a candidate for anything," but "I shall not gratify my enemies by declining what has not been offered." "All that I want is that the Government rule should remain in the hands of those who saved the Union until all the questions growing out of the war are forever settled." When he returned to the States in late March, he again told Washburne he felt "supreme indifference," but now he added, "I owe so much to the Union men of the country that if they think my chances are better for election than for other probable candidates, in case I should decline, I can not decline if the nomination is tendered without seeking on my part."[23]

Thus far, Grant had left the "seeking" on his behalf to others, but they were meeting stiff opposition. More than Sherman, Senator James G. Blaine posed a serious threat. Grant correctly thought that Blaine's alleged ethical lapses in the past would hurt him, but the charismatic "Plumed Knight" enjoyed wide popularity. Blaine's strength showed in the Pennsylvania Republican convention in February, where Cameron barely managed to secure a resolution instructing the state's national delegates to support Grant by a vote of 133 to 113. A few weeks later, Conkling had similar trouble in the New York convention, where an effort to scrap an endorsement of Grant and send an unpledged delegation to the Chicago convention lost by a vote of 180 to 217. Fish thought Grant might withdraw from the contest when he returned from Mexico.[24]

But he did not withdraw. He turned his attention to the South, where his popularity among beleaguered Republicans could offset gaps in his delegate strength in the North. While Grant's backers continued to portray him as a strong leader who would "employ every constitutional power" to protect "the constitutional rights of citizens," the former president assumed a conciliatory posture during a tour of the South. African Americans revered him, but in a series of speeches in several southern cities, he not only appealed to blacks and saluted their progress but also reassured whites that a new Grant presidency would not revive the turmoil of earlier years. At the Louisiana State House, in a visit rich in symbolism, he told the assembled legislators, "We are members of a united and contented family." "It is to be hoped and desired," he said at Vicksburg, "that there may be no more difference between the North and South, sect or color." He maintained this theme when he returned north. In a speech at Springfield, Illinois, he said southerners showed "a returning love for the flag," and he called for "a substantial, solid Union feeling in every section of the country."[25]

In sum, the savior of the Union and champion of Reconstruction projected himself as the avatar of national unity and racial peace. But it was not only political posturing, for Grant had always hoped for true harmony between the sections and the races. By 1880, the severe depression had receded, and Grant saw this as a propitious moment to call on Americans to march forward in harmony toward prosperity for all sections. He confided to Young that he stayed in the race because he thought "he could be the means of ending the 'miserable sectional strifes' between the North and South." Die-hard critics refused to accord him any higher motive than personal ambition, but backers such as Wisconsin senator Timothy Howe believed the applause Grant received in both sections represented "a proffer of reconciliation" that the Republican convention ought to accept.[26]

Although Grant tried to paint his candidacy as a selfless acceptance of a call to duty, as the Republican convention drew near, he privately showed intense interest in his prospects. And his managers engaged in tactics that reeked of raw politics. At the Illinois state convention in mid-May, Logan rammed through a proposal to have that body, dominated by Grant men, bypass the congressional districts, choose all the national convention delegates, and bind them to Grant's support by the unit rule. Logan's victory proved Pyrrhic. It led to loud protests from the supporters of rival candidates, the selection of contesting delegates in several districts, and a credentials fight at the national convention. Grant's political instincts prompted him to focus on the benefits of harmony, but the deep divisions in his party denied him the role of healer.[27]

When the delegates arrived in Chicago, most estimates gave Grant around 300—ahead of all other candidates but shy of the 378 needed for victory. Blaine stood second with about 20 fewer delegates, and Sherman fell further back with a total close to 100. The anti-Grant forces were united in believing that the key to defeating the general was to bar any state's delegation from voting by the unit rule, even if that were the express directive from its state convention. By the unit rule, the majority of a delegation determined the entire vote cast by the state. Both pro- and anti-Grant leaders knew that permitting that rule in New York, Pennsylvania, and Illinois could give the general more than 60 additional votes on the first ballot, taking him close enough to the magic number to spur a movement in his direction and victory on the second or third ballot. If the unit rule were applied to all states' delegations, Grant would lose a few votes from some states but could gain enough elsewhere to put him over the top.[28]

The contest played out during organizing meetings of the Republican National Committee on the eve of the convention. Anti-Grant men controlled the committee and introduced resolutions barring the unit rule. After intense maneuvering, they secured the ban in the convention at large. Undaunted, the Grant men believed they could gain nearly as much from contests over the makeup of individual state delegations, which would be decided by the credentials committee. They were wrong. In the most important case—Illinois—the committee, dominated by Blaine men, recommended seating the minority of anti-Grant delegates who had defied the wishes of the state convention. The resolution carried in the convention. If this and other credentials decisions did not doom the general's candidacy, they did make his managers' task all the more difficult.[29]

The platform committee, headed by Grant's former attorney general Edwards Pierrepont, gave prominence to the southern question in a way that left little doubt about which candidate would be the strongest president when it came to suppressing persistent southern outrages after Hayes's hands-off policy. "The equal, steady, and complete enforcement of laws, and the protection of all our citizens in the enjoyment of all privileges and immunity guaranteed by the Constitution, are the first duties of the Nation. . . . A Nation cannot safely relegate this duty to the States." In his nominating speech for Grant, Conkling made the point explicitly: if Grant were in power, "the poor dwellers in the cabins of the South should no longer be driven in terror from the homes of their childhood and the graves of their murdered dead." But Conkling also carried forward the conciliatory theme of Grant's southern speeches, insisting that he, "more surely than any other man," could carry doubtful southern states as well as New York. The country stood at a crossroads, and only Grant could attract a national coalition to ensure victory. "The election before us is the Austerlitz of American politics," said Conkling. "It will decide for many years, whether the country shall be Republican or Cossack."[30]

Conkling also accentuated Grant's triumphs in office. His inflation veto had cleared the path for resumption, and thanks "to him, immeasurably more than to any other man, . . . every paper dollar is at last as good as gold." The Geneva Arbitration, Conkling said, was "the wisest, the most majestic example of its kind in the world's diplomacy." Moreover, Grant had returned from his trip around the world "a better American than ever, with a wealth of knowledge and experience" added to his "hard common sense." Yet, while exalting the former president, Conkling could not resist maligning his opponents. He vilified the old Liberal Republicans, or independents, as "charlatans, jayhawkers, tramps and guerrillas." Decrying the specious cry of "No Third Term," he said he could conceive of "no department of human reason in which sane men reject an agent because he has had experience, making him exceptionally competent and fit. . . . Nobody now is really disquieted about a third term except those hopelessly longing for a first term, and their dupes and coadjutors." Such discourse could hardly benefit a candidate who needed to look beyond his own core of supporters to amass a winning majority.[31]

Besides Grant, Blaine, and Sherman, the convention heard nominating speeches for three other men: George F. Edmunds, backed by New England independents; William Windom, Minnesota's favorite son; and Elihu Washburne, who favored Grant but whom some saw as a possible alternative if the general should falter. Balloting began on Monday, June 7. In the first round Grant garnered 304 votes to 284 for Blaine, 93 for Sherman, 34 for Edmunds, 30 for Washburne, and 10 for Windom. Nearly 60 percent of Grant's votes came from former slave states, and he picked up another 107 votes from New York, Pennsylvania, and Illinois. But no candidate had a majority, and the balloting continued throughout the day. "There has been more stealing & buying of delegates here than I ever heard of before," Grant's son Fred wrote from Chicago. If that was true, the money was not well spent, for after twenty-eight ballots, the totals showed little change, and the convention recessed for the night.[32]

On the eve of the convention, Grant had written a letter to his managers in Chicago, which Fred Grant passed on to Conkling. According to Fred's later recollection, his father had authorized Conkling and his allies to withdraw his name if Blaine's men agreed to withdraw their candidate, with the understanding that both would throw their support to some dark horse in the interest of party unity. Whether Conkling shared this message with Grant's other managers is unclear, but one of them, George Boutwell, later claimed that he never saw the letter and that Grant had given them "entire freedom to act as we thought wise," as circumstances dictated. On Tuesday, June 8, while the balloting continued, Grant wrote to Fred that among the other named candidates, he "most unquestionably" preferred Edmunds, although he had "an equal or possibly greater preference" for some other men not officially in the running.[33]

Whatever Grant's precise instructions were, Conkling and his comrades stuck with the general. A total of 306 delegates stood by him on the thirty-sixth and last ballot when the anti-Grant men swung to James A. Garfield, who became the dark-horse nominee with 399 votes. Soon after the convention, Orville Babcock saw Grant in Chicago, where he found the general "quiet and philosophical as usual. Mrs. G. not as tranquil." The day after the defeat, Cameron and a Missouri delegate designed a medal to be given to each of the last-ballot loyalists, commemorating the stalwart fortitude of the "immortal 306." But even though the spirit of that steadfast band may have been immortal, the possibility of another presidency of Ulysses S. Grant was dead.[34]

In the end, despite his great popularity in the country and in the Republican Party, Grant's enemies succeeded in using the third term bugbear against him. Moreover, his own efforts to stay on the high road could not allay the apprehension stoked by his opponents that his candidacy represented a return to an unseemly kind of machine politics. All politicians of the day (and of other eras) recognized the value of organization when pursuing power. But Grant's foes tarred his candidacy with "bossism," and his managers' behavior seemed to validate the charge. He was, said Assistant Secretary of State John Hay, "defeated by his friends. Cameron's methods in Pennsylvania, Conkling's in New York, and more especially Logan's in Illinois roused a savage feeling of opposition among thousands of people who were certainly in favor of Grant last fall. The machine was too perfect, and so Grant, who was the *only* candidate less than a year ago, was beaten by a man not dreamed of a week ago."[35]

Grant, of course, had another perspective. He thanked Conkling for his "magnificent and generous support" and that of "the three hundred and odd who stood with you through your week's labors." He told his daughter, "The most unscrupulous means had been resorted to by the friends of other candidates—no doubt by their advice—and even then a good majority of the delegates chosen were for me. But means were resorted to to displace them and give a small majority for all the other candidates combined. Had I been nominated there would have been the most violent campaign eve[r] known in our country made against me. This I have avoided." Even the sober-sided Hamilton Fish thought the Chicago spectacle showed that national nominating conventions were a "farce," where "clap-trap, & temporary furor (not to call it 'insanity') takes the place of judgment, deliberation, & discretion." Fish regretted his old chief's defeat, not only because Grant's nomination would have "ensured the success of our ticket" but also because his election "would have ended the *sectional* division of parties, & the 'solidity' of the South," and resulted in "a division of political parties, on *National* issues & not by geographical lines."[36]

Not long after the disappointment of the convention, a specter from Grant's presidency rose in the form of a scurrilous book entitled *Secrets of the Great Whiskey Ring*, published by St. Louis conspirator John McDonald. The marginally literate McDonald apparently used the services of a ghostwriter, most likely journalist James W. Buel. The work included several letters, some printed in facsimile, written by Orville Babcock and others, to which the "author" applied the most strained and tenuous interpretation to identify Grant as a member of the ring. McDonald added more substantiation of Babcock's guilt, but he failed to prove his claim regarding Grant. Even so, Fish thought McDonald had "mixed up unquestioned facts with insinuations, inferences, & even positive assertions so that refutation may be difficult except by long process." Grant made no comment on the work. Despite its dubious character, the book provided "evidence" for critics, at the time and afterward, who were determined to sully Grant's presidential reputation. Democrats welcomed (and perhaps financially supported) the appearance of the book at this moment, for McDonald included an addendum rehashing Garfield's Crédit Mobilier connection.[37]

Grant soon swallowed his indignation over his treatment by the convention and assured Garfield of his "very deep interest in the success of the republican ticket." He made good on that assurance by agreeing to do what he had long been loath to do: make overtly political speeches. In Garfield's home state he presided at a campaign rally in late September and declared, "I am a Republican as the two great political parties are now divided, because the Republican Party is a national party seeking the greatest good for the greatest number of citizens." Committed to the individual's right to rise, Republicans envisioned a society where "every one has the opportunity to make himself all he is capable of." Grant left unstated his conviction that his own administration had embodied these values.[38]

Near the end of the campaign, Grant made several speeches in critical New York state. He argued that Republican tariff policies protected both capital and labor from foreign competition, but mostly he warned against turning the country over to "Rebel Brigadiers." "Not that we bear any personal enmity toward our late foes," he said, "but we want to bring them to a just sense of the value of a good Government, of a Government where every man has the right to cast his ballot as his conscience dictates, and to have his ballot counted as it was cast." How many voters Grant swayed on his tour is impossible to say, but Garfield won a narrow victory in New York, without whose electoral votes he would have lost to Democrat Winfield Hancock. "The nation has escaped a calamity," Grant told Garfield when he sent his congratulations. He declined to be considered for an appointment: "I want no reward further than the approval of the patriotic people of the land."[39]

But, as matters turned out, he soon concluded that whatever the people thought, he had not won the approval of the new administration. Blaine never got over his belief that, but for Grant's opposition in the convention, *he* would have been president instead of Garfield. Appointed secretary of state by Garfield, Blaine was determined to get his revenge by convincing the president that Grant's supporters were "all the desperate bad men of the party," who should be frozen out of the patronage. Garfield tried to treat the various factions in a balanced fashion, but for the key position of collector of customs in New York, he followed Blaine's suggestion and chose W. H. Robertson, leader of the pro-Blaine, anti-Grant faction of the New York delegation at Chicago. Robertson's appointment entailed the removal of the current collector, Edwin Merritt, who was only halfway through his term. To accommodate Merritt, Blaine proposed making him consul general at London in place of Grant's longtime associate Adam Badeau, whose retention Grant had specifically requested. Blaine and Garfield's plan called for Badeau to replace Michael Cramer, Grant's brother-in-law, as head of the American legation in Denmark and for Cramer to replace Nicholas Fish, the son of Grant's secretary of state, as chargé d'affaires at Bern, Switzerland. The chain of demotions was a scheme breathtaking in its personal vindictiveness against a former president of the same party. "I gave you a hearty and strong support," Grant complained to Garfield. "I ought not to be humiliated by seeing my personal friends punished for no other offence than their friendship and support." He warned the new president that he could not hope to achieve success "by giving the administration over to the settlement of *other people[']s* private grievances." Grant told friends that Blaine was "running" the administration "to destruction fast," and Garfield lacked "the backbone of an Angleworm."[40]

Yet, in conducting a ferocious fight to win Robertson's confirmation over the objections of New York's senators, Garfield was carrying forward the struggle Grant himself had begun in attempting to rebalance relations among the branches of the national government after the Johnson fiasco. Indeed, Grant's supposedly imperious attitude toward the legislature had been a central count in his enemies' indictment against him. Now, in the midst of this struggle, Garfield called in several senators to let them know that Robertson's confirmation was "a test of friendship or hostility to the administration." Grant as Caesar could not have said it better. After a prolonged fight, the Senate confirmed Robertson.[41]

Grant saw the administration's course as a threat to harmony that could "result in a break up of parties and in new alignments."

He suggested that "a new party with good leaders, sound principles, and a platform to suit the times would be popular and receive a heavy following." But the political world was turned upside down on July 2 when Garfield was shot by an insane man who called himself a Stalwart. Charles Guiteau had begged for a federal appointment and had even hounded Grant for a recommendation, which he had refused. Grant denounced Guiteau as "a lunatic who was disappointed because he couldn't get what he wanted." While the president lingered near death, all criticism ended. Grant offered a public defense of Vice President Chester Arthur, a Stalwart and longtime Conkling ally, as "a man of common sense and clear-headed, with good associates—a man of integrity." When Garfield died in September, reporters found Grant "weeping bitterly." Arthur naturally refashioned the cabinet, but the circumstances under which he took office precluded a clean sweep of Blaine's supporters from the public service. Grant soon found Arthur "averse to making any removals, no matter how offensive the parties in place have been to him and his friends."[42]

As Grant's involvement in politics wound down, he gave increased attention to various business enterprises. Impelled by his long-held interest in promoting trade with Latin America, he accepted the presidency of the Mexican Southern Railroad, but insufficient capital funding brought the project to naught. In 1882 Arthur commissioned the former president to negotiate a reciprocal trade agreement with Mexico. In negotiations with his old friend and former minister to the United States Matías Romero, Grant concluded a treaty in January 1883. The Senate approved it in 1884 but attached an amendment requiring legislation for the treaty to take effect. In 1886 (after Grant's death) Republican protectionists and Democrats who preferred a general reduction of tariffs over piecemeal reciprocity agreements banded together to kill the measure.[43]

Arthur's request that Grant negotiate the Mexican treaty did not reverse the growing estrangement between the two men, initially spurred by the president's approach to appointments. In Grant's eyes, Arthur seemed "more afraid of his enemies and . . . more influenced by them than guided either by his judgement, personal feelings, or friendly influences." Arthur's approval of the Pendleton Civil Service Act did not improve their relations, although he gave the chair of the new Civil Service Commission to Dorman Eaton, who had performed the same service during Grant's term. In an ironic twist, Grant came to support a constitutional amendment for a single presidential term with no eligibility for reelection—essentially the position of the Liberal Republicans in 1872.[44]

Beyond his disenchantment over patronage, Grant saw Arthur as a far less assertive chief executive than he had been. Waffling on key issues such as the tariff and the South, Arthur tried to be all things to all people and ultimately found himself with no factional home in the Republican Party. "The republican party to be saved must have a decisive declared policy," Grant wrote in the fall of 1883. "It has now no observable policy except to peddle out patronage to soreheads in order to bring them back into the fold, and avoid any positive declaration upon all leading questions." He scoffed at the idea of running himself in 1884, but he thought nothing was "so important . . . as the breaking down of sectional lines. Any candidate who can best do that I am in favor of." In the spring Grant came out against Arthur's candidacy for the Republican nomination and threw his support to John Logan. Neither man prevailed, and the convention chose Grant's nemesis Blaine, who went on to lose in November.[45]

Grant would have little opportunity to gauge the administration of President Grover Cleveland, the first Democrat to be inaugurated since before the Civil War. Even before Cleveland's election, a sea of personal troubles nearly overwhelmed the ex-president. In late December 1883 he slipped on the ice outside his house in New York and suffered a leg injury that left him an invalid for weeks. In May 1884 he suffered financial disaster with the collapse of the New York investment house where he had placed nearly all his assets. The firm of Grant and Ward—ostensibly a partnership between his son Ulysses and Ferdinand Ward, but actually managed by Ward—turned out to be a gigantic swindle of the type that later generations would call a Ponzi scheme. On the eve of the firm's collapse, Grant thought he was worth $1 million, but in fact he lost everything.[46]

Nearly destitute, Grant turned to writing to make money. He accepted an invitation by *Century Magazine* to write a series of articles on Civil War battles he had fought, but he soon found the work so congenial that he decided to assemble a full account of his military experiences. He began writing in the summer of 1884 and kept at it steadily, despite the irritation of a persistent sore throat. By December, he could barely swallow. His doctors suspected cancer, which was confirmed microscopically in February 1885. The grim prospects made him all the more determined to finish and publish his memoir, not merely to recoup his losses from the Ward fiasco but also to provide for Julia after his death. He signed a contract with the publishing house headed by Mark Twain. On May 23, 1885, the former commander wrote the dedication for the work: to "the American soldier and sailor." He did not say "Union," he told his son, because he meant to include "those we fought against as well as those we fought with. It may serve a purpose in restoring harmony." In mid-June he left his Manhattan home and traveled 100 miles north to enjoy the cool breezes at a friend's Adirondack cottage on Mt. McGregor. There he made the last revisions to his book, and on July 16 he wrote, "There is nothing more I should do to it now." Seven days later he died.[47]

Grant devoted his memoirs almost exclusively to his military career, but toward the end of the 1,100-page work, he offered a few observations that constituted a political testament of sorts. "The President of the United States," he wrote, "is, in a large degree, or ought to be, a representative of the feelings, wishes and judgment of those over whom he presides." This maxim had been at the core of his understanding of the president's role since the promise of his first inaugural address: "I shall on all subjects have a policy to recommend, but none to enforce against the will of the people." Lincoln had embodied that maxim, Grant said, but Johnson's obduracy was its very antithesis, driving Congress to pass "first one measure and then another to restrict his power." Grant conceded that many of those restrictions had been unconstitutional, but they had served an important purpose. Now, in 1885, they were "'a dead letter' upon the statute books of the United States, no one taking interest enough in them to give them a passing thought." He could have added that his own performance in the White House had rendered many of those constraints nugatory.

In his book, Grant described slavery as the root cause of the Civil War. But the war not only preserved the Union and liberated the enslaved; it also showed to European skeptics the viability of America's "republican institutions" and the people's capacity to maintain them. It broke the shackles from the nation's material progress and "begot a spirit of independence and enterprise." Railroad construction opened all regions to the settlement of people and businesses, and as a result, "the country has filled up 'from the centre all around to the sea.'" But, he warned, "growing as we are, in population, wealth and military power," the United States could become the envy of other nations that someday might combine "to crush us out." Hence, "to maintain peace in the future it is necessary to be prepared for war." Worried that "scarcely twenty years after the war, we seem to have forgotten the lessons it taught," he called for an expanded and refurbished navy and construction of the "finest possible" coastal defenses.

Grant's memoirs also warned that "the condition of the colored man within our borders" could someday lead to a domestic "conflict between races." Reprising one of the central themes of his presidency, Grant reminded his countrymen that although blacks had been "brought to our shores by compulsion," their descendants "should be considered as having as good a right to remain here as any other class of our citizens. It was looking to a settlement of this question that led me to urge the annexation of Santo Domingo during the time I was President of the United States." While restating the economic advantages of annexation, he emphasized that African Americans could go there in great numbers and create their own states. "They would still be states of the Union, and under the protection of the General Government; but the citizens would be almost wholly colored."

But neither annexation nor any other strategy for the improvement of "the condition of the colored man" was to be. By the time Grant's memoirs appeared in 1885, two years after the Supreme Court's invalidation of the Civil Rights Act he had signed in 1875, the country was well on its way to submerging African American aspirations in a nationalistic reconciliation of the sections. Joint reunions of the Blue and the Gray showed scant concern for the black. Despite his personal belief in racial equality, at the close of his book and at the close of his life, Grant welcomed the emerging fraternity between North and South. "The war has made us a nation of great power and intelligence," he wrote. "I feel that we are on the eve of a new era, when there is to be great harmony between the Federal and Confederate." As evidence of this growing concord he cited the outpouring of good wishes he had received during his illness from persons and groups throughout the land, regardless of section, nationality, religion, or occupation. "The universally kind feeling expressed for me at a time when it was supposed that each day would prove my last, seemed to me the beginning of the answer to 'Let us have peace.'"[48]

But even though the grave at last brought peace to Ulysses S. Grant, warfare over his legacy as president proved never-ending.

CODA:

RENDERING "THE PRESIDENCY OF
ULYSSES S. GRANT"

Grant's death elicited one of the greatest outpourings of grief in the nation's history. More than one and a half million people lined the streets of New York to witness the former president's funeral procession. Nonetheless, the aspersions that enemies had cast upon him during his time in the White House and the postpresidential years subsided only momentarily, if at all. Old political allies gave eulogies full of praise for their fallen chief, but in their discussion of the presidency, even those eulogies had an air of apologia. Hamilton Fish saluted Grant's magnanimity, firmness, and truthfulness and said that despite having little experience in public affairs, he soon "made himself thoroughly familiar" with them and "applied himself to the great problems of government." But, Fish added, although Grant's knowledge of men was "generally accurate," he "was apt, in this respect, as in others, to reach his conclusions rapidly, and was thus not infrequently led to give his confidence where it was not deserved." During his presidency, said Henry Dawes, Grant showed "calm judgment, clear perception, a comprehensive knowledge of the forces which influence men and nations, and an unflinching firmness in the maintenance of the right." Yet, said Dawes, "mistakes there were." "No one is called upon at this time to defend them," although "in the final estimate of his administration, . . . these mistakes will be deemed trifles and will not weigh in the impartial judgment of history."[1]

But Grant's longtime antagonists insisted that the mistakes were not trifles but the defining element of his presidency. The day after his death the *New York Sun* published a jaundiced biographical article, appearing anonymously but written by Harry Wilson. Having failed several times to receive appointments from Grant, Wilson held the fallen leader in deep contempt. Obsessed with the idea that Grant owed his wartime success largely to his chief of staff John Rawlins, Wilson argued that Rawlins was "the master mind in the Cabinet as he had been on the staff." When the secretary of war died after six months in office, "from that day Grant's political fortunes began to decline." Rawlins "knew an honest or capable man by instinct," but Grant "did not appear to appreciate . . . the difference between virtue and villainy, or between honesty and dishonesty." "In the end grievous mistakes were made, dishonest men secured office, and corruption and scandals came into the Government." Wilson's account of Grant's career said nothing about the Treaty of Washington, the Geneva Arbitration, the Inflation Bill veto, the Specie Resumption Act, the defense of African Americans' rights, or the peace policy. But it did mention the Whiskey Ring, Black Friday, and other scandals. Although conceding that "the President was not directly concerned in most of these affairs," Wilson insisted that "none of them could have occurred against his will; and his responsibility for them caused a lasting injury to his fame."[2]

Wilson and others aimed to make that injury lasting indeed. They made much of Grant's alleged weakness for alcohol. Wilson referred briefly to the charge in his *New York Sun* sketch, but journalist Henry Boynton focused on it in another *Sun* article. Boynton included a melodramatic letter written to Grant in 1863 in which the fanatical teetotaler Rawlins threatened to resign if the general did not give up drinking. Boynton's piece called forth yet another by Sylvanus Cadwallader, a journalist at Grant's army headquarters for three years. Like Wilson, Cadwallader believed Grant gave Rawlins short shrift in his memoirs and thus "deserved to be scourged from the face of the earth." Barring that, he took aim at the general's reputation in his own wartime recollections. Egged on by Wilson, Cadwallader "cut out all superlative adjectives relating to Gen. Grant, and strengthened Rawlins wherever I could." He wrote that on several occasions he had seen Grant drink or exhibit the effects of drinking. Although Wilson privately admitted that, "upon all important occasions either as an officer or civilian, Grant was absolutely abstemious," he nonetheless urged Cadwallader to publish his damning manuscript. The book did not make it into print until 1955, when Cadwallader's allegations spurred heated controversy among historians. By then, however, the image of Grant the drunkard had become fixed in the popular imagination.[3]

Over the years, Wilson's war against Grant continued. In the 1890s he gave an interview to Hamlin Garland, who was preparing one of the earliest semischolarly studies of the general and president. "For two hours," Garland noted, "he battered me with one of the most adroit and copious assaults upon Gen Grant's fame I have met." Wilson condemned Grant as "a d—d ignorant man" and later wrote to Garland that, as a soldier, Grant was "great in some things" and "small in some," but "as a statesman he was scarcely great in anything." Garland dismissed Wilson as "an imperious loud-voiced man" who "mistook bluster for firmness" and "was too intemperate; too unreasonable to succeed in seriously impairing Grant's fame."[4]

But Wilson never gave up trying. He helped pay for the publication of the diary of Gideon Welles, Johnson's secretary of the navy, primarily because he knew that Welles had lacerated Grant in entry after entry. Wilson urged his brother Bluford to tell his version of "the whole vile chapter" of the Whiskey Ring. Bluford declined to enter the recrimination thicket publicly, but he gave Harry documents related to the subject and advised him to read John McDonald's scurrilous and delusive book. Having convinced himself that Grant had sanctioned the Whiskey Ring to advance his ambitions for a third term, the younger Wilson said Grant "was either singularly obtuse or morally blind to the obligations of common honesty and decency in public life."[5]

In 1916 Harry Wilson published a biography of Rawlins. He insisted that his hero was "the only member of the Cabinet who actually knew the capacities and limitations of the President." Had Rawlins lived, Grant's political career would "have been much more successful than it was." If few historians or biographers bought Wilson's portrait of Rawlins's dominance, his book did fuel doubts about Grant's character and leadership. A reviewer for the *American Historical Review* expressed skepticism about Wilson's notions but nonetheless asserted, "There are ample facts to prove that Grant was of too simple and unsuspicious a nature to cope with men of lower type." Grant biographer Louis Coolidge dismissed Wilson's theory as "hyperbole" but added, "It is no great stretch to say that Rawlins was Grant's conscience." If Wilson's exalting of Rawlins eventually faded from historical memory, his portrait of a weak, rudderless, and ethically challenged Grant endured.[6]

Six years after Wilson's book appeared, David Dyer published his autobiography, which included a chapter on his prosecution of the

Whiskey Ring. Softening his earlier attitude, Dyer said that Grant was "an honest man," but the "false representation" of "selfish, dishonest and unprincipled politicians" had "embittered him against Bristow and other officers engaged in unearthing the frauds." Dyer claimed that soon after Grant's death, Bristow told him that the dying general had invited Bristow to his home in New York to make amends. Thirty-seven years after that supposed encounter, Dyer quoted a tearful Bristow quoting Grant: "General Bristow, I have done you a great wrong and I cannot afford to die without acknowledging it to your face. In the prosecution at St. Louis you were right and I was wrong." Although contemporary evidence of this episode is lacking, subsequent writers have often repeated and embellished it.[7]

In concluding his account of this purported encounter, Dyer wrote, "Thus it was that the friendship between the two men was restored." That inference must have been Dyer's fantasy, for Bristow's behavior after Grant's death revealed scant goodwill and no change of heart toward his former chief. One may question whether such a meeting actually occurred, but it is certain that Bristow mounted no effort to spread the word that Grant had, in the end, apologized to him. Among intimates he exhibited no forgiveness of the former president. In a letter to Henry Boynton ten years after the supposed conversation and Grant's death, Bristow still maintained that Grant had "allowed himself to be misled & deceived by a gang of pretended friends into the belief that my efforts to punish a set of thieves were prompted by base & selfish purposes, and hostile to him." Writing to Boynton twenty-seven years closer to the events than Dyer's book, Bristow made no mention of Grant's supposed apology, and he certainly gave no acknowledgment of the part his own ambition for the presidency had played in his cabinet performance. Indeed, Bristow still felt aggrieved. He told Boynton that if Grant "had openly attacked me in any of his various publications I would have replied & given the true facts. But that he never did & now that he is gone I have no wish to open an old sore however grievously I have been wronged." But neither did Bristow show much inclination to *close* the old sore that he still allowed to fester. When journalist John Russell Young approached him for information about the Whiskey Ring, Bristow again showed no eagerness to recount a supposed Grant apology. Fearing that Young planned to write a story sympathetic to the former president, he told Boynton, "I don't care to 'let him see my hand.'"[8]

Other enemies from the presidential years also labored to settle scores with Grant. In 1893 Edward Pierce, Charles Sumner's friend and literary executor, published the last of his four-volume biography of Sumner, in which he replayed the senator's side in the myriad battles waged against the president. Pierce also pushed former interior secretary Jacob Cox to write an article on Grant in the White House. Cox was still nursing a grievance decades after quitting the administration. Promising to "give explicitly the facts which you regarded important" about Grant, Cox told Pierce, "I gave up all attempt at reconciling his acts with plain-dealing."[9]

Cox's article appeared in the *Atlantic Monthly* in August 1895. In it he charged that when Grant moved into the White House, he followed "the pernicious maxim that the end justifies the means." Cox devoted much space to Santo Domingo, and perhaps because of a faulty memory, he offered a distorted account of the affair, including the origins of Orville Babcock's exploratory mission. Although Cox privately told Harry Wilson that he had regarded Rawlins's behavior in the cabinet as "a little shy & observant rather than assertive," his article echoed Wilson's notion of Rawlins as Grant's "living and speaking conscience." After Rawlins died, Cox wrote, "self-seeking men studied General Grant's peculiarities, and took shrewd advantage of them," with the result that by "the later period of his administration, . . . the abuse of his confidence by those who had private ends to gain became deplorably notorious." The article contained several errors, but as a supposed inside account, it influenced much subsequent writing about the administration. Allan Nevins called Cox's article "somewhat untrustworthy" but still quoted from it extensively.[10]

The work by a contemporary enemy that probably did the most damage to Grant's presidential reputation came from the pen of Henry Adams. Published posthumously, *The Education of Henry Adams* appeared in 1918. Adams had written articles criticizing the administration in its first year, and having failed to attain the influence he craved, he grew ever more hostile to Grant. Seven years after the end of the administration, he told Wilson it was a wonder that such a man as Grant could ever have "marched a sergeant's guard out of a potato patch." "In civil affairs he has absolutely *no* mind; there is nothing in him; he is weak, obtuse, narrow and lazy." In old age Adams told his brother, "I have always considered that Grant wrecked my own life, and the last hope or chance of lifting society back to a reasonably high plane."[11]

In *The Education*, Adams got in the last word. "Grant's administration," he wrote, "outraged every rule of ordinary decency." Grant was "pre-intellectual, archaic, and would have seemed so even to the cave-dwellers." Accession to the nation's highest office by such a man "made evolution ludicrous." "The progress of evolution from President Washington to President Grant, was alone evidence enough to upset Darwin." Indeed, Grant "had no right to exist. He should have been extinct for ages." Instead, he ushered in an era in which "one might search the whole list of Congress, Judiciary, and Executive during the twenty-five years 1870 to 1895, and find little but damaged reputation." Of course, Adams himself had done much of the damaging, and his book continued to do so.[12]

As historian Brooks Simpson and others have noted, *The Education* was scarcely an accurate autobiography, let alone a work of history. But as a brooding rumination, it became a classic, and its acerbic depiction of Grant exerts an enduring influence. In 1999 the Modern Library ranked *The Education* at the top of its list of the twentieth century's 100 best nonfiction books written in English.[13]

The efforts of Wilson, Cox, Adams, and others did much to set in stone the damning indictment leveled by Grant's enemies during his presidency. C. Vann Woodward, perhaps the greatest American historian of the twentieth century, put the seal on their judgments: "If any point of reference in American history is fixed in the public imagination it is the Administration of President Ulysses S. Grant. It stands for the all-time low point in statesmanship and political morality in our history."[14]

During his eight years in the White House, Grant was an activist president, winning some policy battles and losing others. To a degree, he remodeled the office of president, traveling extensively, creating a White House staff, and energetically pursuing a legislative agenda. But these steps toward modernity earned scorn from contemporary critics, who set up the cry of Caesarism and thus undermined his contributions to the evolution of the presidency. For many of his opponents, his worst sin as chief executive was his assertiveness—his dominance of politics and governance, grounded in his formidable popularity. But in the end, his political adversaries saw a way to win the public relations battle by stigmatizing his administration with corruption. Over time, corruption has been relatively constant in American public life, but at some times more than others, partisans aggressively deploy allegations of wrongdoing to assault their political adversaries. As Mark Summers has shown, in the post–Civil War era, "corruption had less important consequences than the *corruption issue*." In a period marked by acute if not overwrought sensitivity to "corruption," Grant's administration exhibited enough delinquency to provide his enemies a convenient brush with which to tar his presidential reputation in perpetuity.[15]

In recent years, numerous works have appeared that place Grant's two terms in a more favorable light, especially his efforts in behalf of Reconstruction. H. W. Brands, for instance, hails him as "the man who saved the Union" in peace as well as war. But it remains uncertain whether such treatments will dislodge the damning judgment of his presidency that Woodward saw as "fixed in the public imagination." The operation of confirmation bias exerts a powerful force against the overturning of ingrained understandings of the past. It is said that stereotypes are true until proved otherwise—and then they are still true. As John Russell Young presciently observed, "Calumny has fallen upon the memory of Grant with Pompeiian fury," so that "to tell the truth about him, sounds like unreasoning adulation."[16]

NOTES

CC	Caleb Cushing
CC-LC	Caleb Cushing Papers, Library of Congress
CFA	Charles Francis Adams
CG	*Congressional Globe*
CHK	Chester H. Krum
CR	*Congressional Record*
CS	Charles Sumner
CS-Mf	Charles Sumner Papers, microfilm edition
CSch	Carl Schurz
CSch-LC	Carl Schurz Papers, Library of Congress
DAW	David Ames Wells
DAW-LC	David Ames Wells Papers, Library of Congress
DPD	David P. Dyer
EA	Edward Atkinson
EBW	Elihu B. Washburne
EBW-LC	Elihu B. Washburne Papers, Library of Congress
EMS	Edwin M. Stanton
EMS-LC	Edwin M. Stanton Papers, Library of Congress
EP	Edwards Pierrepont
EP-Yale	Edwards Pierrepont Papers, Yale University Library
ERH	Ebenezer Rockwood Hoar
ERH-CPL	Ebenezer Rockwood Hoar Papers, Concord (Massachusetts) Public Library
ET	Edward Thornton
EWK	E. W. Keyes
EWK-WHS	E. W. Keyes Papers, Wisconsin Historical Society
FHS	Filson Historical Society
FPB	Frank P. Blair
FRUS	*Papers Relating to the Foreign Relations of the United States*, part of the annual compendium of congressional documents published by the Government Printing Office
GFH	George F. Hoar
GFH-MHS	George F. Hoar Papers, Massachusetts Historical Society
GHW	George H. Williams
GSB	George S. Boutwell
GSB-LC	George S. Boutwell Papers, Library of Congress
GW	Gideon Welles
GW-LC	Gideon Welles Papers, Library of Congress
HA	Henry Adams
HF	Hamilton Fish
HF-LC	Hamilton Fish Papers, Library of Congress
HG	Horace Greeley
HG-LC	Horace Greeley Papers, Library of Congress

HG-NYPL	Horace Greeley Papers, New York Public Library
HLD	Henry L. Dawes
HLD-LC	Henry L. Dawes Papers, Library of Congress
HP	Horace Porter
HS	Horatio Seymour
HS-NYHS	Horatio Seymour Papers, New-York Historical Society
JAG	James A. Garfield
JAG-LC	James A. Garfield Papers, Library of Congress
JAG-WRHS	James A. Garfield Papers, Western Reserve Historical Society
JAJC	John A. J. Creswell
JAJC-LC	John A. J. Creswell Papers, Library of Congress
JAL	John A. Logan
JAL-LC	John A. Logan Papers, Library of Congress
JAR	John A. Rawlins
JB	John Bigelow
JB-NYPL	John Bigelow Papers, New York Public Library
JCBD	John Chandler Bancroft Davis
JCBD-LC	John Chandler Bancroft Davis Papers, Library of Congress
JDC	Jacob Dolson Cox
JDC-OCL	Jacob Dolson Cox Papers, Oberlin College Library
JDG	Julia Dent Grant
JGB	James G. Blaine
JGB-LC	James G. Blaine Papers, Library of Congress
JHW	James Harrison Wilson
JHW-LC	James Harrison Wilson Papers, Library of Congress
JHW-USGPL	James Harrison Wilson Papers, Ulysses S. Grant Presidential Library
JLM	John Lothrop Motley
JMH	John Marshall Harlan
JMH-LC	John Marshall Harlan Papers, Library of Congress
JRJ	J. Russell Jones
JRY	John Russell Young
JRY-LC	John Russell Young Papers, Library of Congress
JS	John Sherman
JS-LC	John Sherman Papers, Library of Congress
JSM	Justin S. Morrill
JSM-LC	Justin S. Morrill Papers, Library of Congress
JWF	Joseph W. Fabens
JWF-PEM	Joseph W. Fabens Papers and Fabens Family Papers, Peabody Essex Museum
JWS	Jacob William Schuckers
JWS-LC	Jacob William Schuckers Papers, Library of Congress
KFP-LC	Keim Family Papers, Library of Congress

LC	Library of Congress
LPL	Levi P. Luckey
LT	Lyman Trumbull
LT-LC	Lyman Trumbull Papers, Library of Congress
M and P	James D. Richardson, *Compilation of the Messages and Papers of the Presidents* (Washington, D.C.: Bureau of National Literature and Art, 1903)
MB	Montgomery Blair
MHG	Moses H. Grinnell
MM	Manton Marble
MM-LC	Manton Marble Papers, Library of Congress
NA	National Archives
NPB	Nathaniel P. Banks
NPB-LC	Nathaniel P. Banks Papers, Library of Congress
NYH	*New York Herald*
NYHS	New-York Historical Society
NYPL	New York Public Library
NYS	*New York Sun*
NYT	*New York Times*
NYTr	*New York Tribune*
NYW	*New York World*
OEB	Orville E. Babcock
OEB-NL	Orville E. Babcock Papers, Newberry Library
OEB-USGPL	Orville E. Babcock Papers, Ulysses S. Grant Presidential Library
OPM	Oliver P. Morton
OPM-ISL	Oliver P. Morton Papers, Indiana State Library
PHS	Philip H. Sheridan
PHS-LC	Philip H. Sheridan Papers, Library of Congress
PRO	Public Record Office Microfilm Records, Library of Congress
PUSG	John Y. Simon et al., eds., *The Papers of Ulysses S. Grant* (Carbondale: Southern Illinois University Press, 1967–2012)
RBH	Rutherford B. Hayes
RBH-RBHPC	Rutherford B. Hayes Papers, Rutherford B. Hayes Presidential Center
RBHPC	Rutherford B. Hayes Presidential Center
RC	Roscoe Conkling
RCS	Robert C. Schenck
RG	Record Group
RHJP	Raymond H. J. Perry
RHJP-URI	Raymond H. J. Perry Papers, University of Rhode Island Library
SB	Samuel Bowles
SB-Yale	Samuel Bowles Papers, Yale University Library

SC	Simon Cameron
SC-LC	Simon Cameron Papers, Library of Congress
SJT	Samuel J. Tilden
SJT-NYPL	Samuel J. Tilden Papers, New York Public Library
SPC	Salmon P. Chase
SPC-LC	Salmon P. Chase Papers, Library of Congress
StLGD	*St. Louis Globe-Democrat*
TFB	Thomas F. Bayard
TFB-LC	Thomas F. Bayard Papers, Library of Congress
TOH	Timothy O. Howe
TOH-WHS	Timothy O. Howe Papers, Wisconsin Historical Society
ts	typescript
USG	Ulysses S. Grant
USG-LC	Ulysses S. Grant Papers, Library of Congress
USG-NYHS	Ulysses S. Grant Papers, New-York Historical Society
USG-NYPL	Ulysses S. Grant Papers, New York Public Library
USG-USGPL	Ulysses S. Grant Papers, Ulysses S. Grant Presidential Library
WAR	William A. Richardson
WEC	William E. Chandler
WEC-LC	William E. Chandler Papers, Library of Congress
WEC-NHHS	William E. Chandler Papers, New Hampshire Historical Society
WES	*Washington Evening Star*
WNR	*Washington National Republican*
WQG	Walter Q. Gresham
WQG-LC	Walter Q. Gresham Papers, Library of Congress
WR	Whitelaw Reid
WR-LC	Whitelaw Reid Papers, Library of Congress
WTS	William T. Sherman
WWB	William W. Belknap
WWB-PU	William W. Belknap Papers, Princeton University Library
ZC	Zachariah Chandler
ZC-LC	Zachariah Chandler Papers, Library of Congress

INTRODUCTION: WAR IN PEACE

1. C. Vann Woodward, "The Lowest Ebb," *American Heritage* 8 (April 1957): 53; *NYT*, March 13, 2010.

2. Richard Hofstadter, *The American Political Tradition and the Men Who Made It* (1948; reprint, New York: Vintage Books, 1989), 223. For early exceptions, see Hamlin Garland, *Ulysses S. Grant: His Life and Character* (New York: Doubleday & McClure, 1898); Louis A. Coolidge, *Ulysses S. Grant* (Boston: Houghton Mifflin, 1917).

3. William S. McFeely, *Grant: A Biography* (New York: W. W. Norton, 1981), xii–xiii, 522.

4. Richard N. Current, "Ulysses S. Grant and the Continuing Civil War," in *Ulysses S. Grant: Essays and Documents*, ed. David L. Wilson and John Y. Simon (Carbondale: Southern Illinois University Press, 1981), 8; Brooks Simpson quoted in Nick Baumann, "Ulysses S. Grant Died 130 Years Ago. Racists Hate Him, but Historians No Longer Do," *Huffington Post*, July 23, 2015.

5. Josiah Bunting III, *Ulysses S. Grant* (New York: Times Books, 2004), 6.

6. Joseph A. Rose, *Grant under Fire: An Exposé of Generalship and Character in the American Civil War* (New York: Alderhanna Publishing, 2015), 586.

7. Charles Sumner, *Republicanism vs. Grantism* (Washington, D.C.: F. & J. Rives & Geo. A. Bailey, 1872).

PROLOGUE: A TROUBLED NATION

1. Edward McPherson, *The Political History of the United States of America during the Period of Reconstruction* (Washington, D.C.: Philp & Solomons, 1871), 78.

2. George F. Hoar, *Autobiography of Seventy Years* (New York: Charles Scribner's Sons, 1903), 1:246.

CHAPTER 1. POLITICAL APPRENTICESHIP

1. Brooks D. Simpson, *Ulysses S. Grant: Triumph over Adversity, 1822–1865* (Boston: Houghton Mifflin, 2000), 1–17, 20; U. S. Grant, *Personal Memoirs of U. S. Grant* (New York: Charles L. Webster, 1885, 1886), 1:53.

2. Grant, *Personal Memoirs*, 1:53; John Russell Young, *Around the World with General Grant* (New York: American News, 1879), 2:448; Josiah Bunting III, *Ulysses S. Grant* (New York: Henry Holt, 2004), 21–27.

3. Simpson, *Grant: Triumph over Adversity*, 21, 49–62; Jean Edward Smith, *Grant* (New York: Simon & Schuster, 2001), 84–89; Albert D. Richardson, *A Personal History of Ulysses S. Grant* (Hartford, Conn.: American Publishing, 1868), 137; conversation with Mark Cervi, M.D., September 14, 2014; Grant, *Personal Memoirs*, 1:203; *PUSG*, 1:275–276, 278, 294, 301, 320, 323.

4. Grant, *Personal Memoirs*, 1:210–212; Simpson, *Grant: Triumph over Adversity*, 64–73.

5. Grant, *Personal Memoirs*, 1:212–215; Young, *Around the World with General Grant*, 2:268–269, 446; *PUSG*, 1:347, 352; Simpson, *Grant: Triumph over Adversity*, 70–72.

6. Grant, *Personal Memoirs*, 1:216–217.

7. *PUSG*, 2:3–4; Grant, *Personal Memoirs*, 1:231.

8. Grant, *Personal Memoirs*, 1:231–243; *PUSG*, 2:81, 82, 183.

9. Grant, *Personal Memoirs*, 1:249–251.

10. Grant, *Personal Memoirs*, 1:316–584, 2:17–498; Simpson, *Grant: Triumph over Adversity*, 119–437; *PUSG*, 9:196, 218.

11. *PUSG*, 9:523, 542, 541, 544; *PUSG*, 10:53, 133.

12. Charles A. Dana and J. H. Wilson, *The Life of Ulysses S. Grant* (Springfield, Mass.: Gurdon Bill, 1868), 417; Brooks D. Simpson, *Let Us Have Peace: Ulysses S. Grant and the Politics of War and Reconstruction, 1861–1868* (Chapel Hill: University of North Carolina Press, 1991), xvi–xx.

13. Simpson, *Let Us Have Peace*, 99–116; *PUSG*, 15:266, 358; *PUSG*, 17:224, 227–229.

14. Brooks D. Simpson, "Grant's Tour of the South Revisited," *Journal of Southern History* 54 (August 1988): 433–439; *PUSG*, 15:423, 428; Howard K. Beale, ed., *The Diary of Gideon Welles* (New York: W. W. Norton, 1960), 2:222, 396–398.

15. *PUSG*, 15:434–437; Joseph Schafer, ed., *Intimate Letters of Carl Schurz, 1841–1869* (Madison: State Historical Society of Wisconsin, 1928), 457.

16. *M and P*, 6:372–373; *CG*, 39th Cong., 1st sess., 79–80.

17. *PUSG*, 16:7–8, 69–70; Simpson, *Let Us Have Peace*, 130; Schafer, *Intimate Letters of Schurz*, 356; Edward McPherson, *The Political History of the United States of America during the Period of Reconstruction* (Washington, D.C.: Philp & Solomons, 1871), 68–81.

18. *PUSG*, 16:228, 233–235; Simpson, *Let Us Have Peace*, 136–139.

19. St. George L. Sioussat, "Notes of Colonel W. G. Moore, Private Secretary of President Johnson, 1866–1868," *American Historical Review* 19 (October 1913): 102; Hans L. Trefousse, *Andrew Johnson* (New York: W. W. Norton, 1989), 262–266; McPherson, *Political History during Reconstruction*, 129–141; Beale, *Diary of Welles*, 2:591–593, 595; *PUSG*, 16:307–308, 330; Theodore Calvin Pease and James G. Randall, eds., *The Diary of Orville Hickman Browning* (Springfield: Illinois State Historical Library, 1925–1933), 2:94, 115.

20. *M and P*, 6:445–450; Eric Foner, *Reconstruction: America's Unfinished Revolution, 1863–1877* (New York: Harper & Row, 1988), 262–263; *PUSG*, 16:387, 395.

21. *PUSG*, 17:14, 38, 50, 51; "Partial List of Outrages Committed in Southern States, and Reported to Head Quarters Armies, U.S., during the year 1866," EMS-LC; Beale, *Diary of Welles*, 3:42–46.

22. McPherson, *Political History during Reconstruction*, 176–178, 191–192; *PUSG*, 17:76.

23. *PUSG*, 17:76.

24. *PUSG*, 16:346–347, 350–352; Cyrus B. Comstock, diary, October 23, 24, 1866, March 1, 1867, CBC-LC; Pease and Randall, *Diary of Browning*, 2:103–104; McPherson, *Political History during Reconstruction*, 192–194; OEB, diary, March 25, 26, 1867, OEB-USGPL; *PUSG*, 17:98.

25. OEB, diary, March 5, 6, 1[1], 12, 13, 15, 16, April 4, 1867, OEB-USGPL; Pease and Randall, *Diary of Browning*, 2:135; *PUSG*, 17:80–82; Beale, *Diary of Welles*, 3:62–65.

26. *PUSG*, 17:95–96, 98, 122, 168, 185, 195–196; Simpson, *Let Us Have Peace*, 177–183.

27. John Y. Simon, "Rawlins, John Aaron," *ANB*, 18:199; John A. Logan, John A. Rawlins, et al., Temperance Pledge, October 14, 1862, USG-USGPL; James Harrison Wilson, *The Life of John A. Rawlins* (New York: Neale, 1916), 337–339; HP to JHW, June 28, 1867 (ts), JHW-USGPL.

28. *Speech of Major Gen'l John A. Rawlins* (Washington, D.C.: Chronicle Print, [1868]).

29. *Cleveland Daily Herald*, June 25, 1867; HP to JHW, June 28, 1867 (ts), JHW-USGPL; Beale, *Diary of Welles*, 3:121.

30. McPherson, *Political History during Reconstruction*, 335–336.

31. USG, testimony, July 18, 1867, *PUSG*, 17:210–232; Marcus L. Ward to EBW, August 7, 1867, EBW-LC.

32. Sioussat, "Notes of Colonel W. G. Moore," 107–109; *PUSG*, 17:250–252; Beale, *Diary of Welles*, 3:154–155, 167; Pease and Randall, *Diary of Browning*, 2:155–156.

33. Simpson, *Let Us Have Peace*, 192–193; Beale, *Diary of Welles*, 3:169; Pease and Randall, *Diary of Browning*, 2:158.

34. Beale, *Diary of Welles*, 3:176–181.

35. *PUSG*, 17:277–281.

36. *Philadelphia North American and United States Gazette*, August 27, 1867; Beale, *Diary of Welles*, 3:185–189; Pease and Randall, *Diary of Browning*, 2:159; *PUSG*, 17:301–303; Sioussat, "Notes of Colonel W. G. Moore," 111–113.

37. *Milwaukee Sentinel*, August 28, 1867; *San Francisco Daily Evening Bulletin*, August 27, 1867.

38. *PUSG*, 17:291; *Washington National Intelligencer*, September 6, 1867.

39. Simpson, *Let Us Have Peace*, 206–207; John Niven, *Salmon P. Chase: A Biography* (New York: Oxford University Press, 1995), 416; John Niven, ed., *The Salmon P. Chase Papers* (Kent, Ohio: Kent State University Press, 1993–1998), 5:168, 169.

40. Simpson, *Let Us Have Peace*, 206–208; *Boston Daily Advertiser*, July 27, 1867; Glyndon G. Van Deusen, *Thurlow Weed: Wizard of the Lobby* (Boston: Little, Brown, 1947), 327–328.

41. EBW to JHW, October 4, 1867, USG-USGPL; *Daily Cleveland Herald*, October 8, 1867 (emphasis in original).

42. McPherson, *Political History during Reconstruction*, 353–354, 372; Foner, *Reconstruction*, 313–315; Michael Les Benedict, *Essays on Politics and the Constitution in the Reconstruction Era* (New York: Fordham University Press, 2006), 28–29.

43. *PUSG*, 18:325; M. Russell Thayer to EBW, October 10, 1867, JGB to EBW, October 22, 1867, EBW-LC.

44. Beale, *Diary of Welles*, 3:235.

45. Rachel Sherman Thorndyke, ed., *The Sherman Letters: Correspondence between General and Senator Sherman from 1837 to 1891* (New York: Charles

Scribner's Sons, 1894), 295; M. A. DeWolfe Howe, ed., *Home Letters of General Sherman* (New York: Charles Scribner's Sons, 1909), 362; HP to JHW, November 18, 1867, USG-USGPL.

46. *NYT*, November 26, December 19, 1867; *Boston Daily Advertiser*, November 30, 1867; House Executive Document No. 57, 40th Cong., 2nd sess., 1–2; *PUSG*, 18:445.

47. *NYT*, December 5, 1867; *Boston Daily Advertiser*, December 19, 1867; Alexander H. Rice to EBW, December 24, 1867, EBW-LC; Michael Les Benedict, *A Compromise of Principle: Congressional Republicans and Reconstruction, 1863–1869* (New York: W. W. Norton, 1974), 280; HS to H. Barney, January 17, 1868, JWS-LC.

48. *Chicago Tribune*, December 14, 1867 (emphasis in original); Joseph Medill to EBW, December 16, 1867, EBW-LC.

49. *Washington National Intelligencer*, December 19, 1867; Beverly Wilson Palmer, ed., *The Selected Letters of Charles Sumner* (Boston: Northeastern University Press, 1990), 2:409.

50. Beale, *Diary of Welles*, 3:240; *NYT*, January 3, 9, 1867; Sioussat, "Notes of Colonel W. G. Moore," 114–115; *Journal of the Executive Proceedings of the Senate of the United States of America, 1867–1869* (Washington, D.C.: Government Printing Office, 1887), 128.

51. *PUSG*, 18:106, 116–117.

52. *Journal of Executive Proceedings of the Senate, 1867–1869*, 128–129; *PUSG*, 18:106–107, 116–118, 119–121; Beale, *Diary of Welles*, 3:255–256.

53. *PUSG*, 18:107; Simpson, *Let Us Have Peace*, 227–228.

54. *Journal of Executive Proceedings of the Senate, 1867–1869*, 129–130; *NYT*, January 14, 1868; Sioussat, "Notes of Colonel W. G. Moore," 115; Pease and Randall, *Diary of Browning*, 2:173.

55. *PUSG*, 18:102–103, 107–108, 117–118; E. D. Townsend, *Anecdotes of the Civil War in the United States* (New York: D. Appleton, 1884), 124; Beale, *Diary of Welles*, 3:259; Pease and Randall, *Diary of Browning*, 2:173–174.

56. Beale, *Diary of Welles*, 3:259–261; Pease and Randall, *Diary of Browning*, 2:174–175; Sioussat, "Notes of Colonel W. G. Moore," 115–116; *PUSG*, 18:117–118, 120–121, 124–125, 144–146.

57. *Washington National Intelligencer*, January 15, 1868; *PUSG*, 18:108–109, 116–118, 119–121, 124–126, 144–149; *NYTr*, February 5, 12, 1868.

58. Beale, *Diary of Welles*, 3:269–270; F. C. Ingalls to EBW, February 6, 1868, James Sheldon to EBW, February 6, 1868, EBW-LC; *NYTr*, February 7, 1868.

59. Howe, *Home Letters of Sherman*, 370.

60. J. B. Atkinson to Schuyler Colfax, January 10, 1868, A. Watson to EBW, January 19, 1868, W. B. Johnson to EBW, February 13, 1868, George G. Fogg to EBW, February 4, 1868, EBW-LC; Helen Griffing to Theodore Tilton, January 17, 1868, USG-NYPL; *New York Independent*, February 6, 1868; *Anti-Slavery Standard* quoted in *Newark Advocate*, February 7, 1868; JWS to JRY, May 5, 1868, JRY-LC (emphasis in originals).

61. George G. Fogg to EBW, February 4, 1868, WEC to EBW, February 12, 1868, Marcus L. Ward to EBW, February 3, 12, 1868, EBW-LC; MHG to WEC, February 24, 28, 1868, WEC-LC; *New Hampshire Statesman*, March 13, 1868; Leon Burr Richardson, *William E. Chandler: Republican* (New York: Dodd, Mead, 1940), 84–85; *Congressional Quarterly's Guide to U.S. Elections* (Washington, D.C.: Congressional Quarterly, 1994), 694; Thorndyke, *Sherman Letters*, 314.

62. MHG to WEC, March 16, 18, 23, 30, April 7, 1868, WEC-LC; John Cochrane to EBW, March 25, April 7, 1868, John M. Read to EBW, April 7, 1868, EBW-LC; *NYT*, February 10, March 12, April 8, 1868; *NYH*, April 8, 1868; *NYTr*, April 7, 1868.

63. Michael Les Benedict, *The Impeachment and Trial of Andrew Johnson* (New York: W. W. Norton, 1973), 115–122, 136–137; Niven, *Chase*, 419–427; TFB to James Bayard, March 27, 1868, TFB-LC; Niven, *Chase Papers*, 5:205–211.

64. *NYTr*, March 17, May 14, 1868; B. Gratz Brown to BFW, March 2, 26, 1868, Thomas C. Fletcher to Brown, March 17, 1868, BFW-LC; Horace White to EBW, May 1, 1868, John M. Read to EBW, May 12, 1868, EBW-LC; JDC to JS, March 4, 1868, JS-LC; Benedict, *Impeachment and Trial of Andrew Johnson*, 133–136; Hans L. Trefousse, "Ben Wade and the Failure of the Impeachment of Johnson," *Bulletin of the Historical and Philosophical Society of Ohio* 18 (October 1960): 241–252.

65. H. L. Trefousse, *Benjamin Butler: Radical Republican from Ohio* (New York: Twayne, 1963), 300–301; Simpson, *Let Us Have Peace*, 243–244; *PUSG*, 18:205, 207; Adam Badeau, *Grant in Peace* (Hartford, Conn.: S. S. Scranton, 1887), 136–137; George H. Boker to SC, May 14, 1868, SC-LC; John B. Henderson, "Emancipation and Impeachment," *Century* 85 (November 1912): 207.

66. Beale, *Diary of Welles*, 3:347; William G. Moore, "Large Diary," April 7, 23, 24, 1868 (ts), AJ-LC; Benedict, *Impeachment and Trial of Andrew Johnson*, 137–139; *NYT*, May 16, 1868; *PUSG*, 18:257; *Trial of Andrew Johnson* (Washington, D.C.: Government Printing Office, 1868), 2:486–487, 496–497.

67. JWS to JRY, May 20, 1868, JRY-LC.

CHAPTER 2. "LET US HAVE PEACE"

1. *NYH*, May 20, 1868; *Official Proceedings of the National Republican Conventions of 1868, 1872, 1876, and 1880* (Minneapolis: Charles W. Johnson, 1903), 72–79; *Washington National Intelligencer*, May 22, 1868.

2. *Official Proceedings of the National Republican Conventions*, 64, 85, 97–108.

3. Ibid., 66–72.

4. HP to JHW, May 22, 1868, USG-USGPL; Adam Badeau, *Grant in Peace* (Hartford, Conn.: S. S. Scranton, 1887), 144; *NYTr*, May 23, 1868; *NYT*, May 22, 23, 30, 1868.

5. *NYT*, June 2, 1868.

6. Ibid.; Brooks D. Simpson, *Let Us Have Peace: Ulysses S. Grant and the*

Politics of War and Reconstruction, 1861–1868 (Chapel Hill: University of North Carolina Press, 1991), 246; *PUSG*, 18:294–295.

7. *PUSG*, 18:292–293; Badeau, *Grant in Peace*, 144–145.

8. Theodore Calvin Pease and James G. Randall, eds., *The Diary of Orville Hickman Browning* (Springfield: Illinois State Historical Library, 1925–1933), 2:210–212; Howard K. Beale, ed., *The Diary of Gideon Welles* (New York: W. W. Norton, 1960), 3:363; *PUSG*, 18:292–293.

9. John Niven, ed., *The Salmon P. Chase Papers* (Kent, Ohio: Kent State University Press, 1993–1998), 5:221, 246; TFB to James Bayard, June 10, 1868, TFB-LC; *NYH*, July 10, 1868; John Niven, *Salmon P. Chase: A Biography* (New York: Oxford University Press, 1995), 427–432.

10. Thomas S. Mach, *"Gentleman George" Hunt Pendleton: Party Politics and Ideological Identity in Nineteenth-Century America* (Kent, Ohio: Kent State University Press, 2007), 125–132; William G. Moore, "Large Diary," July 3, 5–9, 1868 (ts), AJ-LC; David M. Jordan, *Winfield Scott Hancock: A Soldier's Life* (Bloomington: Indiana University Press, 1988), 218–221.

11. *Official Proceedings of the National Democratic Convention Held at New York, July 4–9, 1868* (Boston: Rockwell & Rollins, 1868), 4–5, 58, 66–87, 98–161 (emphasis in original); William C. Harris, *Two against Lincoln: Reverdy Johnson and Horatio Seymour, Champions of the Loyal Opposition* (Lawrence: University Press of Kansas, 2017), 192–203.

12. Eric Foner, *Reconstruction: America's Unfinished Revolution, 1863–1877* (New York: Harper & Row, 1988), 340; James D. McCabe Jr., *The Life and Public Services of Horatio Seymour* (New York: United States Publishing Company, 1868), 205, 225, 230–231.

13. FPB to MB, July 1, 1868, BFP-LC; Edward McPherson, *The Political History of the United States of America during the Period of Reconstruction* (Washington, D.C.: Philp & Solomons, 1871), 380–381; *Official Proceedings of the National Democratic Convention*, 39, 58–60, 170; JGB to EBW, July 11, 1868, EBW-LC.

14. *PUSG*, 19:9–13, 23, 50; Ellis Paxson Oberholtzer, *A History of the United States since the Civil War* (New York: Macmillan, 1922), 2:184–185; *NYTr*, July 23, August 3, 1868.

15. *PUSG*, 19:17–18, 26–27, 37–39; Adolph Moses to the editor of the *Quincy Herald*, n.d., in *Daily Cleveland Herald*, October 12, 1868; Jonathan D. Sarna, *When General Grant Expelled the Jews* (New York: Schocken Books, 2012), 7, 21, 50–77; Joseph Medill to EBW, June 16 (ts), 25, 1868, EBW-LC.

16. *PUSG*, 19:47; Leon Burr Richardson, *William E. Chandler: Republican* (New York: Dodd, Mead, 1940), 90–91; Badeau, *Grant in Peace*, 146–147; EBW to WEC, October 25, 1868, AB to WEC, September 15, October 12, 1868, WEC-LC.

17. Memorandum of meeting of the National Republican Committee, July 9, 1868, William Claflin to WEC, July 20, August 6, October 19, 21, 24, 1868, William B. Allison to WEC, August 16, 1868, EBW to Claflin, September 4, 1868, MHG to WEC, September 22, 27, 1868, Jay Cooke to WEC, September 29, 1868, WEC

to "My dear Sir," n.d. [1868], WEC-LC; ATS to WEC, October 20, 1868, WEC-NHHS; WEC to HG, July 15, 1868, HG-NYPL; EBW to HF, September 15, 1868 (ts), MHG to HF, September 24, 1868 (ts, emphasis in original), HF-LC; WEC to AB, September 25, 1868, USG-LC.

18. JRJ to WEC, June 26, 1868, "Plan for Raising Funds," n.d. [1868], William Claflin to WEC, July 27, 1868, Thomas L. Tullock to Claflin, September 4, 1868, Tullock to WEC, September 17, October 9, 26, 1868, WEC-LC; Claflin et al., circular of Union Republican Congressional Committee, to Post Master, Indianola, Texas, July 10, 1868, SPC-LC; Richardson, *Chandler*, 99–100.

19. John Bigelow, ed., *Letters and Literary Memorials of Samuel J. Tilden* (New York: Harper & Brothers, 1908), 1:245; William Claflin to WEC, June 10, 1868, A. H. Conner to WEC, June 20, 1868, William B. Allison to WEC, August 16, 1868, WEC-LC; Silas F. Miller to USG, June 1, 1868, USG-LC; 15 *Statutes at Large*, 125, 167.

20. Alexander Clarence Flick, *Samuel Jones Tilden: A Study in Political Sagacity* (New York: Dodd, Mead, 1939), 181–188; EP to EMS, July 12, 1868, EMS-LC; *NYS*, October 22, 1868; EP to ATS, October 10, 1868, in *WNR*, October 15, 1868; Samuel Ward to MM, July 31, 1868, MM-LC.

21. Bigelow, *Letters and Literary Memorials of Tilden*, 1:219–220 (emphasis in original); FPB to Francis Preston Blair Sr., July 17, 1868, BFP-LC; *Official Proceedings of the National Democratic Convention*, 176–181; *NYH*, July 24, August 11, 1868; *Speech of Gen. F. P. Blair, Democratic Candidate for Vice President, Delivered September 24, 1868, at Indianapolis* (n.p., n.d. [1868]), 6, 9, 11.

22. Charles H. Coleman, *The Election of 1868: The Democratic Effort to Regain Control* (New York: Columbia University Press, 1933), 313; *NYT*, September 5, 1868.

23. W. S. Rosecrans to HS, September 6, 1868, HS-NYHS; *NYT*, September 5, 1868; J. D. Stockton to JRY, September 7, 1868, JRY-LC; AB to WEC, September 15, 1868, WEC-LC.

24. AB to Wickham Hoffman, September 5, 1868, AB to WEC, September 24, 1868, WEC-LC; AB to JRY, September 24, 1868, JRY-LC; WEC to AB, September 21, 25, 1868, USG-LC; David Work, *Lincoln's Political Generals* (Urbana: University of Illinois Press, 2009), 170–171; *NYH*, September 23, 1868.

25. *PUSG*, 18:292–293; Burke A. Hinsdale, ed., *The Works of James Abram Garfield* (Boston: James R. Osgood, 1882), 397–398; *NYTr*, October 2, 1868; John W. Forney and J. R. Welsh to WEC, September 28, 1868, WEC-LC; WEC to AB, October 2, 1868, USG-LC; Bigelow, *Letters and Literary Memorials of Tilden*, 1:247–250; George B. McClellan to Douglas Taylor, October 3, 1868, in *NYT*, October 6, 1868.

26. EMS to JRY, September 19, 1868, JRY-LC; *NYH*, September 26, 1868; Charles A. Dana and J. H. Wilson, *The Life of Ulysses S. Grant* (Springfield, Mass.: Gurdon Bill, 1868), 422; *WNR*, October 28, 1868.

27. A. E. Burr to GW, July 14, 1868, GW-LC; H. H. Savage to N. D. Thompson,

June 16, 1868, Edwin Porter Thompson Collection, FHS; Samuel H. Merrill to Theodore Tilton, October 8, 1868, Letters and Other Material about U. S. Grant, NYPL; *PUSG*, 19:290–291; *WNR*, August 22, 1868; *Frank Leslie's Illustrated Newspaper*, August 29, 1868; *NYH*, October 10, 1868 (emphasis in original).

28. *The Tribune Almanac and Political Register for 1869* (New York: Tribune Association, 1869), 63; Thomas A. Hendricks to HS, September 5, 1868, HS-NYHS; MHG to HF, September 24, 1868 (ts), HF-LC; Schuyler Colfax to WEC, October 6, 7, 1868, A. H. Conner to WEC, June 20, July 2, August 29, 1868, Conner to William Claflin, September 1, October 8, 1868, JRJ to WEC, June 26, July 21, October 6, "Sunday" [October 11], 1868, JRJ to Claflin, September 16, 1868, Godlove S. Orth to EBW, September 1, 1868, Orth to WEC, August 6, September 7, 13, 1868, Orth to HG, September 2, 1868, Conrad Baker to HG, September 1, 1868, John Coburn to Claflin, September 3, 1868, EBW to Claflin, September 4, 1868, WEC to Orth, September 8, October 10, 1868, AB to WEC, September 22, 1868, C. M. Allen to Claflin, October 4, 1868, WEC-LC; WEC to AB, September 25, 1868, JRJ to USG, October 11, 1868, USG-LC.

29. *Tribune Almanac for 1869*, 66, 68–70; WEC to EBW, October 19, 1868, EBW-LC; WEC to AB, October 16, 1868, USG-LC; EBW to WEC, October 18, 1868, F. E. Spinner to WEC, October 14, 1868, WEC-LC (emphasis in original).

30. S. L. M. Barlow to SJT, October 14 (two letters), 1868, W. F. Storey to SJT, October 16, 1868, James T. Athan to August Belmont, October 16, 1868, C. L. Vallandigham to SJT, October 17, 1868, SJT-NYPL; "A Life Long Democrat" to "World," October 15, 1868, C. Rowland to MM, October 15, 1868, SJT to MM, October 20, 1868, MM-LC; Beale, *Diary of Welles*, 3:453–459; *NYW*, October 15, 1868; AB to JRY, October 21, 1868, JRY-LC; Bigelow, *Letters and Literary Memorials of Tilden*, 2:250–251.

31. *NYT*, October 22, 23, 24, 25, 30, 1868; *WNR*, October 24, 1868; Beale, *Diary of Welles*, 3:462; *NYH*, October 23, 24, 25, 27, 28, 29, 31, 1868; EBW to WEC, October 25, 1868, WEC-LC; Harris, *Two against Lincoln*, 205.

32. David Herbert Donald, *Charles Sumner* (1970; reprint, New York: Da Capo, 1996), 2:279; JLM to CS, July 30, 1868, CS-Mf; *NYH*, October 21, 1868; *WNR*, October 22, 1868.

33. Beverly Wilson Palmer, ed., *The Selected Letters of Charles Sumner* (Boston: Northeastern University Press, 1990), 2:443, 446; Theodore Tilton to CS, August 3, 1868, CS to Tilton, August 7, 1868, JRY to CS, September 26, 1868, H. C. Bowen to CS, October 1, 10, 1868, CS-Mf; *Boston Daily Advertiser*, October 30, 1868; Donald, *Sumner*, 2:340–341.

34. CS to the Duchess of Argyll, November 1, 1868, CS-Mf; John H. Caldwell to William Claflin, July 4, 1868, Thomas L. Tullock to Claflin, September 4, 24, 1868, Tullock to WEC, September 17, 24, October 6, 9, 24, 27, 1868, J. C. L. Harris to WEC, September 29, 1868, B. F. Rice to WEC, October 3, 1868, Barbour Lewis to WEC, November 5, 1868, WEC-LC.

35. M. H. Southworth to WEC, October 22, 27, 28, 31, November 5, 1868,

S. P. Packard to WEC, October 30, 1868, Wm. P. Kellogg to WEC, November 8, 1868, WEC-LC; George C. Rable, *But There Was No Peace: The Role of Violence in the Politics of Reconstruction* (Athens: University of Georgia Press, 1984), 68–79.

36. *NYTr*, November 4, 1868; Badeau, *Grant in Peace*, 148–149; EBW to [Mrs. EBW], November 4, 1868, EBW-LC.

37. *Presidential Elections, 1789–2000* (Washington, D.C.: Congressional Quarterly, 2002), 123, 194; William Gillette, *The Right to Vote: Politics and the Passage of the Fifteenth Amendment* (Baltimore: Johns Hopkins Press, 1969), 82.

38. E. H. Derby to EBW, November 10, 1868, EBW-LC; *Harper's Weekly*, November 21, 1868; EA to Hugh McCulloch, November 6, 1868, Hugh McCulloch Papers, LC; Beale, *Diary of Welles*, 3:534, 525.

39. *PUSG*, 19:68–69, 70; *Galena Gazette*, November 5, 1868; *PUSG*, 10:195.

CHAPTER 3. GRANT TAKES COMMAND

1. Charles S. Phelps to CS, January 3, 1869, CS-Mf; AB to JRY, February 20, 1869, JRY-LC; *PUSG*, 25:426; GFH to Ruth Hoar, February 28, 1869, GFH-MHS; *NYH*, February 28, 1869; *WNR*, January 28, 1868.

2. Beverly Wilson Palmer, ed., *The Selected Letters of Charles Sumner* (Boston: Northeastern University Press, 1990), 2:425, 434, 447; Samuel Hooper to CS, November 16, 1868, CS-Mf.

3. J. Medill to EBW, November 30, 1868, JGB to EBW, October 24, 1868 (emphasis in original), EBW-LC.

4. Horace White to EBW, November 28, 1868, EBW-LC; Jacob William Schuckers, untitled, undated memorandum, JWS-LC; Charles Eliot Norton, ed., *Letters of James Russell Lowell* (New York: Harper & Brothers, 1894), 2:233; Palmer, *Selected Letters of Sumner*, 2:447; CS to the Duchess of Argyll, December 29, 1868, CS-Mf; Adam Badeau, *Grant in Peace* (Hartford, Conn.: S. S. Scranton, 1887), 210–211.

5. Badeau, *Grant in Peace*, 210; CFA, diary, December 5, 8, 10, 1868, January 1, 15, February 24, March 16, 1869, AFP-MHS.

6. JLM to AB, December 24, 1868, USG-USGPL; *PUSG*, 19:89; Badeau, *Grant in Peace*, 153; CS to the Duchess of Argyll, December 29, 1868, CS-Mf.

7. J. C. Levenson et al., eds., *The Letters of Henry Adams* (Cambridge, Mass.: Harvard University Press, 1982), 2:20; Charles Richard Williams, ed., *Diary and Letters of Rutherford Birchard Hayes* (Columbus: Ohio State Archaeological and Historical Society, 1924), 3:56–57; P. N. Reed to EBW, February 23, 1869, EBW-LC.

8. *CG*, 40th Cong., 3rd sess., 216; *NYS*, December 5, 12, 24, 1868; *NYH*, January 8, February 18, 1869; *NYTr*, December 14, 1868; Horace White to EBW, October 18, 26, 1868, February 22, 1869, George W. Fogg to EBW, February 1, 1869, Charles B. Atchison to EBW, February 25, 1869, EBW-LC; JGB to Andrew G. Curtin, January 30, 1869, Heartman Collection, NYHS; JB, diary, November 9,

1868 (ts), JB-NYPL; JGB to JRY, December 8, 1868, JRY-LC; JRY to WEC, January 5, 1869, WEC-NHHS.

9. *NYH*, December 21, 1868, February 25, 26, 1869; *WNR*, February 16, 1869; *CG*, 40th Cong., 3rd sess., 77; Horace White to EBW, October 18, 1868, Joseph Medill to EBW, November 30, 1868, March 5, 1869, Damon K. Kilgore to EBW, December 18, 1868, John M. Read to EBW, March 4, 1869, John Cochrane to EBW, November 20, 1868, EBW-LC; J. D. Cameron to JRY, February 23, 1869, JRY-LC; JB, diary, January 19, 1869 (ts), JB-NYPL; William M. Evarts to EP, January 9, February 24, 1869, EP-Yale; Howard K. Beale, ed., *The Diary of Gideon Welles* (New York: W. W. Norton, 1960), 3:464–466.

10. *PUSG*, 19:80–81, 98–100, 107.

11. *CG*, 40th Cong., 3rd sess., 903–904, 1564, 1641; John C. Hamilton to JRY, February 7, 1869, JRY-LC; Hamilton to CS, February 7, 1869, CS-Mf; David Herbert Donald, *Charles Sumner* (1970; reprint, New York: Da Capo, 1996), 2:352–354.

12. O. B. Matteson to EBW, February 25, 1869, EBW-LC (emphasis in original); *CG*, 40th Cong., 3rd sess., 16, 282–283, 568, 936, 1867; *WNR*, February 19, 22, 1869; *NYH*, February 24, 1869; Hans L. Trefousse, *Ben Butler: The South Called Him BEAST!* (New York: Twayne, 1957), 208; Donald, *Sumner*, 2:370.

13. *NYH*, February 14, 1869; *PUSG*, 19:127, 134–135; J. D. Cameron to JRY, February 23, 1869, JRY-LC.

14. *NYT*, February 26, 27, 28, 1869; M. W. Tappan to EBW, February 27, 1869, EBW-LC (emphasis in original).

15. George F. Hoar, *Autobiography of Seventy Years* (New York: Charles Scribner's Sons, 1903), 1:246; George Bancroft to USG, March 5, 1869, USG-LC; G. D. B. Blanchard to NPB, February 27, 1869, NPB-LC; *Harper's Weekly*, March 20, 1869.

16. Beale, *Diary of Welles*, 3:498, 500, 532, 535–538, 540–542.

17. *NYT*, March 5, 1869; *NYTr*, March 5, 1869.

18. Badeau, *Grant in Peace*, 158; JRJ to JHW, October 18, 1886, JHW-LC.

19. *M and P*, 7:6–8; *PUSG*, 19:136–142.

20. *Harper's Weekly*, March 20, 1869; *WNR*, March 5, 1869; CFA, diary, March 4, 1869, AFP-MHS; Beale, *Diary of Welles*, 3:544; *NYH*, March 5, 1869.

21. BM, diary, October 22, 1869, BM-LC; SC to JRY, November 11, 1868, JRY-LC; *PUSG*, 19:143; *NYH*, March 6, 1869; *NYTr*, March 6, 1869.

22. *NYH*, March 6, 1869; *NYTr*, March 6, 1869.

23. *NYH*, March 6, 1869; Joseph Medill to EBW, March 5, 1869, EBW-LC.

24. J. G. Rosengarten to Thomas A. Jenckes, March 12, 1869, Thomas A. Jenckes Papers, LC; Beale, *Diary of Welles*, 3:548; Emory Washburn to EBW, March 8, 1869, EBW-LC.

25. Damon Y. Kilgore to EBW, December 18, 1868, Emory Washburn to EBW, March 8, 1869, EBW-LC; *PUSG*, 19:146; A. E. Borie to George H. Stuart, May 1, 1869, George H. Stuart Papers, LC; HF, diary, April 26, 1875, HF-LC; Beale, *Diary of Welles*, 3:549–550; *NYH*, February 25, 26, 1869; J. D. Cameron to JRY, February 23, 1869, Daniel Dougherty to JRY, March 6, 1869, JRY-LC.

26. JB, diary, January 19, February 27, 1869 (ts), JB-NYPL; MHG to WEC, February 15, 1869, WEC-LC; William M. Evarts to EP, February 24, 1869, EP-Yale; MHG to EBW, March 6, 1869, EBW-LC; CFA, diary, January 22, March 10, 1869, AFP-MHS; Donald, *Sumner*, 2:344–348; *NYTr*, March 6, 1869; Williams, *Diary and Letters of Hayes*, 3:59.

27. *NYT*, March 7, 12, 1869; *NYH*, March 6, 1869.

28. *CG*, 41st Cong., 1st sess., 19–20; *NYT*, March 7, 1869; *NYTr*, March 8, 1869.

29. Henry C. Bowen to CS, March 6, 1869, CS-Mf; *NYH*, March 8, 1869; *NYT*, March 8, 1869.

30. *NYH*, March 9, 10, 1869; *NYTr*, March 9, 10, 1869; *NYT*, March 12, 1869; *NYS*, March 10, 1869; Harry E. Resseguie, "Federal Conflict of Interest: The A. T. Stewart Case: A Century-old Episode with Current Implications," *New York History* 47 (July 1966): 272, 296–298.

31. *NYTr*, March 8, 12, 1869; JGB to JRY, December 8, 1868, JRY-LC; JRY to WEC, December 22, 1868, WEC-NHHS; GFH to Ruth Hoar, February 28, 1869, GFH-MHS.

32. Thomas Shankland to CS, March 7, 1869, CS-Mf; *NYT*, March 4, 1869; Resseguie, "Federal Conflict of Interest," 276–277; CFA, diary, March 10, 1869, AFP-MHS.

33. JB, diary, November 9, 1868, March 13, 1869 (ts), JB-NYPL; *NYH*, March 11, 16, 1869; Horace White to EBW, March 6, 10 (telegram and letter), 1869, EBW-LC.

34. *NYH*, March 7, 10, 1869; *NYT*, March 12, 1869; Palmer, *Selected Letters of Sumner*, 2:455.

35. Charles B. Atchison to EBW, February 25, 1869, EBW-LC; GFH to Ruth Hoar, March 6, 1869, GFH-MHS; John Russell Young, *Around the World with General Grant* (New York: American News Company, 1879), 2:276; *PUSG*, 19:149–152, 180–181; EP to HF, January 20, 1869, HF-LC; G. M. Dodge to JHW, May 6, November 4, 1904, JHW-LC.

36. William H. Seward's comments appear in JB, diary, March 25, 1869 (ts), JB-NYPL; Beale, *Diary of Welles*, 3:546, 551; *NYTr*, March 12, 1869.

37. *PUSG*, 17:49n; *PUSG*, 19:88–89, 90–91, 123, 151–152; WEC to AB, September 25, 1868, USG-LC; *NYH*, February 6, 1869; W. C. Bryant to HF, February 1, 1869 (ts), HF-LC.

38. Young, *Around the World with General Grant*, 2:276–277; JHW to Sylvanus Cadwallader, September 24, 1904, "Referring to page 381," note with Grenville M. Dodge to JHW, November 4, 1904, JHW-LC; *NYH*, March 12, 1869; *NYTr*, March 12, 1869.

39. *Charleston Courier*, March 16, 1869; Beale, *Diary of Welles*, 3:550; *NYTr*, March 12, 1869; Horace White to EBW, March 10, 20, 1869, EBW-LC.

40. JRY to HG, "Sunday" [circa March 14 or 21, 1869], HG-LC (emphasis in original); CS to Charles W. Slack, March 18, 1869, CS-Mf; James G. Blaine, *Twenty Years of Congress* (Norwich, Conn.: Henry Bill, 1884, 1886), 2:449; *NYH*, March 10,

12, 14, 1869; *NYTr*, March 17, 1869; Edward McPherson, *The Political History of the United States of America during the Period of Reconstruction* (Washington, D.C.: Philp & Solomons, 1871), 414; *CG*, 41st Cong., 1st sess., 40, 88, 89.

41. *NYTr*, March 23, 24, 25, 1869; *NYH*, March 24, 25, 1869; *CG*, 41st Cong., 1st sess., 248.

42. *NYH*, March 26, 1869; *NYTr*, March 26, 1869; *CG*, 41st Cong., 1st sess., 286, 288; McPherson, *Political History during Reconstruction*, 414–415.

43. *CG*, 41st Cong., 1st sess., 395, 402, 403; Blaine, *Twenty Years of Congress*, 2:454.

44. HF, diary, April 1, 1869, HF-LC; *NYH*, April 5, 1869; *NYT*, April 6, 1869. In the case of at least one officeholder, the attorney general concluded that "the tenure of the office is [at] the President's pleasure, under the modification prescribed by the recent acts known as the Tenure of Office Acts." On another occasion, however, the administration followed the Senate's interpretation regarding the reinstatement of a suspended officer upon the rejection of a replacement nominee. *PUSG*, 21:468–469; HF, diary, December 15, 1871, HF-LC.

45. Blaine, *Twenty Years of Congress*, 2:455; *PUSG*, 19:160; ET to the Earl of Clarendon, April 19, 1869, PRO.

46. Michael Medved, *The Shadow Presidents: The Secret History of the Chief Executives and Their Top Aides* (New York: Times Books, 1979), 13; William H. Crook, *Through Five Administrations* (New York: Harper & Brothers, 1910), 155–157; *WNR*, March 10, 1869; *WES*, March 10, 1869; BM, diary, December 19, 1872, January 27, 1874, BM-LC.

47. Hiram Barney to Matias Romero, April 20, 1869, USG-USGPL; *CG*, 41st Cong., 3rd sess., 408; HF, diary, March 4, 5, 1875, HF-LC.

48. Brooks D. Simpson, "Babcock, Orville Elias," *ANB*, 1:812–813.

49. Mark Wahlgren Summers, *The Press Gang: Newspapers and Politics, 1865–1878* (Chapel Hill: University of North Carolina Press, 1994), 177, 181; OEB to AB, October 4, 1870, BW to JHW, April 18, July 27, 1875, USG-USGPL; John A. Joyce to OEB, December 16, 1870, OEB to John A. Joyce, December 20, 1870, May 21, 1872, OEB-NL; OEB to ZC, October 21, 1870, ZC-LC; OEB to HF, December 30, 1870 (ts), April 5, 1871 (ts), Donn Piatt to HF, April 29, 1871 (ts), HF to Piatt, May 1 (ts), 8 (ts), 1871, HF to JCBD, September 28, 1874, HF to John H. Clifford, February 17, 1875, HF, diary, September 21, 1874, February 21, 1875, HF-LC; OEB to JCBD, January 9, 1871, OEB to Thomas B. Van Buren, December 16, 1872, USG-LC; OEB to SC, August 16, 1872, SC-LC; OEB to WEC, August 16, 24, September 17, 26, 1872, WEC-LC; *PUSG*, 26:374; *WNR*, February 25, 1874; Cyrus B. Martin to JCBD, July 25, 1876, JCBD-LC.

50. Robert Sobel, ed., *Biographical Directory of the United States Executive Branch, 1774–1977* (Westport, Conn.: Greenwood Press, 1977), 384–385; R. C. Parsons to EBW, June 19, 1876, EBW-LC (emphasis in original).

51. Sobel, *Biographical Directory of the Executive Branch*, 31, 32–33, 75, 77, 115, 169, 283–284; Beale, *Diary of Welles*, 3:540–545.

52. HF, diary, December 20, 1870, May 4, 1875, HF-LC.

53. Hamilton Fish, "General Grant," and Edwards Pierrepont, "Personal Recollections of General Grant," *Independent*, July 30, 1885; HF, diary, March 22, 1870, HF-LC; JCBD, diary, May 30, 1873, JCBD-LC.

54. JRY to HF, November 14, 1870 (ts), HF-LC; JDC to A. F. Perry, July 29, 1870, JDC-OCL; JDC to Murat Halstead, June 16, 1870, Murat Halstead Papers, Cincinnati Historical Society (emphasis in original).

55. JDC to JAG, December 6, 1870, JAG-LC; JDC to HF, November 29, 1870, HF-LC (emphasis in original); HF to JDC, December 27, 1870, ERH to JDC, February 9, 1871, JDC to ERH, September 4, 1872, JDC to William P. Garrison, August 11, 1871, JDC-OCL; Young, *Around the World with General Grant*, 2:154; Jacob Dolson Cox, "How Judge Hoar Ceased to Be Attorney-General," *Atlantic Monthly* 76 (August 1895): 173.

56. *PUSG*, 18:292; HF to George Bancroft, February 11, 1870, HF-LC; Young, *Around the World with General Grant*, 2:265.

57. OEB to George H. Williams, February 8, 1873, USG-LC; HF, diary, November 15, 22, 23, 26, 28, 30, 1869, November 25, 1870, May 4, 1876, HF-LC; JCBD, diary, February 24, 1873, JCBD-LC; *PUSG*, 22:245, 248.

58. OEB to Horace Maynard, February 3, 1873, USG-LC; OEB to ZC, November 9, 1870, ZC-LC; JCBD, diary, February 24, 1873, JCBD-LC; HF, diary, December 9, 11, 1870, May 4, 11, 1872, June 3, 1874, March 2, 4, 1875, January 20, 1877, HF-LC; *PUSG*, 28:156; TOH to Grace Howe, March 8, 1875, TOH-WHS.

59. Young, *Around the World with General Grant*, 2:264; HF, diary, January 7, 10, June 14, 1870, April 28, 1874, HF-LC; C. H. Hill to BHB, March 6, 1874, BHB-LC; William D. Mallam, "The Grant-Butler Relationship," *Mississippi Valley Historical Review* 41 (September 1954): 259–276; Beale, *Diary of Welles*, 3:565; *PUSG*, 28:367.

60. *PUSG*, 20:190, 24:234; S. S. Cox to MM, December 17, 1869 (emphasis in original), Edward Spencer to MM, November 5, 1874, MM-LC; Abram S. Hewitt, "Memorandum of Conversation with President Grant," December 3, 1876, AN-CU.

61. Donald, *Sumner*, 2:564; Young, *Around the World with General Grant*, 2:263–264; CS to S. G. Howe, March 28, 1869, CS to Henry B. Anthony, April 29, 1869, Anthony to CS, May 3, 1869, CS-Mf; Palmer, *Selected Letters of Sumner*, 2:457.

62. CS to S. G. Howe, March 28, 1869, CS-Mf; HF to Justin S. Morrill, September 6, 1870, HF-LC; BHB to JMH, December 24, 1870, JMH-LC.

63. CFA, diary, January 22, 1869, AFP-MHS; *CG*, 41st Cong., 2nd sess., 4194–4195; J. M. Howard to JCBD, June 18, 1870, JCBD-LC (emphasis in original); HF to EBW, February 20, 1871, HF-LC; CS to Anna C. Lodge, [June 8, 1872] (ts), CS to Henry W. Longfellow, June 7, 1872, CS to James Freeman Clarke, [June 7, 1872], CS-Mf; *PUSG*, 28:305.

64. Levenson et al., *Letters of Henry Adams*, 2:10, 13, 15 (emphasis in original); Brooks D. Simpson, *The Political Education of Henry Adams* (Columbia: University of South Carolina Press, 1996), 20–25, 32–40.

65. Levenson et al., *Letters of Henry Adams*, 2:22, 23, 25.

66. Ibid., 2:43, 43n, 50, 51; Henry Adams, "Civil Service Reform," in *The Great Secession Winter of 1860–61 and Other Essays by Henry Adams*, ed. George Hochfield (New York: Sagamore Press, 1958), 97–128; *M and P*, 7:38.

67. Levenson et al., *Letters of Henry Adams*, 2:55, 56.

68. Henry Adams, "The Session. 1869–1870," in Hochfield, *Great Secession Winter*, 193–222.

69. T. O. Howe, *Political History. The Republican Party Defended. A Reviewer Reviewed* (n.p., [1870]); TOH to Grace Howe, December 9, 1870, TOH-WHS; *PUSG*, 20:318; Levenson et al., *Letters of Henry Adams*, 2:95; Simpson, *Political Education of Henry Adams*, 68–70; introduction to "The Session. 1869–1870," in Hochfield, *Great Secession Winter*, 191.

70. HF, diary, February 9, 1870, HF-LC.

71. Janet E. Steele, *The Sun Shines for All: Journalism and Ideology in the Life of Charles A. Dana* (Syracuse, N.Y.: Syracuse University Press, 1993), 101–103; CAD to JHW, October 17, 1869, USG-USGPL; HF to J. Watson Webb, January 1, 1870, HF to Archibald Russell, January 23, 1870, HF to Francis Lieber, September 12, 1870, JCBD to HF, August 9, 1870 (ts), HF, diary, December 23, 1869, June 14, December 5, 1870, HF-LC; Summers, *Press Gang*, 171–188.

72. HF, diary, April 27, 1870, February 3, 1873, December 22, 1874, HF to J. G. Bennett, March 21, 1872 (ts), HF to L. J. Jennings, July 25, 1875, HF to JCBD, January 6, 1875, HF to George Bancroft, January 25, 1870, HF-LC; GFH to Mrs. GFH, June 19, 1870, GFH-MHS; Hasbrouck Davis to JCBD, May 26, 31, [1869], JCBD-LC; OEB to ZC, October 21, 1870, ZC-LC.

73. *PUSG*, 19:119–120; House Report No. 2512, 52nd Cong., 2nd sess.; *WNR*, March 4, 1873, February 12, April 13, 1874, July 23, 1875; WR to Lewis Wallace, March 16, 1873, WR-LC; HF, diary, April 13, 14, 21, June 10, September 9, 22, 1874, July 21, 23, 1875, HF to Thurlow Weed, May 27, 1872, HF-LC.

74. JAJC to ZC, September 9, 1869, ZC-LC; JAJC to "My dear Mother," October 25, 1871, JAJC-LC.

75. JMH to BHB, September 27, 1871, BHB-LC; JB, diary, August 29, 1869 (ts), JB-NYPL; *PUSG*, 30:19; *PUSG*, 26:327.

76. *WNR*, September 20, 1871; *PUSG*, 26:342–344; J. S. Clarkson to OEB, December 2, 1875, USG-LC.

77. HF to RCS, September 28, 1875; HF-LC; *PUSG*, 21:350; *PUSG*, 22:194; DeB. Randolph Keim to J. D. Cameron, September 4, 1869, KFP-LC; *PUSG*, 22:140–142, 155, 157; *PUSG*, 24:190; *PUSG*, 25:186–187; *PUSG*, 26:274, 279.

78. *PUSG*, 30:265; HF, diary, June 25, 1870, HF-LC.

79. Charles Sumner, *Republicanism vs. Grantism* (Washington, D.C.: F. & J.

Rives & Geo. A. Bailey, 1872), 7; James W. Forsyth to JHW, October 7, 1871, JHW-LC; HP to OEB, September 20, 1870, USG-LC; OEB to BHB, July 14, 1874, BHB-LC; *PUSG*, 23:172, 195–196; *M and P*, 7:221.

80. *Journal of the House of Representatives*, 44th Cong., 1st sess., 724; *M and P*, 7:361–366; HF, diary, April 4, 25, May 4, 5, 1876, HF-LC.

81. P. N. Reed to EBW, February 23, 1869, EBW-LC (emphasis in original).

CHAPTER 4. RECONSTRUCTION

1. *PUSG*, 18:292.

2. *M and P*, 7:11; Brooks D. Simpson, *The Reconstruction Presidents* (Lawrence: University Press of Kansas, 1998), 135–139.

3. Edward McPherson, *The Political History of the United States of America during the Period of Reconstruction* (Washington, D.C.: Philp & Solomons, 1871), 395; *Bangor Daily Whig and Courier*, March 20, 1869.

4. W. L. Sharkey to HG, March 30, 1869, HG-LC; William C. Harris, *The Day of the Carpetbagger: Republican Reconstruction in Mississippi* (Baton Rouge: Louisiana State University Press, 1979), 214; *WNR*, April 5, 1869; Jack P. Maddex Jr., *The Virginia Conservatives, 1867–1879: A Study in Reconstruction Politics* (Chapel Hill: University of North Carolina Press, 1970), 58–59; HF, diary, April 5, 1869, HF-LC; *M and P*, 7:11–12.

5. *M and P*, 7:11–12.

6. *CG*, 41st Cong., 1st sess., 633, 635, 653, 656, 661, 662, 699, 700; McPherson, *Political History during Reconstruction*, 408–410.

7. *NYH*, April 9, 10, 1869; CFA, diary, April 12, 1869, AFP-MHS; *CG*, 41st Cong., 1st sess., 607; CS to John M. Forbes, April 14, 1869, CS-Mf.

8. *PUSG*, 19:488–489; Adam Badeau, *Grant in Peace* (Hartford, Conn.: S. S. Scranton, 1887), 26–27; *NYH*, May 2, 1869; *WES*, May 3, 1869; *NYT*, May 4, 1869; William B. Hesseltine, *Ulysses S. Grant: Politician* (New York: Dodd, Mead, 1935), 181.

9. Richard Lowe, *Republicans and Reconstruction in Virginia, 1856–70* (Charlottesville: University Press of Virginia, 1991), 177–179; *NYTr*, July 13, 14, 15, 16, 1869; *NYT*, July 20, 1869; JAG to JDC, July 19, 1869, JDC to JAG, July 26, 1869, JAG-LC; HG to JDC, July 13, 1869, JDC-OCL; *New York Evening Post* quoted in *NYT*, July 20, 1869. See also Allan Nevins, *Hamilton Fish: The Inner History of the Grant Administration* (New York: Dodd, Mead, 1937), 290; Carl H. Moneyhon, *Republicanism in Reconstruction Texas* (Austin: University of Texas Press, 1980), 273n29.

10. *M and P*, 7:16–18; JAJC to ZC, September 9, 1869, ZC-LC; *PUSG*, 19:221–222; Harris, *Day of the Carpetbagger*, 224–257.

11. Thomas B. Alexander, "Political Reconstruction in Tennessee, 1865–1870," in *Radicalism, Racism, and Party Realignment: The Border States during*

NOTES TO PAGES 99–106

Reconstruction, ed. Richard O. Curry (Baltimore: Johns Hopkins Press, 1969), 71–72; Moneyhon, *Republicanism in Reconstruction Texas,* 106–107, 112–123; HP to JHW, October 27, 1869, JHW-LC; Harris, *Day of the Carpetbagger,* 257.

12. Eric Foner, *Reconstruction: America's Unfinished Revolution, 1863–1877* (New York: Harper & Row, 1988), 331–332, 342, 347; Senate Executive Document No. 3, 41st Cong., 2nd sess., 2.

13. *NYT,* September 9, 1869; James Fitzpatrick to BFB, September 17, 1869, BFB-LC; *M and P,* 7:28; HF, diary, January 21, 1870, HF-LC; McPherson, *Political History during Reconstruction,* 609–611; Senate Executive Document 41, 41st Cong., 2nd sess.

14. *M and P,* 7:29; *CG,* 41st Cong., 2nd sess., 325, 362, 502–503; McPherson, *Political History during Reconstruction,* 572–579.

15. *PUSG,* 20:15–16, 133; HF, diary, February 4, March 1, 7, 15, 30, 1870, HF-LC; House Executive Document No. 15, 41st Cong., 2nd sess.; Senate Executive Document No. 63, 41st Cong., 2nd sess.; J. R. Hawley to CS, March 23, 1870, CS-Mf; *NYH,* March 29, 1870; McPherson, *Political History during Reconstruction,* 578; *M and P,* 7:56–57.

16. *M and P,* 7:55–57; GFH draft to USG, March [29], 1870, GFH-MHS; *PUSG,* 32:121.

17. *WNR,* April 2, 1870.

18. HF, diary, March 15, April 15, 1870, HF-LC; *NYH,* April 14, 1870.

19. *NYH,* April 14, 1870; Charles W. Calhoun, *Conceiving a New Republic: The Republican Party and the Southern Question, 1869–1900* (Lawrence: University Press of Kansas, 2006), 19; Simpson, *Reconstruction Presidents,* 151.

20. *CG,* 41st Cong., 1st sess., 3607–3610; McPherson, *Political History during Reconstruction,* 546–550.

21. *PUSG,* 20:18, 426–427; McPherson, *Political History during Reconstruction,* 616–619; *CG,* 41st Cong., 2nd sess., 5123; HF, diary, July 10, 11, 1870, HF-LC.

22. McPherson, *Political History during Reconstruction,* 616–619; *CG,* 41st Cong., 2nd sess., 5121; Calhoun, *Conceiving a New Republic,* 23–24.

23. 16 *Statutes at Large* 162–165; *CG,* 41st Cong., 2nd sess., 3035; Robert M. Goldman, *"A Free Ballot and a Fair Count": The Department of Justice and the Enforcement of Voting Rights in the South, 1877–1893* (New York: Fordham University Press, 2001), 35–37.

24. HF, diary, June 13, 17, 1870, HF-LC; *NYH,* December 16, 18, 23, 24, 1869, June 17, 1870; *WES,* December 28, 1869, January 6, 1870; Moorfield Storey and Edward W. Emerson, *Ebenezer Rockwood Hoar: A Memoir* (Boston: Houghton Mifflin, 1911), 190–193; ERH to JDC, December 25, 1869, JDC to A. F. Perry, July 29, 1870, JDC-OCL; *Journal of the Executive Proceedings of the Senate of the United States,* 41st Cong., 2nd sess., 329–330, 357, 480.

25. William S. McFeely, "Amos T. Akerman: The Lawyer and Racial Justice," in *Region, Race, and Reconstruction: Essays in Honor of C. Vann Woodward,* ed. J. Morgan Kouser and James M. McPherson (New York: Oxford University

Press, 1982), 395–404; Ross A. Webb, *Benjamin Helm Bristow: Border State Politician* (Lexington: University Press of Kentucky, 1969), 21–34, 52–60.

26. Amos T. Akerman to CS, April ?, 1869, CS-Mf; Webb, *Bristow*, 72; McFeely, "Akerman," 405; Calhoun, *Conceiving a New Republic*, 24–25; *PUSG*, 20:251–252; HF, diary, October 18, 21, 24, 28, November 1, 1870, HF-LC; HF to JCBD, November 7, 1870, JCBD-LC.

27. *NYT*, November 8, 9, 10, 1870; Xi Wang, *The Trial of Democracy: Black Suffrage and Northern Republicans, 1860–1910* (Athens: University of Georgia Press, 1997), 79.

28. Allen W. Trelease, *White Terror: The Ku Klux Klan Conspiracy and Southern Reconstruction* (New York: Harper & Row, 1971), 223, 240–242, 270–273, 385–386; Foner, *Reconstruction*, 441–444; Wang, *Trial of Democracy*, 79–80; Kenneth C. Martis, *The Historical Atlas of Political Parties in the United States Congress, 1789–1989* (New York: Macmillan, 1989), 122–125; *M and P*, 7:96, 112.

CHAPTER 5. RECONSTRUCTING THE NATION'S FINANCES

1. *CG*, 40th Cong., 3rd sess., 1880.

2. *M and P*, 7:7; Edward McPherson, *The Political History of the United States of America during the Period of Reconstruction* (Washington, D.C.: Philp & Solomons, 1871), 412–413; 16 *Statutes at Large*, 1.

3. *Report of the Secretary of the Treasury for 1869* (Washington, D.C.: Government Printing Office, 1869), xii; 12 *Statutes at Large*, 545–548; Irwin Unger, *The Greenback Era: A Social and Political History of American Finance, 1865–1879* (Princeton, N.J.: Princeton University Press, 1964), 15n5.

4. Richard H. Timberlake, *Monetary Policy in the United States: An Intellectual and Institutional History* (Chicago: University of Chicago Press, 1993), 88–91; Unger, *Greenback Era*, 42–43, 117; *M and P*, 7:7.

5. Unger, *Greenback Era*, 44, 164–165; *Report of the Secretary of the Treasury for 1869*, xiii–xiv; *Report of the Secretary of the Treasury for 1871* (Washington, D.C.: Government Printing Office, 1871), ix.

6. JRY to HG, "Sunday" [March 14 or 21, 1869], HG-LC; *NYH*, March 20, June 14, 1869; GSB to HG, April 22, 1869, HG-NYPL; Samuel Hooper to CS, September 28, 1869, CS-Mf; George S. Boutwell, *Reminiscences of Sixty Years in Public Affairs* (New York: McClure, Phillips, 1902), 2:137–139; *Report of the Secretary of the Treasury for 1869*, xiii; EBW to GSB, June 19, 1869, EBW-LC; Unger, *Greenback Era*, 164–167.

7. Sidney Andrews to EBW, December 9, 1869, EBW-LC; DeB. Randolph Keim to James Gordon Bennett, September 22, 1869, KFP-LC; *M and P*, 7:29–31; *Report of the Secretary of the Treasury for 1869*, xii–xiii, xv–xviii.

8. *M and P*, 7:30; Sidney Ratner, *American Taxation: Its History as a Social Force*

in Democracy (New York: W. W. Norton, 1942), 73, 85–86, 98, 114, 116; United States Internal Revenue, Annual Taxes, 1869, tax return form, BFP-LC; *Report of the Special Commissioner of the Revenue 1869*, House Executive Document No. 27, 41st Cong., 2nd sess., lxviii–lxx; HF, diary, November 15, 1869, June 28, 1870, HF-LC; *PUSG*, 20:23.

9. *M and P*, 7:30, 37; USG, draft of annual message [December 6, 1869], *PUSG*, 20:23.

10. *Report of the Special Commissioner of the Revenue 1869*, lxxii (emphasis in original); 14 *Statutes at Large* 170–171; *Report of the Special Commissioner of the Revenue for the Year 1868* (Washington, D.C.: Government Printing Office, 1868), 80; Horace White to EBW, October 18, 1868, EBW-LC; White to DAW, December 24, 1869, DAW-LC; Hasbrouck Davis to JCBD, December 30, 1869, JCBD-LC.

11. DAW to MM, June 27, 1869, March 25, April 6, 1870, DAW to J. S. Moore, March 24, 1870, Moore to MM, April 25, 1870, Samuel Ward to [MM], June 2, 1870, MM-LC; J. C. Levenson et al., eds., *The Letters of Henry Adams* (Cambridge, Mass.: Harvard University Press, 1982), 2:68; Horace White to DAW, June 3, 1870, JAG to DAW, June 13, 1870, DAW-LC; *CG*, 41st Cong., 2nd sess., 618.

12. Samuel Ward to [MM], June 2, 1870, MM-LC; *NYH*, June 2, 1870; Charles Nordhoff to CS, June 8, 1870, CS-Mf; Hugh McCulloch to DAW, November 6, 1870, W. C. Bryant to Nordhoff, June 6, 1870, DAW-LC.

13. HF, diary, May 3, 1879, HF-LC; JCBD to Charles Nordhoff, May 4, 1870 [draft], JCBD-LC.

14. *NYT*, July 14, 15, 1870; 16 *Statutes at Large* 256–274; Davis Rich Dewey, *Financial History of the United States* (New York: Longmans, Green, 1903), 394; Edward Stanwood, *American Tariff Controversies of the Nineteenth Century* (Boston: Houghton, Mifflin, 1903), 173; F. W. Taussig, *The Tariff History of the United States* (New York: G. P. Putnam's Sons, 1914), 178–179; McPherson, *Political History during Reconstruction*, 609.

15. *M and P*, 7:7, 39, 40; EBW to HF, December 31, 1869, EBW-LC.

16. *CG*, 41st Cong., 2nd sess., appendix, 78.

17. Ibid., 51. Dawes revealed his meeting with Grant in a subsequent speech (ibid., 78–79).

18. Benjamin F. Butler, *Public Expenditures of Grant's Administration* (Washington, D.C.: Congressional Globe Office, 1870); *CG*, 41st Cong., 2nd sess., appendix, 79; *PUSG*, 20:89–90; *NYH*, January 22, 24, 1870; C. C. Washburn to EBW, February 28, 1870, EBW-LC; HF, diary, January 25, February 9, 1870, HF-LC.

19. SB to HLD, January 20, 1870, HLD-LC; JCBD to William A. Crafts, February 23, 1870, JCBD-LC.

20. Onslow Stearns to BFB, February 11, 1870 BFB-LC; *NYT*, February 21, 1870; *Boston Daily Advertiser*, February 28, 1870; *PUSG*, 20:401.

21. Butler, *Public Expenditures of Grant's Administration*, 15; J. S. Krander to HLD, January 19, 1870, Harrison Homer to HLD, January 22, 1870, W. M. Hilton

to HLD, January 22, 1870, Albert G. Browne to HLD, January 23, 1870, T. W. Stanley to HLD, February 5, 1870, Charles Naylor to HLD, January 23, 1870, HLD-LC.

22. *M and P*, 7:53–55; HF, diary, November 19, 1869, HF-LC; *NYH*, March 25, 1870; Mark Wahlgren Summers, *The Era of Good Stealings* (New York: Oxford University Press, 1993), 130–131; Leonard D. White, *The Republican Era: A Study in Administrative History, 1869–1901* (New York: Free Press, 1958), 58–60; *The Statistical History of the United States from Colonial Times to the Present* (New York: Basic Books, 1976), 1104.

23. *Hepburn v. Griswold*, 8 Wallace 603 (1870); John Niven, ed., *The Salmon P. Chase Papers* (Kent, Ohio: Kent State University Press, 1993–1998), 5:327; Henry Adams, "The Session, 1869–1870," in *The Great Secession Winter of 1860–61 and Other Essays by Henry Adams*, ed. George Hochfield (New York: Sagamore Press, 1958), 209.

24. Unger, *Greenback Era*, 175–177; John G. Sproat, *"The Best Men": Liberal Reformers in the Gilded Age* (New York: Oxford University Press, 1968), 188–189; *CG*, 41st Cong., 2nd sess., 1588; JB, diary, Monday, February 13 [12], 1877, JB-NYPL.

25. "The Legal Tender Cases in 1870," in *Miscellaneous Writings of the Late Hon. Joseph P. Bradley*, ed. Charles Bradley (Newark, N.J.: L. J. Hardham, 1901), 61–74; Charles Fairman, "Mr. Justice Bradley's Appointment to the Supreme Court and the Legal Tender Cases," *Harvard Law Review* 54 (April 1941): 1006; Stephen J. Field to SJT, March 8, 1870, SJT-NYPL.

26. *NYH*, December 16, 18, 23, 24, 1869; *Journal of the Executive Proceedings of the Senate of the United States*, 41st Cong., 2nd sess., 330; *WES*, December 28, 1869, January 6, 1870; ERH to JDC, December 25, 1869, JDC-OCL; Moorfield Storey and Edward W. Emerson, *Ebenezer Rockwood Hoar: A Memoir* (Boston: Houghton Mifflin, 1911), 190–193; Fairman, "Mr. Justice Bradley's Appointment," 1007–1008; HF, diary, January 7, 10, 1870, HF-LC; Bradley, *Miscellaneous Writings*, 61; *NYTr*, February 4, 1870.

27. *Journal of the Executive Proceedings of the Senate of the United States*, 41st Cong., 2nd sess., 359–360; CFA, diary, February 10, 1870, AFP-MHS; Adams, "The Session, 1869–1870," 210–211; T. O. Howe, *Political History. The Republican Party Defended. A Reviewer Reviewed* (n.p., [1870]), 11; ERH to HF, October 26, 1876, HF, diary, October 28, 1876, HF to ERH, October 29, 1876, HF to Sidney Webster, November 15, 1876, HF-LC. For treatments of the Court-packing controversy, see Sidney Ratner, "Was the Supreme Court Packed by President Grant," *Political Science Quarterly* 50 (September 1935): 343–358; Fairman, "Mr. Justice Bradley's Appointment," 977–1034.

28. *PUSG*, 20:56; Fairman, "Mr. Justice Bradley's Appointment," 977–1009.

29. Erwin Stanley Bradley, *Simon Cameron: Lincoln's Secretary of War* (Philadelphia: University of Pennsylvania Press, 1966), 313; Wayne MacVeagh to SC, December 11, 1869, John W. Forney to SC, December 24, 1869, SC-LC; EP to HF,

December 17, 1869 (ts), HF to EP, December 19, 1869, HF-LC; EP to EMS, December 20, 21, 1869, EMS-LC.

30. HF, diary, October 28, 1876, HF-LC. Cf. J. D. Cox's recollection after twenty-five years in JDC to GFH, November 6, 1896, JDC-OCL.

31. HF, diary, November 20, 1869, October 28, 1876, HF-LC; Boutwell, *Reminiscences*, 2:208–210.

32. *Journal of the Executive Proceedings of the Senate of the United States*, 41st Cong., 2nd sess., 402; *NYTr*, March 28, April 1, 1870; Charles Fairman, *Mr. Justice Miller and the Supreme Court, 1862–1890* (New York: Russell & Russell, 1939), 169–173; *Knox v. Lee* and *Parker v. Davis*, 12 Wallace 457 (1871); Boutwell, *Reminiscences*, 2:210.

CHAPTER 6. BRUSH WITH DISASTER

1. *Gold Panic Investigation*, House Report No. 31, 41st Cong., 2nd sess. This report of the congressional investigation into the conspiracy is the essential source for the incident, although some participants who testified had faulty memories or a tendency to distort the facts for self-serving reasons. The evidence is contradictory and requires extrapolation. See also Maury Klein, *The Life and Legend of Jay Gould* (Baltimore: Johns Hopkins University Press, 1986), 99–115. Henry Adams used a selective reading of the House report as the basis for an article published in the *Westminster Review*, "The New York Gold Conspiracy," reprinted in *The Great Secession Winter of 1860–61 and Other Essays by Henry Adams*, ed. George Hochfield (New York: Sagamore Press, 1958), 159–189. A popularized treatment is Kenneth D. Ackerman, *The Gold Ring: Jim Fisk, Jay Gould and Black Friday, 1869* (New York: Harper & Row, 1988).

2. *Gold Panic Investigation*, 135, 152.

3. Ibid., 366; H. D. Cooke to JS, June 18, 1869, JS-LC.

4. *Gold Panic Investigation*, 154; *NYT*, March 29, 1880; *PUSG*, 20:234; John Y. Simon, ed., *The Personal Memoirs of Julia Dent Grant* (New York: G. P. Putnam's Sons, 1975), 160–161, 167n12; House Report No. 414, 35th Cong., 1st sess., 6–9.

5. House Report No. 414, 35th Cong., 1st sess., 6, 7.

6. *Gold Panic Investigation*, 152, 160–161, 163, 243, 314–319, 437–440; Edward G. Longacre, "Butterfield, Daniel," *ANB*, 4:114–116; Simon, *Personal Memoirs of Julia Dent Grant*, 167n12; *PUSG*, 19:258; *NYT*, June 24, 1869.

7. *Gold Panic Investigation*, 245, 152–154, 172.

8. *NYT*, June 17–21, 1869.

9. *Gold Panic Investigation*, 354–355, 366; H. D. Cooke to JS, June 18, 1869, JS-LC; JB, diary, August 29, 1869 (ts), JB-NYPL; *NYT*, August 6, 1869.

10. *Gold Panic Investigation*, 153–154, 243–244; *NYT*, August 14, 16, 18, September 13, 1869; *WNR*, August 14, 19, 1869. A close reading of Gould's testimony,

Corbin's testimony, and contemporary press reports of Grant's movements demonstrates that Gould conflated and reversed the sequence of this August 13 meeting and one with Grant at Corbin's house on September 11.

11. *Gold Panic Investigation*, 172–173, 244; *NYH*, October 4, 1869; *NYT*, October 4, 1869.

12. *Gold Panic Investigation*, 164, 268–269, 272–273, 275–279, 376; *PUSG*, 19:256; *NYT*, August 25, 1869.

13. *Gold Panic Investigation*, 5–6, 276, 354–355, 372–273, 428. What purported to be Boutwell's answer to Gould, dated September 9, 1869, appeared in the *New York Sun* on October 8, 1869.

14. *NYT*, August 25, 26, 1869; *Gold Panic Investigation*, 376.

15. *Gold Panic Investigation*, 162, 246–248, 267, 313, 317; *NYT*, August 31, September 1, 1869.

16. *Gold Panic Investigation*, 358–361 (emphasis added).

17. Adams, "New York Gold Conspiracy," 173–174. In addition, Adams misread Gould's testimony and confused the circumstances surrounding Grant's writing of the September 2 letter with one he wrote to Boutwell on September 12. *Gold Panic Investigation*, 155.

18. JDC to JAG, July 26, 1869, JAG-LC; Burke A. Hinsdale, *The Works of James Abram Garfield* (Boston: James R. Osgood, 1882), 1:629; Jean Edward Smith, *Grant* (New York: Simon & Schuster, 2001), 483. Some grounds exist for doubting that Grant ever wrote the September 2 letter. Under questioning by the investigating committee, Corbin denied that Grant had "countermanded" an order by Boutwell to sell gold, adding, "nor do I believe that there ever was such a transaction." Also, although Boutwell spoke of the letter in his congressional testimony, in his memoirs he made no mention of the September 2 letter, and twice he positively denied receiving such an order. *Gold Panic Investigation*, 249; George S. Boutwell, *Reminiscences of Sixty Years in Public Affairs* (New York: McClure, Phillips, 1902), 2:164–182, especially 169, 171.

19. *Gold Panic Investigation*, 310, 359, 366, 376.

20. Ibid., 151, 163, 168, 253–255.

21. In his later testimony, Gould was confused about the timing of this meeting, but it can be placed on September 11 on the basis of the testimony by Corbin and Porter and by the fact that Gould indicated it took place after the funeral of Secretary of War John A. Rawlins on September 9. Grant arrived in New York on September 10. Gould confused this encounter with one that occurred on August 13. Ibid., 153–155, 244–245, 447–448.

22. Ibid., 153–154, 244, 246, 247, 249, 447–448. Corbin testified that he could not remember whether this incident with the doorman took place in June or September. But at the June meeting Gould had been with several other men, and on September 11 he had come to the house alone. The incident took place on September 11. When Gould and Porter were alone in the room, Gould offered to

buy gold on Porter's behalf, an offer Porter rebuffed. Gould repeated the offer by letter, and Porter again declined. Ibid., 445–447.

23. Ibid., 155, 162, 244, 317, 359, 360.

24. John A. Carpenter, "Washington, Pennsylvania, and the Gold Conspiracy of 1869," *Western Pennsylvania Historical Magazine* 48 (October 1965): 349–350; DeB. Randolph Keim to James Gordon Bennett, September 3, 16, 1869, KFP-LC.

25. DeB. Randolph Keim to James Gordon Bennett, September 16, 25 (telegram), 1869, KFP-LC; *PUSG*, 19:245; *NYH*, October 11, 1869. In Keim's telegram to Bennett and in another to Porter, he mistakenly referred to Grant's letter as being dated September 13.

26. *Gold Panic Investigation*, 155, 249, 313, 317, 339.

27. Ibid., 344, 366; *NYT*, September 17, 1869; *NYH*, September 17, 1869.

28. *Gold Panic Investigation*, 155, 158, 174, 249–250.

29. Ibid., 355, 373.

30. Ibid., 172–173, 258–259, 262. Corbin testified that on July 24 he had purchased $250,000 in bonds and subsequently offered "to let Mrs. Grant in for one half," but she declined. Corbin's step-son-in-law Robert Catherwood later claimed that, according to Corbin, the Grants had given him "a few thousand dollars" left over from their house sale to invest "in what way he thought best." This claim was not substantiated or even explored in subsequent testimony, and Catherwood stated that "outside of Mr. Corbin," he had no knowledge of any member of Grant's family being interested in the sale or purchase of gold. Ibid., 270–271, 443–444.

31. Ibid., 155, 249, 230–233, 250, 444–445, 448–449.

32. No one preserved Julia Grant's letter, but the various recollections of its contents essentially agree. Ibid., 156–159, 251–252, 448; Simon, *Personal Memoirs of Julia Dent Grant*, 182.

33. *Gold Panic Investigation*, 156–159, 251–257 (emphasis in original).

34. Ibid., 12–13, 141–142, 157, 256.

35. Ibid., 13, 165, 175; *NYT*, September 24, 1869.

36. *NYH*, September 24, 1869 (emphasis in original); *Gold Panic Investigation*, 15–17, 161, 167, 181, 202, 205–207, 344–347; *Harper's Weekly*, October 9, 1869.

37. *Gold Panic Investigation*, 158, 175–176, 260–266.

38. Ibid., 176, 266–267, 366, 446–447; *NYH*, September 27, 1869.

39. *Gold Panic Investigation*, 17, 18; Klein, *Life and Legend of Jay Gould*, 114–115.

40. *Gold Panic Investigation*, 187, 209, 290, 333–335; *NYT*, September 30, 1869.

41. *NYH*, September 30, October 4, 1869; *NYS*, October 1, 2, 1869.

42. *NYH*, October 8, 1869; *NYS*, October 5, 6, 7, 8, 11, 1869. Two years later, the *Sun* changed its mind. *NYS*, September 23, 1871.

43. John Covode to WEC, September 21, 1869 (telegram), WEC-LC; *NYH*, October 10, 1869; *Congressional Quarterly's Guide to U.S. Elections* (Washington, D.C.: Congressional Quarterly, 1994), 437, 700, 703; *PUSG*, 19:255–256.

44. EBW to HLD, November 8, 1869, JGB to EBW, October 27, 1869 (emphasis in original), EBW-LC.

45. *NYH*, October 11, 23, 25, 1869.

46. *NYS*, October 20, 1869; *Gold Panic Investigation*, 327–328, 352–353, 379–384; JGB to EBW, October 27, 1869, EBW-LC; *NYT*, November 17, 1869.

47. *M and P*, 7:29.

48. *CG*, 41st Cong., 2nd sess., 99–100.

49. Mary L. Hinsdale, ed., *Garfield-Hinsdale Letters: Correspondence between James Abram Garfield and Burke Aaron Hinsdale* (Ann Arbor: University of Michigan Press, 1949), 157; JDC to JAG, February 1, 1870, JAG-LC; *Gold Panic Investigation*, 471–473.

50. *Gold Panic Investigation*, 1–23.

51. S. S. Cox to MM, December 17, 1869 (emphasis in original), February 27, 1870, MM-LC; *Gold Panic Investigation*, 461–479; HF, diary, June 17, 1870, HF-LC.

52. DeB. Randolph Keim to James Gordon Bennett, September16, 1869, KFP-LC.

53. Ibid.

54. *NYH*, October 5, 1869; D. B. Eaton to JCBD, October 19, 1869, JCBD-LC.

55. Adams, "New York Gold Conspiracy," 159–189; Henry Adams, *The Education of Henry Adams* (1918; reprint, Boston: Houghton Mifflin, 1961), 270, 292; Charles Sumner, *Republicanism vs. Grantism* (Washington, D.C.: F. & J. Rives & Geo. A. Bailey, 1872), 7.

56. JHW to HP, October 12, 1869, JHW to "My dear Friend," October 13, 1869, JHW-LC.

57. JHW to HP, October 12, 1869, JHW-LC; *PUSG*, 19:261 (emphasis in original); Hamlin Garland, "An Interview with General Harry Wilson" (ts), University of Southern California Library; HP to JHW, September 9, 1869, USG-USGPL; HP to WWB, October 10, 1869, WWB-PU; *WNR*, October 14, 1869; Paul Clayton Pehrson, "James Harrison Wilson: The Post-War Years, 1865–1925" (Ph.D. diss., University of Wisconsin, 1993), 119–122.

CHAPTER 7. RECONSTRUCTING AMERICAN FOREIGN POLICY

1. *M and P*, 7:8; *NYH*, March 6, 1869.

2. William B. Hesseltine, *Ulysses S. Grant: Politician* (New York: Dodd, Mead, 1935), 52–53; *PUSG*, 15:186, 206, 285.

3. USG, "Reasons Why San Domingo Should Be Annexed to the United States," [circa 1869], USG-LC; *M and P*, 7:99.

4. Allan Nevins, *Hamilton Fish: The Inner History of the Grant Administration* (New York: Dodd, Mead, 1937), 23–65.

5. Manfred Jonas, "Davis, Bancroft," *ANB*, 6:168–170; Lilian Handlin, "Cushing, Caleb," *ANB*, 5:909–910; Nevins, *Fish*, 117, 863–864.

6. HF to CS, March 13, 1869, CS to S. G. Howe, March 28, April 25, 1869, CS to F. W. Bird, March 30, 1869, CS-Mf; CFA, diary, January 10, 1869, AFP-MHS.

7. JGB to EBW, October 24, 1868, EBW-LC; CFA, diary, March 15, 1869, AFP-MHS.

8. Adrian Cook, *The Alabama Claims: American Politics and Anglo-American Relations, 1865–1872* (Ithaca, N.Y.: Cornell University Press, 1975), 15–65; *FRUS, 1868–1869*, 402–403.

9. Beverly Wilson Palmer, ed., *The Selected Letters of Charles Sumner* (Boston: Northeastern University Press, 1990), 2:454; *NYT*, April 14, 1869; JRY to George W. Smalley, March 2, 1869, WR-LC; USG to HF, April 7, 1869, HF-LC.

10. *NYT*, April 15, 1869.

11. *Journal of the Executive Proceedings of the Senate of the United States*, 41st Cong., special sess., 163; T. L. Smith to CS, April 26, 1869, John E. Addicks to CS, May 27, 1869, Frederick Douglass to CS, April 26, 1869, Cephas Brainerd to CS, April 15, 1869, CS-Mf; Howard K. Beale, ed., *The Diary of Gideon Welles* (New York: W. W. Norton, 1960), 3:578–579; *NYH*, April 15, 16, 1869.

12. J. C. Levenson et al., eds., *The Letters of Henry Adams* (Cambridge, Mass.: Harvard University Press, 1982), 2:33–34; CFA, diary, April 15, June 16, 1869, AFP-MHS.

13. E. Argyll to CS, May [?], 1869, CS-Mf; Palmer, *Selected Letters of Sumner*, 2:462; ET to the Earl of Clarendon, April 19, 1869, PRO; BM, diary, May 1, 3, 13, 1869, BM-LC.

14. *NYH*, June 3, 1869; ET to the Earl of Clarendon, May 17, 1869, PRO; HF to John C. Hamilton, April 22, 1869 (ts), HF-LC.

15. *Journal of the Executive Proceedings of the Senate of the United States*, 41st Cong., special sess., 162; David Herbert Donald, *Charles Sumner* (1970; reprint, New York: Da Capo, 1996), 2:279; Edward L. Pierce to CS, January 8, 1869, CS-Mf; HF to John C. Hamilton, April 22, 1869 (ts), HF-LC.

16. HF to John C. Hamilton, April 22, 1869 (ts), HF-LC; *CG*, 41st Cong., special sess., 730.

17. HF to CS, July 18, 1870, CS-Mf; Palmer, *Selected Letters of Sumner*, 2:509–510; "Memoir J. L. Motley, Washington, 26th April, 1869" (ts), HF-LC.

18. CFA, diary, May 15, 1869, AFP-MHS; HF to BM, December 30, 1870, Senate Executive Document No. 11, 41st Cong., 3rd sess., 28; HF to JLM, May 17, 1869, HF-LC.

19. Nevins, *Fish*, 177–180.

20. HF, diary, March 19, 24, 25, April 6, 19, 20, 1869, HF-LC; *CG*, 41st Cong., 1st sess., 712; *NYH*, April 13, 1869.

21. Fish's draft passage is in "Sumner's Proposed Alteration in the Instructions to Motley, May 1869," HF-LC.

22. Fish's and Sumner's draft passages are in ibid. Fish recounted his argument with Sumner in a conversation with Edward Thornton. See ET to the Earl of Clarendon, May 25, 1869, PRO. A slightly different version of their encounter

appears in J. C. Bancroft Davis, *Mr. Fish and the Alabama Claims: A Chapter in Diplomatic History* (New York: Houghton, Mifflin, 1893), 31–33.

23. Palmer, *Selected Letters of Sumner*, 2:458–461; HF to CS, May 17, 1869, CS-Mf.

24. HF to JLM, May 15, 1869, Senate Executive Document No. 11, 41st Cong., 3rd sess., 2–5. Although discussion and editing of Fish's original draft continued for a few days after May 15, the final instructions bore the date of the draft.

25. ET to the Earl of Clarendon, May 17, 25, 1869, PRO; HF to CS, May 17, 1869, CS-Mf.

26. HF to S. B. Ruggles, May 18, 1869, HF to Francis Lieber, June 10, 1869 (emphasis in original), HF-LC.

27. Palmer, *Selected Letters of Sumner*, 2:463, 465–466, 471–472, 476, 481 (emphasis in original); CS to George Bemis, May 25, 1869, John E. Addicks to CS, May 27, 1869, CS to Theodore Dwight Woolsey, May 31, 1869, CS-Mf.

28. *Liverpool Mercury*, June 1, 1869; *NYH*, June 3, 1869; *NYT*, June 2, 1869; CS to JLM, June 8, 1869, CS-Mf; BM, diary, May 31, June 16, 1869, BM-LC.

29. Samuel Hooper to CS, June 8, 13, 1869, JLM to CS, June 7, 16, 1869 (emphasis in original), CS-Mf.

30. JLM to HF, June 12, 1869, Senate Executive Document No. 11, 41st Cong., 3rd sess., 5–10 (emphasis added); Kenneth Bourne, ed., *British Documents on Foreign Affairs: Reports and Papers from the Foreign Office Confidential Print* (Lanham, Md.: University Press of America, 1986), pt. I, ser. C, vol. 7, 229–230.

31. BM, diary, June 11, 1869, BM-LC.

32. Senate Executive Document No. 11, 41st Cong., 3rd sess., 30–31; ET to the Earl of Clarendon, June 26, 1869, PRO.

33. USG interview, *NYH*, September 25, 1877; Senate Executive Document No. 11, 41st Cong., 3rd sess., 10–11.

34. William Hunter to CS, July 8, 1869, HF to CS, July 10, 1869, CS to the Duchess of Argyll, July 10, 1869, CS-Mf; Palmer, *Selected Letters of Sumner*, 2:482–484.

35. BM, diary, July 10, 15, 16, 1869, BM-LC; Senate Executive Document No. 11, 41st Cong., 3rd sess., 11–13.

36. Senate Executive Document No. 11, 41st Cong., 3rd sess., 13–14, 33.

37. John Rose to CC, June 19, 30, 1869, CC to Rose, June 26, 1869, CC-LC; HF, diary, July 8, 9, 10, 11, 1869, HF to George Bancroft, September 4, 1869, Rose to HF, November 3, 1869 (ts), HF-LC.

38. Palmer, *Selected Letters of Sumner*, 2:484–485, 489; HF to CS, July 19, 1869, HF-LC.

39. HF to John C. Hamilton, September 4, 1869 (ts), HF-LC; HF to CS, October 9, 1869, CS-Mf.

40. CC to HF, September 8 (ts), 17 (ts), 1869, Fish to John C. Hamilton, September 24, 1869, HF-LC; Senate Executive Document No. 10, 41st Cong., 2nd sess., 5–15.

41. BM, diary, October 11, 15, 1869, BM-LC; JLM to HF, October 16, 1869 (ts), HF, diary, November 25, December 21, 1869, HF-LC; Donald, *Sumner*, 2:411; H. C. G. Matthew, ed., *The Gladstone Diaries* (Oxford: Oxford University Press, 1868–1994), 7:153, 155; Senate Executive Document No. 10, 41st Cong., 2nd sess., 17–19; Bourne, *British Documents on Foreign Affairs*, pt. I, ser. C, vol. 7, 240–249, 251.

42. HF, diary, November 4, December 20, 1869, HF-LC; Senate Executive Document No. 11, 41st Cong., 3rd sess., 13–14; BM, diary, October 24, 1869, BM-LC; Matthew, *Gladstone Diaries*, 7:148; HF to CS, October 9, 1869, JLM to CS, September 12, 1869, CS-Mf; ET to the Earl of Clarendon, October 9, 11, 1869, PRO.

43. HF, diary, November 4, 15, December 9, 1869, Schuyler Colfax to HF, December 24, 1869 (ts), HF-LC; ET to the Earl of Clarendon, November 23, December 7, 21, 1869, PRO; Matthew, *Gladstone Diaries*, 7:155; JLM to HF, November 6, 1869 (ts), HF-LC; JLM to CS, December 2, 1869, CS-Mf; *M and P*, 7:32–34; *CG*, 41st Cong., 2nd sess., 238, 305; Senate Executive Document No. 10, 41st Cong., 2nd sess., 8, 11–12.

44. HF, diary, November 4, 1869, HF-LC; HF to CS, November 6, 1869, CS-Mf; Palmer, *Selected Letters of Sumner*, 2:495.

45. HF, diary, November 15, 1869, March 24, 1870, HF-LC.

46. *NYH*, September 23, 1869; HF, diary, November 9, 26, 1869, HF-LC.

47. HF, diary, December 23, 1869, January 4, 6, March 24, 1870, HF-LC.

48. *NYT*, May 24, 25, 26, 1869; *M and P*, 7:85, 91–92; HF, diary, May 24, 25, 29, 30, 31, 1869, September 9, October 7, 9, 1870, HF-LC; *PUSG*, 20:305–306; HF to JCBD, October 13, 1870, JCBD, diary, August 5, 1870, JCBD-LC; Matthew, *Gladstone Diaries*, 7:306.

49. HF, diary, November 15, 1869, June 3, September 18, 1870, HF to Motley, June 10, 27 (ts), 1870, HF-LC.

50. JCBD to HF, July 27 1870 (ts), HF, diary, September 9, October 19, 21, 22, 23, December 6, 1870, HF-LC; JCBD, diary, August 5, September 6, 8, 1870, JCBD-LC; *FRUS, 1870*, 68–69, 193; *M and P*, 7:96–97; HF to JRY, September 24, 1870, JRY-LC; Nevins, *Fish*, 408.

51. HF, diary, July 19, October 10, 11, 14, 16, 17, 19, 1870, George Bancroft to HF, November 3, 1870 (ts), HF-LC; HF to CSch, January 23, 1871, CSch-LC; JCBD, diary, August 5, September 6, 1870, HF to JCBD, October 13, 1870, JCBD-LC; *M and P*, 7:86–91.

52. *Treaties, Conventions, International Acts, Protocols and Agreements between the United States of America and Other Powers, 1776–1909*, Senate Document No. 57, 61st Cong., 2nd sess., 1:631–632, 668–672; Alfred E. Eckes Jr., *Opening America's Market: U.S. Foreign Trade Policy since 1776* (Chapel Hill: University of North Carolina Press, 1995), 25–26 67–68; Edward Stanwood, *American Tariff Controversies in the Nineteenth Century* (Boston: Houghton, Mifflin, 1903), 2:136–137; Cook, *Alabama Claims*, 135–136.

53. HF to JCBD, September 3, 1870, JCBD, diary, September 8, 1870, JCBD-LC; JCBD to HF, September 4, 1870, HF, diary, September 9, 11, 15, 18, 26, November 10, 11, 1870, HF-LC.

54. Foreign Enlistment Act, 1870, www.legislation.uk/ukpga/Vict/33-34/90/enacted; HF, diary, September 15, 18, 1870, HF-LC.

55. HF, diary, September 26, 29, November 17, 1870, HF-LC; Spencer Childers, *The Life and Correspondence of the Right Hon. Hugh C. E. Childers, 1827–1896* (London: John Murray, 1901), 1:173–174; Lucien Wolf, *Life of the First Marquess of Ripon* (London: John Murray, 1921), 1:238; Bourne, *British Documents on Foreign Affairs*, pt. I, ser. C, vol. 7, 290–292.

56. HF, diary, November 15, 1869, November 20, 1870, HF-LC (emphasis in original); ET to Earl Granville, November 22, 1870, PRO.

57. HF, diary, November 30, 1870, HF-LC; *M and P*, 7:102–106; *WES*, December 6, 1870.

58. As it turned out, Boutwell offered several banks, in addition to Morton, Rose, the opportunity to act as agents for the new bonds; then, after lackluster sales, they were handled exclusively by Jay Cooke. John Rose to HF, November 26, 1870 (emphasis in original), HF, diary, December 9, 11, 12, 20, 1870, HF-LC; Bourne, *British Documents on Foreign Affairs*, pt. I, ser. C, vol. 7, 292–299; Matthew, *Gladstone Diaries*, 7:408; Cook, *Alabama Claims*, 152–153; Robert Carlton Clark, "The Diplomatic Mission of Sir John Rose, 1871," *Pacific Northwest Quarterly* 27 (July 1936): 233–238; Jay Sexton, *Debtor Diplomacy: Finance and American Foreign Relations in the Civil War Era 1837–1873* (New York: Oxford University Press, 2005), 211–213, 217–220.

CHAPTER 8. REVOLT IN CUBA

1. CC to CS, June 26, July 8, 1869, CS-Mf; HF to George Bancroft, September 4, 1869 (ts), HF-LC; *NYH*, June 19, 1869; Charles S. Campbell, *The Transformation of American Foreign Relations* (New York: Harper & Row, 1976), 53–55.

2. A. E. Borie to AB, October 3, 1869, *PUSG*, 19:220; *Speech of Major Gen'l John A. Rawlins* (Washington, D.C.: Chronicle Print, [1868]), 15–16; James Harrison Wilson, *The Life of John A. Rawlins* (New York: Neale, 1916), 359–360; Campbell, *Transformation of American Foreign Relations*, 55.

3. HF, diary, July 26, November 5, 1875, HF-LC; John Bassett Moore to JHW, October 4, 1907, JHW-LC. James Harrison Wilson, who became Grant's bitter enemy and a highly sympathetic biographer of Rawlins, denied that Rawlins had received the bonds. Nonetheless, the evidence that Rawlins's papers included Cuban bonds is substantial. Horace Porter, who had been a member of Grant's secretarial staff at the time of Rawlins's death, told the story to Wilson and probably to Secretary of the Treasury Benjamin Bristow. Grant himself told it to Fish and Robeson and also to his friend Judge Walter Q. Gresham. He likely

shared it with additional individuals. Wilson hoped to find conclusive evidence exonerating Rawlins, but failing to do so, he left the bond question out of his laudatory biography. JHW to Charles Francis Adams Jr., October 2, 4, 1902, August 19, 1904, JHW to Moore, October 2, 7, 1907, Adams to JHW, October 10, .1902, August 12, 17, 1904, JHW to Sylvanus Cadwallader, September 8, 24, 1904, S. Cadwallader to JHW, September 17, 1904, Wayne MacVeagh to JHW, October 12, 1906, December 9, 1907, JHW to MacVeagh, October 13, 1906, November 26, December 3, 1907, John L. Cadwalader to JHW, March 15, 1907, JHW-LC; Adams to JHW, August 10, 1904, JHW to Adams, August 15, 1904, USG-USGPL; Wilson, *Life of Rawlins*.

4. *NYH*, May 3, 1869; *NYT*, May 5, 1869; NPB to Mrs. N. P. Banks, May 7, 1869, NPB-LC; HP to JCBD, April 28, 1869, USG-LC; Beverly Wilson Palmer, ed., *The Selected Letters of Charles Sumner* (Boston: Northeastern University Press, 1990), 2:473.

5. *NYH*, May 3, 1869; HF, diary, March 24, 25, April 6, June 21, 1869, HF-LC; William S. McFeely, *Grant: A Biography* (New York: W. W. Norton, 1981), 297–298; ET to the Earl of Clarendon, June 21, 1869, PRO.

6. Paul S. Forbes to USG, June 2, 1869, Forbes to HF, June 3, 1869, HF, "Mem[orandum] Read to the Cabinet & Approved June 4, 1869," Jose Morales Lemus, "Memorandum," June 25, 1869, HF to George Bancroft, September 4, 1869 (ts), HF-LC; ET to the Earl of Clarendon, June 21, 1869, PRO; Palmer, *Selected Letters of Sumner*, 2:485; Allan Nevins, *Hamilton Fish: The Inner History of the Grant Administration* (New York: Dodd, Mead, 1937), 191–194.

7. HF, diary, June 21, 29, 1869, HF-LC; ET to the Earl of Clarendon, June 21, 1869, PRO; JB, diary, August 29, 1869 (ts), JB-NYPL; Nevins, *Fish*, 120, 189–190, 194.

8. HF, diary, June 29, 1869, "Payments on 'President's Approval,'" memorandum filed in diary at February 1, 1870, undated proclamation with Fish notation, HF-LC; JB, diary, August 29, 1869 (ts), JB-NYPL; *PUSG*, 19:235n–236n.

9. Nevins, *Fish*, 236–238; *NYT*, August 4, 5, November 23, 24, 30, December 3, 5, 9, 10, 11, 1869; *NYH*, August 9, December 14, 1869; Manuel Freyre to HF, July 31, 1869, HF to JCBD, August 1, 3, 1869, ERH to HF, August 1, 1869, HF to ERH, August 3, 1869 (ts), JCBD to HF, August 3 (ts), 4 (ts), 1869, unsigned communication from Department of State to Francis C. Barlow, August 4, 1869 (ts), Daniel E. Sickles to HF, September 14, 1869 (ts), HF to Daniel E. Sickles, November 18, 1869, HF, diary, November 4, 7, 11, 13, 15, 16, 18, 19, 20, 24, 25, 27, 28, 29, 30, December 3, 4, 7, 8, 9, 1869, HF-LC; HF to JCBD, August 5, 1869, JCBD-LC; CC to Sidney Webster, December 4, 5, 1869, Webster to CC, December 2, 6, 11, 1869, HF to CC, December 8, 9, 1869, CC-LC.

10. House Executive Document No. 160, 41st Cong., 2nd sess., 16–17; Sidney Webster to HF, July 10, 1869 (ts), HF to Webster, July 14, 1869 (ts), Paul S. Forbes to HF, July 16, 20 (letter, ts), 20 (telegram, ts), 1869, HF to JCBD, July 23, 24 (ts), 1869, HF-LC; HF to JCBD, August 5, 1869, JCBD-LC; JB, diary, August 29, 1869 (ts), JB-NYPL.

NOTES TO PAGES 184–186

11. JB, diary, August 29, 1869 (ts), JB-NYPL; House Executive Document No. 160, 41st Cong., 2nd sess., 13–27; Daniel E. Sickles to HF, July 31, 1869, HF-LC.

12. HF to ET, August 10, 1869, HF-LC; House Executive Document No. 160, 41st Cong., 2nd sess., 25.

13. *PUSG*, 19:234–235, 236; JCBD to HF, August 17 (telegram), 19 (telegram), 1869, HF to JCBD, August 18, 1869 (two telegrams), HF-LC. Fish and Davis had met Porter in New York and made the pitch to withhold the proclamation. Their meeting had an intriguing coda. Davis reported to Fish that a day or two after they met "Porter about the Cuban proclamation," two "gold speculators" called on Davis's brother "stating that they knew that I had in my pocket a proclamation about Cuba, but were uncertain whether it was a proclamation recognizing independence or one recognizing Belligerency." Depending on the nature of the document, it could have a substantial impact on the gold market, and "they said that there was a great deal of money to be made in operating on the information if they could have it accurate." They offered to pay Davis's brother handsomely if he would go to Washington and "ascertain the facts" about the proclamation. He refused. Davis thought the episode indicated a leak in the State Department, where only two staff members other than he and Fish knew "the exact character of that proclamation." But of course, Grant and Porter also knew. August 19 was the day Fisk accosted Grant to press for information about the government's gold-selling intentions. Is it possible that Grant inadvertently made vague mention of the proclamation to Fisk? A likelier culprit was the president's brother-in-law Abel Corbin, who was implicated in the Gold Corner conspiracy with Fisk and Gould. Corbin had accompanied the president on his trip to Pennsylvania and returned with him to New York City on August 19. He may have heard just enough about the proclamation, which was being kept secret, to calculate how it might affect the price of gold and encourage the two "gold speculators" to approach Davis's brother. JCBD to HF, September 10, 1869 (ts), HF-LC; *Gold Panic Investigation*, House Report No. 31, 41st Cong., 2nd sess., 244.

14. *NYH*, August 21, 1869; DeB. Randolph Keim to James Gordon Bennett, August 23, 1869, KFP-LC.

15. USG, memorandum, August 31, 1869, *PUSG*, 19:238; House Executive Document No. 160, 41st Cong., 2nd sess., 16–17, 32, 37–38; HF, diary, September 4, 1869, HF-LC.

16. Sidney Webster to HF, August 30, 1869 (ts), HF to Webster, September 15, 1869 (ts), HF to USG, September 15, 1869, HF-LC; USG to HF, September 17, 1869 (telegram), *PUSG*, 19:247; DeB. Randolph Keim to James Gordon Bennett, September 22, 1869, KFP-LC; WR to EBW, September 11, 1869, EBW-LC; JB to JCBD, "Wednesday" [October 15, 1869], JCBD-LC.

17. D. Sickles to HF, September 14, 1869, HF-LC; House Executive Document No. 160, 41st Cong., 2nd sess., 38–39, 41–43, 46–53, 56–59.

18. HF, diary, November 3, 1869, Paul S. Forbes to HF, October 19, 29 [20],

30, November 10, 12, 1869, HF to Forbes, November 16, 1869 (ts), HF to Daniel E. Sickles, November 18, 1869 (ts), Sickles to HF, December 7, 1869 (ts), HF-LC. Evidence contained in Forbes's letter to Fish dated "29 Octr 69" indicates that he wrote it on October 20 and misdated it.

19. HF, diary, October 25, 26, 1869, HF to George Bancroft, October 26, 27, 1869, HF to Daniel E. Sickles, October 27, 1869, HF to Baron Friedrich von Gerolt, October 27, 1869, HF-LC.

20. HF to George Bancroft, October 27, 1869, HF-LC; HF to CS, December 2, 1869, CS-Mf.

21. *PUSG*, 20:25–29 (emphasis in original); *M and P*, 7:31–33; HF, diary, November 12, 15, 27, 28, 30, December 13, 1869, HF-LC.

22. *M and P*, 7:32.

23. *NYT*, January 20, 1870; Horace Greeley et al. to USG, January 30, 1870, HG-LC; *NYS*, December 28, 1869, January 6, 22, 1870 (emphasis in original).

24. Sidney Webster to CC, January 1, 4 (letter and telegram), 5 (letter and telegram), 6, 7, 8, 1870, CC to Webster, January 3, 4, 5, 6, 7, 1870, CC-LC; CC to HF, January 3, 1870 (ts), HF-LC; Webster to M. Lopez Roberts, January 5, 1870, EP to E. W. Stoughton, January 10, 1870, MM-LC. See also Nevins, *Fish*, 191, 336; James Burke Chapin, "Hamilton Fish and American Expansion" (Ph. D. diss., Cornell University, 1971), 276–280. Chapin was much less charitable toward Fish and Webster than Nevins was.

25. HF to Archibald Russell, January 23, 1870 (ts), Thurlow Weed to HF, January 9, 1870 (ts), HF to John C. Hamilton, January 8, 1870, HF-LC.

26. CC to Sidney Webster, January 5, 6, February 19, 1870, Webster to CC, January 7, 17, 1870, CC-LC; HF, diary, December 3, 1869, February 14, 19, March 10, 1870, Thomas B. Connery to HF, January 7, 1870, HF to J. Watson Webb, January 1, 1870, HF to EP, February 27, 1870, HF to James A. Hamilton, March 13, 1870, HF-LC; *NYH*, January 7, 1870.

27. HF, diary, February 15, 1870, HF-LC.

28. Ibid., February 19, 1870; *CG*, 41st Cong., 2nd sess., 1206.

29. *CG*, 41st Cong., 2nd sess., 1338; NPB to Mrs. NPB, February 17, 1870, NPB-LC; EP to HF, February 23, 1870, HF to EP, February 27, 1870, HF-LC.

30. *CG*, 41st Cong., 2nd sess., 1089; House Executive Document No. 160, 41st Cong., 2nd sess.; *NYTr*, February 23, 1870.

31. *NYH*, March 8, 10, 1870; *WES*, March 10, 1870.

32. *NYH*, March 15, 16, 1870; *NYT*, March 17, 1870; HF, diary, February 14, 19, March 10, 1870, CC to HF, March 3, 1870, HF-LC; Marquis de Chambrun to CC, March 17, 1870, CC-LC.

33. *CG*, 41st Cong., 2nd sess., 3770–3774; *NYH*, May 25, 1870.

34. HF, diary, May 31, June 1, 2, 1870, HF-LC.

35. Ibid., June 2, 1870.

36. *NYH*, June 3, 4, 7, 1870; HF, diary, June 13, 1870, HF-LC; USG, fragment of draft message to Congress, n.d., *PUSG*, 20:167–168. The editors of *PUSG*

speculate that this fragment was dated June 13, 1870. Fish's diary indicates that Grant wrote it before June 13.

37. *New York Evening Post*, June 6, 1870; HF, diary, June 8, 1870, HF-LC; Marquis de Chambrun to CC, "on Wednesday morning" [June 8, 1870], "on Thursday morning" [June 9 (misdated May 9), 1870], CC-LC; *CG*, 41st Cong., 2nd sess., 1617, 4224, 4262, 4314–4316, 4318–4322, 4326, 4331, 4692; House Report No. 104, 41st Cong., 2nd sess.

38. HF, diary, June 10, 12, 17, 1870, HF-LC; CC to JCBD, June 10, 1870, JCBD-LC.

39. HF, "Draft of Message on 'Cuban Belligerency' June 13, 1870," HF, diary, June 13, 17, 1870, HF-LC; USG, fragment of draft message, [June 13, 1870], USG-NYHS.

40. *M and P*, 7:64–69; USG, fragment of draft message, [June 13, 1870], USG-NYHS; HF, "Draft of Message on 'Cuban Belligerency' June 13, 1870," HF-LC.

41. *NYH*, June 14, 1870; *CG*, 41st Cong., 2nd sess., 4383.

42. HF, diary, June 14, 1870; *CG*, 41st Cong., 2nd sess., 4436, 4486–4487, 4506–4507, appendix, 454–465; Edward McPherson, *The Political History of the United States of America during the Period of Reconstruction* (Washington, D.C.: Philp & Solomons, 1871), 619–621.

43. HF, diary, June 17, July 10, 1870, HF-LC.

44. F. M. Grant to NPB, June 15, 1870, NPB-LC; *NYT*, June 17, 1870; *NYH*, June 17, 1870.

45. HF, diary, July 10, 1870, HF-LC.

CHAPTER 9. THE GATE TO THE CARIBBEAN SEA

1. M. M. Gautier, memorandum, March 9, 1869, in JWF to HF, April 1, 1869, Notes from the Legation of the Dominican Republic, Records of the Department of State, RG 59, NA; *NYH*, September 11, 1869; *M and P*, 7: 99; DeB. Randolph Keim, *San Domingo* (Philadelphia: Claxton, Remsen & Haffelfinger, 1870), 316.

2. William Javier Nelson, *Almost a Territory: America's Attempt to Annex the Dominican Republic* (Newark: University of Delaware Press, 1990), 25–39, 53–54; Frank Moya Pons, *The Dominican Republic: A National History* (Princeton, N.J.: Markus Wiener, 1998), 200–225; Senate Executive Document No. 17, 41st Cong., 3rd sess., 4.

3. Senate Executive Document No. 17, 41st Cong., 3rd sess., 4–8, 71.

4. Charles Callan Tansill, *The United States and Santo Domingo, 1798–1873: A Chapter in Caribbean Diplomacy* (Baltimore: Johns Hopkins Press, 1938), 258–260, 343–345; Senate Executive Document No. 9, 42nd Cong., 1st sess., 185–187.

5. Senate Report No. 234, 41st Cong., 2nd sess., 159 (hereafter referred to as Hatch Report); Tansill, *United States and Santo Domingo*, 260–272; *M and P*, 6:689; J. Somers Smith to W. H. Seward, January 9, 18, March 19 (emphasis in original),

1869, Smith to HF, April 9, 1869, Dispatches from US Consuls in Santo Domingo, Records of the Department of State, RG 59, NA.

6. Allan Nevins, *Hamilton Fish: The Inner History of the Grant Administration* (New York: Dodd, Mead, 1937), 255–259; Tansill, *United States and Santo Domingo*, 272–273; JWF to C. K. Garrison, January 6, 1869, quoted in Nevins, *Fish*, 258–259.

7. NPB to JWF, February 17, 1869, JWF-PEM.

8. JWF to BFB, January 11, 1869, BFB-LC; *CG*, 40th Cong., 3rd sess., 317–319, 333–340; Tansill, *United States and Santo Domingo*, 274–277.

9. JWF to NPB, January 18, 1869, NPB-LC; JWF to BFB, January 30, 1869, JWF-PEM; *CG*, 40th Cong., 3rd sess., 769; Tansill, *United States and Santo Domingo*, 277–279; *NYT*, February 2, 1869.

10. J. Medill to NPB, February 4, 1869, NPB-LC; *NYT*, February 10, 1869.

11. William H. Seward to J. Somers Smith, February 15, 1869, Diplomatic Instructions, Special Missions, American Hemisphere, Records of the Department of State, RG 59, NA; Hatch Report, 173–174; NPB to JWF, February 17, 1869, JWF-PEM; JWF to NPB, February 18, March 24 (telegram), 1869, NPB-LC.

12. Charles Callan Tansill, *The Purchase of the Danish West Indies* (Baltimore: Johns Hopkins Press, 1932), 82–83, 89–90; *CG*, 40th Cong., 1st sess., 792–793.

13. Waldemar Raasloff to NPB, February 3, 6, 11, 12, 16, 17, 18, March 2, 3, 10, 12, 16, 17, 19, [20], 22, [23], 25, 27, 1869, JAR to NPB, February 21, 1869, NPB-LC; Edward L. Pierce, *Memoir and Letters of Charles Sumner* (Boston: Roberts Brothers, 1894), 4:620; HF, diary, March 18, 19, 23, 24, April 6, December 7, 23, 1869, March 24, April 14, 1870, HF-LC; Tansill, *Purchase of Danish West Indies*, 130.

14. JWF to NPB, March 24, 1869 (telegram), NPB-LC; JWF to HF, March 27, April 1, 1869, Notes from the Legation of the Dominican Republic, RG 59, NA; HF, diary, April 5, 1869, HF-LC.

15. JWF to [?], April 7, [1869], JWF-PEM. This letter is missing the name of the addressee, but internal evidence suggests it was Mrs. Fabens.

16. HF, diary, April 6, 1869, HF-LC.

17. J. Somers Smith to W. H. Seward, March 9, 1869, Smith to HF, April 9, 1869, Edward Prime Jr. to HF, April 7, 1869, Dispatches from US Consuls in Santo Domingo, RG 59, NA; Tansill, *United States and Santo Domingo*, 350–351; *NYTr*, November 26, 1869; OEB, diary, August 15, 24, 25, 1869, OEB-USGPL; Prime to NPB, April 5, 1869, NPB-LC; Cornelius Cole, *Memoirs* (New York: McLoughlin Brothers, 1908), 324; JWF to HF, April 21, 1869, Notes from the Legation of the Dominican Republic, RG 59, NA. Both Nevins and Tansill misidentified J. P. O'Sullivan as "Peter J. O'Sullivan."

18. JWF to William Cazneau, April 22, 1869, quoted in Nevins, *Fish*, 262–263, and in Tansill, *United States and Santo Domingo*, 354n38; ET to the Earl of Clarendon, May 17, 1869, PRO.

19. *M and P*, 7:129; Senate Executive Document No. 34, 41st Cong., 3rd sess., 2–3; Senate Executive Document No. 17, 41st Cong., 3rd sess., 8. See also Daniel

Ammen, *The Old Navy and the New* (Philadelphia: J. B. Lippincott, 1891), 460, 506–509. Ammen's memory of the sequence of events in the Dominican affair was not entirely accurate.

20. Senate Executive Document No. 34, 41st Cong., 3rd sess., 2–5.

21. T. Bille to NPB, April 29, [1869], JWF to NPB, May 21, June 1, 1869, Spofford, Tileston to NPB, May 22, 1869, NPB-LC; JWF to JCBD, May 27, 1869, JCBD-LC; Senate Executive Document No. 17, 41st Cong., 3rd sess., 8–9. In this document Fish mistakenly referred to Benjamin S. Hunt rather than Benjamin P. Hunt.

22. "Benjamin Peter Hunt," in George Willis Cooke, *An Historical and Biographical Introduction to Accompany the Dial* (Cleveland: Rowfant Club, 1902), 176–180; "The Late Benjamin P. Hunt, of Philadelphia," in *Twenty-Fifth Annual Report of the Trustees of the Public Library, 1877* (Boston: Boston Public Library, 1877), 119–123; [Benjamin P. Hunt], *Why Colored People in Philadelphia Are Excluded from the Street Cars* (Philadelphia: Benjamin C. Bacon, 1866), 26–27.

23. Senate Executive Document No. 17, 41st Cong., 3rd sess., 8–9; HF to Benjamin P. Hunt, June 2, 1869 [misfiled], Diplomatic Instructions, Special Missions, RG 59, NA.

24. JWF to NPB, May 21, June 1, 1869, NPB-LC; *PUSG*, 21:290; Spofford, Tileston to HF, June 8, 1869, HF-LC.

25. M. M. Gautier to JWF, June 22, 1869, JWF to HF, July 1, 9, 1869, Notes from the Legation of the Dominican Republic, RG 59, NA; JWF to CS, July 1, 1869, JWF to HF, July 1, 1869, CS-Mf; CS to JWF, July 8, 1869, JWF-PEM.

26. Affidavit of E. A. Delaney and W. M. Ringwood, July 3, 1869, JWF-PEM; Sumner Welles, *Naboth's Vineyard: The Dominican Republic, 1844–1924* (New York: Payson & Clarke, 1928), 1:368–369; Senate Executive Document No. 34, 41st Cong., 3rd sess., 5–6; M. M. Gautier to JWF, June 22, 1869, JWF to HF, July 9, 1869, Notes from the Legation of the Dominican Republic, RG 59, NA.

27. NPB to Mrs. NPB, June 1, 4, 1869, NPB-LC; JWF to HF, July 9, 1869, Notes from the Legation of the Dominican Republic, RG 59, NA; P. N. Spofford to HF, July 10, 1869, HF-LC.

28. Hatch Report, 35–36, 138; OEB, diary, August 9, 1869, OEB-USGPL.

29. Hatch Report, 138; "Payments on 'President's Approval,'" memorandum filed in HF diary at February 1, 1870, HF-LC; HF to OEB, July 13, 1869, Instructions to Special Agents, Records of the Department of State, RG 59, NA; Senate Executive Document No. 17, 41st Cong., 3rd sess., 9–10.

30. Hatch Report, 35–36; *PUSG*, 20:179; OEB, diary, August 13, 1869, OEB-USGPL.

31. Hatch Report, 36; OEB, diary, July 17, 21, 22, 23, August 24, 25, 1869, OEB-USGPL.

32. OEB, diary, July 24, 25, 1869, OEB-USGPL; OEB to Mrs. Babcock, July 31, 1869, OEB-NL.

33. OEB, diary, "Tuesday, July 26 [27]," 1869, OEB-USGPL; Robert E. May,

"Lobbyists for Commercial Empire: Jane Cazneau, William Cazneau, and U.S. Caribbean Policy, 1846–1878," *Pacific Historical Review* 48 (1979): 383–412. Babcock's diary marks the arrival on "Tuesday July 26th," but July 26 was a Monday, and internal evidence suggests that Tuesday, July 27, was the day the ship landed at Santo Domingo city.

34. OEB, diary, July 28, 29, 1869, OEB to "Mr. Ringwood," July 26, 1869, OEB-USGPL.

35. OEB, diary, July 29, 30, 31, August 1, 2, 3, 1869, OEB-USGPL.

36. OEB to Mrs. OEB, July 31, 1869, OEB-NL; OEB, diary, July 30, August 4, 6, 1869, OEB-USGPL; JCBD to J. Somers Smith, August 7, 1869, Dispatches from US Consuls in Santo Domingo, RG 59, NA.

37. OEB, diary, August 7, 22, 1869, OEB-USGPL; Tansill, *United States and Santo Domingo*, 347–349; Nelson, *Almost a Territory*, 69–70. Babcock erroneously referred to the "Hartman" loan.

38. OEB, diary, August 7, 9, 1869, OEB-USGPL.

39. Ibid., August 13, 1869.

40. Ibid., August 16, 17, 18, 1869.

41. Ibid., August 19, 20, November 29, 1869; Hatch Report, 43, 49; JWF to OEB, September 12, 1869, quoted in Nevins, *Fish*, 276 (emphasis in original).

42. OEB, diary, August 22, 1869, OEB-USGPL.

43. Ibid., August 22, 23, 1869.

44. Ibid., August 24, 25, 1869.

45. Ibid., August 26, 27, 28, 1869.

46. Ibid., August 29, 30, 31, 1869.

47. Ibid., September 1, 1869.

48. Ibid., September 2, 1869; J. Somers Smith to HF, September 2, 1869, Dispatches from US Consuls in Santo Domingo, RG 59, NA.

49. OEB, diary, September 2, 3, 4, 14, 1869, OEB-USGPL.

50. DeB. Randolph Keim to Cornelius Cole, September 3, 1869, Keim to W. A. Read, August 21, 1869, Keim to Wm. M. Courtis, September 4, 1869, Keim to J. Somers Smith, September 5, 1869, Keim to Buenaventura Báez, September 16, 1869, Keim to Mr. Putnam, April 11, 1910, Keim to James Gordon Bennett, September 22, 1869, KFP-LC; *NYH*, July 4, August 3, September 11, 1869.

51. Keim to Wm. M. Courtis, September 4, 1869, Keim to J. Somers Smith, September 5, 16, 1869, KFP-LC; *NYH*, August 13, 1869; JB to "Sir," August 13, 1869, JCBD-LC; JCBD to JB, August 14, 1869, in John Bigelow, *Retrospections of an Active Life* (Garden City, N.Y.: Doubleday, Page, 1913), 4:305–306.

52. HF to USG, September 17, 1869, HF-LC; Nevins, *Fish*, 268; Hatch Report, 188–189; "Memorandum Accompanying Proposition for Annexation," September 4, 1869, in *NYT*, April 30, 1870.

53. HF to USG, September 17, 1869, HF to JLM, September 20, 1869, HF-LC.

54. HF, memorandum for a letter to the Secretary of State of San Domingo, September 22, 1869, Dispatches of Special Agents of the Department of State,

Records of the Department of State, RG 59, NA; OEB to W. L. Cazneau, September, 1869, OEB-NL.

55. Keim to W. A. Read, August 21, 1869, Keim to Wm. M. Courtis, September 4, 1869, Keim to J. Somers Smith, September 5, 1869, KFP-LC; Hatch Report, 109; Smith to HF, September 4, 1869, Dispatches from US Consuls in Santo Domingo, RG 59, NA; "Memorandum Accompanying Proposition for Annexation," September 4, 1869, in *NYT*, April 30, 1870.

56. JLM to HF, October 6, 1869 (ts), HF, diary, December 21, 1869, HF-LC; OEB to HF, October 20, 1869, USG-LC. A month later Motley reported a bit more success in the bond sales, punctuating the need for discretion. JLM to HF, November 11 (ts), 20 (ts), 1869, HF-LC.

57. Hatch Report, 254–257; HF, diary, October 19, 1869, HF-LC; PHS to RHJP, October 7, 1869, H. B. Anthony to USG, October 13, 1869, W. T. Clarke to JAJC, October 19, 1869, RHJP to USG, October 20, 1869, RHJP-URI.

58. Copy of Perry to Grant, 1869, RHJP-URI. This note has "Dec" written on it, but that dating was apparently added later and is clearly mistaken, for Perry was in Santo Domingo in December 1869 and in Washington in October.

59. OEB to HF, October 20, 1869, USG-LC; Hatch Report, 212–218, 253–255; RHJP to "the Select Committee of the US Senate in the case of Hatch imprisonment," June 22, 1870, RHJP-URI.

60. RHJP to HF, October 24, 1869, HF-LC; RHJP to Fannie Perry, November 14, 1869, RHJP-URI; Hatch Report, 19, 30, 176; RHJP to HF, June 7, 1870, Dispatches from US Consuls in Santo Domingo, RG 59, NA.

61. RHJP to OEB, November 16, 1869 (ts), RHJP to HF, November 16, 1869 (ts), RHJP-URI.

62. HF, diary, October 16, 19, 25, 1869, HF-LC.

63. Senate Executive Document No. 17, 41st Cong., 2nd sess., 83–86.

64. Executive Document No. 17, 41st Cong., 2nd sess., 80–82, 94–95; Hatch Report, 19.

65. OEB, diary, November 8, 9, 10, 1869, OEB-USGPL; Hatch Report, 46–58; Ezra J. Warner, *Generals in Blue: Lives of the Union Commanders* (Baton Rouge: Louisiana State University Press, 1964), 245–246.

66. OEB, diary, November 18, 1869, OEB-USGPL; Hatch Report, 19; OEB to Mrs. OEB, November 19, 1869, OEB-NL.

67. OEB, diary, November 19, 22, 24, 25, 26, 27, 28, 1869, OEB-USGPL; Hatch Report, 113–114; Buenaventura Báez to OEB, December 3, 1869, Notes from the Legation of the Dominican Republic, RG 59, NA; Senate Executive Document No. 17, 41st Cong., 3rd sess., 98–102.

68. OEB, diary, August 20, November 29, 1869, OEB-USGPL; Hatch Report, 43, 49.

69. OEB, diary, November 29, 30, December 1, 2, 1869, OEB-USGPL; Hatch Report, 48, 104; Buenaventura Báez to OEB, December 3, 1869, JWF to HF, December 30, 1869, Notes from the Legation of the Dominican Republic, RG 59,

NA; RHJP to HF, December 10, 28, 1869, Dispatches from US Consuls in Santo Domingo, RG 59, NA.

70. HF to EBW, December 24, 1869, EBW-LC; HF to JLM, December 24, 1869, George Bancroft to HF, January 11, 1870 (ts), HF-LC.

71. USG, "Reasons Why San Domingo Should Be Annexed to the United States," [circa 1869], USG-LC. It is impossible to date this memorandum with precision. Grant wrote it on White House stationery with the printed heading "Executive Mansion. Washington, D.C. 186_," suggesting that he wrote it in 1869. He made similar points, though in different language, in his annual message to Congress on December 5, 1870. *M and P*, 7:99–101.

72. USG, "Reasons Why San Domingo Should Be Annexed to the United States," [circa 1869], USG-LC.

CHAPTER 10. THE BATTLE OF SANTO DOMINGO

1. *NYTr*, November 16, 26, December 1, 1869; *NYH*, November 27, December 23, 1869; *WNR*, November 26, 1869.

2. *NYH*, December 29, 1869; *PUSG*, 28:320–321; HF to GSB, November 22, 1877, HF to Benjamin Perley Poore, November 21, 1877, HF-LC.

3. Sources place this encounter at Sumner's house on either Friday, December 31, 1869, or Sunday, January 2, 1870. But the precise date of the interview at Sumner's house was of little consequence compared with the intense controversy over the events of that evening. HF, diary, December 31, 1869, GSB, "Memorandum," November 12, 1877 (ts), HF to GSB, November 22 (emphasis in original), December 1, 1877, GSB to HF, November 28, December 4, 1877, USG to HF, November 14, 1877, HF to Benjamin Perley Poore, November 21, 1877, HF-LC; HF to Editor, October 29, 1877, in *Boston Evening Transcript*, October 31, 1877; OEB to John W. Forney, June 6, 1870, USG to ZC, June 8, 1870, ZC-LC; USG, interview in *NYH*, February 22, 1878; *Bangor Whig & Courier*, October 29, 1877.

4. John W. Forney to OEB, June 6, 1870, OEB-NL; *Bangor Whig & Courier*, October 29, 1877; *NYH*, December 22, 23, 1869, October 5, 1877; GSB, "Memorandum," November 12, 1877 (ts), HF, diary, December 21, 1869, December 23, 1870, HF-LC; USG, interviews in *NYH*, February 22, July 24, 1878; *CG*, 41st Cong., 3rd sess., 243; Edward L. Pierce, *Memoir and Letters of Charles Sumner* (Boston: Roberts Brothers, 1894), 4:433; HF to Editor, October 29, 1877, in *Boston Evening Transcript*, October 31, 1877; Peter F. Stout to CS, December 24, 1869, CS-Mf.

5. *CG*, 41st Cong., 3rd sess., 243; J. M. Ashley to CS, December 19, 1869, CS-Mf; *NYT*, December 19, 1869; *Journal of the Executive Proceedings of the Senate of the United States*, 41st Cong., 1st sess., 120; *PUSG*, 28:321; *Boston Daily Advertiser*, December 20, 1869; Robert F. Horowitz, *The Great Impeacher: A Political Biography of James M. Ashley* (New York: Brooklyn College Press, 1979), 163; GSB, "Memorandum," November 12, 1877 (ts), HF-LC.

6. HF, diary, December 23, 1870, HF-LC; *Bangor Whig & Courier*, October 29, 1877.

7. HF, diary, May 3, 1870, USG to HF, November 14, 1877, GSB, "Memorandum," November 12, 1877 (ts), GSB to HF, November 28, 1877, HF-LC; USG to ZC, June 8, 1870, ZC-LC; *NYH*, December 29, 1869, February 22, 1878.

8. John W. Forney to OEB, June 6, 1870, OEB-NL; Forney to CS, October 20, 1870, CS-Mf; *Washington Daily Morning Chronicle*, January 3, 1870. Forney's reference to his editor's visit to Babcock on January 2 would mean the dinner took place on December 31, 1869. Seven years later, Forney wrote a public statement that on Sunday, January 2, he went home after the dinner at Sumner's and wrote the editorial himself. *NYH*, October 5, 1877. The former scenario seems more plausible, given the closer proximity of the recollection to the event. Whoever wrote the editorial, it represented Forney's endorsement of annexation.

9. John W. Forney to CS, October 20, December 25, 1870, CS-Mf. This source misinterprets the date of the second Forney letter to Sumner as December 28. See J. Macfarland to CS, December 25, 1870, CS-Mf.

10. John W. Forney to OEB, June 6, 1870, OEB-NL; HF to GSB, December 1, 1877, HF-LC; *CG*, 41st Cong., 3rd sess., 243.

11. *CG*, 41st Cong., 3rd sess., 242–244, 253.

12. Ibid., 253–254; HF to Editor, October 29, 1877, in *Boston Evening Transcript*, October 31, 1877; *Journal of the Executive Proceedings of the Senate of the United States*, 41st Cong., 2nd sess., 334–335; *CG*, 41st Cong., 2nd sess., 266; HF, diary, January 15, 1870, TOH to HF, November 8, 1877, GSB to HF, November 28, 1877, HF-LC; CS to HF, "Sat. Morning," [January 29, 1870], CS-Mf.

13. J. M. Ashley to HF, January 23, 1870, TOH to HF, November 8, 1877, USG to HF, November 14, 1877, HF-LC; HF to Editor, October 29, 1877, in *Boston Evening Transcript*, October 31, 1877; *NYT*, March 17, 1870; *Journal of the Executive Proceedings of the Senate*, 41st Cong., 2nd sess., 463, 538–539.

14. USG interview, *NYH*, July 24, 1878; HF to George Bancroft, February 11, 1870, HF-LC; OEB to JCBD, February 21, 1870, JCBD-LC.

15. HF, diary, January 29, February 5, 1870, HF-LC; Senate Executive Document No. 34, 41st Cong., 3rd sess., 11–23.

16. *NYH*, March 2, 12, 16, 1870; *CG*, 41st Cong., 3rd sess., 253–254, 266; CS to OEB, March 10, 1870, OEB-NL; David D. Porter to CS, March 12, 1870, CS-Mf; HF, diary, March 15, 1870, HF-LC; *M and P*, 7:52–53; *Journal of the Executive Proceedings of the Senate*, 41st Cong., 2nd sess., 392, 405–406.

17. OEB to HF, March 16, 1870, USG-LC; *NYH*, March 18, 1870; *NYT*, March 18, 1870; *Boston Daily Advertiser*, April 4, 1870.

18. Beverly Wilson Palmer, ed., *The Selected Letters of Charles Sumner* (Boston: Northeastern University Press, 1990), 2:502; CFA, diary, March 22, 1870, AFP-MHS; *NYT*, March 22, 1870.

19. *NYH*, March 18, 24, April 2, 1870; *PUSG*, 20:123–124.

20. *Journal of the Executive Proceedings of the Senate*, 41st Cong., 2nd sess.,

405–407; *NYH*, March 25, 26, 1870; *NYT*, March 25, 1870; *NYTr*, March 25, 1870; J. R. Hawley to CS, March 25, 1870, CS-Mf (emphasis in original). On the importance of race in the Santo Domingo debate, see Nicholas Guyatt, "America's Conservatory: Race, Reconstruction, and the Santo Domingo Debate," *Journal of American History* 97 (March 2011): 974–1000; Eric T. Love, *Race over Empire: Racism and U.S. Imperialism, 1865–1900* (Chapel Hill: University of North Carolina Press, 2004), 26–72.

21. H. R. Revels to CS, March 30, 1870, CS-Mf; Palmer, *Selected Letters of Sumner*, 2:505; NPB to Mrs. NPB, March 27, 1870, NPB-LC; JCBD to HF, March 27, 1870 (ts), HF, diary, March 30, 1870, HF-LC.

22. *NYH*, March 26, 29, 31, 1870; *NYT*, March 26, 1870.

23. JCBD to HF, March 26, 1870, HF, diary, April 1, 4, 1870, HF-LC; JCBD to RHJP, March 31, 1870, RHJP-URI; *NYH*, March 31, April 2, 1870; *Journal of the Executive Proceedings of the Senate*, 41st Cong., 2nd sess., 410–411; M. M. Gautier to HF, March 17, 1870, Gautier to David Coen, March 17, 1870, Notes from the Legation of the Dominican Republic, John C. Soley to HF, March 30, 1870 (telegram), Dispatches from US Consuls in Santo Domingo, Records of the Department of State, RG 59, NA; ET to the Earl of Clarendon, April 4, 1870, PRO.

24. *M and P*, 7:57. After the Colombian senate amended the treaty to stipulate the canal's neutrality in time of war, the US Senate declined to accept it. Lester H. Brune, *Chronological History of United States Foreign Relations: 1776 to January 20, 1981* (New York: Garland, 1985), 1:321.

25. RHJP to HF, December 10, 28, 1869, February 8, 20, 1870, Dispatches from US Consuls in Santo Domingo, RG 59, NA; RHJP to Fannie Perry, November 14, 1869, RHJP-URI; HF, diary, March 18, 1870, HF-LC.

26. RHJP to OEB, January 20, February 8 (ts), 20 (ts), 1870, RHJP-URI.

27. Senate Report No. 234, 41st Cong., 2nd sess., 135–136 (hereafter referred to as Hatch Report); OEB to RHJP, March 30, 1870 (ts), RHJP-URI.

28. RHJP to OEB, April 15, 1870 (ts), RHJP to USG, March 17, 1870, RHJP-URI.

29. Hatch Report, i–ii, xxviii, 32, 125–126, 150, 169, 182; *NYT*, July 1, 10, 1866; Senate Executive Document No. 54, 41st Cong., 2nd sess., pt. 2, 2; *Journal of the Executive Proceedings of the Senate of the United States*, 39th Cong., 1st sess., 508, 1156–1157; OEB, diary, August 22, 1869, OEB-USGPL. During a later investigation of the Hatch affair, some confusion arose over whether Báez had again nullified Hatch's grant. Gautier to Fabens, March 10, 1869, Notes from the Legation of the Dominican Republic, RG 59, NA; Hatch Report, 191; Senate Executive Document No. 17, 41st Cong., 3rd sess., 92.

30. Hatch Report, iv, 23, 40–41, 69, 185; OEB, diary, August 22, 30, September 1, 1869, OEB-USGPL; Senate Executive Document No. 34, 41st Cong., 3rd sess., 8–9.

31. Senate Executive Document No. 54, 41st Cong., 2nd sess., 4, pt. 2, 1–4; Hatch Report, 20–21, 103, 123, 160, 168.

32. Senate Executive Document No. 54, 41st Cong., 2nd sess., 5–7; RHJP to HF, February 8, 1870, Dispatches from US Consuls in Santo Domingo, RG 59, NA (emphasis in original).

33. Senate Executive Document No. 54, 41st Cong., 2nd sess., 8–9; Hatch Report, 101; RHJP to M. M. Gautier, March 8, 1870 (ts), Gautier to RHJP, March 9, 1870 (ts), RHJP to HF, March 12 (ts), April 4 (ts), 1870, RHJP-URI; RHJP to Gautier, March 9, 1870, Dispatches from US Consuls in Santo Domingo, RG 59, NA; Senate Executive Document No. 34, 41st Cong., 3rd sess., 16–18.

34. Hatch Report, 22, 124, 125; *NYW*, dateline "March 26," [1870], quoted in Hatch Report, 127–128; *CG*, 41st Cong., 2nd sess., 1444, 1774–1775.

35. *CG*, 41st Cong., 2nd sess., 2442, 2495, 2547, 2602, 2660, 2861, 3386, 3977, 4442; *NYT*, April 30, 1870; JWF to Buenaventura Báez, May 4, 1870 (draft), JWF-PEM; JWF to William L. Cazneau, May 4, 1870, quoted in Allan Nevins, *Hamilton Fish: The Inner History of the Grant Administration* (New York: Dodd, Mead, 1937), 325; HF, diary, April 29, May 3, 14, 1870, HF-LC.

36. JWF to Buenaventura Báez, May 4, 1870 (draft), JWF-PEM. In this draft, Fabens wrote and crossed out, "He promises to be active in securing protection to your administration if the present Treaty"; he then substituted the sentence beginning "I have hopes." See also JWF to [HF], n.d. [circa early June 1870], letterpress, JWF-PEM.

37. HF, diary, May 3, 6, 1870, HF to OPM, May 4, 1870 (ts), HF to J. M. Howard, May 10, 1870 (ts), HF-LC; *Journal of the Executive Proceedings of the Senate*, 41st Cong., 2nd sess., 500–501; JCBD to RHJP, May 3, 1870, RHJP-URI.

38. HF to James A. Hamilton, March 13 1870, HF-LC (emphasis in original).

39. NPB to John A. Dix, May 7, 1875, NPB to Mrs. NPB, May 9, 20, 1870, NPB-LC; *NYH*, May 13, 1870; OEB to F. J. Fithian, May 19, 1870, OEB-NL.

40. *NYH*, May 14, 1870; *NYT*, May 14, 1870.

41. HF, diary, May 14, 21, 1870, HF to USG, May 15, 1870, JCBD to HF, May 16, 1870, HF-LC.

42. *M and P*, 7:61–63.

43. RHJP to HF, May 14, 1870, Dispatches from US Consuls in Santo Domingo, M. M. Gautier to HF, May 16, 1870, Notes from the Legation of the Dominican Republic, RG 59, NA; Hatch Report, 89–93.

44. William L. Cazneau to HF, May 17, 1870, with enclosures, M. M. Gautier to HF, May 17, 1870, Notes from the Legation of the Dominican Republic, RG 59, NA; Hatch Report, 255.

45. HF, diary, May 28, June 1, 1870, HF-LC.

46. James D. W. Perry to CS, July 4, 1870, CS-Mf; *NYH*, June 2, 1870; HF, diary, June 3, 4, 1870, HF-LC; Hatch Report, 208–209, 211, 257.

47. *NYH*, June 3, 4, 1870.

48. Fabens recounted his comments in JWF to OEB, June 6, 1870, OEB-NL (emphasis in original).

49. *NYH*, June 7, 1870.

50. JWF to [HF], n.d. [circa early June 1870], letterpress, JWF-PEM (emphasis in original); *NYH*, June 7, 1870; JWF to OEB, June 6, 1870, OEB-NL (emphasis in original).

51. RHJP to HF, June 6, 1870, Dispatches from US Consuls in Santo Domingo, RG 59, NA. A few days later, Perry read this letter to a Senate investigating committee, but he left out several sentences in which he hailed the prospects of annexation. Hatch Report, 194.

52. Hatch Report, 102–107, 194, 258; RHJP "to Prevaricator," June 7, 1870, RHJP-URI.

53. *Journal of the Executive Proceedings of the Senate*, 41st Cong., 2nd sess., 390, 425, 432, 471, 474–479; HF, diary, May 14, 1870, HF-LC.

54. Hatch Report, i–ii, 133; *CG*, 41st Cong., 2nd sess., 4194–4201; NPB to Mrs. NPB, June 9, 1870, NPB-LC; HF to JLM, June 10, 1870, HF-LC.

55. OEB to James W. Nye, n.d. [June 1870], OEB-NL; Hatch Report, 209; *NYH*, June 14, 1870.

56. Hatch Report, 24, 25, 31, 103, 104, 106 198, 210.

57. Ibid., 42–45, 96, 97, 112, 113, 118, 136.

58. Ibid., xxvii, 37, 42, 44, 65–85, 118, 134, 144, 180–181; OEB, diary, September 1, 1869, OEB-USGPL.

59. Hatch Report, 26, 33, 43, 49, 104, 111, 198, 207, 264; OEB, diary, August 20, 1869, OEB-USGPL.

60. Hatch Report, 98–100, 166–175, 178–179, 261–263.

61. RHJP to "Mother and Father," June 13, 1870, RHJP-URI.

62. HF, diary, June 14, 1870, HF-LC; Hatch Report, 212–255.

63. Hatch Report, 105, 207–208, 210, 257, 264–265; RHJP to HF, July 11, 1870, Dispatches from US Consuls in Santo Domingo, RG 59, NA.

64. HF, diary, June 4, 14, 17, 1870, HF-LC; OEB, diary, August 20, 1869, OEB-USGPL; *PUSG*, 20:163 (emphasis in original).

65. Hatch Report, xxii, xlv, xlvi.

66. *PUSG*, 20:164; HF, diary, June 1, 3, 14, 1870, HF-LC; ET to the Earl of Clarendon, June 6, 1870, PRO; USG to ZC, June 8, 1870, ZC-LC.

67. HF, diary, June 13, 14, 15, 17, 1870, HF-LC.

68. ERH to JDC, December 25, 1869, JDC to A. F. Perry, July 29, 1870, JDC-OCL; USG to ERH, June 15, 1870, ERH-CPL; *PUSG*, 20:170. Twenty-five years later, former interior secretary Jacob Cox published an article on Hoar's resignation, but its numerous errors of chronology and fact make it unreliable. Jacob Cox, "How Judge Hoar Ceased to Be Attorney General," *Atlantic Monthly* 76 (August 1895): 162–173.

69. *PUSG*, 20:170, 173; *NYH*, June 17, 1870; HF, diary, June 17, 1870, HF-LC; *PUSG*, 18:292.

70. Palmer, *Selected Letters of Sumner*, 2:507; RBH, diary, July 1, 1870, in *Diary and Letters of Rutherford Birchard Hayes*, ed. Charles Richard Williams (Columbus: Ohio State Archaeological and Historical Society, 1924), 3:111–112. Hayes dated

this entry July 1, but he noted that the encounter at the White House occurred on June 27.

71. Hatch Report, xl, 188; OEB, diary, September 4, 1869, OEB-USGPL; ET to Principal Secretary of State for Foreign Affairs, July 11, 1870, PRO; *PUSG*, 20:179.

72. After the fact, Sumner claimed that Fish made this offer in June 1870, a few weeks before the Senate voted on the treaty. Fish's diary does not confirm this assertion, and his record of events that month makes Sumner's claim as to timing highly unlikely. After the Senate removed Sumner from the Foreign Relations Committee in 1871, the outraged senator incorporated the bribery charge into a speech he intended to give in the Senate. But the speech was so violently anti-administration that associates convinced him not to deliver it. HF, diary, June 25, 1870, HF to George William Curtis, May 14, 1874 (ts), HF-LC; *NYT*, October 20, 1877; HF to Editor, October 29, 1877, in *Boston Evening Transcript*, October 31, 1877; Palmer, *Selected Letters of Sumner*, 2:561–562; Charles Sumner, *Personal Relations with the President and Secretary of State: An Explanation in Reply to an Assault* (Washington, D.C.: n.p., 1871); CS to Anna C. Lodge, April 19, 1871, Edward L. Pierce to CS, May 8, 1871, Henry Wilson to CS, June 6, 1871, CS-Mf; *NYTr*, April 6, 1874.

73. HF, diary, June 27, 1870, HF-LC.

74. Ibid., June 28, 29, 1870.

75. *NYH*, June 30, 1870; Palmer, *Selected Letters of Sumner*, 2:508; *Journal of the Executive Proceedings of the Senate*, 41st Cong., 2nd sess., 500–503.

76. *New-York Standard*, July 1, 1870, quoted in *NYT*, July 2, 1870; *Boston Daily Advertiser*, July 1, 1870.

77. HF, diary, December 20, 1869, July 1, 7, 1870, HF-LC; USG, interview, *NYH*, September 25, 1877; Senate Executive Document No. 11, 41st Cong., 3rd sess., 33; BM, diary, August 22, 1870, BM-LC.

78. HF to CS, October 9, 1869, CS-MF; H. C. G. Matthew, ed., *The Gladstone Diaries* (Oxford: Oxford University Press, 1968–1994), 7:148; BM, diary, May 28, June 21, October 17, 1870, BM-LC; Adam Badeau, *Grant in Peace* (Hartford, Conn.: S. S. Scranton, 1887), 206; J. L. Stackpole to CS, June 25, 1870, CS to Henry Wadsworth Longfellow, [July 26, 1870], CS-Mf; Palmer, *Selected Letters of Sumner*, 2:507–508.

79. BM, diary, June 21, July 14, 15, 17, August 18, 26, November 29, December 3, 1870, BM-LC; Senate Executive Document No. 11, 41st Cong., 3rd sess., 16–17.

80. *PUSG*, 20:191, 192; HF, diary, July 14, 1870, HF-LC; *NYT*, July 15, 1870; *NYH*, July 16, 1870; *Journal of the Executive Proceedings of the Senate*, 41st Cong., 2nd sess., 542, 544–545, 547; RC, manuscript speech notes, July 15, 1870, RC to Frelinghuysen, July 15, 1870 (draft telegram), RC Papers, LC; *Boston Daily Advertiser*, July 16, 1870; CS to TOH, June [misdated; actually July] 27, 1870, TOH-WHS; TOH to CS, August 23, 1870, CS-Mf.

81. HF to USG, July 7, 1870 (ts), HF, diary, November 3, 1869, April 20, June 1, 2, 4, 17, 25, July 8, 10, 1870, HF to R. C. Winthrop, May 31, 1870, HF-LC; CS to CC, July 9, 1870, CS-Mf.

82. HF, diary, September 9, 24, October 4, 21, 1870, HF to Lyman Trumbull, August 5, 1870, HF to Lot M. Morrill, August 8, 1870, George F. Edmunds to HF, August 24, 1870, TOH to HF, September 5, 1870, BFB to HF, October 16, 1870 (ts), HF to BFB, October 18, 1870, HF to AB, October 25, 1870, RC to HF, November 11, 1870, HF-LC.

83. Palmer, *Selected Letters of Sumner*, 2:509–511, 519–523, 526–529; HF to CS, July 18, 19, September 10, 25, 1870, CS-Mf; CS and Samuel Hooper, "Motley's Removal," ts, HF, diary, July 15, 17, 18, 1870, HF-LC.

84. Sumner recounted his comments in CS to CSch, September 15, 1870, CS-Mf. See also Palmer, *Selected Letters of Sumner*, 2:517.

85. JCBD to HF, August 3, 1870 (ts), George Bancroft to HF, October 18, 1870 (ts), JSM to HF, July 18, September 5 (ts), 1870, HF to JSM, August 26, September 6, 1870, TOH to HF, August 23, 1870, HF to AB, October 25, 1870, HF-LC; HF to TOH, August 6, 1870, TOH-WHS; TOH to CS, August 23, 1870, JSM to CS, September 5, 10, 1870, CS-Mf; OEB to ZC, October 8, 1870, ZC-LC (emphasis in original).

86. HF to JSM, August 26, 1870, HF-LC; CS to Anna C. Lodge, November 20, 1870, CS-Mf.

CHAPTER 11. LAUNCHING THE PEACE POLICY

1. *PUSG*, 1:296, 310.
2. *PUSG*, 15:40–41.
3. *PUSG*, 15:486, 16:116–117, 221.
4. *PUSG*, 15:146; House Miscellaneous Document No. 37, 39th Cong., 2nd sess.
5. Theodore Calvin Pease and James G. Randall, eds., *The Diary of Orville Hickman Browning* (Springfield: Illinois State Historical Library, 1925–1933), 2:126; *PUSG*, 17:42–43, 241, 343–344; Howard K. Beale, ed., *The Diary of Gideon Welles* (New York: W. W. Norton, 1960), 3:30, 74, 98–100; *PUSG*, 18:257–262; House Executive Document No. 97, 40th Cong., 2nd sess.; House Executive Document No. 1, 40th Cong., 3rd sess., 831–832; Francis Paul Prucha, *American Indian Policy in Crisis: Christian Reformers and the Indian, 1865–1900* (Norman: University of Oklahoma Press, 1976), 18–23; C. Joseph Genetin-Palawa, *Crooked Paths to Allotment: The Fight over Federal Indian Policy after the Civil War* (Chapel Hill: University of North Carolina Press, 2012), 67–72.
6. *Boston Daily Advertiser*, January 27, 1869; Thomas C. Battey, "Introduction," in Lawrie Tatum, *Our Red Brothers and the Peace Policy of President Ulysses S. Grant* (Philadelphia: John C. Winston, 1899), xvii–xviii; Senate Miscellaneous

Document No. 53, 45th Cong., 3rd sess., 396–397; Robert M. Utley, *The Indian Frontier, 1846–1890*, rev. ed. (Albuquerque: University of New Mexico Press, 2003), 127.

7. *PUSG*, 19:142. The word *christianization* appeared in a handwritten version of the address and in several newspaper accounts, apparently based on copies distributed to reporters. The word's absence from some newspaper accounts and from the official compilation of presidential messages and papers suggests that Grant may have inserted it during his delivery of the address or, alternatively, that it appeared in the prepared text from which he diverged, leaving it out. *M and P*, 7:8; *WES*, March 4, 1869; *NYT*, March 5, 1869; *Cleveland Daily Herald*, March 5, 1869; *Boston Daily Advertiser*, March 5, 1869; *WNR*, March 5, 1869; *Newark (Ohio) Advocate*, March 5, 1869.

8. JDC to ERH, March 19, 1869, JDC-OCL; *PUSG*, 19:197; *Journal of the Executive Proceedings of the Senate of the United States*, 41st Cong., 1st sess., 155, 162, 184, 199; *Philadelphia North American and United States Gazette*, April 17, 1869; *CG*, 41st Cong., 2nd sess., 4083; William H. Armstrong, *Warrior in Two Camps: Ely S. Parker, Union General and Seneca Chief* (Syracuse, N.Y.: Syracuse University Press, 1978), 134–136.

9. *Washington Daily National Intelligencer*, March 16, 1869; *Boston Daily Advertiser*, March 16, 1869; *NYH*, March 16, 1869.

10. *NYH*, March 25, 1869; George H. Stuart, *The Life of George H. Stuart*, ed. Robt. Ellis Thomson (Philadelphia: J. M. Stoddart, 1890), 239–240; JDC to Eli K. Price, William Welsh, et al., March 25, 1869, JDC-OCL; William Welsh to Henry B. Whipple, March 26, 1869, Henry B. Whipple Papers, Minnesota Historical Society; *NYT*, March 26, 28, April 10, 1869; William Welsh, *Summing up of Evidence before a Committee of the House of Representatives Charged with the Investigation of Misconduct in the Indian Office* (Washington, D.C.: H. Polkinhorn, 1871), 60–64; *CG*, 41st Cong., 1st sess., 447–448, 558–561, 590, 628, 647–648; 16 *Statutes at Large* 40.

11. JDC to George H. Stuart, April 13, 1869 (two telegrams), George Hay Stuart Papers, LC; Stuart, *Life of Stuart*, 240–241; *PUSG*, 19:196–197; Utley, *Indian Frontier*, 130–131; Genetin-Palawa, *Crooked Paths to Allotment*, 90–92.

12. JDC to John V. Farwell, April 15, 1869, JDC-OCL; *M and P*, 7:23–24; Utley, *Indian Frontier*, 131; *NYT*, June 8, 1869.

13. Robert H. Keller Jr., *American Protestantism and United States Indian Policy, 1869–82* (Lincoln: University of Nebraska Press, 1983), 76–77; William Welsh to Henry B. Whipple, May 14, 1869, Felix R. Brunot to Whipple, July 3, 1869, Whipple Papers; Welsh, *Summing up of Evidence*, 65; House Executive Document No. 1, pt. 3, 41st Cong., 2nd sess., 488; Welsh to JDC, September 13, 1871, JDC-OCL; *PUSG*, 19:193–197 (emphasis in original).

14. House Executive Document No. 1, pt. 3, 41st Cong., 2nd sess., 487–493.

15. *M and P*, 7:38–39; *Report of the Commissioner of Indian Affairs, 1869*, House Executive Document No. 1, pt. 3, 41st Cong., 2nd sess., 449–450; *NYT*, January 26, 1870.

16. *Report of the Secretary of the Interior, 1869*, House Executive Document No. 1, pt. 3, 41st Cong., 2nd sess., x; *Journal of the Executive Proceedings of the Senate of the United States*, 41st Cong., 2nd sess., 289–292, 326, 348, 463, 545–546.

17. Paul A. Hutton, "Phil Sheridan's Pyrrhic Victory: The Piegan Massacre, Army Politics, and the Transfer Debate," *Montana: The Magazine of Western History* 32 (Spring 1982): 32–43; Genetin-Palawa, *Crooked Paths to Allotment*, 81–82; *CG*, 41st Cong., 2nd sess., 1576–1577, 5402, appendix, 150; *NYT*, March 10, 1870; 16 *Statutes at Large* 360; *Second Annual Report of the Board of Indian Commissioners*, Senate Executive Document No. 39, 41st Cong., 3rd sess., 100–101.

18. 16 *Statutes at Large* 360; *NYH*, June 2, 3, 4, 7, 1870; *NYT*, June 8, 1870.

19. *NYH*, June 4, 8, 10, 1870; *NYT*, June 8, 1870; *Second Annual Report of the Board of Indian Commissioners*, 40–42.

20. *NYH*, June 12, 1870; *Report of the Commissioner of Indian Affairs, 1870*, House Executive Document No. 1, pt. 4, 41st Cong., 3rd sess., 468; Utley, *Indian Frontier*, 144–149.

21. *NYT*, July 16, 1870; *M and P*, 7:79.

22. *CG*, 41st Cong., 2nd sess., 4363–4364; 16 *Statutes at Large* 319; JDC to JAG, August 16, 1870, JAG-LC.

23. *PUSG*, 20:326; *NYT*, October 29, 1870; *Journal of the Executive Proceedings of the Senate of the United States*, 41st Cong., 3rd sess., 619–620; *M and P*, 7:109–110.

24. *Report of the Commissioner of Indian Affairs, 1870*, 474; *Second Annual Report of the Board of Indian Commissioners*, 5, 11; *Report of the Secretary of the Interior, 1870*, House Executive Document No. 1, pt. 4, 41st Cong., 3rd sess., vi; William Welsh to Henry B. Whipple, June 24, 1870, Whipple Papers; Prucha, *American Indian Policy*, 53–58.

25. William Welsh to Henry B. Whipple, December 10, 1870, January 28, 1870 [1871], Whipple Papers; *Second Annual Report of the Board of Indian Commissioners*, 5; *Affairs in the Indian Department*, House Report No. 39, 41st Cong., 3rd sess., ii, vii, 62, 111–122; 16 *Statutes at Large* 568; *PUSG*, 22:71–72; Keller, *American Protestantism*, 82–84; Genetin-Palawa, *Crooked Paths to Allotment*, 100–104; Prucha, *American Indian Policy*, 82–83; Armstrong, *Warrior in Two Camps*, 152–161.

26. 16 *Statutes at Large* 566; Utley, *Indian Frontier*, 132.

27. *PUSG*, 17:40; USG to PHS, December 24, 1868, *PUSG*, 19:99; *M and P*, 7:38, 110.

28. *M and P*, 7:152; Pease and Randall, *Diary of Browning*, 2:103; *NYH*, June 8, 1871.

CHAPTER 12. REFORM AND REVOLT

1. JDC to Edward Cromwell, May 14, 1870, JDC to R. D. Harrison, August 10, 1870, JDC to E. L. Godkin, December 5, 1870, JDC-OCL; *Annual Report of the Commissioner of Patents, 1869*, House Executive Document No. 102, 41st Cong.,

2nd sess., 6–7; *NYT*, December 3, 1870; JDC, "The Civil Service Reform," *North American Review* 112 (January 1871): 100–104; Ari Hoogenboom, *Outlawing the Spoils: A History of the Civil Service Reform Movement, 1865–1883* (Urbana: University of Illinois Press, 1968), 68–69.

2. John Russell Young, *Around the World with General Grant* (New York: American News, 1879), 2:265–266.

3. Hoogenboom, *Outlawing the Spoils*, 9–16, 27–29.

4. Ibid., 9–11; Young, *Around the World with General Grant*, 263–264; Beverly Wilson Palmer, ed., *The Selected Letters of Charles Sumner* (Boston: Northeastern University Press, 1990), 2:457; J. C. Levenson et al., eds., *The Letters of Henry Adams* (Cambridge, Mass.: Harvard University Press, 1982), 2:10, 26; Henry Adams, "Civil Service Reform," in *The Great Secession Winter of 1860–61 and Other Essays by Henry Adams*, ed. George Hochfield (New York: Sagamore Press, 1958), 111; Ari Hoogenboom, "Civil Service Reform and Public Morality," in *The Gilded Age*, ed. H. Wayne Morgan (Syracuse, N.Y.: Syracuse University Press, 1970), 81–86.

5. Hans L. Trefousse, *Carl Schurz: A Biography* (Knoxville: University of Tennessee Press, 1982), 3–174.

6. CSch to EBW, December 10, 1868, EBW-LC (emphasis in original); EBW to CSch, December 29, 1868, CSch-LC; William E. Parrish, *Missouri under Radical Rule, 1865–1870* (Columbia: University of Missouri Press, 1965), 258–267.

7. Trefousse, *Schurz*, 175, 183; CSch to HF, May 16, 1869, AN-CU; CSch to HF, April 1 (ts), 16 (ts), 1869, HF to CSch, May 28, 1869, HF-LC; Frederic Bancroft, ed., *Speeches, Correspondence and Political Papers of Carl Schurz* (New York: G. P. Putnam's Sons, 1913), 1:482–483.

8. HA to JDC, November 8, 1869, JDC-OCL; *CG*, 41st Cong., 2nd sess., 236, 238, 1477, 1595, 2953, 3182–3187, 3221–3225, 3256–3261, 4309; Hoogenboom, *Outlawing the Spoils*, 71–73.

9. *CG*, 41st Cong., 2nd sess., 17, 1077–1078.

10. JDC to CS, June 15, 1869, CS-Mf; Hoogenboom, *Outlawing the Spoils*, 65; *Report of the Secretary of the Interior, 1869*, House Executive Document No. 1, pt. 3, 41st Cong., 2nd sess., xxiv–xxvi; JDC to A. F. Perry, July 29, August 20, 1870, JDC to R. D. Harrison, August 10, 1870, JDC-OCL.

11. *PUSG*, 20:271, 274, 295; HF, diary, October 4, 1870, HF-LC.

12. JDC to J. H. Clendening, July 28, 1870, R. D. Harrison to JDC, May 14, August 3, 1870, JDC to Harrison, August 10, 1870, W. A. Short to JDC, September 7, 1870, JDC to Short, September 8, 1870, JDC-OCL; *NYH*, September 21, 1870.

13. Theodore Tilton to JDC, October 6, 1870, H. Wilson to JDC, October 6, 1870, JDC-OCL; HF, diary, September 25, 1870, HF-LC; *PUSG*, 20:275; *NYH*, November 16, 1870; J. M. Edmunds to ZC, October 16, 1870, ZC-LC. In the many letters Cox wrote justifying his position, he did not accuse Grant of countermanding his stand against assessments. See JDC to E. L. Godkin, December 5, 1870, JDC-OCL; JDC to JAG, December 6, 9, 1870, JAG-LC; JDC to HF, November 29, 1870, HF-LC.

14. *NYT*, September 27, October 5, 1870; *NYH*, November 16, 1870; *PUSG*, 20:294–295.

15. *NYH*, November 16, 1870; *PUSG*, 20:292–293; HF, diary, October 21, 1870, HF-LC.

16. JDC to JAG, December 9, 1870, JAG-LC; *PUSG*, 20:292, 295–296, 298–299.

17. House Report No. 24, 41st Cong., 3rd sess.; *CG*, 40th Cong., 2nd sess., 2388–2390, 2471–2479, 4453; *CG*, 40th Cong., 3rd sess., 1651; *CG*, 41st Cong., 3rd sess., 1450.

18. *NYH*, November 18, 1870; JDC to the Commissioner of the Land Office, August 13, 1870, *WNR*, August 15, 1870. Cox later claimed that Congress regarded the McGarrahan issue as closed after the committee vote, but during the next session the committee's issuance of majority and minority reports, plus debate on a bill to relieve McGarrahan, demonstrated that the issue remained very much alive in Congress after the summer adjournment. JDC, "The McGarrahan Case," in JDC to Charles Nordhoff, December 3, 1870, CSch-LC; House Report No. 24, 41st Cong., 3rd sess., 1–30; *CG*, 41st Cong., 3rd sess., 1402–1414, 1443–1457.

19. *PUSG*, 20:240–241, 243–244.

20. Mark Wahlgren Summers, *The Era of Good Stealings* (New York: Oxford University Press, 1993), 195; JDC to JAG, December 9, 1870, JAG-LC; *PUSG*, 20:241–243, 297; JDC to Charles White, August 23, 1870, USG-LC; HF, diary, October 4, 1870, HF-LC.

21. *PUSG*, 20:297; HF, diary, October 4, 1870, HF-LC.

22. William M. Armstrong, ed., *The Gilded Age Letters of E. L. Godkin* (Albany: State University of New York Press, 1974), 157; *PUSG*, 20:294–298; *Harper's Weekly*, October 29, 1870.

23. Henry V. Boynton, "Mem. of Conversations of Mr. [L. L.] Crounse & J[ohn] R[ussell] Y[oung] with Pres[iden]t as Given by Them to H. V. B," October 1870, Charles Cox to JDC, October 26, 1870, JAG to JDC, October 26, 1870, HA to JDC, October 31, 1870, JDC-OCL; HF, diary, October 21, 1870, JDC to HF, November 29, 1870, HF-LC; *NYH*, October 26, 31, 1870; *NYT*, October 21, 26, 1870; *PUSG*, 20:299–300; JDC to JAG, December 9, 1870, JAG-LC; *WNR*, October 31, November 1, 1870; *Cleveland Daily Herald*, October 31, 1870.

24. Theodore D. Woolsey et al. to JDC, November 4, 1870, JDC to Woolsey et al., November 8, 1870, JDC-OCL; *Boston Daily Advertiser*, November 10, 1870; Henry Wilson to HF, October 31, 1870 (ts), HF-LC; HP to JHW, October 31, 1870, JHW-LC.

25. *NYH*, November 5, 10, 1870; HP to JRY, November 20, 1870, JRY-LC; Henry V. Boynton to JDC, November 15, 1870, JDC-OCL; JMH to BHB, November 10, 1870, BHB-LC (emphasis in original).

26. JDC to Thomas H. Robinson, November 18, 1870, JDC to E. L. Godkin, December 5, 1870, JDC to W. T Spear, December 5, 1870, Henry V. Boynton to JDC, November 15, 1870, HA to JDC, November 11, 1870, Charles Cox to JDC,

November 12, 21, 1870, JAG to JDC, December 7, 17 (and 23), 1870, January 18, February 27, 1871, JDC-OCL; JDC to Charles Nordhoff, December 3, 1870, CSch-LC; JDC to JAG, December 9, 1870, January 12, 19, 23 (two letters), February 14, 24, 1871, JAG-LC; *CG*, 41st Cong., 3rd sess., 1457, appendix, 143.

27. HF to JDC, December 27, 1870, JDC to Edward L. Pierce, May 13, 1895, JDC to John Lynch, March 9, 1871, JDC-OCL; JDC to JAG, March 20, 27, 1871, JAG-LC; Allan Nevins, *Hamilton Fish: The Inner History of the Grant Administration* (New York: Dodd, Mead, 1937), 465, 466.

28. *CG*, 41st Cong., 2nd sess., 3607–3610; *Boston Daily Advertiser*, March 29, 1870; *PUSG*, 20:189, 284.

29. Trefousse, *Schurz*, 190–191; Parrish, *Missouri under Radical Rule*, 292–299; Thomas S. Barclay, "The Liberal Republican Movement in Missouri," *Missouri Historical Review* 21 (October 1926): 75–80.

30. *PUSG*, 20:260, 284, 313–314; *Journal of the Executive Proceedings of the Senate*, 41st Cong., 3rd sess., 556, 570, 576, 613–615; HF to CSch, September 5, 1870, JSM to CSch, October 27, 1870, CSch-LC; Bancroft, *Speeches of Schurz*, 1:520–521; CSch to DAW, October 9, 1870, DAW-LC; Barclay, "Liberal Republican Movement in Missouri," 89–91.

31. Barclay, "Liberal Republican Movement in Missouri," 95–105; Bancroft, *Speeches of Schurz*, 1:521–522; *CG*, 41st Cong., 3rd sess., 714.

32. HF, diary, April 20, June 2, 1870, HF-LC; *Journal of the Executive Proceedings of the Senate*, 41st Cong., 2nd sess., 504, 507, 518, 520, 523–524; *NYT*, July 12, 1870; George Rothwell Brown, ed., *Reminiscences of William M. Stewart of Nevada* (New York: Neale, 1908), 254–257; Hoogenboom, *Outlawing the Spoils*, 75–76; William B. Hesseltine, *Ulysses S. Grant: Politician* (New York: Dodd, Mead, 1935), 211–213; RC to JRY, July 21, 1870, JRY-LC.

33. Summers, *Era of Good Stealings*, 189–191; *PUSG*, 20:142; *NYT*, July 2, 1870.

34. *NYT*, November 9, 10, 1870; Xi Wang, *The Trial of Democracy: Black Suffrage and Northern Republicans, 1860–1910* (Athens: University of Georgia Press, 1997), 79; HP to JRY, November 20, 1870, JRY-LC.

35. Kenneth C. Martis, *The Historical Atlas of Political Parties in the United States Congress, 1789–1989* (New York: Macmillan, 1989), 122–125; Edward McPherson, *A Hand-Book of Politics for 1872* (Washington, D.C.: Philp & Solomons, 1872), 182.

36. *Nation*, November 17, 1870; HA to JDC, November 28, 1870, JDC-OCL; Mahlon Sands to DAW, November 22, 1870, DAW-LC; *NYT*, November 29, 1870; Edward Atkinson to CS, December 1, 1870, CS-Mf; Armstrong, *Letters of Godkin*, 163.

37. HF to Daniel E. Sickles, November 21, 1870, HF-LC; OEB to ZC, November 9, 1870, ZC-LC.

38. JHW to HP, November 4, 1870, JHW-LC; LT to JDC, November 23, 1870, JDC-OCL.

39. *M and P*, 7:109.

40. *NYT*, December 6, 1870; JDC to JAG, December 9, 1870, JAG-LC; HA to JDC, December 8, 1870, JDC-LC; *Nation*, December 8, 1870; *Harper's Weekly*, December 24, 1870.

41. Hoogenboom, *Outlawing the Spoils*, 86–87; *CG*, 41st Cong., 3rd sess., 1935–1936, 1997; *Harper's Weekly*, March 25, 1871.

42. Hoogenboom, *Outlawing the Spoils*, 90–91; *PUSG*, 21:8–9, 13, 83; *Nation*, June 8, 1871; "Minutes of President Grant's Civil Service Commission, 1871–1875," USG-USGPL.

43. HF, diary, October 23, 1870, HF-LC; *M and P*, 7:107–108; *Nation*, December 8, 1870.

44. *NYTr*, December 6, 1870; HA to JDC, December 8, 1870, JDC-OCL; *CG*, 41st Cong., 3rd sess., 70–71, 801; *NYH*, December 13, 1870.

45. HF, diary, November 21, 25, 30, 1870, HF-LC; *M and P*, 7:99–101.

46. HF, diary, December 9, 11, 12, 1870, HF-LC; *PUSG*, 21:78–80, 85, 87; *CG*, 41st Cong., 3rd sess., 53, 66.

47. *Chicago Republican*, November 19, 1870, in *NYH*, November 21, 1870; JRY to HF, November 21, 1870, HF-LC; OEB, diary, August 20, 1869, OEB-USGPL; *CG*, 41st Cong., 3rd sess., 51, 183–187, 291, 416; Senate Executive Document No. 17, 41st Cong., 3rd sess.; JLM to CS, December 8, 1870, Frederick Douglass to CS, December 12, 1870, CS-Mf.

48. *PUSG*, 21:83.

49. *CG*, 41st Cong., 3rd sess., 217–218, 226–271, 381–389, 406–416, 426–431; *Journal of the Senate of the United States*, 41st Cong., 3rd sess., 86, 114.

50. Invoice, F & J. Rives & Geo. A. Bailey, [December 31, 1870], CS-Mf; Charles Sumner, *Naboth's Vineyard. Speech of Hon. Charles Sumner, of Massachusetts, on the Proposed Annexion of "The Island of San Domingo"; Delivered in the Senate of the United States, December 21, 1870* (Washington, D.C.: F. & J. Rives & Geo. A. Bailey, 1870). Inserted passages appear on pages 12 and 13; compare *CG*, 41st Cong., 3rd sess., 230.

51. J. M. Ashley to CS, December 26, 1870, Frederick Douglass to CS, January 6, 1871, CS to S. G. Howe, December 30, 1870, CS-Mf.

52. HF, diary, December 23, 1870, HF-LC; BHB to JMH, December 24, 1870, JMH-LC.

53. ERH to JDC, February 9, 1871, JDC-OCL; HF, diary, January 10, 13, 1871, HF to George Bancroft, January 16, 1871, HF to EBW, January 17, 1871, HF-LC; *PUSG*, 21:132–133; CS to George William Curtis, January 16, 1871, CS-Mf.

54. Senate Executive Document No. 9, 42nd Cong., 1st sess., 31, 36; Charles Richard Williams, ed., *Diary and Letters of Rutherford Birchard Hayes* (Columbus: Ohio State Archaeological and Historical Society, 1924), 3:131; Charles Callan Tansill, *The United States and Santo Domingo, 1798–1873: A Chapter in Caribbean Diplomacy* (Baltimore: Johns Hopkins Press, 1938), 436–438, 438n.

55. Senate Executive Document No. 11, 41st Cong., 3rd sess., 17–26; JLM to CS, December 7, 8, 1870, CS-Mf.

56. HF, diary, January 2, 1871, HF-LC; *CG*, 41st Cong., 3rd sess., 310–311; L. A. Gobright to JCBD, January 9, 1871, JCBD-LC; Senate Executive Document No. 11, 41st Cong., 3rd sess., 27–37.

57. CS to George Bemis, January 20, 1871, JLM to CS, January 20, 1871, CS-Mf; AB to HF, January 26, 1871 (ts), EBW to HF, February 4, 1871 (ts), Thurlow Weed to HF, January 21, 1871 (ts), HF-LC.

58. HF, diary, January 9, 10, 11, 14, 15, 17, 1871, HF-LC; Kenneth Bourne, ed., *British Documents on Foreign Affairs: Reports and Papers from the Foreign Office Confidential Print* (Lanham, Md.: University Press of America, 1986), pt. I, ser. C, vol. 7, 300–306.

59. HF, diary, January 10, 11, 15, 17, 1871, J. W. Patterson to HF, January 12, 1871, HF-LC; Bourne, *British Documents on Foreign Affairs*, pt. I, ser. C, vol. 7, 308–310.

60. CS, "Memorandum for Mr. Fish in Reply to His Inquiries," with Fish's notations, January 17, 1871, HF to CS, January 21, 1871, HF-LC; CS to George Bemis, January 18, 1871, CS-Mf; Palmer, *Selected Letters of Sumner*, 2:542.

61. HF, diary, January 20, 1871, HF-LC; Palmer, *Selected Letters of Sumner*, 2:546; Bourne, *British Documents on Foreign Affairs*, pt. I, ser. C, vol. 7, 315.

62. HF, diary, January 23, 24, 25, 26, 28, 30, February 2, 3, 1871, ET to HF, January 24, 1871 (ts), HF to EBW, February 20, 1871, HF-LC; Bourne, *British Documents on Foreign Affairs*, pt. I, ser. C, vol. 7, 302, 325–329; ET to HF, January 26, February 1, 1871, HF to ET, January 30, 1871, in *NYT*, February 10, 1871; *M and P*, 7:121–122.

63. *PUSG*, 21:173; HF to Thurlow Weed, February 4, 1871, HF-LC.

64. CS to George Bemis, January 20, 24, February 1, 1871, CS-Mf.

65. Edward L. Pierce to CS, February 19, 1871, Richard H. Dana Jr. to CS, February 11, 1871, CS to Francis Vinton, February 20, 1871, CS-Mf; *Journal of the Executive Proceedings of the Senate*, 41st Cong., 3rd sess., 552, 553, 633, 635, 640; HF, diary, February 4, 1871, HF-LC; *NYH*, February 6, 1871.

66. CS to H. W. Longfellow, February 22, 1871, CS to Anna Cabot Lodge, February 22, 1871, Edward L. Pierce to CS, February 21, 25, 1871, Longfellow to CS, February 24, 1871, RHJP to CS, February 28, 1871, Davis Hatch to CS, March 10, 1871, CS-Mf; WR to W. D. Bickham, March 7, 1871, WR-LC; David Herbert Donald, *Charles Sumner* (1970; reprint, New York: Da Capo, 1996), 2:490.

67. HF to Thurlow Weed, February 4, 1871, HF to John Jay, February 25, 1871, HF to EBW, February 20, 1871, HF-LC; D. E. Sickles to JCBD, March 7, 1871, JCBD-LC.

68. HF, diary, March 6, 8, 1871, HF-LC.

69. *CG*, 42nd Cong., 1st sess., 33–53; *NYT*, March 11, 1871.

70. *PUSG*, 21:237–238; *NYH*, March 13, 1871; Edward L. Pierce to CS, March 10, 1871, Charles Nordhoff to CS, March 10, 1871, George William Curtis to CS, March 11, 1871, CS-Mf.

71. CS to Anna Cabot Lodge, March 23, 1871, CS-Mf; *NYH*, March 16, 1871.

72. Richard Smith to HF, March 18, 1871, HF to Smith, March 25, 1871 (draft and letterpress, emphasis in original), HF-LC.

73. Edward L. Pierce to CS, March 15, 1871, Gerrit Smith to CS, March 17, 1871, CS-Mf; *NYH*, March 15, 1871.

74. *WES*, March 22, 1871; BFW to Caroline Wade, February 1, 1871, BFW-LC; BFW to USG, March 6, 1871, BFW Papers, Chicago History Museum.

75. *CG*, 42nd Cong., 1st sess., 294–305.

76. NPB to Mrs. NPB, March 24, 1871, NPB-LC; George M. Robeson to Admiral S. P. Lee, March 21, 1871, in *NYH*, March 28, 1871.

77. *CG*, 42nd Cong., 1st sess., 305–307, appendix, 40–46.

78. *NYH*, March 24, 25, 28, 1871; *M and P*, 7:127–128, 132–133; *CG*, 42nd Cong., 1st sess., 295, 296, 299, 305, appendix, 44.

79. William Lloyd Garrison to CS, March 28, 1871, Wm. Ware Peck to CS, March 28, 1871, Hardy Preer to CS, March 30, 1871, W. McCaulley to CS, March 31, 1871, CS-Mf; G. W. Hazleton to EWK, March 28, 1871, EWK-WHS.

80. *NYT*, March 29, April 10, 1871; TOH to Grace Howe, April 4, 1871, TOH-WHS; *Boston Daily Advertiser*, April 5, 1871; HF, diary, April 9, 1871, HF-LC.

81. Senate Executive Document No. 9, 42nd Cong., 1st sess., 4–34.

82. Ibid., 1–3; OEB, diary, July 17–September 4, 1869, OEB-USGPL.

83. *NYT*, April 6, 1871; TOH to Grace Howe, April 8, 1871, TOH-WHS; William H. C. Bartlett to OEB, April 16, 1871, D. H. Mahan to OEB, April 17, 1871, OEB-NL; HF, diary, March 28, 31, April 8, 1871, HF-LC; OEB to A. M. Clapp, May 9, June 16, 1871, USG-LC; HP to JHW, date missing, USG-USGPL.

84. Palmer, *Selected Letters of Sumner*, 2:552, 565; CS, *Personal Relations with the President and Secretary of State. An Explanation in Reply to an Assault* (Washington, D.C.: n.p., 1871]; HF, diary, April 17, 19, 21, 1871, HF-LC; BFB to CS, April 16, 1871, CS to Anna Cabot Lodge, April 19, 1871, Edward L. Pierce to CS, April 22, May 8, 1871, Henry Wilson to CS, June 6, 1871, CS-Mf (emphasis in originals).

85. TOH to Grace Howe, April 12, 1871, TOH-WHS; Edward L. Pierce to CS, April 22, 1871, CS-Mf.

CHAPTER 13. WAR AT HOME

1. *M and P*, 7:96, 112.

2. *CG*, 41st Cong., 3rd sess., 146.

3. Senate Executive Document No. 16, 41st Cong., 3rd sess., pts. 1 and 2; *NYH*, January 15, 1871.

4. *CG*, 41st Cong., 3rd sess., 570–582, 598, 619.

5. HF, diary, February 14, 1871, HF-LC; 16 *Statutes at Large* 412–413; *M and P*, 7:122–123; 23 *Statutes at Large* 21–22.

6. 16 *Statutes at Large* 433–440; Xi Wang, *The Trial of Democracy: Black Suffrage and Northern Republicans, 1860–1910* (Athens: University of Georgia Press, 1997), 80–81.

7. *CG*, 41st Cong., 3rd sess., 1280, 1637, appendix, 125, 126; Edward McPherson, *A Hand-Book of Politics for 1872* (Washington, D.C.: Philp & Solomons, 1872), 8.

8. Allen W. Trelease, *White Terror: The Ku Klux Klan Conspiracy and Southern Reconstruction* (New York: Harper & Row, 1971), 224–225; *PUSG*, 21:259–260; HF, diary, February 24, 1871, HF-LC.

9. *NYH*, March 9, 1871; *PUSG*, 21:218–219, 263; JAG to JDC, March 23, 1871, JDC-OCL; *NYT*, March 10, 1871.

10. Senate Report No. 1, 42nd Cong., 1st sess., pt. 1, xxxi, pt. 2, 3; *PUSG*, 21:351; *CG*, 42nd Cong., 1st sess., 134–135, 180–182, 534, 537.

11. *PUSG*, 21:266; *NYTr*, March 22, 1871; *NYT*, March 22, 1871.

12. *NYT*, March 15, 16, 1871; *CG*, 42nd Cong., 1st sess., 115–118, 122, 123–125, 152–161, 173–175, appendix, 27–40; BFB, "To the Republicans of the House of Representatives," in *Cleveland Morning Herald*, March 18, 1871; *Milwaukee Sentinel*, March 18, 1871.

13. *WES*, March 23, 1871; *NYH*, March 24, 1871; *M and P*, 7:127–128; "Secretary" to GSB, March 23, 1871, USG-LC; *NYTr*, March 24, 1871; George F. Hoar, *Autobiography of Seventy Years* (New York: Charles Scribner's Sons, 1903), 1:204–206. From the vantage of thirty years, Hoar recalled Grant's reluctance to exercise extraordinary powers without congressional sanction, and he magnified his own influence in persuading the president to send the message.

14. HF, diary, March 24, 1871, HF-LC; *M and P*, 7:132–133; *NYT*, March 25, 1871.

15. *CG*, 42nd Cong., 1st sess., 244–249, 317.

16. Ibid., 367, 409, 687, 335, 487–488; Charles W. Calhoun, *Conceiving a New Republic: The Republican Party and the Southern Question, 1869–1900* (Lawrence: University Press of Kansas, 2006), 26–31; Everette Swinney, *Suppressing the Ku Klux Klan: The Enforcement of the Reconstruction Amendments, 1870–1877* (New York: Garland, 1987), 156–179.

17. *WNR*, April 10, 1871; *NYH*, April 9, 1871.

18. McPherson, *Hand-Book of Politics for 1872*, 87; 17 *Statutes at Large* 13–15; *NYH*, April 25, 1871.

19. HF, diary, April 13, May 2, 1871, HF-LC; *M and P*, 7:134–135; *PUSG*, 21:337, 355; *NYH*, May 18, 1871.

20. *PUSG*, 22:130 (emphasis in original); Gerrit Smith to CS, August 23, 31, September 13, 1871, CS to Smith, August 28, 1871, CS-Mf; *NYH*, June 6, 7, 1871.

21. ATA to J. H. H. Wilcox, August 16, 1871, ATA to E. P. Jackson, August 18, 1871, ATA Letterbooks, Alderman Library, University of Virginia; Robert J. Kaczorowski, *The Politics of Judicial Interpretation: The Federal Courts, Department of Justice and Civil Rights, 1866–1876* (Dobbs Ferry, N.Y.: Oceana Publications, 1985), 83–93; Swinney, *Suppressing the Ku Klux Klan*, 183–197.

22. John Scott to SC, June 28, 1871, SC-LC; HF, diary, September 1, 1871, HF-LC; *NYH*, September 2, 1871; *NYT*, September 1, 2, 1871; *M and P*, 7:163.

23. ATA to Alfred H. Terry, November 18, 1871, ATA Letterbooks; *NYT*, October 31, 1871; JMH to BHB, September 27, 1871, BHB-LC; *PUSG*, 22:162–163.

24. BHB to JMH, October 8, 14, 1871, JMH-LC; JMH to BHB, September 27, 1871, John W. Finnell to BHB, September 14, 1871, BHB-LC.

25. BHB to JMH, October 8, November 7, 1871, JMH-LC (emphasis in original); JMH to BHB, October 11, 1871, BHB-LC.

26. *M and P*, 7:135–138; *PUSG*, 22:178; BHB to JMH, October 14, 1871, JMH-LC.

27. *NYTr*, October 18, 1871; *PUSG*, 22:159–161, 219–224; *M and P*, 7:154; 17 *Statutes at Large* 24, 51.

28. *NYT*, October 31, 1871; *Annual Report of the Attorney General of the United States for the Year 1871*, House Executive Document No. 55, 42nd Cong., 2nd sess., 4–6; Swinney, *Suppressing the Ku Klux Klan*, 213–214, 229–236; ATA to Alfred H. Terry, November 18, 1871, ATA Letterbooks.

29. HF, diary, October 31, December 1, 1871, HF-LC; *NYH*, November 1, 8, 1871; ATA to Benjamin Conley, December 28, 1871, ATA Letterbooks; Brooks D. Simpson, *The Reconstruction Presidents* (Lawrence: University Press of Kansas, 1998), 157; *PUSG*, 21:355–356; *M and P*, 7:150–151, 153.

30. BHB to JMH, October 14, November 7, 1871, JMH-LC; HF, diary, November 24, 1871, HF-LC.

31. *NYH*, December 5, 13, 1871; *Philadelphia Inquirer*, December 13, 1871, *PUSG*, 22:289; HF diary, December 11, 13, 1871, HF-LC; *PUSG*, 22:288–289, 295–296; *NYTr*, December 16, 1871; Allan Nevins, *Hamilton Fish: The Inner History of the Grant Administration* (New York: Dodd, Mead, 1937), 592; ATA to Benjamin Conley, December 28, 1871, ATA Letterbooks.

32. *NYTr*, December 15, 1871; *PUSG*, 22:311–312; *NYT*, December 25, 27, 1871; JMH to BHB, February 2, 1872, JHW to BHB, February 12, 1872, BHB-LC; *PUSG*, 23:283.

33. *PUSG*, 22:297; HF, diary, October 21, 1870, HF-LC; Sidney Teiser, "Life of George H. Williams: Almost Chief Justice," *Oregon Historical Quarterly* 47 (1946): 279; Kathryn Allamong Jacob, *Capital Elites: High Society in Washington, D.C., after the Civil War* (Washington, D.C.: Smithsonian Institution Press, 1995), 95–96; JHW to BHB, December 15, 1871, BHB-LC.

34. *NYH*, December 16, 1871; ATA to Benjamin Conley, December 28, 1871, ATA Letterbooks; Kaczorowski, *Politics of Judicial Interpretation*, 101–103.

CHAPTER 14. PEACE ABROAD

1. HF to Daniel E. Sickles, February 16, 1871, HF-LC; Kenneth Bourne, ed., *British Documents on Foreign Affairs: Reports and Papers from the Foreign Office*

Confidential Print (Lanham, Md.: University Press of America, 1986), pt. I, ser. C, vol. 7, 336; *PUSG*, 21:178.

2. HF, diary, February 3, 7, 8, 14, 1871, HF-LC; *Journal of the Executive Proceedings of the Senate of the United States*, 41st Cong., 3rd sess., 644–645, 651–652.

3. Adrian Cook, *The Alabama Claims: American Politics and Anglo-American Relations, 1865–1872* (Ithaca, N.Y.: Cornell University Press, 1975), 170–171; Montague Bernard, *An Historical Account of the Neutrality of Great Britain during the American Civil War* (London: Longmans, Green, Reader, & Dyer, 1870); HF, diary, February 9, 16, 24, 1871, HF-LC; BM to JCBD, February 10, 1871, JCBD-LC; ERH to JDC, July 4, 1871, JDC-OCL; Phillip E. Myers, *Dissolving Tensions: Rapprochement and Resolution in British-American-Canadian Relations in the Treaty of Washington Era, 1865–1914* (Kent, Ohio: Kent State University Press, 2015), 174–177.

4. Bourne, *British Documents on Foreign Affairs*, pt. I, ser. C, vol. 7, 344–345; Stafford H. Northcote, *Diaries 1869, 1870, 1871, 1875, 1882, of the First Earl of Iddesleigh* (privately printed, 1907), 187–189; Andrew Lang, *Life, Letters, and Diaries of Sir Stafford Northcote, First Earl of Iddesleigh* (Edinburgh: William Blackwood & Sons, 1895), 2:25–26; *NYH*, March 10, 1871; HF, diary, March 28, 1871, HF-LC.

5. Lang, *Life, Letters, and Diaries of Northcote*, 2:23; Northcote, *Diaries*, 196, 210; Stafford H. Northcote to CS, April 27, 1871, CS-Mf; Beverly Wilson Palmer, ed., *The Selected Letters of Charles Sumner* (Boston: Northeastern University Press, 1990), 2:553n; David Herbert Donald, *Charles Sumner* (1970; reprint, New York: Da Capo, 1996), 2:503–504.

6. CFA, diary, February 11, 27, March 4, 5, 10, 1871, AFP-MHS.

7. HF, diary, February 21, March 19, 31, April 7, 13, 19, 1871, JCBD, Treaty of Washington journal (ts), February 26, March 28, April 13, 1871, HF-LC; Bourne, *British Documents on Foreign Affairs*, pt. I, ser. C, vol. 7, 357–358, 366–367, 372; ibid., vol. 8, 3, 8, 20–21; Lang, *Life, Letters, and Diaries of Northcote*, 2:13–15; ERH to JDC, April 7, July 4, 1871, JDC-OCL.

8. JCBD, Treaty of Washington journal (ts), March 4, 26, 1871, HF-LC; Bourne, *British Documents on Foreign Affairs*, pt. I, ser. C, vol. 7, 348–350; HF, diary, March 4, 1871, HF-LC.

9. JCBD, Treaty of Washington journal (ts), March 7, 8, 1871, HF, diary, July 11, 1869, HF-LC.

10. JCBD, Treaty of Washington journal (ts), March 8, 1871, HF-LC.

11. Ibid.

12. Ibid.; Bourne, *British Documents on Foreign Affairs*, pt. I, ser. C, vol. 7, 354–356.

13. JCBD, Treaty of Washington journal (ts), March 8, 9, 13, 14, 1871, HF-LC; Bourne, *British Documents on Foreign Affairs*, pt. I, ser. C, vol. 7, 343–344, 361–363; Northcote, *Diaries*, 192–193; *Treaties, Conventions, International Acts, Protocols and Agreements between the United States of America and Other Powers, 1776–1909*, Senate Document No. 57, 61st Cong., 2nd sess., 1:703.

14. JCBD, Treaty of Washington journal (ts), March 9, 13, 14, 18, 30, April

2, 3, 4, 5, 12, 1871, HF, diary, March 31, 1871, HF-LC; Bourne, *British Documents on Foreign Affairs*, pt. I, ser. C, vol. 7, 347–348; *Treaties, Conventions, International Acts*, 1:703.

15. *Treaties, Conventions, International Acts*, 1:703; JCBD, Treaty of Washington journal (ts), April 14, 1871, HF-LC.

16. Bourne, *British Documents on Foreign Affairs*, pt. I, ser. C, vol. 7, 319, 377; *Treaties, Conventions, International Acts*, 1:701; JCBD, Treaty of Washington journal (ts), April 13, 25, 1871, HF, diary, April 25, 1871, HF-LC; Bourne, *British Documents on Foreign Affairs*, pt. I, ser. C, vol. 8, 3, 9–10, 15.

17. HF, diary, January 17, 1871, JCBD, Treaty of Washington journal (ts), March 8, April 6, 8, 1871, HF-LC; Bourne, *British Documents on Foreign Affairs*, pt. I, ser. C, vol. 8, 5–6, 10–12.

18. Bourne, *British Documents on Foreign Affairs*, pt. I, ser. C, vol. 7, 381–382; ibid., vol. 8, 1, 3, 9–10, 15; JCBD, Treaty of Washington journal (ts), April 24, 25, 1871, HF-LC; *Treaties, Conventions, International Acts*, 1:701, 702.

19. JCBD, Treaty of Washington journal (ts), April 5, 1871, HF-LC; *Treaties, Conventions, International Acts*, 1:701–705.

20. HF, diary, March 29, July 10, 12, December 12, 21, 1869, February 10, March 17, 22, 24, April 14, 21, May 26, September 9, 11, 15, 18, 26, 29, October 16, 19, 30, November 10, 11, 17, 20, 1870, HF-LC; *PUSG*, 20:268; *Treaties, Conventions, International Acts*, 1:631–632, 668–672; Edward Stanwood, *American Tariff Controversies in the Nineteenth Century* (Boston: Houghton, Mifflin, 1903), 2:136–137; Goldwin Smith, *The Treaty of Washington: A Study in Imperial History* (1941; reprint, New York: Russell & Russell, 1971), 4–5; *M and P*, 7:34–35, 102–104.

21. JCBD, Treaty of Washington journal (ts), March 6, 20, 1871, HF, diary, March 6, 1871, HF-LC; Northcote, *Diaries*, 200, 210, 212; Smith, *Treaty of Washington*, 52–54; Bourne, *British Documents on Foreign Affairs*, pt. I, ser. C, vol. 7, 343, 350–352.

22. Northcote, *Diaries*, 198; Smith, *Treaty of Washington*, 54–71, 73–76; Bourne, *British Documents on Foreign Affairs*, pt. I, ser. C, vol. 7, 366, 370–372, 384; JCBD, Treaty of Washington journal (ts), March 20, 27, 1871, HF-LC.

23. HF, diary, April 8, 12, 13, 19, 21, 1871, JCBD, Treaty of Washington journal (ts), April 12, 13, 14, 17, 22, 1871, HF-LC; Bourne, *British Documents on Foreign Affairs*, pt. I, ser. C, vol. 7, 381; ibid., vol. 8, 1–3, 6, 9, 13–14, 24–26, 30–31; Northcote, *Diaries*, 209–210, 212; Smith, *Treaty of Washington*, 77–81.

24. *Treaties, Conventions, International Acts*, 1:708–711; Charles S. Campbell, *The Transformation of American Foreign Relations, 1865–1900* (New York: Harper & Row, 1976), 46–49.

25. *Treaties, Conventions, International Acts*, 1:657; *M and P*, 5:561–563, 666–668.

26. JCBD, Treaty of Washington journal (ts), March 15, 16, 1871, HF-LC; Bourne, *British Documents on Foreign Affairs*, pt. I, ser. C, vol. 7, 354, 357, 363–366; Northcote, *Diaries*, 195; *FRUS, 1872*, 2:50, 52.

27. HF, diary, March 19, April 12, 13, 1871, JCBD, Treaty of Washington journal (ts), March 18, April 12, 14, 1871, HF-LC.

28. Bourne, *British Documents on Foreign Affairs*, pt. I, ser. C, vol. 8, 1, 8, 27–28; JCBD, Treaty of Washington journal (ts), April 19, 22, 1871, HF-LC; *Treaties, Conventions, International Acts*, 1:714–717.

29. HF, diary, March 17, 1871, JCBD, Treaty of Washington journal (ts), March 17, 18, 20, 23, 25, 27, 30, April 14, 15, 22, 23, 24, 25, 26, 1871, HF-LC; John Bassett Moore, *History and Digest of the International Arbitrations to which the United States Has Been a Party* (Washington, D.C.: Government Printing Office, 1898), 1:692–693.

30. HF, diary, May 2, 6, 8, 1871, HF-LC; *Philadelphia North American and United States Gazette*, May 9, 1871; Northcote, *Diaries*, 225–226; Moore, *History and Digest of International Arbitrations*, 1:546.

31. *CG*, 42nd Cong., special sess., 845; *M and P*, 7:132; HF, diary, May 5, 7, 8, 9, 10, 12, 16, 1871, TOH to HF, May 3 (ts), 8 (ts), 1871, HF to TOH, May 4, 1871 (ts), HF to CSch, May 8, 1871 (ts), HF to Editor of the Republican, May 8, 1871, HF-LC; *WES*, May 5, 1871; *WNR*, May 9, 10, 1871; Moore, *History and Digest of International Arbitrations*, 1:546; Cook, *Alabama Claims*, 201; Northcote, *Diaries*, 226–227, 229, 230, 235–236.

32. *NYTr*, May 11, 12, 1871; *WNR*, May 12, 1871; HF, diary, May 16, 1871, HF-LC; Cook, *Alabama Claims*, 201–202; *NYH*, May 9, 18, 1871.

33. Donald, *Sumner*, 2:505–507; CS to George Bemis, May 8 (telegram), 9, 13 (telegram), 1871, F. W. Bird to CS, May 11, 1871 (two letters), CS-Mf; Palmer, *Selected Letters of Sumner*, 2:554–555 (emphasis in original); Northcote, *Diaries*, 226–227, 229, 235–236; *NYH*, May 20, 1871; *CG*, 42nd Cong., special sess., 890.

34. HF, diary, May 16, 18, 21, 22, 1871, HF-LC; *PUSG*, 21:365.

35. *Journal of the Executive Proceedings of the Senate of the United States*, 42nd Cong., special sess., 99–100, 103, 105–108; *CG*, 42nd Cong., special sess., 891; *NYTr*, May 25, 1871; ET to Earl Granville, May 29, 1871, PRO; Cook, *Alabama Claims*, 205–206; Palmer, *Selected Letters of Sumner*, 2:560.

36. ET to Earl Granville, May 29, 1871, PRO; *Journal of the Executive Proceedings of the Senate*, 42nd Cong., special sess., 108–109.

37. *Journal of the Executive Proceedings of the Senate*, 42nd Cong., special sess., 109–114; *NYT*, May 27, 1871.

38. *NYH*, June 3, 1871.

39. Thurlow Weed to HF, May 28, 1871, AN-CU; *New York Evening Post*, May 11, 1871; CFA, diary, June 1, 1871, AFP-MHS; CS to George Bemis, June 5, 1871, CS-Mf.

40. AB to JCBD, May 31, 1871, JCBD-LC; BM, diary, June 9, 11, 1871, BM-LC; HF, diary, June 4, 1871, HF-LC; HF to RCS, June 10, 1871 (telegram), Instructions to United States Ministers to Great Britain, Records of the Department of State, RG 59, NA; HF to ERH, June 18, 1871, ERH-CPL; *PUSG*, 22:51–52; Myers,

Dissolving Tensions, 202–204. As it turned out, the two sides could not agree on the wording of the presentation to the other powers, and the administration closed with no such note transmitted. Senate Executive Document No. 26, 45th Cong., 3rd sess.; Allan Nevins, *Hamilton Fish: The Inner History of the Grant Administration* (New York: Dodd, Mead, 1937), 864–868.

41. HF, diary, January 14, May 29, June 15, 1871, HF-LC; *PUSG*, 22:53–54, 319–320.

42. *PUSG*, 22:106–107, 245–246; HF, diary, November 14, 21, December 4, 5, 6, 20, 1871, HF to USG, December 4, 1871 (ts), Colfax et al. to HF, December 6, 1871 (ts), HF to JCBD, January 8, 1872, HF-LC; HF to Julia Fish, November 14, 1871, AN-CU.

43. HF, diary, December 6, 1871, HF-LC; Charles Sumner, *Personal Relations with the President and Secretary of State: An Explanation in Reply to an Assault* (n.p., 1871), 2; F. V. Balch to CS, August 26, 1871, Gerrit Smith to CS, September 9, 1871, CS-Mf.

44. HF, diary, April 14, June 16, 17, 21, October 11, 1871, HF-LC; *PUSG*, 22:22–25; S. G. Howe to OEB, September 2, 1871, OEB-NL.

45. HF, diary, June 17, October 11, 27, November 10, 14, 1871, HF-LC; *PUSG*, 22:26–27.

46. HF, diary, November 24, 28, 1871, HF-LC; *M and P*, 7:142–155; *Harper's Weekly*, December 23, 1871; U. S. Grant, *Personal Memoirs* (New York: Charles L. Webster, 1885–1886), 2:550.

47. *NYTr*, May 29, 1871; Palmer, *Selected Letters of Sumner*, 2:561, 572; HF, diary, May 29, 31, 1871, HF-LC.

48. HF, diary, May 31, June 15, 1871, HF to Frederick T. Frelinghuysen, July 13, 1871, ERH to HF, July 11, 1871 (ts), HF-LC; HF to ERH, June 18, 1871, JCBD to ERH, July 6, 1871, ERH-CPL; *PUSG*, 22:40, 69–70, 79.

49. CFA, diary, June 22, 24, July 22, August 3, 10, 1871, CFA to HF, August 4, 1871, AFP-MHS; BM, diary, May 8, 1872, BM-LC.

50. HF to JCBD, August 11, 1871, JCBD-LC; JCBD to ERH, June 20, July 6, August 11, November 11, 1871, ERH-CPL; CFA, diary, June 24, August 30, September 4, October 16, 1871, CFA to JCBD, August 23, 1871, AFP-MHS; JCBD to HF, September 11, 1871 (ts), HF-LC; *PUSG*, 22:121; JCBD to TFB, September 2, 6, 1871, TFB to JCBD, September 4, 14, 1871, TFB-LC; *FRUS, 1872*, 4:3–4.

51. HF, diary, July 11, 1869, HF to RCS, April 12, 1871, HF-LC; *FRUS, 1872*, 1:185–190.

52. CFA, diary, December 18, 1871, AFP-MHS; HF, diary, February 3, 1871, HF-LC.

53. BM, diary, January 16, 27, 30, BM-LC; RCS to HF, February 6, 1872, with enclosed press clippings, Despatches from United States Ministers to Great Britain, Records of the Department of State, RG 59, NA; JCBD to HF, January 7 (ts), 19 (ts), 31 (ts), February 6, 16, 1872, HF-LC.

54. *FRUS, 1872*, 2:425–426; ET to Earl Granville, February 3 (two telegrams), 4 (telegram), 6, 1872, PRO; HF, diary, February 3, 1872, HF to RCS, February 3, 1872, HF-LC.

55. ET to Earl Granville, February 7, 1872, PRO (emphasis in original); JCBD to HF, February 5, 1872, HF-LC.

56. *NYH*, February 6, 1872. In fact, the United States had objected to the British submission of the so-called Confederate cotton loan claims. HF to RCS, November 18, 1871 (telegram), Instructions to Ministers to Great Britain, RG 59, NA; BM, diary, November 20, 1871, BM-LC.

57. JB to WR, February 6, 1872, JB-NYPL; *London Times*, February 7, 1872; HF, diary, February 8, 1872, HF to L. P. Morton, February 14, 1872, HF-LC; *NYH*, February 12, 1872.

58. HF, diary, February 6, 1872, HF-LC.

59. CFA, diary, February 22, 23, May 16, 1872, AFP-MHS; HF, diary, February 22, 23, 1872, HF-LC.

60. HF, diary, February 23, 1872, HF-LC; HF to RCS, February 27, 29 (telegram), 1872, Instructions to Ministers to Great Britain, RG 59, NA; Bourne, *British Documents on Foreign Affairs*, pt. I, ser. C, vol. 7, 381–382; ibid., vol. 8, 1.

61. HF to JCBD, March 1, 1872 (ts), JCBD to HF, March 8, 1872 (ts), HF to RCS, March 1, 1872, RCS to HF, March 20, 1872 (ts), HF, diary, February 29, March 1, 1872, HF-LC; RCS to HF, February 14, 1872, Despatches from United States Ministers to Great Britain, RG 59, NA.

62. Bourne, *British Documents on Foreign Affairs*, pt. I, ser. C, vol. 8, 104–105.

63. CFA to HF, March 25, 1872 (ts), HF to Bellamy Storer, April 5, 1872 (ts), RCS to HF, March 28, 1872 (ts), HF to RCS, April 11, 1872 (ts), HF, diary, April 4, 6, 11, 16, 1872, HF-LC; HF to CFA, March 27, 1872, Lord Tenterden to CFA, April 15, 1872, JCBD to CFA, April 15, 1872, AFP-MHS; JCBD to HF, March 29, 1872, JCBD-LC.

64. ET to Earl Granville, April 11, 16, 20 (telegram), 22, 25 (telegram), 1872, PRO; *CG*, 42nd Cong., 2nd sess., 2304; *Boston Daily Advertiser*, April 10, 1872; *Bangor Daily Whig & Courier*, April 12, 1872; HF, diary, February 4, 6, April 19, 27, 1872, HF to JCBD, April 23, 1872 (ts), HF to RCS, February 5, 6, April 23, 26, May 7, 1872 (ts), Levi P. Morton to HF, February 8, March 28, May 4, 1872 (ts), GSB, "Suggestion" (note to HF), May 9, 1872, HF to John C. Hamilton, May 11, 1872 (ts), HF to Morton, February 14, 18, March 30, May 26, 1872, HF to GSB, February 10, 1880, HF-LC; HF to JCBD, August 6, 1872, JCBD-LC; BM, diary, April 24, 1872, BM-LC. Seven years later, during his round-the-world tour, ex-president Grant recalled that Fish had favored including the indirect claims to forestall criticism of the American case by Charles Sumner and to settle the festering question once and for all. "It was a mistake," a reporter quoted Grant as saying in 1879, "but well intended. It is a mistake ever to say more than you mean, and as we never meant the indirect claims, we should not have presented them, even to please Mr. Sumner." John Russell Young, *Around the World with General Grant* (New York: American News, 1879), 2:279–281.

65. HF to RCS, April 11, 1872 (ts), JCBD, Treaty of Washington journal (ts), March 8, April 6, 8, 10, 13, 25, 1871, HF-LC; Bourne, *British Documents on Foreign Affairs*, pt. I, ser. C, vol. 7, 381–382; ibid., vol. 8, 1, 10–12, 15; *FRUS, 1872*, 2:460–474 (emphasis in original).

66. HF, diary, April 15, 20, 1872, GSB to HF, April 22, 1872, HF to JCBD, April 23, 1872 (ts), HF to RCS, April 23, 1872 (ts), HF-LC; CFA, diary, April 22, 1872, AFP-MHS; HF to RCS, April 23, 1872, Instructions to United States Ministers to Great Britain, RG 59, NA.

67. JCBD to HF, April 15, 17, 25, 1872, JCBD-LC; J. C. Bancroft Davis, *Mr. Fish and the Alabama Claims: A Chapter in Diplomatic History* (Boston: Houghton Mifflin, 1893), 97–98.

68. HF, diary, April 25, 26, May 2, 1872, HF to RCS, April 26, May 7, 1872, HF-LC; ET to Earl Granville, April 30, 1872, PRO; *FRUS, 1872*, 2:477–478, 481, 483, 484–486, 491, 493–494 (emphasis in original); BM, diary, May 6, 1872, BM-LC; CFA, diary, May 7, 8, 1872, AFB-MHS; H. C. G. Matthew, ed., *The Gladstone Diaries* (Oxford: Oxford University Press, 1968–1994), 8:150.

69. HF, diary, May 3, 4, 7, 11, 12, 17, 18, 27, 28, 29, 31, June 4, 1872, HF to EBW, April 30, 1872, George F. Edmunds to HF, May 12, 1872 (ts), HF to Edmunds, May 12, 1872 (ts), HF to L. P. Morton, May 26, 1872, HF to John C. Hamilton, May 30, 1872 (ts), HF-LC; *FRUS, 1872*, 2:491, 493–494, 500–502, 525–526, 528–529, 531, 540–542, 555–558, 560; RCS to HF, May 14, 1872, Despatches from United States Ministers to Great Britain, RG 59, NA; Matthew, *Gladstone Diaries*, 8:144n, 149n; ET to Earl Granville, May 13, 20, 26 (telegram), 28, 1872, Granville to ET, May 27, 1872 (telegram), PRO; *Journal of the Executive Proceedings of the Senate of the United States*, 42nd Cong., 2nd sess., 248, 257, 258, 260–263; *PUSG*, 23:144, 156; Bourne, *British Documents on Foreign Affairs*, pt. I, ser. C, vol. 8, 180–182.

70. *FRUS, 1872*, 2:561–562, 566–567, 4:17–18; CFA, diary, June 14, 15, 1872, CFA to HF, September 20, 1872, AFP-MHS.

71. CFA, diary, May 7, 8, June 14, 15, 16, 17, 18, 19, 1872, CFA to HF, September 20, 1872, "Sir Roundell Palmer's 3 Points," June 15, 1872, CFA to RCS, July 2, 1872, CFA to C. E. Norton, July 3, 1872, drafts of arbitrators' statement, June 16, 17, 1872, RCS, draft diplomatic note, circa May 1872, AFP-MHS; Bourne, *British Documents on Foreign Affairs*, pt. I, ser. C, vol. 8, 183–186; Frank Warren Hackett, *Reminiscences of the Geneva Tribunal of Arbitration, 1872: The Alabama Claims* (Boston: Houghton Mifflin, 1911), 238–254.

72. *FRUS, 1872*, 4:19–20.

73. Ibid., 2:577–580; *PUSG*, 23:157; Bourne, *British Documents on Foreign Affairs*, pt. I, ser. C, vol. 8, 189–190.

74. ET to Earl Granville, July 1, 1872, PRO; *NYTr*, June 28, 1872; HF to Daniel Ullman, July 2, 1872, HF-LC; *NYH*, July 9, 18, 1872; *NYT*, July 24, 1872.

75. Cook, *Alabama Claims*, 238–239; Martin Duberman, *Charles Francis Adams, 1807–1886* (Stanford, Calif.: Stanford University Press, 1968), 379–384; *PUSG*, 23:233–234; *FRUS, 1872*, 4:49–54.

76. *NYT*, September 16, 1872; *NYH*, September 19, 1872; Cook, *Alabama Claims*, 241–242.

77. BM, diary, September 21, 1872, BM-LC; RCS to HF, September 26, 1872 (ts), HF-LC.

78. *NYTr*, September 16, 1872.

CHAPTER 15. VINDICATION

1. A. D. Shaw to JCBD, May 17, 1871, AB to JCBD, June 15, 1871, JCBD-LC; *PUSG*, 22:110, 230, 239; *NYH*, July 24, 1878; *PUSG*, 31:98.

2. J. H. Dickson to CS, March 15, 1872, CS-Mf; *NYH*, January 17, 1872; J. M. Scovel to LT, January 28, 1872 (emphasis in original), W. C. Flagg to LT, January 25, 1872, LT-LC.

3. JDC to DAW, July 22, 1871, Amasa Walker to DAW, June 8, 1871, SB to DAW, June 20, 1871, DAW-LC; Frederic Bancroft, ed., *Speeches, Correspondence and Political Papers of Carl Schurz* (New York: G. P. Putnam's Sons, 1913), 2:257–306, 311–312.

4. David M. Jordan, *Roscoe Conkling of New York: Voice in the Senate* (Ithaca, N.Y.: Cornell University Press, 1971), 154–159; RC to SC, October 13, 1871, SC-LC; A. D. Shaw to JCBD, October 9, 1871, JCBD-LC; Edward McPherson, *A Hand-Book of Politics for 1872* (Washington, D.C.: Philp & Solomons, 1872), 142, 145, 182; HF to James R. Partridge, November 20, 1871, HF-LC.

5. *PUSG*, 22:231–232; HF, diary, December 6, 1871, HF-LC.

6. William B. Hesseltine, *Ulysses S. Grant: Politician* (New York: Dodd, Mead, 1935), 256; Jordan, *Conkling*, 172–173; JB to WR, November 22, 1871, JB-NYPL.

7. *M and P*, 7:142–155; Edgar Newham to BHB, December 7, 1871, BHB-LC; *NYTr*, December 5, 1871.

8. DAW to John T. Hoffman, December 25, 1871, Heartman Collection, NYHS; *CG*, 42nd Cong., 2nd sess., 259–260, 354–359; ET to Earl Granville, December 25, 1871, PRO; David Herbert Donald, *Charles Sumner* (1970; reprint, New York: Da Capo, 1996), 2:527–528.

9. Ari Hoogenboom, *Outlawing the Spoils: A History of the Civil Service Reform Movement, 1865–1883* (Urbana: University of Illinois Press, 1968), 101–102; *CG*, 42nd Cong., 2nd sess., 86, 193–194; *NYT*, December 19, 1871.

10. Senate Report No. 227, 42nd Cong., 2nd sess., 1:699–700, 706–712, 719, 723–733, 745–746, 2:322–324, 328, 329, 332, 333, 346, 3:121–125; Mark Wahlgren Summers, *The Era of Good Stealings* (New York: Oxford University Press, 1993), 97–98.

11. Senate Report No. 227, 42nd Cong., 2nd sess., 1:ii, 699–700, 706–712, 719, 723–733, 745–746, 3:349–350.

12. Ibid., 1:9, 22, 2:448–451, 465–466, 3:124–126, 131, 190; *NYH*, January 20, 27, 1872.

13. *PUSG*, 23:56–57; HF, diary, February 13, 1872, HF-LC; GSB to Chester A. Arthur, February 26, 1872, in *WNR*, February 27, 1872; *NYT*, March 11, 1872; *New York Evening Post*, March 11, 1872; *NYTr*, March 11, 1872. Allan Nevins errs in supposing that Grant's call for prosecutions at the February 13 cabinet meeting was related to testimony from the French arms sales investigation. That investigation did not start until early March. Allan Nevins, *Hamilton Fish: The Inner History of the Grant Administration* (New York: Dodd, Mead, 1937), 603–604; Senate Report No. 183, 42nd Cong., 2nd sess.

14. Senate Report No. 227, 42nd Cong., 2nd sess., ii, xvi, xlix, cxliv, cxlv.

15. *CG*, 42nd Cong., 2nd sess., 1008, 1290, 1299, appendix, 58–74; HF, diary, October 14, 16, 17, 19, 1870, HF-LC; HF to CSch, January 23, 1871, WWB to CSch, January 24, 1871, SB to CSch, March 22, 1872, CSch-LC; ET to Earl Granville, February 16, 1872, PRO; Bancroft, *Speeches of Schurz*, 5:34–35; Senate Report No. 183, 42nd Cong., 2nd sess., xiv.

16. Leland L. Sage, *William Boyd Allison: A Study in Practical Politics* (Iowa City: State Historical Society of Iowa, 1956), 112–121; John Sherman, *Recollections of Forty Years in the House, Senate and Cabinet* (Chicago: Werner, 1895), 1:479–480; Rachel Sherman Thorndyke, ed., *The Sherman Letters: Correspondence between General and Senator Sherman from 1837 to 1891* (New York: Charles Scribner's Sons, 1894), 335; DAW to JDC, December 1, 1871, JDC-OCL; Charles Richard Williams, ed., *Diary and Letters of Rutherford Birchard Hayes* (Columbus: Ohio State Archaeological and Historical Society, 1924), 3:186–188; Leon Burr Richardson, *William E. Chandler: Republican* (New York: Dodd, Mead, 1940), 123–125; *NYT*, March 13, April 2, 3, 1872; *The Reform Movement* (Washington, D.C.: F. & J. Rives & Geo. A. Bailey, 1872), 4.

17. Thomas Van Buren to WEC, March 29, 1872, John W. Foster to WEC, April 3, 1872, WEC-LC; Richardson, *Chandler*, 128–129; *NYT*, February 23, 1872; JDC to DAW, March 16, 1872, DAW-LC.

18. *NYT*, February 23, 1872; *M and P*, 7:156–159; minutes for June 29, November 1, 11, 25, 1872, Minutes of President Grant's Civil Service Commission (photocopy), USG-USGPL; *PUSG*, 22:217.

19. *M and P*, 7:157–159; minutes for January 10, 1872, Minutes of the Advisory Board of the Civil Service (photocopy), USG-USGPL.

20. *Reform Movement*, 3; JAG to JDC, January 16, 1872, JDC-OCL.

21. *CG*, 42nd Cong., 2nd sess., 455, 463, 1102; Marcus P. Norton to USG, December 27, 1871, USG-NYPL (emphasis in original); HF, diary, January 23, 1872, HF-LC; Hoogenboom, *Outlawing the Spoils*, 106–107.

22. Minutes for January 20, 1872, Minutes of the Advisory Board of the Civil Service (photocopy), USG-USGPL; *PUSG*, 23:3; *M and P*, 7:180–183; *NYTr*, April 17, 1872.

23. August Belmont to CSch, April 23, 1872, CSch-LC.

24. J. Q. Adams to DAW, April 10, 1872, Charles Francis Adams Jr. to DAW, April 12, 16, 1872, DAW-LC; DAW to CFA, April 17, 1872, CFA to DAW, April

18, 1872, AFP-MHS; *NYT*, April 25, 27, 1872; Martin Duberman, *Charles Francis Adams, 1807–1886* (Stanford, Calif.: Stanford University Press, 1968), 356–359.

25. Mark W. Krug, *Lyman Trumbull: Conservative Radical* (New York: A. S. Barnes, 1965), 271–326; LT to Horace White, January 27, April 24, 1872, LT to Hiram R. Enoch, February 29, 1872, LT to Gustav Koerner, March 9, 1872, LT to John M. Palmer, April 8, 1872, LT to Sinclair Tousey, April 27, 1872, LT-LC; DAW to CFA, April 17, 1872, AFP-MHS; LT to DAW, April 24, 1872, DAW-LC.

26. Frederic Bancroft and William A. Dunning, "Sketch of Carl Schurz's Political Career, 1869–1906," in *The Reminiscences of Carl Schurz* (New York: Doubleday, Page, 1909), 3:345; Norma L. Peterson, *Freedom and Franchise: The Political Career of B. Gratz Brown* (Columbia: University of Missouri Press, 1965), 195–196, 211–213; William E. Parrish, *Frank Blair: Lincoln's Conservative* (Columbia: University of Missouri Press, 1998), 271.

27. *PUSG*, 20:232–233, 21:8, 11–12, 84, 22:231–232; HG to Mrs. R. M. Whipple, February 13, 1872, HG-LC.

28. Earle Dudley Ross, *The Liberal Republican Movement* (1910; reprint, Seattle: University of Washington Press, 1970), 38–39; HG to Beman Brockway, March 13, 1872, HG-LC (emphasis in original); *NYTr*, March 30, 1872; Theodore Cox to JDC, March 14, 1872, SB to DAW, March 25 1872, JDC-OCL; JDC to DAW, March 16, April 4, 1872, DAW-LC.

29. *WNR*, January 11, 1872; *WES*, April 17, 1872; USG to "Gentlemen," May 9, 1872, in *NYT*, May 13, 1872; Charles W. Calhoun, *Conceiving a New Republic: The Republican Party and the Southern Question, 1869–1900* (Lawrence: University Press of Kansas, 2006), 36–39; *M and P*, 7:15, 175–176; *NYT*, February 29, 1872; 17 *Statutes at Large* 32–33.

30. *PUSG*, 22:321–332, 336–350; Brooks D. Simpson, *The Reconstruction Presidents* (Lawrence: University Press of Kansas, 1998), 157–158.

31. *PUSG*, 22:360–361; HF, diary, April 2, 1872, HF-LC; *M and P*, 7:163–164. Grant also reaffirmed his commitment to the peace policy out West by meeting with several Indian delegations. *PUSG*, 22:xxiv, 23:xx–xxi; *WES*, May 27, 28, 1872.

32. *NYT*, March 5, 1872; HF, diary, March 1, 1872, HF-LC; *PUSG*, 23:46–47; *NYH*, February 2, 1872.

33. WR to John D. Defrees, March 11, 1872, HG to WR, March 25, 1872, WR-LC; J. S. Robinson to WEC, April 10, 1872, Russell Errett to WEC, April 12, 1872, S. B. Packard to WEC, April 13, 1872, John W. Foster to WEC, April 18, 1872, WEC-LC; *NYH*, April 11, 1872; *NYTr*, April 18, 1872.

34. *Springfield Daily Republican*, May 1, 2, 3, 4, 8, 1872; *NYTr*, May 1, 2, 3, 4, 1872; HG to WR, May 1, 1872, WR-LC; JDC to Allyn Cox, May 6, 1872, JDC-OCL; Ross, *Liberal Republican Movement*, 88–96.

35. *Proceedings of the Liberal Republican Convention, in Cincinnati, May 1st, 2d, and 3d, 1872* (New York: Baker & Godwin, 1872), 18–21.

36. Ibid., 12, 21; *Springfield Daily Republican*, May 8, 1872; Peterson, *Freedom*

and Franchise, 213–217; Parrish, *Blair*, 279–280; Edward Atkinson to CS, May 23, 1872, CS-Mf.

37. *Proceedings of the Liberal Republican Convention*, 21–36; *Springfield Daily Republican*, May 8, 1872; JDC to Allyn Cox, May 6, 1872, JDC-OCL; SB to CS, May 18, 1872, CS-Mf; Bingham Duncan, *Whitelaw Reid: Journalist, Politician, Diplomat* (Athens: University of Georgia Press, 1975), 43–44.

38. JDC to Allyn Cox, May 6, 1872, JDC-OCL; Bancroft, *Speeches of Schurz*, 2:361–368; Edward Atkinson to CS, June 1, 1872, CS-Mf; CFA, diary, May 4, 1872, AFP-MHS.

39. HF to Thurlow Weed, May 27, 1872 (ts), HF-LC; G. W. Hazelton to EWK, May 11, 1872, EWK-WHS; *PUSG*, 23:139–140.

40. Donald, *Sumner*, 2:519, 539–544; WR to CS, March 28, 1872, WR-LC; Edward Atkinson to CS, April 8, 11, 13, 1872, F. W. Bird to CS, April 11, 15, 23, 27 (telegram), 28, 30, May 1, 1872, CS-Mf.

41. CS to Edward L. Pierce, May 12, 1872, CS to Henry W. Longfellow, May 16, 1872, CS to WR, May 15, 1872, WR to CS, May 16, 1872, SB to CS, May 18, 1872, J. P. Jones to CS, May 22, 1872 (telegram), with CS's draft reply, CS-Mf; Beverly Wilson Palmer, ed., *The Selected Letters of Charles Sumner* (Boston: Northeastern University Press, 1990), 2:591; *NYH*, May 17, 1872; Donald, *Sumner*, 2:547–548 (emphasis in originals).

42. Charles Sumner, *Republicanism vs. Grantism* (Washington, D.C.: F. & J. Rives & Geo. A. Bailey, 1872) (emphasis in original); Donald, *Sumner*, 2:549.

43. *Official Proceedings of the National Republican Conventions of 1868, 1872, 1876, and 1880* (Minneapolis: Charles W. Johnson, 1903), 123–124, 127–143, 149–157.

44. Ibid., 157–165; *NYH*, June 7, 1872.

45. Willard H. Smith, *Schuyler Colfax: The Changing Fortunes of a Political Idol* (Indianapolis: Indiana Historical Bureau, 1952), 333–336, 345–349; *PUSG*, 22:229–231; Palmer, *Selected Letters of Sumner*, 2:582–583; Ernest McKay, *Henry Wilson, Practical Radical: Portrait of a Politician* (Port Washington, N.Y.: Kennikat Press, 1971), 224–225.

46. *NYH*, June 2, 3, 5, 7, 14, 1872; *Official Proceedings of the National Republican Conventions*, 167–175, 177–180.

47. *Official Proceedings of the National Republican Conventions*, 175–177.

48. *NYT*, May 11, 1872; Henry B. Blackwell to Anna Dickinson, June 12, 1872, Matilda Joslyn Gage to WEC, August 18, September 2, 1872, Blackwell to WEC, September 5, 1872, S. B. Anthony to WEC, September 9, 18, 1872, WEC-LC (emphasis in original).

49. August Belmont to CSch, April 1, 23, 1872, MM to CSch, April 23, 1872, SB to CSch, June 18, 1872, CSch-LC; MM to Ivery Chamberlain, May 3, 1872 (two telegrams), D. G. Croly to MM, May 10, 1872, MM-LC; JDC to DAW, May 23, DAW-LC; JDC to John Lynch, July 11, 1872, JDC-OCL; Ross, *Liberal Republican Movement*, 112–114, 120–125.

50. WR to George Peabody, May 8, 1872, WR to E. F. Pillsbury, May 12, 1872, WR to John F. Coyle, June 7, 1872, WR to Cassius M. Clay, May 16, 1872, WR to Walcott Hutchins, May 16, 1872, WR to John D. Defrees, May 20, 1872, WR to B. F. Sawyer, May 16, 1872, WR to William B. Reed, June 25, 1872, WR-LC; *NYT*, June 13, 1872; HG to J. Glancy Jones, June 27, 1872, HG-NYPL; *Official Proceedings of the National Democratic Convention, Held at Baltimore, July 9, 1872* (Boston: Rockwell & Churchill, 1872), 40–72.

51. *NYT*, June 11, 1872.

52. McPherson, *Hand-Book of Politics for 1872*, 208–209, 214.

53. Ross, *Liberal Republican Movement*, 167–171; Sidney Ratner, *American Taxation* (New York: W. W. Norton, 1942), 133–134; *M and P*, 7:176–177.

54. William Lloyd Garrison to CS, May 27, 1872, Lydia Marie Child to CS, June 21, 28, July 9, 1872, Frederick Douglass to CS, July 19, 1872, CS-Mf; Palmer, *Selected Letters of Sumner*, 2:597–599.

55. *Letter to Colored Citizens by Hon. Charles Sumner, July 29, 1872* (Washington, D.C.: F. & J. Rives & Geo. A. Bailey, 1872).

56. HG to CS, July 31, 1872, CS-Mf; *NYT*, August 12, 1872; *NYH*, August 16, 1872; *PUSG*, 23:238; ERH to JDC, August 14, 1872, JDC-OCL.

57. GSB, "Speech at Greensboro, N.C., July 1872," GSB-LC; *NYH*, July 19, 25, 28, 30, 1872; WEC to EWK, July 27, 1872, EWK-WHS; HG to JRY, July 28, 1872, JRY-LC; J. E. West to WEC, August 7, 1872, WEC-LC; OEB to AB, August 8, 1872, USG-USGPL (emphasis in original); *NYT*, September 12, 1872.

58. WEC to E. D. Morgan, July 11, 1872, WEC to John W. Foster, August 16, 1872, WEC to USG, August 16, September 23, 1872, James Harlan to WEC, September 24, 1872, WEC-LC; WEC to EBW, July 19, August 29, 1872, EBW-LC; WEC to EWK, August 21, 1872, EWK-WHS; Richardson, *Chandler*, 143–148; *U. S. Grant and the Colored People* (n.p., [1872]); *Grant's Amnesty Record* (n.p., [1872]); *The Financial Record of President Grant's Administration* (n.p., [1872]).

59. Grenville Dodge to WEC, August 9, 1872, WEC to USG, August 16, 1872, John Pool to WEC, August 20, 1872, John W. Foster to WEC, August 30, 1872, H. C. Page to E. D. Morgan, October 12, 18, 1872, Henry H. Bingham to WEC, September 26, 1872, Ellis H. Roberts to E. D. Morgan, August 10, 1872, WEC-LC; Richardson, *Chandler*, 143; *NYH*, October 9, 1872; *PUSG*, 23:235–236; Henry Clews, *Twenty-Eight Years in Wall Street* (New York: Irving, 1888), 300–306; *Congressional Quarterly's Guide to U.S. Elections* (Washington, D.C.: Congressional Quarterly, 1994), 438, 697.

60. *PUSG*, 23:200, 292–293; *NYT*, June 27, 1872; *NYH*, August 1, September 19, 20, 21, 27, October 21, 22, 25, 1872; USG to George H. Stuart, October 26, 1872, in *NYT*, October 29, 1872.

61. *NYH*, August 6, 1872; *PUSG*, 23:247.

62. HP to John Arthur, January 18, 1870, USG-LC; Marshall Jewell to WEC, September 26, 1872, A. J. French to E. D. Morgan, July 9, 1872, H. T. Sperry to Marshall Jewell, September 11, 1872 (telegram), WEC-LC; WR to William

Lincoln, September 2, 1872, WR-LC; HF to John Carruthers, September 11, 1872 (ts), HF to C. G. Amsden, October 25, 1872 (ts), HF-LC; *NYTr*, August 24, 1872; *NYT*, July 12, 1872; Peterson, *Freedom and Franchise*, 222–224.

63. WR to R. Brinkerhoff, July 26, 1872, WR-LC; *NYTr*, May 17, September 20, 24, October 14, 1872; John Bigelow, ed., *Letters and Literary Memorials of Samuel J. Tilden* (New York: Harper & Brothers, 1908), 1:311.

64. Edward McPherson, *A Hand-Book of Politics for 1874* (Washington, D.C.: Solomons & Chapman, 1874), 228; Emma Lou Thornbrough, *Indiana in the Civil War Era, 1850–1880* (Indianapolis: Indiana Historical Bureau and Indiana Historical Society, 1965), 251–252; Harry James Brown and Frederick D. Williams, *The Diary of James A. Garfield* (East Lansing: Michigan State University Press, 1967–1981), 2:104; *PUSG*, 23:267–268; WR to E. H. House, October 31, 1872, WR to Alfred Wilkinson, November 5, 1872, WR to Murat Halstead, November 19, 1872, WR to George W. Smalley, November 21, 1872, WR-LC.

65. *Presidential Elections, 1789–2000* (Washington, D.C.: Congressional Quarterly, 2002), 113, 123, 124, 195; *NYTr*, November 6, 1872; WR to George W. Smalley, November 21, 1872, WR-LC; James G. Blaine, *Twenty Years of Congress* (Norwich, Conn.: Henry Bill, 1884, 1886), 2:535–536; John G. Sproat, *"The Best Men": Liberal Reformers in the Gilded Age* (New York: Oxford University Press, 1968), 87–88.

66. David D. Porter to SC, November 6, 1872, SC-LC; RCS to USG, November 6, 1872, OEB-NL; *PUSG*, 23:289–290; *M and P*, 7:223.

CHAPTER 16. SECOND TERM WOES

1. *M and P*, 7:184–205; *NYTr*, November 27, 1872; *PUSG*, 23:300–301.

2. *NYH*, November 16, 1872; *PUSG*, 23:331–332.

3. *NYH*, November 16, 1872; *PUSG*, 23:283–284; *NYT*, November 15, 1872; BHB to JMH, November 26, December 4, 1872, JMH-LC.

4. Stanley I. Kutler, "Ward Hunt," in *The Justices of the United States Supreme Court, 1789–1978*, ed. Leon Friedman and Fred L. Israel (New York: Chelsea House, 1980), 2:1221–1222; BHB to JMH, December 4, 1872, JMH-LC; HF, diary, November 30, December 3, 1872, HF-LC; *NYT*, December 12, 1872.

5. HF, diary, December 10, 1872, HF-LC; Edward McPherson, *A Hand-Book of Politics for 1874* (Washington, D.C.: Solomons & Chapman, 1874), 85–87; William Gillette, *Retreat from Reconstruction, 1869–1879* (Baton Rouge: Louisiana State University Press, 1979), 96–99.

6. George Rable, "Republican Albatross: The Louisiana Question, National Politics, and the Failure of Reconstruction," *Louisiana History* 23 (1982): 111–113; McPherson, *Hand-Book of Politics for 1874*, 100–106; HF, diary, December 13, 1872, HF-LC; *NYH*, December 17, 1872; Joe Gray Taylor, *Louisiana Reconstructed, 1863–1877* (Baton Rouge: Louisiana State University Press, 1974), 142.

7. *NYH*, December 17, 20, 1872; Ted Tunnell, *Crucible of Reconstruction: War, Radicalism, and Race in Louisiana, 1862–1877* (Baton Rouge: Louisiana State University Press, 1984), 171; *PUSG*, 24:3; McPherson, *Hand-Book of Politics for 1874*, 108.

8. *CG*, 42nd Cong., 3rd sess., 541–551, 1520–1521; Senate Report No. 457, 42nd Cong., 3rd sess.; Charles W. Calhoun, *Conceiving a New Republic: The Republican Party and the Southern Question, 1869–1900* (Lawrence: University Press of Kansas, 2006), 48–49.

9. *NYH*, February 4, 17, 18, 22, 1872; HF, diary, February 21, 1873, HF-LC; *WES*, February 25, 1873; *NYT*, February 26, 1873.

10. *M and P*, 7:212–213.

11. *CG*, 42nd Cong., 3rd sess., 1872, 1896; *PUSG*, 24:54; OPM to William R. Holloway, [circa March 1873, misdated by archivist "c. 1872"], OPM-ISL; *WES*, February 25, 1873; *NYT*, March 1, 1873.

12. Irwin Unger, *The Greenback Era: A Social and Political History of American Finance, 1865–1879* (Princeton, N.J.: Princeton University Press, 1964), 203–205; 17 *Statutes at Large* 360–366, 482–483; Senate Report No. 242, 42nd Cong., 3rd sess.; *CG*, 42nd Cong., 3rd sess., 1665, 1778, 1780–1781, 2128–2129; HF, diary, December 17, 1872, February 18, 1873, HF to RCS, February 20, 1873, HF-LC; JCBD, diary, February 18, 20, 21, 24, 1873, JCBD-LC; Harry James Brown and Frederick D. Williams, *The Diary of James A. Garfield* (East Lansing: Michigan State University Press, 1967–1981), 2:154; *NYH*, February 20, 1873; *M and P*, 7:208–212.

13. Mark Wahlgren Summers, *The Era of Good Stealings* (New York: Oxford University Press, 1993), 50–54, 226–227, 231–237; JDC to John Hutchins, January 20[?], 1873, JDC-OCL.

14. Ernest McKay, *Henry Wilson: Practical Radical* (Port Washington, N.Y.: Kennikat Press, 1971), 230–233; Summers, *Era of Good Stealings*, 233, 237; *CG*, 42nd Cong., 3rd sess., 1544–1545; *PUSG*, 24:68–69; *NYT*, March 10, 1873; BHB to R. M. Kelly, March 13, 1873, BHB-LC.

15. HF to RCS, February 20, 1873, HF-LC (emphasis in original); JCBD to EBW, February 21, 1873, JCBD to AB, February 20 [21?], 1873, JCBD-LC.

16. *WNR*, November 6, 8, 1872, February 8, 10, 11, 14, 1873; Brown and Williams, *Diary of Garfield*, 2:165; *PUSG*, 24:10–12; House Report No. 59, 42nd Cong., 3rd sess.; 17 *Statutes at Large* 421.

17. McPherson, *Hand-Book of Politics for 1874*, 3–20; Allen Peskin, *Garfield* (Kent, Ohio: Kent State University Press, 1999), 363–366.

18. EBW to Israel Washburn, March 26, 1873, EBW-LC; H. H. Starkweather to WEC, March 25, 1873, WEC-LC; *Congressional Quarterly's Guide to U.S. Elections* (Washington, D.C.: Congressional Quarterly, 1994), 673, 1023, 1027.

19. EBW to William H. Bradley, March 27, 1873, Alexander H. Bullock to EBW, February 15, 1873, EBW-LC; John A. Garraty, *The New Commonwealth, 1877–1890* (New York: Harper & Row, 1968), 1–2; Marvin Felheim, "Introduction," in Mark Twain and Charles Dudley Warner, *The Gilded Age: A Tale of Today*

(1873; reprint, New York: Meridian, 1994), ix; HF to RCS, February 20, 1873, HF-LC; *NYH*, March 4, 1873.

20. *M and P*, 7:221–223.

21. *NYTr*, March 5, 1873; *WNR*, March 5, 1873; *NYT*, March 5, 1873.

22. *NYT*, March 6, 7, 1873; George Rable, *But There Was No Peace: The Role of Violence in the Politics of Reconstruction* (Athens: University of Georgia Press, 1984), 125; Charles Lane, *The Day Freedom Died: The Colfax Massacre, the Supreme Court, and the Betrayal of Reconstruction* (New York: Henry Holt, 2008), 14; *PUSG*, 24:54.

23. *NYTr*, March 29, April 9, 1873; Robert Franklin Durden, *James Shepherd Pike: Republicanism and the American Negro, 1850–1882* (Durham, N.C.: Duke University Press, 1957), 214; Eric Foner, *Reconstruction: America's Unfinished Revolution, 1863–1877* (New York: Harper & Row, 1988), 525–526.

24. Lane, *Day Freedom Died*, 65–109, 265–266.

25. Tunnell, *Crucible of Reconstruction*, 193; Lane, *Day Freedom Died*, 23–24; *WNR*, April 21, 1873; *PUSG*, 24:54–55; Joseph G. Dawson, *Army Generals and Reconstruction: Louisiana, 1862–1877* (Baton Rouge: Louisiana State University Press, 1982), 147–151; *NYH*, May 10, 23, 1873; E. Bruce Thompson, *Matthew Hale Carpenter: Webster of the West* (Madison: State Historical Society of Wisconsin, 1954), 189–191.

26. *M and P*, 7:223–224; Rable, *But There Was No Peace*, 129–131; Gillette, *Retreat from Reconstruction*, 116.

27. HF, diary, January 28, 1873, HF-LC; House Executive Document No. 122, 43rd Cong., 1st sess., 65; Francis Paul Prucha, *American Indian Policy in Crisis: Christian Reformers and the Indian, 1865–1900* (Norman: University of Oklahoma Press, 1976), 86–87; Robert M. Utley, *The Indian Frontier, 1846–1890*, rev. ed. (Albuquerque: University of New Mexico Press, 2003), 168–170.

28. *NYH*, April 15, 17, 18, 1873; *Milwaukee Daily Sentinel*, April 13, 1873; *PUSG*, 24:198.

29. *PUSG*, 24:196–197, 201, 203; HF, diary, October 3, 1873, HF-LC; Utley, *Indian Frontier*, 169–170; Prucha, *American Indian Policy*, 87–88; *Annual Report of the Secretary of the Interior for 1873*, House Executive Document No. 1, 43rd Cong., 1st sess., pt. 5, vol. 1, iii–iv, ix–x.

30. Ari Hoogenboom, *Outlawing the Spoils: A History of the Civil Service Reform Movement, 1865–1883* (Urbana: University of Illinois Press, 1968), 121–123; HF, diary, January 28, 1873, HF-LC; *Journal of the Executive Proceedings of the Senate of the United States*, 41st Cong., 3rd sess., 388, 395; *Harper's Weekly*, October 25, 1873; *NYT*, March 15, April 4, 1873, March 2, 1891, January 15, 1900.

31. *NYTr*, March 17, 1873; *PUSG*, 24:93; Hoogenboom, *Outlawing the Spoils*, 122.

32. *Nation*, April 3, 1873; *PUSG*, 24:104.

33. D. B. Eaton to JCBD, April 4, 5, 8, 16, 26, May 18, 1873, JCBD to Eaton, April 7, 15, 21, 1873, JCBD, diary, May 5, 1873, JCBD-LC; HF, diary, April 15,

1873, HF-LC; Gerald W. McFarland, "Partisan of Nonpartisanship: Dorman B. Eaton and the Genteel Reform Tradition," *Journal of American History* 54 (March 1968): 808–814.

34. D. B. Eaton to JCBD, May 18, 1873, JCBD, diary, May 23, 1873, JCBD-LC; *NYH*, May 25, 1873; HF, diary, May 24, June 4, 20, 1873, HF-LC; McFarland, "Partisan of Nonpartisanship," 815–816; *M and P*, 7:230–235; *Nation*, June 26, 1873; D. B. Eaton, *The Experiment of Civil Service Reform in the United States* (n.p., 1875), 16–18.

35. *M and P*, 7:229; HF to JCBD, May 9, 1873 (telegram, ts), HF-LC; JCBD, diary, May 9, 1873, JCBD-LC; Michael Les Benedict, *Preserving the Constitution: Essays on Politics and the Constitution in the Reconstruction Era* (New York: Fordham University Press, 2006), 143–151.

36. W. H. Bradley to EBW, May 16, 1873, EBW-LC; GSB to HF, September 19, 1873, HF-LC.

37. *NYH*, May 8, 16, 1873; EP to HF, May 19, 1873, HF, diary, May 19, 1873, HF-LC; N. H. Swayne to BHB, September 15, 18, 1873, C. H. Hill to BHB, September 20, [1873], BHB-LC; SC to TOH, July 24, 1873, TOH-WHS; TOH to SC, July 28, 1873, SC-LC; John Y. Simon, ed., *The Personal Memoirs of Julia Dent Grant* (New York: G. P. Putnam's Sons, 1975), 193–194.

38. Unger, *Greenback Era*, 194; James Ford Rhodes, *History of the United States, 1850–1877* (New York: Macmillan, 1912), 7:34; *M and P*, 7:184.

39. *Annual Report of the Secretary of the Treasury for 1872*, House Executive Document No. 2, 42nd Cong., 3rd sess., ix–xxii; *NYH*, December 31, 1872.

40. House Executive Document No. 42, 42nd Cong., 3rd sess.; Senate Report No. 275, 42nd Cong., 3rd sess.; *CG*, 42nd Cong., 3rd sess., 553–554; *NYH*, January 16, 1873; *NYT*, March 15, 1873; Richard H. Timberlake, *Monetary Policy in the United States: An Intellectual and Institutional History* (Chicago: University of Chicago Press, 1993), 100–101.

41. *NYH*, March 12, 14, 1873.

42. HF, diary, March 17, 1873, HF-LC; *NYH*, March 18, 1873; *Journal of the Executive Proceedings of the Senate of the United States*, 42nd Cong., 1st sess., 59, 73; *PUSG*, 24:82–83; ET to Earl Granville, March 18, 1873, PRO; *CR*, 43rd Cong., 1st sess., 704.

43. HF, diary, November 26, 1872, February 3, 1873, HF-LC; Frank Warren Hackett, *A Sketch of the Life and Public Services of William Adams Richardson* (Washington, D.C.: H. L. McQueen, 1898), 56–57, 75–76, lxxi–lxxii.

44. HF, diary, March 16, 1873, HF-LC; *NYT*, March 15, 1873.

45. HF, diary, March 17, 18, 21, 1873, HF-LC.

46. *NYH*, July 7, 1873, July–September 1873 passim; *Harper's Weekly*, August 16, 1873; Mark Wahlgren Summers, *The Press Gang: Newspapers and Politics, 1865–1878* (Chapel Hill: University of North Carolina Press, 1994), 268–270.

47. *NYH*, August 18, 25, September 17, 1873.

CHAPTER 17. CRISES DOMESTIC AND FOREIGN

1. George Bancroft to JCBD, June 8, 1873, JCBD-LC (emphasis in original).

2. Elmus Wicker, *Banking Panics of the Gilded Age* (Cambridge: Cambridge University Press, 2000), 19; James Ford Rhodes, *History of the United States, 1850–1877* (New York: Macmillan, 1912), 7:36–42.

3. *Report of the Secretary of the Treasury for 1873*, House Executive Document No. 2, 43rd Cong., 1st sess., xi–xii; WAR to USG, August 28, 1873, USG-LC.

4. Wicker, *Banking Panics*, 19–21; Rhodes, *History of the United States*, 7:42–43; *NYH*, September 18, 19, 20, 1873; *Report of the Secretary of the Treasury for 1873*, xii; *CR*, 43rd Cong., 1st sess., 2393.

5. Thomas Murphy to USG, September 19, 1873 (telegram), OPM to USG, September 19, 1873 (telegram), WAR to USG, September 19, 1873 (telegram), WAR to Thomas Hillhouse, September 19, 1873 (telegram), OEB to HP, September 19, 1873 (telegram), USG-LC; *WNR*, September 20, 1873; HF to JCBD, September 20, 1873, HF to WAR, September 20, 1873 (telegram), HF-LC. The story that Grant spent the night of September 17 at Cooke's home in Philadelphia and was with him on the morning of the collapse is apocryphal. Contemporary news accounts show that Grant was in Pittsburgh, although he had apparently stayed with Cooke the night of September 15. *NYTr*, September 18, 1873; *NYT*, September 19, 1873; *PUSG*, 24:211. Cf. Ellis Paxton Oberholtzer, *Jay Cooke: Financier of the Civil War* (Philadelphia: George W. Jacobs, 1907), 2:421; Jean Edward Smith, *Grant* (New York: Simon & Schuster, 2001), 575.

6. *NYH*, September 21, 22, 1873; *WNR*, September 23, 1873; *NYT*, September 23, 1873; *Report of the Secretary of the Treasury for 1873*, xii; Frank Warren Hackett, *A Sketch of the Life and Public Services of William Adams Richardson* (Washington, D.C.: H. L. McQueen, 1898), 92–100.

7. HF to WAR, September 22, 26, 1873, HF-LC; *NYT*, September 23, 1873.

8. *NYH*, September 23, 25, 1873; *Report of the Secretary of the Treasury for 1873*, xv; Hackett, *Sketch of Richardson*, 101; *NYT*, October 13, 1873.

9. HF, diary, September 30, 1873, HF-LC.

10. *WNR*, September 29, 1873.

11. *NYH*, October 8, 10, 13, 1873; HF, diary, October 21, 1873, HF-LC; *CR*, 43rd Cong., 1st sess., 700.

12. *NYT*, September 9, November 6, 1873; OPM to John W. Foster, October 30, 1873, John W. Foster Papers, LC; *The American Annual Cyclopaedia and Register of Important Events of the Year 1873* (New York: D. Appleton, 1879), 461, 551–552, 611, 767, 776.

13. *PUSG*, 24:222–224, 229–230; *NYH*, October 24, 1873.

14. *NYT*, October 13, 1873; HF, diary, November 7, 1873, HF-LC; Allen Weinstein, *Prelude to Populism: Origins of the Silver Issue, 1867–1878* (New Haven, Conn.: Yale University Press, 1970), 14–32; *Annual Report of the Secretary of the*

Treasury, 1872, House Executive Document No. 2, 42nd Cong., 3rd sess., xi–xii; *Laws of the United States Relating to Loans, Paper Money, Banking, and Coinage, 1790 to 1895*, Senate Report No. 831, 53rd Cong., 3rd sess., 548–564; *PUSG*, 24:222–224, 226–227; *NYH*, October 13, 25, 27, 28, 29, 30, 1873; *Report of the Secretary of the Treasury for 1873*, xxxii–xxxiii.

15. HF, diary, November 7, 1873, HF-LC; *NYT*, October 13, 1873; Irwin Unger, *The Greenback Era: A Social and Political History of American Finance, 1865–1879* (Princeton, N.J.: Princeton University Press, 1964), 97–100; Floyd William Niklas, "William Kelley: The Congressional Years, 1861–1890" (Ph.D. diss., Northern Illinois University, 1983), 349–350; Gretchen Ritter, *Goldbugs and Greenbacks: The Anti-Monopoly Tradition and the Politics of Finance in America, 1865–1896* (Cambridge: Cambridge University Press, 1997), 98.

16. HF, diary, October 27, November 19, 1870, October 28, December 12, 1872, HF to Daniel E. Sickles, November 25, 1872, HF to Henry S. Hall, October 22, 1873, HF-LC; *FRUS, 1872*, 580–584; Allan Nevins, *Hamilton Fish: The Inner History of the Grant Administration* (New York: Dodd, Mead, 1937), 615–637; Stephen McCullough, "Foreshadowing of Informal Empire: Ulysses S. Grant and Hamilton Fish's Caribbean Policy 1869–1877" (Ph.D. diss., University of Alabama, 2007), 159–195.

17. HF, diary, October 28, November 19, 21, December 2, 12, 22, 1872, January 30, February 14, March 25, 1873, HF to Daniel E. Sickles, November 25, 1872, HF-LC; Nevins, *Fish*, 628–631.

18. HF, diary, February 3, 1873, HF-LC; *CG*, 42nd Cong., 3rd sess., 1053.

19. HF, diary, August 5, 1873, HF-LC.

20. USG to HF, September 8, 1873, HF, diary, September 16, October 21, 1873, HF to Henry C. Hall, October 22, 1873, HF-LC.

21. House Executive Document No. 30, 43rd Cong., 1st sess., 146; *FRUS, 1874*, 922; HF, diary, November 7, 1873, with USG note, HF-LC.

22. McCullough, "Foreshadowing of Informal Empire," 201–206; JCBD to HF, November 9, 1873, HF to JCBD, November 14, 1873, HF-LC.

23. HF, diary, November 11, 12, 14, 1873, HF, draft telegram, n.d., HF-LC; *FRUS, 1874*, 927, 936.

24. HF, diary, November 14, 1873, EP to HF, November 13 (ts), 14(ts), 1873, HF to EP, November 14, 1873 (emphasis in original), HF-LC; 15 *Statutes at Large* 224.

25. HF to William Cullen Bryant, November 17, 1873 (ts), Minister of State to Minister Plenipotentiary at Washington, November 17, 1873 (telegram), HF, diary, November 18, 1873, HF-LC; Nevins, *Fish*, 676–679.

26. HF, diary, November 20, 21, 22, 23, 1873, HF to C. A. Arthur, November 22, 1873, HF-LC; House Executive Document No. 30, 43rd Cong., 1st sess., 74–75; *FRUS, 1874*, 960; ET to Lord Granville, November 24, 1873, PRO; John de la Montagnie to EBW, November 27, 1873, EBW-LC.

27. John de la Montagnie to EBW, November 27, 1873, EBW-LC; HF, diary,

November 27, 28, 29, 30, 1873, HF-LC; House Executive Document No. 30, 43rd Cong., 1st sess., 1–2, 76–82.

28. HF, diary, December 4, 5, 6, 7, 8, 13, 15, 17, 1873, HF-LC; House Executive Document No. 30, 43rd Cong., 1st sess., 2, 145, 208–210; Richard H. Bradford, *The Virginius Affair* (Boulder: Colorado Associated University Press, 1980), 126.

29. House Executive Document No. 30, 43rd Cong., 1st sess., 2; McCullough, "Foreshadowing of Informal Empire," 224–226; Bradford, *Virginius Affair*, 131–132; HF to Louis J. Jennings, December 19, 1873, HF to Hamilton Fish Jr. December 13, 1873 (ts, emphasis in original), WR to HF, December 29, 1873 (ts), HF-LC; Wm. Henry Trescot to JCBD, December 2, 1873, JCBD to [J. Russell] Jones, December 1, 1873, JCBD-LC.

30. *PUSG*, 24:294–295; HF to EBW, February 12, 1874, JCBD to HF, December 23, 26, 1873, HF-LC; BM, diary, December 19, 1873, BM-LC; *FRUS, 1874*, 973–975; Bradford, *Virginius Affair*, 115–118; Nevins, *Fish*, 692–693; *Journal of the Executive Proceedings of the Senate of the United States*, 43rd Cong., 1st sess., 199, 206.

31. HF, diary, November 4, 1873, HF-LC; *PUSG*, 24:253–254; Harry James Brown and Frederick D. Williams, *The Diary of James A. Garfield* (East Lansing: Michigan State University Press, 1967–1981), 2:243; David M. Jordan, *Roscoe Conkling of New York: Voice in the Senate* (Ithaca, N.Y.: Cornell University Press, 1971), 198–202; Louis J. Lang, comp. and ed., *The Autobiography of Thomas Collier Platt* (New York: B. W. Dodge, 1910), 68.

32. JAG to BHB, November 19, 1873, N. H. Swayne to BHB, November 26, 1873, HP to BHB, December 1, 1873, BHB-LC; Brown and Williams, *Diary of Garfield*, 2:246–247; HF, diary, November 28, 30, December 1, 1873, HF-LC.

33. JHW to BHB, December 3, 1873, J. W. Stevenson to BHB, December 8, 1873 (emphasis in original), C. H. Hill to BHB, December 10, 13, 1873, BHB-LC; *Journal of the Executive Proceedings of the Senate*, 43rd Cong., 1st sess., 183, 188; Sidney Teiser, "Life of George H. Williams: Almost Chief-Justice," *Oregon Historical Quarterly* 47 (December 1946): 421–423.

34. Kathryn Allamong Jacob, *Capital Elites: High Society in Washington, D.C., after the Civil War* (Washington, D.C.: Smithsonian Institution Press, 1995), 104–106; "S" to CAD, December 3, [1873] (emphasis in original), CAD to MM, December 4, 1873, TFB to MM, December 26, 1873, MM-LC; HF, diary, November 28, 30, December 1, 1873, HF-LC; C. H. Hill to BHB, December 19, 1873, BHB-LC.

35. BHB to USG, December 22, 1873, HP to BHB, December 18, 1873, BHB-LC; BHB to USG, December 22, 1873, JMH-LC; Philip H. Overmeyer, "Attorney General Williams and the Chief Justiceship," *Pacific Northwest Quarterly* 28 (July 1937): 258–260.

36. C. H. Hill to BHB, December 19, 1873, N. H. Swayne to BHB, December 21, 1873, BHB-LC; James Nesmith to Matthew P. Deady, December 7, 17, 1873, Matthew P. Deady Papers, Oregon Historical Society; Overmeyer, "Attorney

General Williams and the Chief Justiceship," 258–260; HF, diary, December 30, 1873, HF-LC.

37. HF, diary, January 2, 5, 6, 7, 1874, HF-LC.

38. Ibid., January 5, 7, 9, 1874; *Journal of the Executive Proceedings of the Senate*, 43rd Cong., 1st sess., 210; *PUSG*, 24:287.

39. *Journal of the Executive Proceedings of the Senate*, 43rd Cong., 1st sess., 212, 218; *NYH*, January 10, 11, 13, 15, 1874; HF diary, January 9, 13, 14, 1874, HF-LC; CS to Peleg W. Chandler, January 15, 1874, Wendell Phillips to CS, January 12, 1874, CS-Mf; David Davis to BHB, January 13, 1874, BHB-LC; A. Roane to CC, January 16, 1874, CC-LC; Claude M. Fuess, *The Life of Caleb Cushing* (New York: Harcourt, Brace, 1923), 2:364–375; Lilian Handlin, "Cushing, Caleb," *ANB*, 5:909–910.

40. JHW to BHB, January 15, 1874, BHB to USG, January 18, 1874 (draft in another hand), BHB-LC; HF, diary, January 14, 16, 1874, HF-LC; TOH and Hannibal Hamlin to A. B. Cornell, January 18, 1874, RC Papers, LC; Cornell to TOH, January 19, 1874 (two telegrams), USG-LC; TOH to Grace Howe, January 20, 1874, TOH-WHS; TOH to EWK, January 22, 1874, EWK-WHS; ERH to JDC, March 31, 1874, JDC-OCL; CS to SB, circa January 24, 1874, with clipping, SB-Yale; David Herbert Donald, *Charles Sumner* (1970; reprint, New York: Da Capo, 1996), 2:581; *Journal of the Executive Proceedings of the Senate*, 43rd Cong., 1st sess., 222, 225, 226–227.

41. HF to RCS, January 19, 27, 1873, HF-LC; TOH to Grace Howe, January 20, 1874, TOH-WHS; C. H. Hill to BHB, January 10, 1874, BHB-LC; BHB to JMH, January 11, 1874, JMH-LC.

42. Brown and Williams, *Diary of Garfield*, 2:246.

43. *M and P*, 7:242–243, 251; HF, diary, November 18, 1873, HF-LC; 18 *Statutes at Large* 180.

44. *M and P*, 7:244–246.

45. Brown and Williams, *Diary of Garfield*, 2:253.

46. *Report of the Secretary of the Treasury for 1873*, xi–xxi; Unger, *Greenback Era*, 213.

47. Albert D. Shaw to JCBD, November 15, 1873, JCBD-LC (emphasis in original); JSM to John A. Page, April 11, 1873, JSM-LC; Henry Wilson to Francis E. Spinner, March 28, 1873, Henry Wilson Papers, LC; JAL to Mrs. JAL, December 7, 1873, JAL-LC; 18 *Statutes at Large* 4; GW to E. T. Welles, January 29, 1874, GW-LC.

48. HF to EBW, February 17, 1874, EBW-LC (emphasis in original); *CR*, 43rd Cong., 1st sess., 1626–1639, 1667–1681; *PUSG*, 25:32–34, 37–41.

49. George F. Hoar, *Autobiography of Seventy Years* (New York: Charles Scribner's Sons, 1903), 1:207; HF, diary, February 27, 1874, HF-LC; JAG to Burke Hinsdale, March 31, 1874, JAG-WRHS; Brown and Williams, *Diary of Garfield*, 2:306; Edward McPherson, *A Hand-Book of Politics for 1874* (Washington, D.C.: Solomons & Chapman, 1874), 135.

50. McPherson, *Hand-Book of Politics for 1874*, 160–165; *NYTr*, April 15, 1874; HF to John M. Francis, April 18, 1874, HF-LC; Unger, *Greenback Era*, 235–236.

51. Unger, *Greenback Era*, 240–242; McPherson, *Hand-Book of Politics for 1874*, 135–136.

52. HF, diary, April 15, 17, 21, 1874, HF-LC; *PUSG*, 25:65–67; John Russell Young, *Around the World with General Grant* (New York: American News, 1879), 2:153.

53. Young, *Around the World with General Grant*, 2:153–154; HF, diary, April 21, 22, 1874, HF to Gouverneur Kemble, May 9, 1874, HF-LC.

54. *M and P*, 7:268–271.

55. *NYTr*, April 23, 1874; Marshall Jewell to EBW, June 7, 1874, EBW-LC; Joseph R. Hawley to USG, April 22, 1874, USG-LC; JAL to Mrs. JAL, May 7, 1874, JAL-LC.

56. HF to G. L. Schuyler, April 25, 1874, HF-LC; Brown and Williams, *Diary of Garfield*, 2:315–316.

57. *NYTr*, April 23, June 6, 1874; *CR*, 43rd Cong., 1st sess., 3436; McPherson, *Hand-Book of Politics for 1874*, 166; HF, diary, June 1, 3, 4, 1874, HF-LC.

58. *NYTr*, June 6, 1874.

59. *NYTr*, June 8, 1874; ATS to USG, June 8, 1874, USG-LC; HF, diary, June 7, 9, 10, 1874, HF-LC.

60. *NYH*, June 8, 1874; 18 *Statutes at Large* 123–125; *NYT*, June 23, 1874.

61. *NYT*, June 13, 1874; Marshall Jewell to BHB, June 23, 1874, BHB-LC; *Address of the Union Republican Congressional Committee* (Washington, D.C., 1874), 13.

62. House Report No. 559, 43rd Cong., 1st sess., 1–9, 138; Hans Trefousse, *Ben Butler: The South Called Him BEAST* (New York: Twayne, 1957), 228.

63. House Report No. 559, 43rd Cong., 1st sess., 6–9, 87–88, 91, 140; HF to JCBD, April 3, 1874, JCBD-LC; HF, diary, April 10, 15, 1874, HF to EBW, April 20, 1874 (emphasis in original), HF-LC; Ari Hoogenboom, *Outlawing the Spoils: A History of the Civil Service Reform Movement, 1865–1883* (Urbana: University of Illinois Press, 1968), 131.

64. HF to JCBD, April 3, 1874, JCBD to ?, fragment, n.d. [circa May 1874], JCBD to AB, May 14, 1874, JCBD-LC; [HP] to BHB, May 16, [1874], BHB-LC; *PUSG*, 25:172; HF, diary, April 15, 24, 25, May 1, 5, 1874, HF-LC; BHB to JMH, March 27, April 7, 14, May 3, 1874, JMH-LC; WEC to EBW, May 4, 1874, HF to EBW, May 5, 1874 (telegram), George M. Robeson to EBW, May 5, 1874 (telegram), EBW to HF, May 6, 1874 (telegram), EBW-LC.

65. BHB to JMH, March 27, 31, April 7, 14, 17, 22, June 2, 1874, JMH-LC; JHW to BW, April 6, 1874, JHW-LC; [HP] to BHB, May 16, [1874], BHB-LC; Young, *Around the World with General Grant*, 2:155; HF, diary, June 1, 1874, HF-LC; *Journal of the Executive Proceedings of the Senate*, 43rd Cong., 1st sess., 311, 334.

66. BHB to E. W. Stoughton, June 6, 1874, BHB Papers, Filson Historical Society; John H. Ferry to JMH, June 10, 1874, JMH-LC; David Davis to BHB,

June 15, 1874, JHW to BHB, June 7, July 8, 20, 1874 (emphasis in original), BHB to JHW, July 18, 1874 (ts), BHB-LC.

67. BHB to JMH, July 22, September 4, 8, 1874, JMH-LC; George M. Robeson to BHB, August 1, 8, 25, 1874, USG to BHB, August 11, 1874, OEB to BHB, August 11, 14, 1874, George F. Edmunds to BHB, August 15, 1874, BHB to Robeson, August 28, September 10, 1874, JMH to BHB, August 28, 1874, BHB-LC; *PUSG*, 25:170–171, 182–186, 204–205; *NYT*, December 14, 1874.

68. JMH to BHB, December 14, 1874, JHW to BHB, September 8, November 30, 1874, G. C. Wharton to BHB, October 28, 1874, BHB-LC; JHW to AB, December 5, 1874 (ts), JHW-LC; *PUSG*, 25:136–137; 140; *NYT*, January 12, 14, 1875.

69. BHB to JMH, September 8, 1874, JMH-LC.

CHAPTER 18. RECONSTRUCTION UNDER SIEGE

1. Nicolas Barreyre, "The Politics of Economic Crises: The Panic of 1873, the End of Reconstruction, and the Realignment of American Politics," *Journal of the Gilded Age and Progressive Era* 10 (October 2011): 403–423.

2. *Slaughter-House Cases*, 83 U.S. (16 Wall.) 36 (1873) at 78; *CR*, 41st Cong., 1st sess., 4116; BHB to OPM, May 6, 1873, BHB-LC.

3. *M and P*, 7:255; *CR*, 43rd Cong., 1st sess., 2, 97; Edward McPherson, *A Hand-Book of Politics for 1874* (Washington, D.C.: Solomons & Chapman, 1874), 205–206; *WES*, December 10, 12, 1873.

4. *NYH*, January 7, 1874; Barnas Sears to Robert C. Winthrop, January 8, 1874, in J. L. M. Curry, *A Brief Sketch of George Peabody, and a History of the Peabody Education Fund through Thirty Years* (Cambridge, Mass.: John Wilson & Son, 1898), 64–65; Alfred H. Kelly, "The Congressional Controversy over School Segregation, 1867–1875," *American Historical Review* 64 (April 1959): 552–554; *CR*, 43rd Cong., 1st sess., 456–457.

5. *NYTr*, March 14, 1874.

6. *NYTr*, April 6, 1874; Charles Sumner, *Personal Relations with the President and Secretary of State: An Explanation in Reply to an Assault* (Washington, D.C.: n.p., 1871); CS to Anna C. Lodge, April 19, 1871, Edward L. Pierce to CS, May 8, 1871, Henry Wilson to CS, June 6, 1871, CS-Mf; TOH to Grace Howe, March 13, April 15, 1874, TOH-WHS; HF to JCBD, April 6, 1874, JCBD-LC; HF to Thomas E. Vermilye, April 18, 1874, HF-LC.

7. *CR*, 43rd Cong., 1st sess., 3451–3454, 4081–4083, 4115–4116, 4147–4152, 4176, 4242–4243, 4439, 5162–5163, 5328–5329, appendix, 358–361; McPherson, *Hand-Book of Politics for 1874*, 207–209.

8. BM, diary, July 10, 1873, BM-LC; HF to Henry C. Wayne, November 16, 1873, HF-LC; Michael Perman, *The Road to Redemption: Southern Politics, 1869–1879* (Chapel Hill: University of North Carolina Press, 1984), 160–164; *NYH*, January 18, 1874.

9. Charles Lane, "Edward Henry Durell: A Study in Reputation," *Green Bag* 13 (Winter 2010): 164–166; Matt Carpenter to H. C. Warmoth, May 7, 1873, March 16, 1874, G. A. Sheridan to Warmoth, January 30, 1874 (telegram), Henry C. Warmoth Papers, Southern Historical Collection, University of North Carolina at Chapel Hill; *CR*, 43rd Cong., 1st sess., 1215; *NYH*, January 18, 1874.

10. WEC to USG, January 22, 1874 (draft), WEC to Wm. P. Kellogg, n.d. (draft telegram), Kellogg to WEC, January 22, 1874 (telegram), WEC-LC; S. B. Packard to USG, January 23, 1874 (telegram), USG-LC; Kellogg to OPM, January 17, 1874, OPM-ISL; HF, diary, January 27, 1874, HF-LC; *CR*, 43rd Cong., 1st sess., 3270.

11. Carl H. Moneyhon, *Republicanism in Reconstruction Texas* (Austin: University of Texas Press, 1980), 191–194; *NYT*, January 13, 1874; McPherson, *Hand-Book of Politics for 1874*, 112; *PUSG*, 25:11–12.

12. Earl F. Woodward, "The Brooks and Baxter War in Arkansas, 1872–1874," *Arkansas Historical Quarterly* 30 (Winter 1971): 315–323.

13. McPherson, *Hand-Book of Politics for 1874*, 87–100; HF, diary, April 17, 21, May 5, 8, 12, 14, 1874, HF-LC; *M and P*, 7:272–273; Woodward, "Brooks and Baxter War," 326–334.

14. HF, diary, March 26, 27, 1874, HF-LC; *NYT*, February 20, 1874; *NYTr*, March 31, 1874; *Georgia Weekly Telegraph and Georgia Journal & Messenger*, April 10, 1874; Wm. Henry Trescot to JCBD, April 3, 1874, JCBD-LC.

15. USG, "Civil Service Reform," [draft, December 1, 1873], USG-LC; *M and P*, 7:255; *CR*, 43rd Cong., 1st sess., 57, 74; Ari Hoogenboom, *Outlawing the Spoils: A History of the Civil Service Reform Movement, 1865–1883* (Urbana: University of Illinois Press, 1968), 128.

16. *Journal of the Executive Proceedings of the Senate of the United States*, 43rd Cong., 1st sess., 251, 259, 260; *NYT*, February 17, 18, 1874; George F. Hoar, *Autobiography of Seventy Years* (New York: Charles Scribner's Sons, 1903), 1:210–211; George S. Boutwell, *Reminiscences of Sixty Years in Public Affairs* (New York: McClure, Phillips, 1902), 283–284; Hoogenboom, *Outlawing the Spoils*, 132; *Harper's Weekly*, March 7, 1874.

17. *NYT*, January 23, February 14, 28, April 20, May 7, 1874; *CR*, 43rd Cong., 1st sess., 766, 4888–4889; *M and P*, 7:263; Hoogenboom, *Outlawing the Spoils*, 129–130.

18. *PUSG*, 24:163–164; *WNR*, May 22, 1874; Jesse R. Grant, *In the Days of My Father General Grant* (New York: Harper & Brothers, 1925), 176; Harry James Brown and Frederick D. Williams, *The Diary of James A. Garfield* (East Lansing: Michigan State University Press, 1967–1981), 2:325; Christopher Gordon, "A White House Wedding: The Story of Nelly Grant," *Gateway* 26 (Summer 2005): 9–19.

19. Robert J. Kaczorowski, *The Politics of Judicial Interpretation: The Federal Courts, Department of Justice and Civil Rights, 1866–1876* (Dobbs Ferry, N.Y.: Oceana Publications, 1985), 179–184, 187–189.

20. Edward McPherson, *A Hand-Book of Politics for 1876* (Washington, D.C.:

Solomons & Chapman, 1876), 40; OPM to Henry Wilson, August 23, 1874, OPM-ISL; *PUSG*, 25:188; JMH to BHB, August 18, 1874, BHB-LC; George C. Rable, *But There Was No Peace: The Role of Violence in the Politics of Reconstruction* (Athens: University of Georgia Press, 1984), 133–136; Ted Tunnell, *Crucible of Reconstruction: War, Radicalism, and Race in Louisiana, 1862–1877* (Baton Rouge: Louisiana State University Press, 1984), 198–202.

21. *NYH*, September 4, 6, 1874.

22. *NYH*, September 16, 1874; HF, diary, September 15, 16, 1874, HF-LC; *PUSG*, 25:213–214; Marshall Jewell to EBW, September 19, 1874, EBW-LC.

23. *NYH*, September 16, 17, 18, 1874; HF, diary, September 16, 1874, HF-LC; Marshall Jewell to EBW, September 19, 1874, EBW-LC; McPherson, *Hand-Book of Politics for 1876*, 25.

24. EBW to JCBD, September 20, 1874 (ts), HF-LC; Marshall Jewell to EBW, September 19, 1874, EBW-LC.

25. C. C. Sniffen to HF, September 19, 1874, HF, diary, September 21, 1874, HF-LC; *PUSG*, 25:246–247.

26. HF to John L. Cadwalader, October 5, 1874, HF, diary, October 24, 1874, HF to JCBD, September 28, 1874, HF-LC; HF to JCBD, November 11, 1874, JCBD-LC.

27. HF, diary, September 21, October 24, 1874, HF-LC.

28. Charles W. Calhoun, *Conceiving a New Republic: The Republican Party and the Southern Question, 1869–1900* (Lawrence: University Press of Kansas, 2006), 59; Frederic Bancroft, ed., *Speeches, Correspondence and Political Papers of Carl Schurz* (New York: G. P. Putnam's Sons, 1913), 3:93; John Sherman, *Selected Speeches and Reports on Finance and Taxation from 1859 to 1878* (New York: D. Appleton, 1879), 452–465; HLD, manuscript speech, October 8, 1874, HLD-LC; Irwin Unger, *The Greenback Era: A Social and Political History of American Finance, 1865–1879* (Princeton, N.J.: Princeton University Press, 1964), 249–250.

29. WR to L. Clarke Davis, July 13, 1874, WR to T. S. Lang, August 13, 1874, WR to JB, August 20, 31, September 7, 1874, WR to Thurlow Weed, September 11, 1874, WR to John Cochrane, September 11, 1874, WR to John A. Dix, September 11, 1874, WR-LC; JB, diary, July 24, 1874, JB-NYPL; *NYTr*, September 14, 1874; *NYH*, July–November 1874; *NYT*, September 24, 1874; HF, diary, October 24, 1874, HF-LC; David M. Jordan, *Roscoe Conkling of New York: Voice in the Senate* (Ithaca, N.Y.: Cornell University Press, 1971), 214–215.

30. *NYH*, October 13, 1874; JB, diary, November 3, 1874, JB-NYPL.

31. *PUSG*, 25:252–259; *Cleveland Daily Herald*, October 16, 1874.

32. *American Annual Cyclopaedia and Register of Important Events of the Year 1874* (New York: D. Appleton, 1875), 415, 669; Emma Lou Thornbrough, *Indiana in the Civil War Era, 1850–1880* (Indianapolis: Indiana Historical Bureau & Indiana Historical Society, 1965), 289–294; Unger, *Greenback Era*, 250; J. Q. Smith to JS, October 22, 1874, JS-LC; *NYT*, October 17, 1874; HF, diary, October 24, 1874, HF-LC; *NYH*, October 26, 27, 28, 1874.

33. JHW to BHB, October 20, 1874, BHB-LC; HF, diary, October 27, 1874, HF-LC.

34. *WNR*, October 28, 1874; HF, diary, October 28, 1874, HF-LC.

35. *NYTr*, November 4, 1874; HF to Henry Crosby, November 7, 1874, HF-LC; Kenneth C. Martis, *The Historical Atlas of Political Parties in the United States Congress, 1789–1989* (New York: Macmillan, 1989), 126–129, 428–435.

36. *NYH*, November 4, 1874; JB to WR, November 4, 1874, JB-NYPL; *NYTr*, November 4, 1874; HF, diary, November 8, December 2, 1874, HF-LC; Marshall Jewell to JCBD, December 26, 1874, JCBD-LC; Jewel to EBW, December 5, 1874, EBW-LC.

37. BHB to Z. M. Sherley, November 9, 1874, BHB-LC; HF, diary, December 2, 1874, HF-LC; BW to JHW, January 31, 1875, USG-USGPL.

38. *PUSG*, 25:269–270; HF, diary, December 1, 4, 1874, HF-LC.

39. *M and P*, 7:296–299.

40. Rable, *But There Was No Peace*, 148–149; *M and P*, 7:322–323; McPherson, *Hand-Book of Politics for 1876*, 28.

41. James T. Otten, "The Wheeler Adjustment in Louisiana: National Republicans Begin to Reappraise Their Reconstruction Policy," *Louisiana History* 13 (Fall 1972): 357; Tunnell, *Crucible of Reconstruction*, 204; HF, diary, December 29, 1874, HF-LC.

42. McPherson, *Hand-Book of Politics for 1876*, 30–31; *NYT*, January 16, 1875; *CR*, 43rd Cong., 2nd sess., 366.

43. *NYT*, January 6, 7, 1875; *NYTr*, January 6, 7, 1875.

44. HLD to SB, January 7, 1875, SB-Yale; Wendell Phillips to WWB, January 9, 1875, WWB-PU; EP to USG, January 10, 1875 (emphasis in original), with news clipping, USG-LC; *CR*, 43rd Cong., 2nd sess., 248, 370.

45. HF, diary, January 5, [8], 10, 11, 1875, HF-LC.

46. Otten, "Wheeler Adjustment in Louisiana," 358–359; HF, diary, January 10, 11, 12, 1875, HF-LC; BHB to JMH, January 11, 1875, JMH-LC; USG to WWB, January 9, 1875, WWB-PU; PHS to WWB, January 10, 1875 (telegram), USG-LC.

47. HF, diary, January 12, 1875, HF-LC; TOH to Grace Howe, January 18, 1875, TOH-WHS (emphasis in original).

48. *M and P*, 7:305–314; *PUSG*, 26:3–16.

49. TOH to Grace Howe, January 14, 1875, TOH-WHS; *NYT*, January 14, 1875; JGB to USG, January 14, 1875, ERH to USG, January 14, 1875, USG-LC; JB to SJT, February 2, 1875, SJT-NYPL.

50. *NYT*, January 16, 1875; *NYH*, January 16, 24, 25, 1875.

51. *M and P*, 7:314; *CR*, 43rd Cong., 2nd sess., 879; *WES*, January 16, 1875; *NYT*, January 18, 19, 1875.

52. Otten, "Wheeler Adjustment in Louisiana," 359–361; Calhoun, *Conceiving a New Republic*, 69–72.

53. HLD to SB, February 2, 1875, SB-Yale.

54. Calhoun, *Conceiving a New Republic*, 72–73; House Report No. 127, 43rd Cong., 2nd sess.

55. HF, diary, November 17, December 4, 1874, January 22, 1875, HF-LC; *M and P*, 7:298; A. H. Garland to USG, January 13, 1875 (telegram), USG-LC; *NYH*, January 22, 1875; *NYT*, January 22, 1875.

56. House Report No. 127, 43rd Cong., 2nd sess., 15–16; *CR*, 43rd Cong., 2nd sess., 922.

57. HF, diary, May 5, 1874, HF-LC; *M and P*, 7:319; *PUSG*, 26:52–53.

58. BHB to JMH, February 14, 1875, JMH-LC; HF, diary, February 9, 11, 1875, HF-LC; Mark W. Summers, *Railroads, Reconstruction, and the Gospel of Prosperity: Aid under the Radical Republicans, 1865–1877* (Princeton, N.J.: Princeton University Press, 1984), 259–260; JMH to BHB, February 16, 1875, BHB-LC.

59. *M and P*, 7:319; *CR*, 43rd Cong., 2nd sess., 2093; HF, diary, February 9, 1875, HF-LC.

60. BHB to JMH, February 14, 21, 1875, JMH-LC.

61. HF, diary, February 21, 1875, HF-LC.

62. *CR*, 43rd Cong., 2nd sess., 1055–1056, 1078, 2086–2118; HF to L. J. Jennings, March 4, 1875, HF, diary, March 9, 1875, HF-LC.

63. *CR*, 43rd Cong., 2nd sess., 1645–1652; McPherson, *Hand-Book of Politics for 1876*, 36–40; Otten, "Wheeler Adjustment in Louisiana," 360–364.

64. *NYT*, February 14, 15, 1875; *CR*, 43rd Cong., 2nd sess., 1453; McPherson, *Hand-Book of Politics for 1876*, 13–18.

65. *CR*, 43rd Cong., 2nd sess., 1791–1798, 1861–1870; McPherson, *Hand-Book of Politics for 1876*, 8–11; 18 Part 3 *Statutes at Large* 335–337; John C. Patterson, "Marshall Men and Marshall Measures in State and National History," *Michigan Historical Collections* 38 (1912): 270; James M. McPherson, "Abolitionists and the Civil Rights Act of 1875," *Journal of American History* 52 (December 1965): 508–510; *NYTr*, April 1, 1875.

66. EP to HF, March 10, 1875, HF-LC (emphasis in original).

CHAPTER 19. SOUND MONEY, CROOKED WHISKEY

1. HF, diary, November 11, 1874, HF-LC; JHW to BHB, November 13, 1874, BHB-LC.

2. *PUSG*, 25:284; Edward McPherson, *A Hand-Book of Politics for 1874* (Washington, D.C.: Solomons & Chapman, 1874), 193–200; *Address of the Union Republican Congressional Committee* (Washington, D.C., 1874), 14; Harry James Brown and Frederick D. Williams, eds., *The Diary of James A. Garfield* (East Lansing: Michigan State University Press, 1967–1981), 2:399, 400; Mary L. Hinsdale, ed., *Garfield-Hinsdale Letters: Correspondence between James Abram Garfield and Burke Aaron Hinsdale* (Ann Arbor: University of Michigan Press, 1949), 300; *M and P*, 7:301; *Annual Report of the Secretary of the Treasury, 1874*, House Executive Document No. 2, 43rd Cong., 2nd sess., xvii.

3. HF, diary, November 11, 1874, HF-LC; *M and P*, 7:285–287, 293–294; *Annual Report of the Secretary of the Treasury, 1874*, xi–xvii.

4. Floyd W. Nicklas, "William Kelley: The Congressional Years, 1861–1890" (Ph.D. diss., Northern Illinois University, 1983), 356–360, 366–371; *CR*, 43rd Cong., 2nd sess., 20–26, 44–49; Brown and Williams, *Diary of Garfield*, 2:400–401; S. S. Cox to MM, December 8, 1874, MM-LC.

5. John Sherman, *Recollections of Forty Years in the House, Senate and Cabinet* (Chicago: Werner, 1895), 1:509; *NYT*, December 14, 1874; TOH to Grace Howe, December 14, 1874, TOH-WHS; Irwin Unger, *The Greenback Era: A Social and Political History of American Finance, 1865–1879* (Princeton, N.J.: Princeton University Press, 1964), 252–253.

6. *NYT*, December 20, 1874; Edward McPherson, *A Hand-Book of Politics for 1876* (Washington, D.C.: Solomons & Chapman, 1876), 125; HF to JCBD, January 6, 1875, JCBD-LC; *M and P*, 7:314.

7. *CR*, 43rd Cong., 2nd sess., 161, 186–188, 194–208, 317–319; McPherson, *Hand-Book of Politics for 1876*, 125–127; *PUSG*, 25:313–314.

8. HF, diary, January 11, 1875, HF-LC; *PUSG*, 26:35–38; *M and P*, 7:314–316.

9. HF, diary, January 19, 1875, HF-LC; *NYT*, January 20, 1875.

10. *CR*, 43rd Cong., 2nd sess., 1984, 2065; 18 Part 3 *Statutes at Large* 339–340; HF, diary, March 2, 1875, HF-LC; TOH to Grace Howe, March 8, 1875, TOH-WHS.

11. HF, diary, November 18, 25, December 5, 24, 1874, January 4, 5, 7, 15, 19, 20, 22, February 1, 12, 27, March 11, 16, 19, 1875, HF-LC; *NYT*, February 25, 1875; Charles S. Campbell, *The Transformation of American Foreign Relations* (New York: Harper & Row, 1976), 68–70; James Burke Chapin, "Hamilton Fish and American Expansion" (Ph.D. diss., Cornell University, 1971), 524–539, 543–544.

12. HF, diary, March 5, 1875, HF-LC; *Report of the Secretary of the Treasury, 1875*, House Executive Document No. 2, 44th Cong., 1st sess., xxv; Richard H. Timberlake, *Monetary Policy in the United States: An Intellectual and Institutional History* (Chicago: University of Chicago Press, 1993), 111–112.

13. Marshall Jewell to EBW, October 17, 1874, EBW-LC.

14. *M and P*, 7:300–301.

15. HF, diary, March 9, 1875, HF-LC; *NYH*, March 12, 1875; *Harper's Weekly*, December 26, 1874, March 27, 1875; Frederic Bancroft, ed., *Speeches, Correspondence and Political Papers of Carl Schurz* (New York: G. P. Putnam's Sons, 1913), 6:148.

16. *NYT*, May 15, 1875; D. B. Eaton to JCBD, November 25, 1875, JCBD-LC (emphasis in original).

17. *PUSG*, 28:184, 265; John Russell Young, *Around the World with General Grant* (New York: American News, 1879), 2:263–266.

18. HF, diary, December 19, 30, 1874, January 2, 1875, HF-LC.

19. *PUSG*, 26:106–107; *NYH*, August 19, 1876; *NYT*, September 9, 1874; H. C. Whitley, *In It* (Cambridge, Mass.: Riverside Press, 1894), 257–261; *Whisky Frauds*, House Miscellaneous Document No. 186, 44th Cong., 1st sess., 406–407.

20. *PUSG*, 26:106–107; HF, diary, March 12, 1875, HF-LC.

21. HF, diary, April 12, 1875, HF to EBW, April 14, 1875 (ts), HF-LC.

22. HF, diary, April 12, 26, 1875, HF to EP, April 26, 1875 (ts), HF-LC; *NYT*, April 29, 1875; EP to BHB, February 4, 6, 1875, BHB-LC.

23. BHB to JMH, February 21, March 14, 1875, JHW to JMH, April 1, 1875, JMH-LC; BW to JHW, April 18, 1875, USG-USGPL; JMH to BHB, February 17, March 9, 1875, JHW to BHB, March 9, 1875, BHB-LC; HF, diary, February 21, 1875, HF-LC.

24. BHB to WQG, December 18, 1874, BHB to JMH, February 8, 1875 (ts), BHB-LC; BHB to JMH, February 14, March 3, April 4, 1875, JHW to JMH, April 1, 1875, JMH-LC; HF, diary, January 5, February 21, 1875, HF-LC; BW to JHW, March 16, 1875, USG-USGPL; Brown and Williams, *Diary of Garfield*, 2:43.

25. HF, diary, December 19, 1874, January 5, February 21, 1875, HF-LC; BHB to William Cassius Goodloe, March 29, 1875, Frank Wolcott to BHB, March 14, 24, 1875, USG to BHB, April 6, 1875, BHB-LC; House Report No. 794, 44th Cong., 1st sess., i–vii, 1–4, 37.

26. House Report No. 794, 44th Cong., 1st sess., ii, v, 1–4, 23–29, 44; BW to JHW, April 18, 1875, USG-USGPL; HF, diary, April 26, 29, 1875, HF-LC.

27. HF, diary, April 26, 29, May 17, 1875, HF-LC; JHW to BHB, April 7, 1875, BHB-LC; BHB to JMH, May 17, 1875, JHW to JMH, May 15, 1875, JMH-LC; *NYH*, April 23, 1875; *PUSG*, 26:274, 308–309, 329.

28. *PUSG*, 26:168–170; BHB to JMH, September 10, 1875, JHW to JMH, August 28, 1875, JMH-LC; HF, diary, June 16, July 25, September 11, 1875, HF-LC; *NYH*, July 24, October 20, 1875; BW to JHW, July 27, 1875, USG-USGPL; BHB to John Feland, June 25, 1875, BHB-LC.

29. HF, diary, January 19, 1875, HF-LC; *M and P*, 7:293; 18 Part 3 *Statutes at Large* 339–340.

30. *Whisky Frauds*, 70, 330–332, 376–377; HF, diary, July 26, 1875, HF-LC; "Sylph" [OEB] to John A. McDonald, December 13, 1874 (telegram), BHB-LC.

31. *Whisky Frauds*, 70–71, 438–439, 453, 455; *PUSG*, 27:31–32, 26:235.

32. *Whisky Frauds*, 71, 84–85, 332–333, 345, 357, 438–439, 479; *PUSG*, 26:235; "Sylph" to O. E. Babcock, February 3, 1875 (telegram, copy), BHB-LC; [John Joyce] to John McDonald, February 6 (telegram), 8, 1875, in John McDonald, *Secrets of the Great Whiskey Ring* (Chicago: Belford, Clarke, 1880), 124–125.

33. *Whisky Frauds*, 353; JHW to JMH, April 1, 1875, BHB to JMH, May 10, 1875, JMH-LC; JHW to BHB, April 7, 1875, George C. Buchanan to Will S. Stewart, March 27, 1875, BHB-LC; BW to JHW, March 16, April 18, 1875, USG-USGPL.

34. *Whisky Frauds*, 332–333, 353–354, 393, 466–467, 479, 504–505; BW to Myron Colony, March 1, 1875, BW to George W. Fishback, March 2, 1875, Colony to BW, March 15, 1875, BHB-LC; BHB to JMH, May 10, 1875, JMH-LC; Mark Wahlgren Summers, *The Press Gang: Newspapers and Politics, 1865–1878* (Chapel Hill: University of North Carolina Press, 1994), 185, 285; Ross A. Webb, *Benjamin*

Helm Bristow: Border State Politician (Lexington: University Press of Kentucky, 1969), 188–189; H. V. Boynton, "The Whiskey Ring," *North American Review* 123 (October 1876): 282–284.

35. HF, diary, April 13, 21, 1875, HF-LC; *Whisky Frauds*, 354–355, 481–482; BHB to JMH, May 10, 1875, JMH-LC; BHB to D. D. Pratt, April 29, 1875, BHB-LC; McDonald, *Secrets of the Great Whiskey Ring*, 131–156.

36. *Whisky Frauds*, 355–356, 482; BHB to JMH, May 10, 1875, JMH-LC.

37. "Horace Houghton" to John McDonald, May 7, 1875, OEB to McDonald, May 7, 1875, in McDonald, *Secrets of the Great Whiskey Ring*, 159–164 (emphasis in original); BHB to JMH, May 10, 1875, JMH-LC.

38. Boynton, "Whiskey Ring," 299–300; BHB to E. W. Stoughton, May 13, 1875, BHB-LC; *PUSG*, 26:115–116; David P. Dyer, *Autobiography and Reminiscences* (St. Louis: William Harvey Miner, 1922), 138–139, 151–152; DPD to JHW, June 27, 1875, JHW-LC (emphasis in original).

39. *PUSG*, 26:118, 239, 285–286; BHB to DPD, June 30, July 10, 1875, DPD to BHB, July 3, 18, 23, 1875, "Sylph" [OEB] to John McDonald, December 13, 1874 (telegram), BHB to Walter Q. Gresham, July 14 1875, BHB-LC; HF, diary, July 26, 1875, HF-LC; *WES*, July 8, 1875.

40. HF, diary, July 26, 1875, HF-LC.

41. *PUSG*, 26:232–233; USG, endorsement, July 29, 1875, USG-LC; *Whisky Frauds*, 357; *WES*, August 17, 1875.

42. *Whisky Frauds*, 358–360, 363, 489–490; JHW to BHB, August 26, 1875, BHB-LC; BW to JHW, September 2, 1875, USG-USGPL; HF, diary, September 17, 1875, HF-LC.

43. BHB to USG, September 1, 1875, BHB-LC; HF, diary, September 17, 1875, HF-LC; BHB to JMH, September 10, 1875, JMH-LC (emphasis in original).

44. BW to John B. Henderson, September 24, 1875, BHB-LC (emphasis in original); *Whisky Frauds*, 360–361, 364, 488–489.

45. *Whisky Frauds*, 26–27, 35, 43; George F. Stagg to BW, October 15, 1875, BHB-LC.

46. Robert M. Utley, *The Indian Frontier, 1846–1890*, rev. ed. (Albuquerque: University of New Mexico Press, 2003), 171–173; *PUSG*, 26:119–120, 138–145, 159, 163; "Agreement between the United States and the Sioux for the Relinquishment of Hunting Rights in Nebraska," in House Executive Document No. 1, pt. 5, vol. 1, 681–682; *M and P*, 7:352.

47. *PUSG*, 26:203–204, 208–209, 224–225, 302; Francis Paul Prucha, *The Great Father: The United States Government and the American Indians* (Lincoln: University of Nebraska Press, 1984), 1:587–588; *NYT*, November 2, 1875.

48. *Appletons' Annual Cyclopaedia and Register of Important Events of the Year 1875* (New York: D. Appleton, 1877), 219, 346–349; 417; *NYH*, April 7, 1875; Marshall Jewell to EBW, April 23, 1875, EBW-LC; Brown and Williams, *Diary of Garfield*, 2:39; BHB to JMH, May 17, 1875, JMH-LC.

49. *Appletons' Annual Cyclopaedia 1875*, 617; HF, diary, May 30, 1875, HF-LC; *PUSG*, 26:128–129, 132–134.

50. USG to Harry White, May 29, 1875, in *WNR*, May 31, 1875.

51. John Y. Simon, ed., *The Personal Memoirs of Julia Dent Grant* (New York: G. P. Putnam's Sons, 1975), 185–186; George Bancroft to JCBD, June 4, 1875, JCBD-LC; *NYH*, May 31, 1875; HF to EBW, June 2, 1875, HF-LC; Frederick Douglass to OEB, May 31, 1875, USG-LC.

52. *Appletons' Annual Cyclopaedia 1875*, 606, 607; JAG to RBH, June 24 1875 (ts), RBH-RBHPC; Unger, *Greenback Era*, 266–280.

53. HF, diary, July 8, 1875, HF-LC; *PUSG*, 26:177–178; ZC to BHB, July 2, 1875, BHB-LC (emphasis in original); John L. Cadwalader to JCBD, August 20, 1875, JCBD-LC.

54. *PUSG*, 26:270–272, 327.

55. Ward M. McAfee, *Religion, Race, and Reconstruction: The Public School in the Politics of the 1870s* (Albany: State University of New York Press, 1998), 177–180; Edward F. Noyes to BHB, September 5, 1875, BHB-LC; *PUSG*, 26:342–344; Brown and Williams, *Diary of Garfield*, 3:120; JGB to A. T. Wickoff, October 2, 1875, JGB-LC; Tyler Anbinder, "Ulysses S. Grant: Nativist," *Civil War History* 43 (June 1997): 119–132.

56. BHB to JMH, August 27, 1875, BHB-LC; Charles Richard Williams, ed., *Diary and Letters of Rutherford Birchard Hayes* (Columbus: Ohio State Archaeological and Historical Society, 1924), 3:286; EP to Alphonso Taft, June 25, 1875, William Howard Taft Papers, LC.

57. *WES*, September 8–10, 1875.

58. McPherson, *Hand-Book of Politics for 1876*, 40–42; *PUSG*, 26:295–297; *WES*, September 10, 1875; *NYT*, September 10, 11, 1875.

59. USG to EP, September 13, 1875, EP-Yale.

60. *NYT*, September 9, 1875; EP to Adelbert Ames, September 14, 1875, in *WES*, September 16, 1875 (emphasis in original).

61. EP to USG, September 15, 1875, USG-LC; McPherson, *Hand-Book of Politics for 1876*, 43; *NYTr*, September 17, 1875; proclamation and warrant signed by USG, September 1875, EP-Yale.

62. Blanche Ames, *Adelbert Ames, 1835–1933: General, Senator, Governor* (New York: Argosy-Antiquarian, 1964), 431–434; Adelbert Ames to USG, September 25, 1875 (with USG endorsement to EP, September 27, 1875), Ames to EP, October 16, 1875, G. K. Chase to EP, May 4, 1877, EP-Yale; EP to Ames, October 23, 1875, Letters Sent, Records of the Department of Justice, RG 60, NA; Senate Report No. 527, 44th Cong., 1st sess., 2:1801–1804, 1810.

63. *NYT*, October 13, 1875; G. K. Chase to EP, May 4, 1877, EP-Yale; EP to Adelbert Ames, October 28, 1875 (telegram), EP to Chase, October 28, 1875, Letters Sent, RG 60, NA; George C. Rable, *But There Was No Peace: The Role of Violence in the Politics of Reconstruction* (Athens: University of Georgia Press, 1984), 158–161; Senate Report No. 527, 44th Cong., 1st sess., 2:92.

64. *Appletons' Annual Cyclopaedia 1875*, 564, 618; Brown and Williams, *Diary of Garfield*, 3:176; *NYT*, November 7, 1875.

65. EP to JCBD, November 4, 1876, JCBD-LC; *NYT*, November 4, 1875.

CHAPTER 20. THE PRESIDENT UNDER FIRE

1. G. M. Dodge to J. S. Clarkson, November 4, 1875, James S. Clarkson Papers, LC; E. R. Chapman to BW, November 5, 1875 (telegram), BHB-LC; *NYT*, November 4, 5, 6, 7, 1875.

2. Harry James Brown and Frederick D. Williams, eds., *The Diary of James A. Garfield* (East Lansing: Michigan State University Press, 1967–1981), 3:204; TOH to Grace Howe, December 11, 1875, TOH-WHS; James C. Madigan to Charles P. Kimball, November 11, 1875, SJT-NYPL (emphasis in original); *CR*, 44th Cong., 1st sess., 228; Edward McPherson, *A Hand-Book of Politics for 1876* (Washington, D.C.: Solomons & Chapman, 1876), 143–144.

3. *M and P*, 7:332–356; HF, diary, October 29, November 5, 27, 30, December 3, 5, 1875, HF-LC.

4. *CR*, 44th Cong., 1st sess., 205; McPherson, *Hand-Book of Politics for 1876*, 240–241; HF to Wickham Hoffman, March 4, 1877, HF-LC.

5. *NYT*, November 5, 6, 1875; BHB to JMH, November 7, 1875, JMH-LC (emphasis in original); JMH to BHB, November 7, 1875, BHB-LC.

6. *Whisky Frauds*, House Miscellaneous Document No. 186, 44th Cong., 1st sess., 361; BHB to JMH, November 7, 1875, JMH-LC; BW to EP, November 10, 11, 1875 (telegrams), DPD to BW, November 10, 1875, BW to BHB, November 10, 1875, BHB-LC.

7. *Whisky Frauds*, 358–362, 540–542.

8. BW to JHW, November 18, 1875, BHB to JHW, November 20, 1875, USG-USGPL; BW to Lucien Eaton, November 17, 1875, OEB to John Joyce, December 5, 1874, quoted in Eaton to BW, November 19, 1875 (telegram), "J" to Babcock, December 3, 1874, quoted in Eaton to BW, November 29, 1875 (telegram), BHB-LC.

9. BW to DPD, November 20, 1875, BHB-LC.

10. Lucien Eaton to BW, November 22, 23, 29, 1875 (telegrams), BW to Eaton, November 23, 29, 1875 (telegrams), BHB-LC; *StLGD*, November 30, 1875; *Whisky Frauds*, 36–37.

11. *Whisky Frauds*, 2–4, 23, 37, 38.

12. OEB to USG, December 2, 1875, *PUSG*, 26:375; [WWB], "Memorandum," [December 3, 1875], WWB-PU; HF, diary, December 2, 3, 1875, HF-LC; Lucien Eaton to BW, December 6, 1875 (telegram), BHB-LC; *Whisky Frauds*, 5, 39–40.

13. LPL to EBW, March 8, 1876, EBW-LC; BW to JHW, December 8, 1875, USG-USGPL; *Whisky Frauds*, 360–362, 364, 366, 490.

14. *StLGD*, December 4, 1875; *Whisky Frauds*, 5–6, 70; Lucien Eaton to BW, December 6, 7, 1875 (telegrams), BW to BHB, December 10, 1875, BHB-LC; HF, diary, December 7, 10, 1875, HF-LC; EP to DPD, December 9, 1875 (telegram), USG-LC; BHB to JHW, December 11, 1875, USG-USGPL; BHB to JMH, December 10, 1875, JMH-LC (emphasis in original).

15. *Whisky Frauds*, 5–6; James L. Blair, *An Address on the Life and Character of Samuel T. Glover* (Kansas City, Mo.: Kansas City Bar Association, 1897); *PUSG*, 26:380, 427–428; DPD to EP, December 11, 1875 (telegram), EP to USG, December 13, 1875, EP-Yale; *NYH*, December 11, 12, 1875; DPD to JHW, December 26, 1875, JHW-LC.

16. Lucien Eaton to BW, December 7, 9, 1875 (telegrams), BHB-LC; DPD, *The Indictment* (St. Louis, 1875), in OEB-NL; *PUSG*, 26:380–381, 384–385; *Whisky Frauds*, 40–41, 335–342.

17. *Whisky Frauds*, 44–45, 53–54, 110–140, 363, 365, 487 (emphasis in original) ; *PUSG*, 26:430.

18. *Whisky Frauds*, 366, 487.

19. Ibid., 366, 375, 378, 487; BHB to JMH, December 16, 1875, A. E. Willson to JMH, December 19, 1875, JMH-LC; BW to JHW, December 23, 1875, USG-USGPL.

20. John Krum to OEB, December 13, 15, 17, 1875, CHK to OEB, December 22, 24, 27, 1875, January 11, 1876, OEB-NL.

21. *Whisky Frauds*, 7–12, 19, 38, 40–43, 366–368, 445, 448, 462–463; HF, diary, February 1, March 7, 1876, HF-LC; *PUSG*, 27:219–220.

22. HF, diary, February 6, 1876, HF-LC (emphasis in original); BHB to JMH, February 3, 1876, A. E. Willson to JMH, February 7, 1876, JMH-LC; BW to JHW, February 7, 1876, USG-USGPL; *Whisky Frauds*, 445.

23. A. E. Willson to JMH, February 7, 1876, JMH-LC; BW to JHW, February 7, 1876, USG-USGPL.

24. HP to USG, February 4, 1875 [1876], USG-LC (emphasis in original); *PUSG*, 27:23.

25. DPD to BW, February 1, 1876 (telegram), BW to DPD, February 1, 1876 (telegram), BHB-LC; HF, diary, February 8, 1876, HF-LC.

26. *NYH*, February 13, 1876; *PUSG*, 27:27–35, 44–45.

27. *PUSG*, 27:35–44, 50.

28. HF, diary, February 14, 1876, HF-LC; BW to DPD, February 9, 1876, BHB-LC.

29. *NYH*, February 11, 1876; *StLGD*, February 9–13, 15–16, 18, 1876.

30. *StLGD*, February 17–19, 1876; *Whisky Frauds*, 90–91.

31. *StLGD*, February 20, 22, 23, 24, 1876; *NYT*, February 15, 1876; *NYH*, February 15, 1876; Lucien Eaton to BW, February 22, 1876 (telegram), BW to DPD, February 22, 1876 (telegram), BHB-LC.

32. OEB to Annie Campbell Babcock, February 23, 1876, OEB-NL.

33. *StLGB*, February 25, 26, 1876 (emphasis in original); *NYT*, February 25, 1876.

34. *NYTr*, February 25, 1876; *NYT*, February 25, 1876; *NYH*, February 25, 1876; HF, diary, February 22, 1876, HF-LC; BHB to Richard Smith, February 28, 1876, BHB-LC.

35. HF, diary, February 25, 29, March 1, 4, 5, 1876, HF-LC; *Whisky Frauds*, 1; LPL to EBW, March 8, 1876, EBW-LC; *PUSG*, 27:63; *NYT*, April 16, 1876; Alan Lessoff, *The Nation and Its City: Politics, "Corruption," and Progress in Washington, D.C., 1861–1902* (Baltimore: Johns Hopkins University Press, 1994), 95–96, 169–172.

36. House Report No. 579, 44th Cong., 1st sess., i–xvi, 4–8, 310; HF, diary, November 24, 28, 1871, August 5, 6, 1873, HF to RCS, August 6, 1873 (draft not sent), HF-LC; BM, diary, February 15, 1873, BM-LC; *PUSG*, 24:179.

37. HF, diary, February 9, 11, 14, 15, 22, March 3, May 20, 22, 1876, HF to RCS, February 14, 1876, RCS to HF, March 2, 1876 (telegram), HF-LC; House Report No. 579, 44th Cong., 1st sess., i–ii, xvi.

38. House Report No. 186, 44th Cong., 1st sess., 3–4, 7–8; *Proceedings of the Senate Sitting for the Trial of William W. Belknap* (Washington, D.C.: Government Printing Office, 1876), 571; *NYTr*, February 16, 1872; WR to Z. L. White, February 20, 1872, WR-LC; Edward S. Cooper, *William Worth Belknap: An American Disgrace* (Madison, N.J.: Fairleigh Dickinson University Press, 2003), 164–166, 293.

39. *NYH*, February 9, 10, 1876; House Report No. 186, 44th Cong., 1st sess., 2, 4–7; *NYT*, March 4, 1876; Cooper, *Belknap*, 32.

40. BHB to JMH, March 4, 1876, JMH-LC; HF, diary, March 2, 1876, HF-LC; *PUSG*, 27:53–54; *NYH*, March 4, 1876.

41. HF, diary, March 3, 7, 1876, HF-LC; BHB to JMH, March 4, 1876, JMH-LC; Brown and Williams, *Diary of Garfield*, 3:243–244; *NYH*, March 3, 4, 1876.

42. WWB to Anna Mary Belknap, March 20, 1876, WWB-PU (emphasis in original); Cooper, *Belknap*, 240.

43. WTS to JDC, March 19, 1876, JDC-OCL; WTS to JS, March 10, 1876, in *The Sherman Letters: Correspondence between General and Senator Sherman from 1837 to 1891*, ed. Rachel Sherman Thorndyke (New York: Charles Scribner's Sons, 1894), 348–349; *NYT*, March 6, 1876; W. T. Sherman, *Memoirs* (New York: Charles L. Webster, 1892), 2:444–455.

44. HF, diary, March 3, 5, 1876, HF-LC; JHW to JMH, March 2, 1876, BHB to JMH, March 8, 1876, JMH-LC; A. E. Willson to JMH, March 2, 1876, BHB-LC; Linda C. A. Przybyszewski, "Taft, Alphonso," *ANB*, 21:250–251; *NYT*, March 12, 1876; Sherman, *Memoirs*, 2:454–455.

45. HF, diary, March 14, 21, 31, 1876, HF-LC; Cooper, *Belknap*, 285–308; House Report No. 791, 44th Cong., 1st sess.; WWB to Anna Mary Belknap, August 3, 1876, WWB-PU.

46. Cooper, *Belknap*, 243–252; HF, diary, March 21, 31, 1876, HF-LC; WWB

to Clara B. Wolcott, May 21, 1876, WWB-PU; *PUSG*, 27:61–62; *NYT*, February 9, 1877.

47. Hamilton Fish, "General Grant," *Independent*, July 30, 1885; O. H. Tiffany, *Pulpit and Platform: Sermons and Addresses* (New York: Hunt & Eaton, 1893), 206–207; *PUSG*, 31:70.

48. HLD to SB, March 5, 1876, SB-Yale; *NYT*, January 18, 1876; HF, diary, February 15, 1876, HF-LC.

49. *M and P*, 7:361–366, 380–381; HF, diary, April 4, 7, 25, May 4, 5, 1876, HF-LC; *NYTr*, May 5, 1876.

50. John L. Cadwalader to JCBD, April 14, 1876, HF to JCBD, April 23, 1876, JCBD-LC.

CHAPTER 21. SECURING THE SUCCESSION

1. *PUSG*, 18:292–293.

2. John H. Ferry to JMH, June 10, 1874, JMH-LC; David Davis to BHB, June 15, 1874, JHW to BHB, June 7, July 8, 20, 1874, BHB-LC; BW to JHW, December 30, 1875, USG-USGPL.

3. Henry Cabot Lodge to CSch, February 14, 15, 16, 18, 24, 1876, Horace White to CSch, February 17, 1876, CSch-LC; J. C. Levenson et al., eds., *The Letters of Henry Adams* (Cambridge, Mass.: Harvard University Press, 1982), 2:247, 249–258; Ross A. Webb, *Benjamin Helm Bristow: Border State Politician* (Lexington: University Press of Kentucky, 1969), 220–223.

4. Frederic Bancroft, ed., *Speeches, Correspondence and Political Papers of Carl Schurz* (New York: G. P. Putnam's Sons, 1913), 3:226, 228–229, 240–248; BHB to CSch, April 3, 1876, Newton Booth to SB, March 29, 1876, CSch-LC; Booth to SB, April 3, 1876, SB-Yale; Hans L. Trefousse, *Carl Schurz: A Biography* (Knoxville: University of Tennessee Press, 1982), 227–228.

5. Horace White to CSch, March 10, 1876, Charles Nordhoff to CSch, March 8, 1876, CSch-LC.

6. HF, diary, March 6, 1876, HF-LC; House Report No. 784, 44th Cong., 1st sess., 152–153, 160–161, 195, 198; House Miscellaneous Document No. 170, 44th Cong., 1st sess.; *NYH*, July 22, 1876.

7. HF, diary, April 20, 1876, HF-LC; House Report No. 800, 44th Cong., 1st sess., xlii, liii; *NYH*, April 20, 22, 28, 1876; *NYT*, February 12, 1894.

8. Newton Booth to SB, April 3, 1876, SB-Yale; *NYT*, April 2, 1876; *Whisky Frauds*, House Miscellaneous Document No. 186, 44th Cong., 1st sess., 69, 71, 140–144, 550–553; HF, diary, April 5, 1876, HF-LC.

9. *WNR*, March 23, 1876; Mark Wahlgren Summers. *The Era of Good Stealings* (New York: Oxford University Press, 1993), 266; R. R. Hitt to OPM, April 21, 1876, Robert R. Hitt Papers, LC.

10. James Burke Chapin, "Hamilton Fish and American Expansion" (Ph.D.

diss., Cornell University, 1971), 535–536; HF, diary, February 7, 10, March 10, 21, April 21, October 12, December 8, 1876, January 4, 5, February 2, 8, 1877, HF-LC; Charles S. Campbell, *The Transformation of American Foreign Relations* (New York: Harper & Row, 1976), 62.

11. Charles W. Calhoun, *Conceiving a New Republic: The Republican Party and the Southern Question, 1869–1900* (Lawrence: University Press of Kansas, 2006), 91–93; JAG to Burke Hinsdale, April 4, 1876, JAG-WRHS; *NYH*, April 6, 1876; *NYT*, April 8, 1876.

12. Joseph Medill to EBW, March 15, 1876, EBW-LC; *NYH*, April 6, May 23, 1876; *NYT*, April 8, 1876; HF, diary, April 20, 1876; BHB to JMH, May 8, 1876, DPD to JMH, May 3, 1876, BW to JMH, May 23, 1876, C. H. Hill to JMH, June 7, 1876, JMH-LC; BW to JHW, April 6, 1876, USG-USGPL; John Russell Young, *Around the World with General Grant* (New York: American News, 1879), 2:273–275; JCBD to John L. Cadwalader, April 13, 1876, JCBD to HF, May 23, 1876, Cadwalader to JCBD, April 14, May 25, 1876, HF to JCBD, June 12, 1876, JCBD-LC.

13. *NYH*, May 23, 1876; *Official Proceedings of the National Republican Conventions of 1868, 1872, 1876, and 1880* (Minneapolis: Charles W. Johnson, 1903), 304–305, 307, 320–327.

14. HF, diary, February 22, 29, March 1, 6, 14, April 5, 29, May 22, 1876, HF to ERH, March 18, 1876, HF-LC; HF to ERH, March 14, 1876, ERH-CPL; HF to SC, March 14, 1876, SC-LC; *NYH*, May 23, 1876.

15. BHB to E. G. Sebree, April 20, 1876, BHB to C. H. Hill, April 24, 1876, JHW to BHB, May 30, 1876, BHB-LC; BHB to JMH, April 22, 23, May 3, 14, 19, 21, 25, 28, 29, June 1, 1876, R. W. Healy to BW, May 31, 1876, JMH-LC.

16. HF, diary, February 9, May 15, June 6, 1876, HF-LC; WEC to "My dear Judge," May 7, 1876, WEC Papers, RBHPC; BW to JMH, May 30, June 6, 1876, JHW to JMH, June 7, 8, 9, 12, 1876, BHB to JMH, June 5, 8, 1876, JMH-LC; JHW to BHB, June 9, 13, 1876, BHB-LC; *StLGD*, June 14, 1876; *NYH*, June 19, 1876.

17. *Official Proceedings of the National Republican Conventions*, 279–281.

18. Ibid., 288–301, 319–327; *PUSG*, 27:133.

19. *PUSG*, 27:136–137; BW to USG, June 20, 1876, USG-LC; HF, diary, October 12, 1876, HF-LC.

20. HF, diary, June 29, 1876, HF-LC; *NYH*, July 1, 1876; *PUSG*, 27:161–162; C. C. Sniffen to Secretary of the Treasury, July 1, 1876, USG to Lot Morrill, July 10, 1876, USG-LC; *NYT*, July 1, 1876.

21. *Whisky Frauds*, 322–328, 343–344, 353–373, 400–420, 479–504; BHB to JMH, July 6, 8, 9, 18, 30, 1876, JHW to JMH, July 17, 1876, JMH-LC; *PUSG*, 27:185–186; *WNR*, July 21, 22, 1876; *NYH*, August 18, 1876.

22. *M and P*, 7:368–370; 19 *Statutes at Large*, 65, 78, 95, 122, 131; *NYT*, July 26, 1876.

23. *NYT*, July 26, 1876; HF, diary, June 27, 28, 30, July 10, 11, 1876, HF-LC; *NYH*, September 12, 1876.

24. *WNR*, July 8, 20, 1876; HF, diary, June 30, July 21, 25, 28, 1876, HF-LC; *M and P*, 7:373–375, 377–378.

25. *M and P*, 7:377–378; Allan L. Damon, "Impoundment," *American Heritage* 25 (December 1973): 22–23; *NYT*, August 15, 1876; *NYH*, August 21, 1876.

26. *M and P*, 7:376; 19 *Statutes at Large* 376.

27. Robert M. Utley, *The Indian Frontier, 1846–1890*, rev. ed. (Albuquerque: University of New Mexico Press, 2003), 174–175; Paul Andrew Hutton, *Phil Sheridan and His Army* (Lincoln: University of Nebraska Press, 1985), 298–303; *PUSG*, 27:170–172.

28. Hutton, *Sheridan*, 306, 308; *NYH*, February 9, 10, March 30, 1876; House Report No. 799, 44th Cong., 1st sess., 152–164; Edward S. Cooper, *William Worth Belknap: An American Disgrace* (Madison, N.J.: Fairleigh Dickinson University Press, 2003), 279–283.

29. *PUSG*, 27:71–74, 170–179; Hutton, *Sheridan*, 310–318.

30. *NYH*, September 2, 1876; Utley, *Indian Frontier*, 178–181.

31. HF, diary, August 1, 1876, HF-LC; *PUSG*, 27:180–183; 19 *Statutes at Large* 192, 254–264; Senate Executive Document No. 9, 44th Cong., 2nd sess.; Richmond L. Clow, "The Sioux Nation and Indian Territory: The Attempted Removal of 1876," *South Dakota History* 6 (Fall 1976): 456–469.

32. *M and P*, 7:401; House Executive Document No. 9, 44th Cong., 2nd sess., 1; 19 *Statutes at Large* 254–264.

33. *PUSG*, 28:168.

34. Donald Bruce Johnson and Kirk H. Porter, comps., *National Party Platforms, 1840–1872* (Urbana: University of Illinois Press, 1975), 49–51, 53–55; Michael F. Holt, *By One Vote: The Disputed Presidential Election of 1876* (Lawrence: University Press of Kansas, 2008), 98–101; *Official Proceedings of the National Democratic Convention, Held in St. Louis, Mo., June 27th, 28th and 29th, 1876* (St. Louis: Woodward, Tiernan, & Hale, 1876), 129.

35. Johnson and Porter, *National Party Platforms*, 54; BHB to JMH, July 6, 1876 (emphasis in original), JMH-LC; *PUSG*, 27:133; JDC to RBH, June 20, 1876, JDC-OCL.

36. Edward McPherson, *A Hand-Book of Politics for 1876* (Washington, D.C.: Solomons & Chapman, 1876), 212–213.

37. *PUSG*, 27:167, 275–276.

38. *PUSG*, 27:259; William B. Hesseltine, *Ulysses S. Grant: Politician* (New York: Dodd, Mead, 1935), 408–409; James N. Tyner to ZC, November 1, 1876, ZC-LC; Holt, *By One Vote*, 128, 158–159.

39. George Rable, *But There Was No Peace: The Role of Violence in the Politics of Reconstruction* (Athens: University of Georgia Press, 1984), 163–168; *NYT*, July 14, 20, 1876; *PUSG*, 27:199–202; *NYH*, July 20, 1876; HF, diary, July 18, 26, 28, 1876, HF-LC; Senate Executive Document No. 85, 44th Cong., 1st sess.; Senate Miscellaneous Document No. 48, 44th Cong., 2nd sess., 2:30–31.

40. Abram S. Hewitt to SJT, July 19, 1876, Scott Lord to SJT, July 31, 1876,

SJT-NYPL; McPherson, *Hand-Book of Politics for 1876*, 218; *CR*, 44th Cong., 1st sess., 5419–5422; RBH to JAG, August 5, 6, 12, 1876, JAG-LC; Charles Richard Williams, ed., *Diary and Letters of Rutherford Birchard Hayes* (Columbus: Ohio State Archaeological and Historical Society, 1924), 3:340 (emphasis in original).

41. *NYH*, September 12, 1876; *PUSG*, 27:318.

42. *NYH*, August 17, 18, September 5, 25, 1876.

43. Rable, *But There Was No Peace*, 171–182; John L. Cadwalader notes, HF, diary, October 12, 17, 1876, HF-LC; House Executive Document No. 30, 44th Cong., 2nd sess., 16–22, 99–102; *NYH*, November 7, 1876.

44. Brooks D. Simpson, "Ulysses S. Grant and the Electoral Crisis of 1876–77," *Hayes Historical Journal* 11 (Winter 1992): 5–6. For a detailed treatment of the crisis, see Calhoun, *Conceiving a New Republic*, 105–136.

45. Keith Ian Polakoff, *The Politics of Inertia: The Election of 1876 and the End of Reconstruction* (Baton Rouge: Louisiana State University Press, 1973), 207–210; Ari Hoogenboom, *The Presidency of Rutherford B. Hayes* (Lawrence: University Press of Kansas, 1988), 27–28; *PUSG*, 28:17–20; HF, diary, [November 9, 10, 1876], HF-LC; *NYH*, November 11, 20, 21, 1876; G. J. Pillow to SJT, November 18, 1876, SJT-NYPL (emphasis in original); John Davis to JCBD, November 25, 1876, JCBD-LC.

46. HF, diary, November 26, 27, 30, December 1, 1876, HF-LC; Edward McPherson, *A Hand-Book of Politics for 1878* (Washington, D.C.: Solomons & Chapman, 1878), 77; Alphonso Taft to RBH, December 6, 1876 (ts), RBH-RBHPC; *PUSG*, 28:58–59.

47. Abram S. Hewitt, memorandum of conversation with President Grant, December 3, 1876, AN-CU.

48. *PUSG*, 28:73; *NYH*, December 4, 11, 1876; HF, diary, December 5, 1876, HF-LC.

49. *PUSG*, 28:67; HF, diary, December 4, 1876, HF-LC; *M and P*, 7:411.

50. Calhoun, *Conceiving a New Republic*, 107–108, 117; OEB, diary, January 12, 1877, OEB-NL; Polakoff, *Politics of Inertia*, 269–271.

51. RBH to W. K. Rogers, December 31, 1876, JS to RBH, January 3, 8, 1877, RBH-RBHPC; Williams, *Diary and Letters of Hayes*, 3:395, 400; Calhoun, *Conceiving a New Republic*, 114–115; J. Thomas Spriggs to SJT, November 19, 1876, W. T. P[elton] to SJT, "Friday night" [February 16, 1877?], SJT-NYPL; James C. Welling to MM, January 10, 1877, MM-LC; JB, diary, February 9, [12], [14], 1877, JB-NYPL; Bancroft, *Speeches of Schurz*, 3:341–343, 351, 353, 360, 379–383.

52. JAG to RBH, December 9, 1876, JS to RBH, December 9, 21 (ts), 22, 1876, John D. Defrees to RBH, December 14, 1876, A. Taft to RBH, December 24, 31 (ts), 1876, Edward F. Noyes to RBH, December 26, 1876, George W. Childs to RBH, January 2, 1877, RBH-RBHPC; RBH to USG, December 25, 1876, USG-LC; *PUSG*, 28:106.

53. James M. Comly to RBH, January 8, 1876, RBH-RBHPC (emphasis in original).

54. McPherson, *Hand-Book of Politics for 1878*, 60–65; HF, diary, January 2, 7, 9, 12, 16, 1877, HF-LC; OEB, diary, January 15, 1877, OEB-NL; *NYH*, January 16, 1877; Uncle Sam [Ward] to SJT, January 16, 1877, SJT-NYPL.

55. HF, diary, January 17, 1877, HF-LC; *M and P*, 7:6.

56. G. F. Edmunds to CSch, January 2, 1877, CSch-LC; Williams, *Diary and Letters of Hayes*, 3:404; HF, diary, January 20, 26, 27, 28, 1877, HF-LC; McPherson, *Hand-Book of Politics for 1878*, 9–10; *NYH*, January 27, 1877; *M and P*, 7:422–424; R. P. Buckland to RBH, January 29, 1877, RBH-RBHPC.

57. House Executive Document No. 30, 44th Cong., 2nd sess.

58. *M and P*, 7:425–427.

59. *NYS*, November 23, 1876; *WNR*, November 24, 25, 1876; Henry V. Boynton to BHB, November 23, 26, 1876, BHB-LC.

60. HF, diary, October 31, November 18, 1876, HF-LC; *PUSG*, 27:13–17.

61. Chester Krum to OEB, April 14, 16, July 12, October 18, December 3, 13, 21, 30, 1876, John Joyce to OEB, July 16, October 2, 1876, January 1, 1877, John McDonald to Krum, December 29, 1876, OEB, diary, January 11, 1877, OEB-NL; HF, diary, February 27, 1877, HF-LC; *PUSG*, 27:14–17; John McDonald, *Secrets of the Great Whiskey Ring* (Chicago: Belford, Clarke, 1880), 305–326. McDonald recovered and lived until 1912. Joyce eventually received a pardon from President Hayes.

62. OEB, diary, January 8, 11, 25, 26, 27, 29, 30, 31, February 6, 7, 10, 14, 15, 16, 19, 21, 24, 26, March 1, 4, 5, 1877, USG, order, March 1, 1877, OEB-NL. While still serving as a lighthouse inspector in 1884, Babcock drowned in a severe storm off the coast of Florida. *NYT*, June 4, 6, 28, 1884.

63. OEB, diary, January 22, 23, 24, 25, 26, February 1, 2, 3, 5, 6, 7, 9, 10, 12, 13, 15, 16, 17, 19, 20, 21, 22, 23, 24, 25, 26, 27, 28, March 1, 2, 4, 5, 1877, OEB-NL; Calhoun, *Conceiving a New Republic*, 118–129; *PUSG*, 28:160; *NYT*, February 26, 1877. On the actions of the southerners, see Michael Les Benedict, "Southern Democrats in the Crisis of 1876–1877: A Reconsideration of *Reunion and Reaction*," *Journal of South History* 46 (November 1980): 489–524.

64. Calhoun, *Conceiving a New Republic*, 123–135.

65. Polakoff, *Politics of Inertia*, 230; *NYT*, February 26, 1877; House Miscellaneous Document No. 31, 45th Cong., 3rd sess., vol. 3, 618; HF, diary, February 20, 1877, HF-LC; McPherson, *Hand-Book of Politics for 1878*, 80; Calhoun, *Conceiving a New Republic*, 129–135.

66. *PUSG*, 28:164–165; McPherson, *Hand-Book of Politics for 1878*, 67–68; House Miscellaneous Document No. 31, 45th Cong., 3rd sess., vol. 3, 626–630; *NYH*, March 3, 4, 1877. Grant drafted the dispatch that went to Packard over Sniffen's name. HF, diary, March 1, 1877, HF-LC.

67. Williams, *Diary and Letters of Hayes*, 3:426; *NYT*, March 6, 1877; Harry James Brown and Frederick D. Williams, eds., *The Diary of James A. Garfield* (East Lansing: Michigan State University Press, 1967–1981), 3:454.

CHAPTER 22. THIRD TERM DREAMS

1. *M and P*, 7:399–400; *NYT*, December 6, 1876.

2. *M and P*, 7:400; *PUSG*, 28:67; HF, diary, December 4, 5, 1876, HF-LC.

3. *M and P*, 7:400–413.

4. *NYH*, March 4, 1877.

5. *NYH*, March 10, 1877; *M and P*, 7:444–445; *PUSG*, 28:191; *WES*, March 7, 8, 1877; Ari Hoogenboom, *Rutherford B. Hayes: Warrior and President* (Lawrence: University Press of Kansas, 1995), 301–302; Edward L. Pierce to CSch, March 13, 1877 (ts), CSch-LC.

6. William M. Ferraro, "Engagement Rather than Escape: Ulysses S. Grant's World Tour, 1877–1879," in *A Companion to the Reconstruction Presidents, 1865–1881*, ed. Edward O. Frantz (Chichester, U.K.: Wiley Blackwell, 2014), 353–380; *PUSG*, 28:233.

7. *PUSG*, 28:207, 233, 237, 271–272, 275, 277, 290–291, 29:275.

8. *PUSG*, 29:151–157, 202–204, 206–208, 213–226; Ferraro, "Engagement Rather than Escape," 379.

9. *PUSG*, 29:211–212.

10. *PUSG*, 28:327, 368 (emphasis in original); *Chicago Inter-Ocean*, August 15, 1878; *NYT*, December 7, 1878.

11. *NYH*, June 15, 1877; *NYTr*, June 16, 1877.

12. *PUSG*, 28:306, 329; *NYH*, September 25, 1877.

13. *NYH*, October 5, 19, 20, 29, November 10, 11, 12, 13, 17, 28, 1877, January 4, 9, February 22, 23, July 24, 1878; *Boston Evening Transcript*, October 31, 1877; *PUSG*, 28:268–269, 320–322; HF to GSB, November 28, December 4, 1877, HF to JCBD, December 31, 1877 (ts), HF-LC; *Harper's Weekly*, December 8, 1877.

14. *PUSG*, 28:251–254, 363.

15. John Russell Young, *Around the World with General Grant* (New York: American News, 1879), 2:359–365.

16. *PUSG*, 28:267, 355, 359, 367 (emphasis in original); *NYH*, September 25, 1877.

17. *PUSG*, 28:262, 297.

18. *PUSG*, 28:456; C. A. Boynton to William Henry Smith, August 8, 1878, William Henry Smith Papers, Ohio Historical Society.

19. *NYT*, July 7, 1878; *PUSG*, 28:440; Charles W. Calhoun, *Conceiving a New Republic: The Republican Party and the Southern Question, 1869–1900* (Lawrence: University Press of Kansas, 2006), 153–160; *PUSG*, 29:38.

20. *PUSG*, 29:9, 93–94 (emphasis in original); Archibald E. H. Anson, *About Others and Myself 1745 to 1920* (London: John Murray, 1920), 362.

21. Calhoun, *Conceiving a New Republic*, 169–170; J. Donald Cameron to TOH, February 19, 1880, TOH-WHS; *PUSG*, 29:234, 297; HLD to Mrs. HLD, December 15, 1879, HLD-LC (emphasis in original).

22. *PUSG*, 29:355–356; Charles Richard Williams, ed., *Diary and Letters of*

Rutherford Birchard Hayes (Columbus: Ohio State Archaeological and Historical Society, 1924), 3:582, 583; RBH to AB, December 13, 1887, AB Papers, LC; Hoogenboom, *Hayes*, 415–416, 429.

23. *PUSG*, 29:352–353, 359, 371.

24. *Appletons' Annual Cyclopaedia and Register of Important Events of the Year 1880* (New York: D. Appleton, 1883), 573, 616–617; J. Donald Cameron to TOH, February 19, 1880, TOH-WHS; JGB to Edward McPherson, February 6, 1880, Edward McPherson Papers, LC; HF to Nicholas Fish, March 5, 1880 (ts), HF-LC.

25. George S. Boutwell, "General Grant and a Third Term," *North American Review* 130 (April 1880): 384; *NYT*, March 22, April 1, May 6, 1880; *PUSG*, 29:376, 381.

26. *PUSG*, 29:411; Thurlow Weed to SC, April 29, 1880, SC-LC; TOH to JGB, April 14, 1880, JGB-LC.

27. Adam Badeau, *Grant in Peace* (Hartford, Conn.: S. S. Scranton, 1887), 320; *PUSG*, 29:408; James Pickett Jones, *John A. Logan: Stalwart Republican from Illinois* (Tallahassee: University Presses of Florida, 1982), 133–135; J. J. S. Wilson to EBW, May 22, 1880 (telegram), EBW-LC; James Ford Rhodes, *History of the United States from Hayes to McKinley, 1877–1896* (New York: Macmillan, 1919), 114.

28. George F. Hoar, *Autobiography of Seventy Years* (New York: Charles Scribner's Sons, 1903), 1:389–390; *Proceedings of the Republican National Convention Held at Chicago, . . . 1880* (Chicago: Jno. B. Jeffrey, 1881), 198.

29. *NYT*, June 2, 1880; *NYTr*, June 2, 1880; Harry James Brown and Frederick D. Williams, eds., *The Diary of James A. Garfield* (East Lansing: Michigan State University Press, 1967–1981), 4:425; *Proceedings of the Republican National Convention Held at Chicago, 1880*, 93–125, 151–160; Hoar, *Autobiography*, 1:390–393; Leon Burr Richardson, *William E. Chandler: Republican* (New York: Dodd, Mead, 1940), 252–255.

30. *Proceedings of the Republican National Convention Held at Chicago, 1880*, 162–163, 180–181.

31. Ibid., 162–163, 180–181.

32. Ibid., 175–179, 184–194, 198–251; F. D. Grant to JRY, June 7, 1880, JRY-LC.

33. GSB to Fred D. Grant, May 28, June 1, 1897 (and enclosed extract), [F. D. Grant] to Boutwell, May 30, 1897, USG-USGPL; George S. Boutwell, *Reminiscences of Sixty Years in Public Affairs* (New York: McClure, Phillips, 1902) 2:266–272; *PUSG*, 414–415; *Proceedings of the Republican National Convention Held at Chicago, 1880*, 252–271. Julia Grant later recalled, probably erroneously, that Grant had directed the supposed withdrawal letter to Cameron. John Y. Simon, ed., *The Personal Memoirs of Julia Dent Grant* (New York: G. P. Putnam's Sons, 1975), 321–322.

34. *Proceedings of the Republican National Convention Held at Chicago, 1880*, 271; OEB to AB, June 27, 1880, AB-LC; *NYT*, April 29, 1888.

35. John Hay to JRY, June 9, 1880, JRY-LC (emphasis in original).

36. *PUSG*, 29:416, 428–429; HF to Israel Washburn Jr., July 6, 1880 (ts), HF-LC (emphasis in original).

37. John McDonald, *Secrets of the Great Whiskey Ring* (Chicago: Belford, Clarke, 1880); HF to JCBD, August 13, 1880, HF-LC. Buel is identified as McDonald's ghostwriter in D. W. Lusk, *Politics and Politicians: A Succinct History of the Politics of Illinois from 1856 to 1884* (Springfield, Ill.: H. W. Rokker, 1884), 288–289.

38. *PUSG*, 29:440, 446, 468–469, 477–479.

39. *PUSG*, 30:58, 59, 60, 74–75.

40. Allen Peskin, *Garfield* (Kent, Ohio: Kent State University Press, 1999), 517, 553–561, 563–564; *PUSG*, 30:180, 203–205, 209–210, 215, 218 (emphasis in original).

41. Brown and Williams, *Diary of Garfield*, 4:568; Peskin, *Garfield*, 569–572.

42. *PUSG*, 30:223, 233, 250–251, 303–308, 358; *NYT*, September 20, 1881.

43. David M. Pletcher, *Rails, Mines, and Progress: Seven Promoters in Mexico, 1867–1911* (Ithaca, N.Y.: Cornell University Press, 1958), 160–179; David M. Pletcher, *The Awkward Years: American Foreign Relations under Garfield and Arthur* (Columbia: University of Missouri Press, 1962), 338–339.

44. *PUSG*, 31:22, 136; Thomas C. Reeves, *Gentleman Boss: The Life of Chester Alan Arthur* (New York: Alfred A. Knopf, 1975), 324–327.

45. Badeau, *Grant in Peace*, 552; *PUSG*, 31:98–99, 115, 117–118, 119, 130, 241–242; *NYTr*, September 20, 1884.

46. *NYT*, December 28, 29, 1883; *PUSG*, 31:109, 323–333. For the Grant and Ward episode, see Geoffrey C. Ward, *A Disposition to Be Rich* (New York: Alfred A. Knopf, 2012).

47. *PUSG*, 31:170, 185–186, 244, 291, 295, 410, 437; John H. Douglas, journal (ts), 24–30, 41–47, John Douglas Papers, LC; *NYT*, March 1, 1885; U. S. Grant, *Personal Memoirs of U. S. Grant* (New York: Charles L. Webster, 1885, 1886).

48. Grant, *Personal Memoirs*, 2:510–512, 523–524, 542–554; *M and P*, 7:6.

CODA: RENDERING "THE PRESIDENCY OF ULYSSES S. GRANT"

1. Joan Waugh, *U. S. Grant: American Hero, American Myth* (Chapel Hill: University of North Carolina Press, 2009), 243; Hamilton Fish, "General Grant," *Independent*, July 30, 1885; *Boston Daily Advertiser*, August 10, 1885.

2. *NYS*, July 24, 1885; JHW to Hamlin Garland, February 25, 1897, JHW-LC.

3. *NYS*, January 23, 28, 1887; *StLGD*, February 11, 1887; Henry V. Boynton to JHW, March 17, 1885, Sylvanus Cadwallader to JHW, February 18, 25, 1887, June 21, 1897, August 31, September 17, October 4, 1904, May 4, 1905, December 2, 1907, JHW to Cadwallader, September 24, October 12, 1904, Grenville M. Dodge to JHW, November 4, 14, 1904, JHW to Dodge, November 8, 1904, JHW to Boynton, February 17, 1905, JHW-LC; JHW to Cadwallader, February 13, 1887, September 8, 1904, Sylvanus Cadwallader Papers, LC; Sylvanus Cadwallader,

Three Years with Grant, ed. Benjamin P. Thomas (Lincoln: University of Nebraska Press, 1996). For a refutation of Cadwallader's depiction of Grant's alleged drinking on a trip to Satartia, Mississippi, during the Vicksburg campaign, see Brooks D. Simpson, "Introduction to the Bison Books Edition," in Cadwallader, *Three Years with Grant*, v–xviii.

4. Hamlin Garland, "An Interview with General Harry Wilson" (ts), University of Southern California Library; JHW to Garland, February 25, 1897, JHW-LC; Paul Clayton Pehrson, "James Harrison Wilson: The Post-War Years, 1865–1925" (Ph.D. diss., University of Wisconsin, 1993), 250; Hamlin Garland, *Ulysses S. Grant: His Life and Character* (New York: Doubleday & McClure, 1898).

5. Pehrson, "Wilson," 244; JHW to BW, September 25, 1906, BW to JHW, December 24, 1906, JHW-LC.

6. Pehrson, "Wilson," 259–265; James Harrison Wilson, *The Life of John A. Rawlins* (New York: Neale, 1916), 358, 380–381; Eben Swift, review of *The Life of John A. Rawlins*, in *American Historical Review* 22 (April 1917): 718; Louis A. Coolidge, *Ulysses S. Grant* (Boston: Houghton Mifflin, 1917), 124–125; Allan Nevins, *Hamilton Fish: The Inner History of the Grant Administration* (New York: Dodd, Mead, 1937), 136–137, 247.

7. David P. Dyer, *Autobiography and Reminiscences* (St. Louis: William Harvey Miner, 1922), 161, 164, 170; William B. Hesseltine, *Ulysses S. Grant: Politician* (New York: Dodd, Mead, 1935), 451; Helen Todd, *A Man Named Grant* (Boston: Houghton Mifflin, 1940), 587–588; Ross A. Webb, *Benjamin Helm Bristow: Border State Politician* (Lexington: University Press of Kentucky, 1969), 294–295; Jean Edward Smith, *Grant* (New York: Simon & Schuster, 2001), 626. Helen Todd apparently invented dialogue between the two men and admitted that when she could not verify "facts," she offered "what seemed to me the probabilities." Todd, *Man Named Grant*, unpaginated front matter.

8. Dyer, *Autobiography*, 170; BHB to Henry V. Boynton, November 7, 1895, BHB to JRY, November 14, 23 (telegram), 1895, BHB-LC; Webb, *Bristow*, 294–295.

9. Edward L. Pierce, *Memoir and Letters of Charles Sumner* (Boston: Roberts Brothers, 1893); JDC to H. E. Scudder, March 19, 1895, JDC to Edward L. Pierce, April 2, 18, May 13, 1895, JDC-OCL.

10. Jacob Dolson Cox, "How Judge Hoar Ceased to Be Attorney General," *Atlantic Monthly* 76 (August 1895): 162–173; JDC to JHW, September 19, 1895, JDC-OCL; Nevins, *Fish*, 264, 268–269; Hesseltine, *Grant*, 209–210; William S. McFeely, *Grant: A Biography* (New York: W. W. Norton, 1981), 364–365; Smith, *Grant*, 500–501, 689n32.

11. Henry Adams, *The Education of Henry Adams* (1918; reprint, Boston: Houghton Mifflin, 1961); HA to JHW, May 20, 1884, JHW-LC (emphasis in original); J. C. Levenson et al., eds., *The Letters of Henry Adams* (Cambridge, Mass.: Harvard University Press, 1982), 6:480.

12. Adams, *Education*, 262, 265–266, 280, 294.

13. Brooks D. Simpson, "Henry Adams and the Age of Grant," *Hayes*

Historical Journal 8 (Spring 1989): 5–6, 20–21; Brooks D. Simpson, *The Political Education of Henry Adams* (Columbia: University of South Carolina Press, 1996), ix–xi, 112–114; Waugh, *Grant,* 104–105; *NYT,* April 30, 1999.

14. C. Vann Woodward, "The Lowest Ebb," *American Heritage* 8 (April 1957): 53.

15. Mark Wahlgren Summers, *The Era of Good Stealings* (New York: Oxford University Press, 1993), x (emphasis in original).

16. H. W. Brands, *The Man Who Saved the Union: Ulysses S. Grant in War and Peace* (New York: Doubleday, 2012); Woodward, "Lowest Ebb," 53; John Russell Young, *Men and Memories: Personal Reminiscences* (New York: F. Tennyson Neely, 1901), 2:469.

BIBLIOGRAPHICAL ESSAY

Given the tendentiousness and inaccuracy of much of the secondary literature concerning Ulysses S. Grant and his presidency, reevaluation of his years in the White House requires resort to the relevant primary sources. Fortunately, they are abundant. The starting point is the thirty-two-volume collection *The Papers of Ulysses S. Grant*, produced under the editorial hand of the late John Y. Simon. Volumes 19 through 31 cover the presidential and postpresidential years and contain nearly everything of historical significance that Grant wrote. Superb editorial annotations expand on the Grant documents and include lengthy passages from letters to and about him, as well as other material such as diaries, news reports, and government documents. Beyond the published papers, the Ulysses S. Grant Presidential Library under the direction of John F. Marszalek houses a massive treasure trove of material, including photocopies of papers from numerous repositories throughout the country. The Manuscript Division of the Library of Congress holds the largest body of original Grant papers. Most of that collection is available on microfilm.

Equally indispensable is the collection of Hamilton Fish's papers at the Library of Congress. In addition to Fish's voluminous correspondence, the collection includes the secretary's diary during his eight-year tenure. Although one wishes Fish had registered a fuller appraisal, his journal nonetheless presents an invaluable record of cabinet meetings, interactions with the president, conversations with diplomats and other officials, and the unfolding of events during the administration. Other useful collections in the Manuscript Division include the papers of Nathaniel P. Banks, Thomas F. Bayard, James G. Blaine, the Blair Family, George S. Boutwell, Benjamin H. Bristow, Benjamin F. Butler, Sylvanus

Cadwallader, Simon Cameron, William E. Chandler, Zachariah Chandler, Salmon P. Chase, John A. J. Creswell, Cyrus B. Comstock, Caleb Cushing, J. C. B. Davis, Henry L. Dawes, John H. Douglas, James A. Garfield, Horace Greeley, Walter Q. Gresham, John Marshall Harlan, Andrew Johnson, the Keim Family, John A. Logan, Manton Marble, Benjamin Moran, Justin S. Morrill, Whitelaw Reid, Jacob William Schuckers, Carl Schurz, Philip H. Sheridan, John Sherman, William T. Sherman, Edwin M. Stanton, Lyman Trumbull, Benjamin F. Wade, Elihu B. Washburne, Gideon Welles, David Ames Wells, James Harrison Wilson, and John Russell Young. The Manuscript Division also has a microfilmed edition of British Foreign Office correspondence from the Public Records Office in London. The National Archives preserves official correspondence and other documents generated during the Grant administration.

Several other institutions hold collections relevant to Grant's presidency. Allan Nevins donated to the Columbia University library a substantial collection of letters from the period, including many related to Fish. Yale's library holds the papers of Edwards Pierrepont and Samuel Bowles. The Adams Family Papers and the papers of George F. Hoar are at the Massachusetts Historical Society. The Concord, Massachusetts, Public Library maintains Ebenezer Rockwood Hoar's papers. The New York Public Library houses the papers of Horace Greeley, John Bigelow, and Samuel J. Tilden and also has a small Grant collection. The New-York Historical Society holds a few Grant documents as well as the Horatio Seymour Papers.

The Princeton University library houses the papers of William W. Belknap. A substantial collection of William E. Chandler's papers at the New Hampshire Historical Society complements that at the Library of Congress. The Western Reserve Historical Society has a small Garfield collection. The papers of Timothy O. Howe, an important congressional ally of Grant, are at the Wisconsin Historical Society, along with the papers of E. W. Keyes and Lucius Fairchild. Oliver P. Morton's papers are at the Indiana State Library, as are the papers of Daniel D. Pratt. The University of Virginia library holds the Amos T. Akerman Papers. The bulk of Orville Babcock's papers are at the Newberry Library, but the Grant Presidential Library houses a small Babcock collection that includes the diary of his Santo Domingo trips. The Jacob Dolson Cox Papers at the Oberlin College library have been microfilmed. The Peabody Essex Museum holds the Joseph W. Fabens Papers and the Fabens Family Papers. The voluminous Rutherford B. Hayes Papers at the Hayes Presidential Center are available in a microfilm edition, and the center holds several smaller relevant collections as well. The Raymond H. J. Perry Papers are at the University of Rhode Island library. The endnotes refer to additional manuscript collections.

A significant portion of Charles Sumner's correspondence is accessible in *The Selected Letters of Charles Sumner* (Boston: Northeastern University Press, 1990), edited by Beverly Wilson Palmer. Palmer also assembled a comprehensive microfilm edition based on Sumner's papers in the Harvard University

Library and numerous other collections. Other important document publications include J. C. Levenson et al., eds., *The Letters of Henry Adams* (Cambridge, Mass.: Harvard University Press, 1982–1988); Kenneth Bourne, ed., *British Documents on Foreign Affairs: Reports and Papers from the Foreign Office Confidential Print* (Lanham, Md.: University Press of America, 1986); Theodore Calvin Pease and James G. Randall, eds., *The Diary of Orville Hickman Browning* (Springfield: Illinois State Historical Library, 1925–1933); John Niven, ed., *The Salmon P. Chase Papers* (Kent, Ohio: Kent State University Press, 1993–1998); *Papers Relating to the Foreign Relations of the United States,* part of the annual compendium of congressional documents published by the Government Printing Office and known as the US Congressional Serial Set; Harry James Brown and Frederick D. Williams, eds., *The Diary of James A. Garfield* (East Lansing: Michigan State University, 1867–1981); Mary L. Hinsdale, ed., *Garfield-Hinsdale Letters: Correspondence between James Abram Garfield and Burke Aaron Hinsdale* (Ann Arbor: University of Michigan Press, 1949); H. C. G. Matthew, ed., *The Gladstone Diaries* (Oxford: Oxford University Press, 1968–1994).

Additional useful document collections include Charles Richard Williams, ed., *Diary and Letters of Rutherford Birchard Hayes* (Columbus: Ohio State Archaeological and Historical Society, 1924); Edward McPherson, *A Hand-Book of Politics* (Washington, D.C.: various publishers, 1872–1878); McPherson, *The Political History of the United States of America during the Period of Reconstruction* (Washington, D.C.: Philp & Solomons, 1871); Stafford H. Northcote, *Diaries 1869, 1870, 1871, 1875, 1882, of the First Earl of Iddesleigh* (privately printed, 1907); Andrew Lang, ed., *Life, Letters, and Diaries of Sir Stafford Northcote, First Earl of Iddesleigh* (Edinburgh: William Blackwood & Sons, 1895); Joseph Schafer, ed., *Intimate Letters of Carl Schurz, 1841–1869* (Madison: State Historical Society of Wisconsin, 1928); Frederic Bancroft, ed., *Speeches, Correspondence and Political Papers of Carl Schurz* (New York: G. P. Putnam's Sons, 1913); Rachel Sherman Thorndyke, ed., *The Sherman Letters: Correspondence between General and Senator Sherman from 1837 to 1891* (New York: Charles Scribner's Sons, 1894); M. A. DeWolfe Howe, ed., *Home Letters of General Sherman* (New York: Charles Scribner's Sons, 1909); John Bigelow, ed., *Letters and Literary Memorials of Samuel J. Tilden* (New York: Harper & Brothers, 1908); Howard K. Beale, ed., *The Diary of Gideon Welles* (New York: W. W. Norton, 1960).

Grant's messages to Congress appear in James D. Richardson, comp., *Messages and Papers of the Presidents, 1789–1902* ([Washington, D.C.]: Bureau of National Literature and Art, 1903). This compilation of the official messages should be supplemented by drafts appearing in *The Papers of Ulysses S. Grant.* Annual reports of cabinet members and other administration officers, as well as other executive publications, are printed in the Congressional Serial Set. Congressional debate and action can be followed in the *Congressional Globe,* the *Congressional Record,* the *Journal* of each house, the *Journal of the Executive Proceedings of the Senate of the United States,* and *Statutes at Large.* Each house published its own documents and reports as well as executive and miscellaneous documents. Special reports of investigations often included testimony.

One must exercise care when examining the sometimes unreliable newspapers from this period. I consulted numerous publications but relied most heavily on the *New York Times, New York Herald, New York Tribune, New York Sun, New York World, Boston Daily Advertiser, Washington National Republican, Washington Evening Star, St. Louis Globe-Democrat, Harper's Weekly,* and *Nation.* Targeted searching of newspapers is available through the website Nineteenth Century U.S. Newspapers from Gale Cengage Learning. Mark Wahlgren Summers, *The Press Gang: Newspapers and Politics, 1865–1878* (Chapel Hill: University of North Carolina Press, 1994), presents a discussion of the vagaries of political journalism in the Grant era.

Memoirs, reminiscences, and autobiographies contain much valuable information and insights, but they are often compromised by the frailties of human memory, ideology, or amour propre. Where possible, I weighed them in tandem with contemporary sources. Among the most useful works of this type are Blanche Ames, *Adelbert Ames, 1835–1933: General, Senator, Governor* (New York: Argosy-Antiquarian, 1964); Adam Badeau, *Grant in Peace* (Hartford, Conn.: S. S. Scranton, 1887); James G. Blaine, *Twenty Years of Congress* (Norwich, Conn.: Henry Bill, 1884, 1886); George S. Boutwell, *Reminiscences of Sixty Years in Public Affairs* (New York: McClure Phillips, 1902); J. C. Bancroft Davis, *Mr. Fish and the Alabama Claims: A Chapter in Diplomatic History* (Boston: Houghton, Mifflin, 1893); David P. Dyer, *Autobiography and Reminiscences* (St. Louis: William Harvey Miner, 1922); Jesse Grant, *In the Days of My Father General Grant* (New York: Harper & Brothers, 1925); John Y. Simon, ed., *The Personal Memoirs of Julia Dent Grant* (New York: G. P. Putnam's Sons, 1975); Frank Warren Hackett, *Reminiscences of the Geneva Tribunal of Arbitration, 1872: The Alabama Claims* (Boston: Houghton Mifflin, 1911); Moorfield Storey and Edward W. Emerson, *Ebenezer Rockwood Hoar: A Memoir* (Boston: Houghton Mifflin, 1911); George F. Hoar, *Autobiography of Seventy Years* (New York: Charles Scribner's Sons, 1903); Frank Warren Hackett, *A Sketch of the Life and Public Services of William Adams Richardson* (Washington, D.C.: H. L. McQueen, 1898); John Sherman, *Recollections of Forty Years in the House, Senate and Cabinet* (Chicago: Werner, 1895); Edward L. Pierce, *Memoir and Letters of Charles Sumner* (Boston: Roberts Brothers, 1894); and John Russell Young, *Around the World with General Grant* (New York: American News, 1879).

As one might expect, most biographies of Grant give much more coverage to his service in the army than to his presidency. Many authors are drawn to Grant by his military career and exhibit less interest in or understanding of the complicated issues of politics and governance of the 1870s. Some biographers—for whom Grant is simply one of many varied individuals they have examined over the years—offer important insights into his character, but they slight or misconstrue the nuance and detail of the political context in which the eighteenth president operated. Only two works present comprehensive evaluations focused on Grant's presidential years. Both are outdated and otherwise flawed. According to Allan Nevins's laudatory biography *Hamilton Fish: The Inner History of the Grant Administration* (New York: Dodd, Mead, 1937), the noble secretary of state saved the administration and the country from Grant's supposed ineptitude. Tacitly partaking of Fish's racism, Nevins execrates Grant's support for Reconstruction as his worst mistake. In *Ulysses S. Grant: Politician* (New York: Dodd, Mead, 1935), William B. Hesseltine seeks to redeem Grant from some of the condemnation of his contemporary critics, but he portrays Grant as insufficiently wary of rapacious capitalism and an ally of reactionary interests.

The best modern scholar who specializes in Grant is Brooks D. Simpson, whose works include *Let Us Have Peace: Ulysses S. Grant and the Politics of War and Reconstruction, 1861–1868* (Chapel Hill: University of North Carolina Press, 1991) and *The Reconstruction Presidents* (Lawrence: University Press of Kansas, 1998). The first volume of Simpson's biography, *Ulysses S. Grant: Triumph over Adversity, 1822–1865* (Boston: Houghton Mifflin, 2000), carries the story through Appomattox, and a projected second volume will cover the presidency. Simpson provides an indispensable corrective to such critical works as William S. McFeely, *Grant: A Biography* (New York, W. W. Norton, 1981); Michael Korda, *Ulysses S. Grant: The Unlikely Hero* (New York: HarperCollins, 2004); and Joseph A. Rose, *Grant under Fire: An Exposé of Generalship and Character in the American Civil War* (New York: Alderhanna, 2015).

Other recent works on Grant—widely varying in their accuracy and usefulness—include Ronald C. White, *American Ulysses: A Life of Ulysses S. Grant* (New York: Random House, 2016); H. W. Brands, *The Man Who Saved the Union: Ulysses Grant in War and Peace* (New York: Doubleday, 2012); Joan Waugh, *U. S. Grant: American Hero, American Myth* (Chapel Hill: University of North Carolina Press, 2009); Josiah Bunting III, *Ulysses S. Grant* (New York: Times Books, 2004); Jean Edward Smith, *Grant* (New York: Simon & Schuster, 2001); Frank J. Scaturro, *President Grant Reconsidered* (Lanham, Md.: University Press of America, 1998); and Geoffrey Perret, *Ulysses S. Grant: Soldier and President* (New York: Random House, 1997).

For additional biographical studies and other works pertaining to individuals and events connected with Grant, I refer the reader to the endnotes.

INDEX